BURLINGTON HOUSE

HOME OF THE ROYAL ACADEMY OF ARTS

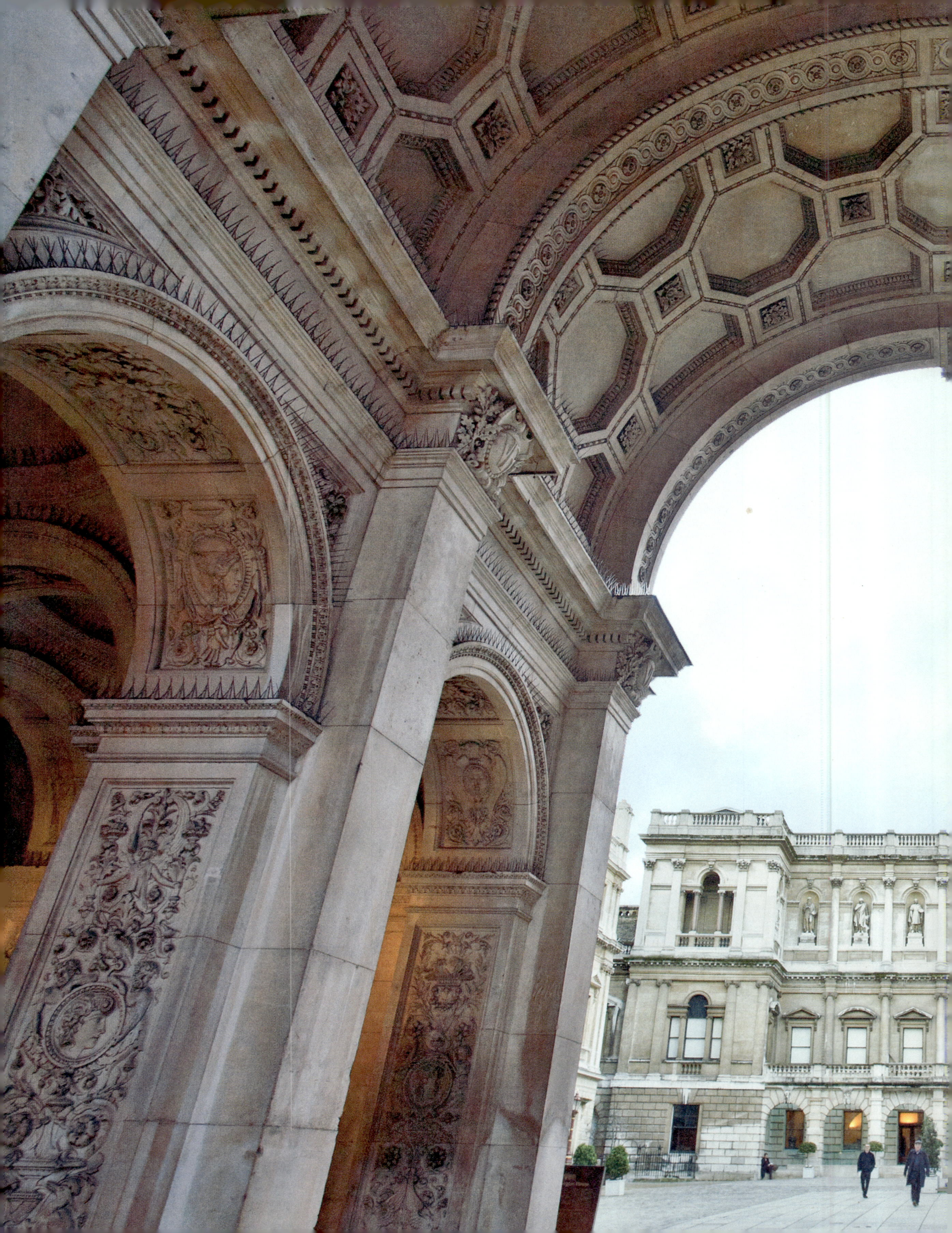

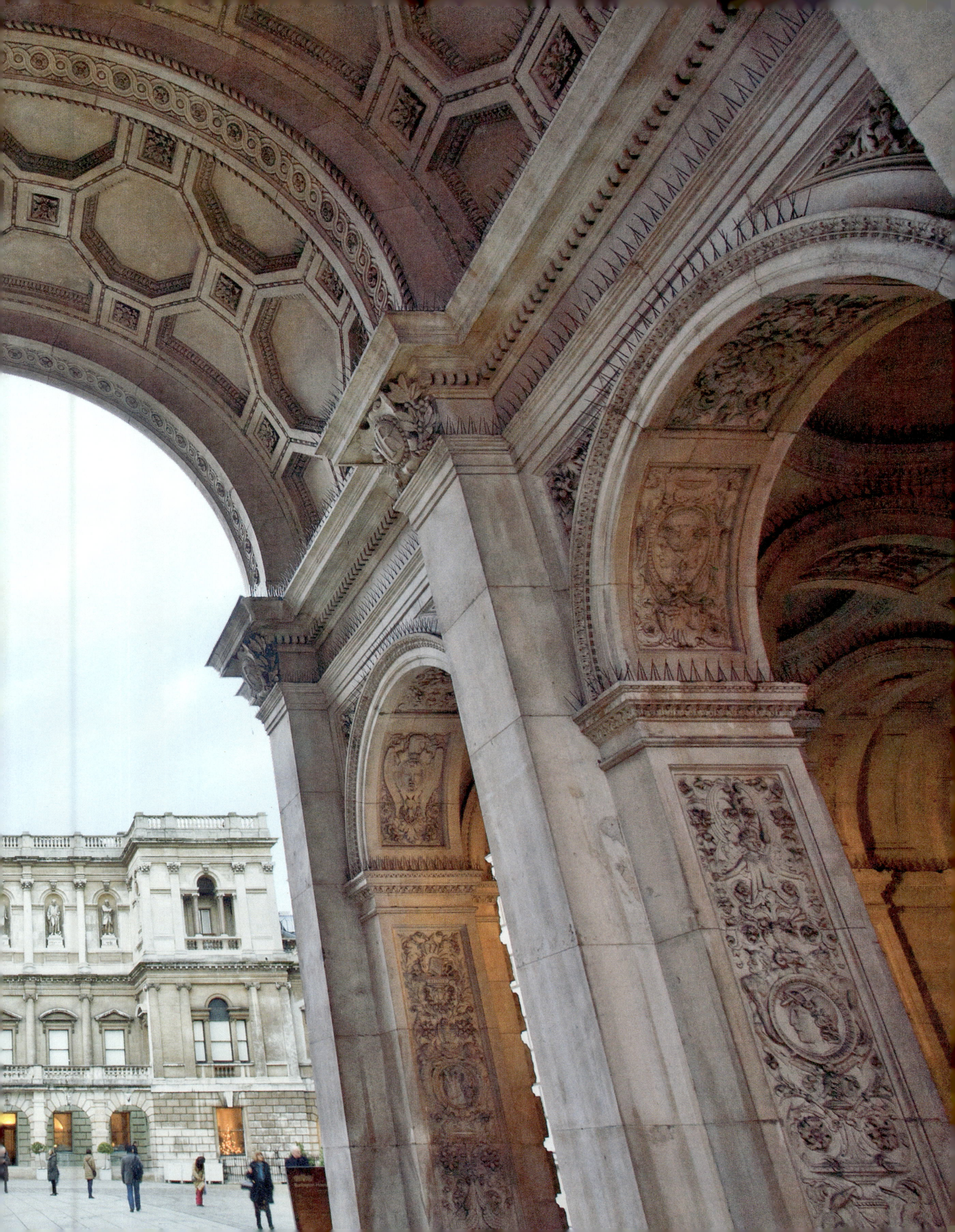

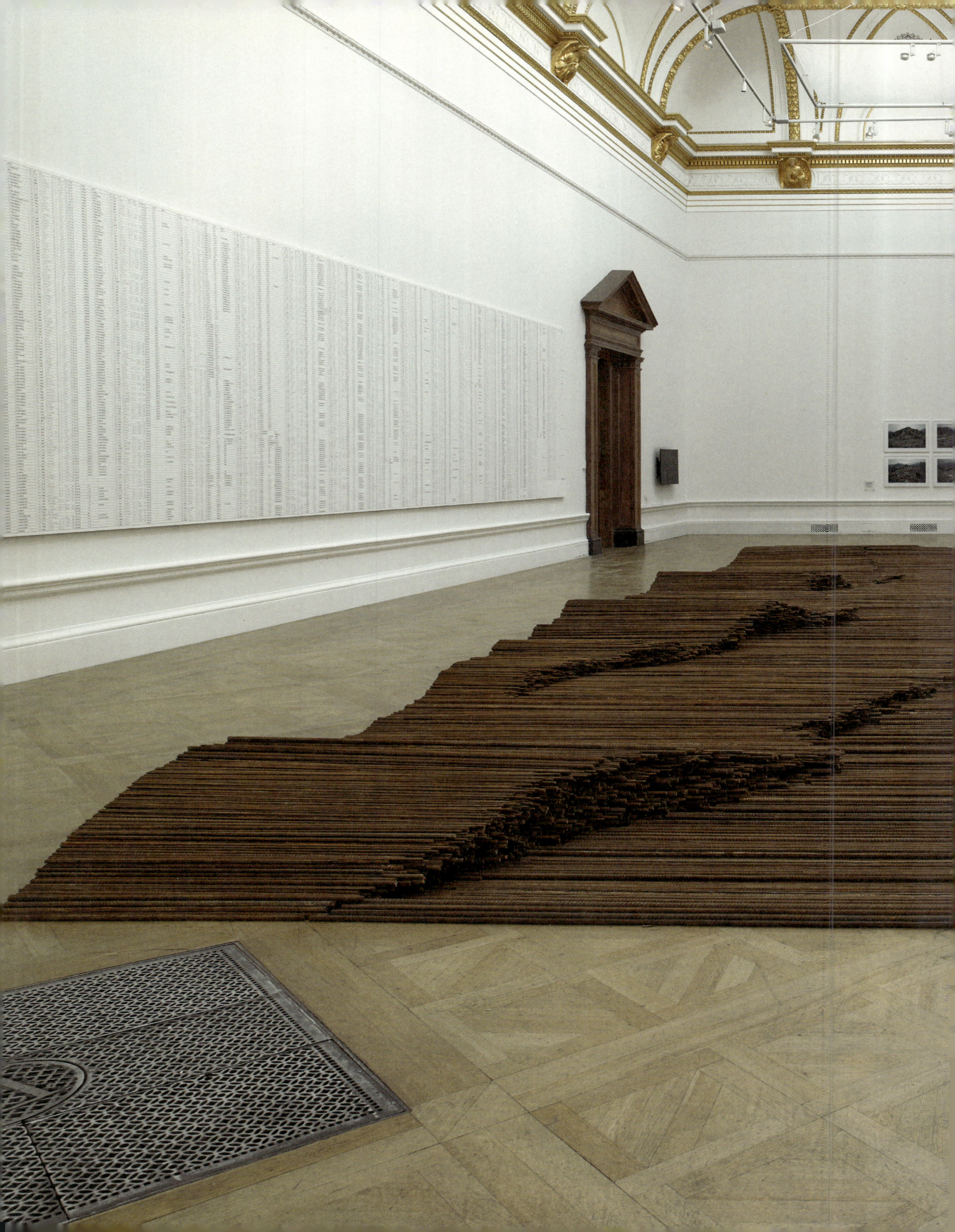

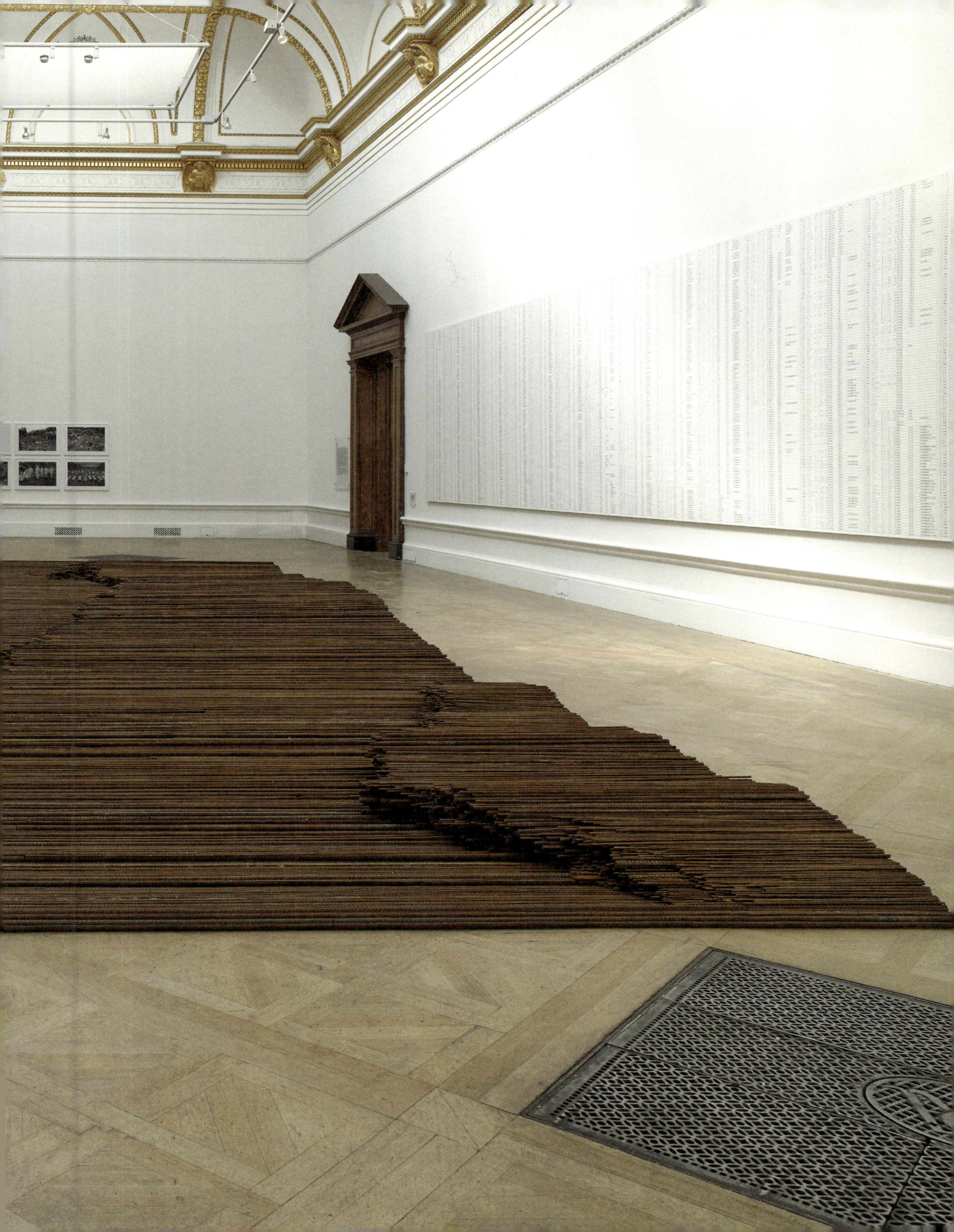

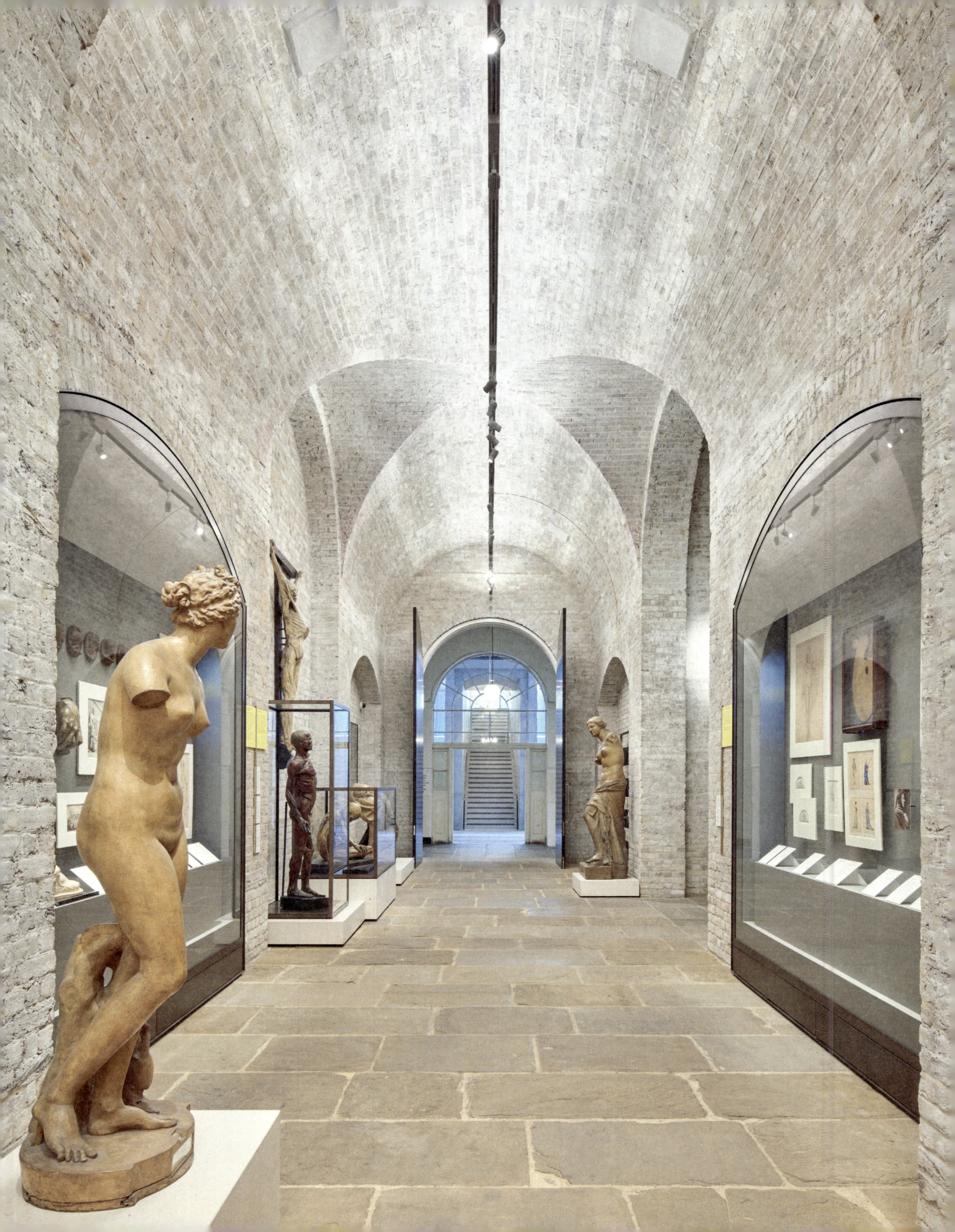

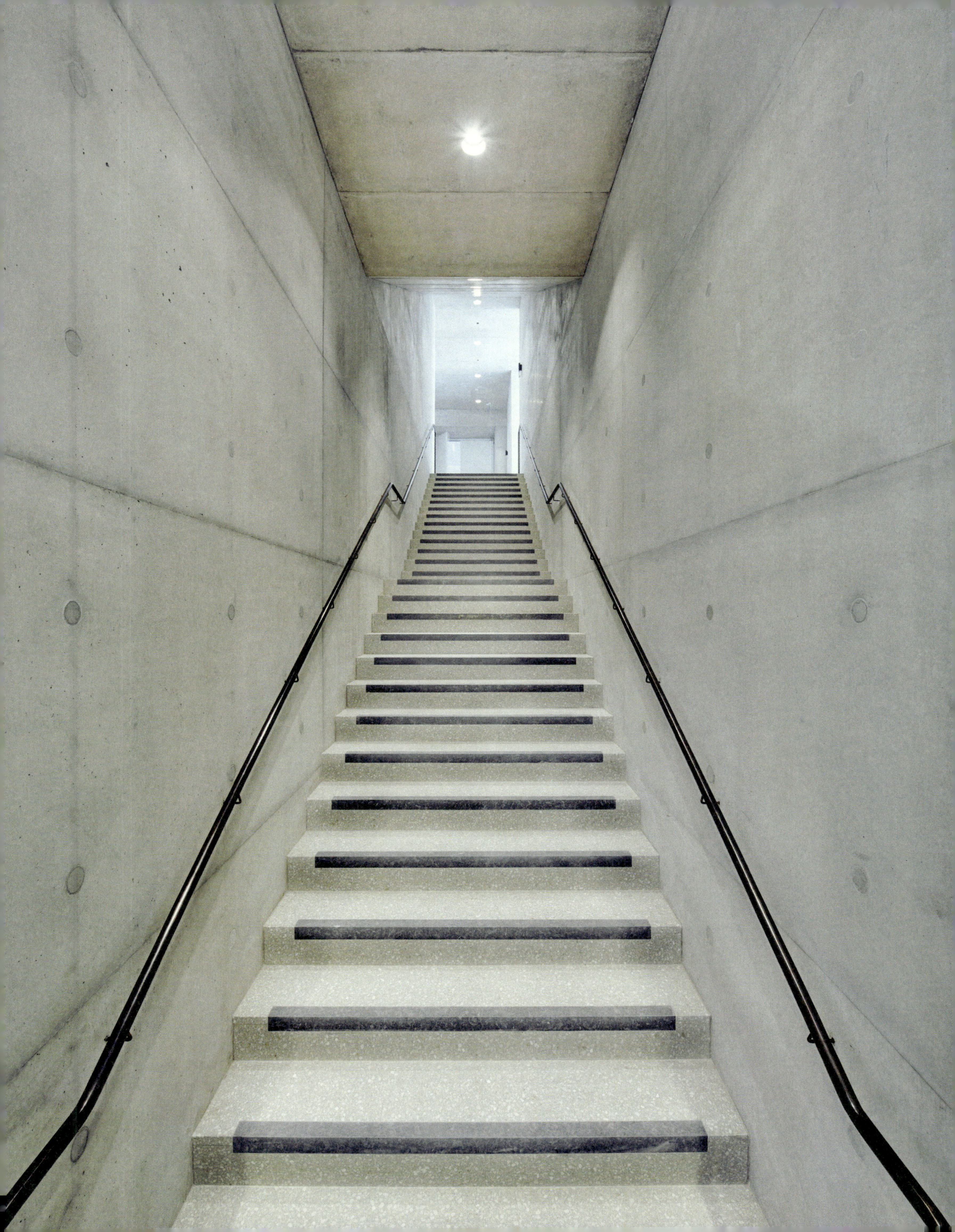

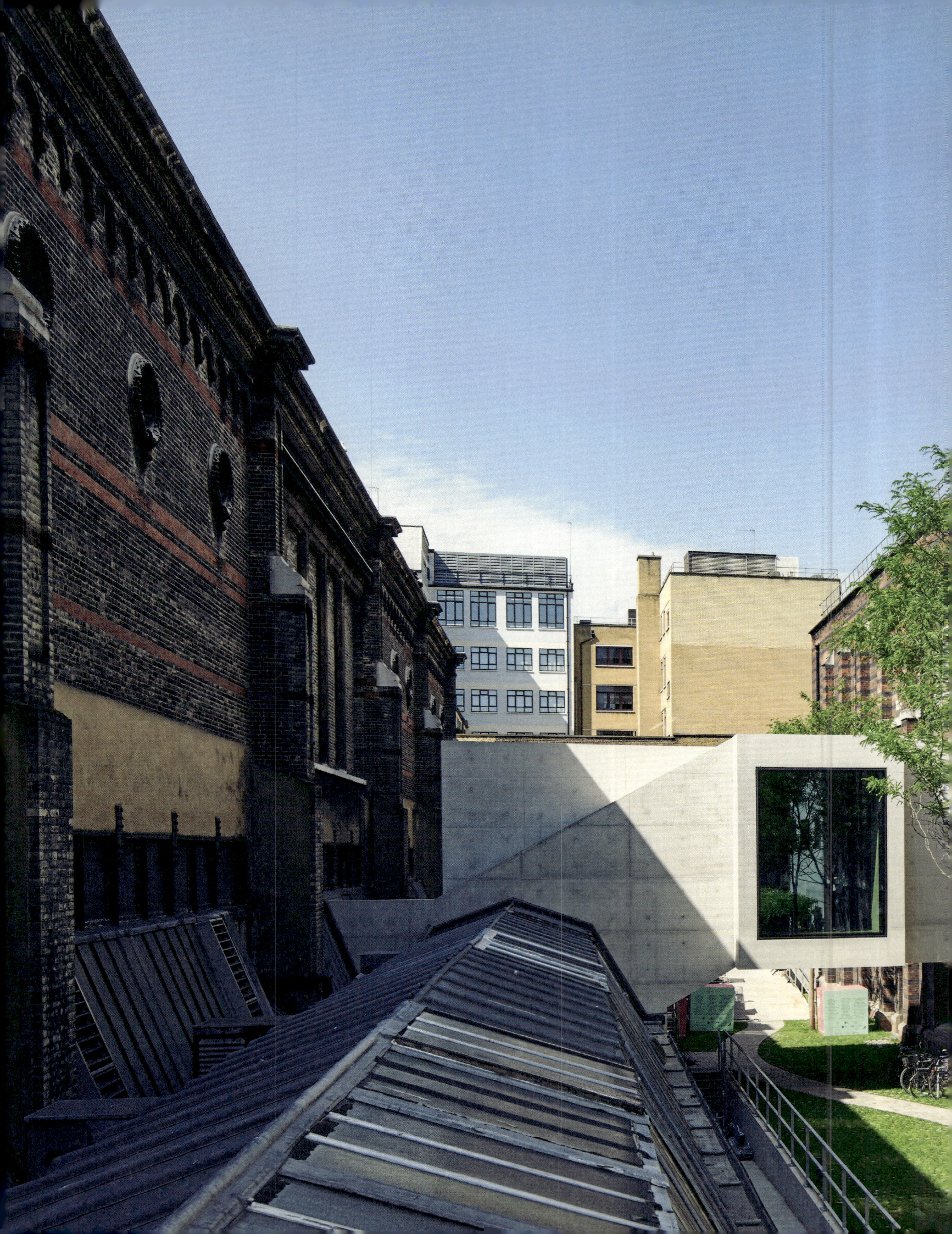

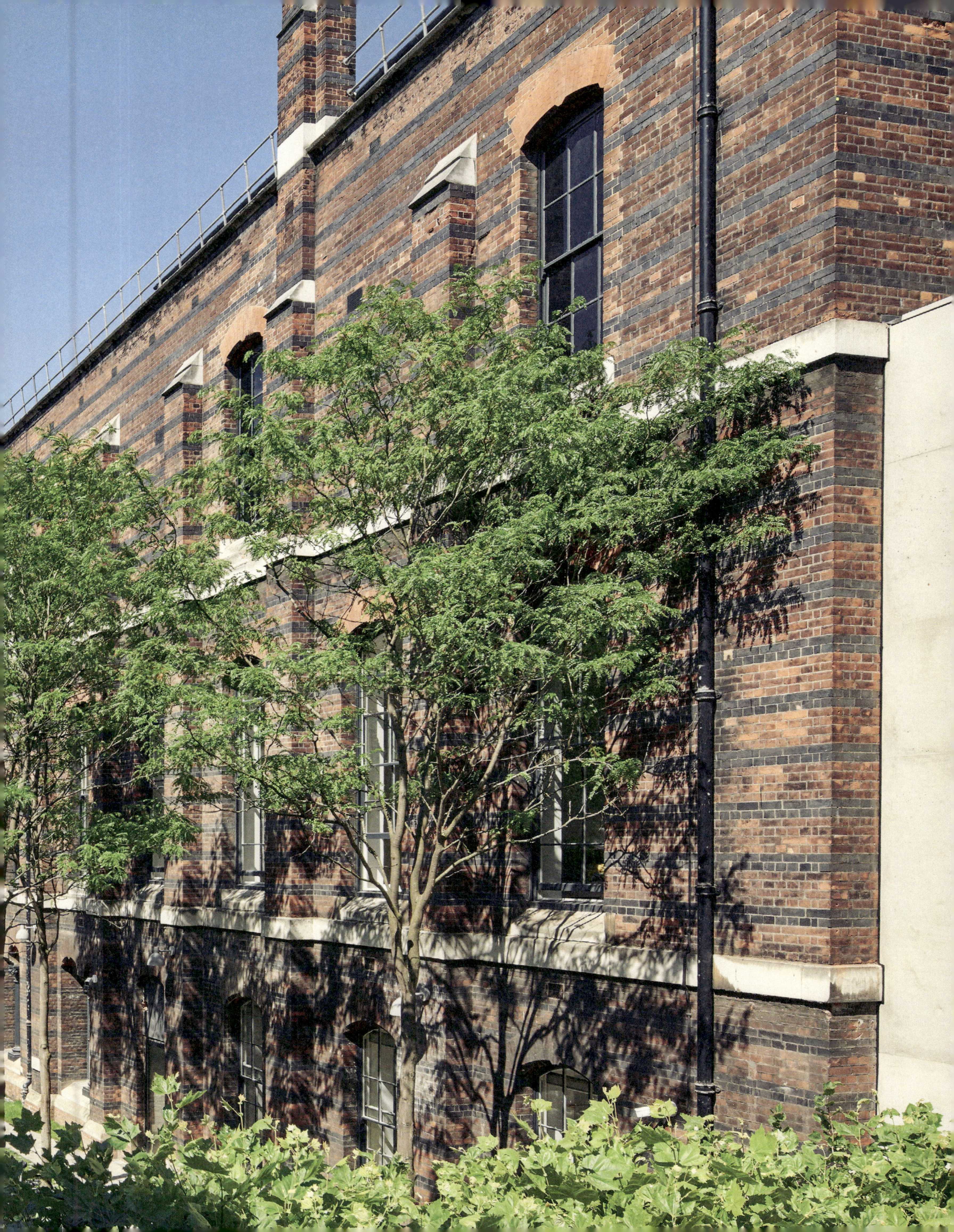

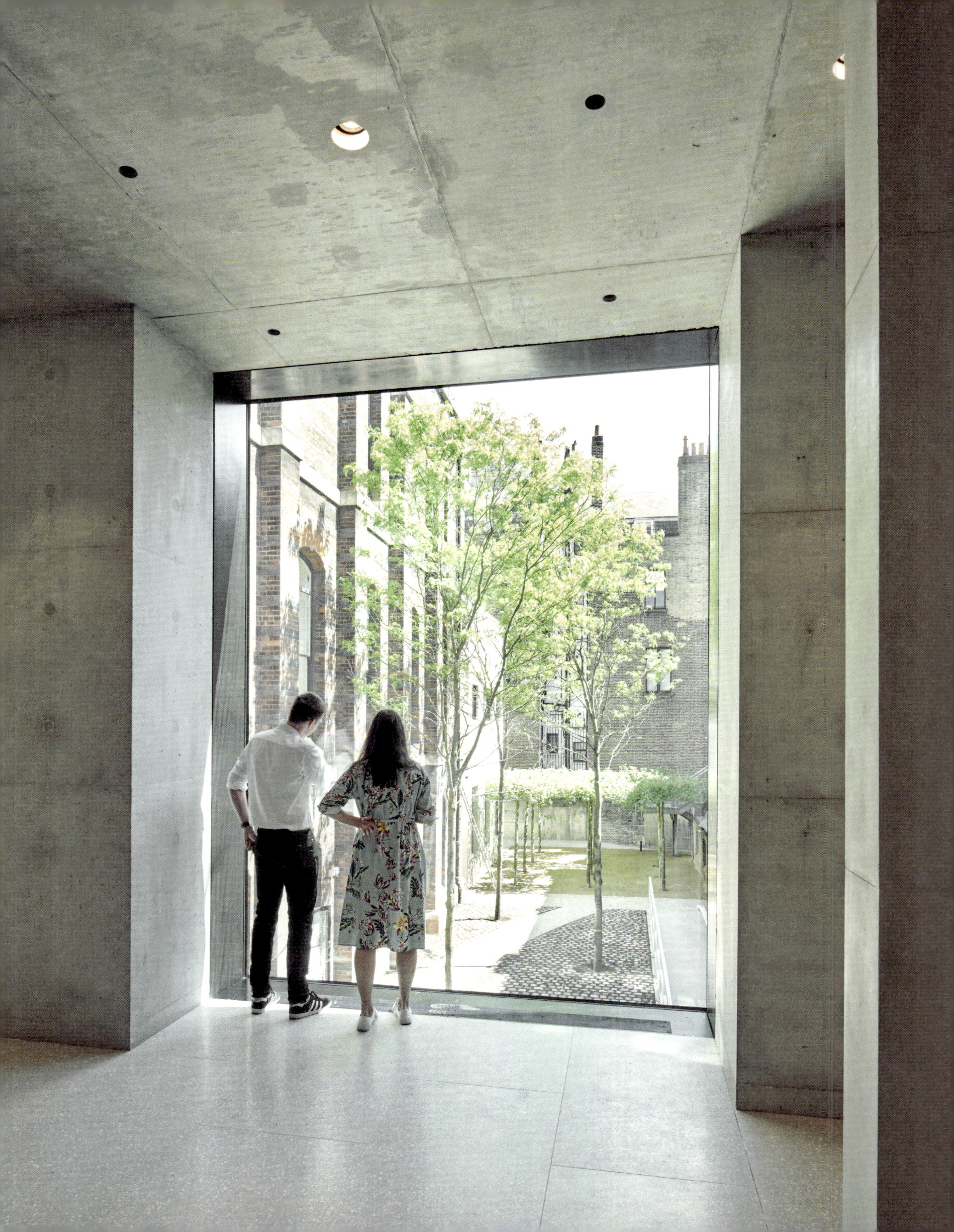

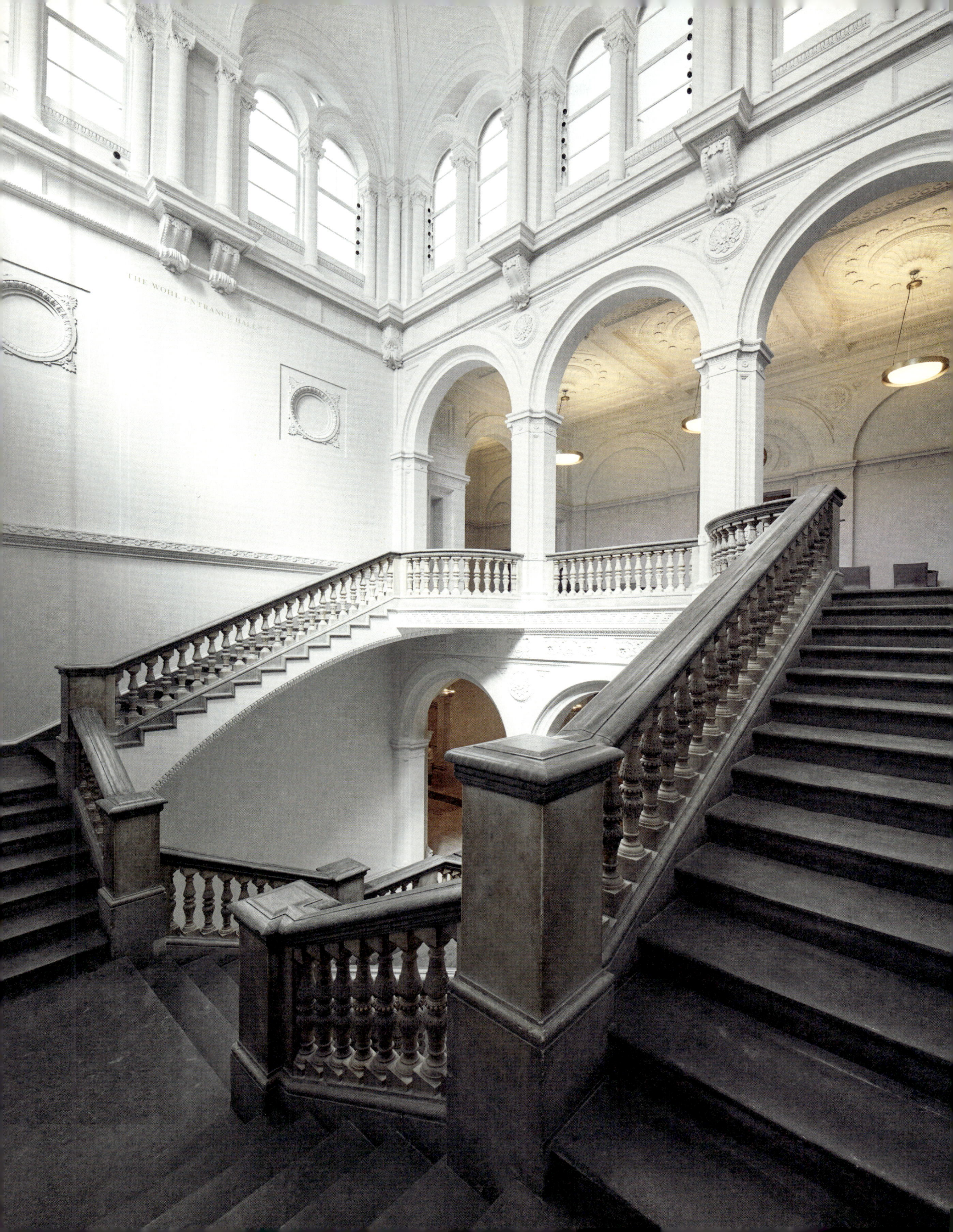
THE WOHL ENTRANCE HALL

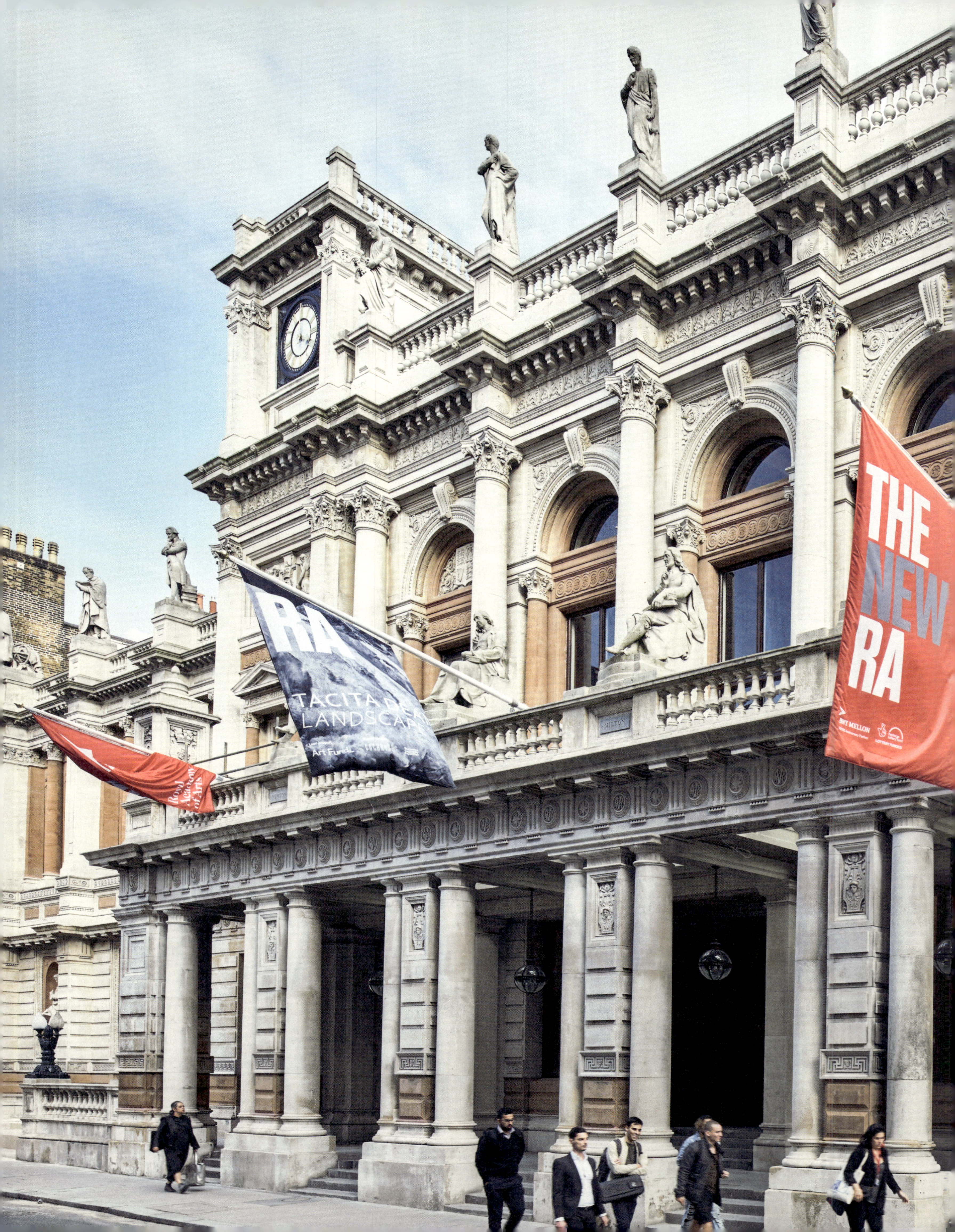
THE
NEW
RA
BNY MELLON
RA
Art Fund
MILTON

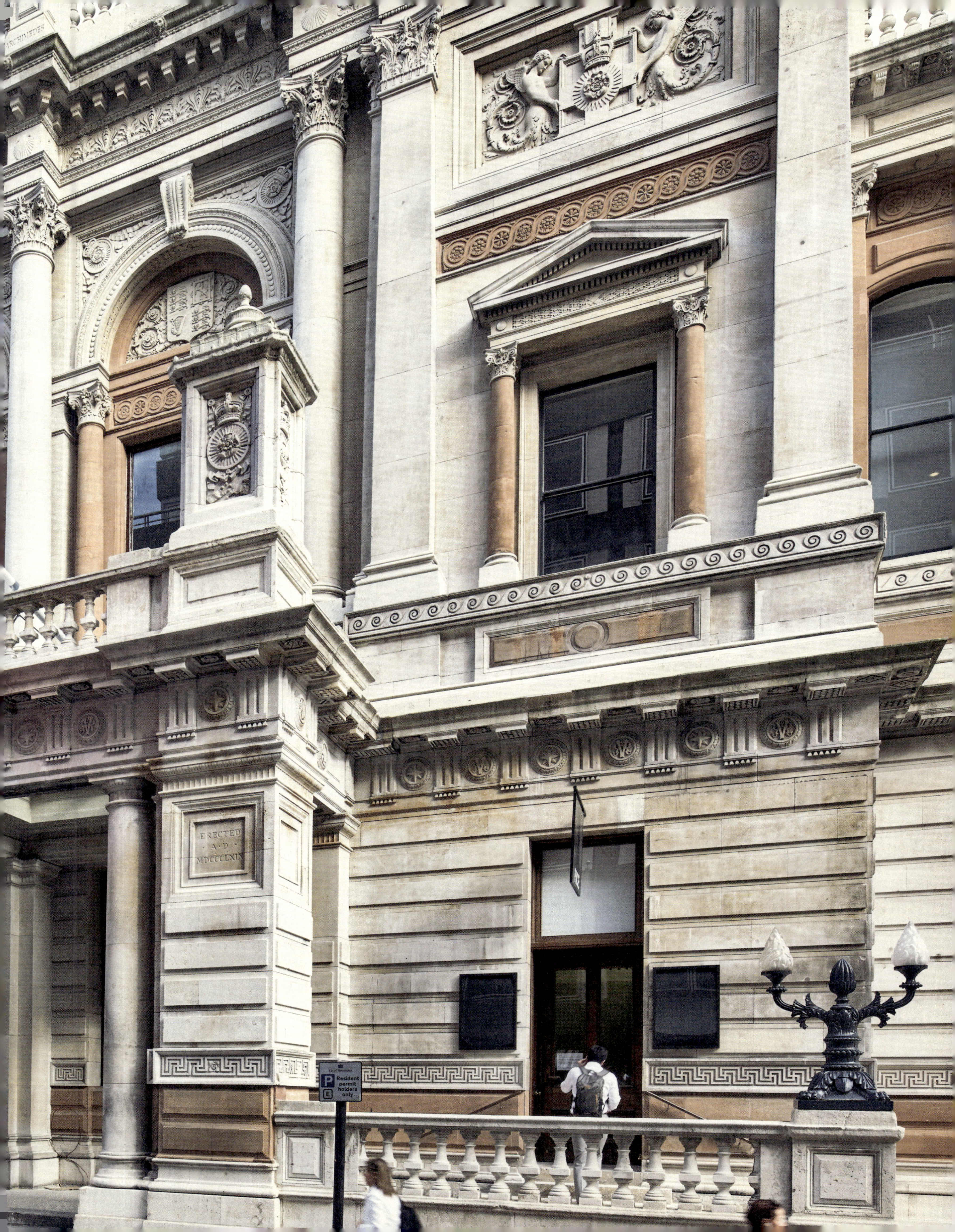
ERECTED
A·D
MDCCCLXIX
Resident permit holders only

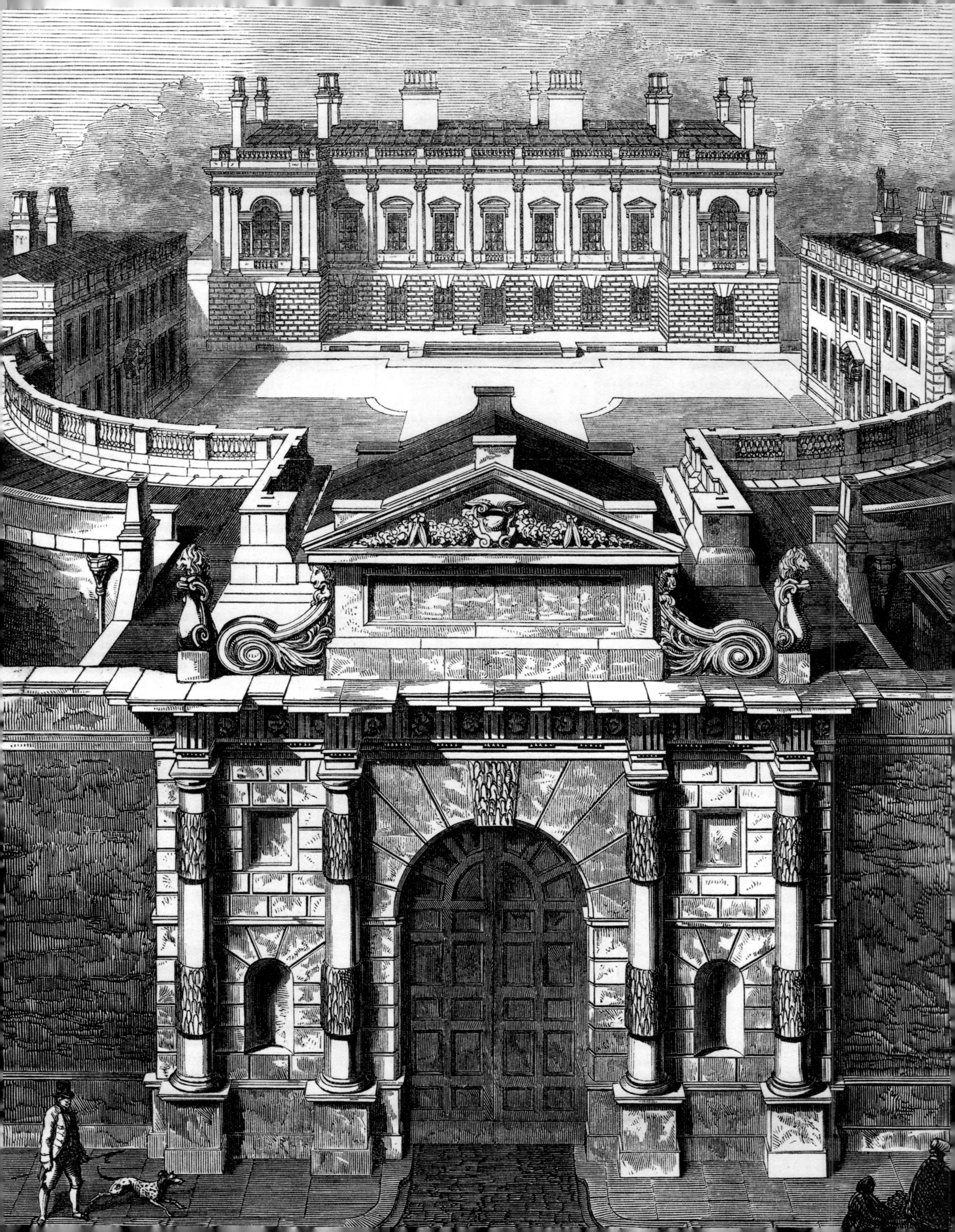

BURLINGTON HOUSE
HOME OF THE ROYAL ACADEMY OF ARTS

Nicholas Savage

ROYAL ACADEMY OF ARTS

The Royal Academy is grateful to The Pollen Estate for its generous support, which has assisted with this book's photographic costs.

THE POLLEN ESTATE
EAST MAYFAIR

Royal Academy Publications
PUBLISHER Nick Tite
EDITORIAL DIRECTOR Peter Sawbridge
PRODUCTION MANAGER Carola Krueger
PRODUCTION CO-ORDINATOR Florence Dassonville

PROJECT EDITOR Tom Neville
PICTURE RESEARCH Sara Ayad
INDEX Hilary Bird
DESIGN Philip Lewis
COLOUR ORIGINATION Gomer Press

Printed in Wales by Gomer Press

British Library Cataloguing-in-Publication Data
A catalogue record for this book is available from the British Library

ISBN 978-1-910350-80-5

Distributed outside the United States and Canada by ACC Publishing Group, Sandy Lane, Old Martlesham, Woodbridge, Suffolk IP12 4SD

Distributed in the United States and Canada by ARTBOOK | D.A.P., 155 Sixth Avenue, New York NY 10013

CHAPTER OPENINGS
Pages 20–21: detail of Fig. 11
Pages 40–41: detail of Fig. 45
Pages 74–75: detail of Fig. 141
Page 142–143: detail of Fig. 205
Page 212–213: detail of Fig. 277

IMAGES
Pages 2–3: the south front of Burlington House viewed from Piccadilly.
Pages 4–5: Gallery III during the 2015 exhibition 'Ai Weiwei': on the floor, the artist's *Straight*, 2008–12; on the side walls, his *Names of the Student Earthquake Victims Found by the Citizens' Investigation*, 2008–11; and, on the end wall, his *Sichuan Earthquake Photographs*, 2008.
Page 6: the vaults beneath the Main Galleries, restored by Sir David Chipperfield in 2018, are lined with historic casts from the Royal Academy Schools.
Page 7: the staircase that rises through the Weston Bridge, designed by Sir David Chipperfield and completed in 2018.
Pages 8–9: the exterior of the Weston Bridge, linking Burlington House, on the left, to Burlington Gardens. The daylit studios of the Royal Academy Schools can be seen in the foreground, with the Lovelace Courtyard to their right, adjoining Burlington Gardens.
Page 10: looking out onto the Lovelace Courtyard from the Weston Bridge.
Page 11: Sir James Pennethorne's nineteenth-century staircase in the Wohl Entrance Hall.
Pages 12–13: the north front of Burlington Gardens, designed by Sir James Pennethorne in 1868–70 and restored by the Royal Academy in 2018.
Page 14: Charles William Sheeres, after B. Sly, View into the courtyard of Burlington House from the house opposite, 1854 (detail), from *The Builder*, 28 October 1854, vol. XII, no. 612, p. 559. RIBA Collections
Pages 16–17: Soane office, Burlington House, south front and offices, RA Lecture drawing, 1811 (detail). Sir John Soane's Museum, London, 17/4/8

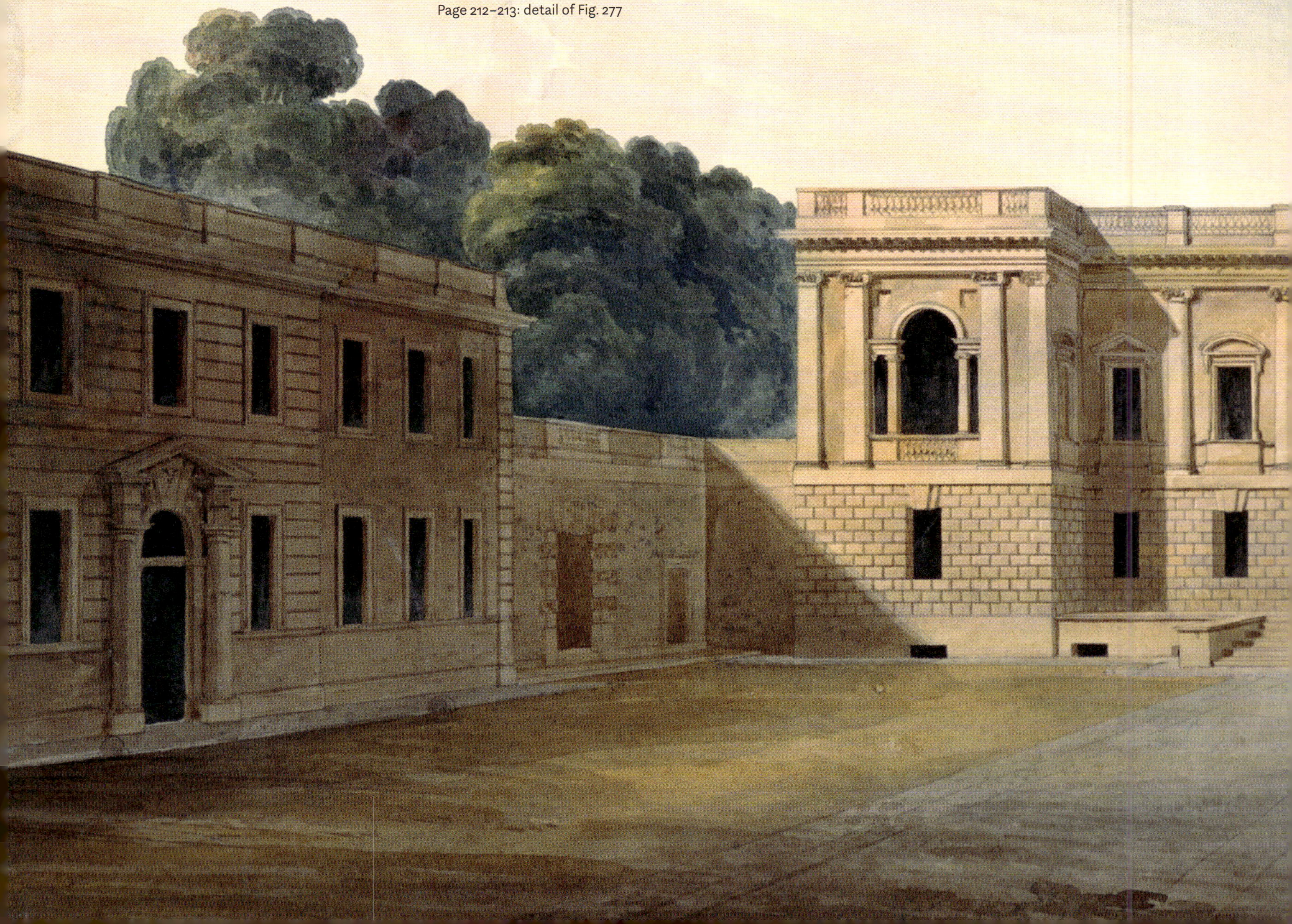

CONTENTS

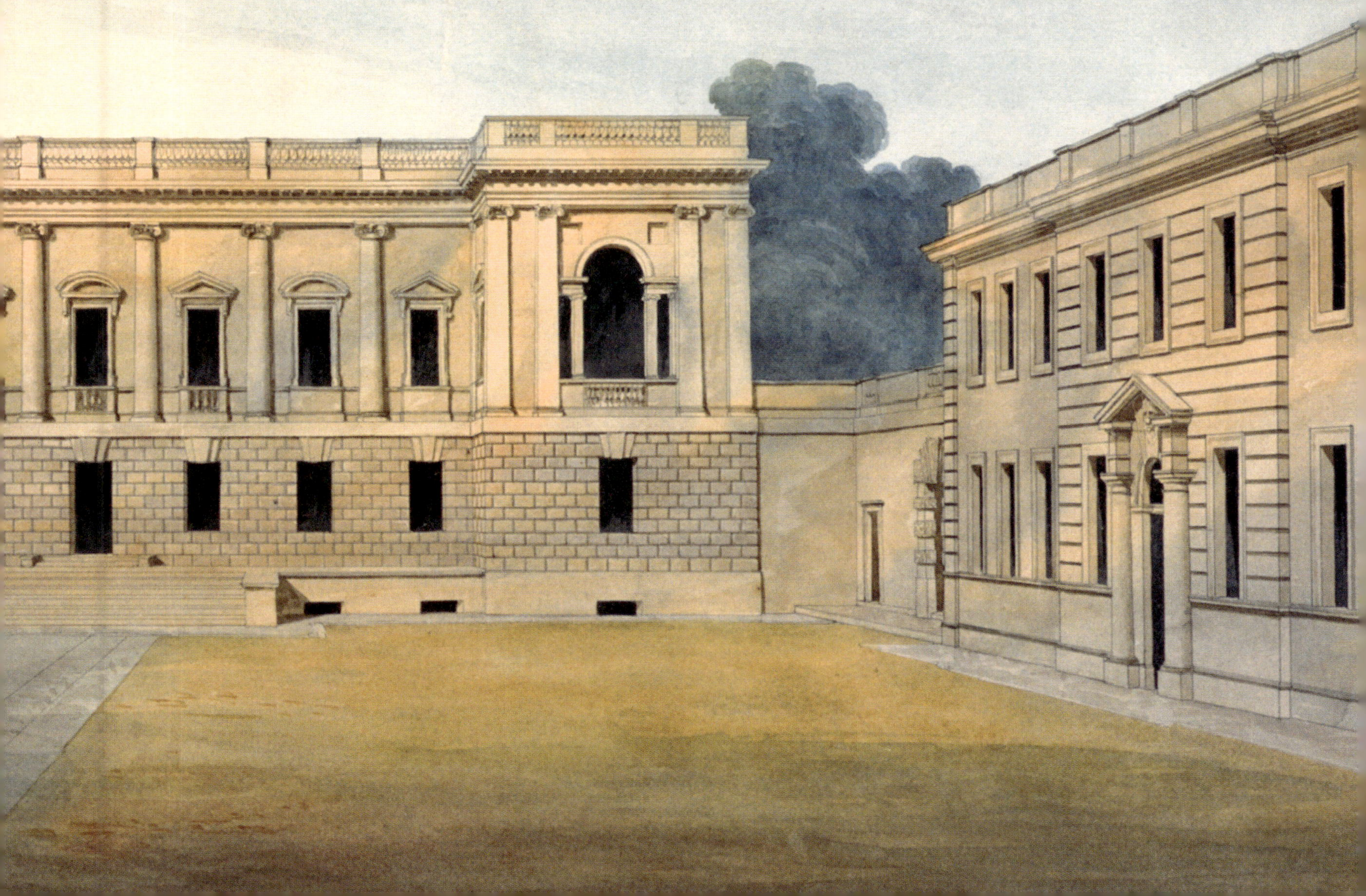

PREFACE

LORD BURLINGTON'S HOUSE on Piccadilly is the last seventeenth-century aristocratic mansion of its kind left in London. Why it should have survived for 350 years when every other private town house of the period fronted by a *cour d'honneur* has long since disappeared is not an easy question to answer. The criteria upon which its present-day Grade II* listing is based certainly did not figure in William Gladstone's thinking when he advocated the purchase of its three-and-a-half-acre site 'for the public service' in 1854, since he was in no doubt then that 'it would be impossible to retain the mansion as it stood.' In the century before that there was scarcely a moment when it would not have made more financial sense to demolish it and lay out new streets on its site linking the Burlington-Cavendish estate to the north with Piccadilly and St James's to the south – a town-planning improvement publicly mooted as early as 1766. Indeed, so often did the fate of the house hang by a thread, its survival in any form seems little short of miraculous.

From the very beginning powerful *genii loci* have watched over the gently sloping 10-acre meadow known as Stone Conduit Close, from which fresh spring water had been piped to the royal palace of Whitehall since Henry VIII's time. Burlington House itself might never have been built in such a *locus amoenus* had the court favourites to whom Charles II granted the freehold of this Crown land pursued their original idea to build an enclave of ten or twelve grand terrace houses to rival those currently being built close-by in St James's Fields – an unrealised property-developer's dream that has haunted the site ever since. But for quotidian mishaps of insanity, insolvency, war, pestilence, adultery, and possible murder by poison, the subject of this book might well have been Denham rather than Burlington House. Likewise, had Charles Boyle, the 2nd Earl of Burlington, not recommended in his will that his widow, the Countess Juliana, keep in her employ Richard Graham, a noted art connoisseur and the son of his grandfather's most trusted agent, his nine-year-old heir – the celebrated 'Architect-Earl' – is unlikely to have grown up in a house decorated by three of the most celebrated Venetian painters in Europe. Without such spectacular paintings on its walls, Burlington House would have not inspired the panegyrics of poets of the calibre of John Gay and Alexander Pope, Handel would have not composed *Silla*, *Teseo* or *Amadis of Gaul* under its hospitable roof, and half a century later Horace Walpole would not have remembered looking outside his bedroom window one morning to find a fairytale vision of its famous colonnade 'rais'd by genii in a night's time'.

Contingencies of this kind suggest the guiding hand of providence but in reality, of course, the history of Burlington House has been shaped by the hopes and dreams of the people who have owned and used it. Beginning with the poet Sir John Denham's impossible dream of finding there the 'happinesse of sweete retir'd content / … at once secure, and innocent', and the 1st Earl of Burlington's pious injunction that his heirs should not 'intermeddle' with his house in any way, its architectural history can only be understood in the light of the motives of those who have been able to decide to alter it, or not, as the case may be. Far from being a matter of chance therefore, its fate has been determined by such specific human factors as the widowed Countess of Burlington's determination to protect and promote her son's inheritance; the 3rd Earl's momentous rediscovery of the principles of ancient classical architecture in the drawings of Palladio and Inigo Jones; the Duke of Portland's tightrope political career at the head of the Whig opposition and final apostasy as a turncoat Tory Prime Minister; the 5th Duke of Devonshire's filial attachment to his mother's ancestral London house; Lord George Cavendish's deeply poisonous relationship with his eldest surviving son; a progressive Tory administration's short-lived hopes of uniting a gamut of academic, scientific and artistic institutions on the site; the twice-defeated attempt to use it instead to build a new, much larger National Gallery; the University of London's embarrassment at having to resort to a corrugated-iron shed in the garden to conduct its exams; the 'vacillation, uncertainty, costliness, extravagance, meanness, and all the conflicting vices' with which Gladstone in opposition excoriated the Office of Works over its mishandling of the site; and last, but not least, Sir Francis Grant's brass-necked campaign to secure it as the Royal Academy's first permanent home in defiance of the wishes of both the Queen and the Prime Minister.

It is due to frustrations and imperatives such as these, arising out of specific situations, that Burlington House has survived in the way it has. It is perhaps only in the 'biography' of a building of this kind that it is possible to grasp what it is that drives architectural history at grass-roots level, rather than as a reflection of abstract social, economic and political forces, aesthetic movements, or phases in an architect's career. However, this book is an account of the Burlington House site, and consequently is concerned with the lives of the families and institutions for whom it has provided or still provides a home only insofar as these have materially affected the site's architectural history.

Although this is the first monograph on Burlington House, it stands on the shoulders of P. A. Bezodis and Walter Ison's anonymous chapter in the St James's Piccadilly volume of the *Survey of London*, which more than fifty years ago set the gold standard for all subsequent attempts to tackle the subject. While differences in approach and emphasis are to be expected, the extent to which I have relied on their meticulously researched foundations will be abundantly evident. Insofar as more facts have come to light since then, this is largely thanks to the research of Richard Hewlings, who was the first to point out that the 3rd Earl by no means abandoned his Piccadilly residence for Chiswick after 1733; of Tim Knox, who was the first to unearth the documentary evidence for the 3rd Duke of Portland's extensive alterations; and of Neil Bingham, who was the first to catalogue properly the drawings relating to Burlington House held at the Royal Academy, including the important collection of drawings by Samuel Ware deposited on indefinite loan by Lord Chesham in 1956. For pointing me towards additional sources and resolving difficulties of interpretation, I am also much indebted to Ian Blackburn, David Blissett, Ian Bristow, John Harris, Nick Hill, David McKinstry, Philip Pearce, Joanna Price, Andrew Saint, and Peter Schmitt.

I would like to thank Lady Chesham for kindly allowing me to consult and quote from the original building accounts for Ware's work at Burlington House, as well as from Charles Compton Cavendish's correspondence with his agent relating to its sale and other important documents in the Chesham family archive relating to the Cavendish family's period of ownership. Quotations from material held in the Devonshire Manuscripts Collection have been made by kind permission of the Duke of Devonshire and the Chatsworth House Trust. Grateful acknowledgement is also due to the University of Nottingham Manuscripts and Special Collections, the University of London Senate House Library, and the libraries of the Royal Society of London, the Geological Society of London, the Linnean Society, the Society of Antiquaries, the British Academy, and the Royal Academy of Arts. For practical help in accessing archival material held in their collections I am grateful to James Towe and Aidan Haley at Chatsworth; Caroline Lam, archivist of the Geological Society; Liz McGow, archivist of the Linnean Society; Keith Moore, head of Library and Information Services at the Royal Society; Karen Syrett, archivist and librarian of the British Academy; Heather Rowland, head of Library and Collections at the Society of Antiquaries; and Charles Harrowell, Special Collections administrator, and Richard Temple, archivist of the Senate House Library. This book could not have been written or as handsomely illustrated without the unfailing help of my former colleagues in the Collections and Library of the Royal Academy, in particular the librarian Adam Waterton, the information assistants Andrew Potter and Karine Sarant-Hawkins, the archivist Mark Pomeroy, the collections manager Morgan Feely, the senior curator Helen Valentine, and the picture librarians Laura Valentine, Jennifer Camilleri, Trine Lyngby-Trow and Milena Harrison-Gray.

This book has been the brainchild of Peter Sawbridge, editorial director of Royal Academy Publications, who suggested that I might like to write it without knowing that it was something I had thought I might do one day when I started work at the Academy more than thirty years ago.

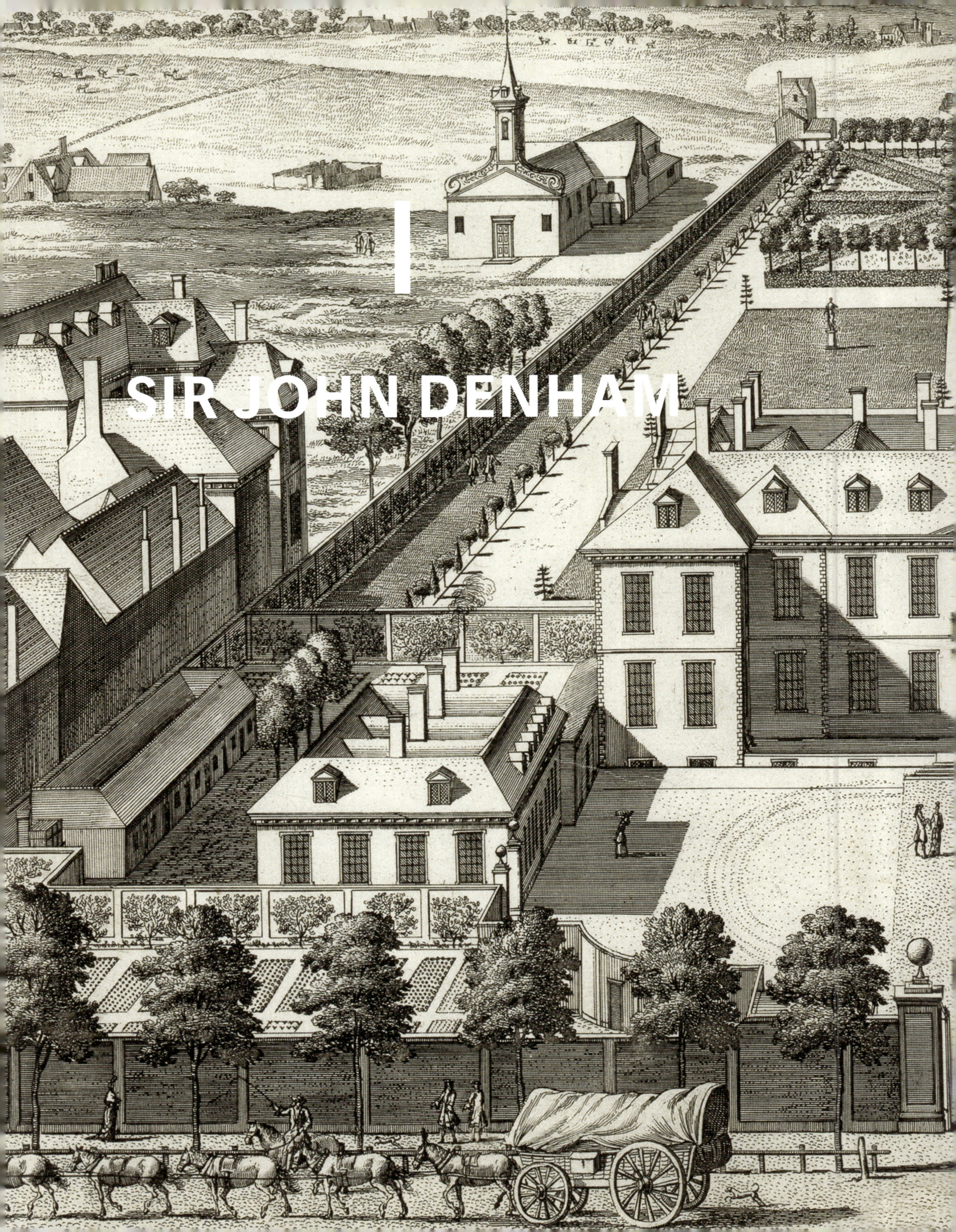

I

SIR JOHN DENHAM

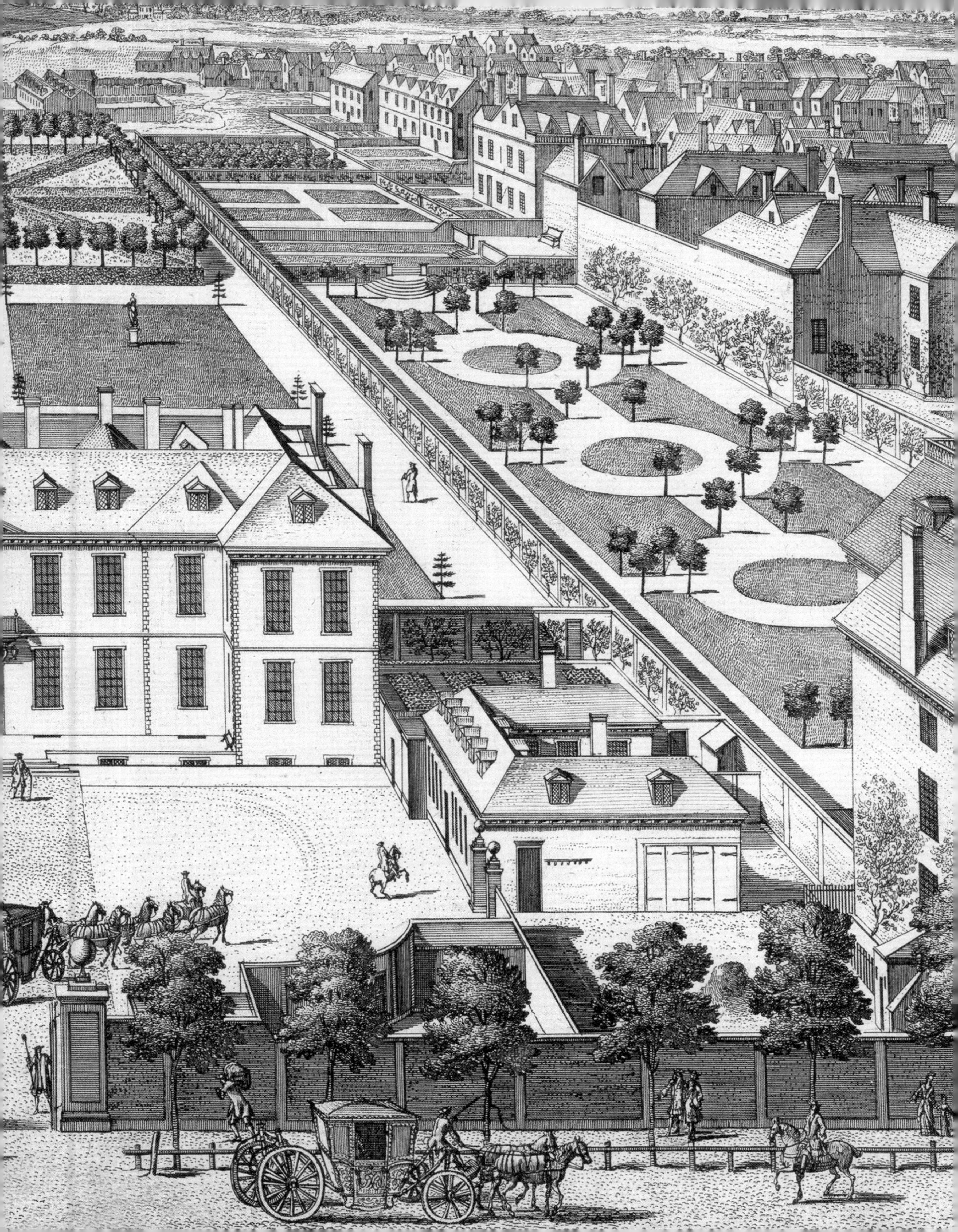

'... the dreamingst young fellow'.
JOSIAS HOWE[1]

ALMOST FROM THE MOMENT HE BEGAN TO BUILD a house on Piccadilly to the day he sold it, Sir John Denham's life was marked by tragedy. His troubles stemmed not so much from the problems that can afflict all building projects – bad weather, shortage of materials, ballooning costs, unreliable workmen – but rather from his rash marriage to a beautiful and flirtatious young woman half his age. Whatever Denham may have at first envisaged doing with his new house, by the time he married Margaret Brooke on 25 May 1665 there seems little doubt the couple intended to live there in grand style (Figs 1, 2).[2] However, this was not to be, for in the wake of a severe bout of insanity between April and August 1666, and the scandal of his wife's flagrant appearance at court that summer as the Duke of York's latest mistress, the final blow – her death on 6 January 1667 from what she claimed was a cup of poisoned chocolate – was followed twelve days later by Denham's sale of his unfinished house and its three-and-half-acre plot to Richard Boyle, 1st Earl of Burlington.[3]

Given such a classic tale of hubris it is hardly surprising that the generally accepted moral is that it reveals the vanity of a middle-aged man who embarks at one and the same time on a doomed second marriage and a house he can't afford to build. That Denham overstretched his means is certainly evident from the fact that six of the building tradesmen he employed on the house lodged a petition in the Court of Chancery in February 1671, some two years after his death, seeking arrears of £707 from his estate in payment for the work they had carried out 'in or about 1666'. The petitioners claimed that, on being 'much pressed and importuned', Denham 'did att length acquaint your Orators that he would sell the said house and Land with the appurtenances and out of the money which he should raise thereby would pay and satisfie the same.'[4]

However, it needs to be stressed that Denham was no novice builder forced to quit when the stakes got too high, but the Surveyor General of the King's Works, and as such a key player in the post-Restoration metropolitan building world. Nor was building his Piccadilly house the only time that he took advantage of the priority of access to building materials, skilled labour and credit terms that his post afforded. The eponymous 'Sir John Denham's Buildings' in Middle Scotland Yard, a three-storey range of brick lodgings built in the manner of barristers' chambers on land adjacent to the Surveyor General's official residence in the precincts of Whitehall Palace, had already shown how profitable such ventures could be. Erected at Denham's own expense, on a site leased from the King on 3 March 1661 at a ground rent of £5 per annum, a year's rental income from this one building could almost triple his salary as Surveyor General.[5] Moreover, as the administrative head of the Office of Works, Denham was responsible for the care of all royal buildings, and consequently ideally placed to promote both his own interests and those of the Crown in this way. Before we attribute the fate of Denham's house on Piccadilly solely to his private misfortunes therefore, it would be worth examining the circumstances that led him to build it where he did, and considering what other factors are likely to have influenced the course of events during his ownership of the site.

The earliest record we have of Denham's new house is an entry in Samuel Pepys's diary dated 20 February 1665:

> ... Rode into the beginning of my Lord Chancellor's new house, near St. James's: which the common people have already called Dunkirke-house, from their opinion of his having a good bribe for the selling of that towne. And very noble I believe it will be. Near that is my Lord Barkeley beginning another on one side, and Sir J. Denham on the other.[6]

These three neighbouring mansions were set in 30 acres of gently sloping arable land on the north side of 'Portugal Street', as this stretch of Piccadilly was then called in honour of the queen consort, Catherine of Braganza (Fig. 3). Comprising three fields, known locally as Stone Conduit Close, Penniless Bank and Stone Bridge Field, this was farmland that had been Crown property since its purchase by Henry VIII in 1536 as part of a strategy for piping uncontaminated spring water to his new palace at Whitehall.[7] On 23 August 1664, some six months before Pepys's visit, Charles II had granted all this land in fee to 'my Lord Chancellor' (i.e. Edward Hyde, 1st Earl of Clarendon) and his son

Fig. 1
William Dobson, *Portrait of an Old and a Younger Man* (John Taylor and John Denham), 1640–45.
The Courtauld Gallery, London

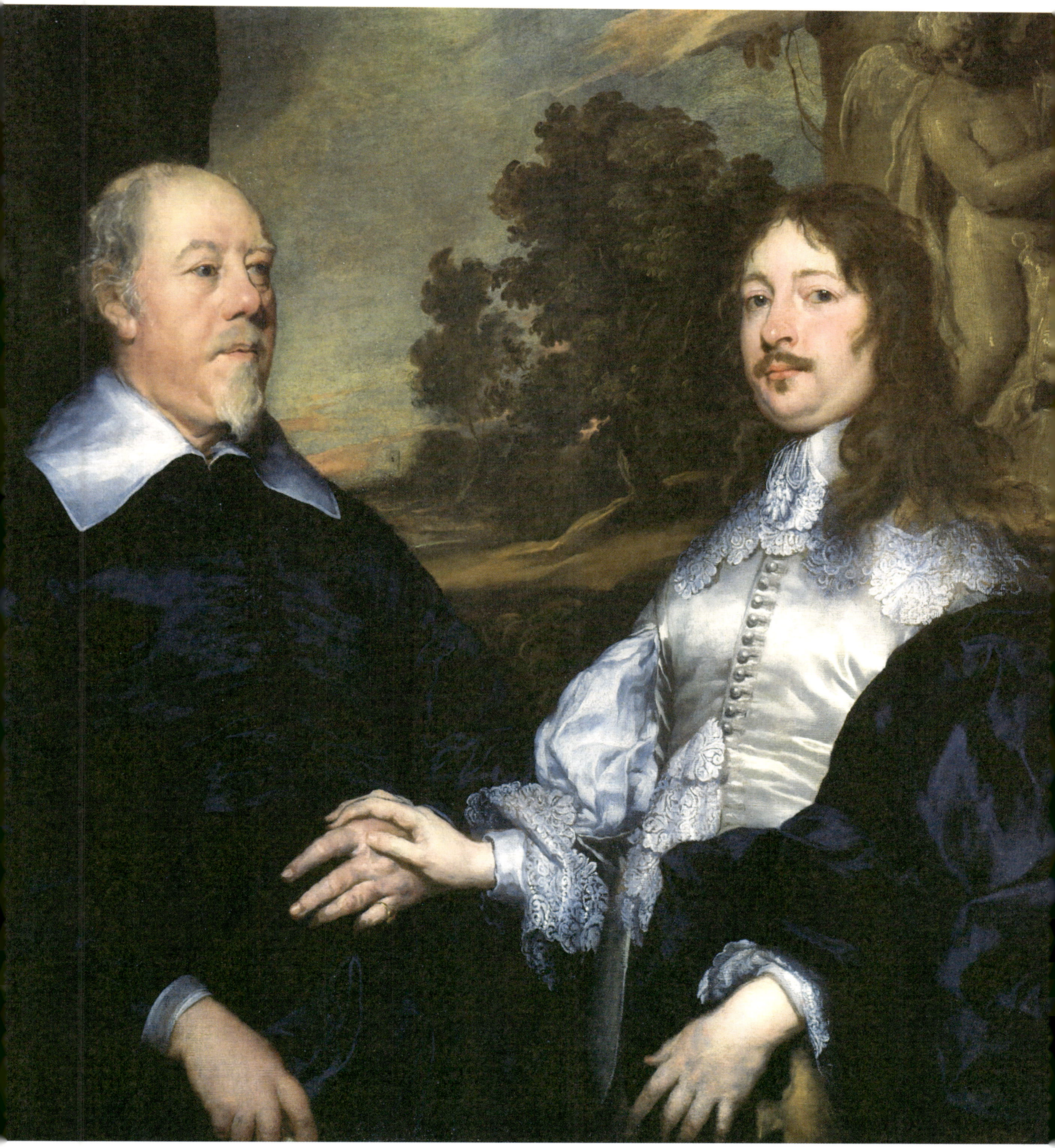

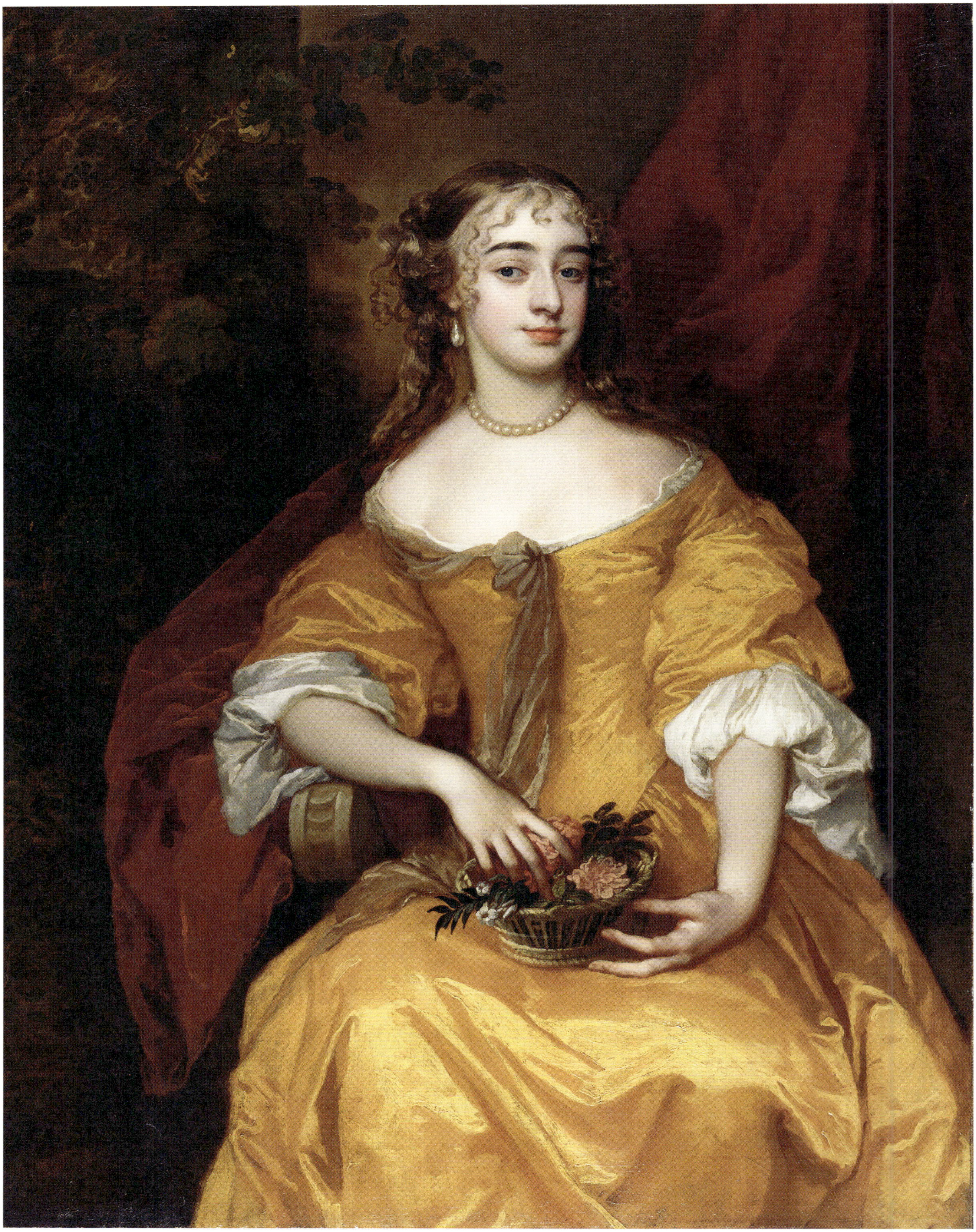

Fig. 2
Sir Peter Lely, *Margaret, Lady Denham*, c. 1664–65.
Royal Collection, Hampton Court Palace, RCIN 401212

Viscount Cornbury, a transaction that would seem to lend some weight to the cynical opinion of 'the common people' reported by Pepys.[8] Despite this gossip, which was to grow more virulent as building work progressed, Pepys could well have taken comfort, as its embattled owner was destined never to do, from the fact that, bribe or no bribe, Clarendon House turned out to be not only 'very noble' but also, in the words of a leading architectural historian, 'one of the most influential buildings in the history of English domestic architecture' (Fig. 4).[9]

From the perspective of any sensible plan for the growth of the city, however, the simultaneous building of Clarendon House and its westerly neighbour Berkeley House (Fig. 5), each with its own spacious forecourt on Piccadilly and six or seven acres of garden behind, was little more than ribbon development on a grand scale in an area of prime land at the edge of the city that had been a hot spot of illegal and haphazard new building for well over fifty years. Until now the main culprits had been the somewhat disreputable owners of a shop-cum-lodging house in Great Windmill Street, a large isolated building which the locals had nicknamed 'Pickadilly Hall' because it was then 'the outmost or skirt house of the Suburbs that way' and Robert Baker, the man who

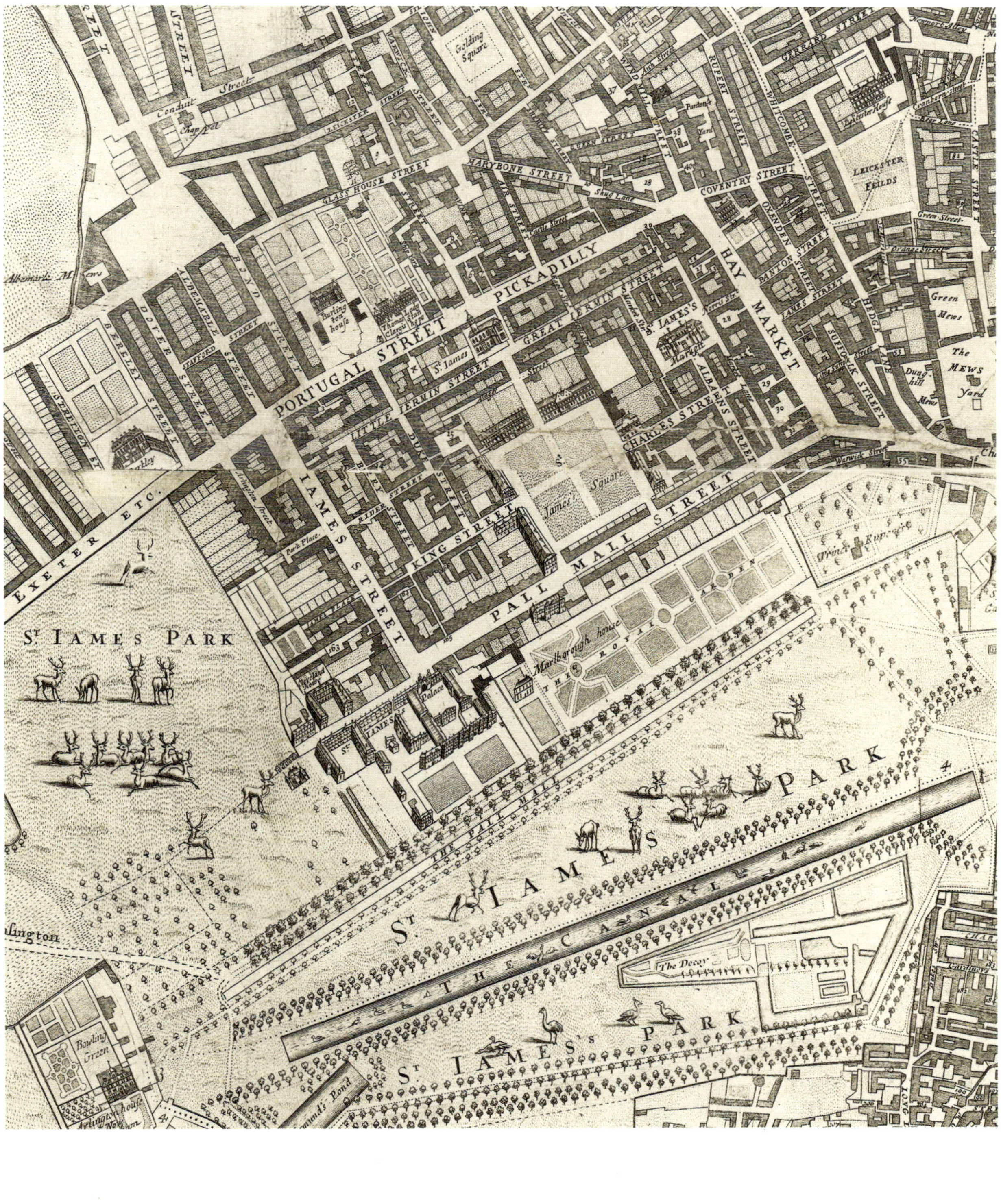

Fig. 3
Piccadilly, St James's Park and the surrounding district, from a map by William Morgan, 1681.
British Library, London, Maps Crace Port. 2.60

Fig. 4
William Skillman, after Johann Spilberg II, *Prospect of the Famous House of the Illustrious Duke of Albemarle* (formerly Clarendon House), published in 1724.
Government Art Collection

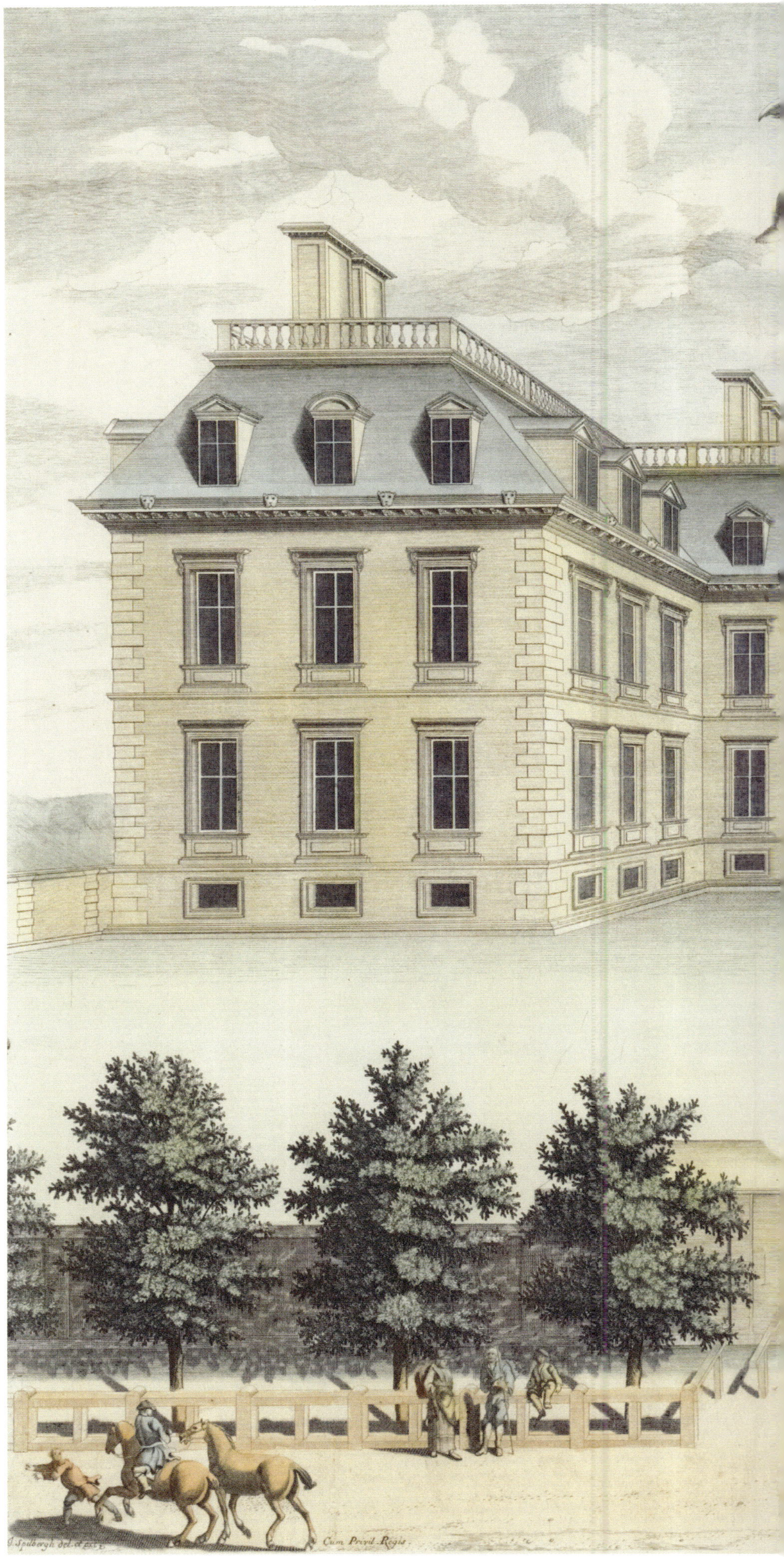

originally built it in about 1611–12, happened to have been a tailor who had made his fortune from selling fringes for outer garments called 'piccadillies'.[10] As grandee newcomers, Clarendon and his fellow Privy Councillor Lord John Berkeley of Stratton seem to have had no interest in the future development of the neighbourhood beyond the obvious one of keeping it at a suitable distance from their door. Although it is true that Clarendon's architect, Sir Roger Pratt, stipulated that 'the middle point of the house is to be put exactly to the middle of St James' Street,' and 'be set in a right angle to the street, and also parallel to the court wall before it', this careful alignment was mainly to ensure that 'the two grand stories of the house may below at St James' be perfectly seen' (an unintended symbol of his influence over the King that Clarendon was soon to regret).[11] In fact, the centring of Clarendon House at the top of St James' Street not only blocked the possibility of continuing that street northwards, it also meant that any other street in that direction would have to begin beyond Clarendon's boundary wall to the east and Berkeley's to the west. Some awareness of this consequence may perhaps be deduced from the fact that the royal grant of 23 August was part and parcel with a deed signed the next day conveying the freehold of seven acres of Stone Conduit Close to the east of Clarendon's plot jointly to Sir John Denham, the King's Surveyor General, and the former leaseholder of most of the land covered in the grant, Sir William Pulteney.[12] As 'professionals' rather than grandees, Denham and Pulteney could perhaps have been expected to adopt a more considered approach to urban planning.[13]

Evidence of where such an approach might have led can be found in the agreement that Denham and Pulteney came to five days later on 29 August 1664, in which they divided ownership of their land by the unusual expedient of each taking a 100-foot-wide strip and holding the remainder in common.[14] The key to understanding why they did this lies in the fact that, by a stroke of providence, their plot consisted of a natural square. When therefore, about a month later on 1 October, they obtained a royal licence 'to build 10 or 12 houses, each to cost not less than 1,000 l., on a square of 560 feet

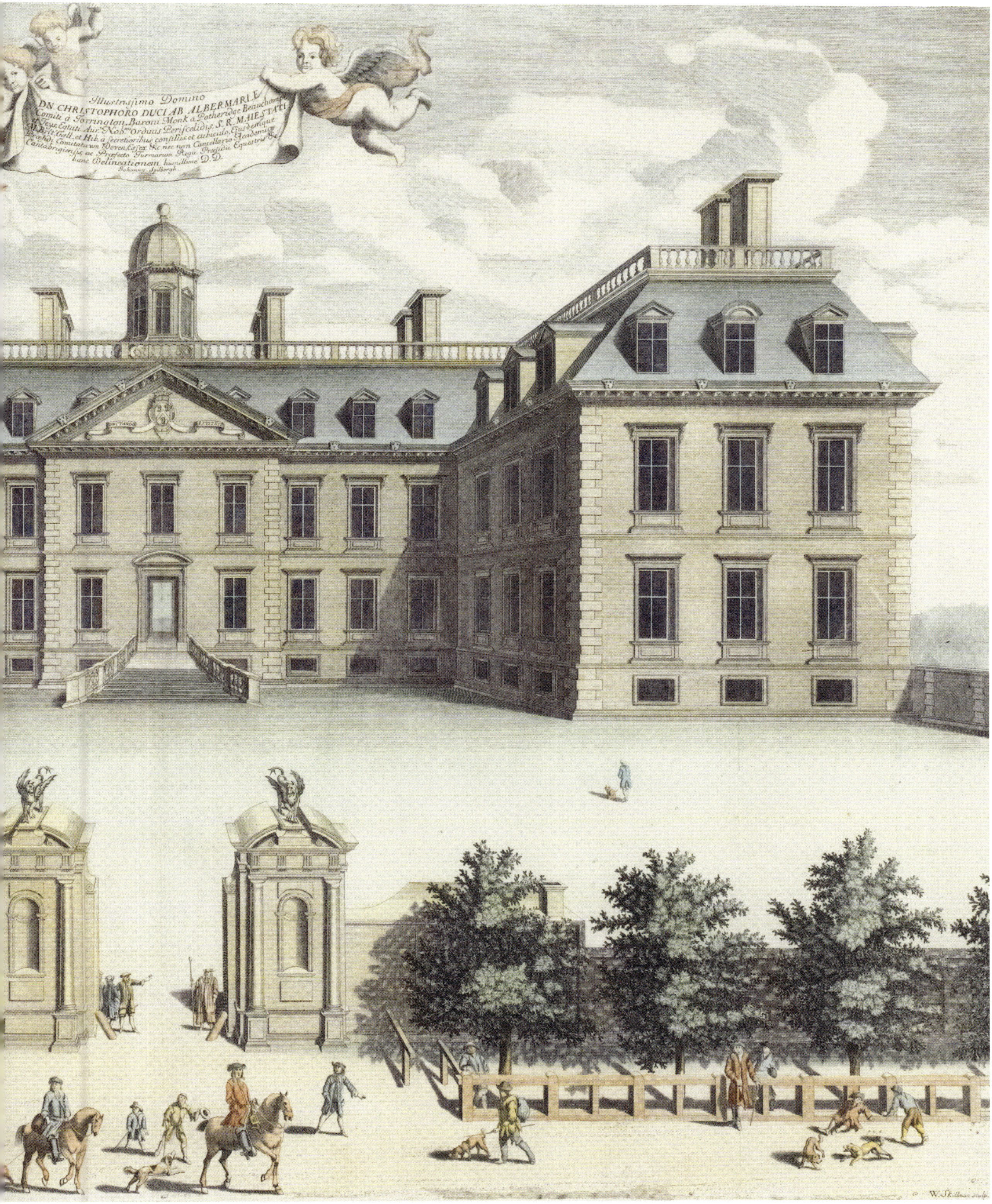
Illustrissimo Domino
DN. CHRISTOPHORO DUCI AB ALBERMARLE
Comiti à Torrington, Baroni Monk a Potheridge Beauchamp
et Teys, Equiti Aur. Nob.mi Ordinis Periscelidis, S.R. MAIESTATI
M. Brit. Gall. et Hib. à secretioribus consiliis et cubiculo, Eiusdemque
Praesidi Comitatuum Deven, Essex &c. nec non Cancellario Academiae
Cantabrigiensis, ac Praefecto Turmarum Regii Praesidii Equestris &c.
hanc Delineationem humillime D.D.
Johannes Spilbergh.
W. Skillman sculp.

Fig. 5
A bird's-eye view of Berkeley House, Piccadilly, 1735–45.
British Museum, London
1880,1113.2026

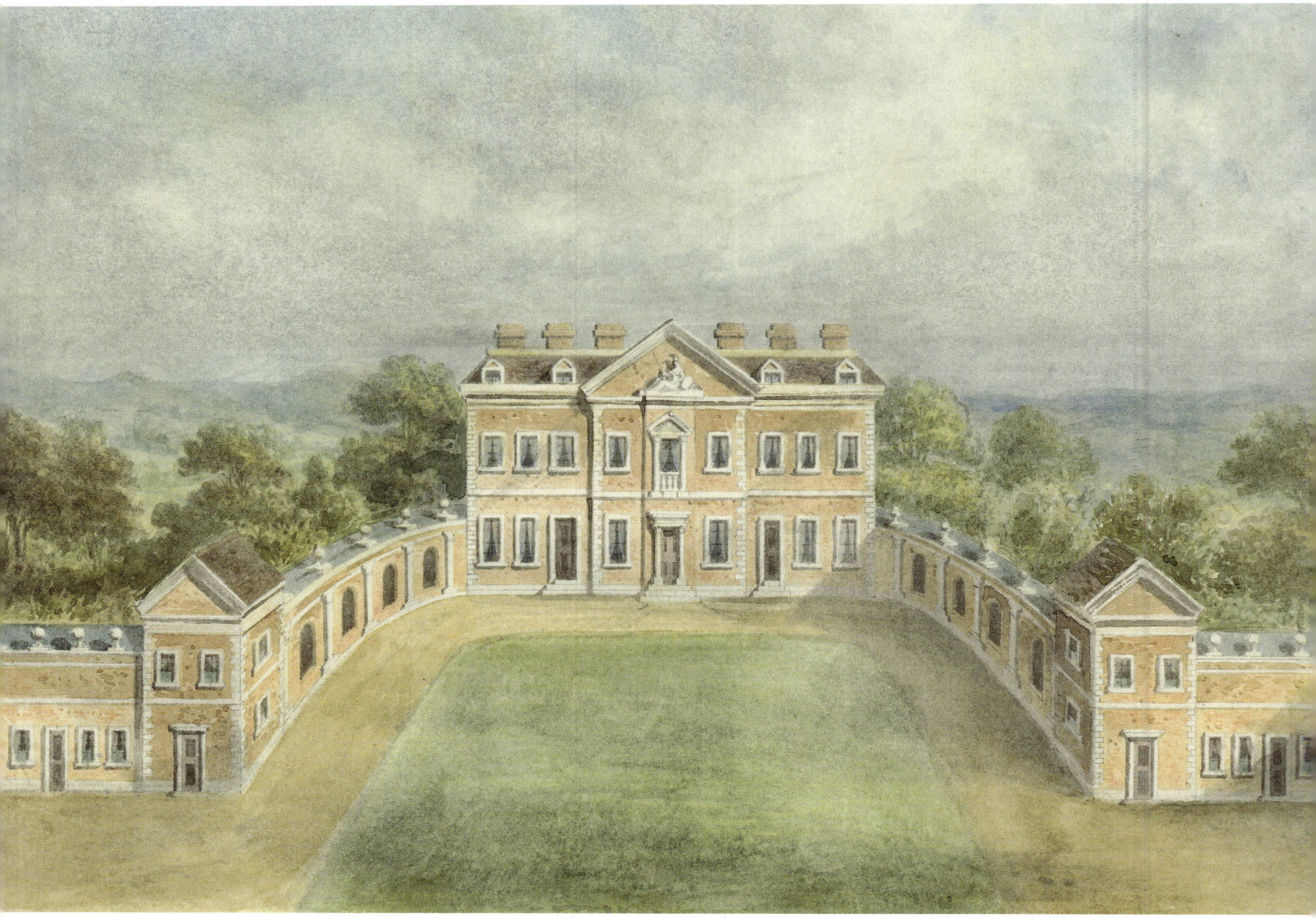

of ground, next the Earl of Clarendon's', there can be little doubt that their intention was to erect two rows of five (or six) large houses facing each other across a communal square bordered by Piccadilly to the south and open fields to the north.[15] It was a vision of *rus in urbe*, inspired by the *locus genii* of a preordained open space, that has haunted the site ever since. It was also exactly the kind of royally sanctioned improvement of the city's suburbs that John Evelyn so ardently hoped to encourage in dedicating his translation of Fréart de Chambray's *Parallel of the Antient Architecture with the Modern* (1664) firstly to Charles II and secondly to 'Sr John Denham … Superintendent and Surveyor of His Majestie's Buildings and Works' (Fig. 6). While by his own admission Evelyn found it 'hard not to slide into the Panegyric', his tribute to Denham 'for the reformation of a thousand deformities in the streets', was perfectly sincere. Despite his private opinion that the Surveyor General was 'a better Poet than Architect',[16] there can be no doubt that Evelyn fully shared Denham's concern to tackle the problems of London's squalid and dangerous streets in a practical way:

> But neither here must I forget what is alone due to you Sir … as by your introducing that incomparable form of Paving, to an incredible advantage of the Publick … which is begun in Holborn … for the saving of Wheels and Carriages, the cure of noysom Gutters, the deobstruction of Encounters, the dispatch of Business, the cleanness of the Way, the beauty of the Object, the ease of the Infirme, and the preserving of both the Mother and the Babe; so many of the fair-Sex and their Off-spring having perish'd by mischances (as I am credibly inform'd) from the ruggedness of the unequal streets, &c. … Sure I am, that more has been done for the Ornament and Benefit of the Publick in two years' time, that your Self, with the Commissioners who undertook the Inspection, have acted, than in five hundred before.[17]

Behind the hyperbole lies Evelyn's genuine belief that the restoration of the monarchy under Charles II, a 'paragon' to 'the great Augustus', heralded a renaissance of the arts and sciences in England, and that to judge from what had

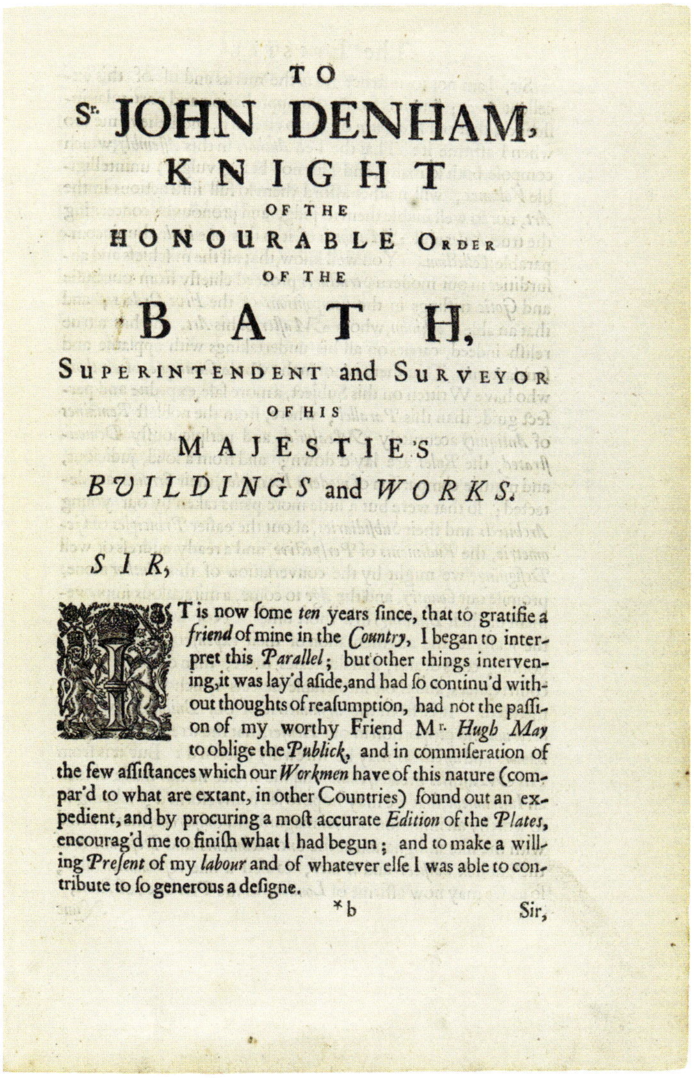

TO
Sr. JOHN DENHAM,
KNIGHT
OF THE
HONOURABLE ORDER
OF THE
BATH,
SUPERINTENDENT and SURVEYOR
OF HIS
MAJESTIE'S
BUILDINGS and *WORKS*.

SIR,

IT is now some *ten* years since, that to gratifie a *friend* of mine in the *Country*, I began to interpret this *Parallel*; but other things intervening, it was lay'd aside, and had so continu'd without thoughts of reasumption, had not the passion of my worthy Friend Mr. *Hugh May* to oblige the *Publick*, and in commiseration of the few assistances which our *Workmen* have of this nature (compar'd to what are extant, in other Countries) found out an expedient, and by procuring a most accurate *Edition* of the *Plates*, encourag'd me to finish what I had begun; and to make a willing *Present* of my *labour* and of whatever else I was able to contribute to so generous a designe.

*b Sir,

Fig. 6
John Evelyn's dedication to Sir John Denham, from Roland Fréart, sieur de Chambray, *A Parallel of the Antient Architecture with the Modern*, 1664.
RIBA Collections, RIBA112301

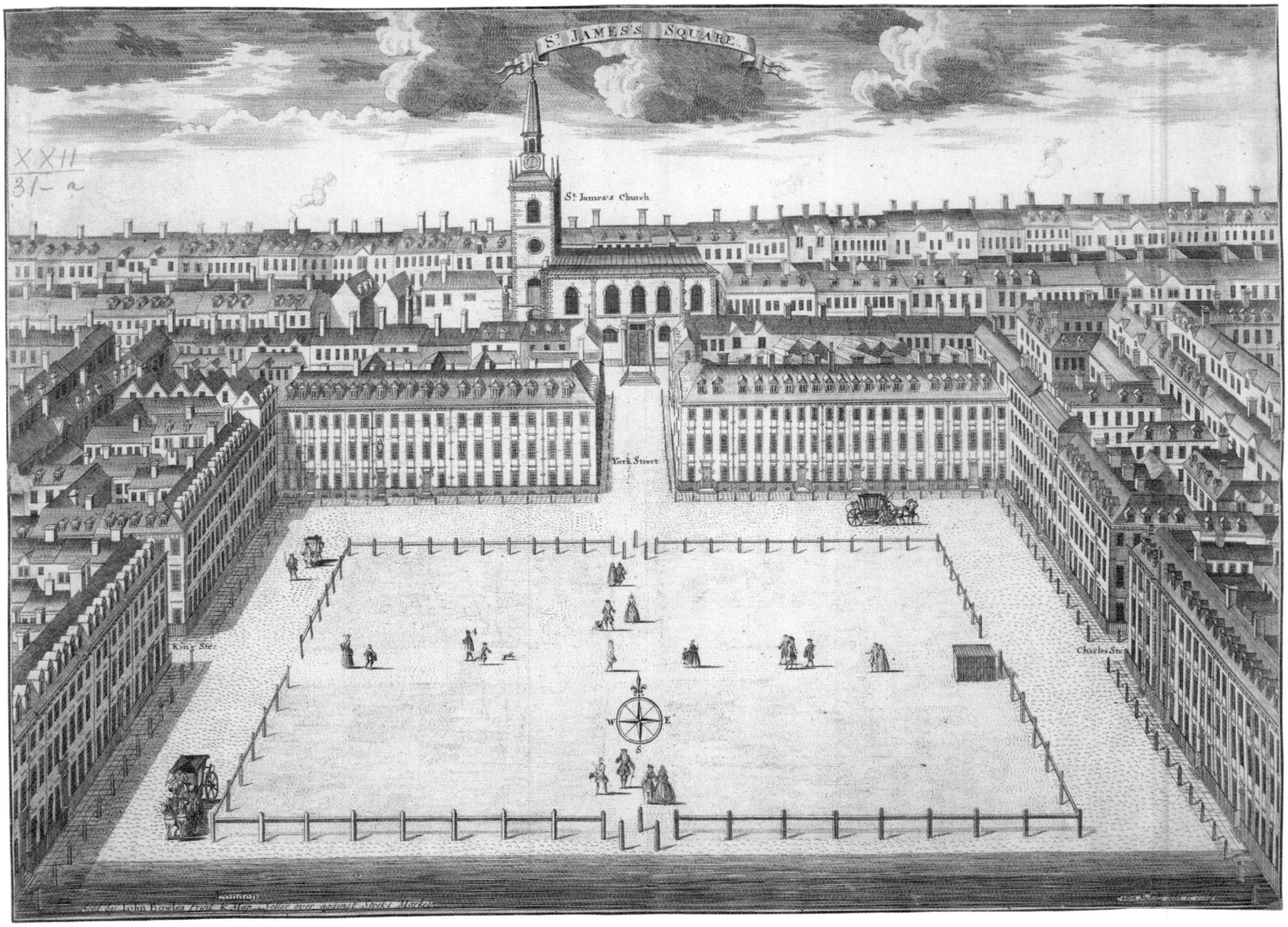

already been done to improve the city, London would soon be worthy of comparison with present-day Paris and even ancient Rome:

> They were not a foolish or impolitick People, who from the very Principles of humanitie, destin'd for the ease of their Subjects, so many spacious Waies, cool Fountains, shady Walks, refreshing Gardens, and places of publick Recreation, as well as stately Temples, and Courts of Justice, that Religion and the Laws might be published with the more pomp and veneration: And if his Majesty, with your pains and industry, hath contributed to something of all this, it is that for which the whole Nation becomes obliged, as the promoting of such publick and useful Works (and especially that of Building) [is] a certain Indication of a prudent Government of a flourishing and happy People.[18]

Although Evelyn could perhaps be alluding here to the building of Greenwich Hospital, the context suggests that he is more probably referring to royal support for the Earl of St Albans's projected square on St James's Field, work on which had started in 1663. This is made all the more likely by the dramatic contrast that he then goes on to draw with other parts of the city's suburbs:

> … how infinitely were it to be wished, that whilst the beautie and benefit of the City is increased in one part, the Deformity and apparent Ruine of it might cease on the other: But this we are to hope for, when, to bring this monstrous Body into shape and scatter these ungovernable enormities, either the restraint of Building irregularly shall polish the Suburbs, or (which I rather could wish) some royal Purchase contract and demolish them.

Evelyn's hope for 'some royal Purchase' to 'scatter these ungovernable enormities' was no mere fantasy but grounded on common knowledge of the influence that the King was currently exerting over the development of St James's Square by virtue of the fact that the land

Fig. 7
Sutton Nicholls, Bird's-eye view of St James's Square, looking towards York Street and St James's Church, with King Street on the left and Charles Street on the right, 1728.
The British Library, London

on which it was being built was leased from the Crown. His preference for this solution, rather than for further ineffectual attempts to legislate against 'Building irregularly', also suggests that he knew of, and would have whole-heartedly supported, the printed petition of the 'Builders in and near St. James's Fields' against a further bill of this kind introduced into the House of Commons in June 1663. Basing their case on the King's personal approval of building in this district – 'his Majesty intending those Places near his Majestie's Pallaces of White-Hall and St. James's for the conveniency of the Nobility and Gentry who were to attend upon his Majestie's Person, and in Parliament, and for the better Ornament of the Place' – the petitioners stated explicitly that they had had 'his Majestie's Officers for the Plotters, Designers and Contrivers of the said Buildings'.[19] There can be little doubt that Evelyn was aware that this current demonstration of the benefits of royal intervention in the design of new buildings in London was due to the fact that St Albans's Crown lease required his assignees to 'frame erect alter take downe new build and sette up' any houses to be built there 'according to such designes and plotts as … his … Majestie his heirs or Successors … and his or their Surveyor Generall shall approve.'[20] What Denham may as a result have contributed personally to the restrained architectural character and generous proportions of St James's Square is unclear, although he was certainly responsible as the King's representative for superintending and approving its overall design and would have been fully aware of its merits in terms of urban planning (Fig. 7).

St James's Square succeeded as a commercial enterprise largely because the Earl of St Albans's well-heeled friends and relations were attracted by the prospect of taking up residence in an elegant enclave of well-constructed town houses 'built more for the Convenience of their opulent and noble Possessors, than for causing Surprize in the Beholders'.[21] As a model for aristocratic city dwelling it offered a sober but commodious alternative to the ostentation and expense of Clarendon's palace, which had incited not merely surprise in the beholder, but vandals to cut down his trees, break his windows, and paint graffiti on his front door.[22] Also, in contrast to the coterie that gathered around St Albans, it was unfortunately the case that neither of the Lord Chancellor's neighbours could count on him as a friend: Denham he had always distrusted, and he had had a longstanding quarrel with Berkeley over the beautiful Anne Villiers, with whom they were both in love.[23] There could be no question therefore of Denham and Pulteney's project eliciting any support from Clarendon, whose first thought had been to build a brick wall on the boundary between their properties.[24]

It should not be assumed that it was merely vanity or a desire to please his new wife that prompted Denham to abandon the idea of a square and build instead a single house on the western half of the site he shared with Pulteney. Rather, it was a decision that made sound business sense in the light of the competition Denham and Pulteney were facing a stone's throw away to the south of Piccadilly, especially once the King had acceded in principle on 23 September 1664 to the Earl of St Albans's repeated requests for the grant of the freehold of St James's Square, and thereby eliminated what had been the unique selling-point of their Piccadilly site (Fig. 8).[25] In fact, it is noticeable that Pulteney – a seasoned property developer and building contractor who had made a fortune from the sand and gravel pits of Soho – did not erect any buildings on his own account on his half of the site. Instead, four years later in 1668, he sold off a 100-foot-wide strip (the present-day site of Albany) for his friend Sir Thomas Clarges to build a house almost as large as Denham's, and divided the remainder of his plot between three tenants, one of whom, Robert Chipp, was to build a new street in 1671 on the eastern perimeter of Stone Conduit Close (the site of present-day Sackville Street).[26]

Pulteney's reluctance to make any direct investment in his own plot may also be partly accounted for by the fact that he had already acquired a stake in the equity of Denham's proposed house, probably at the time they agreed to divide the land equally between them.[27] This in turn suggests that, to begin with at least, the house was intended to be sold for their joint profit, and that if Denham had lived in it himself, he would have had to come to a different arrangement with Pulteney before

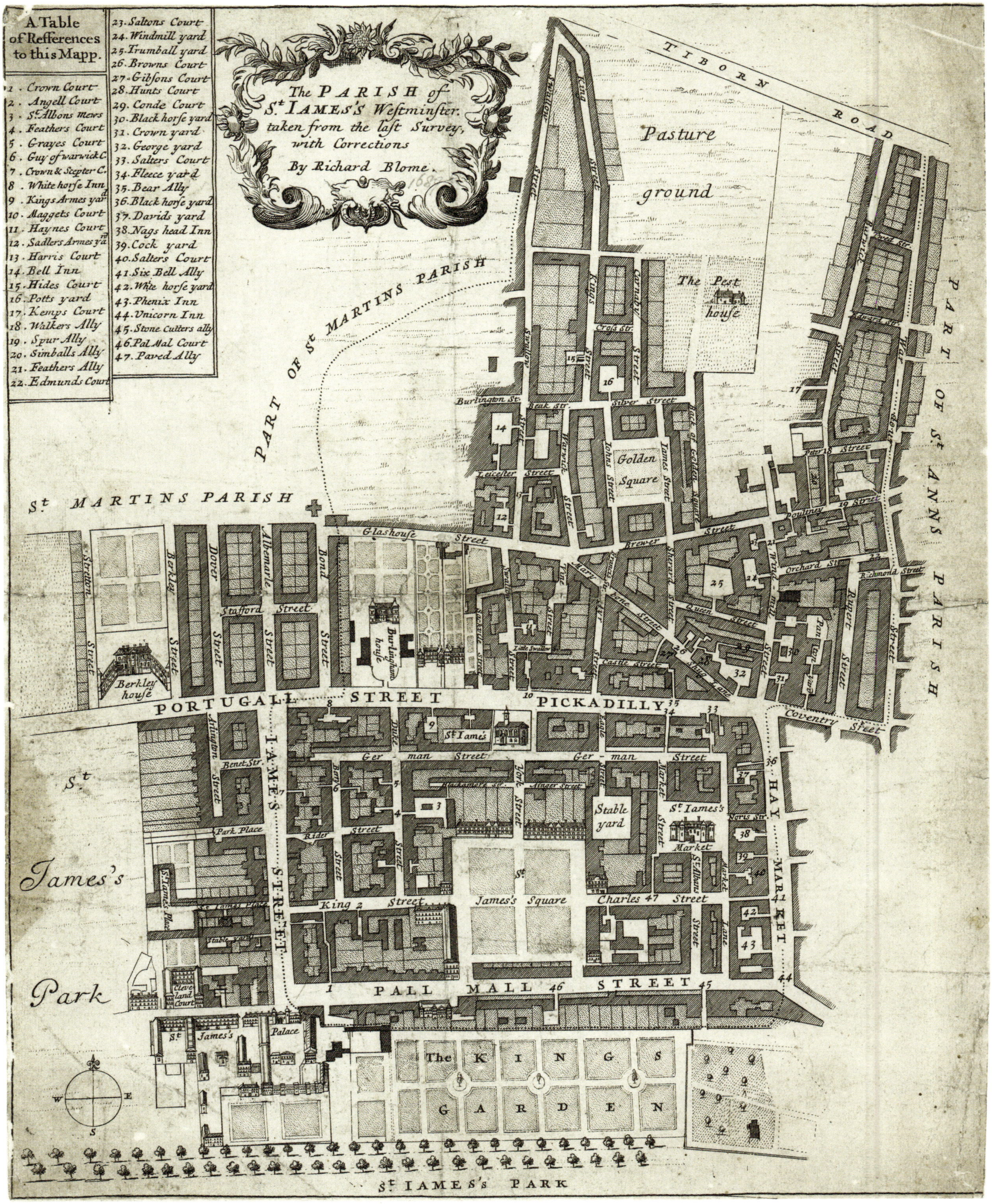
A Table of Refferences to this Mapp.
1. Crown Court
2. Angell Court
3. S.t Albons mews
4. Feathers Court
5. Grayes Court
6. Guy of warwick C.
7. Crown & Scepter C.
8. White horse Inn
9. Kings Armes yard
10. Maggets Court
11. Haynes Court
12. Sadlers Armes yard
13. Harris Court
14. Bell Inn
15. Hides Court
16. Potts yard
17. Kemps Court
18. Walkers Ally
19. Spur Ally
20. Simballs Ally
21. Feathers Ally
22. Edmunds Court
23. Saltons Court
24. Windmill yard
25. Trumball yard
26. Browns Court
27. Gibsons Court
28. Hunts Court
29. Conde Court
30. Black horse yard
31. Crown yard
32. George yard
33. Salters Court
34. Fleece yard
35. Bear Ally
36. Black horse yard
37. Davids yard
38. Nags head Inn
39. Cock yard
40. Salters Court
41. Six Bell Ally
42. White horse yard
43. Phenix Inn
44. Unicorn Inn
45. Stone Cutters ally
46. Pal Mal Court
47. Paved Ally
The PARISH of S.t IAMES'S Westminster. taken from the last Survey, with Corrections
By Richard Blome.
TIBORN ROAD
Pasture ground
The Pest house
PART OF S.t MARTINS PARISH
S.t MARTINS PARISH
PART OF S.t ANNS PARISH
Golden Square
Glashouse Street
Burlington house
Berkley house
PORTUGALL STREET
PICKADILLY
S.t James's
German Street
Stable yard
S.t James's Market
S.t James's Park
IAMES'S STREET
King Street
S.t James's Square
Charles Street
HAY MARKET
PALL MALL STREET
S.t James's Palace
The KINGS GARDEN
S.t IAMES's PARK

Fig. 8
Richard Blome's map of the parish of St James's, Westminster, 1685.
The British Library, London
Maps Crace Port. 12.2

doing so. It is very likely therefore that the house was designed at the outset to be an affordable, scaled-down version of its much larger neighbours, built as a profitable speculation rather than to meet any unrealistic social aspirations on Denham's part. In this connection, it is worth stressing that Denham was neither very wealthy nor aristocratic: his position at court carried no political influence; his family's claim to the status of gentry could be traced no further back than his paternal grandfather, a successful City goldsmith; and although he could readily obtain credit terms in the building trade by virtue of his position as Surveyor General, he could never on his own account have raised the very large capital sum of £30,000 to £35,000 that Berkeley and Clarendon reportedly spent on their houses. The fact that the 1st Earl of Burlington was to buy Denham's unfinished house for £3,300, and needed only £1,700 more to complete it, is a measure of the comparative economy with which it was built and belies any suggestion that vanity had deluded Denham into aping the splendour of his aristocratic neighbours.[28] A more probable motive for Denham to want to live in the house himself – a motive obviously brought into focus by the circumstance of his new marriage – would have stemmed quite simply from a natural desire to put down roots again after more than two decades of peripatetic exile and homelessness.

However, it must also be admitted that Denham's marriage to Margaret Brooke opened a particularly unsettling chapter in his life, predicated to some degree on her excessive ambition and his self-delusion, and it would not be surprising if, as work progressed on his house, he started to deceive himself into thinking they could actually afford to live there. This alternative outcome could readily coexist in his mind for as long as the house was being built, and would account for his reluctance to admit to his creditors that he intended to sell it after all. Whether this decision in the face of their importunate demands was a factor in precipitating his mental breakdown in April 1666, or a sign of his recovered sanity four months later, there is no way of telling. In either case, however, it would have been a wake-up call, shattering an illusion that the restoration of the exiled King, for which Denham had long conspired but with less practical effect than he liked to imagine, could also bring about the restoration of the life he remembered before the Civil War turned his world upside down.

To understand what was at stake here, it is necessary to take into account what Denham's modern literary biographer has called his 'emblematic habit of mind' as a poet.[29] Contrary to standard assumptions about Restoration court poets, Denham was no amateur versifier, but a significant pioneer of the great age of English Augustan poetry, whose much admired and imitated *Coopers Hill* (1641–42; revised 1655 and 1668) was acclaimed by his fellow poet and rival John Dryden as 'a Poem which … for the Majesty of the Style, is, and ever will be the exact Standard of good Writing'.[30] As one of the earliest poems in the English language to make the topography of a real place central to its structure, *Coopers Hill* is sometimes mistakenly read as simply a celebration of the commanding view of the Surrey countryside that can still be enjoyed on a clear day from this vantage point above Denham's home town of Egham. In fact, as Brendan O Hehir has amply demonstrated, it is really a political-didactic meditation on the currently perilous state of the King's realm and the need for the naturally opposed forces of royal prerogative and the rights of subjects to be brought into harmony with each other through the balancing action of self-imposed restraint. This political imperative is expressed in the poem through an emblematising of key features seen from the hill, so that Windsor Castle, St Anne's Hill and St Paul's Cathedral in the distance, and Runnymede and the flood meadows of the Thames in the foreground, become as it were 'hieroglyphics' of the past events with which they are associated and from which the poet is able to 'read' lessons for the present. Denham's model for this new type of political poem – Edmund Waller's 'Upon His Majesties repairing of Pauls' (*c.* 1639–41) – had shown how the physical presence and location of a particular building could become the focus for a wide range of moral and political analogies. Although how Denham thought about Windsor Castle and St Paul's Cathedral as a poet may now seem irrelevant to the practical work on their repair he was later to oversee, it is difficult to see how anyone at the time could have failed to make the connection, or to have been unaware that Charles II had appointed him Surveyor General in recognition of the emblematic importance given to royal works and buildings in his best-known poem.

In the light of this 'emblematic habit of mind', it is worth considering what building a house for himself on Piccadilly might have meant to Denham personally. Clarendon and Berkeley were clearly set on having the best modern town house that they could afford, modelled on the smart Parisian *hôtel* familiar from their years in exile and equivalent in aristocratic grandeur to the now *démodé* Tudor and Jacobean mansions on the south side of the Strand (Fig. 9). However, unlike the Earl of Southampton, who was probably the first person in London to build a residence of the new Parisian type fronted by an open courtyard, Clarendon and Berkeley were, as we have seen, not interested in a house that connected to its urban surroundings in the way that Southampton House and its *cour d'honneur* occupied the north side of Bloomsbury Square (Fig. 10). Instead, they adopted a tradition more typical of the siting of a gentleman's country seat, cordoning their houses off from the edge of the city rather than integrating them into its growth, and consequently prizing above all the view of open country beyond their gardens. Here the model was not in any sense urban or modern, but somewhat old-fashioned, replicating, for instance, the way that the garden of Berkshire House (where Clarendon stayed in 1666–67 while his new house was being built) gave out on to Green Park, preserving a haven of rural retirement insulated from the rigours and pollution of the city.

Fig. 9
Jan Kip, after Leonard Knyff, Bird's-eye view of Somerset House and its gardens from the south, from *Britannia Illustrata*, 1707
British Museum, London, 1880,1113.1421

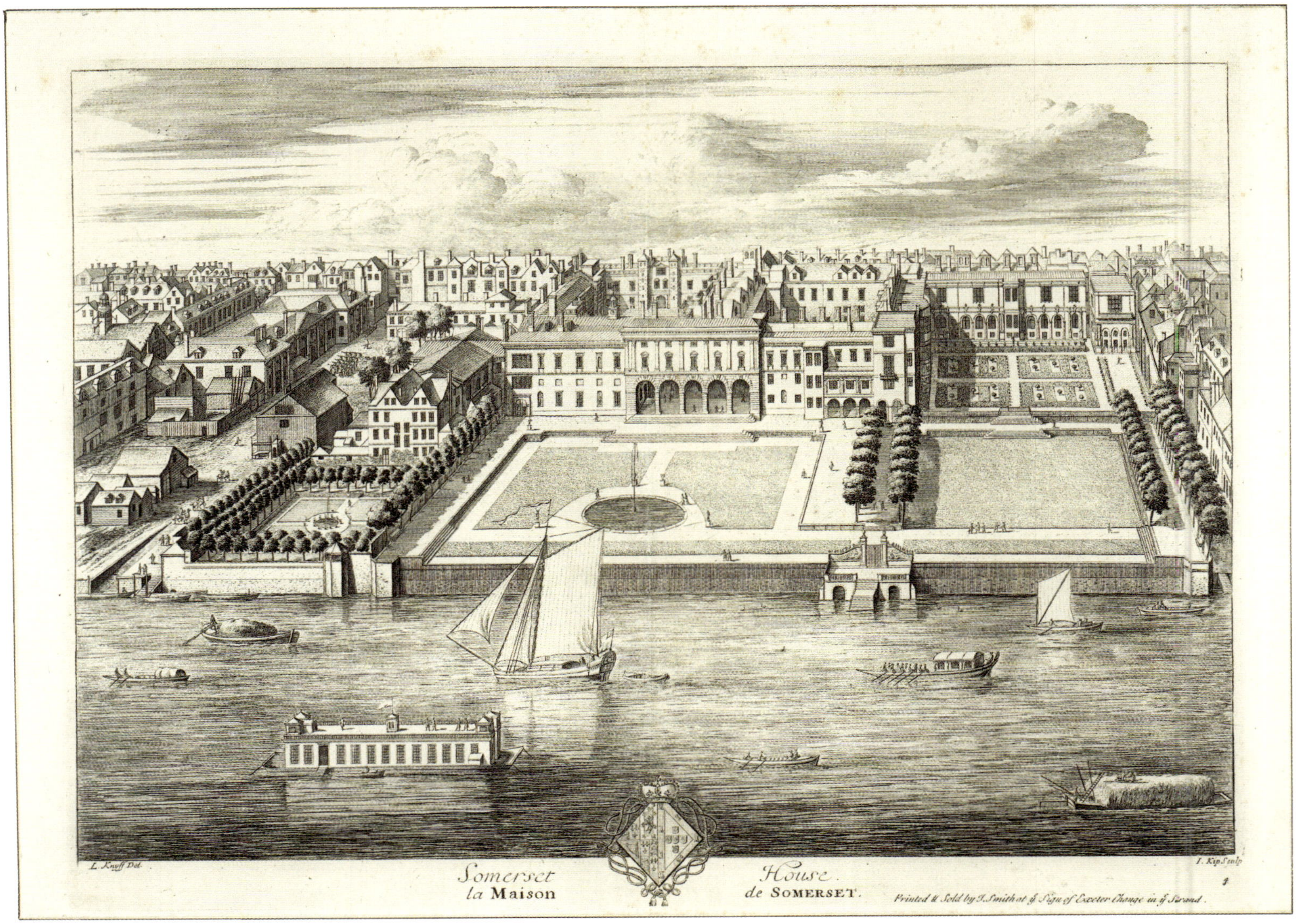

Fig. 10
Sutton Nicholls, Bird's-eye view of Southampton (or Bloomsbury) Square, looking north towards Bedford House from Vernon Street, with Hampstead and Highgate in the distance, *c.* 1725.
British Museum, London, 1880,1113.4405

To appreciate how the rural character of Stone Conduit Close is likely to have turned Denham's thoughts in the direction of building a house for himself rather than for profit, it is worth recalling the nostalgia for the happy days of his youth that John Aubrey records in his 'brief life' of the poet:

> Memorandum: – the parsonage-house at Egham (vulgarly called The Place) was built by baron Denham; a house very convenient, not great, but pretty, and pleasantly scituated, and in which his son Sir John, (though he had better seats), did take most delight in. He sold it to John Thynne esq. In this parish is a place called Cammomill-hill, from the cammomill that growes there naturally; as also west of it is Prune-well-hill (formerly part of Sir John's possessions), where was a fine tuft of trees, a clear spring, and a pleasant prospect to the east, over the levell of Middlesex and Surrey. Sir John took great delight in this place, and was wont to say (before the troubles) that he would build there a retiring-place to entertain his muses; but the warres forced him to sell that as well as the rest.[31]

'The rest', Aubrey might have added, included numerous farms and manors in Essex, Suffolk, and Gloucestershire inherited from his father in 1639, as well as estates in Buckinghamshire and Carmarthenshire left to him by his first wife Anne Cotton in about 1646, all of which were eventually sold, sequestered or gambled away during the Interregnum. The loss of these patrimonial and matrimonial estates represented not merely a loss of financial security,

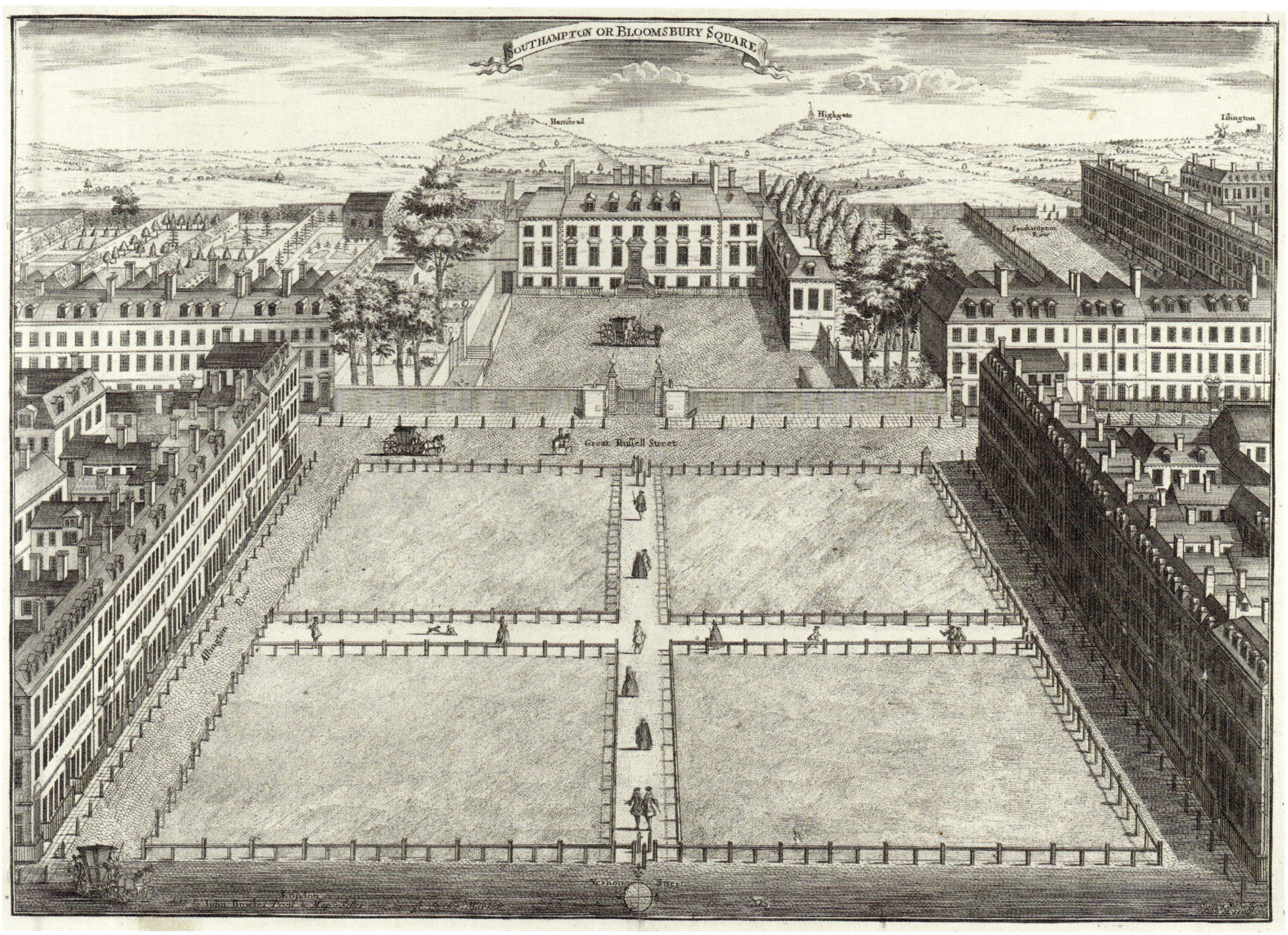

but took its toll on the poet's psyche. As O Hehir has pointed out, 'every version of *Coopers Hill* contains, at the end of Section II ("London"), a couplet that expresses Denham's inmost desire, in a context that demonstrates his awareness of the impossibility of its attainment: "Oh happinesse of sweete retir'd content! / To be at once secure, and innocent."'[32] It is no coincidence that Denham invokes this unattainable state of innocent retirement in direct contrast to the negative consequences of living in the city:

So rais'd above the tumult and the crowd
I see the City in a thicker cloud
Of businesse, then of smoake; where men like Ants
Toyle to prevent imaginarie wants;
Yet all in vaine, increasing with their store,
Their vast desires, but make their wants the more.
As food to unsound bodies, though it please
The Appetite, feeds onely the disease;
Where with like haste, though severall waies they runne:
Some to undoe, and some to be undone:
While Luxurie, and wealth, like Warre and Peace,
Are each the others ruine, and increase;
As Rivers lost in Seas some secret veine
Thence reconveies, there to be lost againe.[33]

Despite its total transformation in the nineteenth century, the courtyard of Denham's house remains to this day emblematic not only of a poet's desire for 'sweete retir'd content' but also of a viewpoint, equivalent to Cooper's Hill itself, from which to see the city's endlessly self-defeating busyness in true perspective. In physical terms this need to apprehend the city from a proper distance is symbolised by Denham's placing of his house 240 feet back from Piccadilly. The fact that he dug the foundations of the house somewhat to the east of the site's centre line seems to indicate a deliberate choice on his part not to dimension his entrance courtyard in proportion to the full width of the site, but rather to emphasise the focal effect produced by limiting its width to that of the house itself. Because his site had less than half Clarendon or Berkeley's frontage, this deep recession from the street created a greater sense of seclusion than was the case with either of their houses, where the service wings formed the short rather than long sides of a much wider courtyard. Indeed, Denham's rather unusual decision to site the main house at the end rather than along the side of a rectangular courtyard is probably the single most important contribution he made to establishing its distinctive seclusion from the city, which arguably was to have a more lasting influence on the subsequent alteration of this space than any other factor in the history of the site. While it is necessary to bear in mind that neither the service wings nor the street boundary wall had been built by the time the house was sold, it is also clear that its new owner carried out Denham's original plan, in spirit at least, by laying out immediately inside the street wall a stable yard to the east and a walled kitchen garden to the west of the entrance gateway (Fig. 11).[34] The interior screening of these utility areas with concave quadrant walls was to inspire the great Doric courtyard colonnade erected fifty years later by Burlington's great-grandson.

It has been suggested that Burlington's employment of Hugh May, Paymaster of the Office of Works and a practised architect, to supervise the completion of his newly purchased house could indicate that May had previously provided or assisted Denham with its design.[35] Although the absence of documentary or graphic evidence to support this hypothesis cannot be taken as conclusive, there are nonetheless more reasons for discounting than accepting it. Firstly, while the design of Denham's house is similar in some respects to other double-pile country houses on which May is known to have worked at around this time – in particular Eltham Lodge in Kent (1664) and, to a lesser extent, Cornbury House in Oxfordshire (1663–68) – this similarity is also characteristic of what Walter Ison aptly described as 'the quiet virtues of many other Restoration houses', such as Field Place, Warnham in Sussex and Groombridge Place, near Tunbridge Wells in Kent, both of which were probably designed by their owners. Secondly, if Denham did feel the need for help in designing his house (which is questionable), he is more likely to have consulted architectural cognoscenti in his social circle, such as John Evelyn or Sir Roger Pratt, the learned and much respected architect of Clarendon House, in preference

Fig 11
Johannes Kip, after Leonard Knyff, Burlington House in Piccadilly, from *Britannia Illustrata*, 1707, plate 29.
Royal Academy of Arts, London, 05/3704

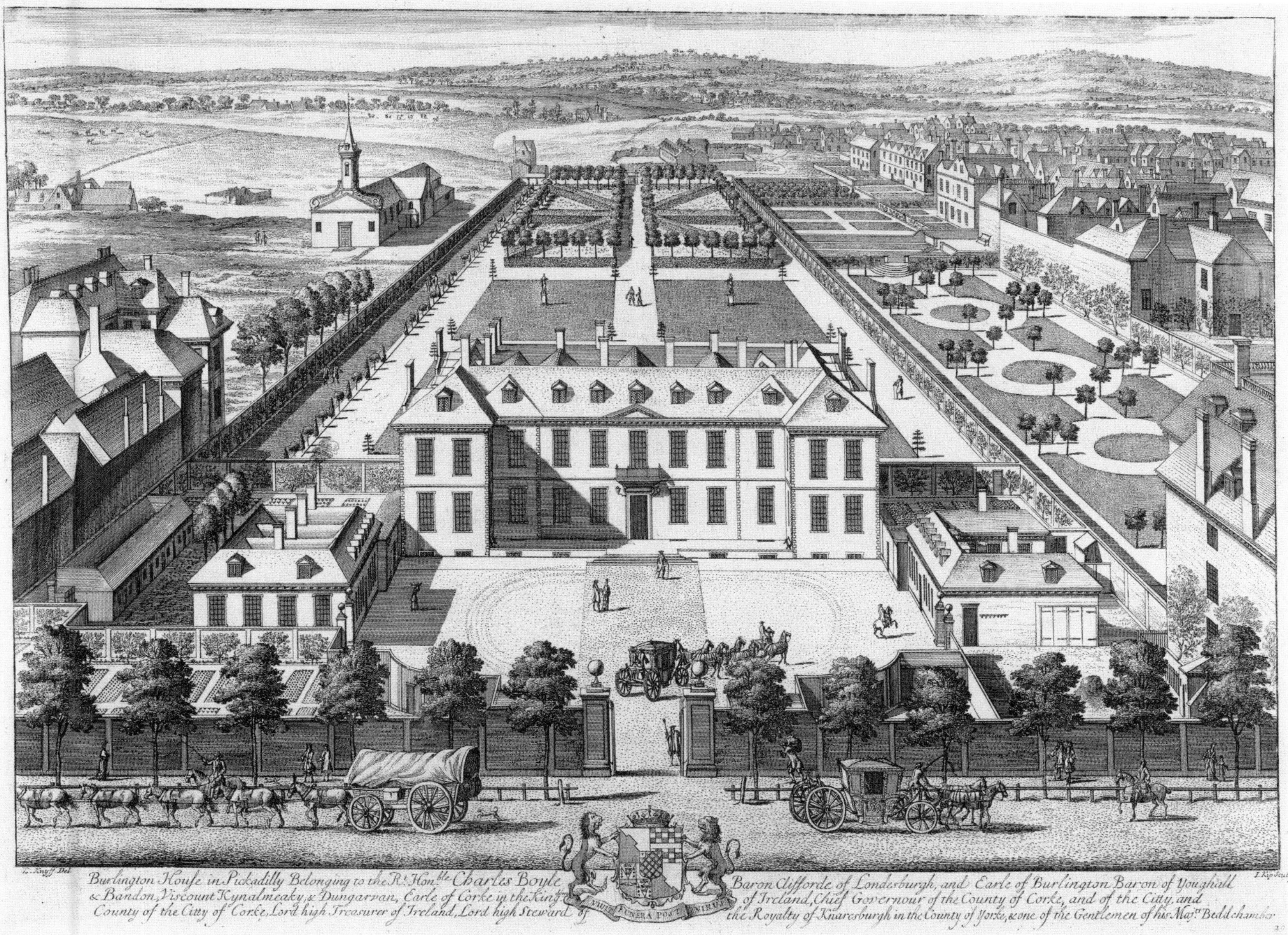

to his second-in-command at the Office of Works, whom he knew to be highly ambitious and covetous of his position. A connection with Pratt is also quite likely in the light of the fact that Denham assisted Pratt during the latter's work on Clarendon House by supplying a copy of the terms of a carpenters' contract that Denham had drawn up for work to be carried out on St James's Friary in February 1665.[36] And thirdly, as Pratt's tacit acknowledgement of Denham's expertise implies, there was no aspect of managing construction work with which he would have been unfamiliar, and therefore no practical need for him to employ someone to communicate his intentions to building operatives. Indeed, he may well have avoided employing an architect for the same reason that Pratt advised the builder of a new house against having its design drawn up for him by 'a home-bred Architect for want of his better experience, as is daily seen'.[37]

Another reason for Denham to act as his own architect was almost certainly to save money. While his finances were much less precarious than they had been during his rootless years of exile and royalist delinquency, his annual salary as Surveyor General amounted to a fairly modest £382 5s. 8d. Although, as we have seen, he was able to augment this considerably with rent from his buildings in Scotland Yard, the latter was evidently subject to wide variation, due no doubt to the uncertainty of finding and retaining reliable tenants.[38] In the hope of securing a steadier source of income than this rent, on at least three occasions in 1665 and 1666 Denham made unsuccessful attempts to sell his Scotland Yard buildings to the Crown in exchange for a lump sum of £7,000 or an annuity of £1,225 for his and his wife's lifetime. It is not clear why negotiations broke down since both parties were apparently keen to come to an agreement – the Crown because of the increased demand for government office space and Denham because of his outgoings on his new house – though one possible reason might have been Treasury objection to Denham's cautious but wise stipulation that his annuity 'be charg'd upon some certain fonde'.[39]

Denham's failure to secure a steadier income might not have threatened the financial viability of his house on Piccadilly so seriously had it not been for the economic impact of the outbreak of the Second Anglo-Dutch War on 4 March 1665 and the catastrophe of the Great Plague that killed roughly 15% of London's population during the course of that year and the next. The impact of these two events on construction costs is vividly evident in a letter Pratt wrote to the Earl of Clarendon on 13 February 1666 explaining why he had far exceeded the £18,000 budget initially allowed for completing his lordship's house. Having recited fairly standard unforeseen problems with water-logged foundations, hidden pipes, and 'walles so wholly shattered by ye wett, & Frost of ye last winter, yt both endes of ye howse were forced to bee taken up againe, & much of ye stone worke of ye fronts likewise', Pratt goes on to explain that:

> … two of our master brick makers dying successively of ye Plague, & many other of theire servants … wee were forced to sollicite Sr Nicholas Crispe to furnish us from his Clamps, wch though hee had at as reasonable rates, as they could by law bee had at in other places, yet at ye layeing them downe in ye yard they cost at ye least 15sh p 1000 & some more for rubbing &c. so yt what with waste & also tales I count ye price of ye bricks neere double to what they were at 1st proposed.
>
> As for ye Tymber ye Dutch warre comeing on, ye Price of it increased; ye Carpenter by yt time hee had framed & raised ye 1st floore professed himselfe to bee utterly undone by soe greate an undertaking; refused to goe forward, & humbly submitted himelfe to yr Lordshippes mercy, to deale with him as you pleased.
>
> At this time ye towne was highly infected, the workmen every where dyed, & where to finde a more active or able master Carpenter, was very difficult, & uncertaine … Whereupon twas thought ye best, by faire words & promises to incourage him to persist in his beegun undertakeings, wch yet hee would not doe without first making new propositions, … wch thing hath now brought his accounts to one third at ye least more, than his former bargaine.[40]

We will never know the clinical causes of the life-threatening seizure that struck Denham at the beginning of April 1666 while travelling on official business to inspect the King's quarries on the Isle of Portland in Dorset. Having been carried, probably unconscious, to a friend's house in Somerset – the initial reports to reach London and Oxford a day or two later claimed that he was either on the point of death or already dead – on the return journey he seems to have fallen into a state of complete delirium, insisting on trying to collect rent from properties in Hounslow long since sold, and going before the King to claim he was the Holy Ghost.[41] O Hehir rather too readily dismisses on purely chronological grounds Aubrey's assertion that 'Sir John's distemper of madness' was triggered by his wife's love affair with the Duke of York. Although no-one at the time made any such connection, and Pepys's first mention in his diary of Lady Denham as the Duke's new mistress does not occur until 10 June, it is perfectly possible that their affair predated Denham's Portland journey and that he was aware of it by then. On the other hand, O Hehir's broader hypothesis, 'that Denham suffered in March and April of 1666 a psychological functional breakdown' that had several other root causes apart from that of sexual jealousy, is surely correct. However, in addition to the deep-seated stresses that O Hehir traces to flaws in Denham's personality and an 'adolescence' prolonged by the chaos of the Civil War and the undercover intrigues of the Interregnum years, some account should also be taken of the trauma of the Great Plague of 1665–66. To see the streets of London, which as a parliamentary commissioner of sewers and highways Denham had worked hard to improve and which had earned him the sincere praise of Evelyn, to see these same streets filled with corpses must truly have been a vision of hell and the futility of all human endeavour. Although Denham would not have been alone in succumbing to religious mania in the face of such terrible evidence of divine retribution, for his contemporaries it was all the more shocking to behold in someone who had prided himself on his logical mind and ready wit. As one witness wrote to a friend in Dublin not long after the onset of Denham's illness:

> Sir John Denham, that great master of wit and reason, is fallen quite mad, and he who despised religion, now in his distraction raves of nothing else. I pray God divert his judgments from us and send us health, which I wish you.[42]

The Great Fire of London that broke out on 2 September 1666 and destroyed the 'monstrous Body' and 'ungovernable enormities' that Evelyn had execrated in the old city, seems to have brought about a personal catharsis in Denham, an act of God that literally brought him to his senses. Although the recovery of his sanity had no doubt been gradual under the specialist care of Dr Lentall in the Charterhouse, the real test came when he agreed that the roof of his buildings in Scotland Yard should be torn off to hinder the westwards progress of the fire towards the Palace of Whitehall.[43] Throwing himself, like so many others, into the herculean task of rehousing the inhabitants of the city, his own half-built house on the outskirts of town must have seemed almost an irrelevance.

II

THE EARLS OF BURLINGTON AND CORK

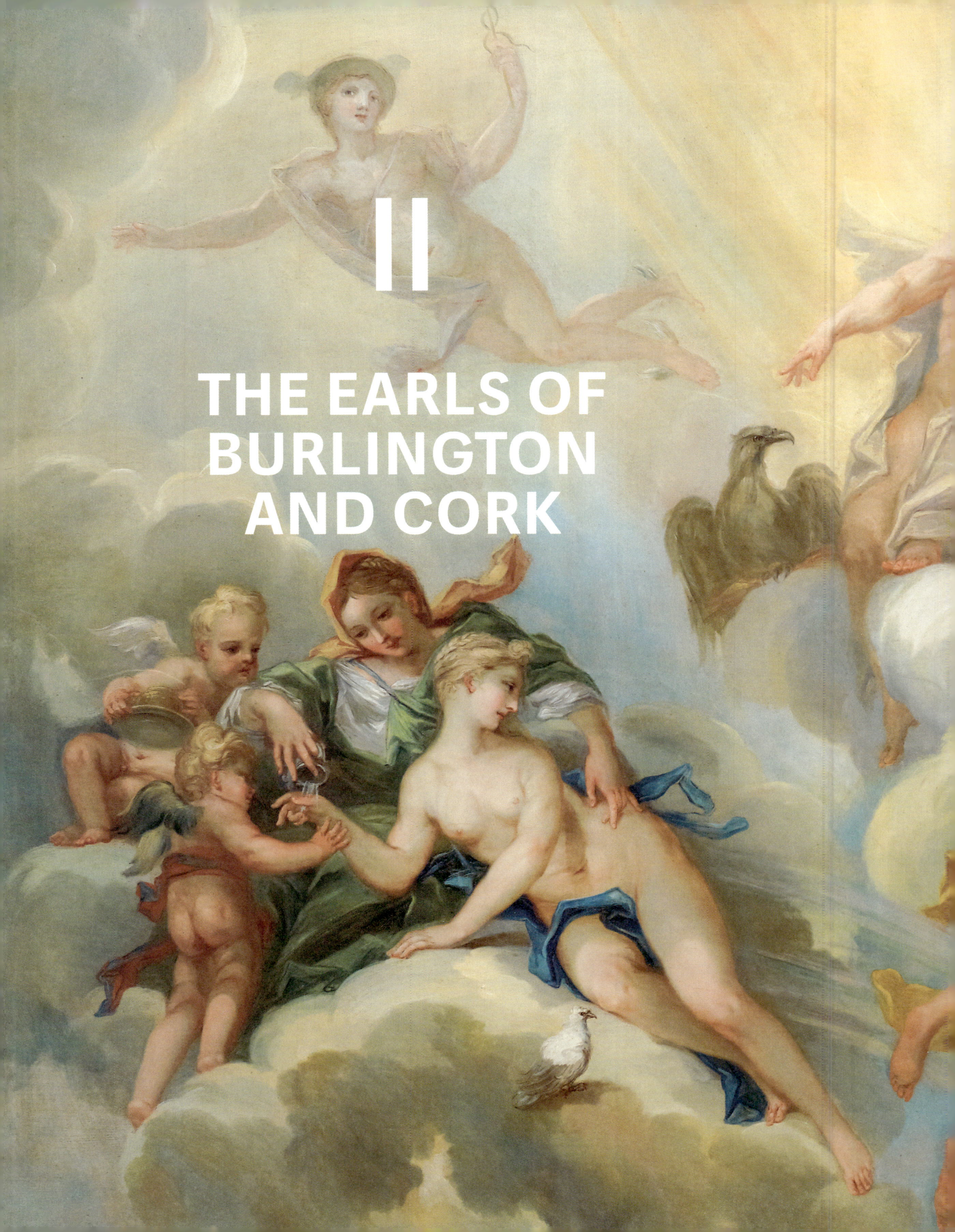

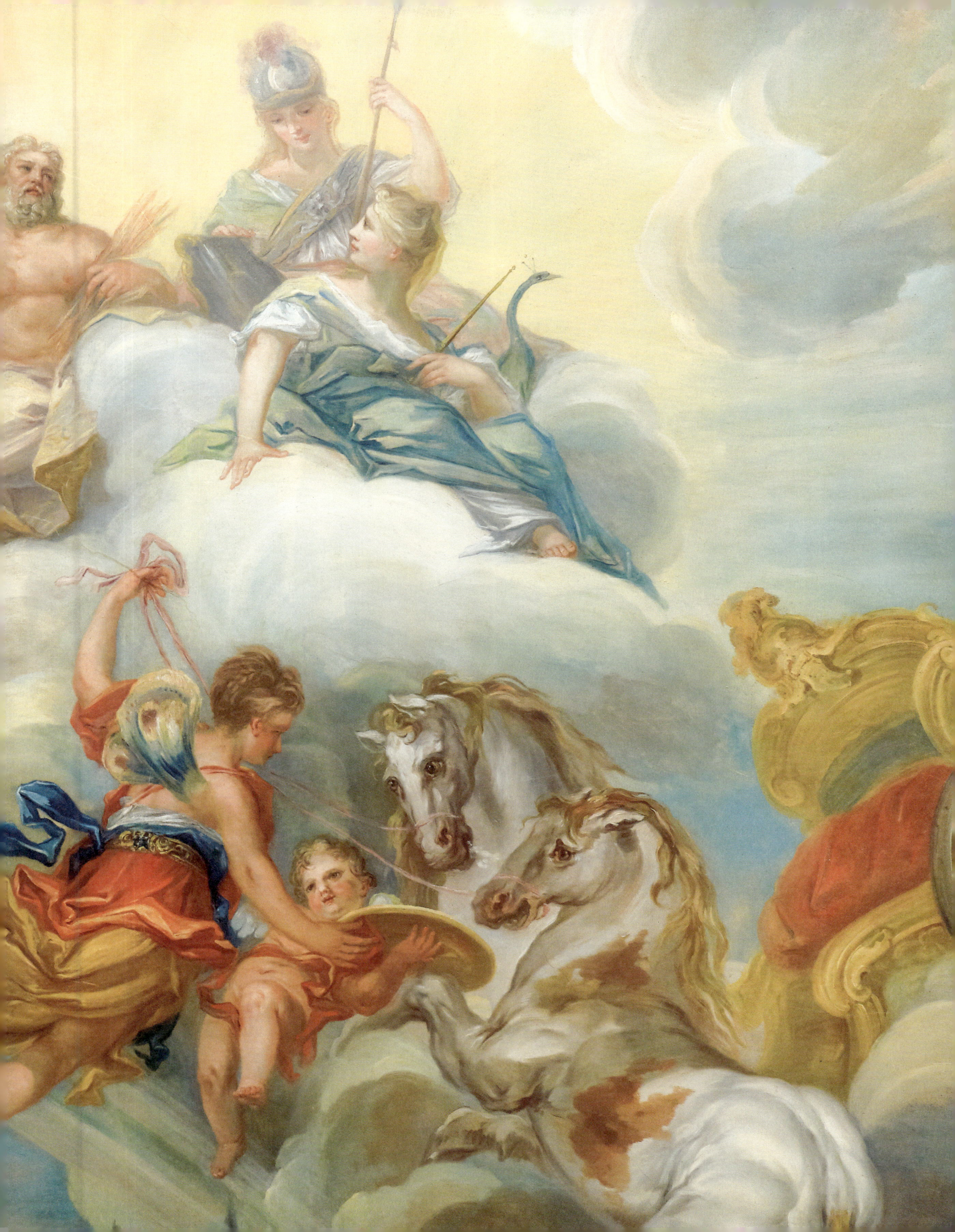

This day I was carried out of my chamber at Stanhope house ... to my new house ... I beseech god I may in it sence him constantly and that hee will blesse us in it and confirme it to my family.
1st Earl of Burlington's diary, 16 April 1668[1]

FOR THE FIRST HUNDRED YEARS OF ITS HISTORY the largest room in Burlington House was a chapel. Double-height, with a gallery for the family accessible at ground-floor level, it originally took up two-thirds of the basement and ground floor of the east wing. The reason consecrated space was given such prominence in the house is not hard to discover since its new owner, Richard Boyle, 1st Earl of Burlington and 2nd Earl of Cork, was a genuinely religious man for whom prayer and devout observance of the Anglican liturgy was integral to daily life. Indeed, the importance he attached to providing for the spiritual needs of family and servants in his new home is evident both from frequent references in his diary to religious service and the point he made of stipulating in his will that:

> all my Plate gilt with gold belonging to my Consecrated Chappell at Burlington house together with the Ornaments thereof shall be and hereafter remain to the perpetuall use and usage of the said Chappell and not for other use or usage whatsoever and for that end onely and for noe other I give and bequeath to the said Charles Lord Viscount Dungarvan & Lord Clifford for his life and afterwards to such person or persons as shall be in possession of Burlington house by virtue of or under any settlement or settlements thereof by me at any time or times heretofore made.[2]

Given the Earl's close acquaintance with Clarendon House next door – his daughter Henrietta had married Laurence Hyde, the Lord Chancellor's younger son, on 18 July 1666 and was living there by April the following year – it cannot be coincidental that both houses had large chapels in their south-east wings. Unfortunately, Sir John Denham's incomplete double-pile building came without the inestimable advantage of Clarendon House's exceptionally lucid internal planning (Fig. 12). There it had been comparatively straightforward to slot a double-height chapel into one of its four great corner pavilions without in the least disrupting circulation elsewhere in the building. By contrast, shoehorning almost as large a

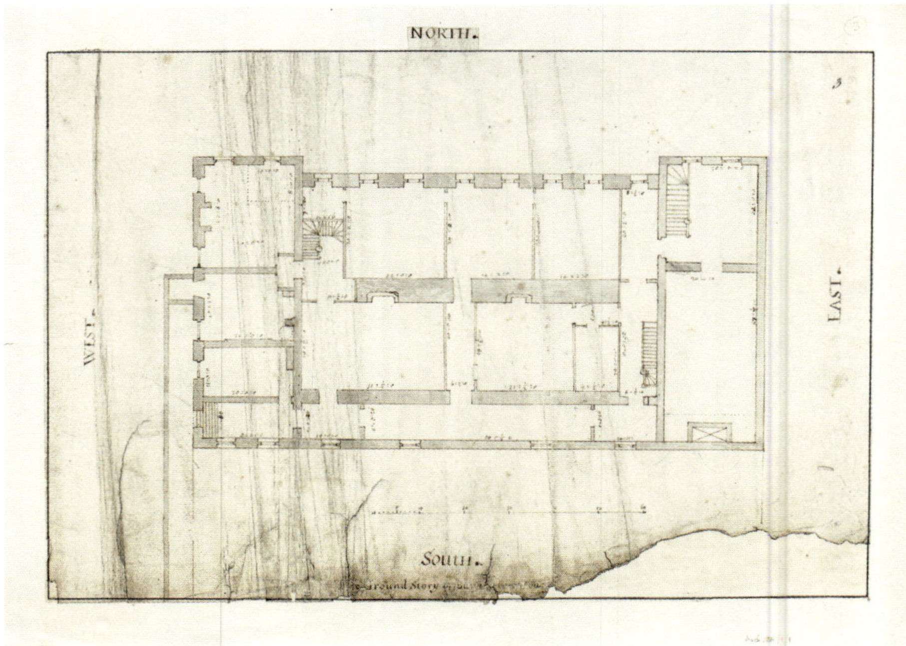

Fig. 12 (above)
Burlington House: ground-storey (i.e. basement) plan, c. 1710.
Royal Academy of Arts, London, 06/4958

OPPOSITE

Fig. 13
Burlington House: first-storey (i.e. ground-floor) plan, c. 1710.
Royal Academy of Arts, London, 06/4959

Fig. 14
Burlington House: second-storey (i.e. first-floor) plan, c. 1710.
Royal Academy of Arts, London, 06/4960

Fig. 15
Burlington House: garret-storey plan, c. 1710.
Royal Academy of Arts, London, 06/4961

chapel into the east wing of Burlington House immediately isolated its north-east corner and created several difficulties for its main staircase. Thus, providing access to the chapel gallery from the ground floor of the staircase compartment meant that the staircase needed to have reached sufficient height at the point where the two spaces communicated. Similarly, providing a necessary route from the front of the house at ground-floor level to the service stairs in the north-east wing meant imposing a half-landing on the north side of the staircase compartment, from which a short flight of backstairs could then lead to the first floor on the east side of the house. Meeting these constraints meant in turn that a suitable gradient to the stair could only be maintained if it began its ascent up against the window wall (Fig. 13). Although perhaps acceptable in an old house, this was an egregious fault in a new one, affecting its most important ceremonial feature and visible moreover to anyone approaching the house from the courtyard.

It is odd that these problems were not avoided by simply placing the main staircase in the centre of the

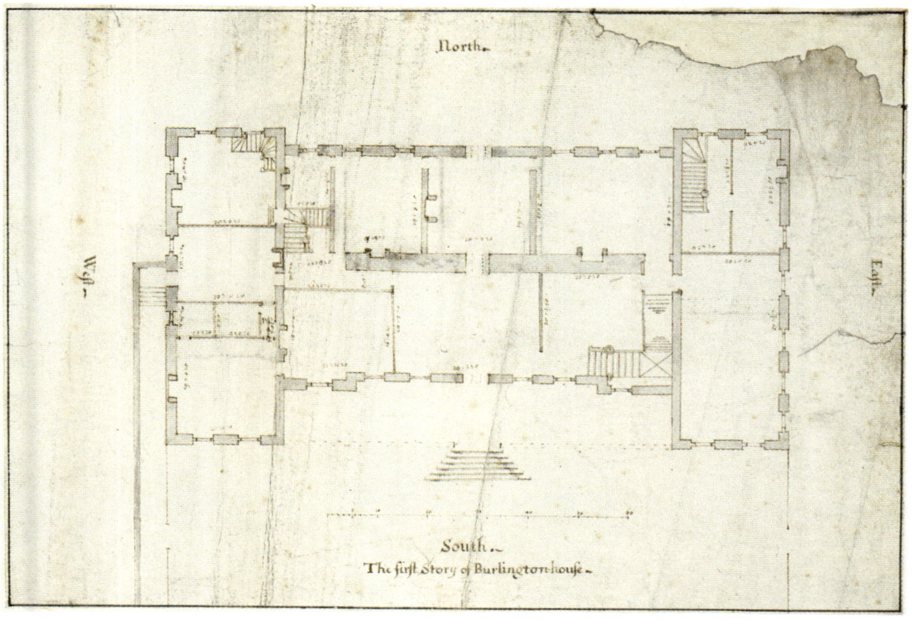

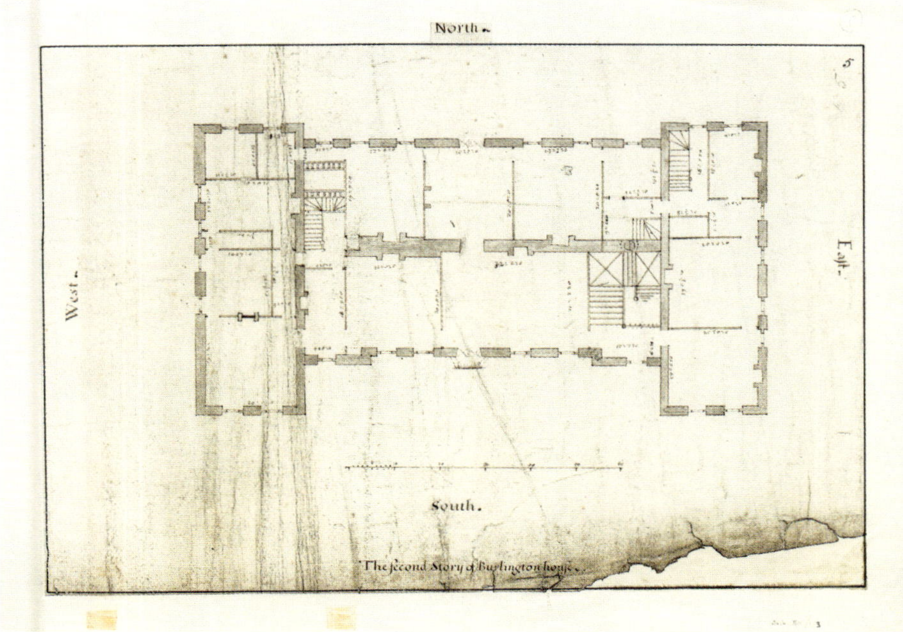

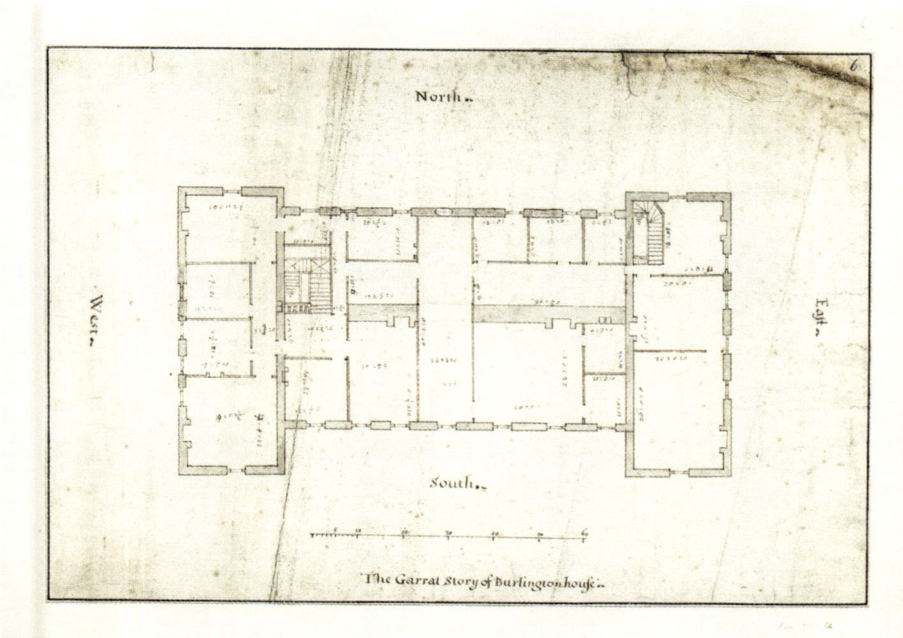

house, something that the absence of windows in the central hallway lobby to the garden suggests Denham had originally intended. Here again, perhaps, the influence of the house next door is detectable since a clear view of the garden through the centre of Clarendon House's entrance hall was an important feature of its much-admired design. It is also possible that awareness of the need to circumnavigate the chapel in Burlington House had the effect of pulling the main staircase over to that side of the building. Indeed, to judge from a set of floor plans probably dating from about 1710, it is clear that problems with the original interior of Burlington House were not confined to its unsatisfactory principal staircase. For instance, while the absence of communication between the chapel gallery and the backstairs in the north-east wing was probably deliberate (to avoid creating a transit route through consecrated space), it is difficult to understand why there was also no communication between these stairs and the important ground-floor room to its west. Similarly, it is hard to see why the only way in and out of the equivalent room in the north-west wing was via an awkwardly configured winder on the backstairs (Figs 13, 14)

One factor that needs to be taken into account is the probable attitude of the house's new owner (Fig. 16). Having inherited from his father, the rapacious 'Great Earl' of Cork, many thousands of acres in southern Ireland and married Lady Elizabeth Clifford, sole heiress of the 5th Earl of Cumberland's almost equally extensive estate in Yorkshire, the 1st Earl of Burlington was one of England's wealthiest peers, with an annual income in the 1670s said to be close to £30,000. However, as can often be the case with the very rich, he constantly fretted about ways to prevent the slightest waste or unnecessary expense, pestering his Irish agents about putting down cakes of rat poison in his Youghall house or retrieving broken chairs and worn pewter dishes that had been borrowed by poorer members of the family.[3] His approach to building projects is likely therefore to have been determined by an overriding concern to avoid making any alterations to what had already been constructed. As a result, he probably failed to take heed of professional architectural advice in the finishing of Denham's house,

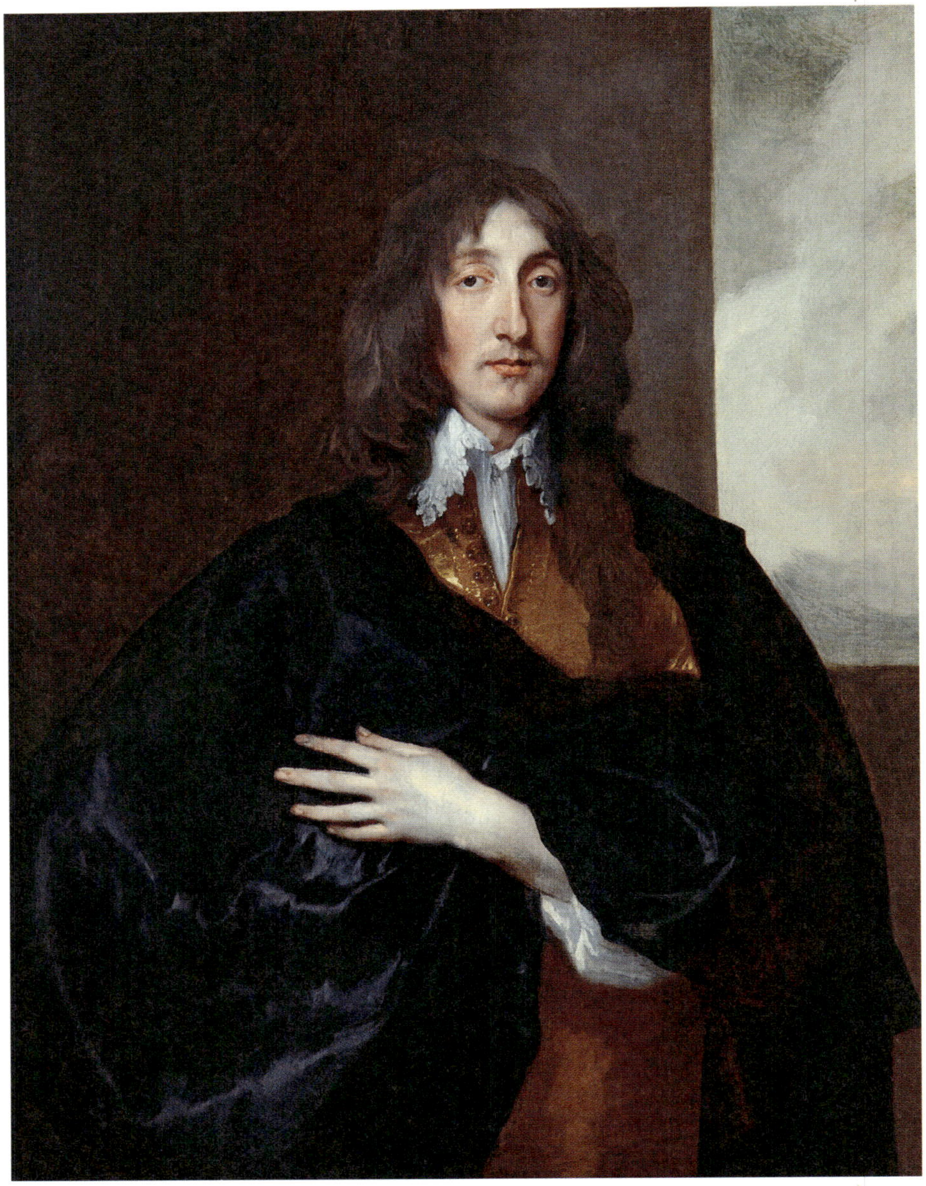

Fig. 16
Anthony van Dyck, *Richard Boyle, 1st Earl of Burlington and 2nd Earl of Cork*, c. 1640.
Devonshire Collection, Chatsworth House, Derbyshire

despite having the advantage of Hugh May's highly experienced supervision of the work, and thereby lost an opportunity to nip in the bud faults in its planning. Instead, perhaps understandably, the ever-cautious Earl was more concerned to maintain continuity in the workforce, keep costs down, and generally hurry the work along, all of which May, as the Paymaster of the Office of Works under Denham, was ideally placed to do despite chronic shortages of timber and manpower caused by the Second Anglo-Dutch War (1665–67). However, a letter from Laurence Hyde to his mother-in-law the Countess of Burlington, written fourteen months after the family had finally moved in, hints that she at least may have been less happy with the outcome than her husband:

> However your Ldy.p may be pleased there at first, I assure you Burlington house is a fine place, & by that time you have made some alterations there, I believe you will thinke upon this againe with delight ... I hope we may give your Ldy.p some divertisment amongst all the trouble, if we can but order the matter soe, as to come just when your Ldy.p hath made an end of some little alterations in your house, that you may have occasion to change againe for our reception.[4]

Hyde's tactful, if rather convoluted reassurance implies that there had been some friction in the family about how well the house had turned out. Whatever the nature of the 'little alterations' carried out at the Countess's behest, however, they would certainly have been finished in time for the consecration of the Earl's chapel in 1674.

WHEN THE 1ST EARL DIED on 15 January 1698 at the advanced age of 85, he was succeeded by his eldest surviving grandson Charles Boyle (Fig. 17), who inherited estates said to be worth £22,000 per annum, a Jacobean mansion near the Thames at Chiswick, a large country seat at Londesborough in the East Riding of Yorkshire and, last but not least, his grandfather's house on Piccadilly.

Fig. 17
Sir Godfrey Kneller, *Charles Boyle, 3rd Earl of Cork and 2nd Earl of Burlington*, 1695.
National Trust, Hardwick Hall, Derbyshire

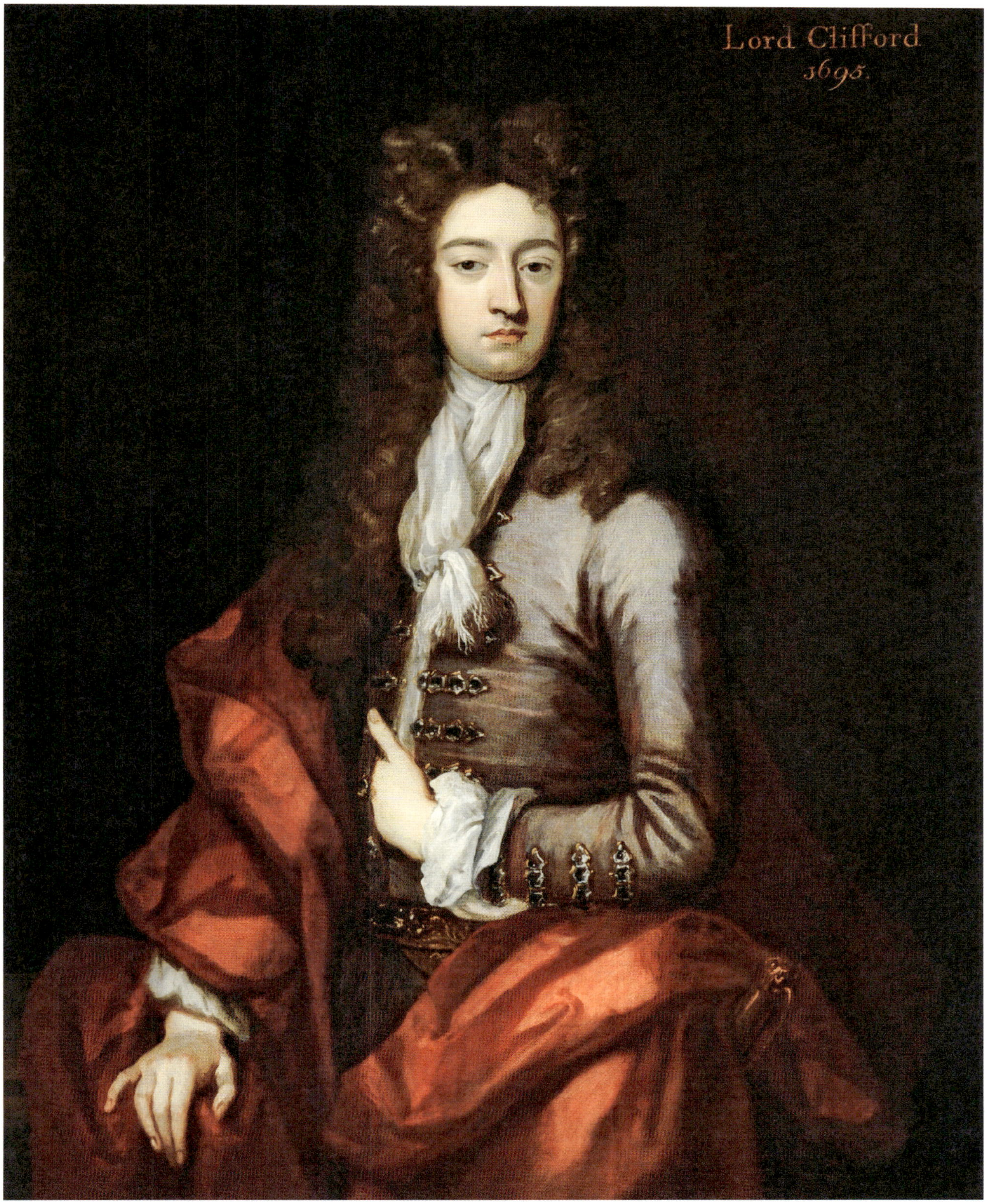

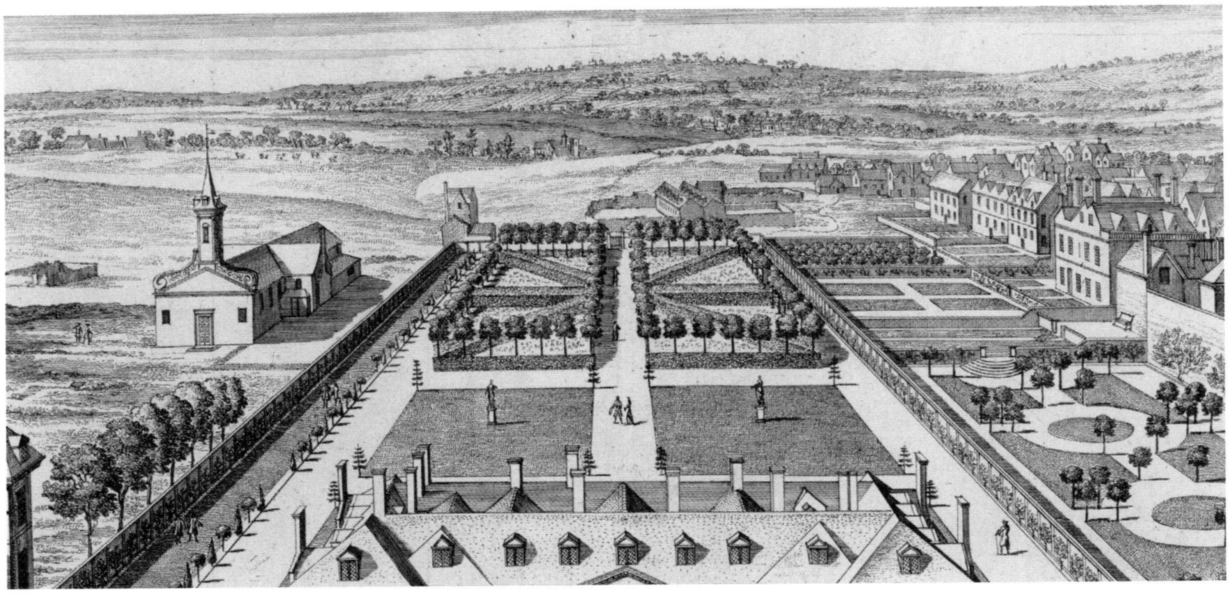

Fig. 18
Johannes Kip, after Leonard Knyff, Bird's-eye view over the extended gardens of Burlington House *c.* 1700, from *Britannia Illustrata*, 1707, detail of plate 29.
Royal Academy of Arts, London, 05/3704

In the thirty years that the 1st Earl had lived there, he (and no doubt his grandson) would have seen the city press inexorably closer to their garden, and although Thomas Clarges's neighbouring land to the east buffered the immediate effect of the building of Robert Chipp's new houses along the forerunner of Sackville Street, this was small comfort when compared to the melancholy events that had occurred on their western boundary. The sale and demolition of Albemarle (formerly Clarendon) House in 1683 to make way for speculative street development only 21 years after it had been built must rank as one of the greatest losses in the history of English architecture. For Burlington, however, it would have been far more than that, not only because its previous owner had been a close friend and his most important political ally, but because the shock of the house's destruction, its sudden and total erasure, cannot but have been deeply affecting for someone of his temperament. With hardly a trace of it remaining to remind passers-by of the fickleness of political fortune, the loss of Clarendon House dramatised above all the way in which a nobleman's home was a physical expression not only of what he owed to his ancestors but also of what he in turn could contribute to succeeding generations. This connection is still evident in the genealogical use of the word 'house' to mean family, and the 1st Earl's awareness of it clearly lies behind both his pious concern to safeguard his chapel's plate in perpetuity, and his further stipulation that the house that bore his name should remain as he left it:

> And I strictly hereby enjoyne my said Grandson and such other person or persons as shall be possessed of the said [i.e. Burlington] house not to intermeddle therewith.[5]

How the 1st Earl's said grandson, his granddaughter-in-law Juliana, and his great grandson the 'Architect Earl', consciously or unconsciously reinterpreted the intention of this injunction over the next two and a half decades was to prove crucial to the future of Burlington House.

To begin with, while it still rang freshly in their ears, it was no doubt taken more or less literally. Therefore, when the 2nd Earl wrote to his Irish agents in July 1699 urgently demanding cash, being 'at a great charge in altering my house, which must be done with ready money', insofar as this might relate to Burlington House rather than to Londesborough or Chiswick, he is likely to be referring not to the house itself, but to an idea for doubling the length of its garden in the manner shown in Leonard Knyff's bird's-eye view of 1698–99 (Fig. 18).[6] This scheme may perhaps have been envisaged in the 1st Earl's lifetime and it is not impossible that its realisation after his death was carried out in his memory. It was he after all who had had the foresight as early as May 1670 to obtain a 56½-year lease of the six acres or so of pasture land on the other side of Glasshouse Street (now called Burlington Gardens) that were directly visible from the north front of his house.[7] Unfortunately, the 2nd Earl's application for letters patent to reroute the intervening highway was unsuccessful, so the old and the new garden never did connect seamlessly and, for as long as the latter existed, visitors would have had to make do with what was probably a private footbridge to cross the intervening road.[8]

Despite appearances to the contrary, there was more to the 2nd Earl's new garden than a futile attempt to resist forthcoming engulfment by the city. It is worth noticing that Knyff's view shows Clarges's long narrow garden next door extended in the same manner as the Earl of Burlington's, so that the two neighbouring gardens formed a mutually supportive 'green belt' at their northern end. Since this extension of Clarges's garden would have occupied some of the additional land leased by the 1st Earl in March 1683, the idea of enlarging both their gardens was clearly part of a conscious strategy, not just for the 'protection' of Burlington House, but for improving the quality of life in its neighbourhood generally. As is usual in 'house portraits' of this kind, Knyff's bird's-eye view was purposely flattering, suppressing the reality of 'noisome' trades typical of the ragged, half-rural half-urban fringes of a rapidly expanding city. On two occasions in 1693–94 for instance, the 1st Earl had complained to the parish vestry of St James about 'the place behind his Lordship's House and Garden where they shoot the Night Stuffe and Boyle for Salt Peter.'[9] From around the mid-1670s the owners of this flourishing business had been performing an important public service in recycling the city's waste to extract saltpetre (potassium nitrate) for the manufacture of glass (hence the probable derivation of the name 'Glasshouse Street'). Unfortunately for the neighbours, however, one of their operations entailed boiling up large vats of shit; while his lordship might lodge as many complaints as he liked, unless he owned a controlling interest over the land where it was taking place, or could prove that it was being carried out in illegally constructed buildings, for all his wealth and status there was practically nothing that he nor anyone else could do about it. His only recourse was to set a good example as a landlord, not only by insisting on covenants that prevented tenants from causing such nuisances, but by actively encouraging the building of houses that would attract residents prepared to invest in improving the amenities of the neighbourhood. It would have been for this reason, rather than only for profit, that the 1st Earl obtained a licence in January 1688 to build an eponymous 'Burlington Street' approximately where New Burlington Mews is today.[10] Ten or eleven years later his grandson was to extend the garden of Burlington House so that it met the end of this street, suggesting an awareness of how the house itself might begin to influence its surroundings rather than *vice versa*.

The 2nd Earl's garden project is known to have been carried out in some form because twenty years later a Private Bill was introduced into the House of Lords to enable the grant of building leases of land 'lying behind Burlington-House Garden, now inclos'd with a Brick Wall, and used as a Garden'.[11] Although some minor alterations might have been undertaken in the house itself, it is very probable that the 2nd Earl heeded his grandfather's injunction against 'intermeddling', if only because of a continuing lack of 'ready money'. Throughout the 1690s the disastrous state of the Irish economy in the wake of the Williamite War (1688–91) seriously affected the ability of many of the 1st Earl's tenants to pay their rents in full or on time. In the following decade, English embargoes on the export of Irish produce during the War of the Spanish Succession (1700–14) tended to depress agricultural prices even further, to the point where landlords were 'forced to take cattle and butter at such rents as the tenants will please to give them and after being at the expense to bring them to Dublin [to] sell them at five or six shillings in the pound less.'[12] It was the notorious difficulty of extracting money from Irish tenants in particular, more than extravagant expenditure, that was most to blame for the accumulation of debts that encumbered the 2nd Earl's estate by the time his nine-year-old son Richard succeeded him in 1704 as the 3rd Earl of Burlington and 4th Earl of Cork. The fact that three years later the 2nd Earl's widow, the Dowager Countess Juliana, was told that still 'upwards of £15,000' was owed to her son in rent arrears – equivalent to almost a whole year's income – attests to the scale of the difficulties she faced in shouldering sole responsibility for the 'care and management' of his far-flung patrimony 'untill he shall attaine his age of one and twenty yeares.'[13]

The picture of Countess Juliana that emerges from Rachel Wilson's recent study, *Elite Women in Ascendancy Ireland, 1690–1745*, is of a determined, forthright and energetic woman (she was only 31 when her husband died), who rose to the challenge of managing a pyramid of 'commissioners, collectors, lawyers, surveyors, seneschals, bailiffs and sergeants of woods' – equivalent, as one historian has recently claimed, to a government department – with a tenacity worthy of the 1st Earl himself (Fig. 19).[14] Tireless in defence of her son's physical property and hereditary rights, she was just as concerned as his ancestor had been to stamp out unnecessary expense. Anxious, for example, that unwarranted costs were being incurred at Lismore Castle, she wrote from London in 1704 to complain to her son's agents there, that 'I told you plainly before that I would not allow firing, candles, or an assistant, and I wonder that you will trouble me again on the same subject, for I think it a needless expense to my son.'[15] However, where Juliana differed fundamentally from the 1st Earl was in her absenteeism – she is said to have never set foot on Irish soil – and in her decision therefore to make London the centre of her operations.

From this metropolitan perspective, by far the most important priority for Juliana was to be seen to be securing her son's future as the 3rd Earl. Uncertainty over whether he would live long enough to reach his majority had to be addressed therefore by commissioning the poet laureate, Nahum Tate, to compose and publish *The Muse's Memorial of the Happy Recovery of the Right Honourable Richard Earl of Burlington, from a Dangerous Sickness* (1707). And to counter the rumours flying around that her husband's debts had brought his family close to ruin, she steadily but surely began to make improvements to Burlington House, for it was here that her son was most in the public eye and where evidence of his continuing prosperity could be most easily demonstrated.[16] It was here also, however, that legal as well as financial constraints dictated to a large extent what she could do, because, as she was well aware and as she frequently reminded her agents in Ireland and Yorkshire, for as long as her son was a minor they were both barred by the Court of Chancery from authorising expenditure from his estate except for its maintenance and preservation. As a contemporary of Juliana was categorically informed by her legal advisor in March 1718, in relation to her proposed architectural projects at Dromoland Castle, County Clare, this meant:

> you ought not to lay out any of your son's money in building or other improvements, [as] you cannot answer expending a minor's money in any way but in preserving and keeping in repair what is already built and done.[17]

As a consequence of this legal constraint on the one hand and the need to signal the rejuvenation of the family's fortunes on the other, it is not surprising that Juliana began by making improvements to the interior of Burlington House that were non-structural and spectacular.

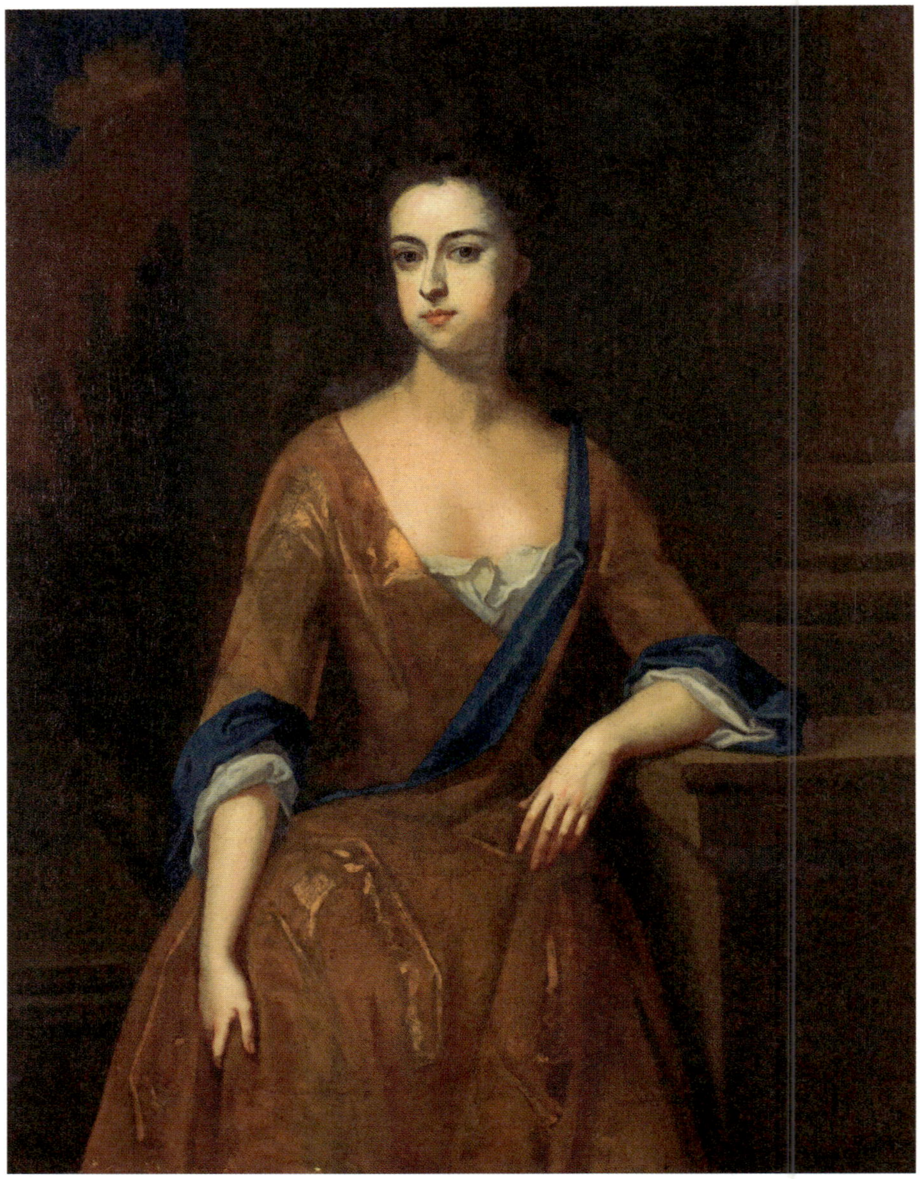

APART FROM A memorandum by Sir James Thornhill dated 24 August 1717, in which 'Signor [Giovanni Antonio] Pellegrini' is reported as having received 'Of Lord Burlington for the sides of his hall £200', the only information we have about the Dowager Countess's first major alteration to Burlington House is a confused entry in George Vertue's notebooks, probably dating from 1716, in which he credits Pellegrini with the decoration of 'the hall and Staircase & one of two of the great rooms. at the Lord Burlington his hall.'[18] Despite this slender evidence, Pellegrini's recent biographer George Knox has made a convincing case for crediting a longstanding but previously discounted tradition that his paintings for Burlington House were given away by the 3rd Earl to his friend and probable mentor Sir Andrew Fountaine.[19] Through close analysis of canvas structure, matching dimensions and correlated subject-matter, Knox has identified a coherent group of six large mythological paintings at Narford Hall, the Fountaine family's ancestral

Fig. 19
Studio of Sir Godfrey Kneller, *Juliana Noel, Countess of Burlington*, c. 1695.
Althorp, Northamptonshire, P360

Fig. 20
Giovanni Antonio Pellegrini, *Europa and the Bull*, c. 1709–10.
Private collection

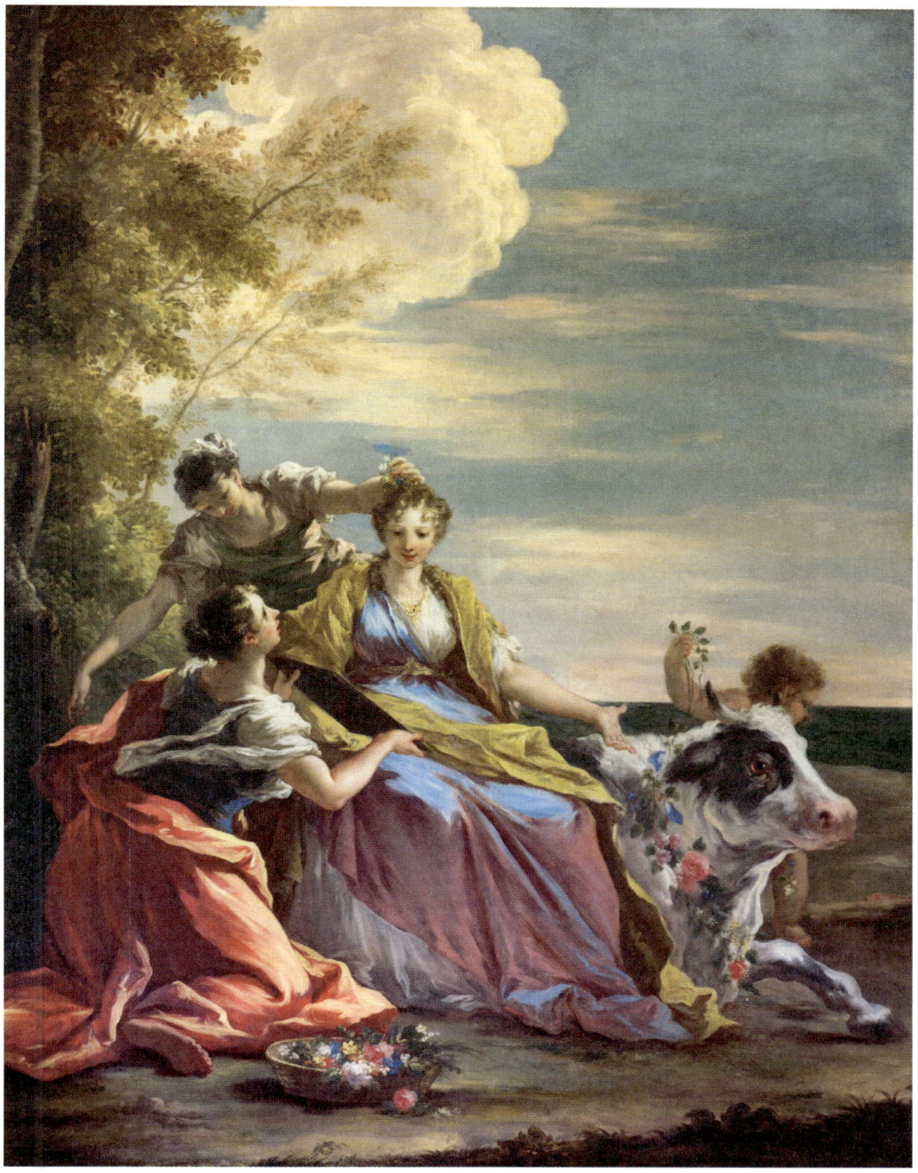

home in Norfolk, as almost certainly those commissioned originally for the 'hall' at Burlington House. If Knox's identification is correct, the fact that this is a clearly defined group attributable on stylistic grounds to Pellegrini's early collaboration in England with Marco Ricci, means that Juliana's commission must date from between the two artists' arrival in London in late 1708 and Marco's departure for Venice in the summer of 1711 (Fig. 20).

Several factors are likely to have influenced the Countess's decision to commission Pellegrini and Marco Ricci to paint this particular group of canvases for Burlington House at this time. The first and most important attraction for her would have been the high esteem in which Pellegrini was held, since, as Knox has pointed out 'from the moment he set foot in England, [he] was clearly recognized as a leading, perhaps the leading contender, for the most important commission of the age in this country', namely the decoration of the dome of St Paul's Cathedral.[20] Both Pellegrini and Marco Ricci must in fact have come to Juliana's attention not long after their arrival in London since, as an avid supporter of Italian opera, she is certain to have seen the Haymarket Theatre production of Scarlatti's *Pyrrho & Demetrio* that opened on 2 April 1709, on which the two artists had collaborated as scenery painters. Juliana's choice of Ovid's *Metamorphoses* as the main source of subject-matter for the decoration of her hall was similarly 'a la mode', reflecting the increasing popularity of this celebrated treasure-trove of classical mythology in early eighteenth-century England. The topicality of her choice is evident also from the fact that a few years later she was to be one of the fifteen aristocratic women to whom the publisher Jacob Tonson dedicated the full-page 'sculptures' (i.e. engravings) that embellished his sumptuous 1717 edition of Ovid's poem.[21] And last but not least, in January 1710 there was finally good news from Ireland, where the embargo on the export of Irish corn was lifted, thanks in part to Juliana's successful lobbying of the Chancellor of the Exchequer four months earlier (it helped that he was her brother-in-law, Henry Boyle, later Lord Carleton).[22]

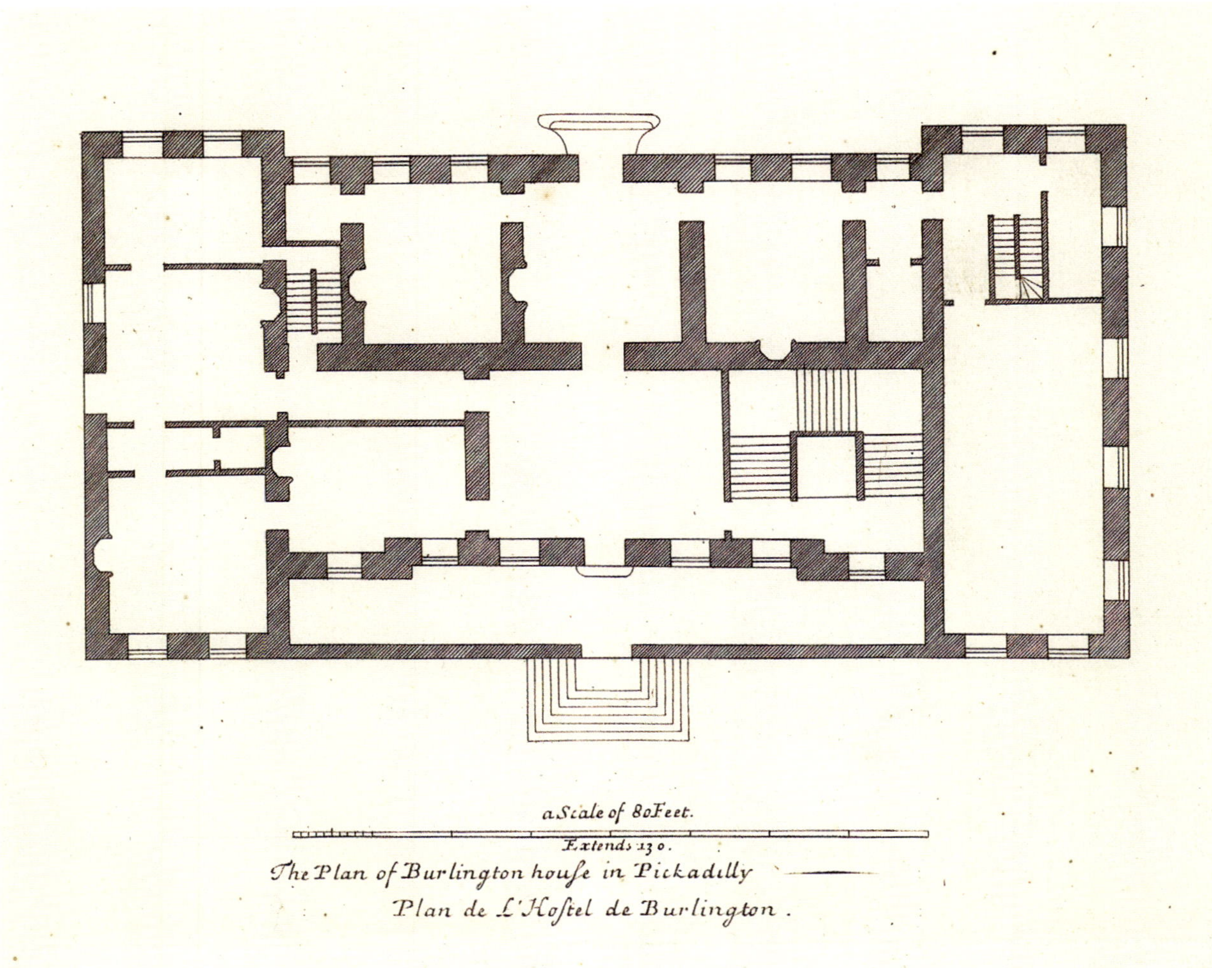

Fig 21
After Colen Campbell, Ground-floor plan of Burlington House, from *Vitruvius Britannicus*, 1715, vol. I, plate 31 (detail of lower half).
RIBA Collections

It is something of a paradox that Juliana's obligation not to spend her son's money on building work, except as was necessary for the repair and preservation of an existing structure, in a sense compelled her to make purely aesthetic improvements to the interior of Burlington House, since this could be justified as legitimate expenditure, while any major alteration of its fabric could not. There is little doubt that she was positively encouraged in this stratagem by the one person who might have otherwise been expected to restrain her, namely her lawyer Richard Graham. The son of Richard Graham of Clifford's Inn, who had served for many years as the 1st Earl's secretary, this 'Richard Graham of the parish of St. Dunstan Esq.r' was one of the two people that the 2nd Earl had particularly recommended in his will that his wife should retain in her service (if she 'shall think fitting') to assist her in managing their son's estate.[23] Juliana's most trusted advisor for legal and estate business was also a well-known art collector, the author of a collection of the lives of 'the most eminent painters, both ancient and modern', and a founder member of the Society of the Virtuosi of St Luke, probably the earliest artists' society in Britain and, according to George Vertue who joined in 1726, 'one of the 'Tip-Top Clubbs of all, for men of the highest Character in Arts & Gentlemen lovers of Art'.[24] As such it can hardly be doubted that Graham played a major role in guiding and encouraging Juliana's interest in commissioning artists of the highest repute to decorate Burlington House.

The Countess's newly decorated hall was probably conceived alongside and as part of work to address more mundane longstanding problems in the house such as poor communication between the wings and the main body of the building and, in particular, the pokey staircases. Almost any reasonably competent master builder and joiner could have sorted out these quite basic problems, but since they had arisen through previously misplaced reliance on executant craftsmen's advice, Juliana probably felt that it would be better to call in an architect. Our evidence for this remedial work comes from an engraving of the ground-floor plan published in volume I of Colen Campbell's *Vitruvius Britannicus* (May 1715; Fig. 21). A comparison of this with the hand-drawn plans of *c.* 1710 (see Figs 12–15) shows quite clearly that the staircases throughout the house have been replaced and repositioned; a ground-floor window in both the west and east fronts has been removed and the fenestration of the east wall of the chapel altered; several fireplaces have been moved to different positions or, in the case of the east front, replaced by a window; new doorways have

Fig. 22
Sebastiano Ricci, *The Marriage of Bacchus and Ariadne*, *c.* 1713–15.
Chiswick House, London

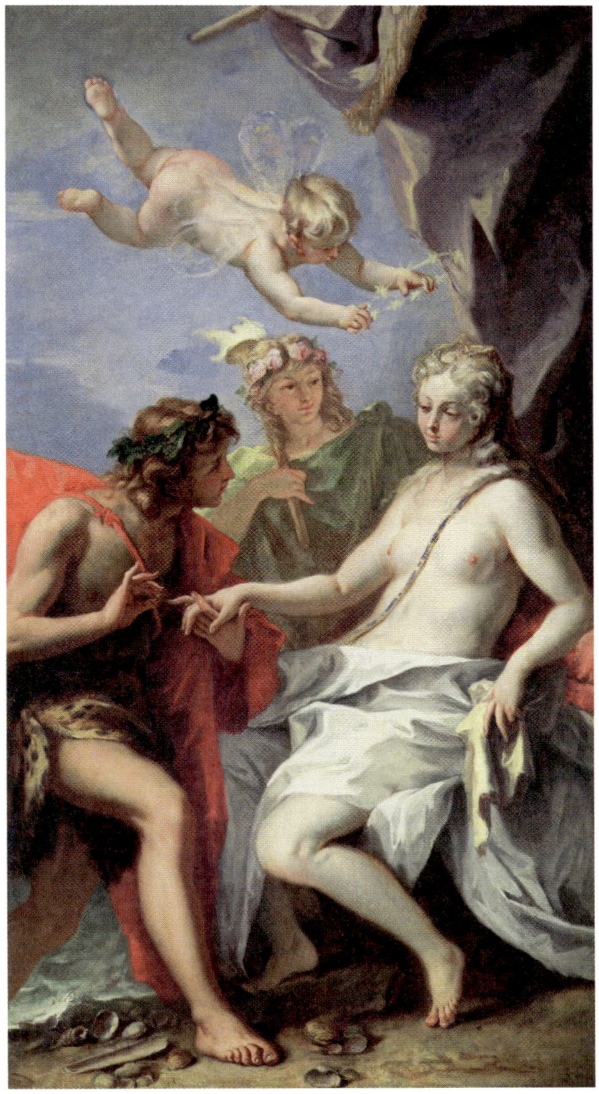

been opened to create an enfilade between the ground-floor rooms in the west wing and to connect the east backstairs for the first time with the main body of the house; and lastly, a new double-height compartment has been formed to accommodate a much grander main staircase. Since this latter alteration meant requisitioning a third of the dining room above, this was probably also the moment when the latter was centralised over the entrance hall below it, a relocation of internal walls that determined for the first time the present-day position and dimensions of what later became known as the 'Saloon'.

Despite some minor inaccuracies in Campbell's engraving, in particular relating to load-bearing walls, its omission of any indication of the chapel gallery may well be evidence that this room had been raised to ground-floor level by early 1715 at the latest. Certainly, the new spacing of the windows in the chapel's east wall would be consonant with such reconstruction. However, whether or not this rebuilt chapel was double-height is impossible to determine on the basis of existing knowledge. That it may have been, and might even have had a vaulted ceiling incorporating the garret above, is perhaps suggested by a comparable chapel of the period at Grimsthorpe Castle in Lincolnshore (*c.* 1722). There, in placing a large *serliana* or Venetian window over the altar, Vanbrugh was not only paying homage to Inigo Jones's Queen's Chapel at St James's Palace, but quite possibly acknowledging Campbell's use of this motif at Burlington House. However, until new evidence emerges, it has to be accepted that when, by whom and in what form the chapel at Burlington House was first rebuilt remain questions for which there are no answers. Whatever did happen, insofar as it affected the chapel we may be sure the admonitory ghost of the 1st Earl was watching.

Fortunately, we have a more solid foundation for re-imagining Sebastiano Ricci's decoration of the upper walls and ceiling of Burlington House's new staircase with what have been described as some of 'the largest mythologies in the history of Venetian painting' (Figs 22–26).[25] In 2004, thanks to the survival of four of these canvases (albeit in two cases cut down), and of two drawings recording the still extant structure of the staircase in 1812, the Royal Academy's surveyor Peter Schmitt was able to produce a convincing reconstruction of the effect Ricci's paintings would have had in their original location.[26] The iconographic decipherment of Ricci's paintings has been the subject of much debate and, although they take as their starting point Annibale Carracci's great fresco cycle in the Galleria Farnese in Rome, has tended to create the impression that they would have seemed 'a slightly outrageous display of pin-ups to most English taste of the time'.[27] What has been rather ignored in the discussion so far is the importance of the fact that Sebastiano (probably working with his

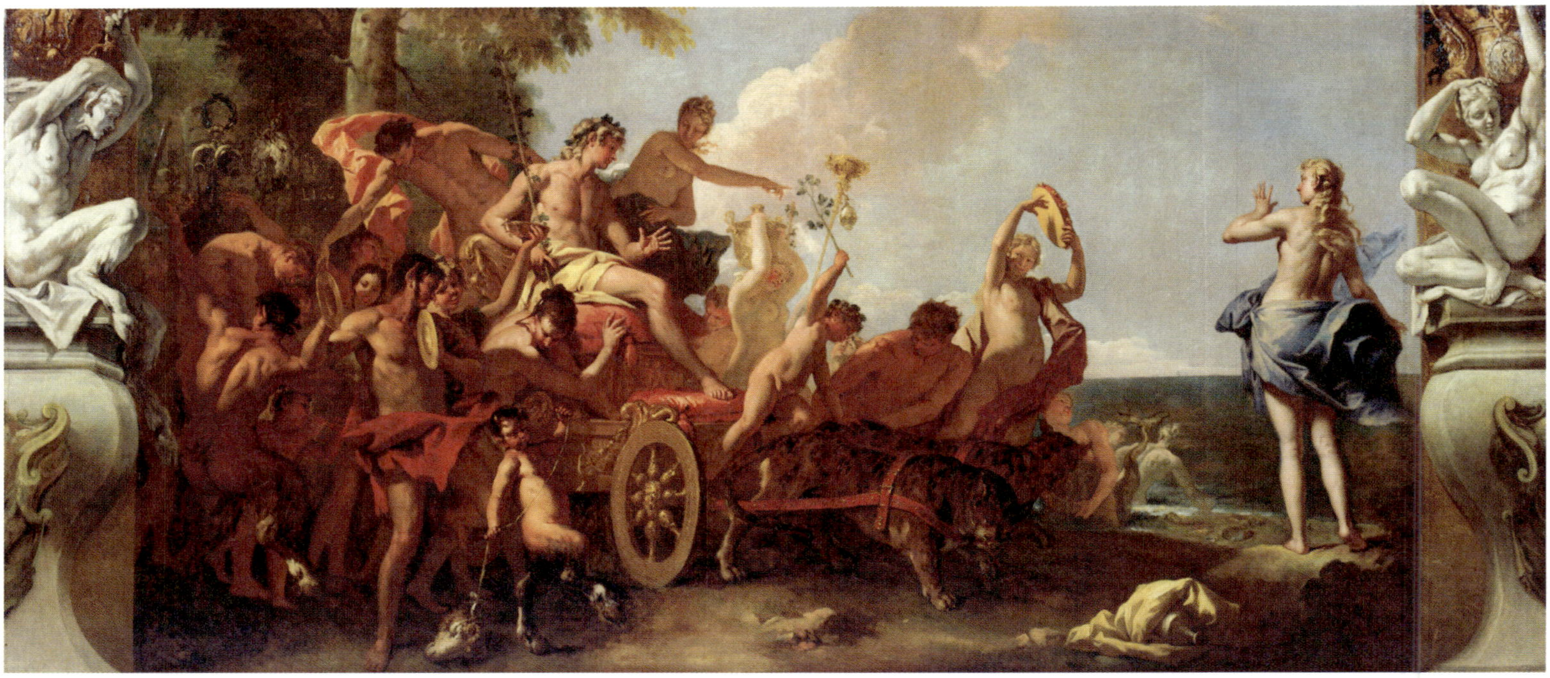

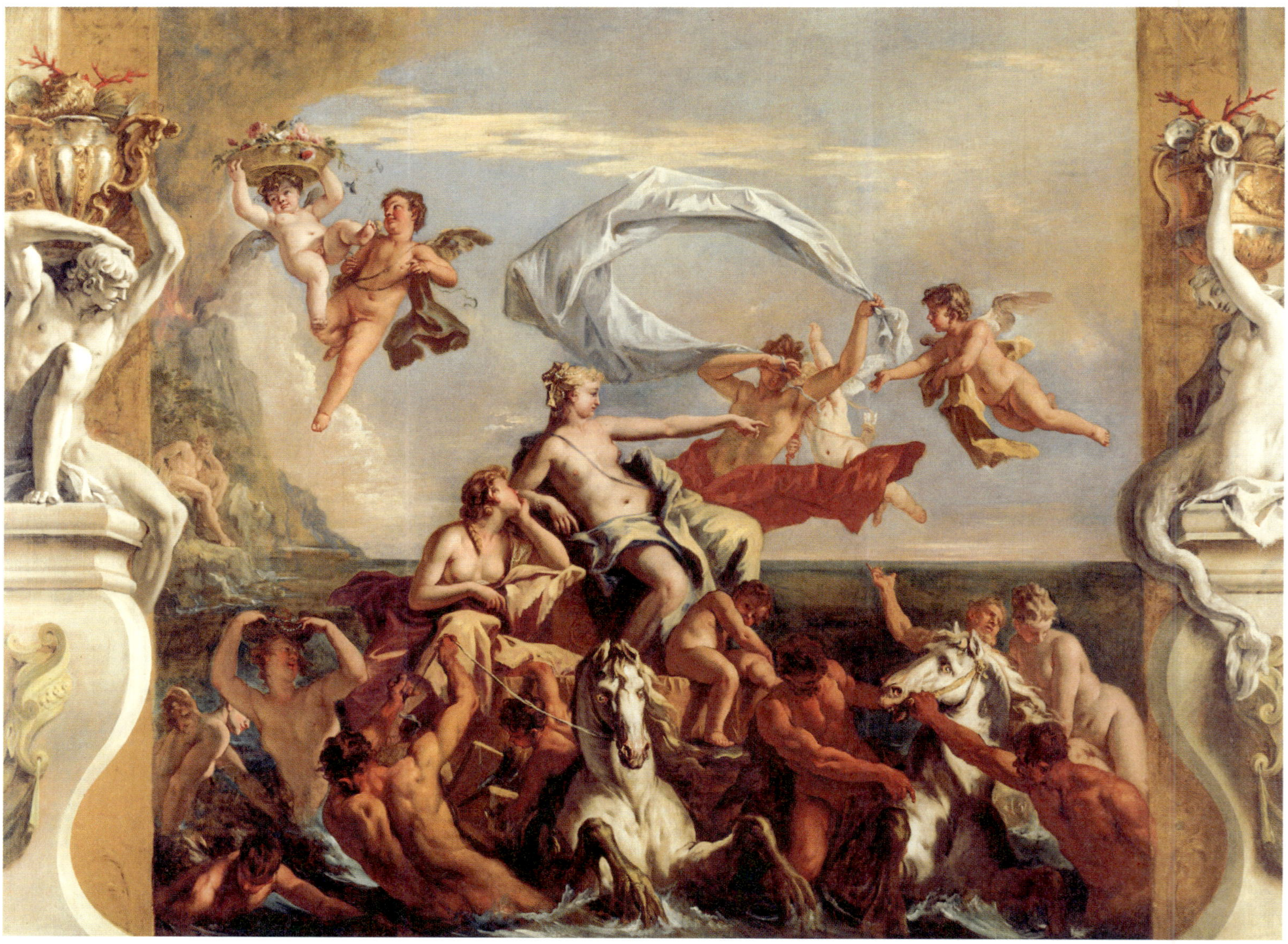

Fig. 23
Sebastiano Ricci, *The Meeting of Bacchus and Ariadne*, c. 1713–15.
Royal Academy of Arts, London, 03/214

Fig. 24
Sebastiano Ricci, *The Triumph of Galatea*, c. 1713–15.
Royal Academy of Arts, London, 03/188

Fig. 25
Sebastiano (and Marco?) Ricci, *Diana and Her Nymphs Bathing*, c. 1713–15.
Royal Academy of Arts, London, 03/187

nephew Marco) was commissioned by a noblewoman consciously looking forward to an event that, when it came, would be of the greatest significance both for her and her son. Whereas the various subjects of Pellegrini's canvases had a common theme in the skill, courage and fortitude of women in adversity (Arachne, Europa, Dejanira; Fig. 20) and their role in the nurturing of gods and heroes when children (*The Infancy of Achilles*, *The Nursing of Jupiter*), and therefore in one way or other paid subtle homage to the qualities that Juliana had needed to bring up her son alone, there can be no doubt that the overarching theme of Ricci's cycle – the power and constancy of love – was also a prediction of the happiness and good fortune that would attend her son once he had married. It was particularly appropriate therefore that what is generally agreed to have been the first of the large canvases in Ricci's sequence – associated no doubt with the overdoor painting of *The Marriage of Bacchus and Ariadne* (Fig. 22) now at Chiswick House – was

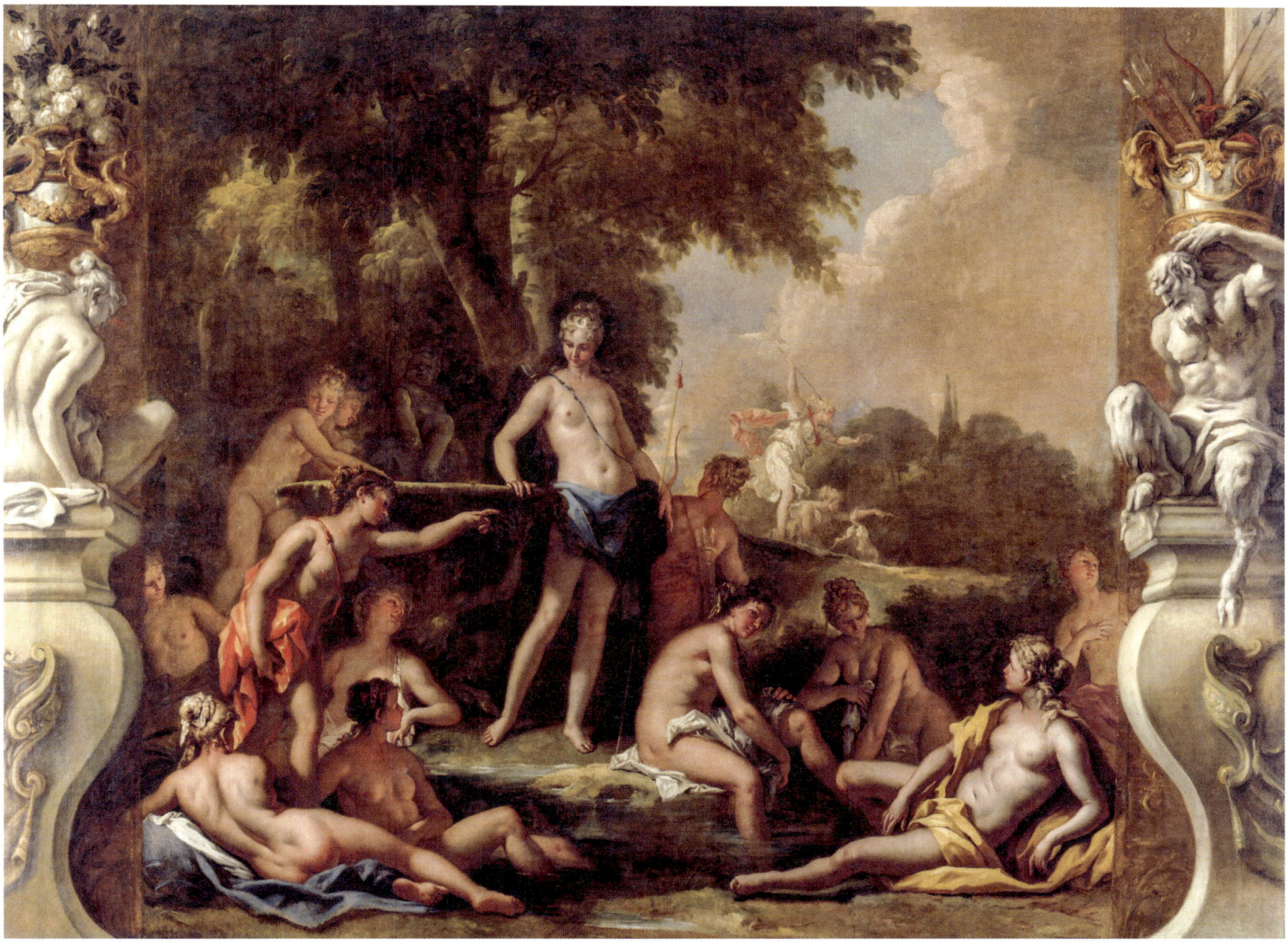

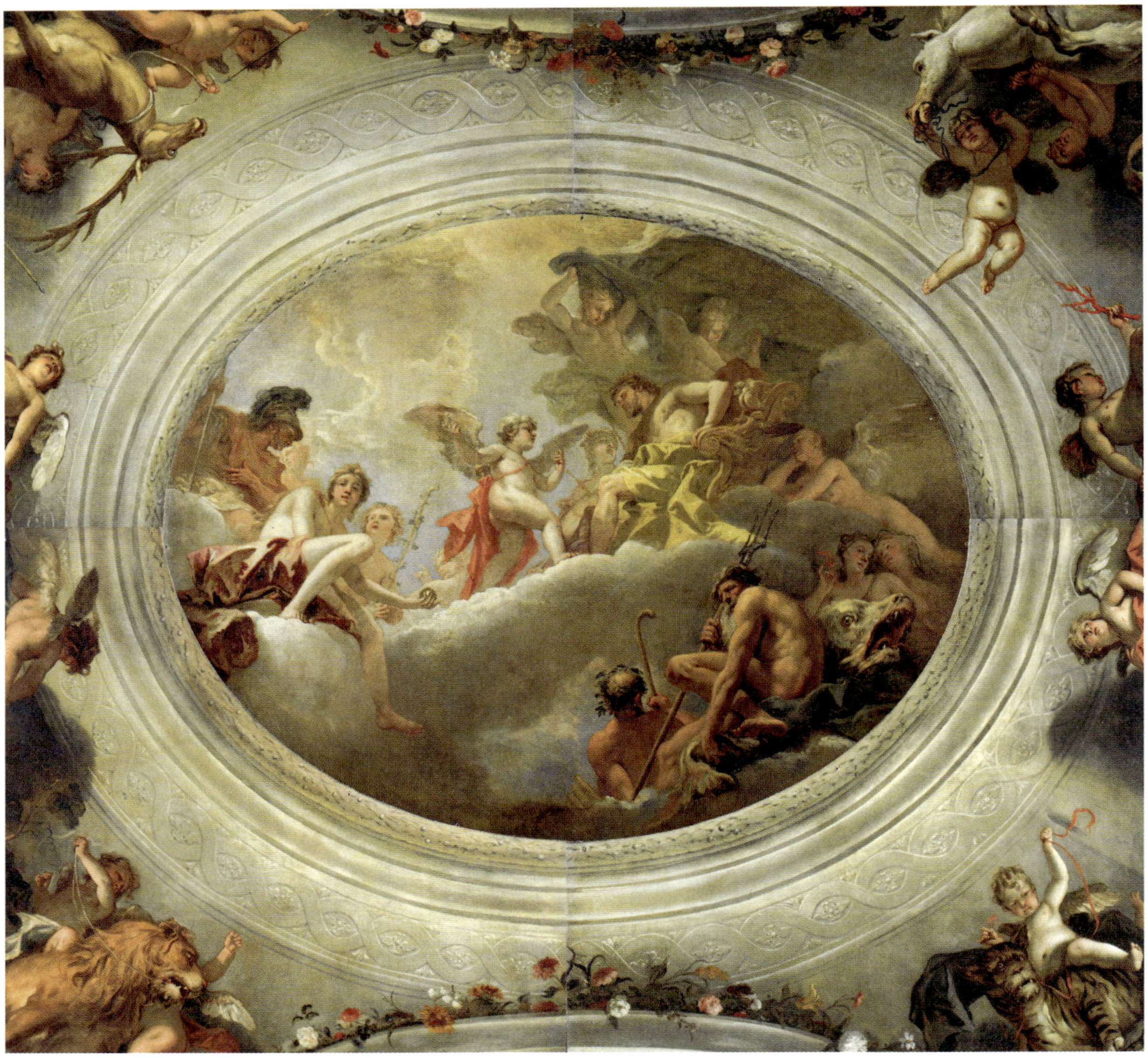

Fig. 26
Sebastiano Ricci, *Cupid Before Jupiter* (detail of the central section), c. 1713–15.
Royal Academy Arts, London, 03/201

a version of the so-called *Triumph of Bacchus* that takes as its subject the far from triumphant moment of Ariadne's abandonment by the god (Fig. 23). Not only did these two paintings make a fitting tribute to the faithfulness of Juliana's love for her husband in widowhood, they also forged a direct thematic link with Pellegrini's canvases next door.

WHEN THE 3RD EARL OF BURLINGTON arrived back in London on 2 May 1715, after almost a year away on his 'Grand Tour' and accompanied by no less than 878 items of luggage, he would have crossed the threshold of Burlington House for the first time as an adult, having reached the age of 21 only a week before (Fig. 27).[28] Although he had of course been the 3rd Earl since his father died, it was only now that he was the master of his own 'house' and head of the family. It is worth bearing in mind also that this coming of age had exceptional significance, both for himself and for everyone around him, because it had always been the predicted moment when he would come into his inheritance – the moment for which, in the old cliché, his life so far had been a preparation. Awareness of this fact had lent a peculiar urgency to his absorption of influences, ideas and taste, especially from those whom his mother had taken care to introduce into his circle. His early and lasting appreciation of the arts of painting, music and literature, for instance, was not something that he just happened to have in common with her, but had been carefully and deliberately nurtured in him by her patronage of the leading artists, writers and musicians of the day. It was indeed fortunate that she had had the taste and discrimination to engage painters of the calibre of Ricci and Pellegrini to decorate Burlington House, and the foresight to encourage the likes of Alexander Pope and John Gay, the Queen's physician Dr Arbuthnot, and the greatest musical genius of the age George Frideric Handel, to treat it as their home.

In one important art, however, it had been more difficult for Juliana to influence her son's taste. Exactly when and from whom the young Earl first contracted the virus that was to become his deepest intellectual passion

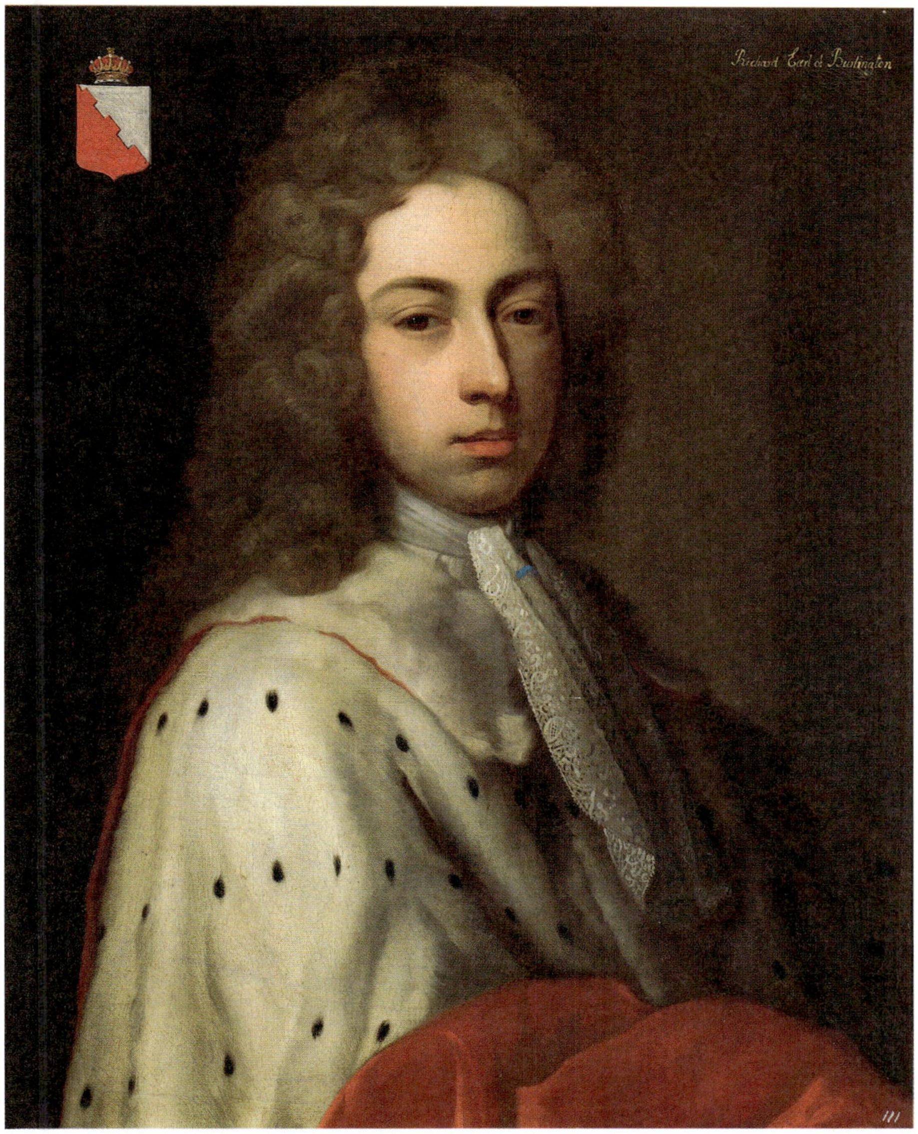

Fig. 27
English School, *Richard Boyle, 3rd Earl of Burlington*, c. 1715–20.
National Trust, Oxburgh Hall, Norfolk

will never be known. As has often been pointed out, neither the account of his purchases nor his itinerary reveal any particular interest in architecture during his first tour of Italy and the Continent. However, the seventeen weeks he spent in Rome between 29 September 1714 and 4 February 1715 was by far the longest of his sojourns anywhere, and although he was apparently ill for some of the time it is hard to believe that it was not there in the Eternal City that, perhaps without realising it at the time, he fell in love with architecture.[29] As his ears sought out the rich and enticing sounds of Italian music and song, his eyes were filled with all the vestigial glories of ancient Rome, awakening a creative sensitivity to the corresponding harmonies of proportion in the two arts that led eventually to his becoming not simply his own architect but an architect with a burning mission.

In his book *Earls of Creation* (1962), James Lees-Milne was the first to point out the irony that James Gibbs, the first architect known to have altered Burlington House – a building that Colen Campbell, his immediate successor and rival, was soon to transform into a cynosure of neo-Palladian reform in English architectural taste – had trained in Italy under Carlo Fontana, a pupil of Bernini no less, and the leading living exponent of Italian baroque architecture.[30] The fact that Gibbs was a practising Roman Catholic, a suspected Jacobite, and in secret correspondence with the attainted rebel Earl of Mar, may also seem to some historians indicative of the 3rd Earl's true political sympathies, which it is claimed he kept hidden for the whole of his life in order to work undercover for the Jacobite cause.[31] However, it is worth considering whether there might have been a more straightforward explanation for Gibbs's employment at Burlington House, namely that it was probably not the 3rd Earl who was responsible for employing him there in the first place.

It may be coincidental, but at around the time the Dowager Countess would have been looking for someone to sort out Burlington House's interior-planning problems – i.e. 1710–11 – Gibbs happened to be an exceptionally well-trained, hard-up architect recently returned from Italy who, having built nothing as yet, would have been quite prepared to take on almost any work he could find. It so happened also that his only commission to date had been to divide up a house in the Privy Gardens, Whitehall, into separate dwellings for John Erskine, 11th Earl of Mar, and his joint Secretary of State for Scotland, Hugh Campbell, 3rd Earl of Loudoun. Modest though it was, this job gave Gibbs just the kind of experience in re-planning an interior that the Countess needed, and moreover in a building just across Green Park should she have wanted to appraise the quality of his work. Furthermore, unknown as he was, Gibbs had been canny enough to enrol as a founder member of Sir Godfrey Kneller's new drawing academy in 1711. Here, as the first British architect to be trained abroad, there can be little doubt that he would have immediately attracted the notice of one of its founding directors, Antonio Pellegrini.

There are only scraps of evidence linking James Gibbs reliably to Burlington House. The most informative comes in a partly autobiographical 'Manuscri by Mr. Gibbs Memorandums &c.' preserved in the library of Sir John Soane's Museum. Here it is stated, without any indication of date, that 'the Earl of Burlington had him to build and adorne his house and offices in piccadilly, they are all built w^{t} solid portland stone, as is likewise the fine circular colonad fronting the house.'[32] While 'adorne' could include making alterations to the interior of the house – such as the design and installation of a new main staircase and chapel – more telling is the stress placed on the use of Portland stone throughout to transform its exterior, including the 'offices' in the forecourt and the 'colonad fronting the house'. This strongly suggests that, despite the fact that some of these elements were in the end built to a different design by a different architect (i.e. Colen Campbell), they were *recollected* by Gibbs as a unified ensemble. As Walter Ison pointed out in his chapter on Burlington House in the *Survey of London*, 'it is feasible to assume that Gibbs (or whoever Campbell's immediate predecessor was) provided designs for transforming the whole group of buildings, and that the stables, colonnade, and some changes within the house were all that were finished when Burlington turned against the "modern Italian" style exemplified by Gibbs ... and transferred his patronage to Campbell.'[33] But if this were the case, one might ask why Gibbs's proposed transformation began with the stable block and then proceeded to the non-essential colonnade when it would have surely been more logical to attend to both offices first, along with the façade of the house itself. A possible explanation for this odd sequence is suggested by the awkwardness of the conjunction of the cornice of the colonnade with the pilaster on the corner of the stable block (Fig. 28). As this was something that Gibbs would have been careful to resolve had these two elements been designed and built together, they must represent discrete stages in the new forecourt's evolution. In addition, there were no doubt pragmatic reasons for tackling the stables first, since this would have been less disruptive to the general life of the house than the demolition and reconstruction of its laundry and kitchens. Also, it could well be that work started here, probably either just before or during the 3rd Earl's tour in 1714–15, because by then he was fast approaching his majority and Juliana could feel justified in authorising a start to the external improvements to the house, particularly one that would contain and screen from view the unavoidable mess associated with a stable yard. And finally, it is also not hard to imagine that it would only have been later that Gibbs, keen to demonstrate his abilities, dazzled his client one day with a drawing of the arms of Bernini's colonnade in the piazza of St Peter's, Rome, somehow magically transported to her front door (Fig. 29).[34]

Another reference to what can only be Burlington House occurs in a letter written to Gibbs on 16 April 1716 from Avignon by his exiled friend and former patron the Earl of Mar, in which Mar remarks upon Gibbs having 'work enough upon your hands in Piccadilly.'[35] Although Mar's information may have been a little out of date, his comment certainly implies that Gibbs's undertakings at Burlington House amounted to a good deal more than Campbell was prepared to admit in his 'Explanation' of

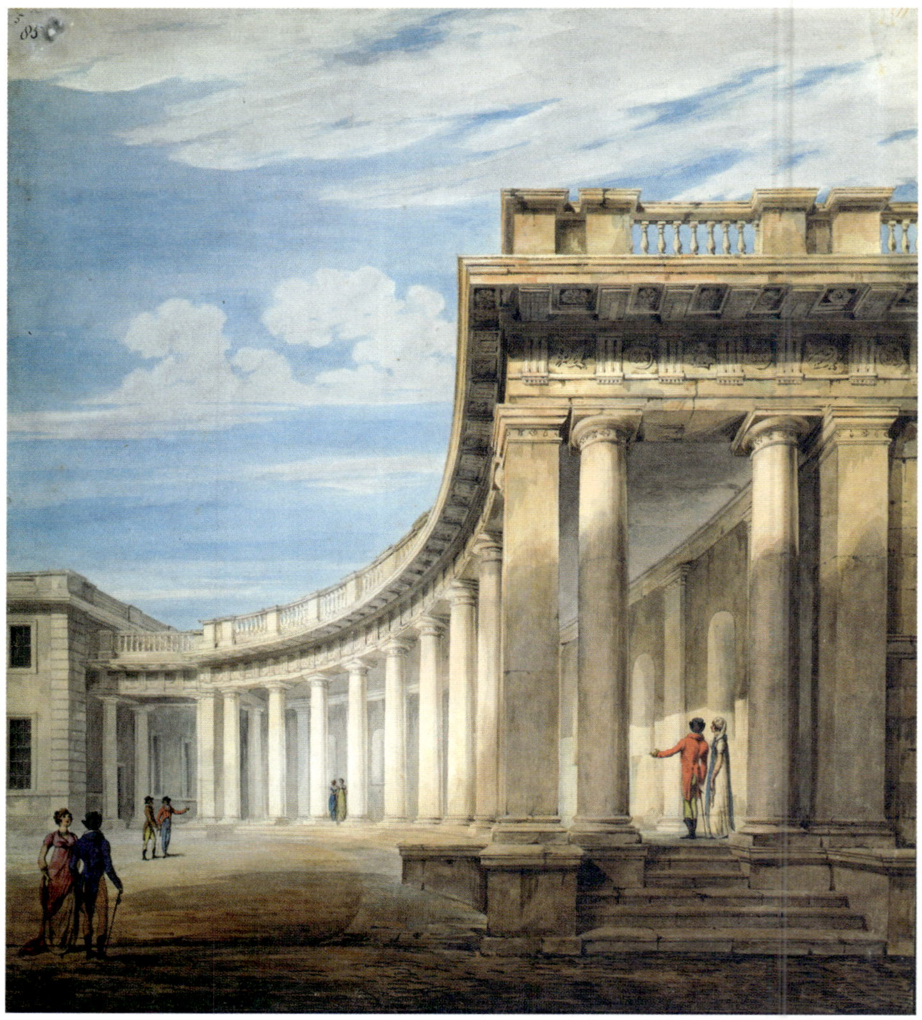

Fig. 28
Soane office, East quadrant of the Burlington House colonnade, RA Lecture drawing, 1811.
Sir John Soane's Museum, London, 17/4/10

its transformed appearance in volume III of *Vitruvius Britannicus* (1725). Here, by a piece of mischievous legerdemain, Campbell suppressed any indication that his predecessor had designed and built the forecourt colonnade (which he showed in plan only), pointing out merely that, 'the Stables [on the east side of the forecourt] were built by another Architect before I had the Honour of being called to his Lordship's Service, which obliged me to make the Offices opposite, conformable to them' (Figs 30, 31).[36]

The only known mention of Gibbs in connection with payment for work undertaken for the 3rd Earl is an entry in Richard Graham and Jabez Collier's account

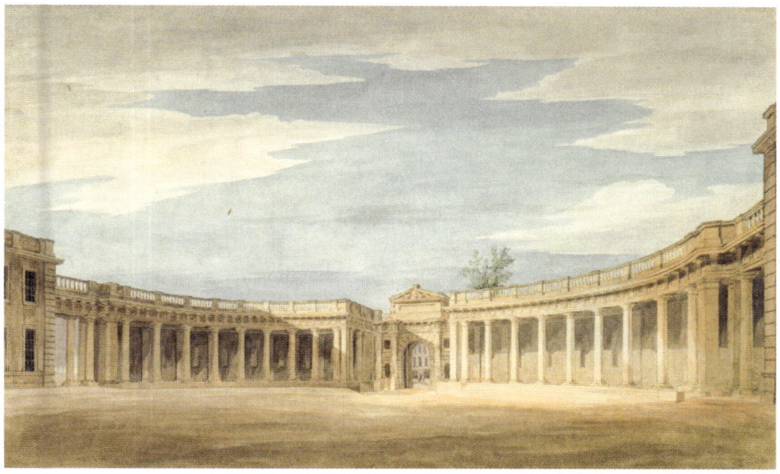

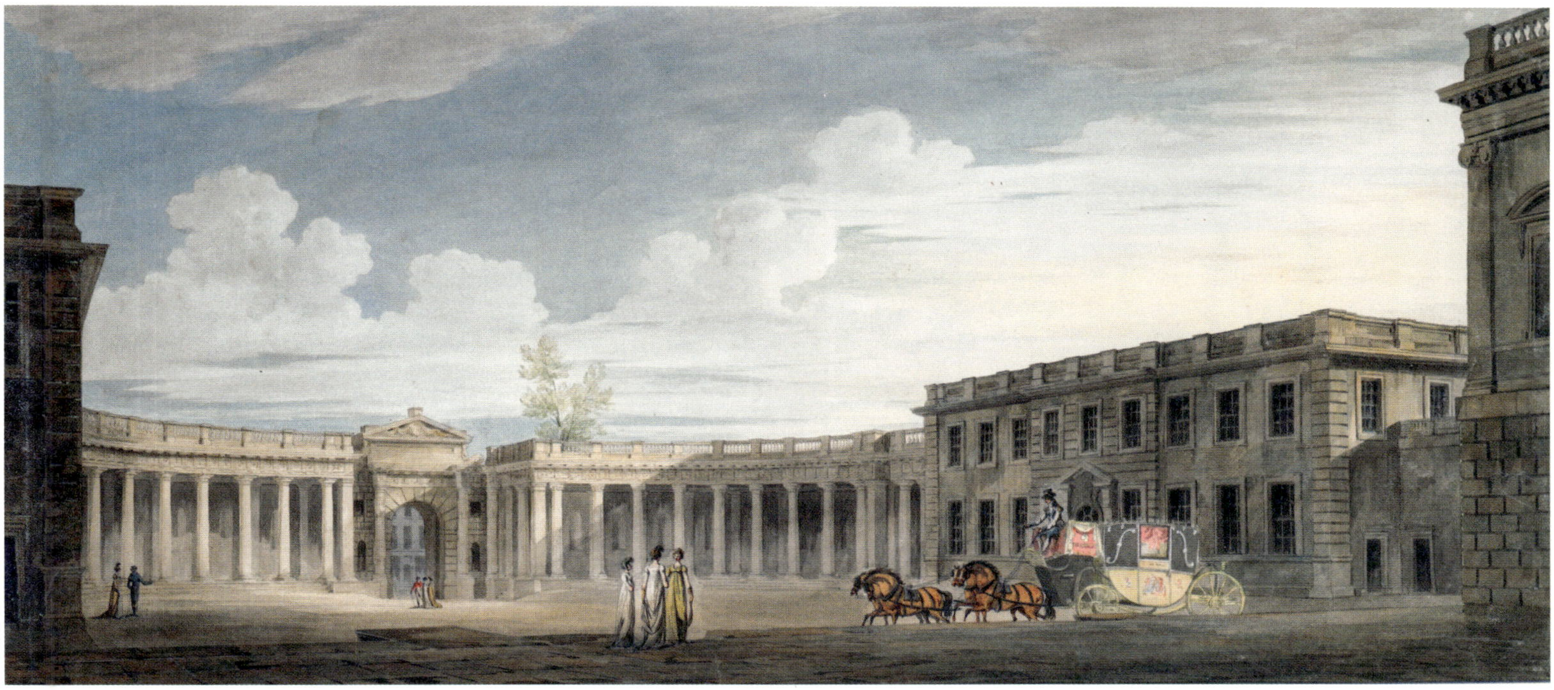

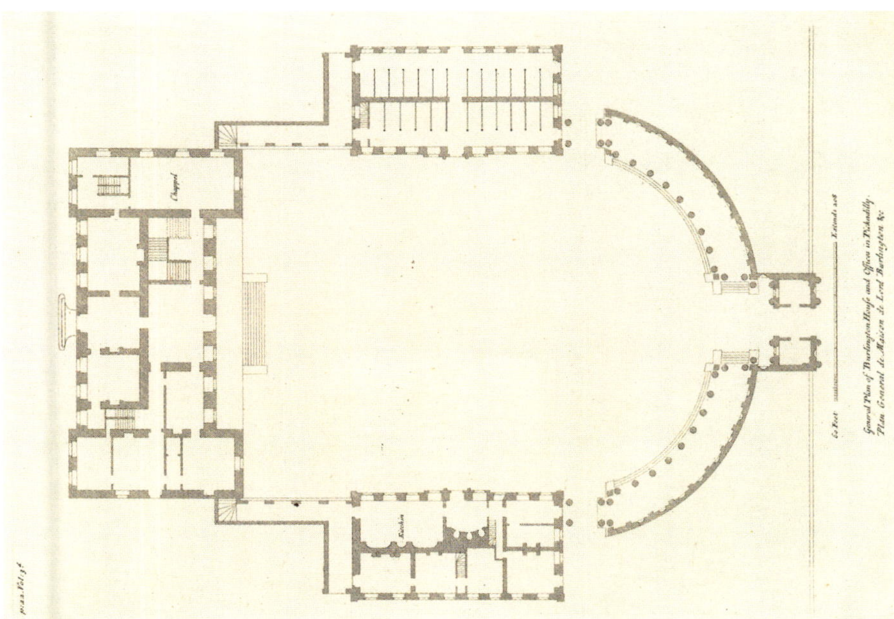

Fig. 29
Soane office, Perspective of the Burlington House colonnade looking south-east, RA Lecture drawing, 1811.
Sir John Soane's Museum, London, 17/4/9

Fig. 30
Soane office, Perspective of the Burlington House courtyard looking south-west, RA Lecture drawing, 1811.
Sir John Soane's Museum, London, 17/4/7

Fig. 31
After Colen Campbell, Burlington House, general plan of the house and offices, from *Vitruvius Britannicus*, 1725, vol. III, plate 22.
RIBA Collections

book recording Samuel Gunn's receipt of 9 guineas on 11 September 1719, 'being in full of a Bill for measuring the Masons and other work as by a Bill of Particulars signed by Mr Gibbs'.[37] Although this bill might perhaps relate to Chiswick rather than Burlington House, the fact that it was paid at least two years after Campbell had supplanted his rival is a reminder of the incremental, overlapping, stop-start nature of the building process, especially when 'ready money' is an issue. The financial crisis that came to a head when the 3rd Earl's agents informed him in 1717 that his debts amounted to upwards of £23,000, almost certainly brought further building work to a halt.[38] It also probably marked the end of that first, euphoric phase in the artistic life of Burlington House to which Richard Graham drew enthusiastic attention in his dedication of the second edition of Dryden's translation of Du Fresnoy's *The Art of Painting* (1716),[39] and that John Gay immortalised in his poem *Trivia: or, The Art of Walking the Streets of London,* published in January that year:

> Yet Burlington's fair palace still remains;
> Beauty within, without Proportion reigns.
> Beneath his Eye declining Art revives,
> The Wall with animated Picture lives;
> There Handel strikes the Strings, the melting Strain
> Transports the Soul, and thrills through ev'ry Vein;
> There oft' I enter (but with cleaner Shoes)
> For Burlington's belov'd by ev'ry Muse.
> (Book II, lines 493–500)

It may well have been this enforced hiatus in building operations as much as a Damascene change of heart that prepared the way for the 3rd Earl's conversion to the neo-Palladian cause. Given the circumstances it may not have been irrelevant that a design that adhered to the more austere 'reformed' style of classical architecture promoted in Campbell's *Vitruvius Britannicus* – the second volume of which was ready for delivery to subscribers on 30 March 1717 – was less reliant on exterior carved ornament and might therefore be cheaper to execute than a design in more baroque taste. By about the middle of 1717 also, the second book of the Venetian architect Giacomo Leoni's *The Architecture of A. Palladio; In Four Books* (1715–20) – the first complete English translation of Andrea Palladio's *I Quattro Libri d'Architettura* (1570) – was attracting numerous new subscribers, including the 3rd Earl himself. Although he was later to be critical of inaccuracies in this edition, the fact that his mother had been among its original subscribers (by a strange coincidence proposals for its publication had appeared on the day of his arrival back in England), and Sebastiano Ricci had supplied the design for its handsome allegorical frontispiece (as well as for a spurious portrait of the author), suggests that it would have found much favour in Burlington House at that time (Fig. 32). Certainly, its fashionable success as an unprecedentedly lavish English architectural book cannot be unconnected to the 3rd Earl's initial conversion to neo-Palladianism and his determination as a result to refashion Burlington House into the first exemplar of reformed architectural taste in London.

In view of his credentials Leoni might have expected to be in the running for this task. Instead he had to be content with the consolation prize of designing the large house that faced the bottom of the Earl's garden (Queensberry, later Uxbridge House, also known as No. 7 Burlington Gardens, which was built in 1721–23). The fact was, Campbell had gained a decisive advantage over Leoni by securing for publication in the second volume of *Vitruvius Britannicus* what were then supposed to be Inigo Jones's designs for Whitehall Palace (they were actually by Jones's assistant John Webb). This coup consolidated in spectacular fashion Campbell's careful presentation of himself in his first volume as a faithful

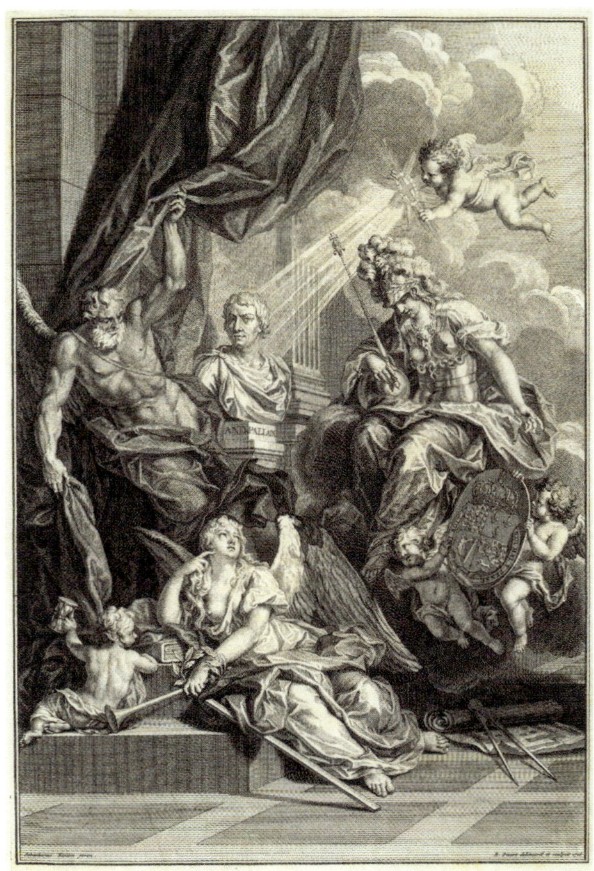

Fig. 32
Bernard Picart, after Sebastiano Ricci, Frontispiece for *The Architecture of A. Palladio; In Four Books*, 1715.
RIBA Collections

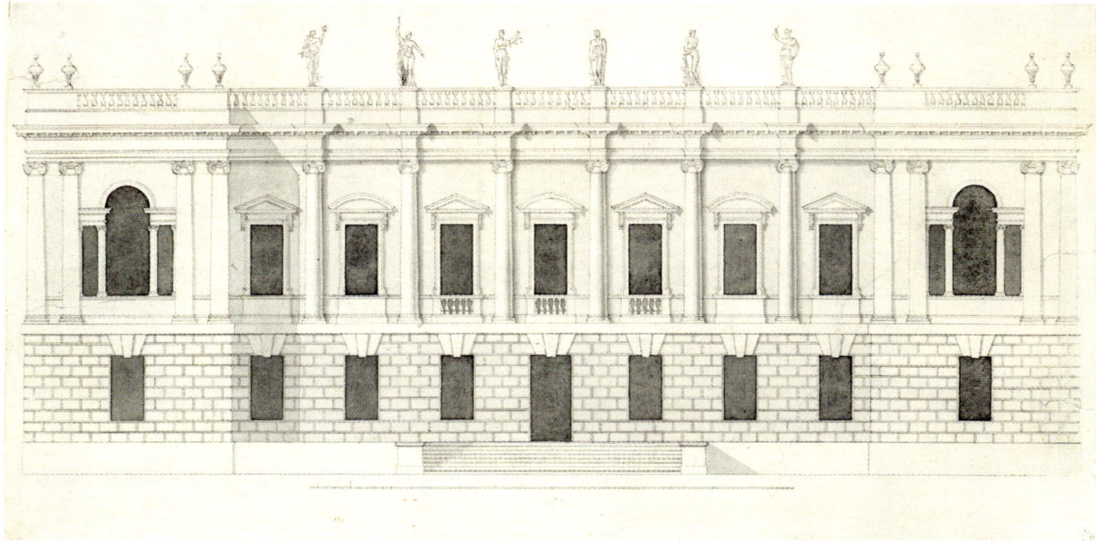

Fig. 33
Colen Campbell, Design for remodelling and refacing Burlington House: elevation of the south front almost as executed, 1717.
RIBA Collections, SC10/1(3)

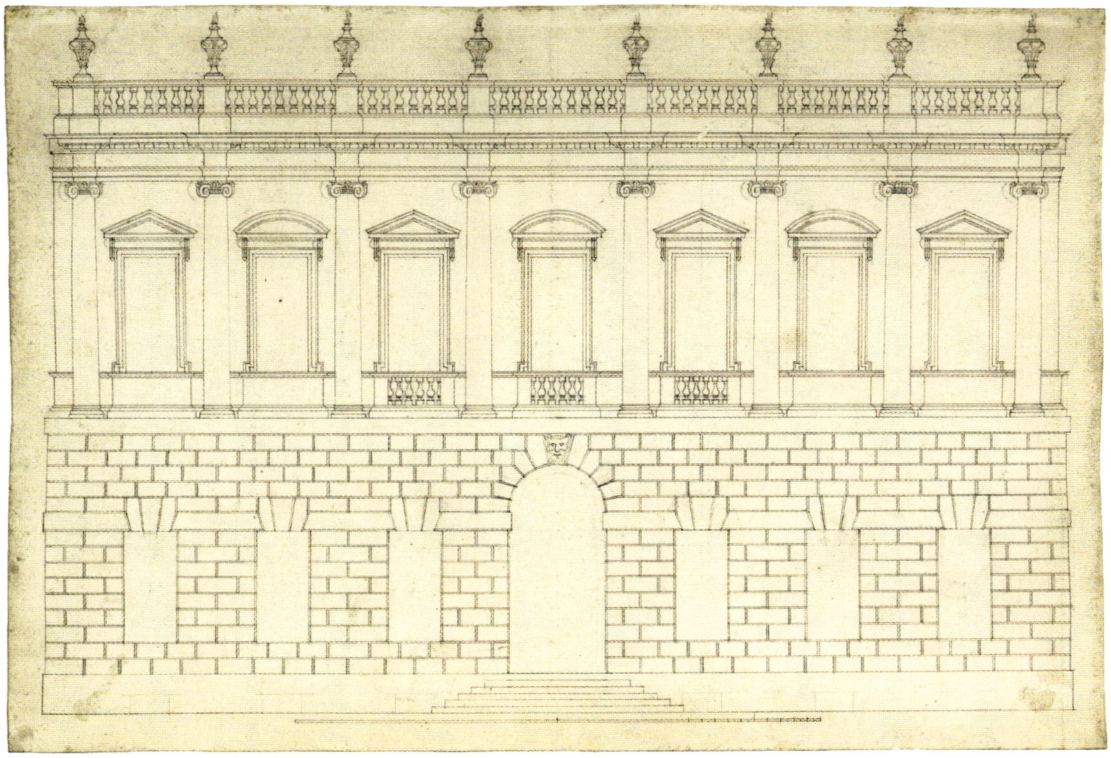

Fig. 34
Colen Campbell, Unexecuted design for a house for Archibald Campbell, 1st Earl of Islay: entrance façade elevation, drawing for *Vitruvius Britannicus*, 1715, plate 54.
RIBA Collections, VOS/49 folio 50

and knowledgeable follower of Jones, whose Banqueting House in Whitehall he had no hesitation in declaring 'without Dispute, the first Structure in the World'. Particularly in this first volume Campbell had deliberately juxtaposed plans and elevations of buildings by (or presumed to be by) Jones alongside buildings of a more baroque complexion. These contrasts he then resolved with strategically placed examples of his own designs which, though Palladian in inspiration, often owed more to Jones's example. Indeed, it was Campbell's championing of Jones as the 'British Vitruvius' and Palladio's equal, that was ultimately responsible for the success of *Vitruvius Britannicus* as the key manifesto of the neo-Palladian movement in England. Thus, it was no accident that the façade of the first building the 3rd Earl designed himself – the so-called 'Casina' or 'Bagnio' in the garden at Chiswick, which Campbell made a point of publishing alongside Burlington House in volume III of *Vitruvius Britannicus* as 'the first Essay of his Lordship's happy invention, Anno 1717' – was made up almost entirely of elements taken directly from Campbell's just published engravings of Jones's presumed designs for Whitehall.

It is hardly surprisingly therefore that the presiding genius of Campbell's transformation of the exterior of Burlington House between 1717 and 1719 proved in the end to be not Palladio but Inigo Jones (Fig. 33). Close to his unexecuted 'Design for the Earl of Islay', published in the first volume of *Vitruvius Britannicus* (plate 54; see Fig. 34), and, like that, distantly related to Palladio's design for the Palazzo di Iseppo da Porto in Vicenza, the derivation

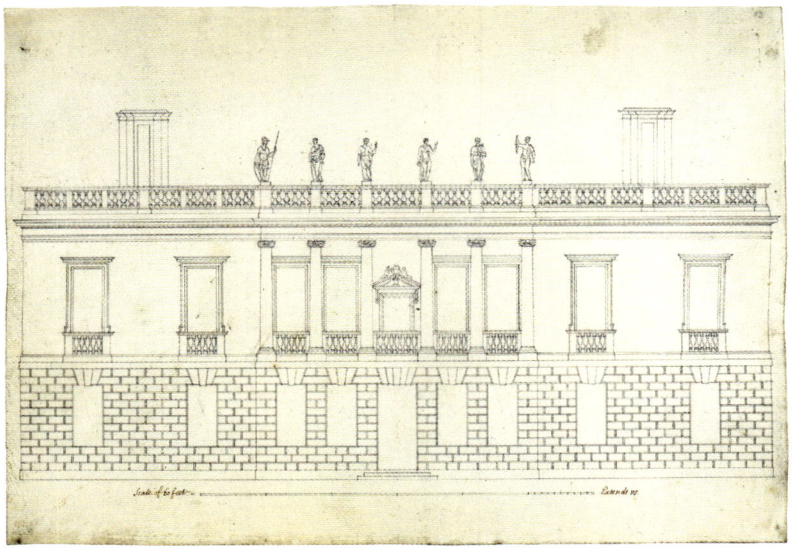

Fig. 35
Colen Campbell, Queen's House in Greenwich: elevation to the park, drawn for *Vitruvius Britannicus*, 1715, vol. I, plate 15.
RIBA Collections, VOS/49 folio 13

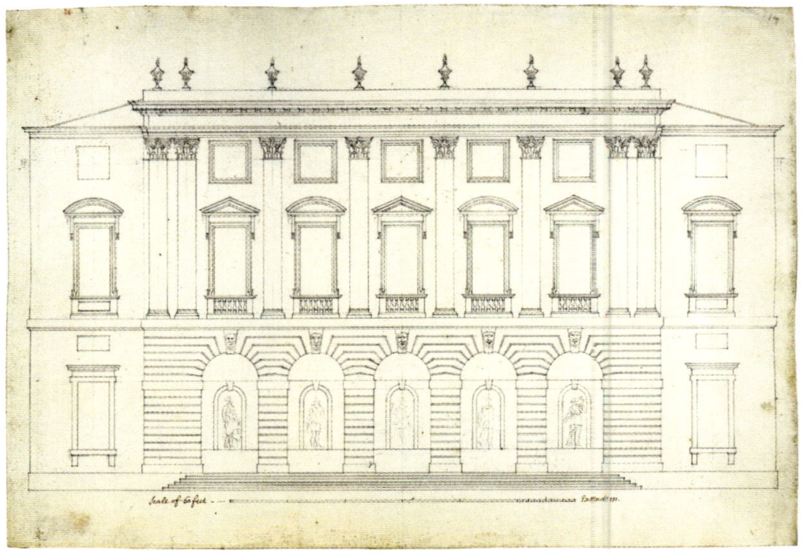

Fig. 37
Colen Campbell, Somerset House in the Strand: elevation of the Great Gallery facing the Thames, drawn for *Vitruvius Britannicus*, 1715, vol. I, plate 16.
RIBA Collections, VOS/49 folio 14

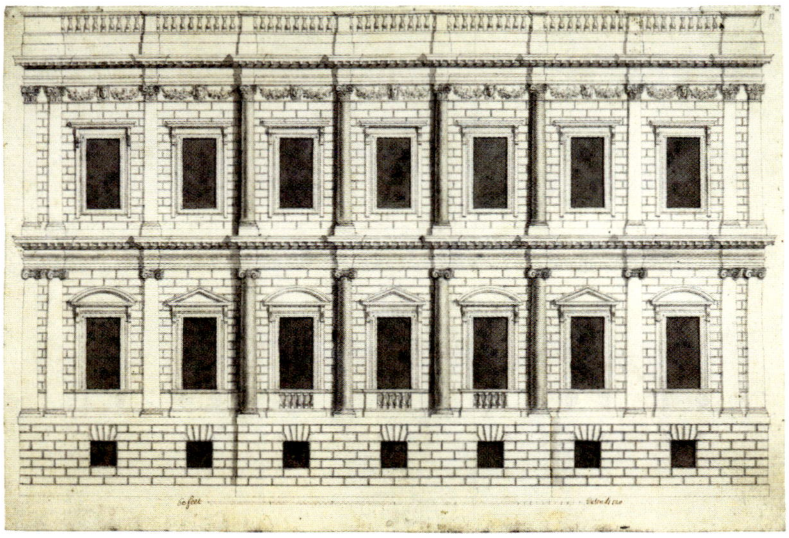

Fig. 36
Colen Campbell, Banqueting House, Whitehall: elevation, drawn for *Vitruvius Britannicus*, 1715, vol. I, plate 13.
RIBA Collections, VOS/49 folio 11

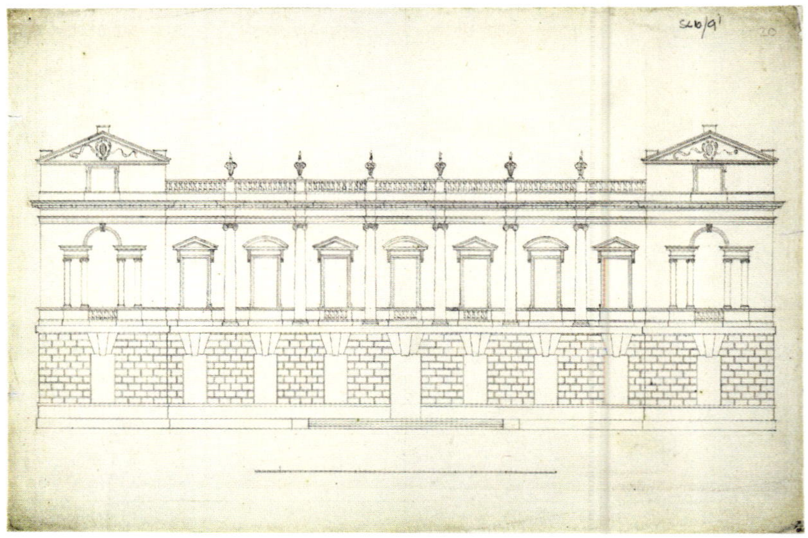

Fig. 38
Colen Campbell, Design for remodelling and refacing Burlington House: elevation of the south or court front with pedimented angle towers, 1717.
RIBA Collections, SC10/1(1)

of Campbell's new south front for the house was not dissimilar from that of the 3rd Earl's Chiswick 'Bagnio', in that its distinctive features were borrowed from several of the key buildings by Jones lauded in Campbell's book. Thus, from the Queen's House, Greenwich (Fig. 35), Campbell took the idea of a rustic basement-cum-ground storey; from the Banqueting House, Whitehall (Fig. 36), an Ionic colonnaded main storey that only varied significantly from its source by having walls faced in plain ashlar rather than rusticated masonry; and from the Great Gallery at Old Somerset House (Fig. 37), windows dressed with enriched architraves, scrolled consoles, pulvinated friezes and alternate triangular and segmental pediments. Campbell's homage to Jones is evident also in his little-known alternative design for Burlington House in which he proposed raising the east and west wings of the building into squat pedimented towers reminiscent of the south front of Wilton House (Fig. 38). With its supposed Jonesian pedigree, this idea was to be soon taken up by the 3rd Earl in his design for his brother-in-law's house at Tottenham Park, Wiltshire, in 1721, and thereafter became almost as much a leitmotif of the neo-Palladian movement as the *serliana*, the so-called 'Venetian' or 'Palladian' tripartite window. And although not quite the first *serlianas* in an English house – Vanbrugh had pipped him to the post by building an example in the west loggia at Kings Weston House, Bristol, in 1717–18 – the fact that Campbell used them to give emphasis to the wings of Burlington House was another similarly overt evocation of Jones, since it was he who had pioneered this motif in England, first in the Queen's Chapel at St James's Palace (1623–25) and then in his supposed Whitehall designs.

However, the dramatic refacing of the front of his London house in the idiom of a Vicentine palazzo was not the most visible statement of the 3rd Earl's new architectural allegiance. More prominent still was the erection of a triumphal gateway on Piccadilly (Fig. 39) modelled on the York House Water Gate, yet another much-admired building believed to have been designed by Inigo Jones. Although Campbell dated his designs for the new south front and 'Great Gate' to 1717 and 1718 respectively, the latter had probably been executed before work finally began on altering the front of the house in August 1719. By the end of that month, the 3rd Earl had left for a second tour of Italy, this time to study with his own eyes and far greater knowledge not only the precious legacy of Palladio's actual buildings but any other traces he could find of that great master's life and work. As a result, his second homecoming from Italy – he was back at Burlington House by 10 December that year – was to have an even greater impact than his first.[40]

IN A WAY, it was a repeat performance, for once again the 3rd Earl arrived back in London thoroughly fired up by what he had seen in Italy. This time he returned with a very specific goal in mind and precisely the means to achieve it. The story of how he found a collection of Palladio's drawings of ancient Roman baths at the Villa Maser, where the great architect had died nearly a century and a half earlier, is probably romantic embroidery on what really happened. However, there is no question that, despite some of the worst floods in living memory, the 3rd Earl did manage to buy a cache of drawings in Venice, and that this set him on the way to amassing within the next eighteen months the largest collection of drawings by Palladio and Inigo Jones in existence. What the 3rd Earl learnt by studying these drawings has been described by the architectural historian John Harris as 'cataclysmic' in its effect. In short, they taught him not *what* the Renaissance masters had derived from antique models but *how* they had done so. With that came the realisation, shared by no-one else at the time apart from Nicholas Hawksmoor, that Inigo Jones had evolved an entire vocabulary of interior ornament from studying

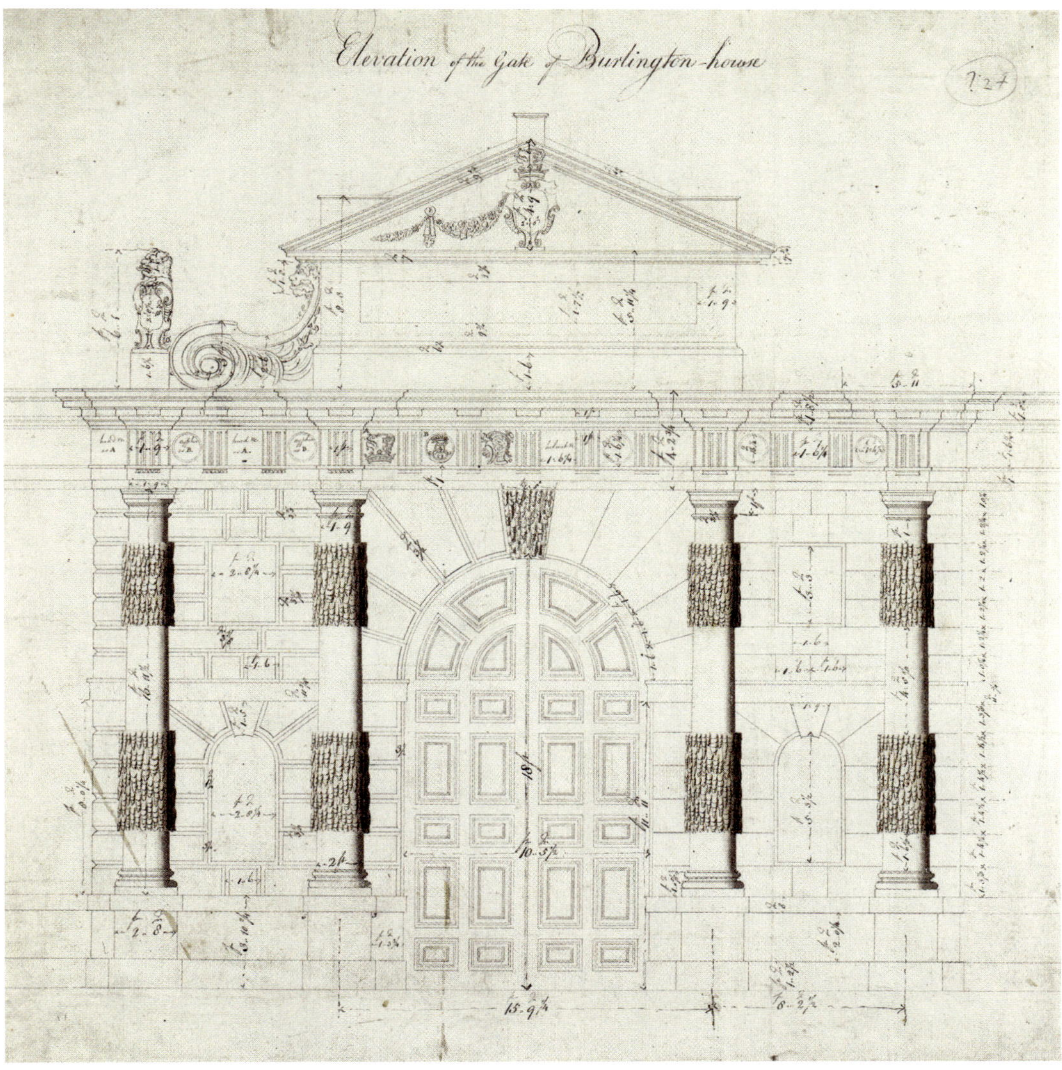

Fig. 39
George Meredith, Measured drawing of the Great Gate, Burlington House: south elevation to Piccadilly, *c.* 1782.
Royal Academy of Arts, London, 05/472

Fig. 40
William Aikman, *William Kent*, *c.* 1710–20
Government Art Collection

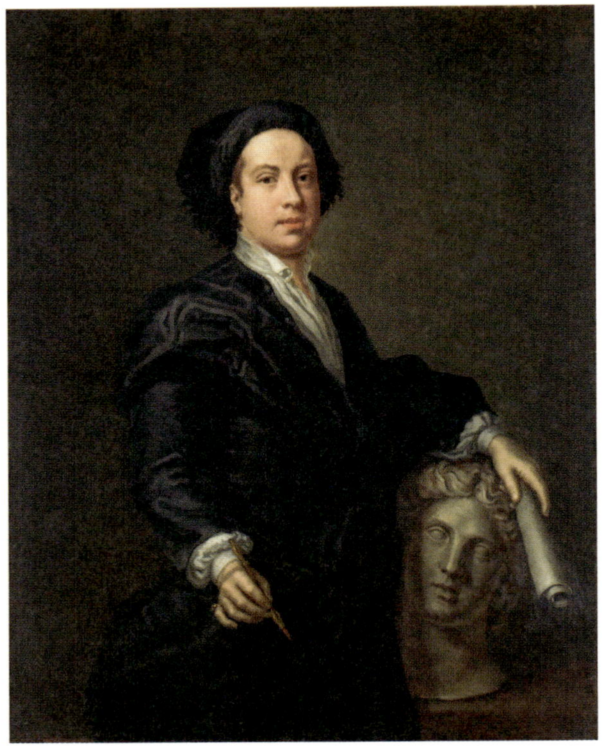

Palladio's reconstructions of ancient Roman monuments in Book II of *I Quattro Libri*. Yet again, it was Jones who showed the true path, a path that, as Harris points out, would lead the Earl back to ancient Rome, since his 'adoption of this new grammar of ornament would become a distinguishing mark of his progress from being a neo-Palladian architect to a neo-classic one.'[41]

The most immediate architectural problem the 3rd Earl faced on returning to Burlington House was how to create an interior that corresponded to its magnificent new 'Palladian' façade. There is little doubt he believed he had found an important part of the answer by bringing back with him an ebullient, ambitious Yorkshireman who, after ten years of study as a painter in Rome, had acquired an inexhaustible fund of ideas for designing interiors 'al Italiano,' as well as all the natural charm of a true-born Italian gentleman or 'Signor', as William Kent was to be affectionately nicknamed by the Earl's family for the rest of his life (Fig. 40). The architectural imprint of Kent's long residence in Burlington House is impossible to gauge today, despite the fact that it was from here that he launched a comet-like career that was to draw into its wake almost every aspect of early Georgian architecture and design. Initially, however, it is clear that his contribution was strictly that of a decorative painter. Thus despite a stinking cold, within six weeks of his arrival in London he wrote to his friend and former patron Burrell Massingberd, 'I have made a sketch in collers for the great roome in the front, and all the rest of the ornements yt are, to be al Italiano, I waite only to get my things & then hope shall set to work' (Fig. 42).[42] Kent's mention of 'all the rest of the ornements yt are' is almost certainly a reference to what is probably his *trompe l'œil* decoration of the cove in the Saloon, a small section of which was revealed in 2001–04 under fourteen layers of oil-based overpaint.[43]

It is also clear that, at this critical moment of Kent's arrival, Campbell's reputation was riding high, however much he may have annoyed the Earl's agents by refusing to abate building tradesmen's bills by the full amount they wanted in order to curry his lordship's favour.[44] Kent's remark to Massingberd about 'being quite a stranger to the extravigant tast of ye English vertuosi in painting sculpt: arch that I don't [k]now w[h]ere I am when I am once [out] of the gates of L:d Burlingtons house w[h]ere I think you may see a true Palladian front'[45] is clearly an echo of the opinion of the house's owner, who like Kent was seeing it for the first time in built form. Far from treating Kent as a rival, therefore, it is much more likely that Campbell would have welcomed the chance of borrowing ideas from him for improving on the old-fashioned bolection panelling he had proposed for the interior of Wanstead House, Essex, the 'Palladian answer to Blenheim and Castle Howard' that he had begun to design for Sir Richard Child from about 1714.[46]

Located at the centre of the *piano nobile* of its new principal front, and probably at this date the only room in the south range to be given a raised ceiling and cove, the 'Saloon' (an anglicising of the Italian 'salone') was now architecturally the most important space in Burlington House. As such it corresponded precisely to what Palladio had termed a 'hall'. 'Every well-order'd House', he wrote, 'ought to have in the middle, or chief part, some place with which all the other parts of the House have an easy Communication. Those places in the Ground-Story are vulgarly call'd Entries, Lobbies, or Passages; and above they are Halls. They serve in a House as publick places. The Entries serve for those who attend, or wait on the Master to salute him, or to do any business with him. ... The Halls serve for all sorts of ceremonial Feasts, as Weddings, Banquets, Comedies, and such other Pastimes.'[47] Since neither Palladio nor his follower Vincenzo Scamozzi had provided any visual guidance on the subject of interior decoration, the Saloon at Burlington House became in effect a test bed for establishing the appropriate neo-Palladian 'prototype' of a room of this kind. Given the circumstances and faced with having to create something so new, it is hard to believe the three of them – an increasingly knowledgeable and exacting client, an ambitious painter-decorator just returned from ten years in Rome, and the architect most closely associated with the new taste in architecture – didn't sit down and thrash out their ideas together. It is likely too, that at some point early on they were joined by Giovanni Battista Guelphi, a rather opinionated Italian sculptor of whom the 3rd Earl had high hopes, and who may well have come up with the happy notion of decorating the pediments of doorcases with pairs of reclining *putti*.

Here for the first and perhaps only time at Burlington House, there was also a real opportunity for the 3rd Earl to turn architect, not it should be noted in the absence of professionals, but by working alongside them. Although there is no documentary evidence to show how the design of the Saloon evolved, Ian Bristow's chemical analysis of the composition of the gold size used in the 3rd Earl's time on the tabernacle wall frames and their corresponding dadoes has indicated that these belong to a distinct and probably later phase of construction as compared with the pedimented 'Van Dyck' pier-glass frames and other architectural elements in the room bearing gold leaf of the same era.[48] Given the room's priority as a 'prototype' it is hardly surprising to find recurrences of its most distinctive components featuring in many later designs by Kent and Campbell. However, perhaps the most intriguing echo of the Saloon wall frames is to be found in the unexecuted design of the upper wall panels in the interior of the Tribuna at Chiswick House. Not only is this room in effect the fully realised equivalent of the Palladian 'hall' at Burlington House, but the similarity of these panels raises the possibility that the 3rd Earl may have been responsible for their design in both cases, since the engraving of the Chiswick Tribuna design is signed categorically 'Burlington Architectus' (Fig. 41).[49]

Kent's awareness of the Saloon as the *pièce de résistance* of the house and the attention it would therefore attract spurred him to attempt the most ambitious ceiling painting of his career (Fig. 42). In taking as his subject Raphael's *The Wedding Feast of Cupid and Psyche* in the Loggia di Psiche of the Villa Farnesina, Rome, one of the most celebrated syntheses of architecture and painting of the Italian Renaissance, he probably felt he was aiming no higher than the occasion demanded. Kent tended to have a rather literal appreciation of classical

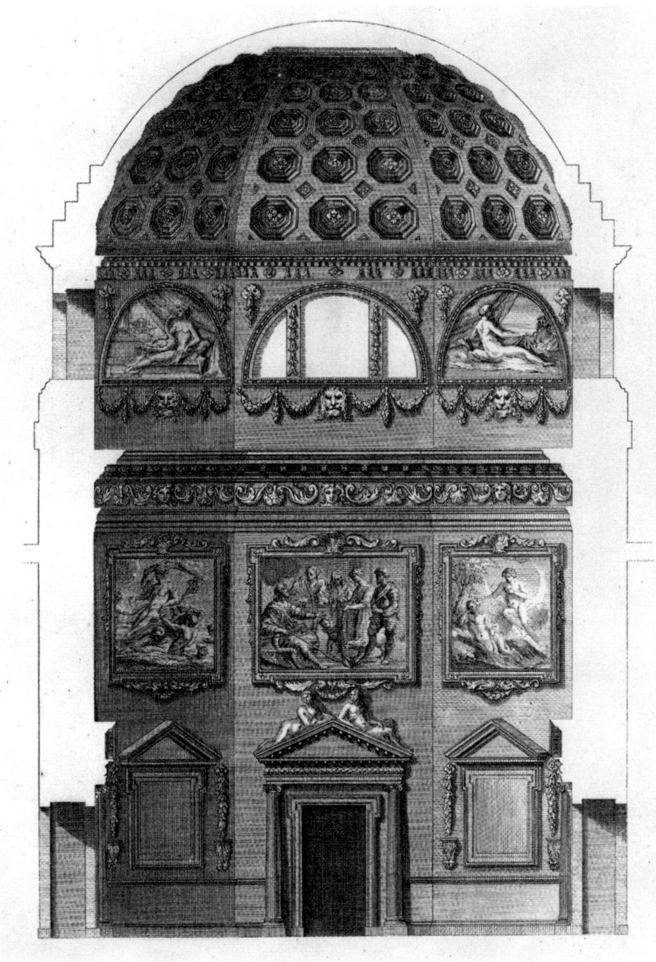

Fig. 41
Paul Fourdrinier after William Kent, The Octagonal Hall at Chiswick House designed by the 3rd Earl of Burlington, from *The Designs of Inigo Jones* ..., 1727, vol. 1, plate 72.
RIBA Collections, EW E.d.181/1

Fig. 42
William Kent, *Banquet of the Gods* (or *The Wedding Feast of Cupid and Psyche*), 1720
Royal Academy of Arts, London, 03/1095

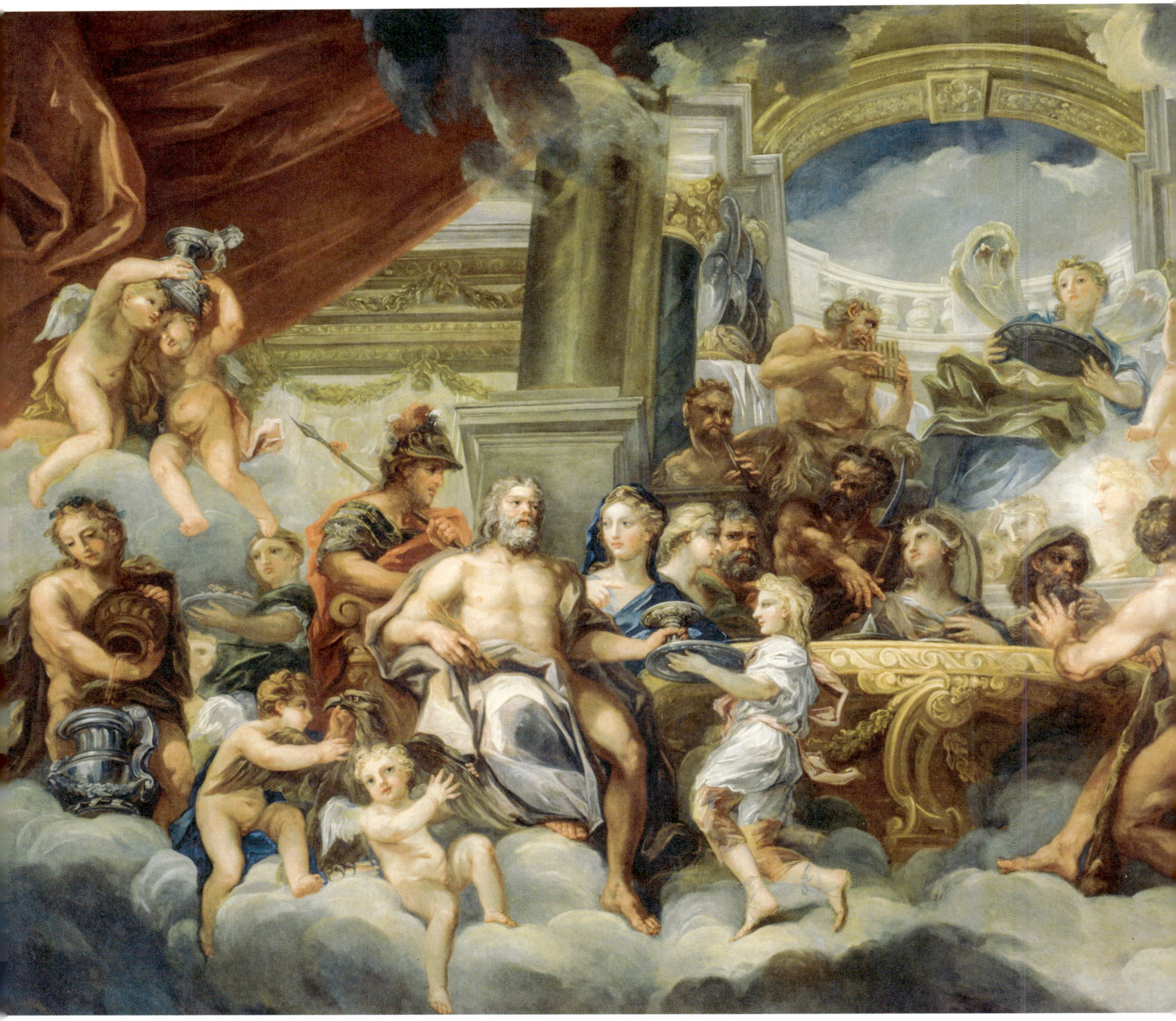

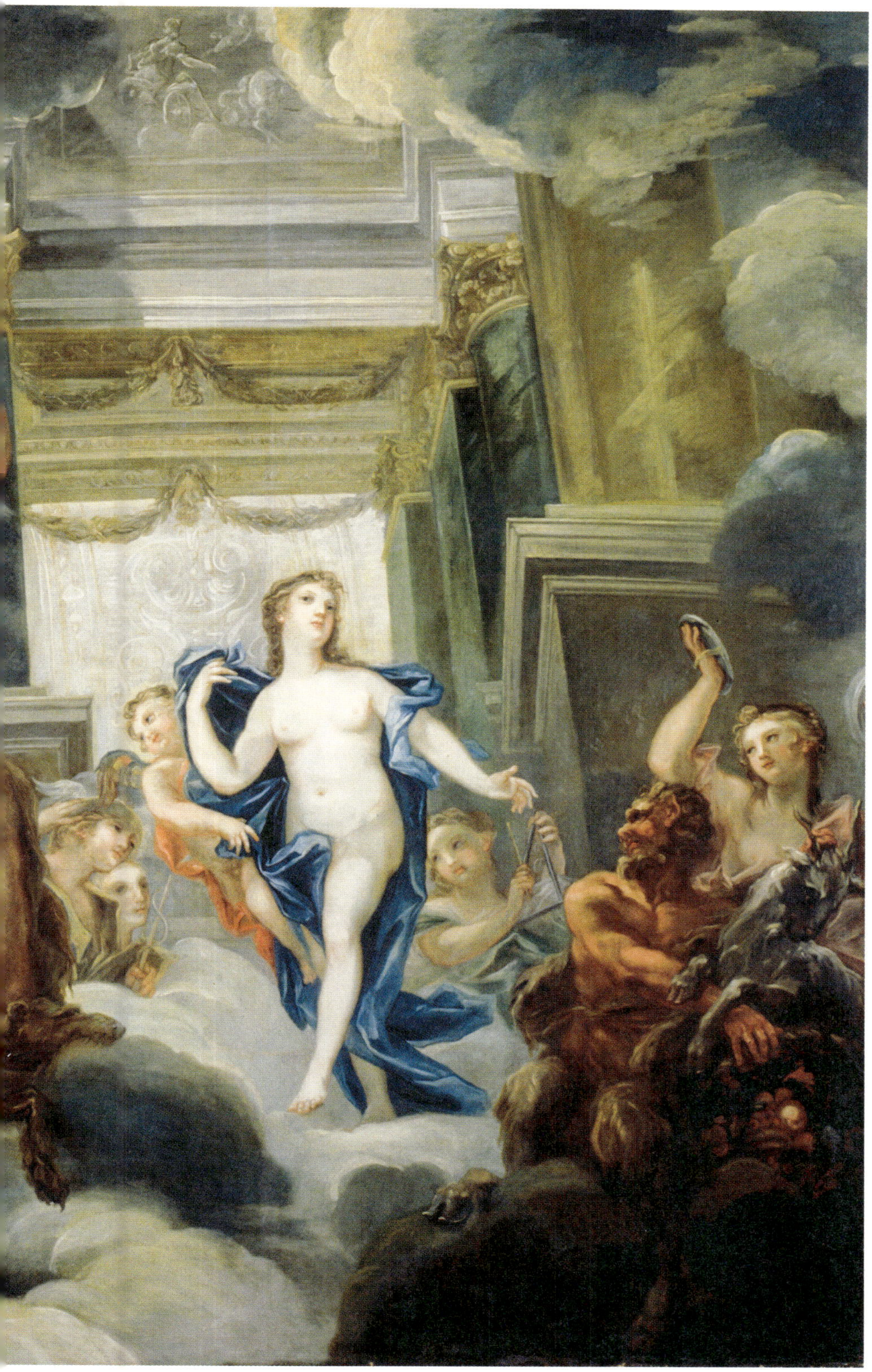

myths – he liked them in the way children like fairy stories – and deeper meanings mostly passed him by. For this reason, he was probably unaware of the underlying moral theme of Ricci's cycle of paintings on the staircase leading up to the Saloon or of its relevance to the 3rd Earl's upbringing and responsibilities. This is why, no doubt, he took his cue from what he almost certainly saw as a depiction of 'Jupiter's consent to the marriage of Cupid and Psyche' on the staircase (now Council Room) ceiling (see Fig. 26) even though the context of Ricci's cycle makes its subject more probably 'Cupid called before the gods to account for his misdemeanours' – an interpretation that Kent would by all accounts have found less appealing. It would also explain why, to judge from the fragment revealed in 2001–04 of what may be a rare depiction of Jupiter and Semele, in decorating the cove he appears to have not felt the need for iconographic consistency with the Cupid and Psyche story, and to have introduced instead more generalised scenes of the loves of the gods.

Although Campbell had already made his name as the author of *Vitruvius Britannicus*, the architect of Wanstead House (built 1715–21) and, less happily, as a short-lived Deputy Surveyor of the Office of Works (1718–19), he was to return frequently to the Saloon at Burlington House as a touchstone for the design of interiors, so much so that he made the motif of doorcases supporting reclining *putti* almost a personal trademark though, as we have seen, this does not necessarily mean that he thought of it first. For Kent on the other hand his work in Burlington House proved such a successful springboard that within six months of his arrival in England he was writing to Massingberd 'I am at present upon ye greatest works in England. Lord Burlington's Ld Duck Shandoe's [i.e. Duke of Chandos at Cannons] & Lord Castellmaine's' [at Wanstead].[50] And for the Earl also, the experience of fashioning a 'model' for a new style of classical interior in his London home can reasonably be claimed to have sparked the obsession that would culminate in his building a fully realised 'statement' of his architectural credo alongside his old Jacobean house at Chiswick. For all three the Saloon was a provisional creation, in the sense that it served a particular purpose at a

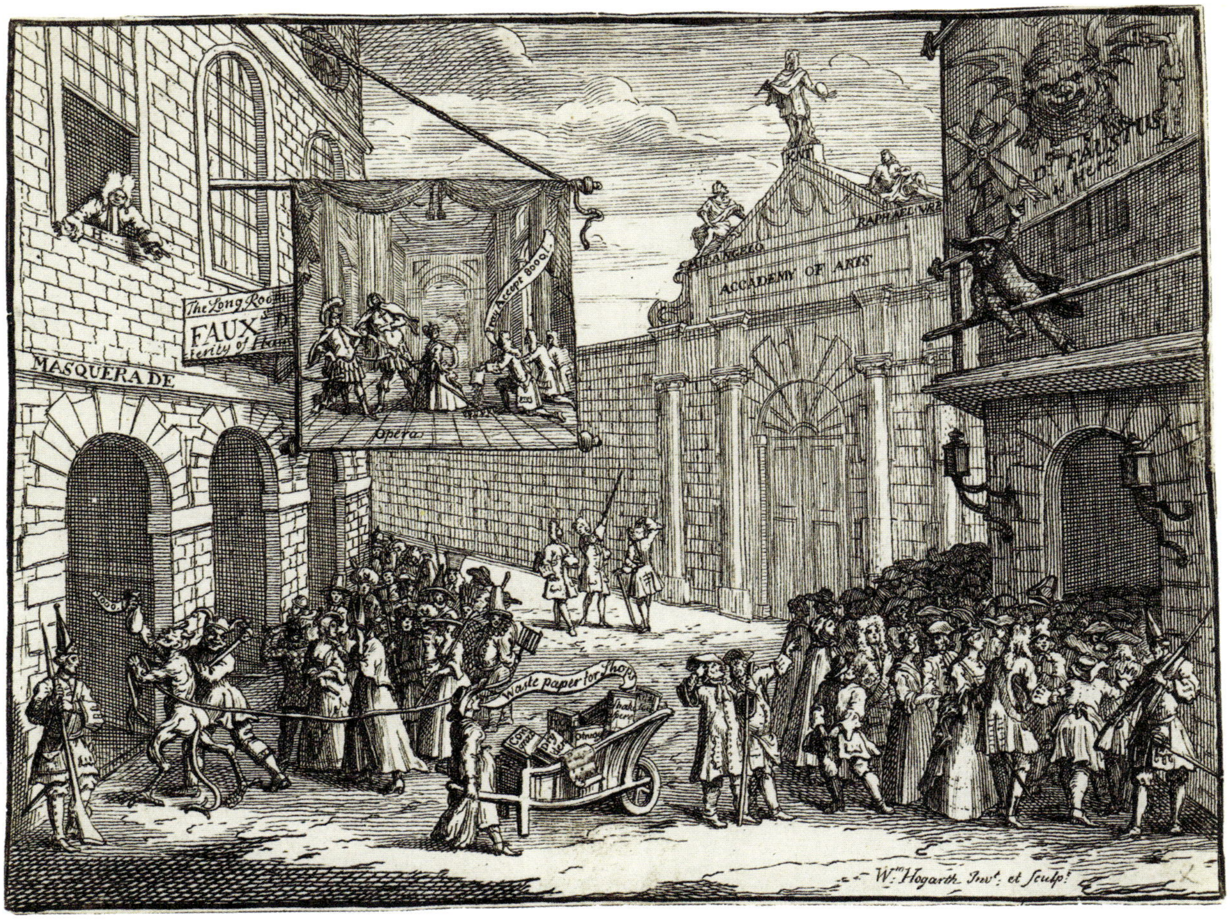

Fig. 43
William Hogarth, *Masquerades and Operas*, 1724.
British Museum, London, 1868,0808.3471

particular time, and as with all prototypes the process of its evolution was more important than its completion. Just as the 3rd Earl never got around to 'Palladianising' the north front of the house – in a sense the point had already been made on its south front – so Kent never got around to filling the Saloon tabernacle frames with paintings. In both cases the analogy is with the incompleteness of an architectural drawing, where what matters is the indication of a design rather than an image of its full realisation.

For the world beyond the Earl's circle all that was visible of Burlington House was a 28-foot-high brick and stone wall on Piccadilly, Campbell's 'Great Gate', and two rusticated archways providing wide service entrances to the stable yard on the east side of the forecourt and the kitchen court on the west. In William Hogarth's satirical print *Masquerades and Operas* (1724; Fig. 43) this total seclusion of Burlington House from the street becomes symbolic of what he sees as the utter failure of aristocratic patronage to recognise and support true merit in the arts. Hogarth's primary target is the debasement of the great traditions of English theatre – the works of Shakespeare, Dryden, Otway, Congreve and others are being carted away as scrap paper – in favour of such mindless and meretricious spectacle as actor-manager John Rich's lavish and immensely profitable staging of *The Necromancer: or, Harlequin Doctor Faustus* at his Lincoln's Inn Fields theatre, and the conjurer Isaac Fawkes's animal and puppet shows in the Long Room of Queen Anne's Tavern during Southwark Fair. Burlington House was implicated in all this for two reasons. Firstly, its owner was a director and prominent patron of the Royal Academy of Music, a joint-stock company that had squandered huge sums of money on staging expensive Italian operas sung by grossly overpaid actors in a language few could understand. Worse still, much of this money had been raised by the stratagem of hiring out the King's Theatre in the Haymarket for subscription 'masquerades' of dubious reputation. Secondly, it was where a third-rate painter by the name of KNT so ruled a roost of mutual admirers that even Michelangelo and Raphael looked up in awe as the house poet showered him with absurd praise:

> There on the walls let thy just labours shine,
> And Raphael live again in thy design.
> Yet stay awhile; call all thy genius forth,
> For Burlington unbyass'd knows thy worth:
> His judgement in thy master-strokes can trace
> Titian's strong fire and Guido's softer grace … [51]

Hogarth sums up the false values and cronyism that he saw as emanating from Burlington House with the prophetic words 'ACCADEMY OF ARTS' over a travesty of its entrance gate. He was of course no more 'unbyass'd'

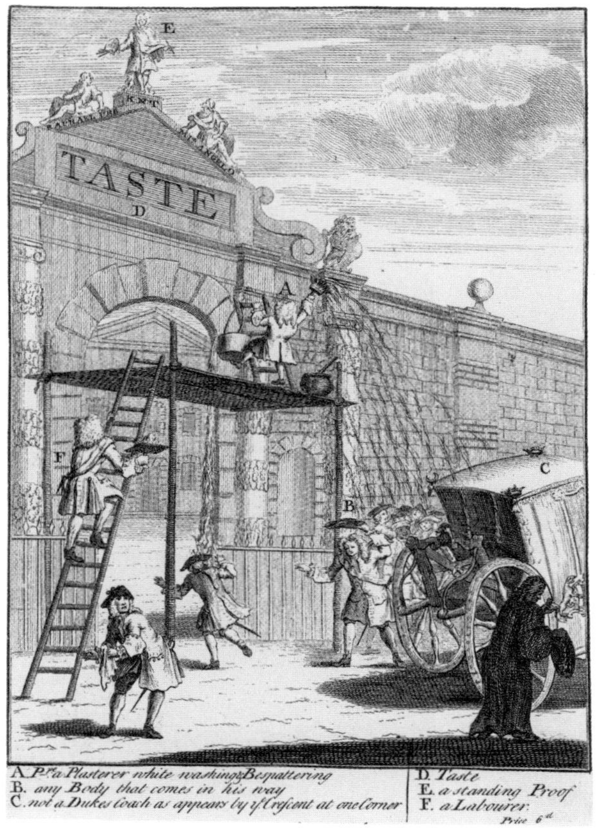

Fig. 44
Formerly attributed to William Hogarth, *Taste, or Burlington Gate*, 1732.
British Museum, London, Cc,1.114

in his opinion of Kent than the 3rd Earl had been in arranging for his protégé to paint the Cupola Room in Kensington Palace over the rightful prior claim of Sir James Thornhill. More interesting from the point of view of the history of the house is how Campbell's high wall and massive gate on Piccadilly immediately gave it the air of a citadel, whether seen from the inside as a protected (and protective) haven of aristocratic values within a potentially hostile city; or from the outside as the bastion of an arbitrary 'rule of taste', as in the anonymous engraving *Taste: or Burlington Gate*, a satire on Pope's *Epistle to Burlington* (1731; Fig. 44).

What Hogarth and Pope's *Dunciad* adversaries did not realise was that Burlington House had indeed become a kind of academy, not as they liked to imagine for bad painters, sycophantic poets and Italian musicians, but rather for a new pedigree of well-trained and highly competent English architects. The first of these, Henry Flitcroft – or 'Burlington Harry' as he became known – was working as a joiner at Burlington House in the early part of 1719 when he fell off a scaffold and broke his leg. Having paid a surgeon to attend to his recovery, the 3rd Earl is said to have accidentally come across the injured workman drawing and, 'noticing his more than ordinary talent', taken him into his service as a draughtsman.[52] The experience Flitcroft gained over the next ten years, working in various capacities on the Earl's architectural projects, and with Kent in preparing the drawings selected for publication at the Earl's expense in *The Designs of Inigo Jones* (1727), laid the foundations for an extensive architectural practice and stellar career in the Office of Works, where he succeeded Kent as Master Mason and Deputy Surveyor in 1748 and Thomas Ripley as Comptroller of the Works in 1758. A similar, if less plausible sequence of events is said to account for the transformation of Isaac Ware from a chimney-sweeper's boy to one of the most successful and well-informed architects of his generation. Although it is highly improbable that the Earl of Burlington was 'the gentleman of considerable taste and fortune' who is said to have discovered him one day chalking an elevation of the Banqueting House on the pavement of Whitehall, it is certainly the case that Ware came into Earl's orbit as a young man and may well have been able to travel to Italy as a result of his patronage.[53] And it was therefore not by chance that Ware went on to publish, not only a pattern book of *Designs by Inigo Jones and Others* (1731) that included chimneypieces designed by Kent and the 3rd Earl, but also the only English translation of Palladio's *Four Books of Architecture* (1738) to meet the Earl's exacting standards.

Ware had been apprenticed to Thomas Ripley and therefore from early on attached to the Office of Works, so is unlikely to have ever been given board and lodging at Burlington House in the way that Flitcroft and Daniel Garrett certainly were. Another protégé plucked from obscure and no doubt humble origins, Garrett was to rise so high in the estimation of his master that, when called upon to recommend a source of advice on completing the Mausoleum at Castle Howard, Sir Thomas Robinson wrote to Lord Carlisle in 1736 that 'My Ld Burlington has a much better opinion of Mr Garret's knowledge and judgement than Mr Flitcroft's or any person whatever, except Mr Kent, he lives in Burlington House and has had care and conduct of the Duke of Richmond's house [in Whitehall], my Ld Harrington's [at Peterborough] and all my L^{ds} designs he ever gave.'[54]

Three factors made the character of the architectural training on offer at Burlington House and Chiswick unique in Britain at this time: the first and most important was the high seriousness of the Earl's commitment to the study of architecture as the 'Mother of the Arts'; the second was undoubtedly the access that his 'students'

Fig. 45
William Kent, *Assembly of the Gods*, 1719–20.
Royal Academy of Arts, London, 03/264

were given to the finest collection of architectural drawings and books in the country; and the third is something so fleeting and of the moment that it can now only be guessed at, namely the excitement and energy that is sparked when vast differences in rank, experience and knowledge are set aside in pursuit of a common artistic goal. The whole model and pattern for this last vital ingredient was almost certainly set by Kent, whose extraordinary ability to cross all artificial boundaries of this kind was so evident in his relationship to the Earl.

ON 21 MARCH 1721, the 3rd Earl took a hint from Ricci's staircase paintings and married Lady Dorothy Savile, co-heiress with her sister Mary to the estates of William Savile, 2nd Marquess of Halifax, her paternal grandfather. Hoping no doubt that this would generate new projects, Kent had written excitedly to Massingberd: 'Lord Burlington is going to be marry'd to Lady Doroty Savile. So I hope ye vertu will grow stronger in our house and archetecture well floresh more.'[54] Unfortunately, a gap in the Earl's accounts between 1721 and 1725 makes it impossible to know how much work on Burlington House might have continued in these years immediately after his marriage. If, as seems likely, Lady Dorothy encouraged her husband (and Kent) to confine building work to one of their homes at a time, the fact that the first phase in the Earl's redesign of the gardens at Chiswick had probably come to an end by February 1719 (when Pope asked for permission to take a group of his friends around) and that building the new house there probably didn't start until 1727, makes it likely that it was during this period that most work was done at Burlington House to bring it more into line with the new aesthetic proclaimed in the Saloon and on its south front. Equally, with the appointment of Lady Dorothy in 1727 as one of Queen Caroline's Ladies of the Bedchamber, and the Earl's closer connection with the court party from March 1723 (he was first sworn of the Privy Council on 15 May 1729), Burlington House must have been a more convenient *pied-à-terre* than Chiswick whenever the court was in residence at St James's Palace – door to door they are less than 600 yards apart. It is unlikely also that the Earl and Countess would have planned a grand ball and dinner party there for the Prince and Princess of Wales in 1729 unless any ongoing alterations to the interior of the house were by then more or less complete.

Apart from the Saloon, the only other room in Burlington House that has survived reasonably unaltered from this period is a former bedroom or dressing-room immediately to its west, known since its restoration by the Royal Academy in 2004–05 as the Lee and James C. Slaughter Room. It was probably formed from two smaller rooms at the time the main staircase was replaced and the Saloon (the original dining room) centred over the entrance hall. The architectural historian Richard Hewlings has suggested that the richly carved and gilded compartmented framework of the ceiling in this room, which unusually is constructed of wood rather than moulded in plaster, might be a survival from the 1st Earl's era. Tim Knox, however, has pointed out its strongly Jonesian character, and suggested instead that its similarity to a ceiling at Chiswick makes it 'seem highly probable' that it was designed by the 3rd Earl himself.[56] Hewlings's hypothesis is perhaps somewhat weakened by Ian Bristow's report on the composition of the gold size associated with its original appearance, which reveals the same addition of red pigment as was found in equivalent samples taken from the entablature and doorcases in the Saloon. Unlike the *Banquet of the Gods* that he painted for the Saloon, Kent's ceiling painting for this private room did not have to relate in strictly iconographic terms to the Ricci staircase canvases, since it would not have been publicly visible in the original sequence of reception rooms in the house. It is probably for this reason that its subject has so far eluded any really convincing explanation, despite a recent valiant attempt to interpret it as 'Psyche created Immortal (on her Wedding Night) before an Assembly of the Gods' (Fig. 45).[57]

The only graphic evidence we have for the alterations that Campbell, Kent or the 3rd Earl himself may have designed for other parts of the house are two engravings after designs by Kent published in his book *The Designs of Inigo Jones* (1727). These show, respectively, a chimneypiece with pedimented overmantel, swags, Vitruvian scroll decorative moulding and a lion's mask (vol. I, plate 67,

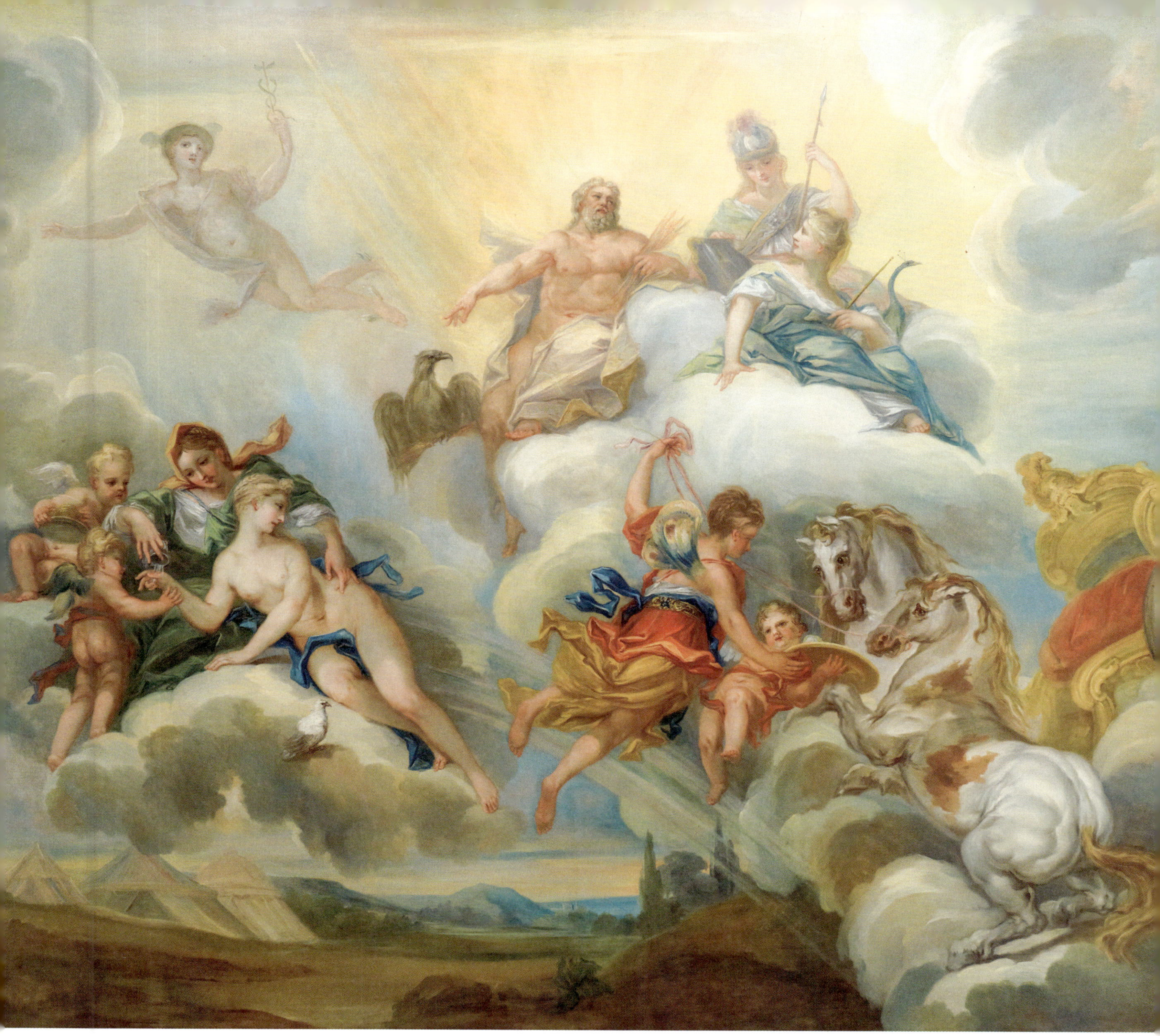

lower image); and a room elevation with panelled walls, plain cove, and a central panel surmounted by a broken pediment and garlanded cartouche that is repeated on flanking doorcases (vol. I, plate 63, first image on left; Figs 47, 48). Both designs are described in the text as simply 'for Lord Burlington's house' and there is no evidence to indicate that either was executed. However, the wall dimensions shown in the latter elevation (approximately 13 feet high by 20 feet wide) do correspond roughly with those of the east and west walls of the ground-floor entrance hall, so it is not impossible that this engraving is a proposal by Kent for the end walls of that room. If this supposition is correct, this design represents not only one of the earliest known instances of Kent working as an architect rather than painter, but also, as a substitution for Pellegrini's canvases, is particularly revealing of the 3rd Earl's keenness to express architectural values immediately inside the house that would correspond better with the expectations raised by its exterior.

Apart from the absence of a fireplace (which may be partly explained by the way the practical function of the room was secondary to its rehearsal of an architectural statement), the most extraordinary feature of the Saloon at Burlington House is the monumental Corinthian doorcase on its north wall (Fig. 46).[58] After the experience of walking up Ricci's staircase, this was truly bringing 'Architecture' indoors. Nowadays we tend to enter the Saloon back to front and generally only notice this wonderful doorcase on our way out. For the 3rd Earl, however, it was the propylaeum to the house's inner sanctum. We know this thanks to a series of surreptitious sketches made in September 1815 by John Carter, the patron saint of English architectural conservation, who was as passionately fond of 'the Divine Melodies of the immortal Handel' as he was devoted to the preservation of England's medieval architecture. 'Nervous, irascible and eccentric', and motivated perhaps as much as anything by the fact that the 3rd Earl had shared his great fondness for music, and that his greatest musical hero was thought to have composed some of his best operas while living in Burlington House, Carter managed to get his foot in the front door on the spurious pretext that he needed to sketch the colonnade as part of a treatise he was preparing on 'the rise and progress of our national architecture'.[59] In fact, he was perfectly well aware that the house was about to be gutted and this was the last chance anyone would have to record its current state. Apart from the two survey drawings of the main staircase already mentioned, Carter's tiny, hurried sketches of

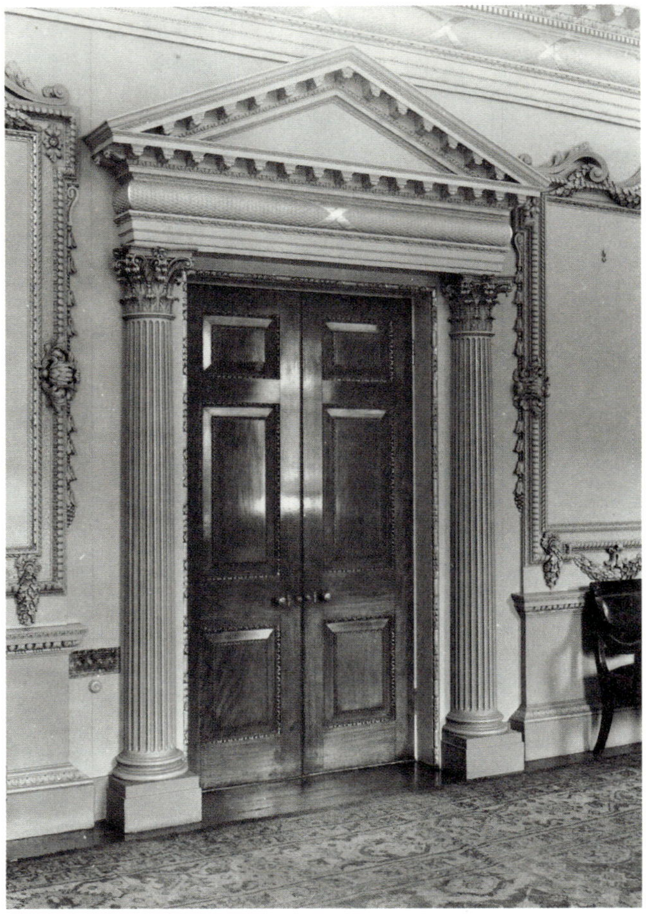

Fig. 46
The Corinthian doorcase in the Saloon at Burlington House.
LCC Photograph Library, London Metropolitan Archives (City of London)

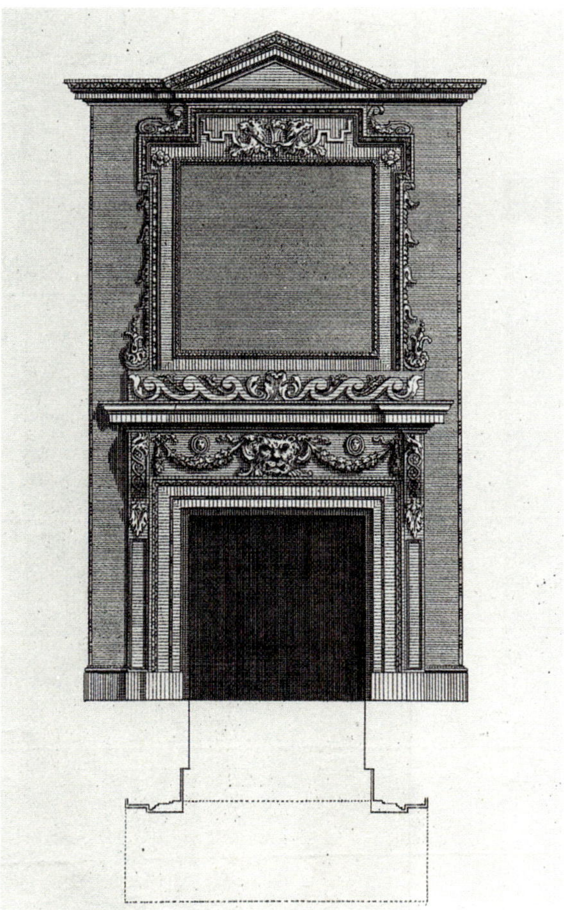

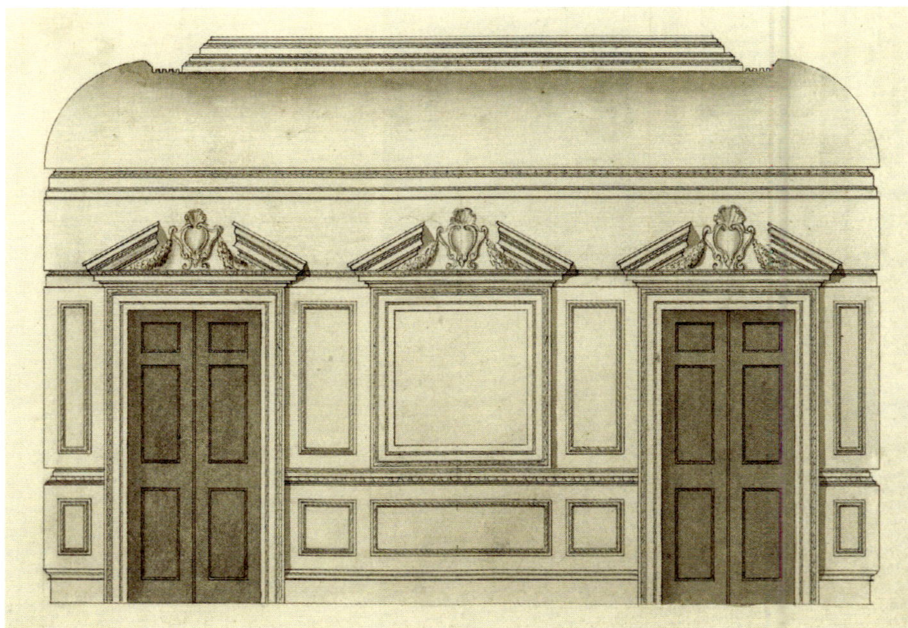

Fig. 47
Paul Fourdrinier, after Henry Flitcroft, Chimneypiece designed by William Kent for Burlington House, from *The Designs of Inigo Jones* ..., 1727, vol. II, plate 63 (detail).
RIBA Collections

Fig. 48
Paul Fourdrinier, after Henry Flitcroft, Elevation of an unidentified room (possibly the entrance hall, since demolished) in Burlington House designed by William Kent, from *The Designs of Inigo Jones* ..., 1727, vol. II, detail of plate 67.
RIBA Collections

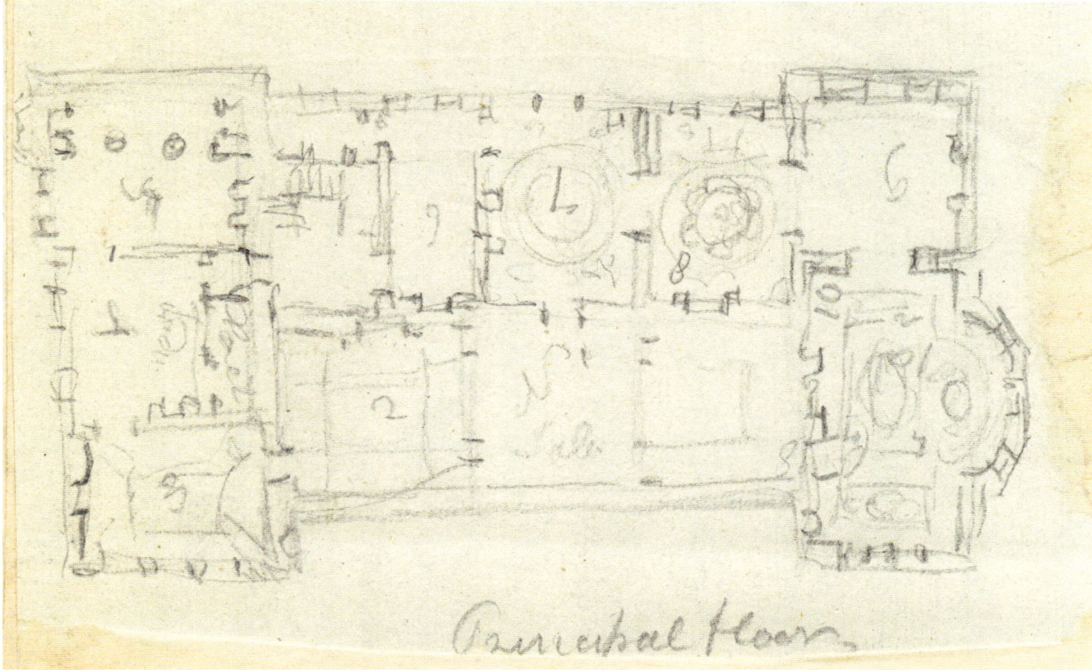

Fig. 49
John Carter's sketch plan of the principal (first) floor of Burlington House, with ceilings and numbered key to rooms, 1815.
Royal Academy of Arts, London, 06/2157 (verso)

three of its first-floor rooms and his scrappy floor plan showing the outline of the ceilings on this storey constitute the only known visual record of the appearance of the interior of the house before 1815 (Fig. 49).

It is Carter's plan in particular that enables us to identify what was in the room on the other side of the Saloon door, since the large roundel it shows in the centre of its ceiling (numbered '7') indicates that it was here, in the heart of the house, that Kent's painting *The Glorification of Inigo Jones* looked down on those worthy to enter (Fig. 50). This paid personal homage not only to Jones himself (whose original drawings Flitcroft may perhaps have copied in this room since it had the largest window in the house with north light), but also quite specifically to Burlington House as in some sense an academy.[60] Thus, Architecture points with her dividers not only to a drawing of the house's new front, but also to the portico of the ancient temple of Fortuna Virilis in Rome from which Campbell's use of the Ionic order derived its ultimate authority. Similarly, with her set square in her other hand, she acknowledges not only the tribute of the portrait of the 'British Vitruvius' brought to her by Painting, but also the contribution of Sculpture bearing a statuette of Minerva and, behind them, the beauty of the modern Roman Doric order recently exemplified in Burlington House's forecourt colonnade.

Kent's recognition of sculpture's contribution to architecture may be connected to his designs for the well-known statues of Jones and Palladio that now guard the entrance to Chiswick House but which were originally intended to be placed in the first-floor niches on the inside returns of the façade of Burlington House (Fig. 51). Here they would have faced, not inwards looking towards each other as at Chiswick, but outwards looking across the forecourt towards the oncoming visitor, Jones on the left and Palladio on the right. Although according to Campbell's description of Burlington House in the third volume of *Vitruvius Britannicus* (1725) these statues had been placed as intended in the 'two Niches in Flank, fronting each other', a French visitor to Chiswick in 1727 (or 1728) saw them in one of the garden buildings there, possibly the 'Casina' or 'Bagnio' where the 3rd Earl is said to have set up a drawing office.[61] On one level their removal may be taken as symbolic of a decisive shift that had occurred by then in the focus of the Earl's architectural ambitions, away from further tinkering with the interior of Burlington House, and towards the astonishing idea of designing and building a revolutionary new house for himself in the garden of his old-fashioned Jacobean mansion at Chiswick. On another, more prosaic level, however, it is also possible that Palladio in particular hadn't been especially comfortable in his niche on the outside of Burlington House, since it afforded him only 166 mm headroom. A not-unheard-of blunder of this kind could perhaps have been one of the reasons why Giovanni Battista Guelphi, the sculptor probably responsible for carving the statues, was to fall out of the Earl's favour by the mid-1720s.

Following the Earl's dramatic, and to his contemporaries somewhat inexplicable, resignation of all his court posts on 3 May 1733, it is often asserted that he signalled his complete retirement from the political arena by 'moving all his principal possessions to Chiswick'. However, there is no evidence that he abandoned Burlington House, either then or at any time later.[62] And although it is true that the construction of the

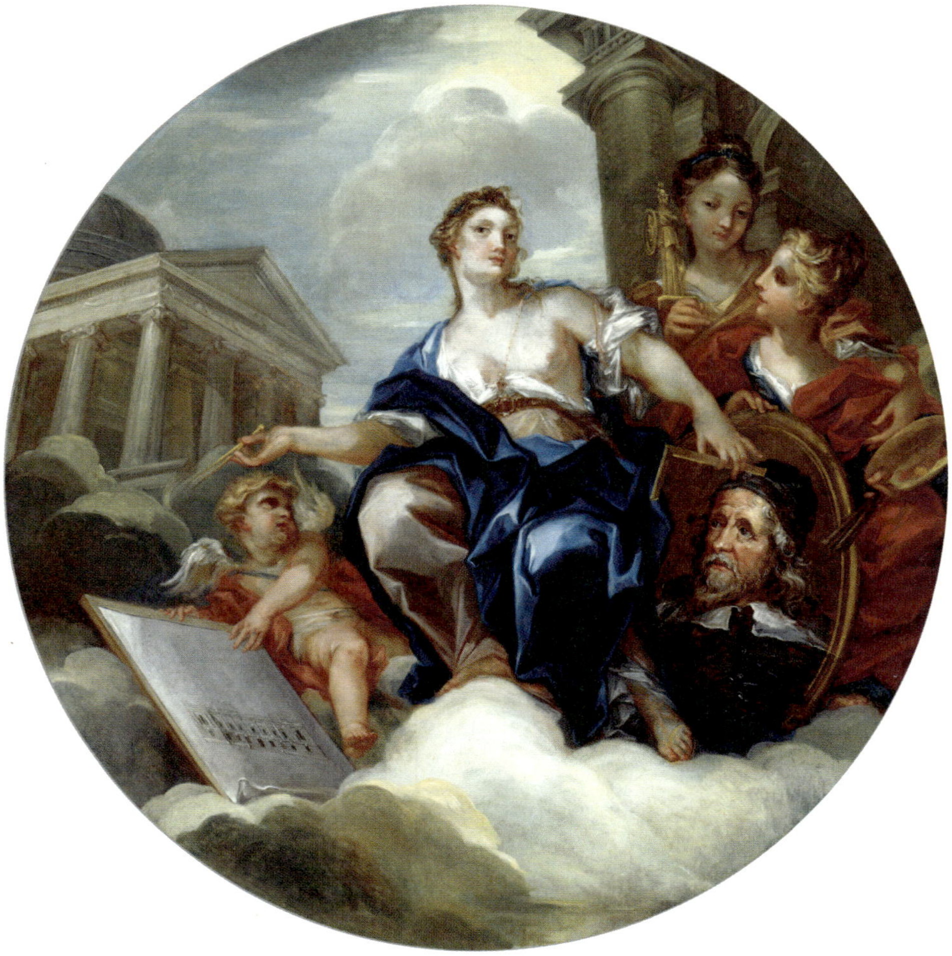

Fig. 50
William Kent, *The Glorification of Inigo Jones*, 1719–20.
Royal Academy of Arts, London, 03/186

so-called 'Link Building' at Chiswick in 1732–33 enabled more convenient use of the old and new house, this certainly does not mean that the family moved out of London. For one thing, there would have been occasions, particularly in 1733–36, when Kent's earth-moving operations in the garden at Chiswick probably made Burlington House seem quite peaceful. Furthermore, although it was rumoured at the time of the Earl's resignation that Lady Dorothy would follow her husband's example, she in fact continued to serve at court as one of the Ladies of the Bedchamber until Queen Caroline's death in December 1737. It is not surprising therefore that the Earl's accounts for 1745–53 show not only that Burlington House remained his principal residence in the last eight years of his life, but that he was also making numerous payments for building work there. Thus, at various dates between 1746 and 1748, Joseph Pickford was paid a bill of £53 10s. 6d. for mason's work; Joseph Pratt bills of £68 13s. 10d. and £19 10s. 10d. for bricklaying; John Marsden bills of £63 16s. and £68 5s. for joinery and carpenter's work; Thomas Clark bills of £94 11s. and £26 2s. for plastering; Edward Cock bills of £48 19s. 6d. and £5 15s. 4d. for plumber's work; John Wilkins and Thomas Lovett a bill of £58 2s. for paviour's work; Richard Brewerton bills of £33 8s. and £18 9s. 10d. for smith's work; James Loton a bill of £7 15s. 6d. for glazier's work; and Edward Wetherby, painter, was paid £32 12s. and £53 10s. on 22 March and 9 August 1748 respectively.[63] These quite substantial sums are too concentrated in time not to relate to a project of some kind, and although unspecified work at Chiswick is included in some of the bills listed above they were all charged to the 'Burlington House' account. What such a project might have involved there is no way of telling, although it does suggest that even late in life the 'Architect Earl' could not resist the temptation to tinker with his London house.

What may perhaps have been one result of such tinkering was later to catch the critical eye of the eminent architect Sir William Chambers, who in nearly every other respect was an enthusiastic admirer of Burlington House and its forecourt. On the warpath against such slavish imitation of archaisms in ancient architecture as the making of doors and windows narrower at the top than at the bottom, Chambers expressed 'surprise that a person of such refined taste as the Earl of Burlington should have introduced a couple of these ill-formed doors in the cortile of his

Fig. 51
Chiswick House, London: the grand staircase to the entrance portico by night, with a statue of Inigo Jones by Giovanni Battista Guelphi. Photograph by Eric de Maré, 1958.
Architectural Press Archive / RIBA Collections, AP Box 801 Chiswick

house in Piccadilly.'[64] In fact, clearly fascinated by the Vitruvian authority for such doorways, the 3rd Earl had inserted pairs of them not only in the screen walls of the passages linking the main house to the service wings, but also in the side entrances to the wings themselves (see Fig. 30). What other experiments in advanced Neoclassicism he might perhaps have 'introduced' elsewhere we have no way of knowing. Indeed, so little is known of the interior of Burlington House during the remaining thirty or so years that its most celebrated owner lived there that we have no way of telling, for example, where the following work was carried out:

> 21 March 1749 Paid Mr Stephen Wright The Sum of Thirty Pound Seventeen Shillings for Cleaning mending and pricking in of the Grotesque Ceiling in the Dineing and Glass Rooms and for measureing and makeing up the Artificers bills for the years 1747 and 1748 &c. &c. &c.[65]

Nor should we assume that Kent was not allowed near the garden. Thus, on 12 September 1745 he wrote to the Earl, not just to pass on the latest news about who had joined the Young Pretender, but to explain a recent instance of his taking matters into his own hands at Burlington House:

> You'll say I'm always in trouble but its over now, the new Buildings in Bond Street was going to use your wall, which I have stop'd I sent for Pratt and rais'd your wall above two ft. & new cop'd it, on[e] reason I rais'd it was, the wooden things & sheds they had stop'd up the ends of your wood sheds &c.: & being taken away the light was quite through, so raising the wall has shut all close – the gravil walks are all layd down in y^{e} Garden – [66]

There will always be parts of 'Burlington's fair Palace' and garden where no-one may enter however clean their shoes.

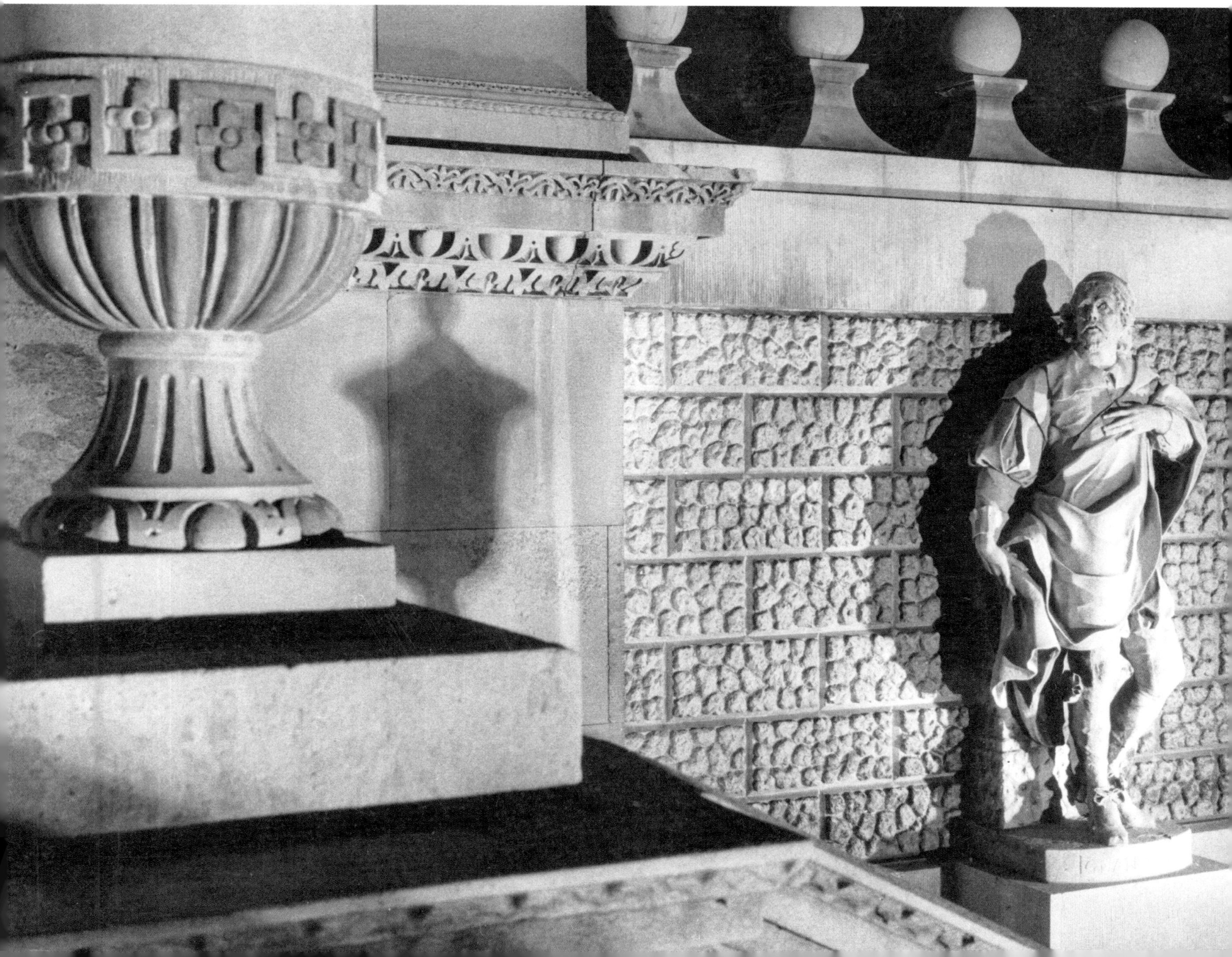

III

THE CAVENDISH FAMILY

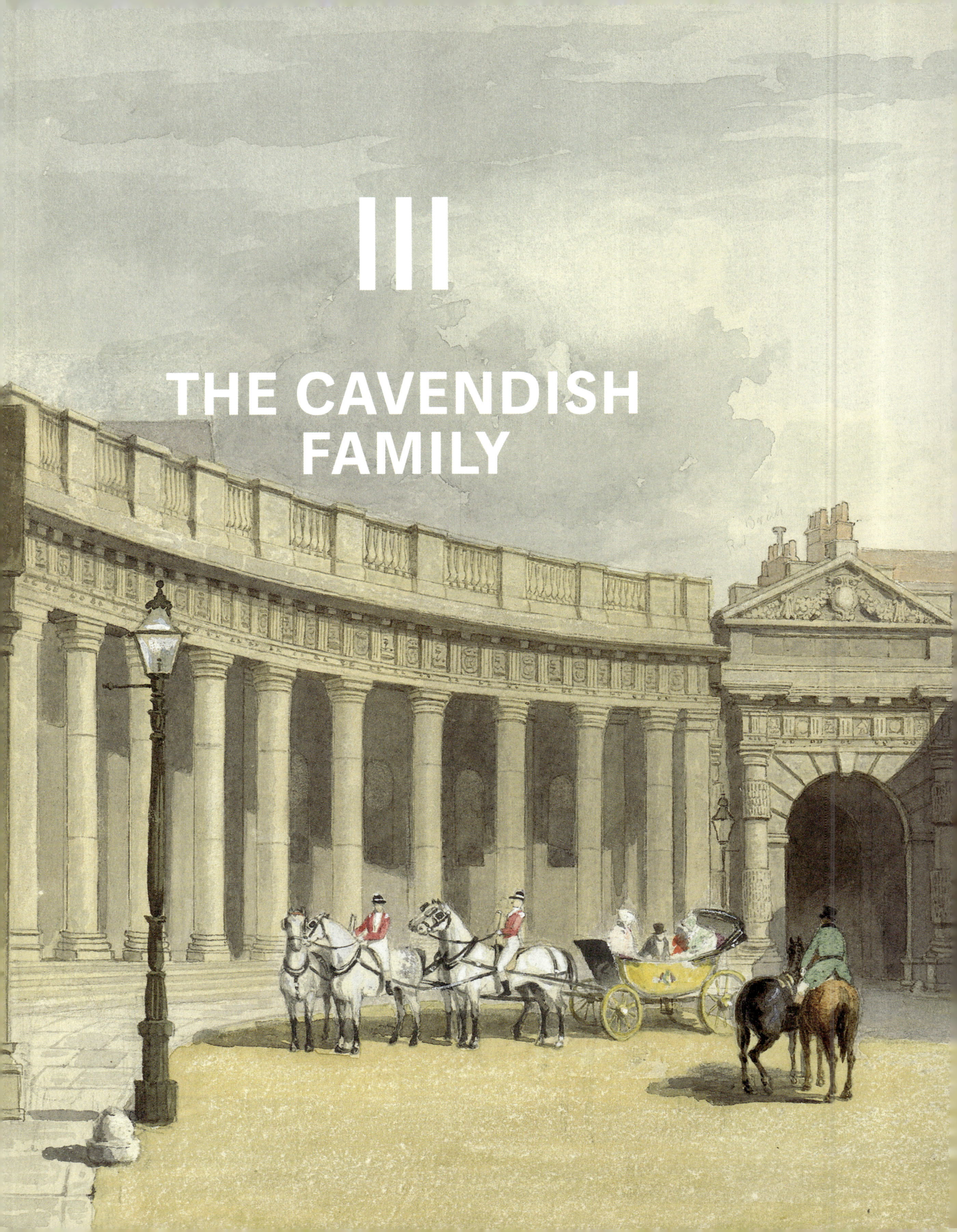

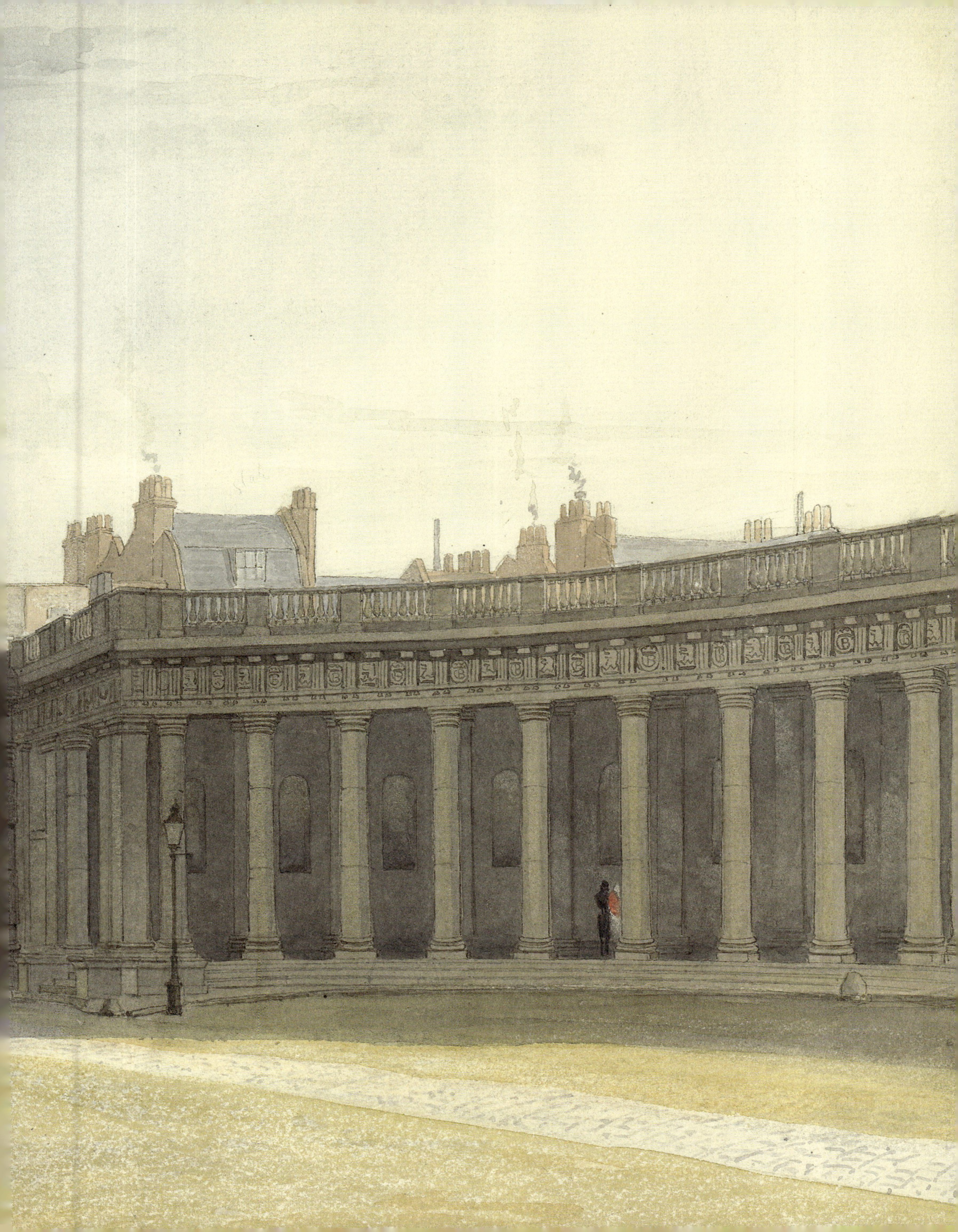

'Persons feeling all the architectural beauties of this classical spot would consider the possession desirable at thousands per annum; – whilst others, without such feelings would regard the occupancy of the premises, for a limited time, and with covenants to maintain them agreeably to their original destination, a very heavy tax!'
John Soane, 1811[1]

LIKE HIS GRANDFATHER BEFORE HIM, WILLIAM Cavendish, Marquess of Hartington, was nine years old when he inherited Burlington House from his grandmother Dorothy, Countess of Burlington, following her death in September 1758. In the same year, his father, the 4th Duke of Devonshire, commissioned the architect James Paine to build at Chatsworth, the Cavendish ducal seat in Derbyshire, a new stable block with a carriage entrance modelled on the Great Gate of Burlington House.[2] While obviously concerned to meet practical needs, by choosing this particular design for 'probably the grandest private stables ever built in Britain',[3] the Duke was also commemorating his late wife Charlotte, the 3rd Earl of Burlington's last surviving daughter, who had died of smallpox in December 1754 aged only 23, having borne four children in less than six years and brought to the Cavendish family the entire Burlington inheritance.

Since no decisions affecting the future of his inheritance could be made before the Marquess came of age on 14 December 1769, Burlington House entered a period of limbo in the 1760s that stands in marked contrast to its lively history during the 3rd Earl's minority fifty years earlier. Then Juliana, the Dowager Countess of Burlington, had done all she could to focus attention on her son's Piccadilly house, largely ignoring his Jacobean manor at Chiswick, and indeed her own equally old-fashioned family residence at Campden House in Kensington.[4] The Duke of Devonshire, on the other hand, could scarcely be expected to prefer Burlington House, however renowned its associations, when Devonshire House, a magnificent modern town mansion built at great expense after Berkeley House had burnt down in 1733, was only a couple of hundred yards down Piccadilly.

The cloud hanging over the future of Burlington House was to grow still darker when the 4th Duke died in October 1764, since that removed the hope that it might have become the Marquess's London residence after he had come of age. It was probably awareness of its perilous situation, gathered perhaps from their close friend and neighbour Paine, that led John Gwynn, a passionate advocate of metropolitan improvements, to propose in *London and Westminster Improved* (1766) that

> ... the ground on which Burlington-House stands is laid out into elegant streets, viz. from Burlington-Street to Pall-Mall, from Piccadilly through Saville-Row into Conduit-Street, and from Piccadilly through Cork-Street to Conduit-Street Chapel ...

Admitting 'the demolition of Burlington-House may be thought an extraordinary proposition', he argued that:

> ... when it is considered, what a prodigious improvement will be made in those streets about Burlington-Gardens ... that the rents of those very streets will be considerably augmented, and that the public will lose nothing in point of elegance but the removal of the dead-wall in Piccadilly, every objection that will be made to this alteration it is imagined will entirely vanish.[5]

Gwynn is being deliberately provocative. As he and his readers were well aware, behind that 'dead-wall in Piccadilly' lay what William Chambers, the leading architectural authority of his day, had just recently described as 'one of the finest pieces of Architecture in Europe'.[6] And although, like Chambers, Gwynn could have caught sight of Burlington House only when the porter happened to open its Great Gate to let a carriage pass through, he could scarcely plead ignorance of its merit 'in point of elegance' since he was currently sharing lodgings with Samuel Wale, the only artist of the time known to have drawn the house as it was built rather than as it appeared in *Vitruvius Britannicus* (Fig. 52). Equally disingenuous is Gwynn's sly dig about 'augmented' rents, the insinuation being that since the landlord of the Burlington Gardens estate and the owner of Burlington

Fig. 52
Benjamin Green, after Samuel Wale, Burlington House, from *London and Its Environs Described*, 1761, vol. 2, p. 57.
British Museum, London, 1880,1113.5895

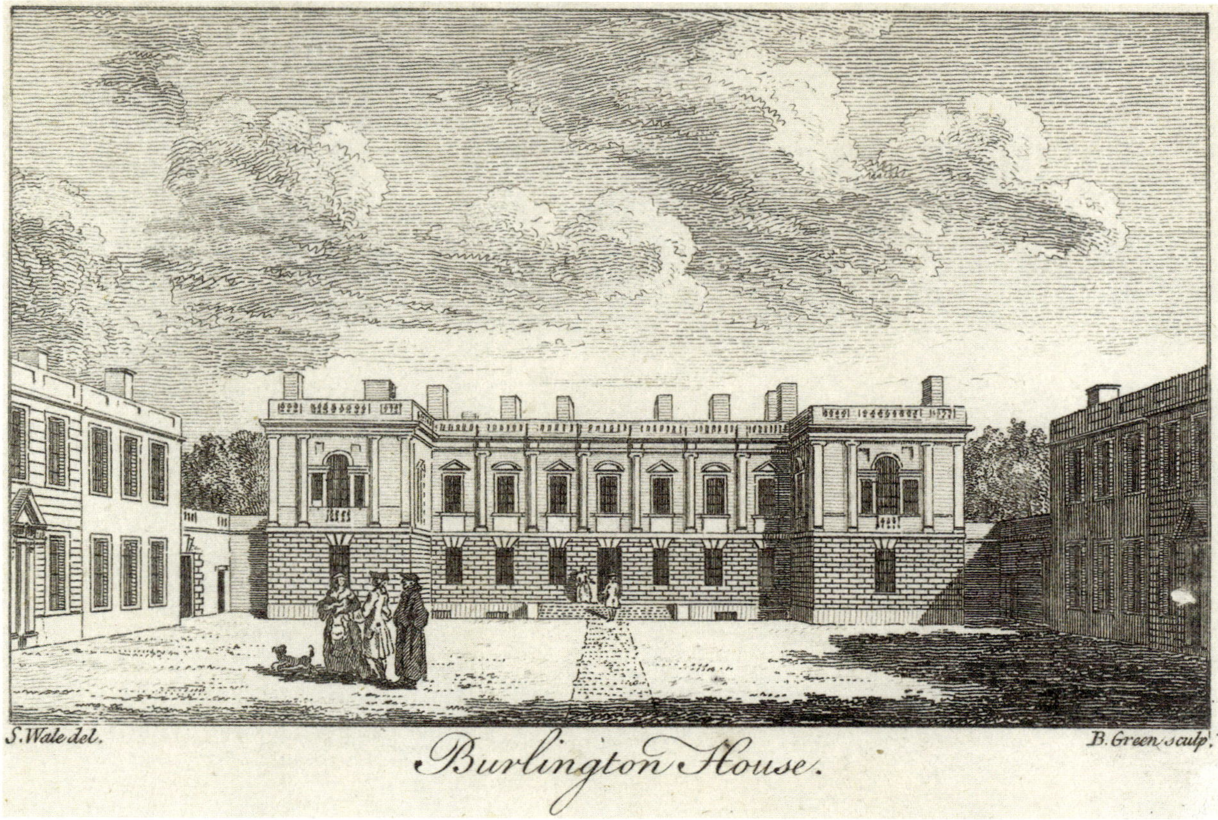

House was one and the same person, he could be counted upon to sacrifice for private gain what his 'dead-wall' had for so long denied to public benefit. In the late 1760s it must have seemed therefore that Horace Walpole's dawn vision of the colonnade as 'one of those edifices in fairy-tales that are raised by genii in a night's time' might be about to vanish as quickly as it came.[7]

On reaching his majority, the 5th Duke's response to pressure to decide on the future of the house was to become standard during its Cavendish years, namely by agreeing that a valuation needed to be made based on a scheme for building on all or parts of its site. On one level this was simply what any land agent would have advised to assess the relative advantages of retaining the property or selling it. At a deeper level, however, the airing of these schemes acted as a safety valve since, right up to the final agonised decision to sell in 1853, the Cavendish answer to the 'problem' of Burlington House was invariably to maintain the *status quo* regardless of whether it made sense financially. As a result, contrary to appearances, each new scheme for its redevelopment became progressively less likely to materialise than the last. The question of what to do with Burlington House was therefore never simply a matter of property management, but brought into play sentiments that the 1st Earl of Burlington would have recognised, and indeed expected to have found passed down by his descendants. As a result, more radical alterations were to be made to the house in the interests of preserving it than could have ever been acceptable for reasons of financial gain.

The scheme for building on the Burlington House site that James Paine is said to have prepared for the 5th Duke in 1770 has not been traced.[8] However, on '30 May and following Days 1770', the appraisers John Wicksted and Roger Bennett compiled an inventory and valuation of the house's contents that is the only surviving evidence for how it was furnished during the Burlington era. Their detailed listing of the 'goods and chattels' in 43 different rooms included in the chapel, 'A Pulpit, four forms, a pair of Steps, Thirty three Hassocks, a Communion Table with a Velvet Cover four Crimson Velvet Vallences Twenty Velvet Cushions, Eight Walnuttree back Stool Chairs Cover'd with Crimson Velvet, a Side Lanthorn and Burner in the Passage'; and, among the household silver, 'Two Chalices Gilt, one Cup and Cover Gilt, One Patten Gilt, a large Salver Gilt, Two Porringers with Covers & a Gilt Spoon.' The gardener had managed to keep everything in order with 'An Iron Roller, a Stone Ditto, two S[c]ithes, a Spade, A Rooting Ax, an Edging Iron, [and] a paddle', and to water his plants from 'a lead Cistern with a Waist pipe, a Brass Cock & Pump'. Oddly, the appraisers found little to record where they started in the attic ('No. 1 The Garret's & Cock Loft') apart from a small quantity of disused furniture and 'A suit of Armour, A Sumpter Cloth Laced & fringed with Gold & Silver, A Bridle, 2 Stirrups, a Sword, a Scabbard & a pike'. In room 'No. 42', however, 'Mrs Ferret's Apartment', they came across an occupational hazard – 'a four post Bedstead with blue furniture' that had to be taken out and 'Burnd for Buggs'.[9]

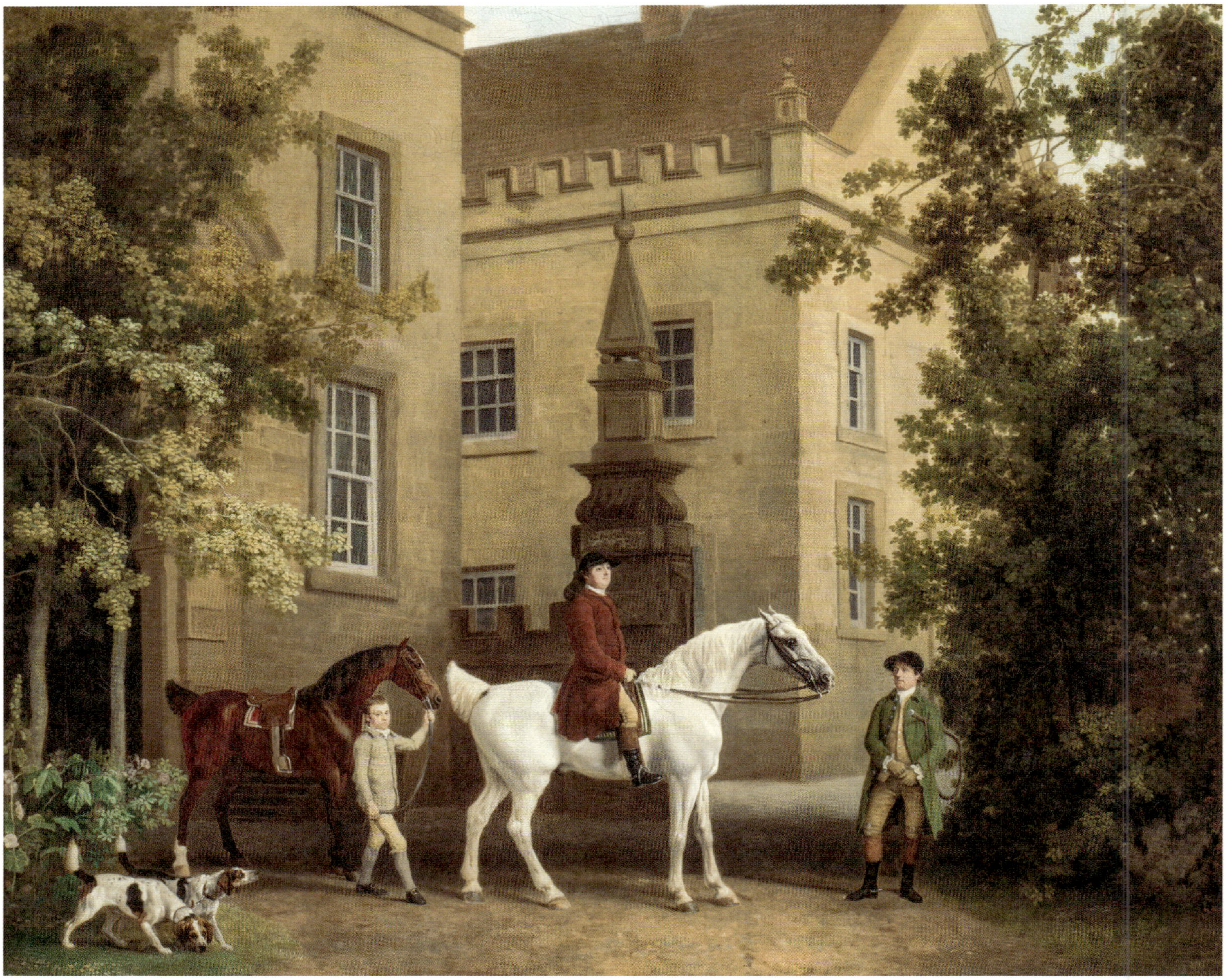

This valuation was probably compiled for accounting purposes following the Duke's coming of age, rather than because it had been agreed by then that his brother-in-law, William Cavendish-Bentinck, 3rd Duke of Portland, would take the house on as his London residence. This neat solution to the problem of how to keep it in the family's hands may have been mooted as far back as Portland's marriage to the 5th Duke's sister in November 1766. However, it was not until April 1771 that Portland was informed that he could move in, the current caretakers, Mr Clementson and Mr Evans, having by then agreed to 'leave Burlington House as soon as they conveniently can.'[10] Two months later, John Hinchcliffe, Bishop of Peterborough, wrote to Portland recommending a local builder whom he had employed the previous year 'in some alterations & in making a new room' in his house in nearby Conduit Street:

> The man is indeed no more than a common Joiner & frequently works himself at his business, but he has a good knowledge of the executive part of building, & some taste. Should your Grace want such a person at Burlington house to do necessary repairs or make alterations for convenience, I think he woud answer better for the purpose than a professed Architect. He made me an estimate of all I required to be done, & I question not woud contract to take the whole upon himself. His name is Sims at No. 13 Somerset Street, Oxford Road.[11]

The well-intentioned bishop probably misjudged his Grace on this occasion, for it was not in Portland's character to economise on building projects, particularly when they might offer scope for 'improvements'. In his twenty-year collaboration with Humphry Repton on ambitious schemes to re-landscape the surroundings of

Fig. 53
George Stubbs, *The 3rd Duke of Portland, Welbeck Abbey*, 1767.
Harley Gallery, Welbeck Abbey, Nottinghamshire

his country houses at Welbeck Abbey in Nottinghamshire and Bulstrode in Buckinghamshire; in his sensitivity to the picturesque potential of judicious tree-planting and felling on his recently enclosed estates in Sherwood Forest; and in his insistence on the adoption of the latest techniques in crop rotation, animal husbandry and livestock breeding; in all these traditional concerns of a great eighteenth-century landowner, Portland demonstrated that he was 'self-consciously an improver' (Fig. 53).[12]

Although he never owned nor it seems formally leased Burlington House, Portland used it as his London residence between mid-1771 and March 1782 and again from late 1785 or early 1786 until his death in October 1809, apparently on the basis of an understanding that he kept the building and its 'appurtenances' in repair. Despite the informality of this arrangement, the impact of Portland's occupation of the house was both extensive and completely transitory in as much as no trace of it can be seen today. To make matters worse, scarcely any documentary evidence survives that might indicate, for instance, when he undertook the major structural additions to the east wing that show up in Richard Horwood's map of London and Westminster published in June 1792.[13] While a few tradesmen's bills have been found, they date only from 1774 to 1776, and relate either to repairs and regilding or to minor works, such as the replacement of marble chimneypieces and mahogany doors, and the supply of small quantities of carved ornament and decorative plasterwork.[14] And while there are some references in a letter from the architect John Carr of York dated 27 October 1771 indicating that he had by then designed 'stucco pannels' and a chimneypiece for the new 'Dining Room at Burlington House' ('with a fluted Architrave round the chimney, & with columns to it much like that in the draw.g Room at Welbeck'), and that he suggested the monumental mason John Devall could design a similar chimneypiece for the 'drawing Room of about £60 Value', these do not add up to evidence that he had supplied designs for structural alterations.[15] It is clear, however, that at least the first phase of the work carried out for Portland in the early 1770s was executed under the direction of the prominent Pimlico building contractor Richard Dixon, who wrote to the Duke three times between May 1772 and January 1775 pleading with increasing desperation for payment of bills amounting to at least £1,800.[16] Dixon and his brother Joseph had gained considerable experience in altering and rebuilding houses in Pall Mall during the 1760s, and either individually or in partnership would have been quite capable of providing and working to their own designs.[17]

In view of the dearth of contemporaneous evidence about alterations to the house dating from Portland's occupancy, it is fortunate that detailed floor plans were made by the architect Samuel Ware in October 1811 (see Figs 54, 55).[18] These drawings show that the east wing in particular was altered by Portland not just to reflect current taste in interior decoration, but to meet his needs during different phases of his career as a high-ranking politician. When Portland first moved into Burlington House in 1771 it was as a rising star of the aristocratic, Rockingham wing of the Whig party. Although he was no longer living there by the time he served for a few months as Prime Minister in 1783, when he returned to the house in 1785/86 it was as the party's new leader in opposition. It was in this role that he became a consummate fixer, working tirelessly behind the scenes to hold the party's warring factions together until the final split with Charles James Fox in 1793. Thereafter Portland lived in Burlington House as a prominent government minister, serving first as a notably ruthless Home Secretary in William Pitt's coalition administration of 1794–1801; and then, from March 1807 until his death two and a half years later, as an aged, gout-afflicted Prime Minister, whose failure to prevent internecine plotting in his own Cabinet culminated in the famous duel on Putney Heath between George Canning and Viscount Castlereagh. During the first of these phases Portland needed above all a suitable London house in which to entertain his fellow Whig grandees; during the second it became important to have somewhere private to conduct confidential party business; and in his career's last stressful phases, he no doubt appreciated the comforts of a secluded town mansion that afforded a high degree of privacy and security, particularly at tense times during the food riots of 1795–96 and 1800–01 and in the late

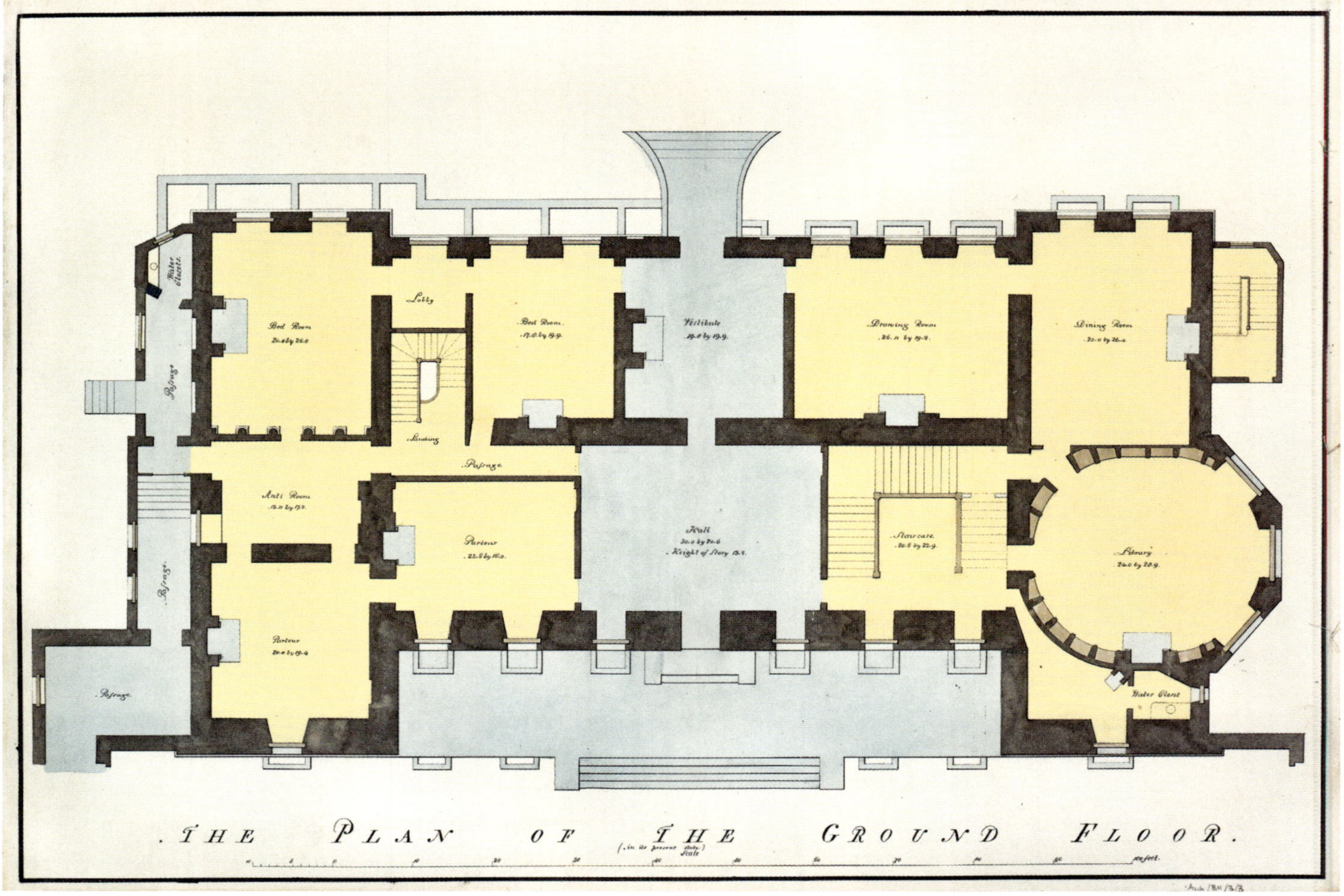
Water Closet
Bed Room
20.8 by 26.0
Lobby
Bed Room
17.0 by 19.9
Vestibule
19.8 by 19.9
Drawing Room
26.11 by 19.2
Dining Room
30.0 by 26.0
Passage
Landing
Passage
Anti Room
12.11 by 17.2
Parlour
22.6 by 16.0
Hall
30.0 by 20.6
Height of Story 13.9
Staircase
26.6 by 22.9
Library
24.0 by 28.9
Passage
Parlour
20.0 by 19.4
Passage
Water Closet
THE PLAN OF THE GROUND FLOOR.
(in its present state)
Scale
feet

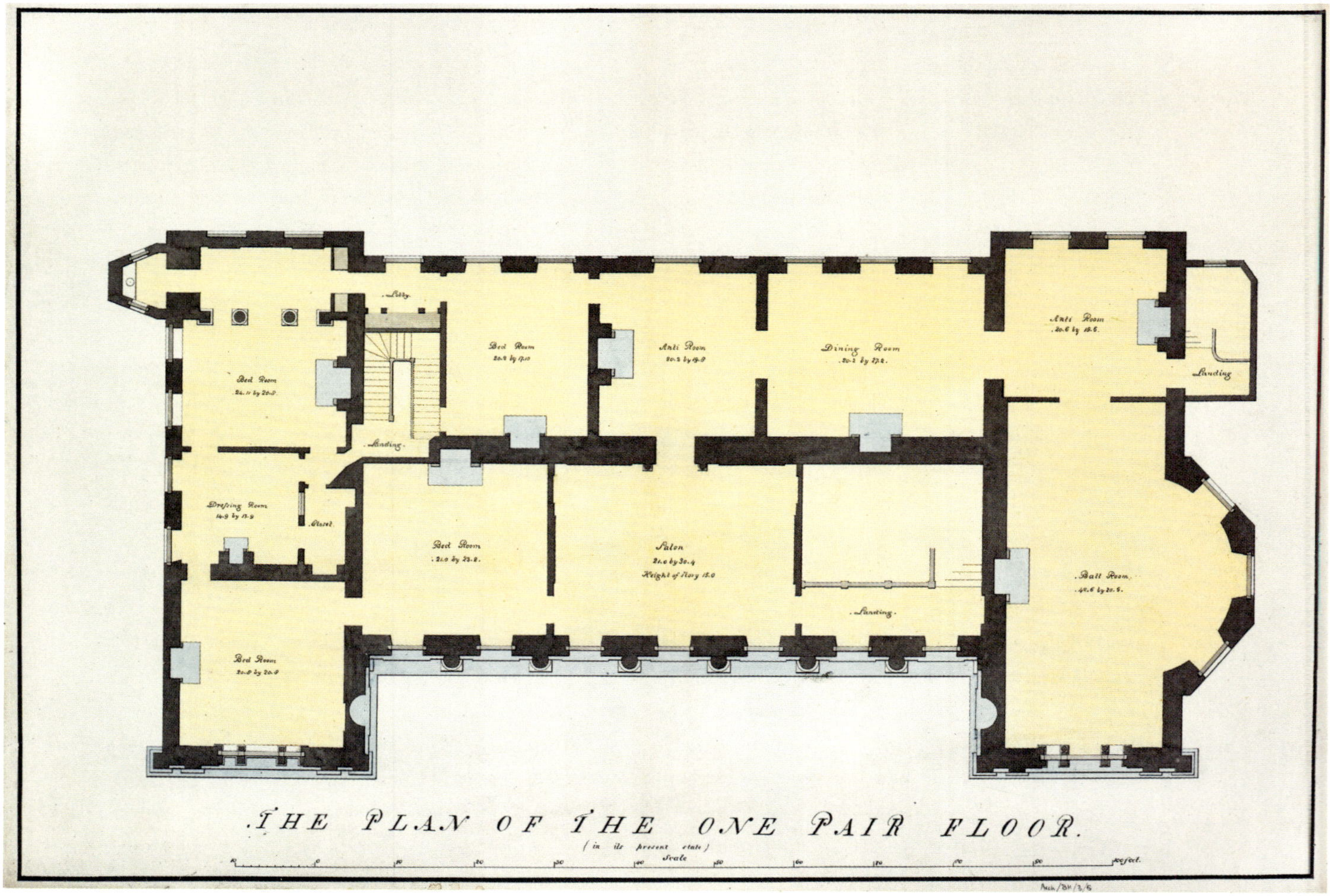
Lobby
Bed Room
20.2 by 17.10
Anti Room
20.2 by 19.8
Dining Room
20.2 by 27.2
Anti Room
20.6 by 19.6
Bed Room
24.11 by 20.8
Landing
Landing
Dressing Room
14.9 by 13.9
Closet
Bed Room
21.0 by 23.2
Salon
21.0 by 30.4
Height of Story 15.0
Ball Room
40.6 by 20.5
Landing
Bed Room
20.0 by 20.9
THE PLAN OF THE ONE PAIR FLOOR.
(in its present state)
Scale
feet

Fig. 54
Samuel Ware, Burlington House: ground-floor plan, 1811.
Royal Academy of Arts, London, 06/4337

Fig. 55
Samuel Ware, Burlington House: first-floor plan, 1811.
Royal Academy of Arts, London, 06/4339

1790s when Burlington House became the nerve centre of the government's counter-revolutionary secret service.[19]

To create a sequence of grand reception rooms Portland not unnaturally capitalised on the existing splendours of the Ricci staircase and the Saloon, both of which he left unaltered apart from renewing the carved ornament on the window shutters in the latter room (without gilding) and probably painting over Kent's decoration of the ceiling cove.[20] For Portland, however, the Saloon was never the principal room on the *piano nobile* as it had been in the Burlington era, but rather a transitional space on the way to the central 'anti-room' on the north front. From here an enfilade of double doors led eastwards, through the middle of a large three-bayed drawing room (used later as a dining room) into a further anti-room in the north-east corner of the house. And from there guests could make a suitably dignified entrance into the most impressive space in the building, a 42½ × 20½-foot vaulted banqueting-cum-assembly room with a 24-foot-wide, externally splayed bow window overlooking Lord Melbourne's garden to the east (Fig. 55).

A peculiar feature of Portland's ceremonial route through the house was that, although it described an almost complete circle, unless a guest was prepared (or wanted) to take the service stairs and leave clandestinely via the basement, no exit was possible without exactly retracing one's steps. This oddity arose from the need to centre the new banqueting room's fireplace on the bow window opposite, which directly interfered with the existing door at the top of the main staircase. The fact that Portland was prepared to accept the consequence of sealing up this doorway illustrates how very different modern considerations of convenience are from the way an aristocrat's house was expected to function during this period. Indeed, for someone as closely in touch as Portland was to current notions of the picturesque, what seems to us supremely impractical probably induced pleasurable illusions of being in a much larger house. It is not surprising therefore that he ordered a showy new chimneypiece from John Devall in July 1776 for the 'Center Room North Front' as this formed a major focal point for departing guests.[21]

It is clear from the 1770 inventory that Portland's banqueting/assembly room was formed by amalgamating three smaller rooms listed there as 'No 11', '12' and '13'. This is why a later hand wrote 'Ball Room' against 'No 11', ran a cancelling line through the contents of 'No 12' and 'No 13', and endorsed them as 'Not to be Found'. To judge from their contents 'No 12' had been an important, richly furnished bedroom with two east windows and a closet, 'No 11' a small dressing or lady's maid's room adjacent to the backstairs, and 'No 13' a larger, south-facing dressing or drawing room. Similarly, Portland's new north-east anti-room (endorsed later as the 'North east Room') was created by combining 'No 10', a small room lying to the east of the backstairs, with the space freed up by moving these stairs out into an annexe on the east side of the building. If, as Tim Knox has suggested, the 'huddle of small rooms' that evidently still existed in this part of the house in 1770 reflects the original seventeenth-century layout, this would mean that the raising of the chapel to ground-floor level in about 1711–15 had *not* impinged on the first floor, and therefore it was probably Portland who was the first to heighten the ceilings of these rooms by colonising the garret space above.[22]

Pushing out the great bow window on the first floor obviously impacted on the room below, so Portland's new library underneath was almost certainly created at the same time (Fig. 54). A distinctive feature of this oval room within a room is its insulation from the rest of the house – it was probably the only place where confidential meetings and business could be conducted without risk of domestic interruption. Just as remarkable was its flexibility of access, for in addition to having a public entrance from the staircase hall centred on its bow window opposite, there was also a jib door in its north-west corner should the Duke need to slip in or out unseen. Although, rather unfortunately, the Duke's new water closet was situated close to where the altar had been, it appears that he did not dare risk angering the 1st Earl's ghost by eradicating his chapel altogether. Instead, just as Carr had modernised rather than removed the medieval chapel at Welbeck in 1763–65, a reduced version of the chapel at Burlington House seems to have been reinstalled in the 20 × 26-foot space that had been created, like the north-east anti-room above it, as a result of moving the service stairs into an external annexe. Perhaps as a consequence of this relocation, a dilapidations report carried out in July 1782 noted of the chapel that its 'wainscoting in many places wants to be made good'.[23] However, this was to prove only a short reprieve for the spiritual heart of the old house since by 1811 it had become the family dining room. By then also the former principal dining room in the north-west wing, which in 1770 had been called the 'Great Dining Parlour' and by 1782 was known as the 'Old Dining Parlour' (no doubt to distinguish it from the new first-floor banqueting room), had been demoted to a bedroom, despite the fact it was the grandest room on the ground floor and, because of its proximity to the kitchen service wing, much the most practical dining space in the house.

On hearing in July 1807 that the Duke of Devonshire was thinking of selling Burlington House, Portland wrote to reassure his brother-in-law that he was ready to give it up at short notice, and also to convey his gratitude for the long 'use of the most comfortable habitation in all London, which I hope will not be found the worse for having been occupied by me ...'.[24] Insofar as Portland's praise of the comforts of the house was justified he had himself to thank, for he had spent considerable sums modernising it without any prospect of a return on his outlay. From today's perspective, it is hard not to regret some of his 'improvements', not least because his successor eradicated them all so thoroughly that it is difficult to know what may have been unaltered, particularly on the west side of the house. It was precisely this that John Carter had hoped to find out in relation to the first-floor rooms, but unfortunately his scrappy sketches and indecipherable jottings are now of frustratingly little help.[25] It is possible to deduce, however, from the fact that it was replaced by Portland's banqueting/assembly room, that the 'Great Dining Parlour' on the ground floor, with its 'steel pillar stove' in a large old-fashioned fireplace and its grand columned south wall, had probably survived more or less unaltered from the Burlington era. The master bedroom above it on the other hand – called in the 1770 inventory the 'Velvet Bed Room' – seems to have received Portland's early attention. In November 1772 Adam Price, the Duke's steward at Burlington House, mentioned that he had written 'to her Grace last week about the Chimney piece in the little room next that design'd for the Bedchamber', and in February the following year reported that 'the Chintz Bed & Curtains were put up last week'.[26] After 1782, this room seems to have been called the 'Pillar Bed Room', indicating perhaps that the columnar screen at its northern end was introduced during the Duke's second period of occupation.[27] Behind this screen lay what was probably a bath alcove, the provision of which entailed blocking up both windows at the northern end of the room. To compensate for this loss, the garden could be seen instead from one of two small windows in the adjoining water closet, which projected in a small canted bay on the west wall. The trouble taken to accommodate the latter convenience – another was installed immediately below it and, as we have seen, a third was tucked behind the south wall of the Duke's library – suggests that it employed the most advanced technology available. This was probably also true of the 'patent stove' that Devall installed in the Duchess's dressing room in February 1776 and certainly so of the 'large Cast Iron Buzaglo Stove' placed in the entrance hall downstairs, the Duke's acquisition of which may have been influenced by the claim of its inventor to have discovered a cure for gout.[28]

As his recent biographer David Wilkinson has noted, 'shielded by a high wall facing on to Piccadilly, Burlington House was entirely in keeping with Portland's image: secluded from the vulgar gaze yet easily accessible' to friends and associates, it 'fulfilled every expectation of the residence of a Whig grandee, and thus helped to bolster Portland's status as the aristocratic head of the party.'[29] As a consequence of his residence, the house became the *de facto* headquarters of the Whig party and, in combination with the effect of Fox's long association with Devonshire House further down Piccadilly, brought to the street such a lively demand for political literature that between them John Debrett and John Stockdale, two prolific publisher-booksellers with premises located 'opposite Burlington House', were to dominate the rapidly expanding market for political pamphlets throughout the 1780s and '90s. *Bardolph Badger'd or The*

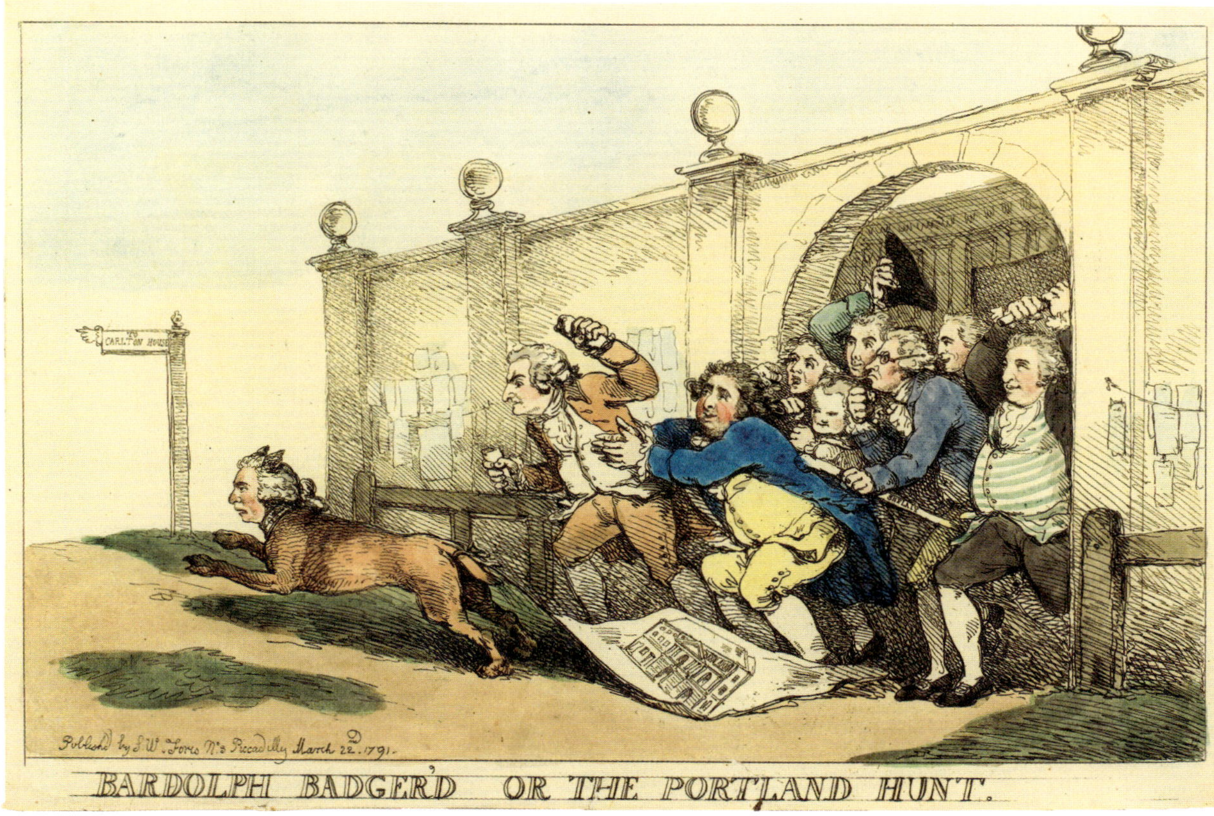

Fig. 56
Thomas Rowlandson, *Bardolph Badger'd, or the Portland Hunt*, published by S. W. Fores, 22 March 1791.
Royal Collection, RCIN 810411

Portland Hunt (1791) by Thomas Rowlandson is likewise typical of the vast number of political satires emanating in this period from the printshops of S. W. Fores at No. 3 Piccadilly and Mrs Hannah Humphrey just round the corner in Old Bond Street (Fig. 56). This particular example, satirising the dissensions in the party caused by Richard Brinsley Sheridan's toadying to the Prince of Wales, shows the Duke of Portland and his fellow Whig leaders, including Fox and Burke, angrily driving the miscreant hound/thief Sheridan away from the gate of a mansion that is reminiscent both of Burlington House and Devonshire House. As a misleadingly 'composite' mansion, this may have been intended to symbolise the false unity of the party under Portland's leadership, the true nature of which was revealed in the festoons of pamphlets and broadsides hung up for sale by hawkers along its street wall. This was probably a common enough sight outside Burlington House since, conveniently for street traders, its Piccadilly boundary wall lay about eleven feet north of the present building line.[30] On the other side of this wall Portland was free to cultivate aristocratic aloofness from the 'rough and toilsome business' of politics, preserving the illusion of life on his estate at Welbeck where he always claimed he preferred to be.[31] It was surely for this reason, rather than out of any real need, that he built a chicken coop and cow sheds in the grounds of Burlington House, and converted the front half of Gibbs's stable block into a riding school (Figs 57, 58).

ON LADY DAY 1807, shortly after Portland had become Prime Minister for the second time, another countdown began on the future of Burlington House. The problem was not only the poor health of its eminent occupant, which was a cause of concern for the whole country, but the less visible consequence of the fact that in two years' time the Cavendish head lease interest in the adjoining Burlington Gardens estate would finally fall in. While this did not affect Burlington House directly, the imminent loss of £10,400 per annum rent from the streets to its north and north-east developed by the 3rd Earl of Burlington in 1718–24 and 1732–39 respectively, highlighted the failure so far to derive income from the house itself or financial benefit from the rise in the value of the land it occupied. In addition to this, the accountants' discovery that the 5th Duke's first wife Georgiana, the great socialite Duchess of Devonshire, had racked up debts of £109,135 by the time she died in 1806, brought new pressure on his financial advisors to devise ways to stem the tide of debt engulfing the estate. Despite their best efforts, during this period the aggregate debt secured on Devonshire property was to escalate from a worrying £310,298 in 1790 to an alarming £593,000 in 1814, by which time interest payments and annuities were consuming no less than 60% of the Duke's annual income.[32]

Given the apparent severity of this financial situation (which was to pale into insignificance once the 6th Duke started to take advantage of the fact that he could legally

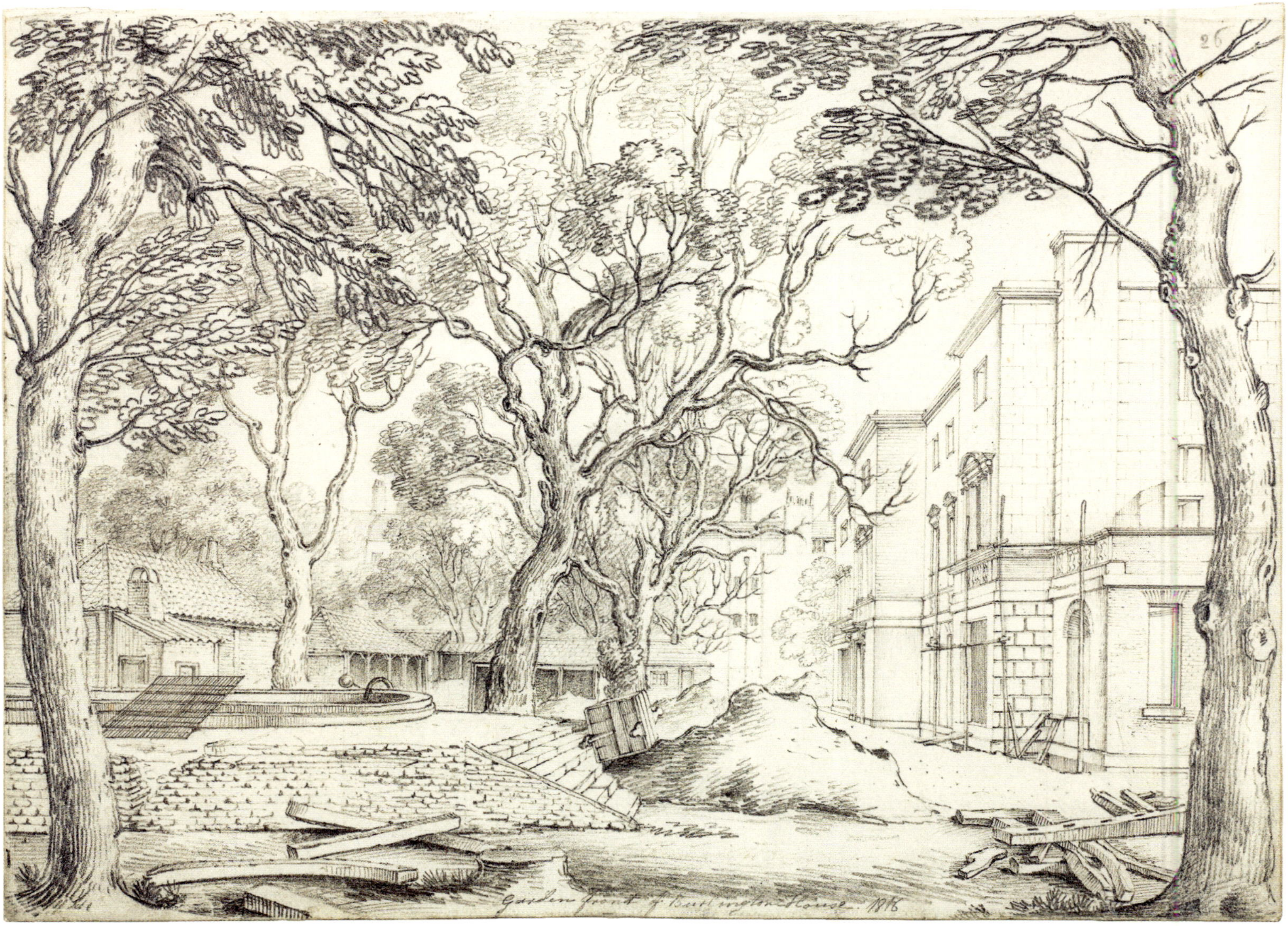

sell parts of the estate to finance his overspending), it was probably John Heaton, the 5th Duke's resident auditor for the Burlington Gardens properties and, as it happened, also one of Portland's principal business advisors, who urged most strongly that a proper commercial approach now needed to be taken to Burlington House as a financial asset. In fact, almost as soon as Portland declared he was happy to give the house up at short notice in July 1807, Heaton seems to have taken it upon himself to prepare a brief for redeveloping the site into a so-called 'Burlington Place'. This brief was evidently predicated on demolishing the house and replacing it with a self-contained enclave of 'first-rate' houses, including private stables, coach-houses and a chapel, together with shops and further houses along the Piccadilly and Vigo Lane street fronts. A tell-tale sign of Heaton's involvement in drawing up this brief is the fact that the architects he approached all found space in their designs for a well-appointed 'Auditor's House', together with a secure 'Evidence Room' for the safe-keeping of the cash, title deeds and other legal documents in his care.

Another sign that it was Heaton who took the lead in the 'Burlington Place' project is the large number of proposals it generated, for which there would have been little need had it not been necessary to persuade the 5th Duke of its merits. Having had long experience of advising on projects of a similar nature to alleviate the even worse state of the Duke of Portland's finances, Heaton not surprisingly called on the expertise of the latter's surveyor John White, who had been responsible for laying out the new streets on Portland's Marylebone estate from 1787 onwards. No doubt aware of Heaton's need to present multiple options, White in turn called on the assistance not only of his son John White junior, but also of Richard Wooding, an experienced London surveyor with whom he undertook the arduous task of measuring and valuing the materials of the existing buildings on the site. Between them these three architect-surveyors were able to submit eight variant designs for Heaton's consideration by the middle of March 1808.

As might have been expected, all four of Wooding's options took it as read that the site needed to be cleared

Fig. 57
John Claude Nattes (attrib.), Garden front of Burlington House with the sheds built by the Duke of Portland, 1816.
London Metropolitan Archives (City of London)

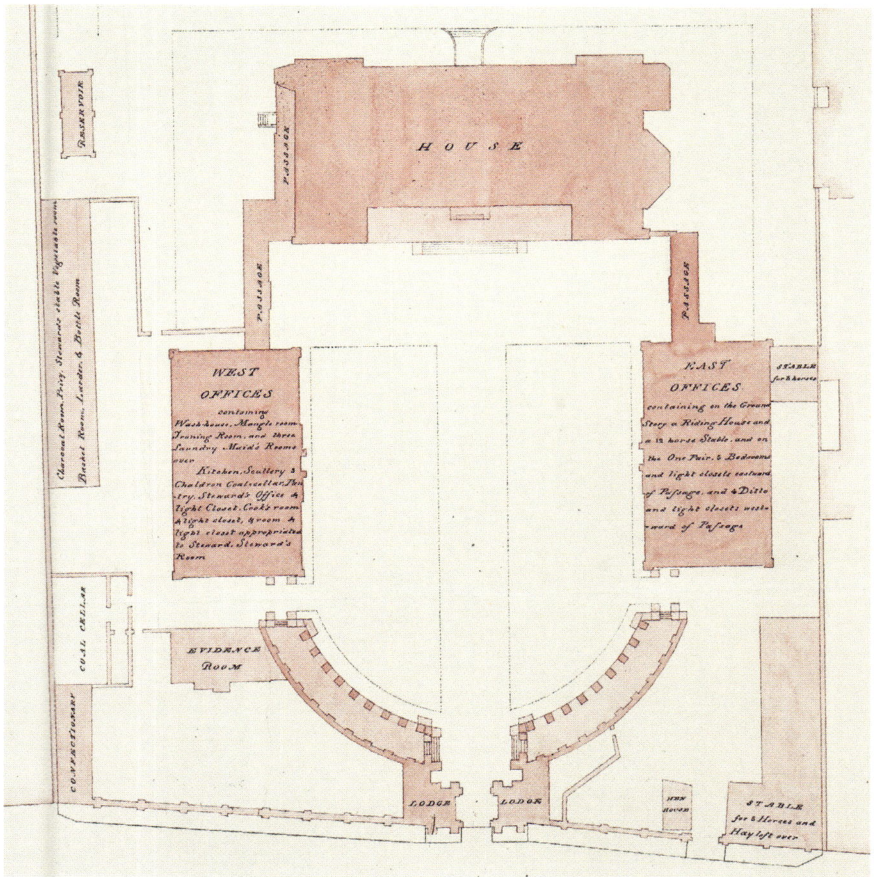

Fig. 58
Samuel Ware, Burlington House: detail of site plan, c. 1812.
Royal Academy of Arts, London, 06/4924

Fig. 59
Richard Wooding, Perspective sketch of the Piccadilly elevation of Burlington Place, 1808.
Royal Academy of Arts, London, 07/175

completely of existing buildings. Rather than concern himself with varieties of architectural effect, he made a point of posing the more fundamental question of whether it was better to build one 60-foot-wide street of large houses with or without a chapel, or two narrower streets that would include some smaller 'second-rate' houses and possibly a connecting 'Cross Street' (Fig. 59).[33] The Whites, on the other hand, being perhaps more sensitive to the architectural quality of the site in its present state, contrasted their own proposal for a single street of terraced houses along its whole length (a more articulated version of Devonshire Place), with a much less densely developed shorter street consisting of eighteen

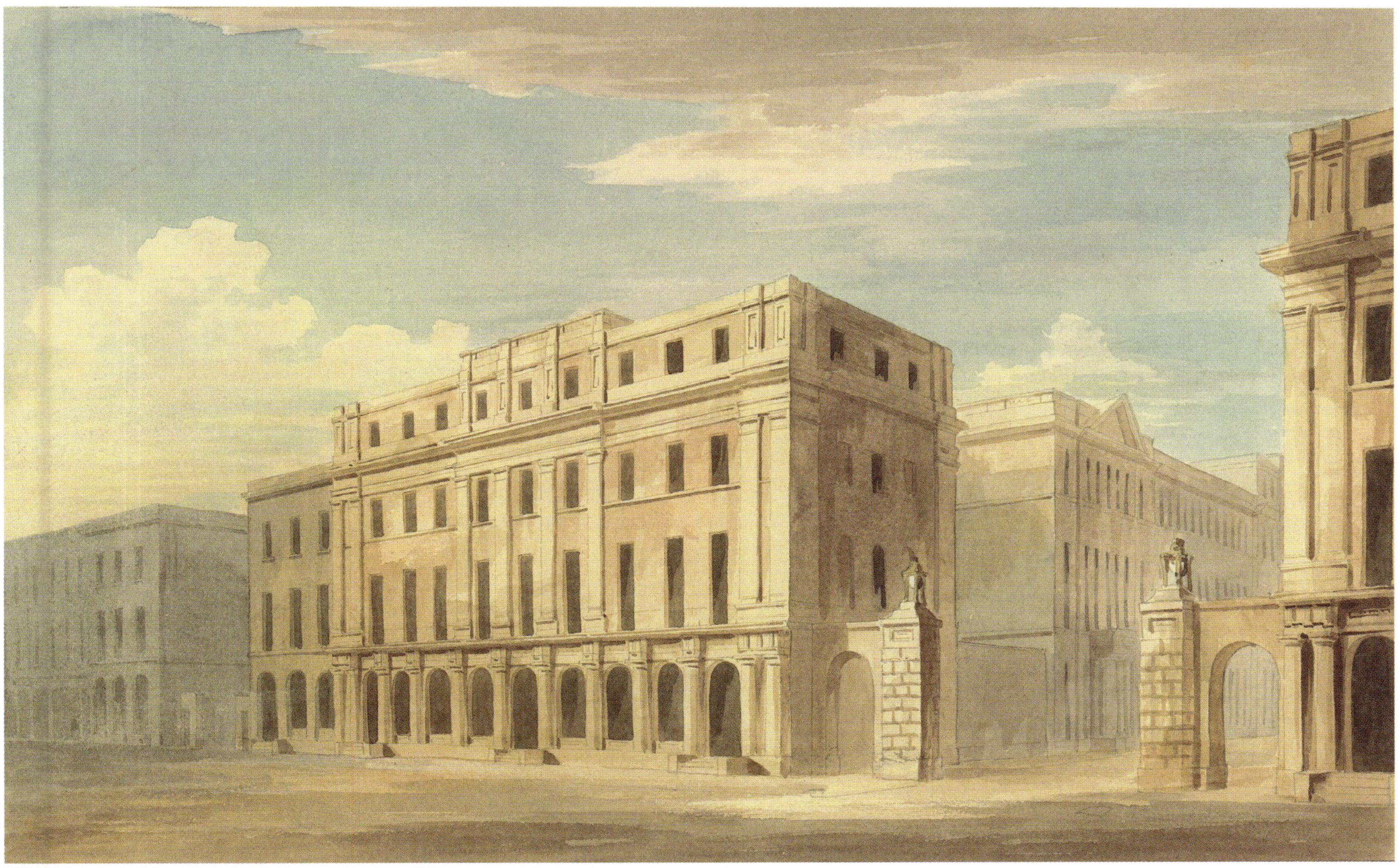

as opposed to thirty-four houses (Figs 60, 61). This second option demonstrated a way of preserving the original colonnade, the Great Gate and both the east and west service wings, the latter of which they proposed to convert into a chapel. In a further scheme, submitted by John White junior on his own account, it was proposed instead to retain no original buildings and to compensate for their architectural loss by rebuilding the colonnade along the front of the shops on Piccadilly and erecting at the centre of the Vigo Lane front a small domed chapel with a semi-circular porch. Of the two drawings of White junior's proposals that are known to have survived, his site plan (signed and dated 10 February 1808) shows this porch facing south; while in what is probably his design for the Vigo Lane elevation it faces north, forming the centrepiece of a colonnaded frontage of shops with living accommodation above that presumably matched a missing design for the Piccadilly elevation.[34]

In addition to approaching these specialists in residential development, Heaton invited designs from

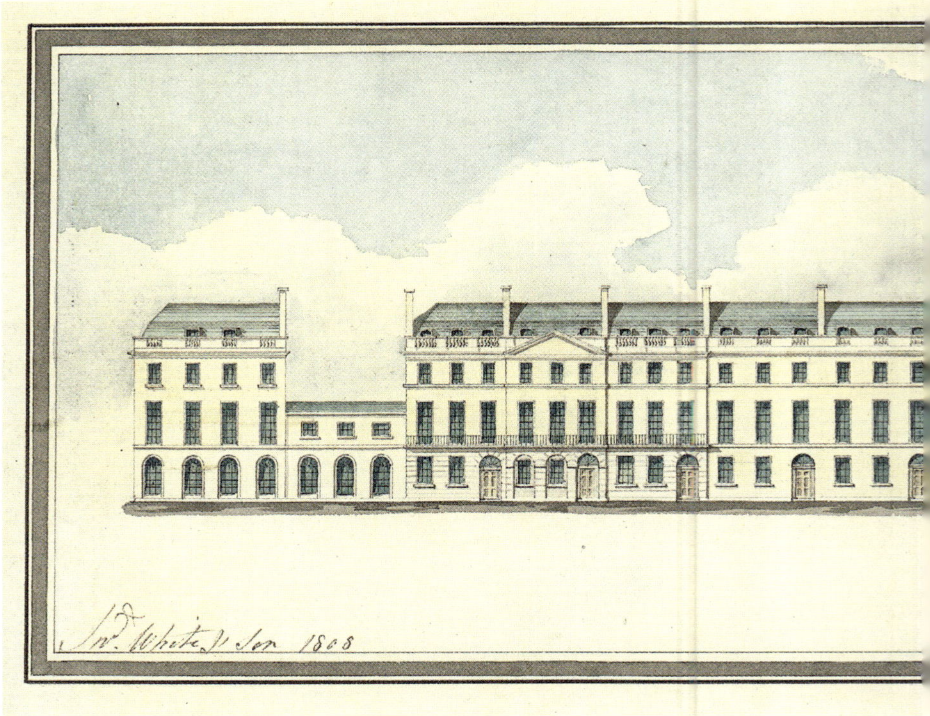

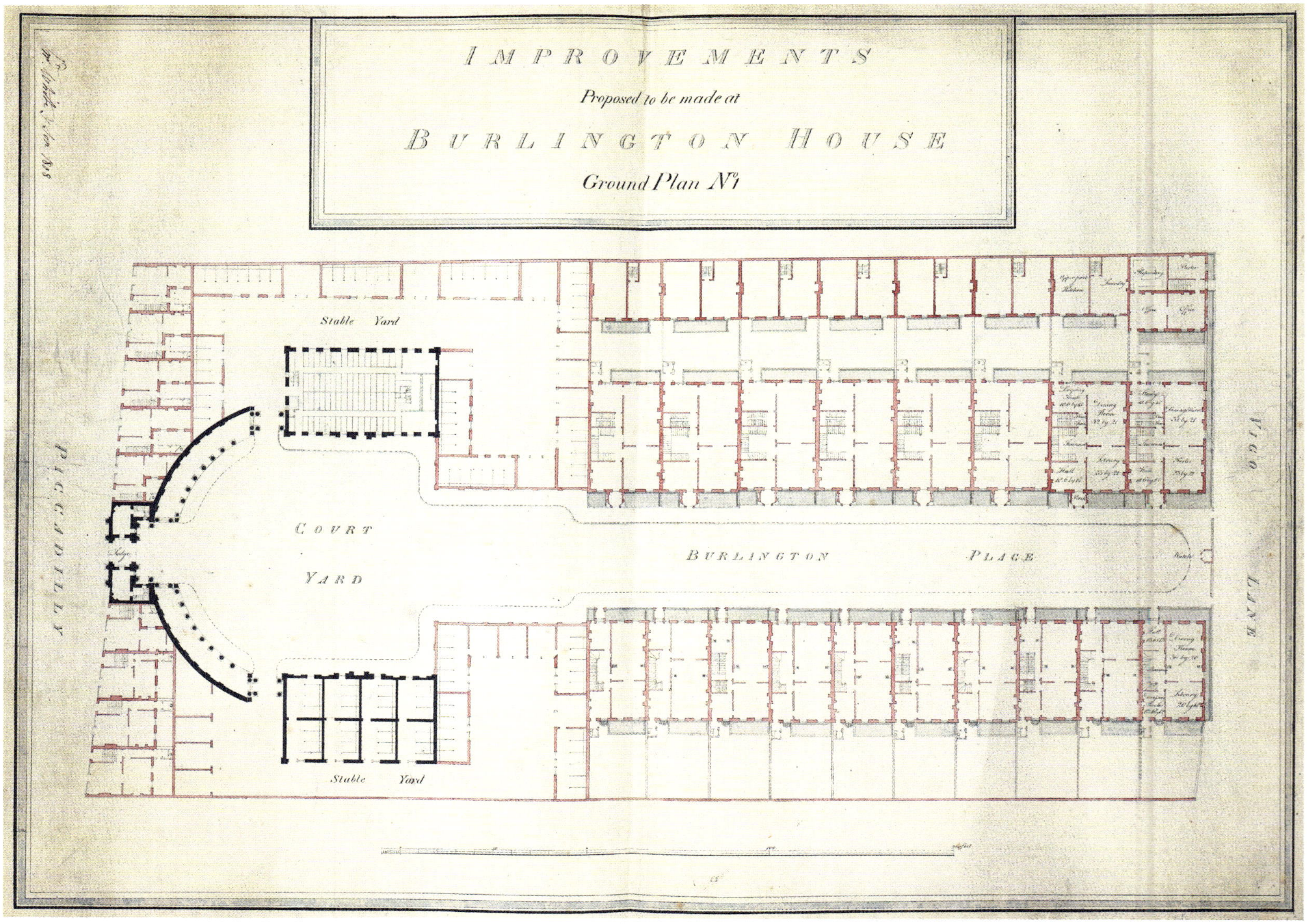

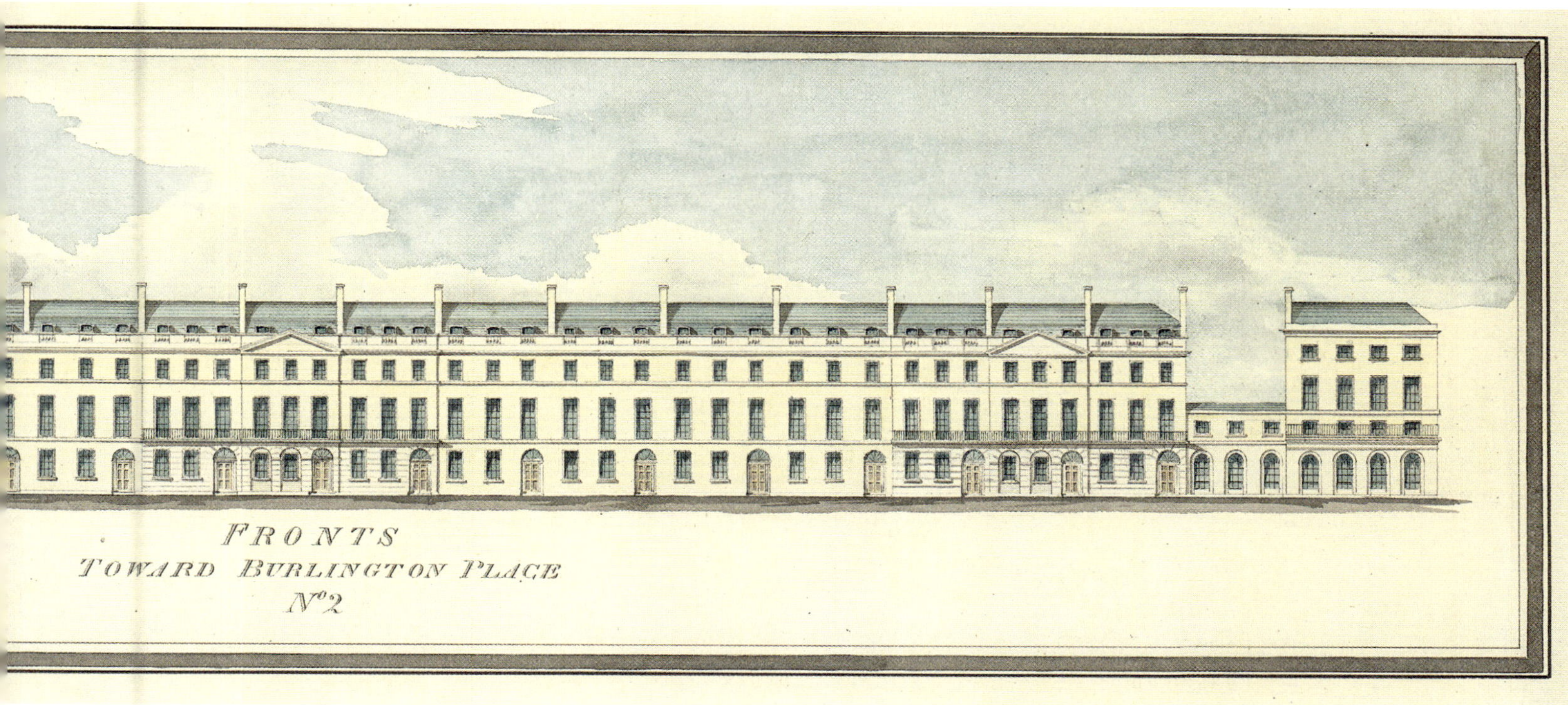

Fig. 60 (above)
John White Sr and John White Jr, Terrace houses on 'Burlington Place': elevation, 1808.
Royal Academy of Arts, London, 07/209

Fig. 61 (left)
John White Sr and John White Jr, First 'Burlington Place' scheme: ground plan, 1808.
Royal Academy of Arts, London, 07/202

a more unexpected quarter. Neil Bingham has suggested that Humphry Repton's beguiling proposal for the 'greening' of Burlington Place, which he and his son John Adey Repton presented in watercolours imbued with all their usual seductiveness, may have come about through the intervention of Portland himself.[35] Nicely ironic as this would have been, a more likely scenario is that Heaton was only too familiar with the Reptons' persuasive 'Red Book' designs for relandscaping the parks at Welbeck and Bulstrode, and hoped that on this occasion their blandishments could be turned to profitable account by demonstrating the benefits of sacrificing Burlington House (Figs 62–64). From Heaton's point of view, however, the picturesqueness of the Reptons' proposal was to backfire since it highlighted instead the advantage of retaining as many of the existing buildings as possible. Perhaps aware of this, and in the light of this initial round of submissions, Heaton invited yet another, younger architect of his acquaintance to work up a design that he must have thought could combine the attractiveness of the Reptons' scheme with the commercial potential of the more intensive development proposals submitted by the Whites and Wooding.

Samuel Ware was still an architectural student in the Royal Academy Schools when in 1804–05 Heaton first engaged him for what was probably routine surveyor's work on the Burlington Gardens estate.[36] The opportunity this gave Ware to examine at first hand buildings designed by the 3rd Earl of Burlington and the architects in his circle may account to some degree for the sympathetic knowledge he was to bring ten years later to the most important commission of his career. On 26 July 1814, not long before he landed this great prize, Ware wrote to Heaton recounting in typically methodical fashion the previous occasions that he had been called upon to assist in matters relating to Burlington House. The earliest that he recalled was when 'through your kindness in 1808 I had the honour to be employed in making Plans and Estimates for the disposal of Burlington House and Grounds for the information of the late Duke of Devonshire.'[37] This was an important break for Ware and the trouble he took over it is evident from the ambitious scale and fine draughtsmanship of the two sets of finished drawings he made of his proposals, both of which are currently held in the Royal Academy's collection (Figs 66–70).

The key to Ware's scheme was his removal of the east and west offices and the retention of the colonnade and Great Gate to form a compressed oval 'Colonnade Court' at the entrance to a long 70-foot-wide '——— Place'. This enabled him to preserve the architectural grandeur of the existing courtyard and gateway while at the same time allowing room for a more intensive development than had been possible in either the Whites' or Reptons' low-density options. Presented in two variants, comprising either 22 four-bay houses of five storeys or 30 smaller three-bay houses of four, and including at the centre of each terrace a slightly recessed five-bay mansion with a Doric palace-front, Ware's design extracted the maximum possible 'first-rate' residential space from the site. In the two awkward residual areas behind his oval entrance court he tucked a chapel and vestry to the west and additional

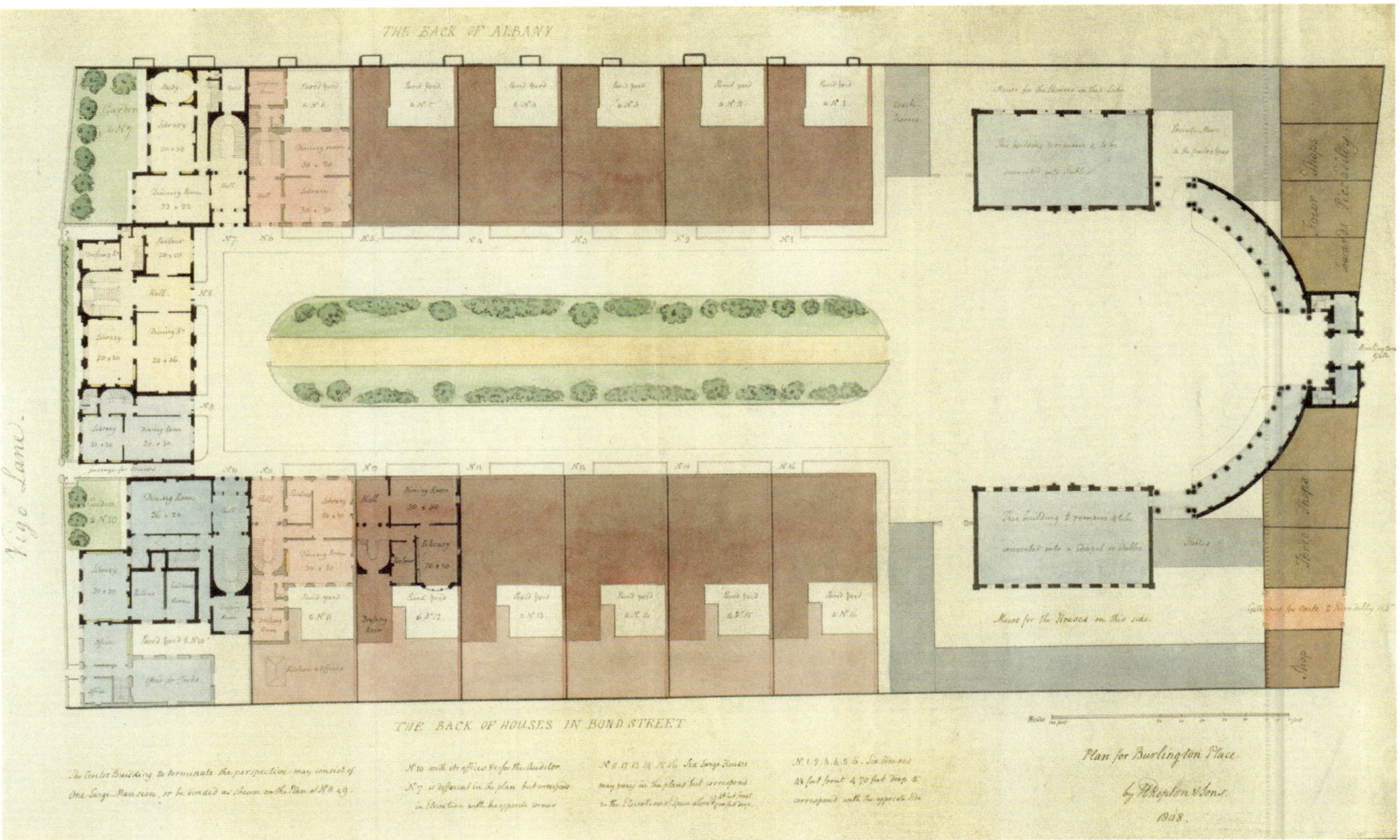

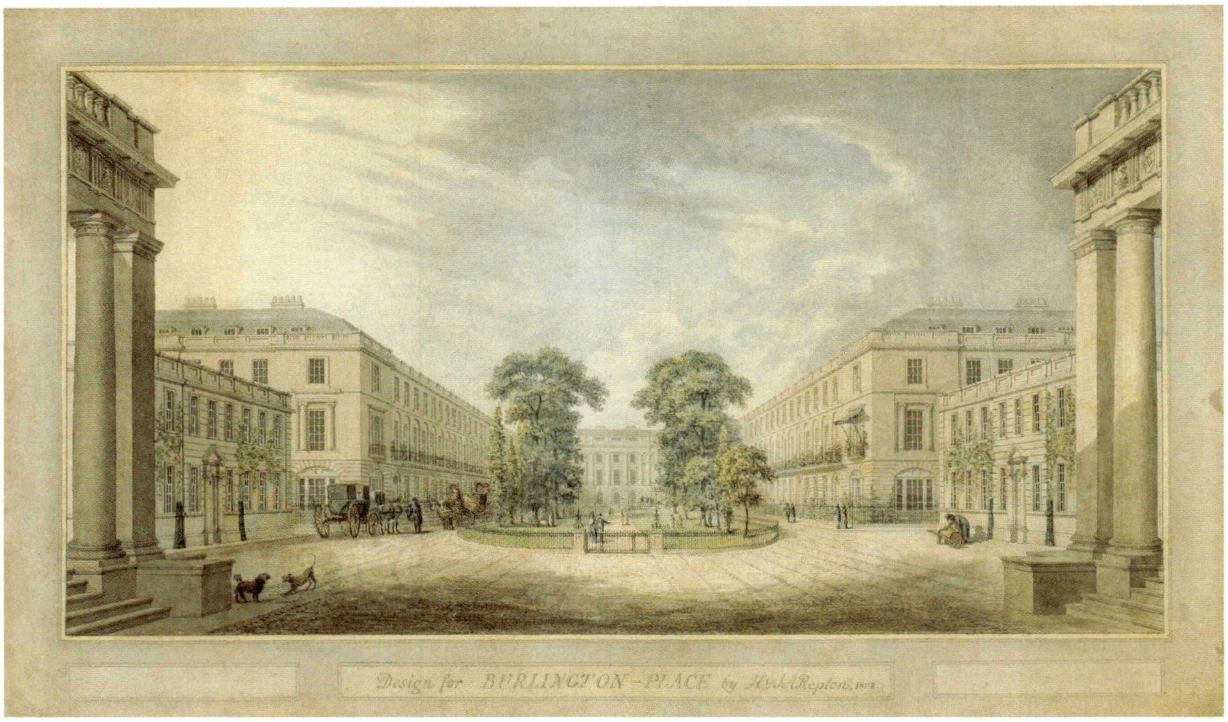

Fig. 62
Humphry Repton and John Adey Repton, Burlington House site redevelopment ('Burlington Place'): ground-floor plan with overlay of first-floor part-plan, 1808.
Royal Academy of Arts, London, 07/197

Fig. 63
Humphry Repton and John Adey Repton, Burlington House site redevelopment: perspective looking north, 1808.
Royal Academy of Arts, London, 07/198

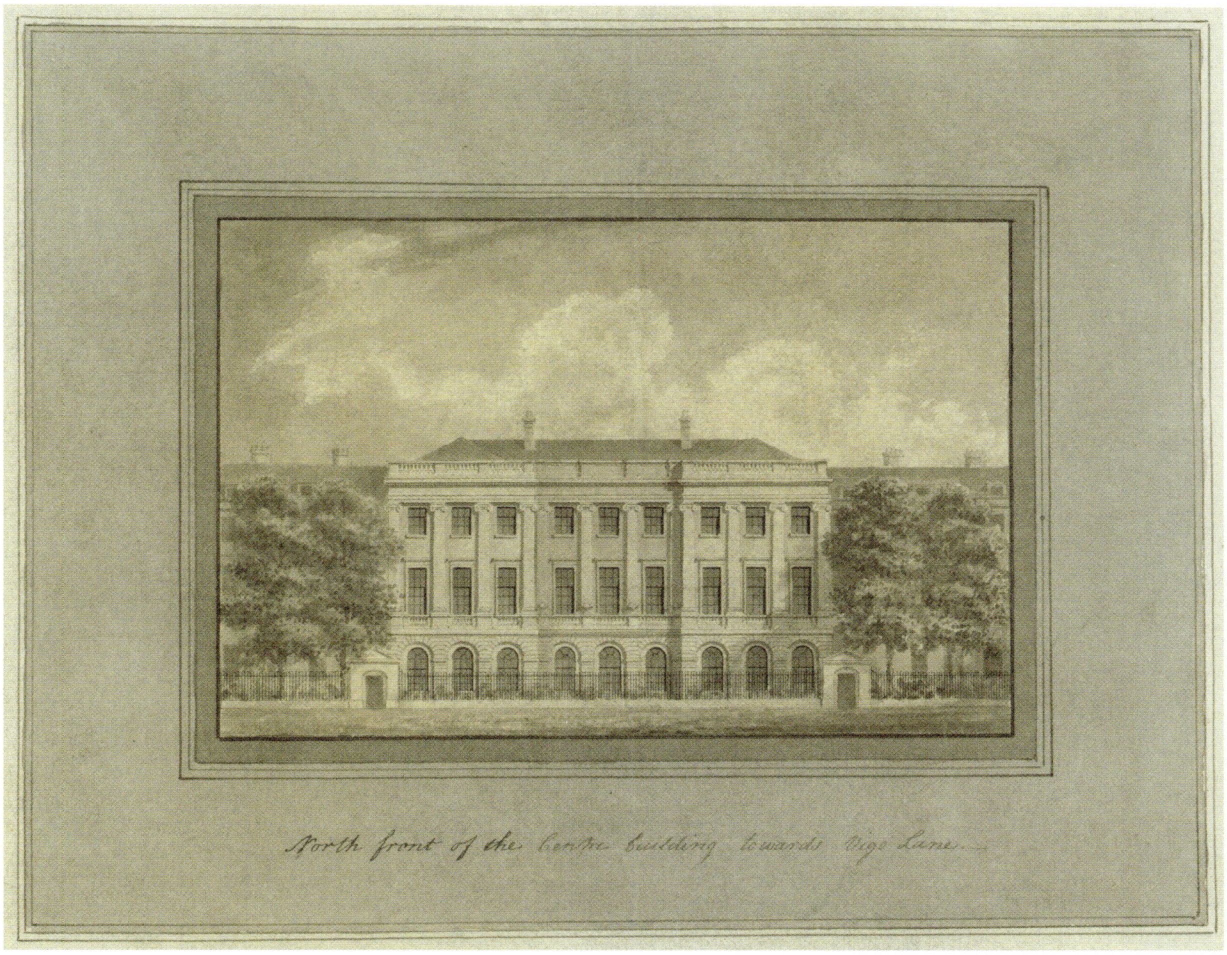

Fig. 64
Humphry Repton and John Adey Repton, Burlington House site redevelopment: north elevation to Vigo Lane, 1808.
Royal Academy of Arts, London, 07/199

stabling and coach houses to the east. This orientation was probably inherited from the Whites' 'preservationist' option since it ignored the logical consequence of the most innovative, and indeed prophetic aspect of Ware's overall plan, namely his placing of the main mews along the western perimeter to centralise the whole site on the Great Gate. Ware was to reverse the respective positions of the chapel and additional stabling when, in July 1811, he redrew his scheme 'to a small scale' for the purposes of a valuation according to three 'different modes of disposing' of the site.[38]

Although there are many indications of Ware's fluent command of the vocabulary of both early and late Georgian architectural ornament in the detail of his designs, his scheme brings a rather chilling monumentality to the homely Georgian terrace that is not far removed from what the pupil of an advanced Neoclassical French architect of the period might have offered in his place (Fig. 67). It is also only too apparent from the six-foot-long elevation he drew showing how old and new related, that his immense terrace would have dwarfed the colonnade and Great Gate (Fig. 65). It was probably no accident, therefore, that he suppressed in this drawing the flank of the western block of five-storey shops, which, together with their eastern counterparts, loom over the Great Gate and its sympathetically designed pedestrian entrances in his accompanying drawing of the 'Elevation in Piccadilly' (see Fig. 70).

The 5th Duke of Devonshire's response to this avalanche of proposals, commissioned ostensibly for his 'information' only, may be gauged by the fact that the future of Burlington House was still undecided when Portland died in October 1809. The expiry of the Burlington Gardens lease having come and gone to no avail, this was another moment for Heaton to stress again the necessity of a decision, not least because Portland's eldest son, the former Marquess of Titchfield and now 4th Duke, needed to know on a practical level how long he might be able to stay in the house.

William Atkinson, the sixth and final architect commissioned to design a 'Burlington Place', took up Ware's idea of a 70-foot-wide street prefaced by concave arcaded screen walls mirroring the colonnade, but followed the Reptons in retaining the east and west service blocks, perhaps in the belief that, unlike Ware's flattened oval, this would preserve the proportions and atmosphere of the original courtyard (Figs 71–74). A more experienced architect than Ware, with a promising country-house practice in the Manchester area, Atkinson staked everything on the skilful interior planning he had learnt

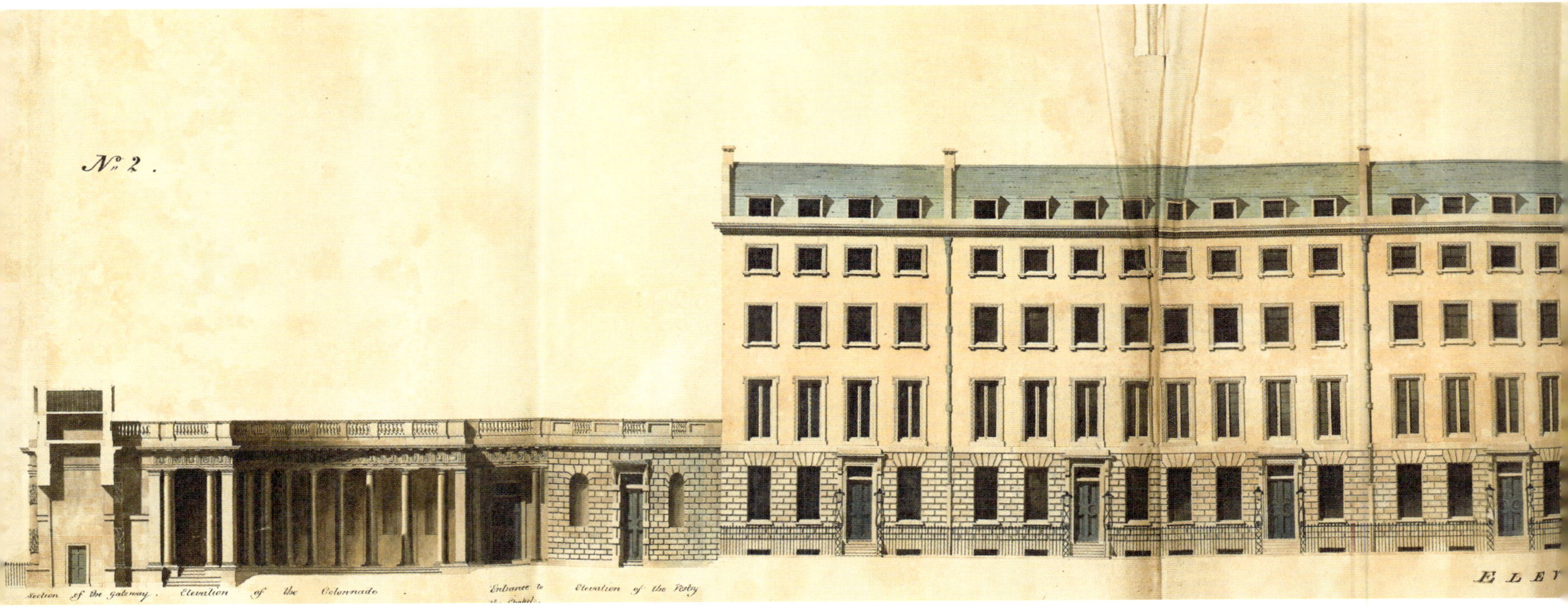

Fig. 65 (above)
Samuel Ware, Burlington House site redevelopment: section through the great gate and contiguous elevation of the west side of the colonnade and houses, first scheme, 1808.
Royal Academy of Arts, London, 07/461

Fig. 66 (below)
Samuel Ware, Burlington House site redevelopment: ground plan, first scheme, 1808.
Royal Academy of Arts, London, 07/460

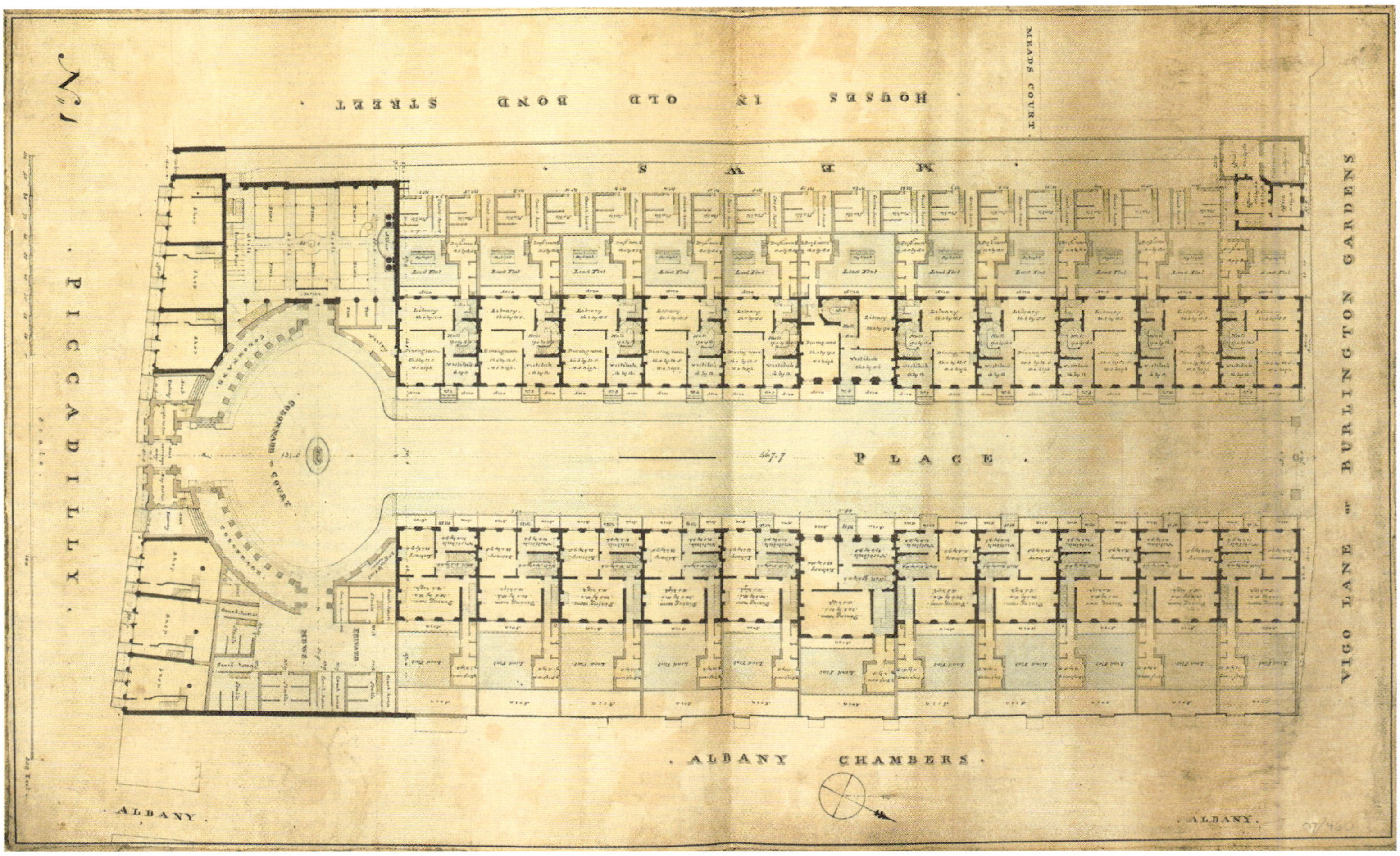

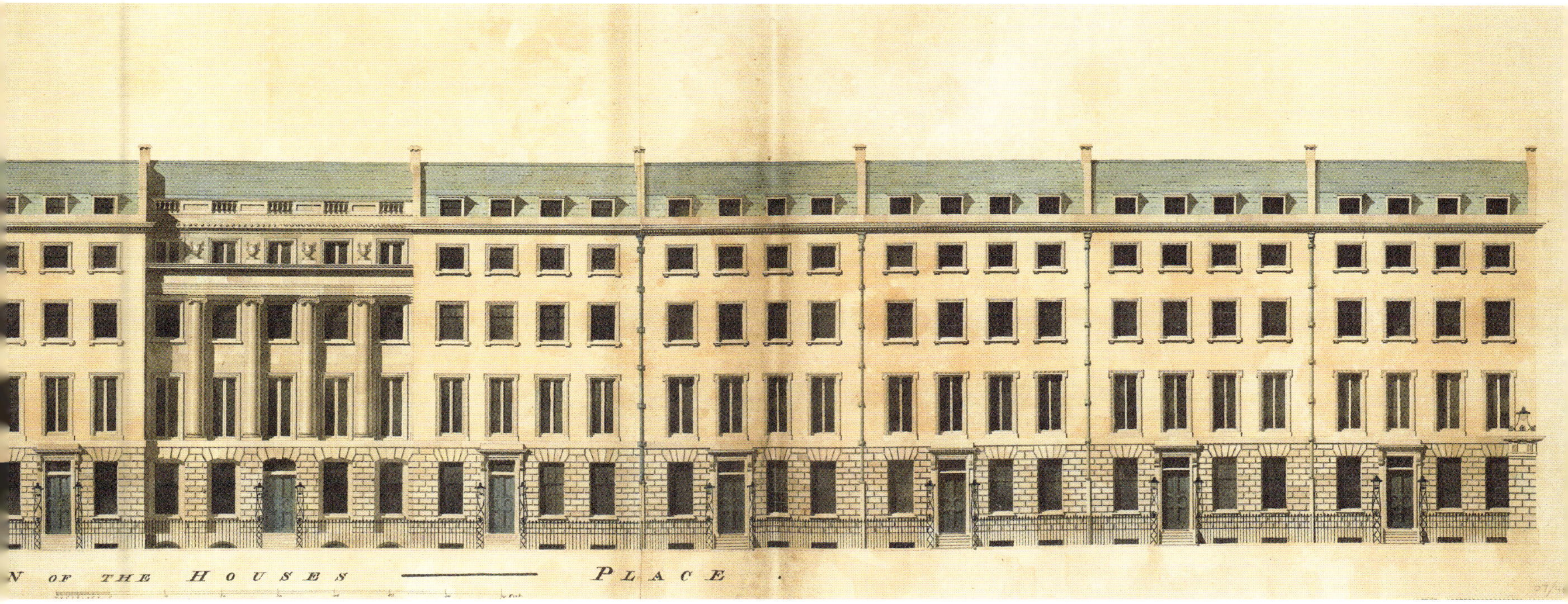

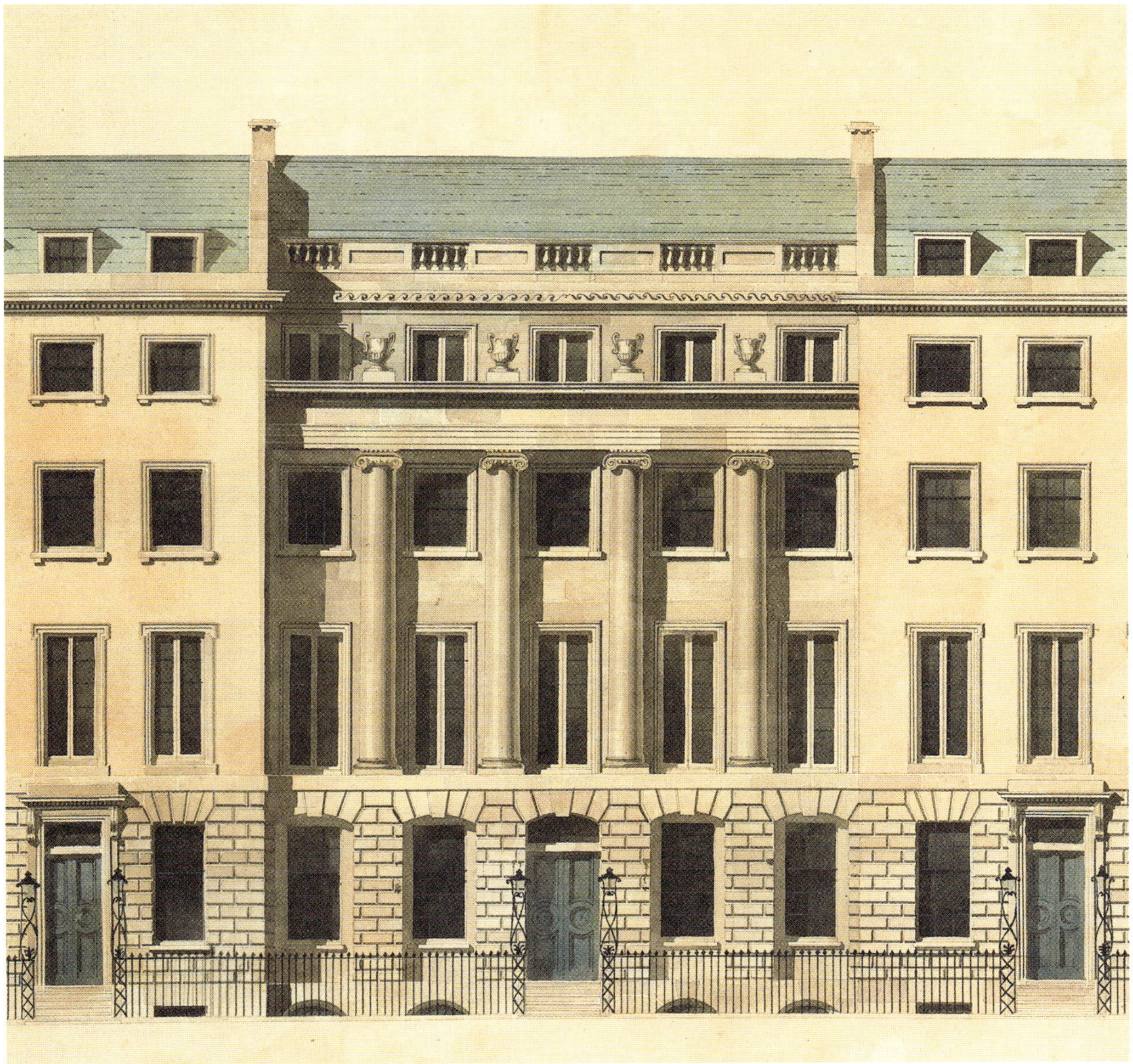

Fig. 67
Samuel Ware, Burlington House site redevelopment: detail of elevation showing the central houses, first scheme, 1808.
Royal Academy of Arts, London, 07/461

Fig. 68
Samuel Ware, Burlington House site redevelopment: elevation to Vigo Lane (also known as Burlington Gardens), first scheme, 1808.
Royal Academy of Arts, London, 07/463

Fig. 69
Samuel Ware, Burlington House site redevelopment: part-plan and part-elevation of 'Burlington Place' houses, second scheme, 1808.
Royal Academy of Arts, London, 07/464

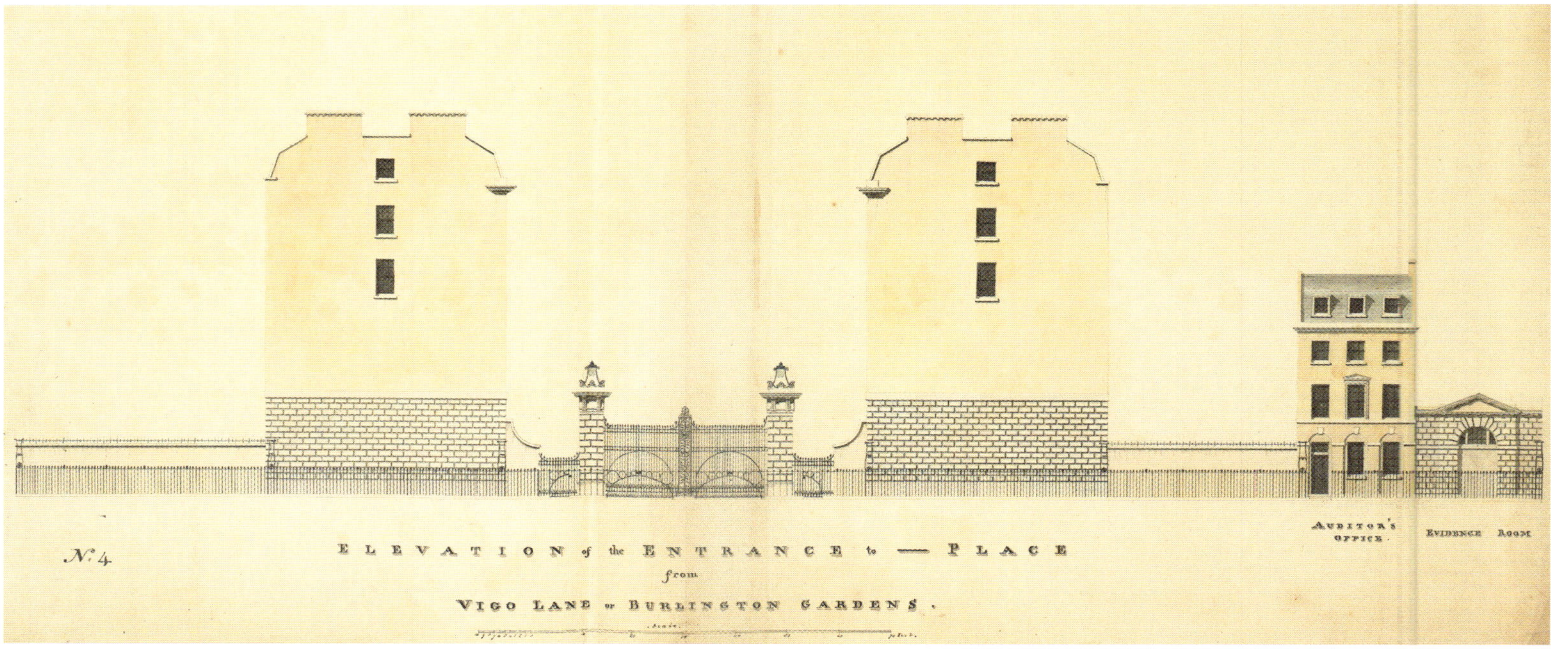

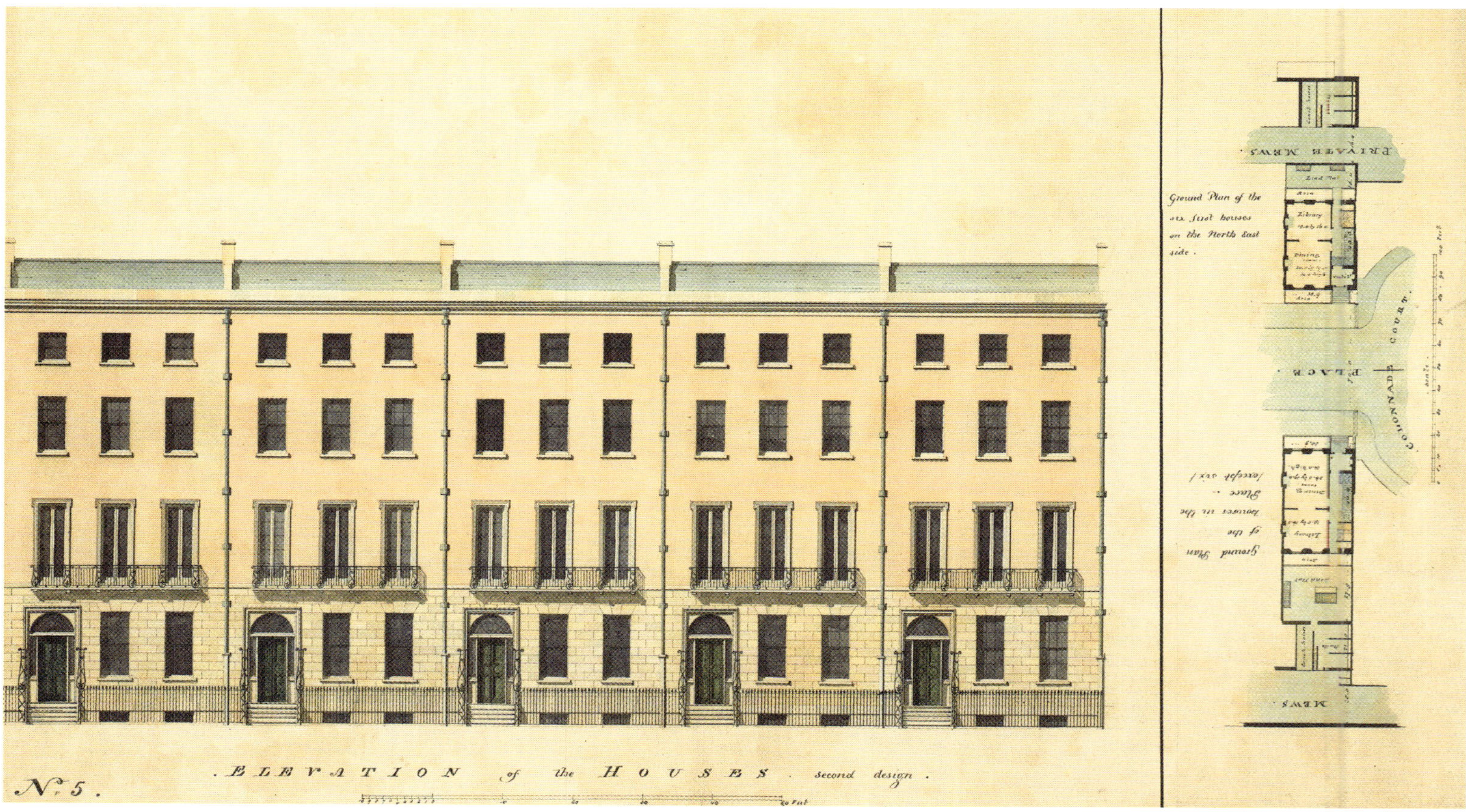

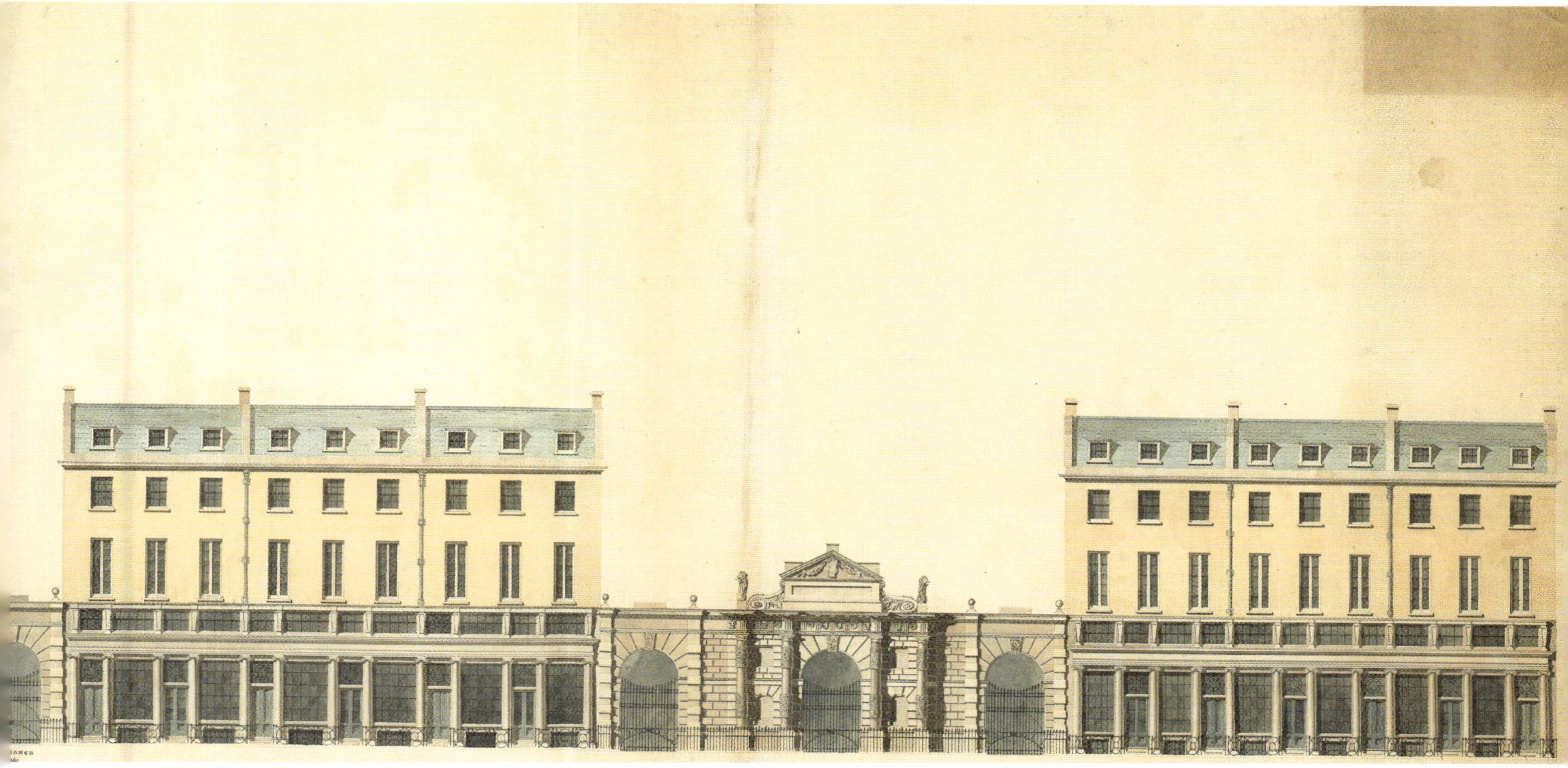

Fig. 70
Samuel Ware, Burlington House site redevelopment: Piccadilly elevation showing the great gate flanked by shops, 1808.
Royal Academy of Arts, London, 07/462

as a pupil in the office of James Wyatt. For a site no bigger than the footprint of Burlington House and its garden (the former is shown in outline on his block plan), Atkinson produced no less than eight intricate varieties of layout for a total of nineteen houses, his objective being presumably to avoid the kind of uniformity of interior planning that might offend the wealthier prospective tenant. He was also able to improve on Ware's scheme by replacing the cliff-like end gables in the latter's Vigo Lane elevation with independent Doric mansions facing the street, as the Reptons had suggested (Fig. 73).

Perhaps because of the time he needed to elaborate so many different floor plans, Atkinson's design for the shops on Piccadilly is dated a year later than (and somewhat revises) his 1809 scheme (Fig. 74). Once again he set out to improve on Ware's design, this time by straightening the historic kink in the existing building line and redesigning the Piccadilly side of the Great Gate in the watered-down modern Doric he had adopted for his Burlington Place and Vigo Lane elevations. The result was even less satisfactory than Ware's out-of-scale shop frontage in that it sacrificed the Piccadilly elevation of Campbell's gate for an entrance that was not only feebler in architectural effect but skewed everything else in relation to the proposed new building line.[39] Despite this, however, Atkinson's earlier block plan of 1809 (Fig. 71), which had shown the Great Gate unaltered, was prophetic in that it hinted for the first time at the possibility of continuing the Piccadilly shop frontage northwards to form short alleys at the sides of the site, an idea that was to bear fruit a few years later in Ware's design for the Burlington Arcade.

Given the steady progression towards more preservationist proposals in successive schemes for 'Burlington Place', it is hardly surprising that the reaction to Atkinson's final iteration was to abandon the idea of demolishing Burlington House altogether and to invite proposals instead for building only on those parts of the site that would leave the existing structures unaffected. Accordingly, the Whites were approached again in July 1810 to make 'a particular Ground Plan of the House and Offices with a view to convert them into two mansions and to build upon the front of the ground towards Piccadilly and to Vigo Lane'.[40] At the same time, they were asked to make 'a design agreeably thereto' and estimate 'the produce as a rental & for the Freehold'. Although

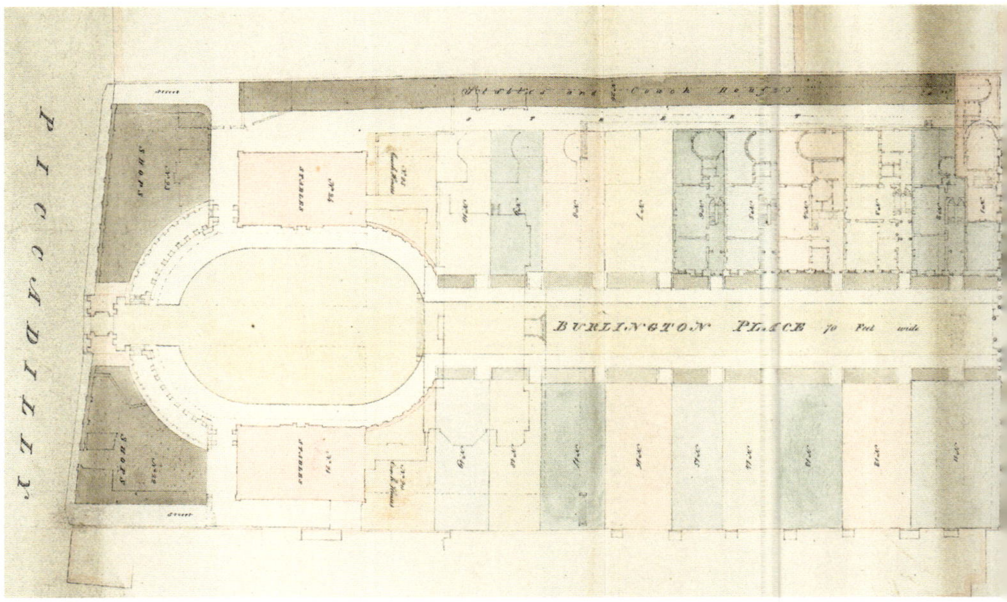

Fig. 71
William Atkinson, Burlington House site redevelopment: block plan, 1809.
Royal Academy of Arts, London, 07/376

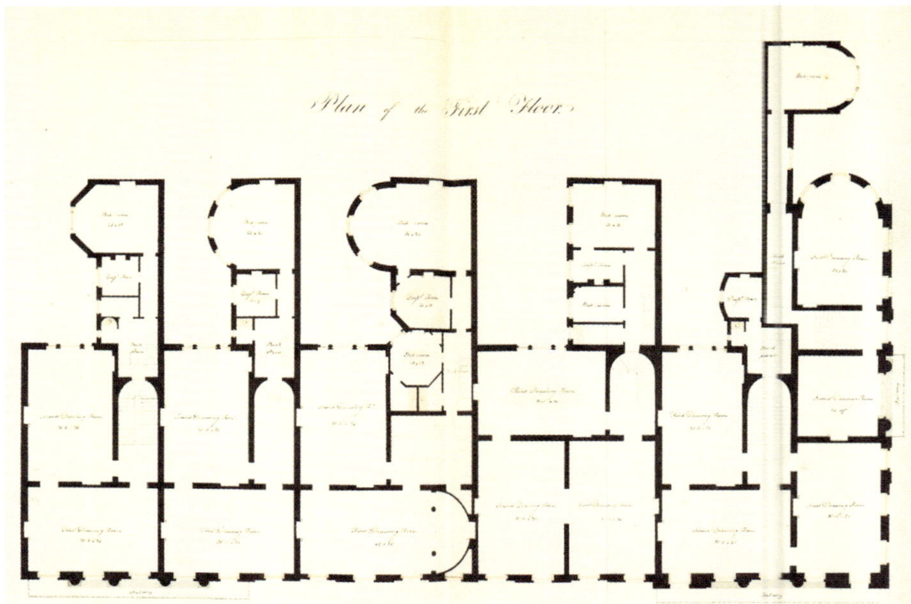

Fig. 72
William Atkinson, Burlington House site redevelopment: first-floor plan of houses, 1809.
Royal Academy of Arts, London, 07/379

the Whites' design for this scheme is not known to have survived, their estimate that it would produce £1,730 *less* net profit than could be achieved by leaving all the existing buildings *in situ* and letting the house as a single dwelling must have been a revelation.[41] Suddenly the most 'preservationist' solution turned out to be also the most profitable. In the light of their estimate, the Whites prepared later on that year 'a further design made at the suggestion of His Grace for Building two lines of Houses at the back of Burlington House instead of one line fronting towards Vigo Lane'. It was presumably in connection with this last proposal that the Whites received by the end of the year 'applications from Mr. Copland [the proprietor of Albany, the bachelors' chambers recently built along the length of Lord Melbourne's former garden to the east], Mr. Harrison, Mr. Neill, [and] Mr. Baxter to build upon [the site], and from Mr. Marsh, who was desirous of obtaining the Premises for the erection of a new theatre.'[42]

The Whites had based their estimate of the profitability of letting Burlington House and building on its garden and Piccadilly frontage on the assumption that, despite the loss of these amenities, a tenant would be willing to pay an annual rent of £2,000 for the privilege of living there. The closer the prospect of such a tenant being found, however, perhaps the less attractive it seemed since, during the course of 1811, three members of the Cavendish family put themselves forward as possible future occupants. One of these, unsurprisingly, was the 4th Duke of Portland who, according to Heaton, in November 1811 had told John White that he 'would give any Rent for Burlington House, and enter into any Engagement for Repairs that might be proposed ... being much attached to the Spot'.[43] As we shall see, Heaton was probably exaggerating this possibility in an attempt to clinch a deal with another member of the family. In fact Portland was hardly in a position to rent the house on any such terms (he and his family had left it finally early in the week of 10 June 1811) at a time when he was faced with debts on his father's estate of more than £500,000.[44] A more realistic contender for the privilege was (once again) the current Marquess of Hartington who, to judge from the draft of his father's letter to him on the subject

Fig. 73
William Atkinson, Burlington House site redevelopment: elevation to Vigo Lane, 1809.
Royal Academy of Arts, London, 07/380

Fig. 74
William Atkinson, Burlington House site redevelopment: elevation to Piccadilly showing nine shops with housing over, set in two blocks on either side of the central gated entrance to 'Burlington Place', 1810.
Royal Academy of Arts, London, 07/383

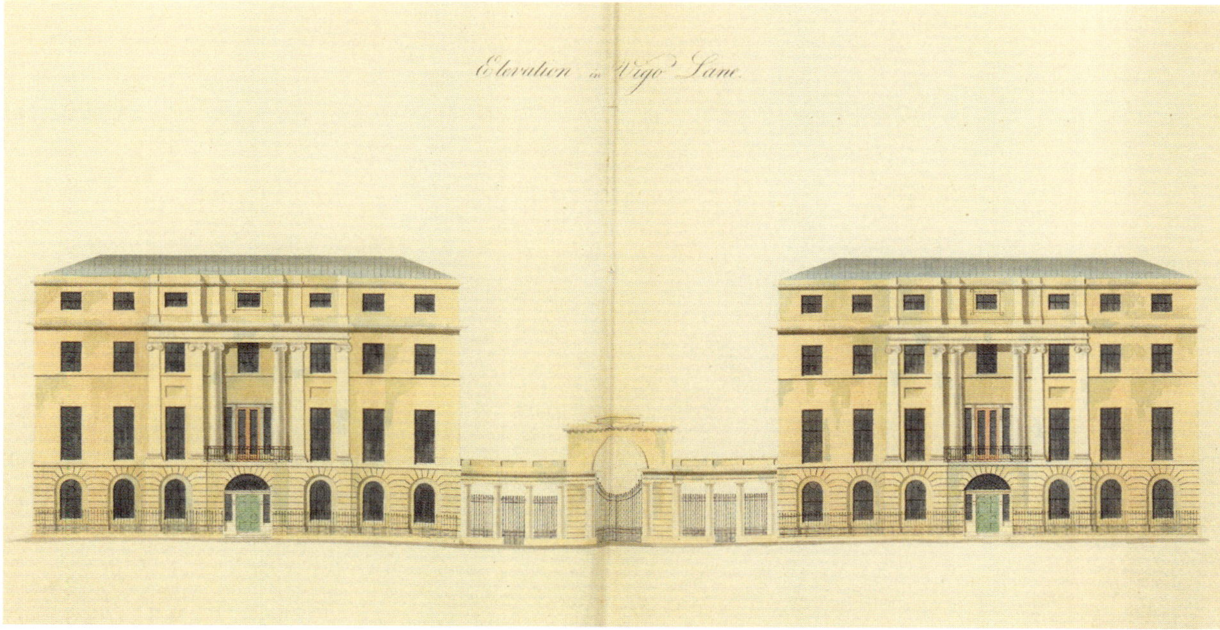

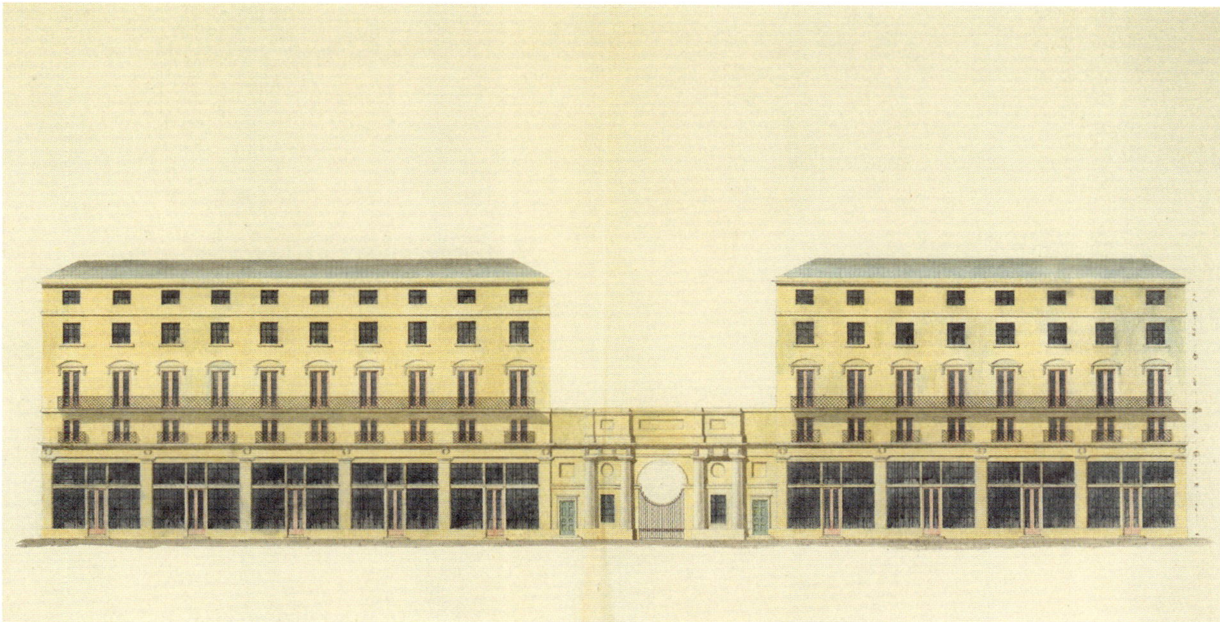

(written by no coincidence on 10 June), seems to have hoped to establish himself at Burlington House following his coming of age on 21 May 1811.[45] By then, however, the Duke's younger brother, Lord George Augustus Henry Cavendish – the other member of the family mentioned above – had set the cat among the pigeons by offering to buy the house outright. Had the Duke not died little more than six weeks after writing to his son about wanting to accept this offer, there is little doubt that the sale of the house to Lord George would have gone ahead and at a stroke dispelled the uncertainty that continued to cloud its future for another four years.

Far less concerned than his father about the escalating debts of the Devonshire estate, the 6th Duke was in no hurry to sell Burlington House to his uncle, nor indeed to pursue the Whites' latest proposal for redeveloping parts of its site. Aware that his youthful new employer wanted to keep his options open, Heaton tried hard to interest Lord George in leasing the house instead. With this in mind, in November 1811 Heaton instructed Ware to obtain the opinions of three well-known architects 'on what may be a proper Rent for Burlington House, Offices and Gardens to be let on a Repairing Lease for 25 Years, the Tenant to be subject to all Taxes except the Landlords' Property Tax'. While George Saunders and William Porden came up with figures in line with the Whites' estimate of £2,000 per annum, John Soane, the Royal Academy's Professor of Architecture, complicated matters by stressing the degree to which the rentable value of the house depended upon the sentiments of its prospective occupant.[46] Filled with dread at the prospect of a great work of art facing imminent destruction, Soane turned what should have been a straightforward assessment of its rentable value into a paean to its incalculable worth as architecture:

> I must premise that of all the places to which I have ever been requested to affix a rent, I have never experienced so much difficulty and difference of opinion as in the case of Burlington House and its appurtenances: – these premises to be let on a repairing lease, set all calculation at defiance; this superb and unique residence although not 'raised by Genii in a nights time' is a creation of such rich fancy and refined taste that persons feeling all the Architectural beauties of this classical spot would consider the possession desirable at thousands per annum, – whilst others, without such feelings would regard the occupancy of the premises, for a limited time, and with covenants to maintain them agreeably to their original destination, a very heavy tax!

Fearing for the survival of the house, Soane may have hoped that setting its rentable value to between £800 and £1,000 per annum made it less likely to come on to the market and therefore increased its chances of continuing in Cavendish ownership. Soane's impassioned response to what would have normally been simply a chore – his preliminary notes and draft cover nine foolscap pages cogitated over three weeks and refer feelingly to Burlington House as 'a national organism that I hope will never be destroyed' – cannot but have resonated in Ware's memory when he later found himself making a far greater contribution to the house's future than he could have ever imagined.[47] For while Heaton's hopes of tempting Lord George with a 25-year repairing lease came to nothing, Soane's concern for the preservation of Burlington House, expressed though it was in the dry context of a valuation report, was to become a decisive influence four years later (Fig. 75).[48]

By then, however, a rather different influence on the future of the house had also begun to emerge, prefiguring the more public uses that would eventually fill the vacuum of its faltering viability as a private dwelling.

THE FIRST USE OF Burlington House for the exhibition of works of art, or indeed for a public attraction of any kind, arose as a consequence of the 5th Duke having given permission a few weeks before he died in July 1811 for a makeshift shed behind the west quadrant of the colonnade to be used to house the Elgin Marbles.[49] With negotiations for the government's purchase of the collection at a standstill, Lord Elgin's Park Lane house no longer available for its display, and a proposal for its exhibition under the aegis of the British Institution recently rejected, it was a stroke of good fortune that the 6th Duke's reluctance to sell Burlington House prolonged an arrangement intended to last five months into as many years. Because Elgin had at first invited only a few artists to make drawings from the marbles, B. R. Haydon and the then president of the Royal Academy Benjamin West in particular liked to exaggerate the exclusivity of their

Fig. 75
Soane office, Burlington House, south front and offices, RA Lecture drawing, 1811.
Sir John Soane's Museum, London, 17/4/8

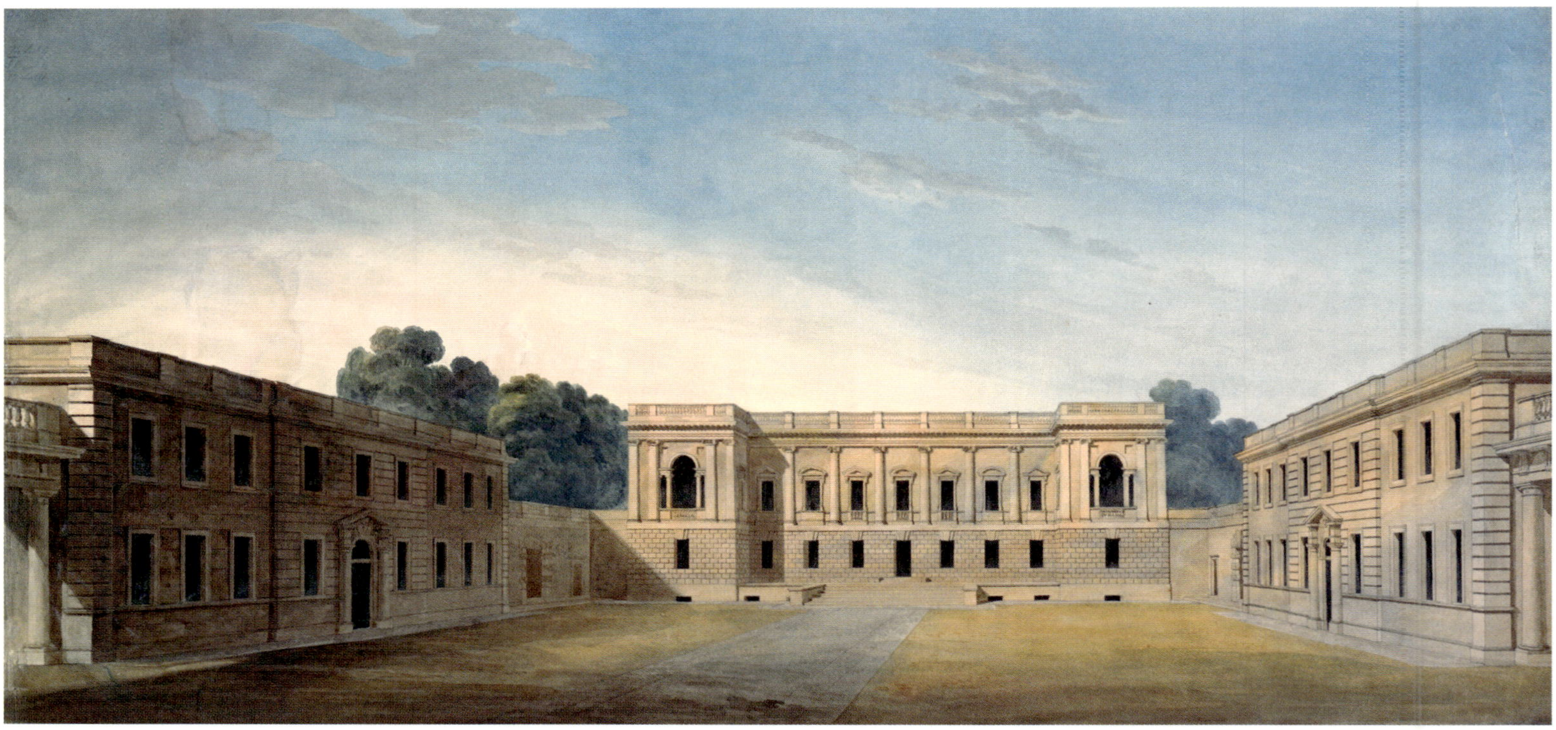

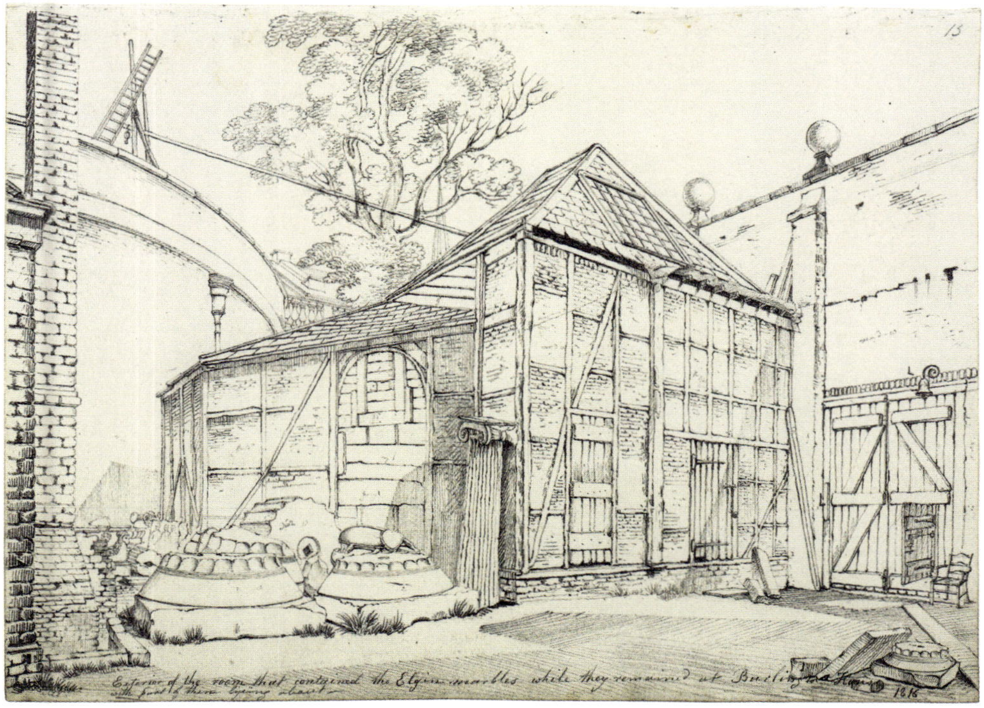

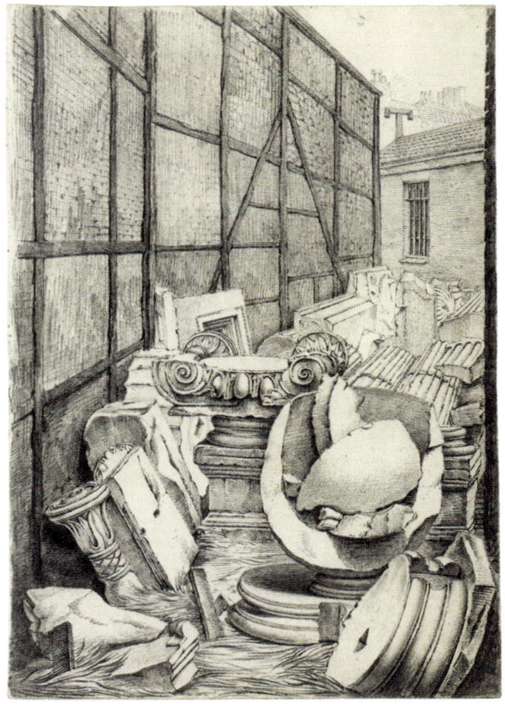

Fig. 76
J. C. Nattes (attrib.), The shed behind the western quadrant of the Burlington House colonnade, with parts of the Elgin Marbles lying about, 1816.
London Metropolitan Archives (City of London)

Fig. 77
J. C. Nattes (attrib.), Some of the Elgin Marbles stored behind a shed at Burlington House, 1816.
London Metropolitan Archives (City of London)

privilege. In typical schoolmasterly fashion West took it upon himself to restrict Elgin's open invitation for students of the Royal Academy Schools to draw from the marbles at Burlington House by limiting tickets of admission to prize-medal winners only.[50] In a similarly possessive fashion, Haydon claimed to be not only the first English artist to have studied the Parthenon sculptures at such close quarters, but also the first to have truly communed with their grandeur and beauty:

> I used to go down in the evenings with a little portfolio, and bribe the porter at Burlington House to which the Elgin Marbles were now removed, to lend me a lantern, and then locking myself in, take the candle out and make different sketches till the cold damp would almost put the candle out. As the light streamed across the room, and died away into obscurity, there was something solemn and awful in the grand forms and heads and trunks, and fragments of mighty temples and columns that lay scattered about in sublime insensibility – the remains, the only actual remains of a mighty people. The grand back of the Theseus would come towering close to my eye, and his broad shadow spread over the place a shade of mystery and awe.[51]

Although it slightly muddles the sequence of events leading up to the collection's purchase by the government in 1816, Joseph Nollekens's memory of frequent visits to draw the Elgin Marbles at Burlington House probably reflects more accurately their growing accessibility and reputation during this period:

> [The marbles] were shortly afterwards moved to the side premises of Burlington-house, where they remained until a temporary gallery could be prepared for them in the British Museum by Government, which had purchased them for the use of the public, and the advancement of Art. During the time these marbles were Lord Elgin's property, Mr. Nollekens, accompanied by his constant companion, Joseph Bonomi, … paid them many visits; and indeed at that time, not only all the great artists, but every lover of the Arts, were readily admitted. The students of the Royal Academy, and even Flaxman, the Phidias of our times, and the venerable President West, drew from them for weeks together.[52]

There is no known record of how the marbles were arranged inside their 'gallery' at Burlington House. However, three drawings of its exterior, made about a year after building work had necessitated its closure in April 1815, include one in which the attendant's empty chair and the bell to attract his attention from the street appear to be still in place, suggesting that 'lovers of the Arts' continued to call at the Piccadilly side gate in the hope of gaining admission (Fig. 76). The overflow of large, mainly architectural fragments stacked outside was due to the arrival of a second shipment of 68 cases from Malta in July 1812 (Fig. 77).[53]

Elgin did not pursue a proposal, first mooted in November 1811, that the 6th Duke might agree to a better exhibition space being built on the site – had he done so the British Museum could have had an outpost in the gardens of Burlington House a century and a half before its Ethnographic Department moved there in 1969.[54]

However, the precariousness of the marbles' accommodation in a ramshackle shed off Piccadilly probably in the end served Elgin's purpose better by shaming politicians into realising the need to provide a worthier home for them on English soil. This would have certainly been the case once it became known that the celebrated Italian sculptor Antonio Canova, and Ennio Quirino Visconti, Napoleon's curator of antiquities at the Louvre, had both made special journeys to view the marbles in their hut, and pronounced them to be among the greatest masterpieces of classical sculpture in existence.[55]

In the victorious summer of 1814 London became almost overnight the party capital of Europe and Burlington House one of its most spectacular venues. White's Club kicked off on 20–21 June with a grand 'Fete' held in honour of the state visit of the allied sovereigns, at which 2,500 distinguished guests were served supper at 2 a.m. in one of three rose-and-white muslin-lined marquees in the garden. The walls of the grandest of these – the 'Royal Room' – were 'covered with a fine panoramic painting of the arrival of the Sovereigns at Dover – the roof hung with azure blue', while the 'platform at the upper end, set apart for the principal guests, represented the quarter-deck of the ship in which they came over.' The temporary ball room, where the Emperor of Russia was reported to have danced till five in the morning, was described in *The Times* the following day as

> … divided into three grand walks, by two rows of pillars reaching to the roof, and covered with white muslin, in large flutings: the ceiling was à *la marquée*, in strong folds, varied with rosettes of white, from which chandeliers hung, and light drapery borders. Fifty-four immense white curtains hung from the ceiling, fastened with pink rosettes, and draped. The pillars from their length and lightness, gave the entire vast hall a peculiar impression of elegance.[56]

Ten days later, Watier's Club held a masquerade ball on the same site in honour of the Duke of Wellington. The managers, 'under the direction of several noblemen of high distinction', clearly set out to put White's party in the shade by erecting an even more elaborate set of temporary buildings behind Burlington House. The following Monday a still giddy *Morning Post* reporter found it quite impossible to convey

> … the beauty of [the] scene, either in close examination or in perspective from the hall of Burlington House. At the entrance to the *allee vert*, on the right and left, a noble archway was constructed; the one on the right communicated with the ball-room, that on the left commanded a view of the banqueting-room. Entering the ball-room the eye was first directed to a stage at the upper end, possessing a style of conception and a character quite out of the common way, irradiated by a glory. To Mr. FARLEY's taste the managers were thus far indebted. Here was a scaffold erected for rope-dancing, and scenery for a Grand Ballet. The attention was next arrested by a shop, erected near the centre, in a recess, occupied by a *marchande des modes*, and lined with costly articles of plate. The floor, for dancing, displayed a greatness of idea, a sublimity of character, worth of the Hero who occupied the leading situation; it was WELLINGTON and his coat of arms … Quitting the Ball, we again entered the Promenade, and thence got into the Supper Room. The improvements challenged our warmest panegyric. Instead of three supper-rooms we beheld … no less than seven tables, placed in parallel lines, running north and south, and extending upwards of 200 feet.[57]

White's fete had been marred by 'insupportable' heat in the marquees, generated by the rammed crowd and 'probably not less than a hundred' of the 'most superb and numerous sets of chandeliers that perhaps have ever been used on one occasion'. The managers of Watier's ball learnt from their predecessors' mistake by introducing mirrors to reflect more light from fewer chandeliers and opening a continuous vent in the cornices of the marquees. They were also careful to follow White's example in advertising detailed access and parking instructions in the press:

> It is earnestly requested … that Gentlemen will order their Carriages to get into the line of approach to Burlington House, in Davies-street, Berkeley-square; proceed along the eastern side of Berkeley-square,

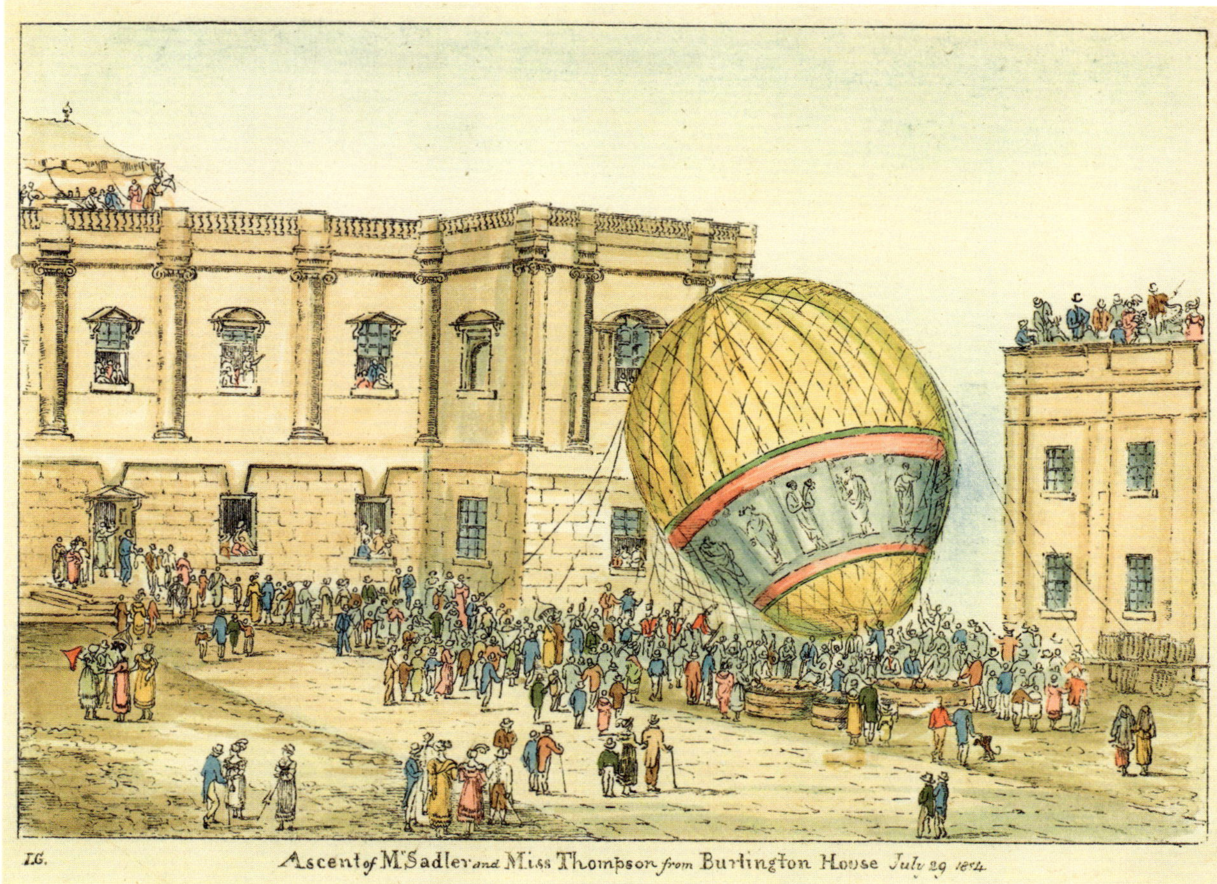

Fig. 78
James Gillray, *Ascent of Mr Sadler and Miss Thompson from Burlington House, 29 July 1814.*
London Metropolitan Archives (City of London)

> up Berkeley-street, into Piccadilly. Carriages will enter by the centre gate of Burlington House, turn to the left on entering the court-yard, and go out at the eastern gate. No carriages excepting those of the Royal Family will be permitted to approach Burlington House in any other way, or to remain in the court-yard. All chairs to enter at the door made for that purpose, in Vigo-lane, where carriages will not be allowed to set down. The carriages coming to take up must range their hind wheels against the pavement, and their horses' heads towards the centre of the street, this preserving a clear way down the centre. Except those of the Royal Family, no carriages to enter the yard of Burlington House until called for.[58]

Although White's organised a further sumptuous dinner in honour of Wellington on 6 July and a 'Grand Military Fete' followed on 18 July, it was Watier's 'Masquerade' that a correspondent writing in the *Morning Post* a week later felt sure was destined to go down in history

> ... as equal if not superior to anything of the kind ever before given in this country. Who will not rejoice at some future period, at having been present at this *fete*, given expressly to celebrate the return of an Officer, who by his brilliant succession of victories unparalleled in history, has immortalised his name as long as the world shall exist, and brought his country to a pitch of military glory and renown hitherto unexampled.[59]

It was not just extravagant parties that put Burlington House in the limelight this heady summer, for on 15 July Britain's first aeronaut, the veteran balloonist James Sadler and his seventeen-year-old son Windham made the first of their two ascents from the courtyard that month. Despite meeting contrary winds at Gravesend, they landed safely in a grass field near Whalley in Essex, having travelled an estimated 47 miles in an hour and five minutes – an astonishing speed for the time.[60] This, however, was only a trial run for the showstopper that came a fortnight later when Sadler's son repeated the exploit accompanied by a Miss Thompson, who thereby became apparently the first English woman to undertake a balloon flight in Britain. The Duke of Devonshire rose to the occasion by serving a picnic for fifty friends from a tent pitched on the roof of Burlington House and allowing the house itself to be used as a grandstand for visitors prepared to pay half a guinea for the view. This extraordinary spectacle brought the whole of Piccadilly to a standstill – according to one report Vigo Lane was clogged with more than three hundred noblemen's carriages – and was to be immortalised in a Gillray print showing Sadler's balloon 'revolving continually' in the north-east corner of the courtyard, 'the wind being high [and] occasioning some trouble to the undertakers'

(Fig. 78).[61] Considering the extreme concentrations of naked flame to which the whole site was repeatedly exposed, the early morning high jinks of thousands of inebriated party-goers, and the vast quantity of coal gas needed to inflate the Sadlers' balloon twice over, it was a small miracle that Burlington House – and the Elgin Marbles with it – did not go up in flames in the summer of 1814.

THREE DAYS BEFORE the Sadlers made their second ascent, Ware responded to a letter from Heaton 'desiring a Statement of the several Valuations which have been made of Burlington House; and my opinion of its value at this time.'[62] Heaton's request is the first clear indication that negotiations for Lord George's purchase of the house had resumed after a two-year hiatus following the failure to persuade him to take it on a 25-year lease. No evidence has come to light to suggest that the Duke had evolved any plans of his own for its future during this interval beyond continuing to use it as a convenient party venue. Nor, conversely, was it for want of progress on Lord George's part that the house remained in limbo. As early as 26 September 1811 he had sent his nephew an outline of the alterations he was planning to make to the house that presaged virtually everything that would be carried out four years later;[63] and by the end of October that year Ware had undertaken a careful survey of the house, prepared 'a detailed estimate of the necessary repairs', and made 'drawings shewing sundry Improvements proposed by the Right Honourable Lord George Cavendish'.[64]

So, what went wrong? One does not need to delve far into his poisonous relationship with his eldest surviving son Henry, or read many of his painfully pompous letters to his nephew the 6th Duke, to realise that Lord George Cavendish was not just a difficult man, he was impossible. When crossed by some thing or person that offended his exaggerated sense of family pride, resentful anger would tie him up in knots from which he found it almost impossible to break free. On discovering, at the end of August 1811, that his nephew had agreed, without consulting him first, to attend Henry's forthcoming wedding in October to Sarah Fawkener, Lord George exploded in fury. As the head of the Cavendishes, the Duke had not only seriously undermined Lord George's implacable objection to the marriage (based apparently on the grounds that 'from her behaviour her character is somewhat blown') but worse still, this had positively encouraged the misguided couple's defiance and in the process harmed his own and Lord George's reputation.[65] Although the row did eventually blow over enough for the sale of Burlington House to take place on 25 March 1815[66] (at Ware's July 1814 valuation of £70,000), the Duke's difficult relationship with his uncle is evident from the frankness of his agent James Abercromby's bitter complaints about how impossible Lord George was to deal with, and the Duke's own comment on hearing of his aunt's death in April 1835: 'Poor Aunt George, only one year of happiness'.[67]

Samuel Ware's neat handwriting and superb draughtsmanship are almost enough on their own to explain why he was ideally suited to handle such a prickly character. Although he may have achieved no great fame as an architect either in his lifetime or since, he was an excellent businessman with a clear understanding of what was needed to ensure the successful outcome of a complex architectural project. Ware's organisational skills are evident for instance in the agreement he drew up with the building contractor Wilson, Woolcot & Co. 'for performing that part of the business which belongs to the tradesman in the alterations and additions to Burlington House', a draft of which he sent for Heaton to vet on 12 April 1815.[68] Here he sets out with great care the responsibilities of the contractor 'for purchasing, sorting and distributing the materials, hiring and selecting men, and in arranging the works from the drawings, specifications and directions of the architect'; the authority invested in Thomas Dudly, the clerk of the works he had taken on the previous week, for examining and booking in deliveries, timekeeping, weekly accounting, and workforce discipline; and even the routine that the porter, Dudly's son, needed to adopt to maintain site security, including ringing 'a bell … at the several times of coming and going from the works.'[69] The agreement limited the contractor's profit to 2½% on bricks, plaster, laths, lime and sand; 5% on timber, deals, glass, stone, and exchanged lead; 7½% on

Fig. 79
Sir Thomas Lawrence, *The Three Children of Lord Cavendish* (George, Anne and Williiam), 1790.
Städel Museum, Frankfurt am Main

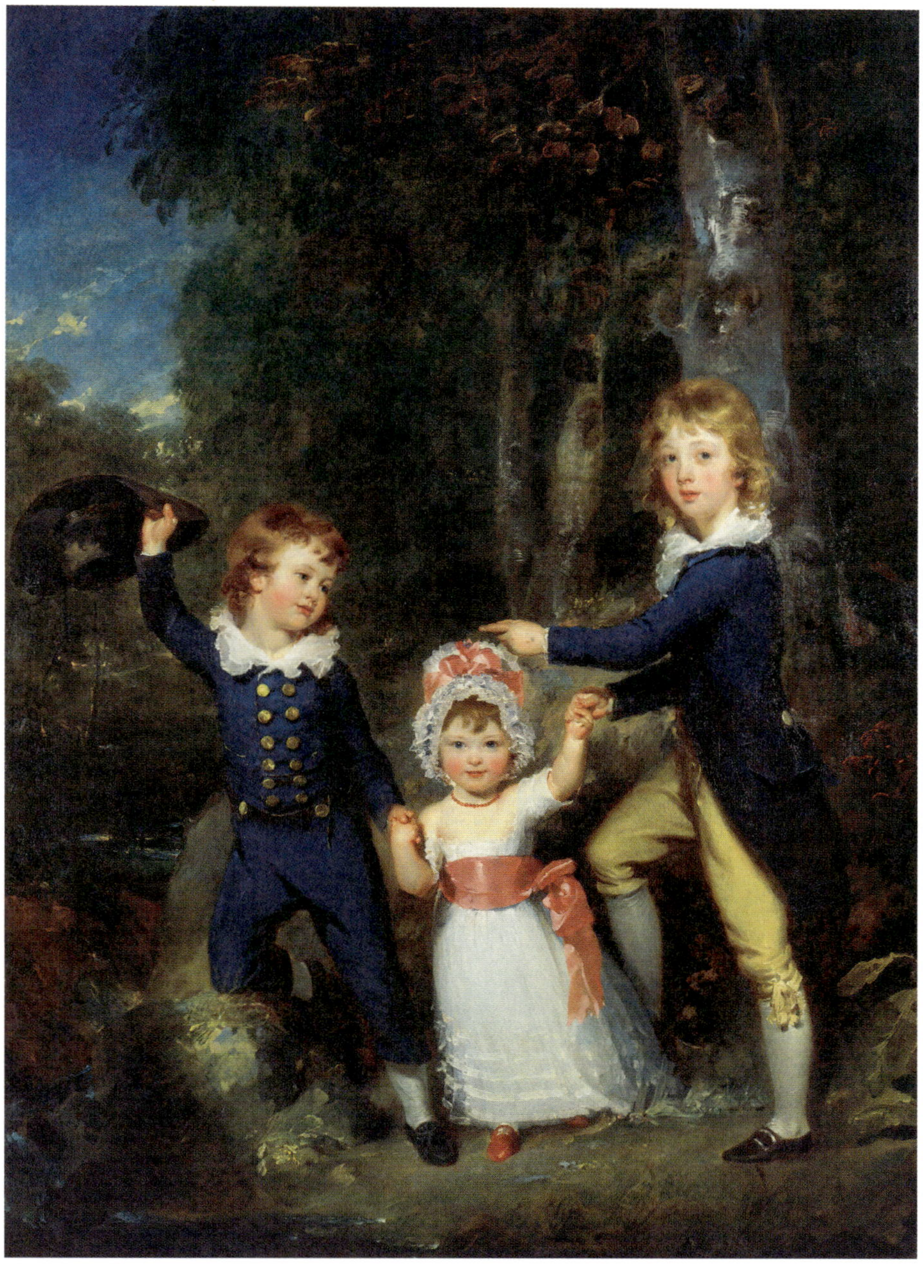

labour; and 10% 'on all works of nicer manufactory where superior seasoned materials are required & which may be necessary to have done at their shops'. 'I think', Ware wrote in his accompanying letter, 'the arrangement described in the agreement highly advantageous in a pecuniary point of view and that it affords great facility in the performance of the works.'

Another important advantage, from both the architect's and client's points of view, was the fact that they had had four years in which to refine what needed to be done. This was why enabling works could begin on 5 April 1815, less than a fortnight after the house was formally conveyed into Lord George's hands. It was also why reports of the new owner's intentions had appeared in the press a month earlier:

> Burlington House came to the hammer a few days ago, and was knocked down for £75,200. The purchaser is supposed to be a Nobleman, who means to make this princely mansion his own residence, without any alteration in its present magnificent order or structure.[70]

Slight as it is, there is a grain of truth in this garbled account of Lord George's long-digested plans, since it is the earliest indication that these had evolved into a project to preserve his grandfather's house in all 'its present magnificent order or structure'. Perhaps in the light of Soane's report, Ware may have already played some part in persuading his client to take this preservationist approach. However, it was more Lord George's pride in owning Burlington House, rather than Ware's compunction in altering it, that led them to undertake what became the first historical restoration of a neo-Palladian building in Britain.

Lord George's motives for wishing to own his grandfather's house, and to restore it in a way that he must have hoped would have pleased his ancestor, cannot be disassociated from the fact that it was where he and his wife, Lady Elizabeth (née Compton), had lived for the first three years of their marriage, during which time the two eldest of their eleven children, William and George, had been born in 1783 and 1784 respectively (Fig. 79). The tragic death of both sons in early adulthood –

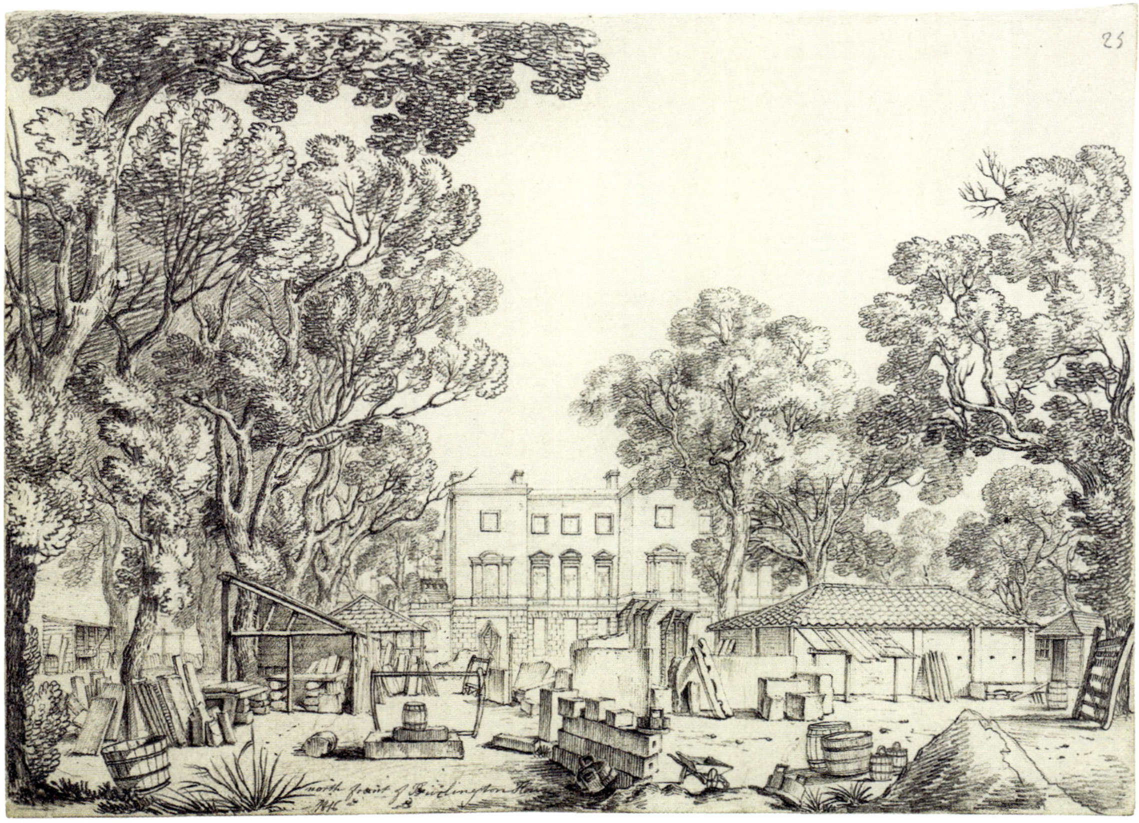

Fig. 80
J. C. Nattes (attrib.), North front of Burlington House under construction, 1816.
London Metropolitan Archives (City of London)

George, a major in the 7th Dragoons, had drowned in January 1809 when his transport ship sunk in a storm off the Cornish coast, and William had died three years later after being thrown from a carriage while driving in Holker Park – must have affected their father deeply and may well have been a factor in poisoning his relationship with his third son Henry, who was doomed never to make up for the loss of his elder siblings. It is not too far-fetched to see Lord George's return to Burlington House as in some sense a substitute for disappointed dynastic hopes, an attempt to revive the glories of his part of the family's past when the promise of future ones had apparently faded. At the celebration of his marriage to Lady Elizabeth in Trinity Chapel, Conduit Street, on 27 February 1782, and on their first setting up home together in high style at Burlington House a fortnight later, everyone had expected that he would be the 'begetter of future dukes', his flamboyant sister-in-law Georgiana having at that point had no children despite seven years of marriage.[71] Fate having apparently denied him this prospect, Burlington House would become as it were his true legacy, a restored monument to his famous forebear more lasting than flesh and blood.

Although the circumstances of Lord George's departure from Burlington House, probably towards the end of 1785 or the beginning of 1786, are unclear, it is likely that maintaining the grandeur of such an establishment proved beyond his means, partly because his wife's £10,000 a year was not included in their marriage settlement, and partly also because of some truth in George Selwyn's gossip that 'her head runs upon nothing but dress, and expense.'[72] Evidence that the couple might have overstretched themselves can be found in a small, pink silk-covered pocket notebook in which Lady Elizabeth totted up their household expenses for the first six months of 1782.[673] Quite apart from the astonishing £3,529 5s. 6d. that she had paid from her private account for her wedding clothes, she calculated that furnishing Burlington House with new linen had cost £650 8s. 3d.; that equipping themselves with a 'landau compleat' including 'seats & town harness', a 'fine sedan chair', and supplying their coachmen, footmen, chairmen and grooms with suitable liveries, had come to a further £807 10s. 0¼d.; and that 'tradesmen extra bills besides total for this first ½ year' had amounted to £3,206 19s. It must have been a disappointment when the family had to move out to No. 1 Savile Row three years later, and for another thirty years to be reminded of their former splendour every time they saw the garden of Burlington House from a first-floor window. It was only after inheriting the bulk of his uncle Lord Frederick Cavendish's estate in 1803 and a third of his distant cousin Henry Cavendish's vast fortune in 1810 that Lord George became sufficiently wealthy to buy and restore Burlington House.[74] The day that he and Lady Elizabeth moved back in would have seemed like the fulfilment of a long-postponed destiny.

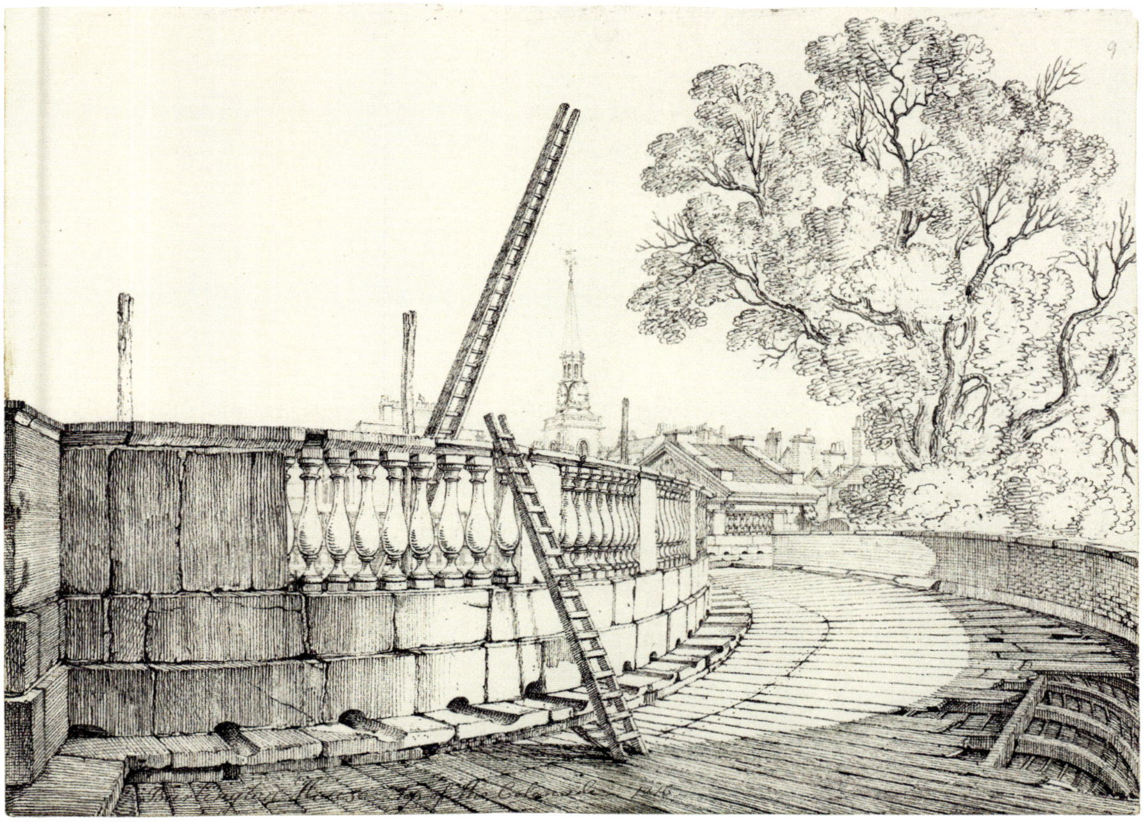

Fig. 81
J. C. Nattes (attrib.), Top of the Burlington House colonnade under repair, 1816.
London Metropolitan Archives (City of London)

Fig. 82
J. C. Nattes (attrib.), East end of the Burlington House colonnade, with the entrance from the courtyard to the stable and coach house, 1816.
London Metropolitan Archives (City of London)

In sharp contrast to all previous work carried out on the fabric of Burlington House, the extent and nature of Ware's building operations for Lord George are abundantly clear. Not only do we have the benefit of a series of 26 superbly detailed construction-site drawings made in around August 1816 (probably by the topographical artist John Claude Nattes; see Figs 80–82),[75] but also an authoritative 'general statement of the works performed … to Burlington House, buildings & walls, exclusive of the last coats of paint, papering & gilding', that Ware himself sent his client on 2 May 1818.[76] After reminding Lord George of the terms that had been agreed with Wilson, Woolcot & Co. on 6 May 1815, Ware gives a characteristically clear and concise account of what had been done:

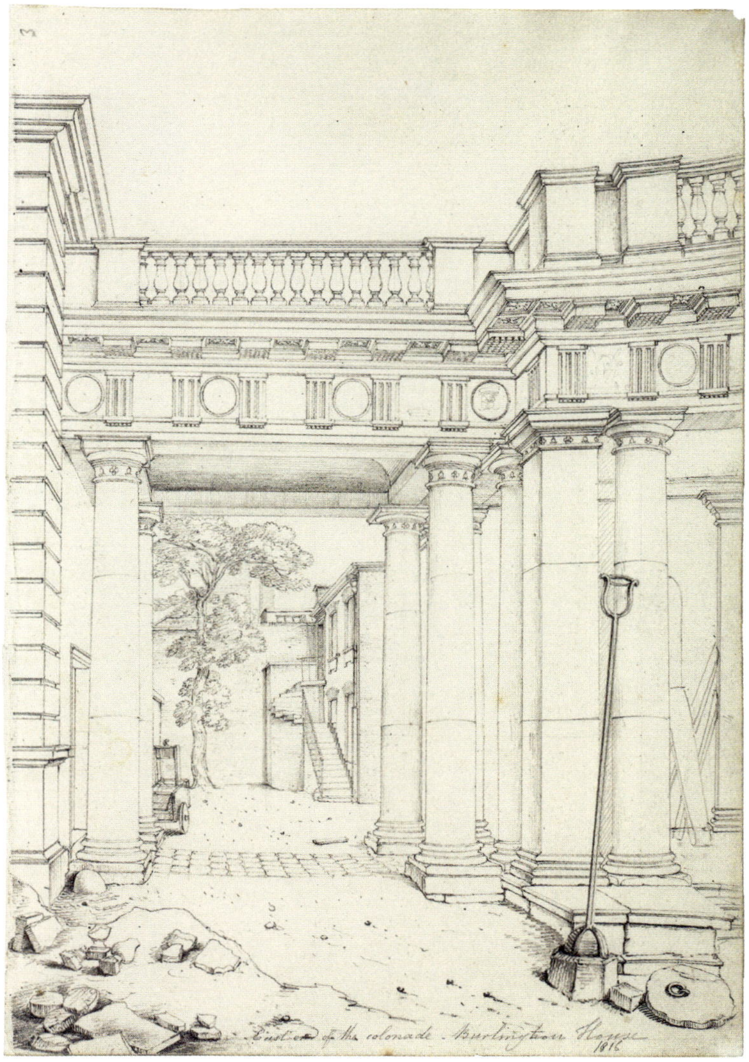

> The south façade, the façades of the wings & colonnade forming the entrance court, the gateway & wall erected by the late Lord Burlington have been repaired throughout, & by your lordship's direction, scrupulous attention has been paid to preserve them entire.
>
> The whole of the house (except the salone and room adjoining it westward) north of the façade which had been built at an earlier period and originally of very bad materials and which was found to be decayed and dangerous, has been taken down and rebuilt and the same stile of architecture, as that of the entrance court, has been attempted to be maintained throughout.

The back front of the west wing has been taken down and the whole of the interior made new.

The east wing which consisted of one long room and stables (except the main walls) has been taken down rebuilt and converted into a dwelling house and offices attached to it have been erected.

The stables and coach-houses have been repaired and a new stable has been erected.

The roofs of all the buildings with the exception of part of the west wing & part of the stable building have been covered in lead.

There has been also in the east wing and in the offices a considerable expense in fixtures.

Ware's emphasis on the fact that the house was in such poor condition that it had had to be almost completely rebuilt sounds like an architect's standard justification for exceeding his estimates. Although parts of the fabric of the seventeenth-century house may well have been in a bad state structurally, this was certainly not the only reason why Lord George had proposed in the autumn of 1811:

> To throw an Attick over the North front.
> To take down [probably] the Bow window at the East end of the House & open the window to the South Front, making a room of equal size on the ground floor to that above.
> To make a large room at the West end of the House up one pair of Stairs for dining Room.
> To alter the offices below stairs, to open an area to the North from which they will receive light & make the Cellars under the South part.
> To alter the situation of the Staircases, Water closets &c. The great stairs to be placed in the lobby of the North Front.[77]

'To throw an Attick over the North front' was the project's starting point, not merely because the seventeenth-century brick façade may have been in a visibly poor state, but because bringing it into architectural harmony with the stone-clad south front was the most obvious improvement to the house that the 3rd Earl would have made in Lord George's place (Fig. 83). It is not surprising therefore that both of Ware's initial designs for a new north front – which were probably those he recalled making in October 1811 – take their cue from Inigo Jones: the first by directly evoking Campbell's south front of the house as executed; and the second by quoting a distinctive window-surround from the garden front of Wilton House (Figs 84, 85). By pure coincidence it seems, Campbell had employed this same motif in the wings of his own unexecuted design for the north front almost a century earlier (Fig. 86).

The reason for Lord George's hesitation over whether or not to remove Portland's bow window in the ball room and library – the word 'probably' is interpolated – may have been connected to Ware's suggested solutions to the problem of obtaining a better alternative source of daylight in these rooms. These all entailed quite major changes to the fenestration on the south front, *viz.* enlarging the ground-floor windows, replacing Campbell's first-floor *serlianas* in the wings with larger pedimented tripartite windows, and opening up four new windows in the return walls. Lord George must have decided, however, that it would be better to put up with gloomier rooms than interfere in any way with the south façade. Accordingly, Ware was in the end to leave this front unaltered apart from, tellingly, correcting the misalignment of the *serlianas* with the other first-floor windows, a deviation from Campbell's published design

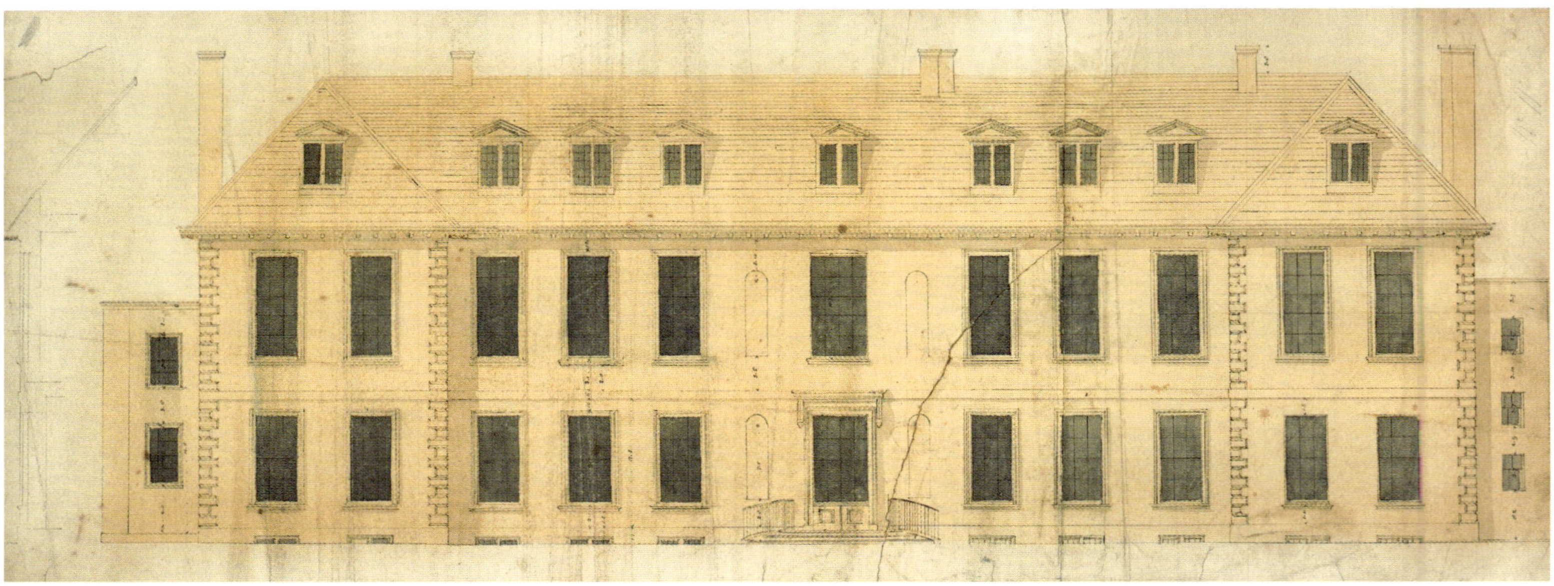

Fig. 83
Samuel Ware, Burlington House: existing north front elevation, 1811.
Royal Academy of Arts, London, 06/4383

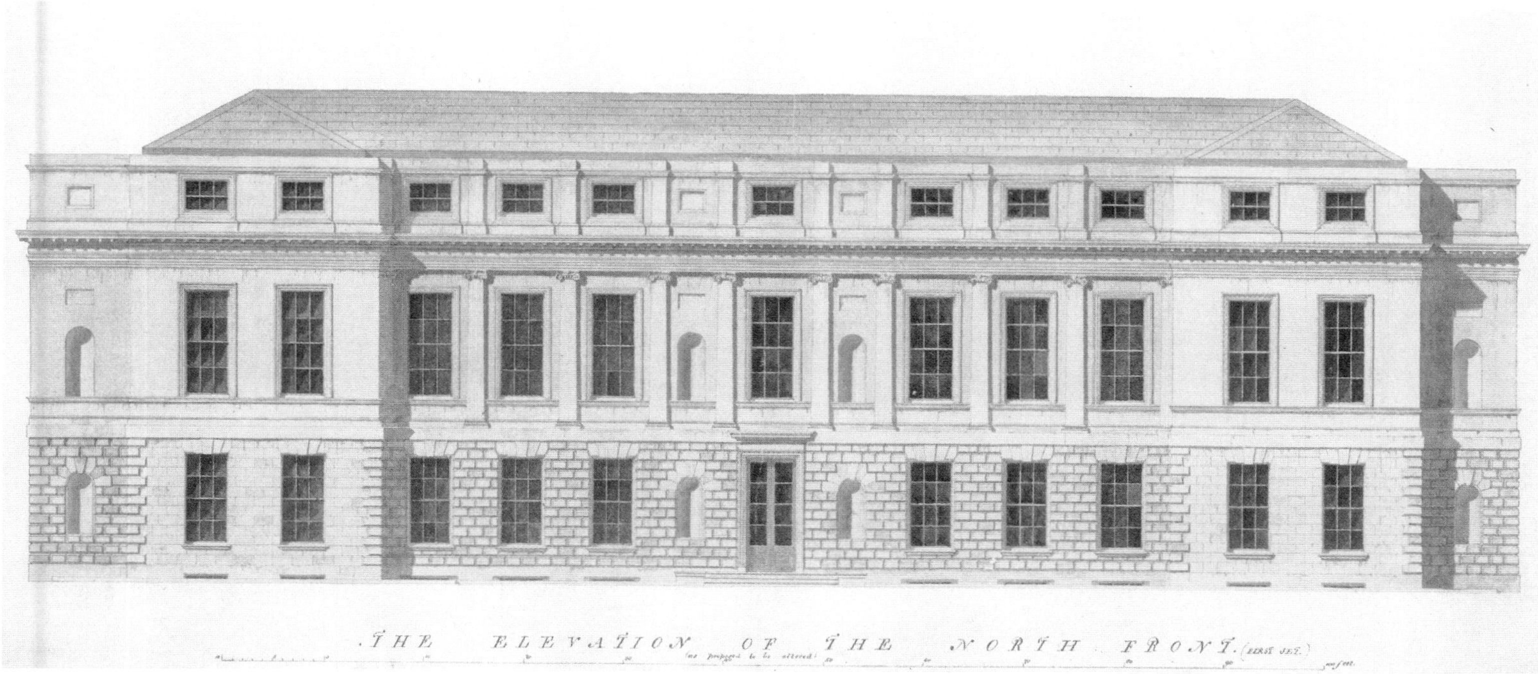

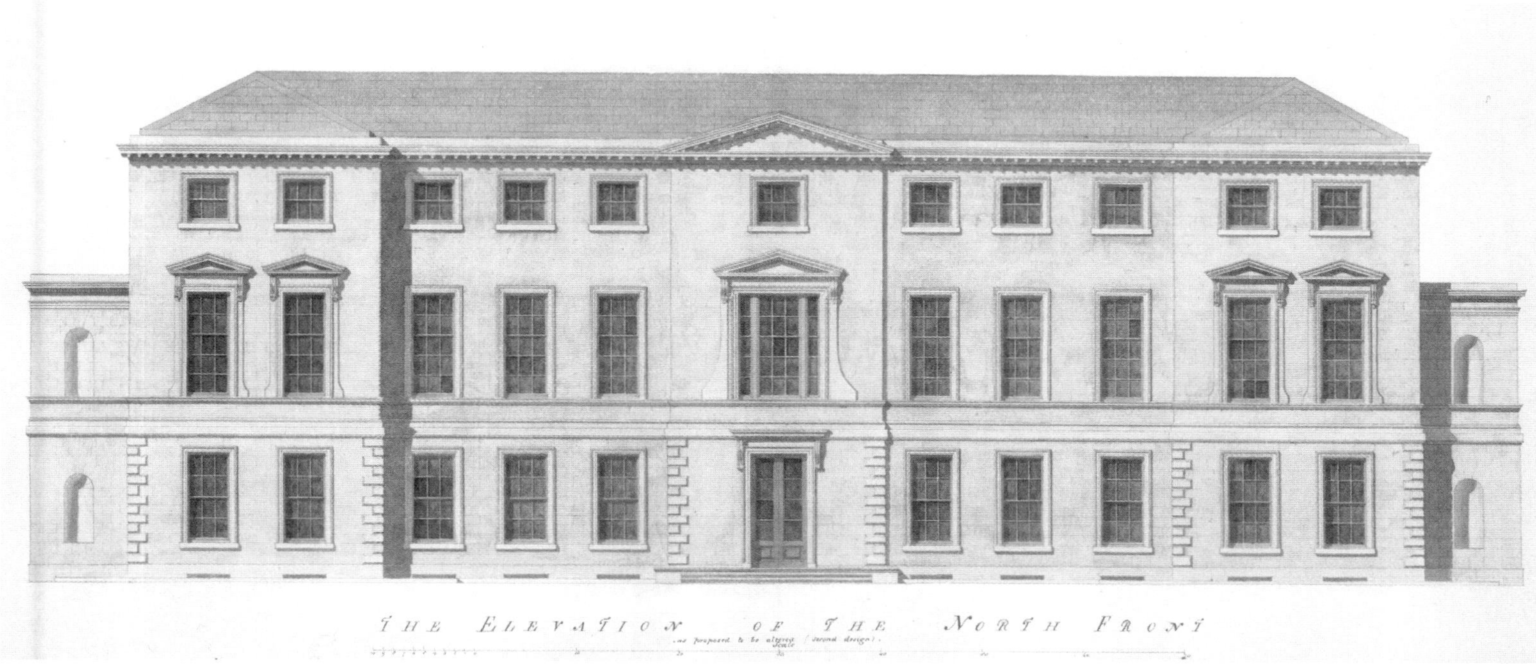

Fig. 84
Samuel Ware, Preliminary design for remodelling the north front of Burlington House: elevation, *c.* 1811.
Royal Academy of Arts, London, 06/5832

Fig. 85
Samuel Ware, Alternative preliminary design for remodelling the north front of Burlington House: elevation, *c.* 1811.
Royal Academy of Arts, London, 06/5833

Fig. 86
Colen Campbell, Unexecuted design for remodelling and refacing the north front of Burlington House: elevation, 1717.
RIBA Collections, SC10/1(2)

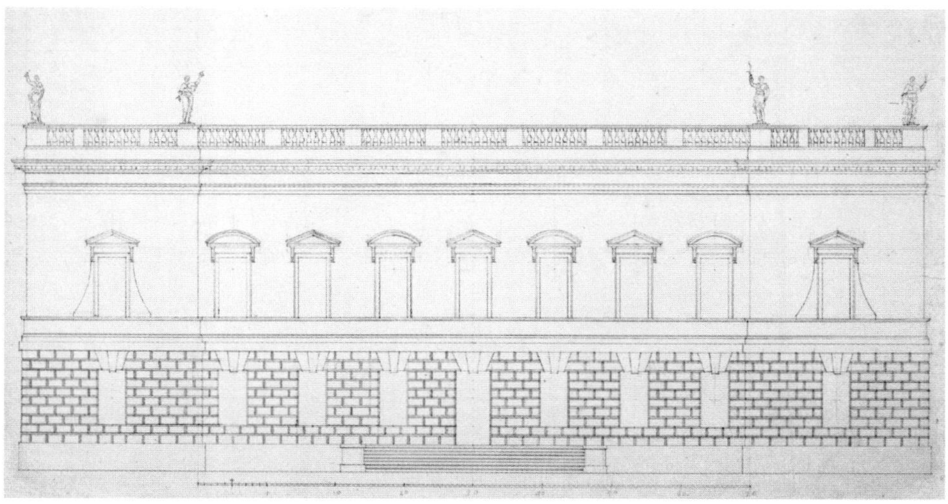

that apparently even the 3rd Earl had been powerless to prevent (Figs 87, 88). Since Ware's drawing is the only known representation of the house to show this fault it is perhaps not surprising that only one particularly sharp-eyed commentator – the indefatigable topographer John Britton – noticed its correction:

> In 1815, Burlington House was purchased of the Duke of Devonshire by his uncle Lord George Cavendish, who repaired all those parts of the building erected by Lord Burlington; and by raising the Venetian windows of the south front to the height of the others, completed his design for this façade.[78]

Ware was only able to do this by sacrificing the arch in the middle light of the *serlianas* when seen from inside the house. It is clear from his survey drawing showing the original relationship of inside to outside in these windows that their failure to align correctly on the façade was due to the insufficient ceiling height on the interior (Fig. 88). Ware's drawing is unique evidence of the profile of the Ionic columns that, as his 1811 survey plan shows

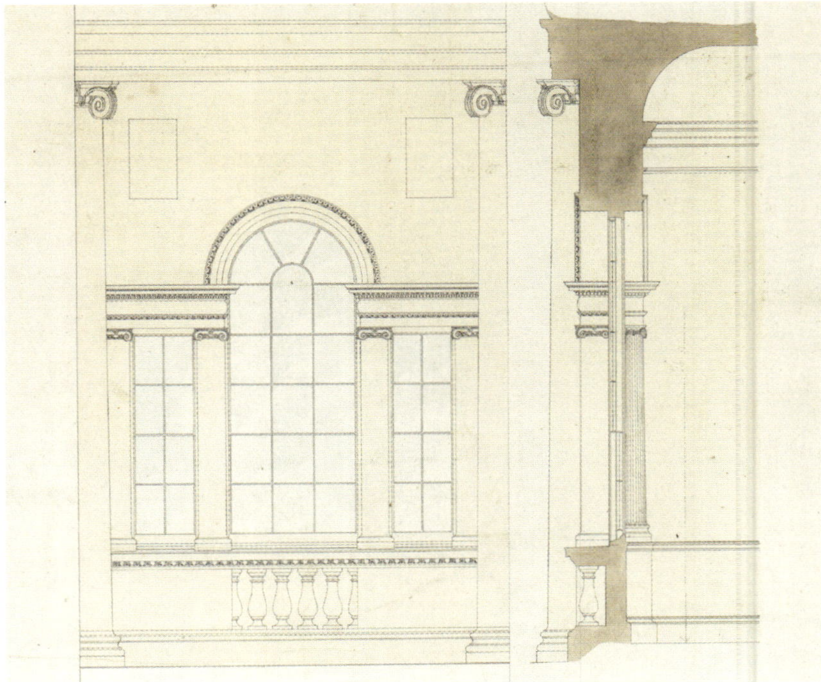

Fig. 87 (below)
Samuel Ware, Unexecuted design for remodelling the south front of Burlington House: elevation, *c.* 1815.
Royal Academy of Arts, London, 06/5830

Fig. 88 (above)
Samuel Ware, Palladian window on the south front of Burlington House: exterior elevation and section, *c.* 1815.
Royal Academy of Arts, London, 06/5064

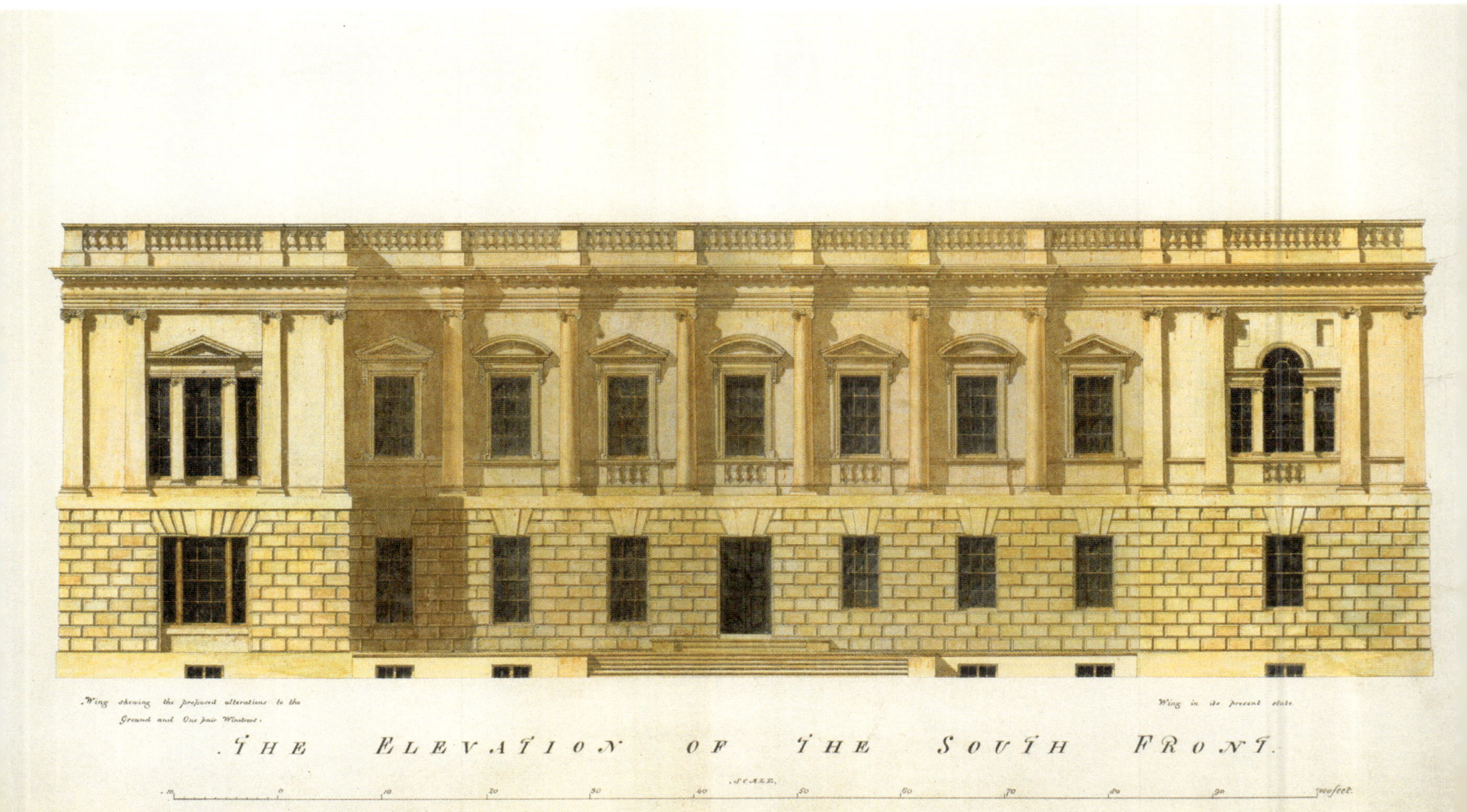

Fig. 89
Samuel Ware, Preliminary design for alterations and additions to Burlington House, first scheme: first-floor plan without overlay, *c.* 1812.
Royal Academy of Arts, London, 06/4340

Fig. 90
Samuel Ware, Preliminary design for alterations to Burlington House, second scheme: first-floor plan with overlay, *c.* 1812.
Royal Academy of Arts, London, 06/4340

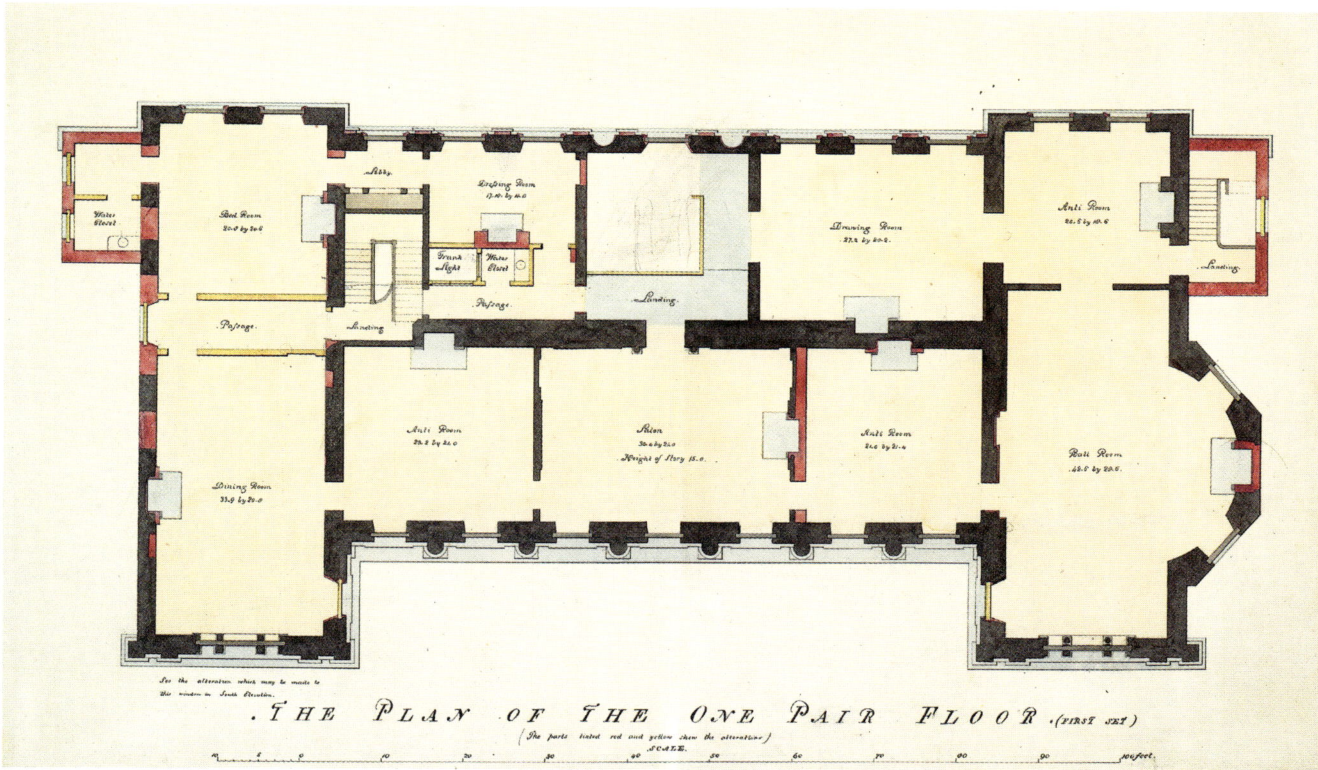

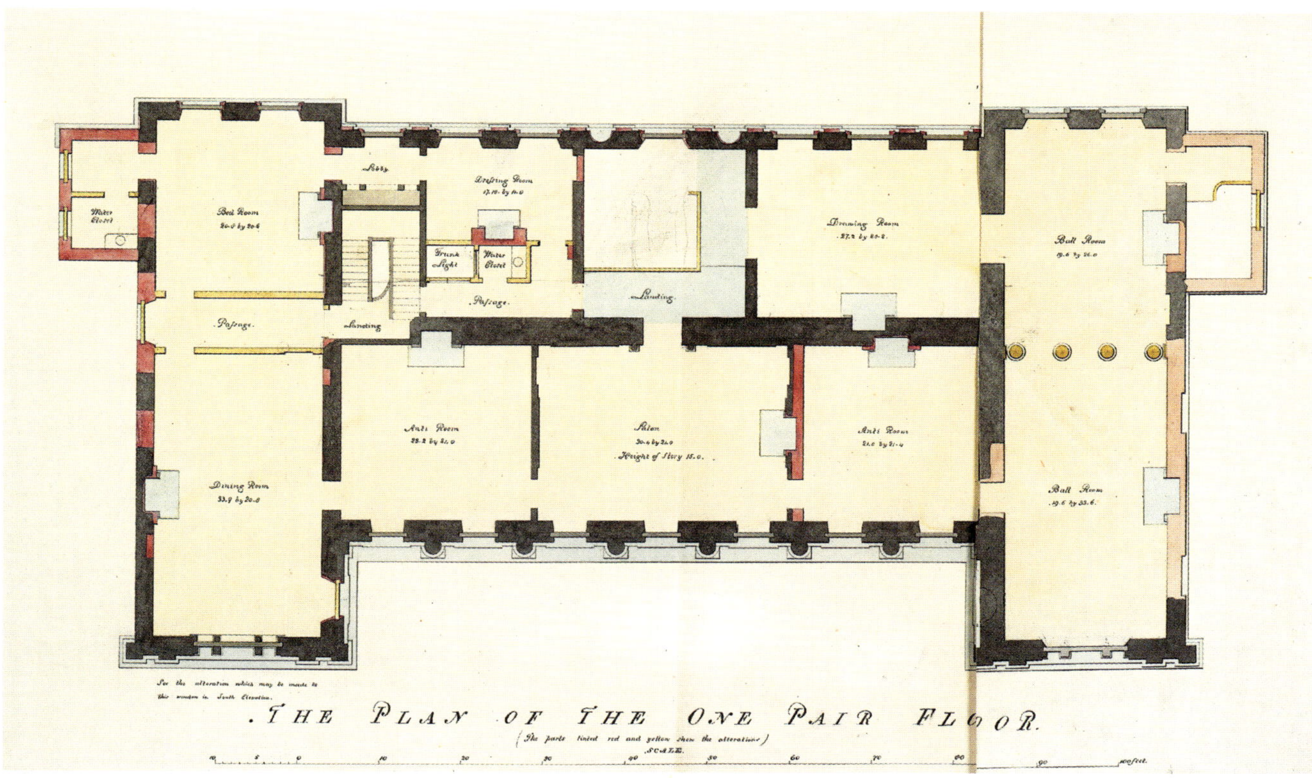

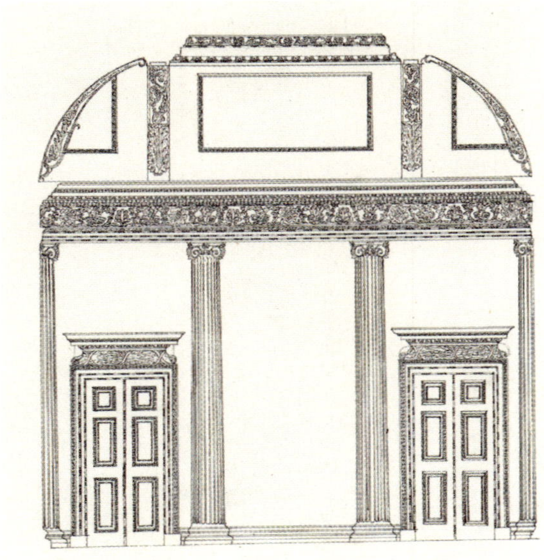

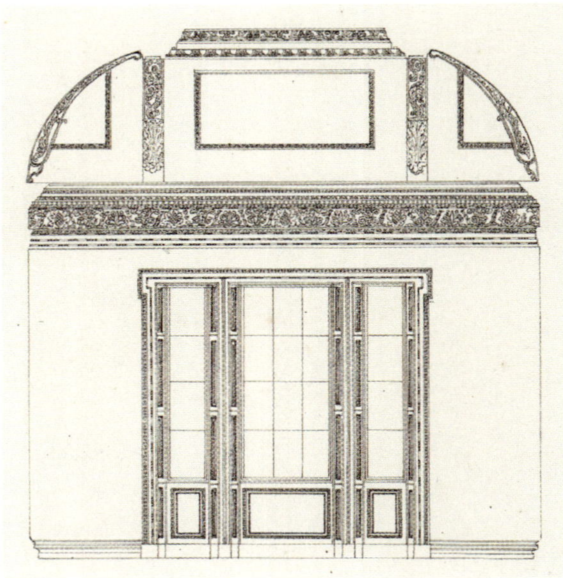

Fig. 91
Samuel Ware, Burlington House: elevation of the north or south wall of the ball room as executed, *c.* 1820.
Royal Academy of Arts, London, 06/5766

Fig. 92
Samuel Ware, Burlington House, State Dining Room: elevation of the south wall as executed, *c.* 1820.
Royal Academy of Arts, London, 06/5767

Fig. 93
Samuel Ware, Staircase at Burlington House: elevation looking north, 1811.
Royal Academy of Arts, London, 06/4703

(see Fig. 55), framed the middle light of the *serliana* in Portland's assembly/ball room. Although he may have considered them to be part of Portland's remodelling, he must also have had doubts about sweeping them away since they were included not only in his proposal for a new ball room retaining Portland's bow window but also (originally at least) in his alternative design showing the latter removed (Figs 89, 90).[79] In fact, the perfect correspondence of the interior order with that of the exterior suggests that this was indeed the original internal form of Campbell's *serliana*. Ware's solution to the problem of how to raise the *serlianas* was not one of which the 3rd Earl would have approved, but it was to prove useful as a way of enabling the interiors of these windows to match their equivalents on the north front without involving any necessity for their exteriors to correspond exactly (Figs 91, 92).

Of all Ware's alterations to the interior, much the most radical was his removal of the main stairs to the centre of the house (Fig. 94). Not only did this impact on the whole building rather than on just one part, it introduced for the first time a staircase that could serve rooms from the central spine of the house rather than via its periphery. It was also in historical terms the most problematic of his interventions, in that it entailed dispersing the Ricci cycle, justly celebrated as one of the great glories of the interior and just as obviously a relic of the 3rd Earl's era as the Saloon. Memories of having to live with Portland's nonsensical 'ceremonial' route to his assembly/ball room may well have played some part in Lord George's determination to improve the 'situation' of the staircases in general and of the main stairs in particular. It is likely, too, that Ware was in favour of moving the main staircase to the centre of the garden front, not only on the grounds of obvious

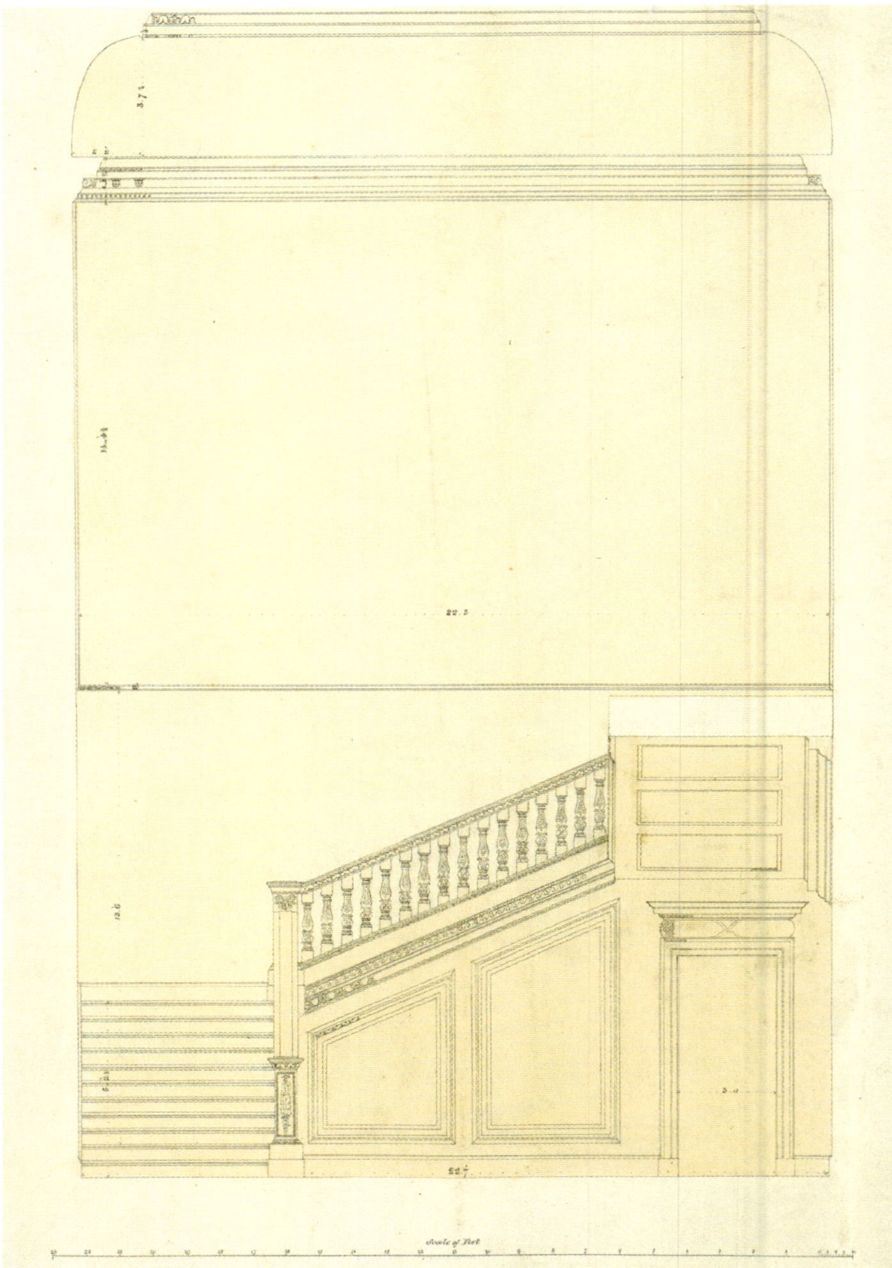

Fig. 94
Samuel Ware, Burlington House and Burlington Arcade: detail of ground plan as executed, c. 1820.
Royal Academy of Arts, London, 06/4949

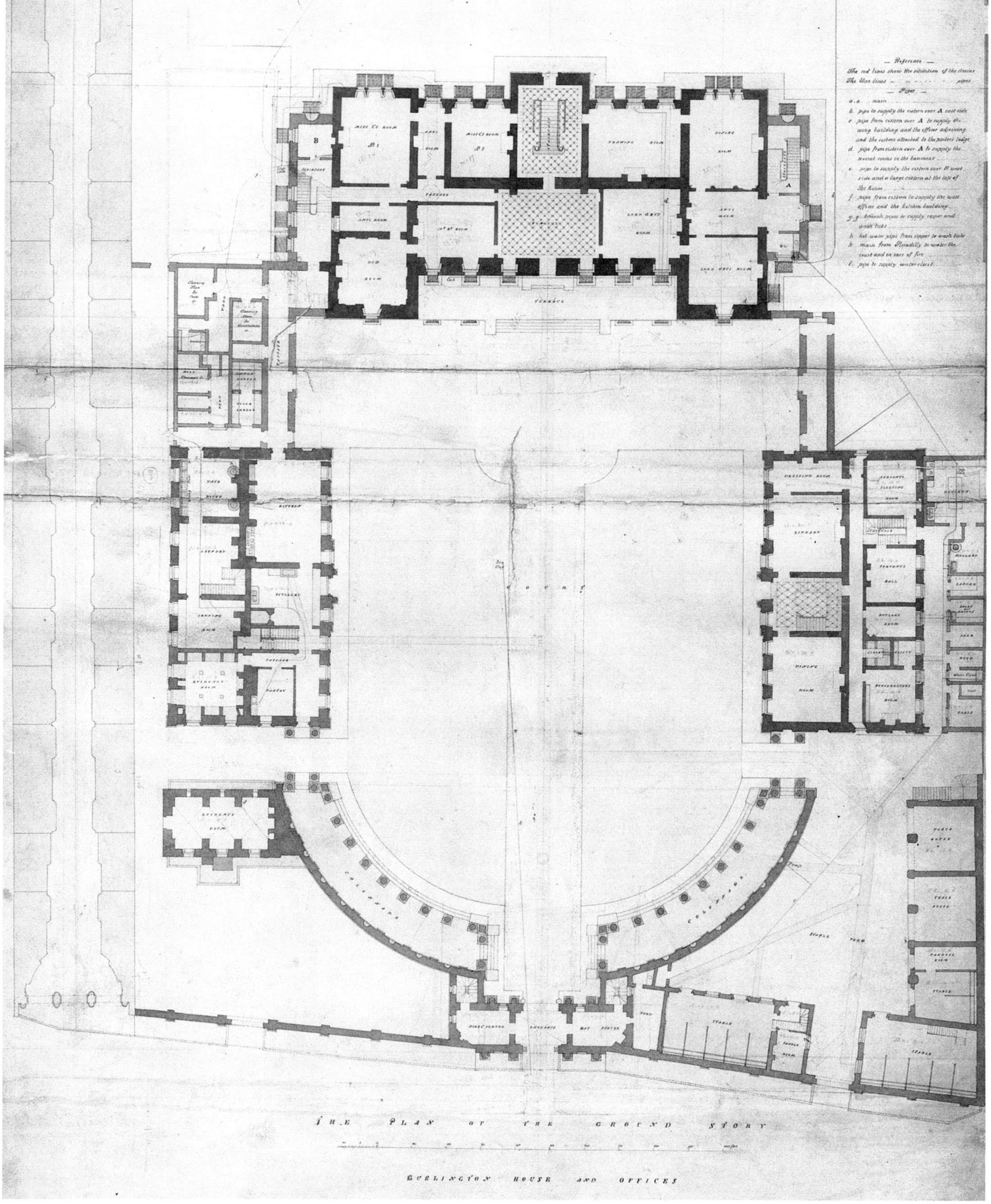

Fig. 95
Samuel Ware, Alternative designs for alterations and additions to Burlington House: ground-floor plan, *c.* 1812.
Royal Academy of Arts, London, 06/4338

Fig. 96
Samuel Ware, Alternative preliminary designs for alterations and additions to Burlington House: ground-floor plan, *c.* 1812.
Royal Academy of Arts, London, 06/4338

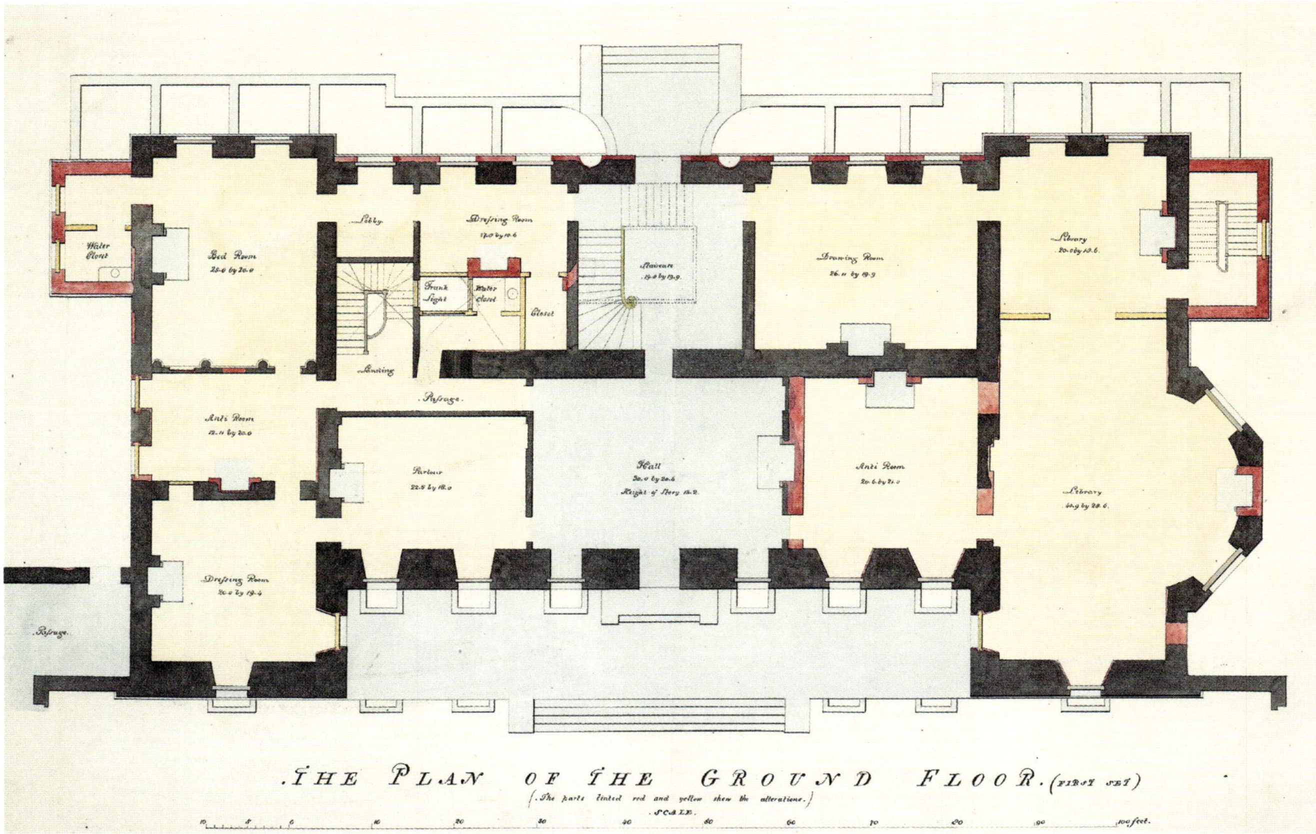

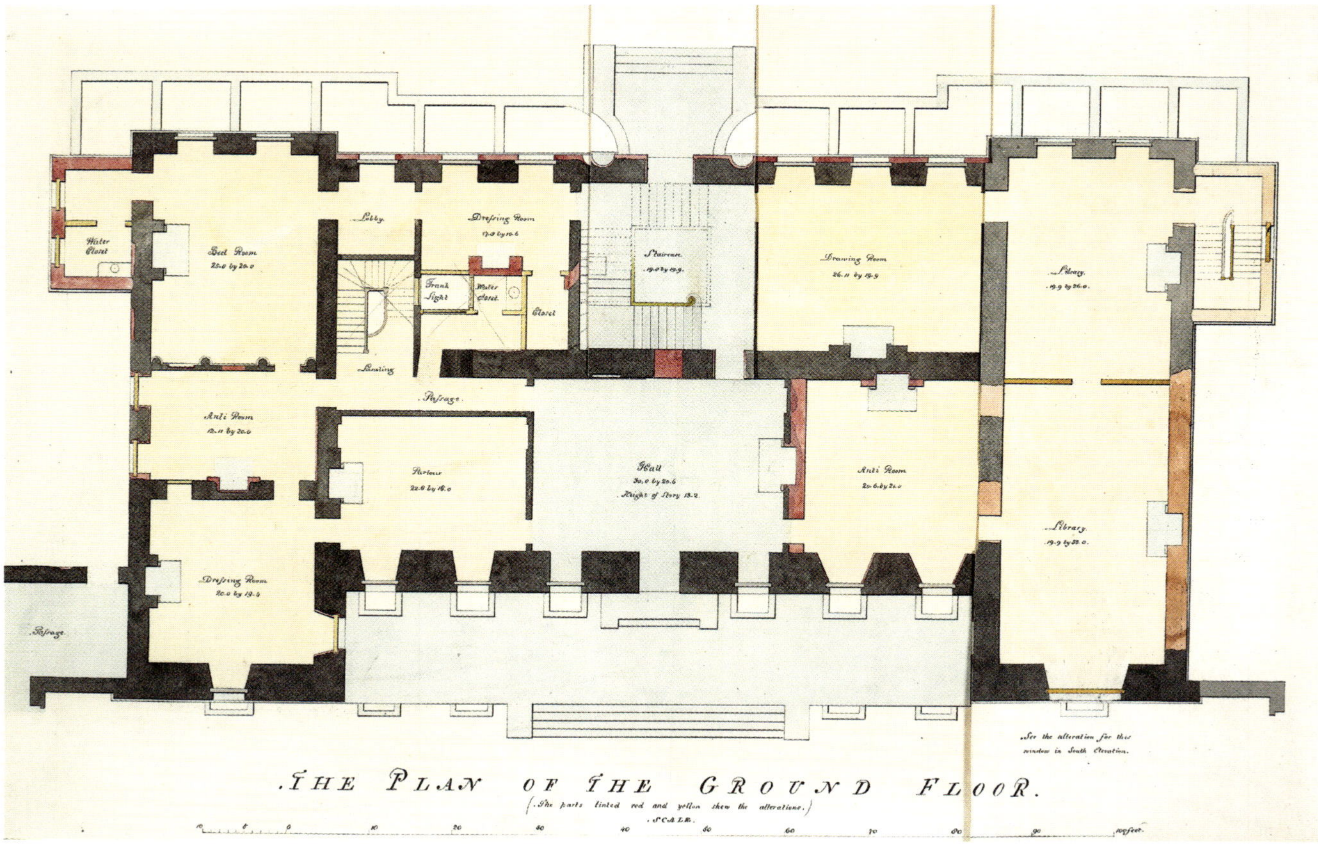

Fig. 97
Samuel Ware, Design, as executed, for iron panel decoration of the Great Staircase in Burlington House, 1817.
Royal Academy of Arts, London, 06/5011

neo-Palladian precedent, but also because early floor plans (see Figs 12–15), which he may well have found in the house, showed that its anomalous position predated the 3rd Earl's time and was therefore something that the latter might well have wanted to rectify.

No doubt conscious of the conflicting priorities of improvement and preservation in this situation, Ware initially proposed adapting the existing main staircase to its new location (Figs 93, 95). However, this proved unworkable because the central position of the doorway from the entrance hall prevented the curtail step from being placed sufficiently distant from the west wall to allow for the first flight to form a reasonable incline. Some thought was given to moving the entrance-hall door east to solve this problem, but disturbing the symmetry of the hall defeated the point of centralising the staircase in the first place (Fig. 96). Abandoning the idea of reinstalling the old stairs, Ware proposed instead an open-well top-lit staircase more suited to the available space, with the advantage that it could be made to rise through the whole height of the building (Fig. 98). Lord George's objection to this alternative design idea was probably a combination of dislike of the way its skylight broke the roofline of the new garden front, and concern that its ceremonial importance might be somewhat compromised if it was seen to continue to the servants' quarters in the attic. Faced with this impasse, someone came up with the idea of an imperial staircase, a symmetrical form of ceremonial stairs with divided flights ideally suited to such a central location in the building. This was a perfect solution: not only was it sure to meet Lord George's wish to combine ceremony with practicality, it also drew upon Ware's specialist knowledge of structurally efficient vaults and arches, a subject about which he had published a pioneering treatise in 1809 and which remained a lifelong interest.[80] It is not surprising therefore that more drawings have survived relating to Ware's great staircase than for any other part of the house, reflecting the considerable trouble he took over its design. These reveal, for instance, that an earlier idea for 'S' balusters was rejected in favour of a grander balustrade formed from large cast-iron decorative panels (Figs 97, 99).

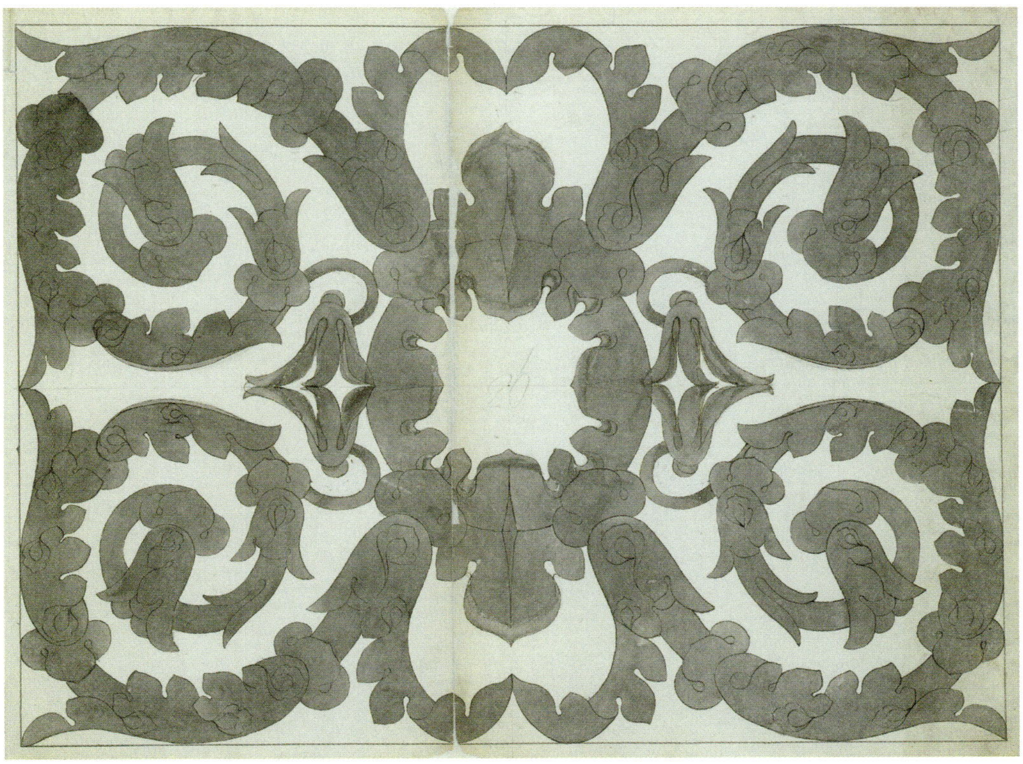

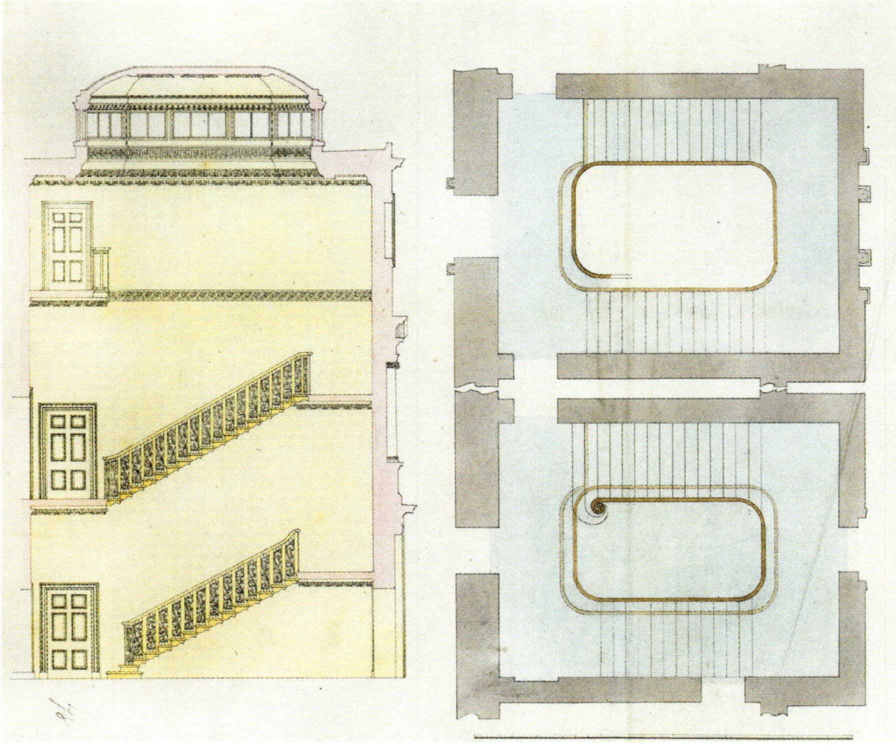

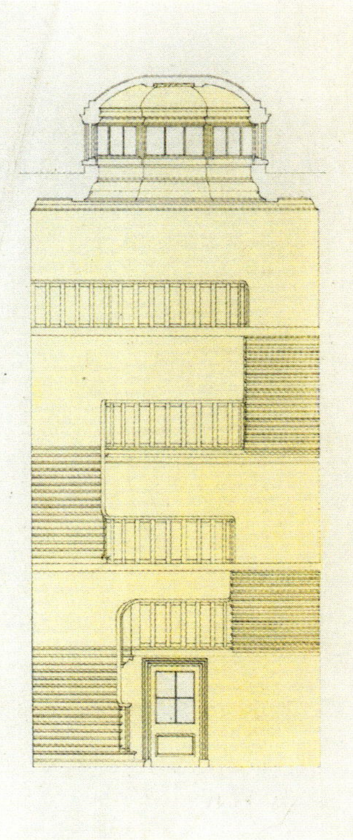

Fig. 98 (left)
Samuel Ware, Unexecuted design for the Great Staircase with cupola in Burlington House: ground- and first-floor plans and sections looking west and north through the full height of the building, *c.* 1816,
Royal Academy of Arts, London, 06/4707

Fig. 99 (below)
Samuel Ware, Great Staircase, design for cast-iron support and S-scroll balusters, *c.* 1816
Royal Academy of Arts, London, 06/4829

Fig. 100 (right)
Samuel Ware, Great Staircase, as executed: section looking west, 27 March 1817.
Royal Academy of Arts, London, 06/4835

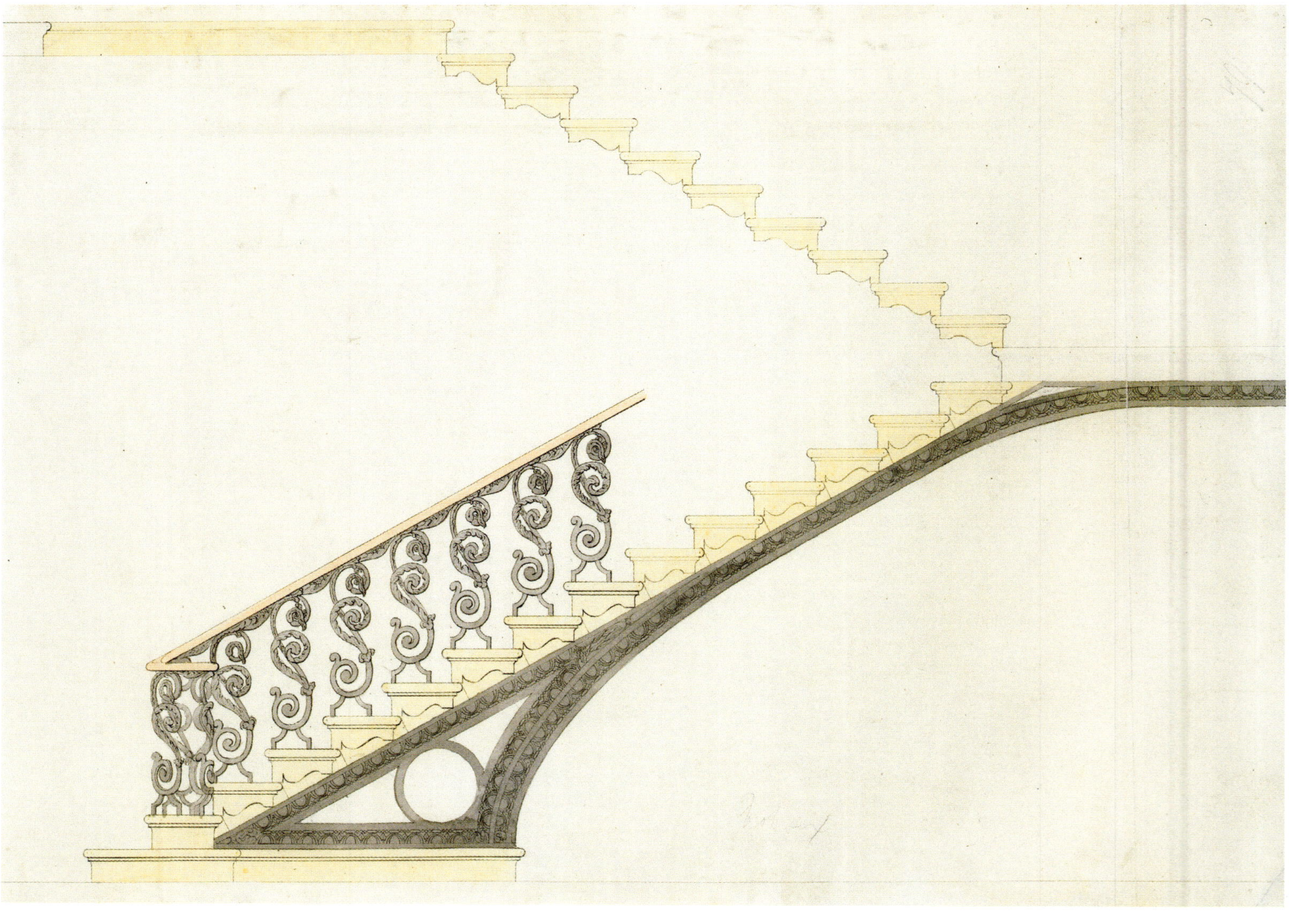

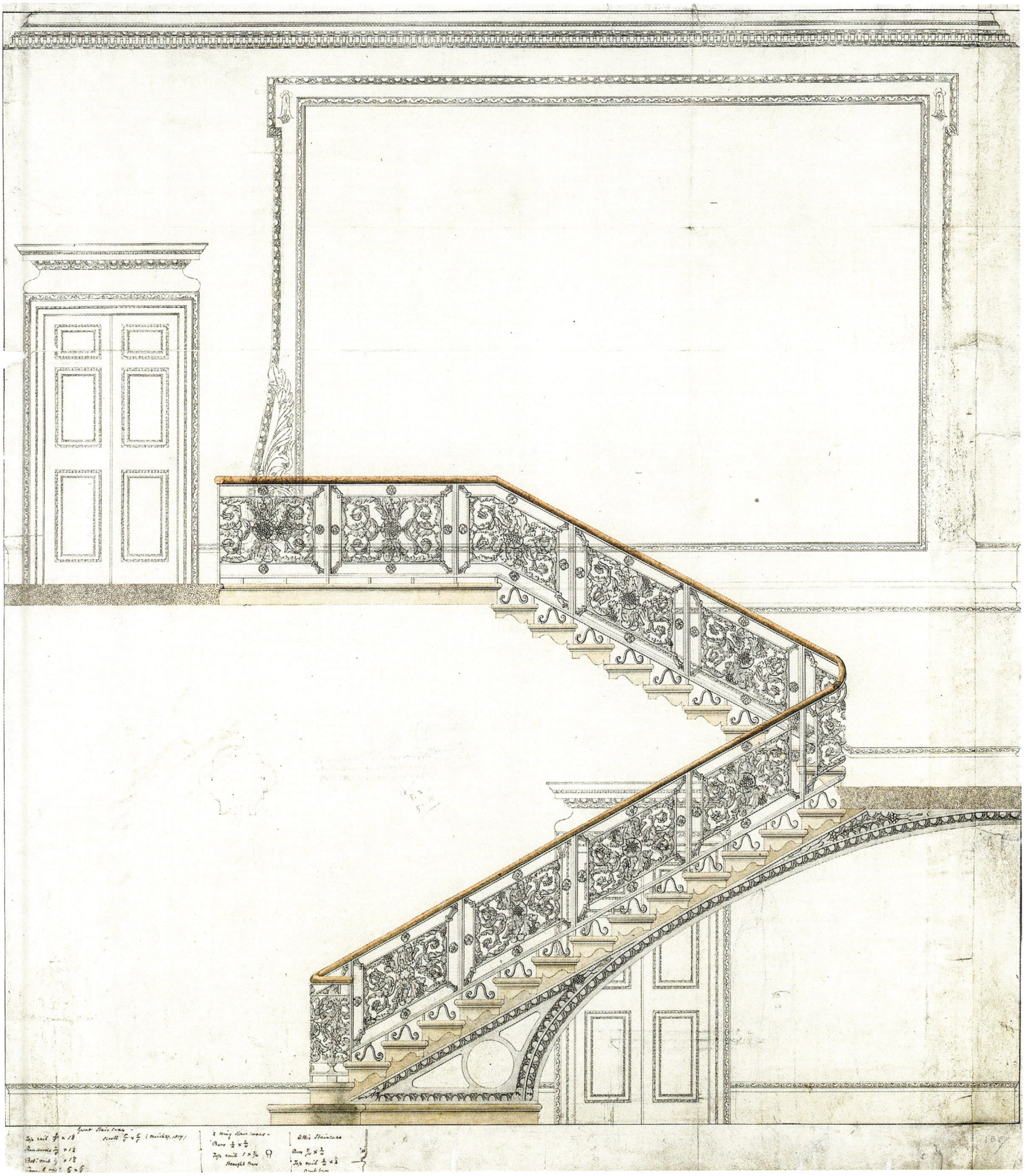

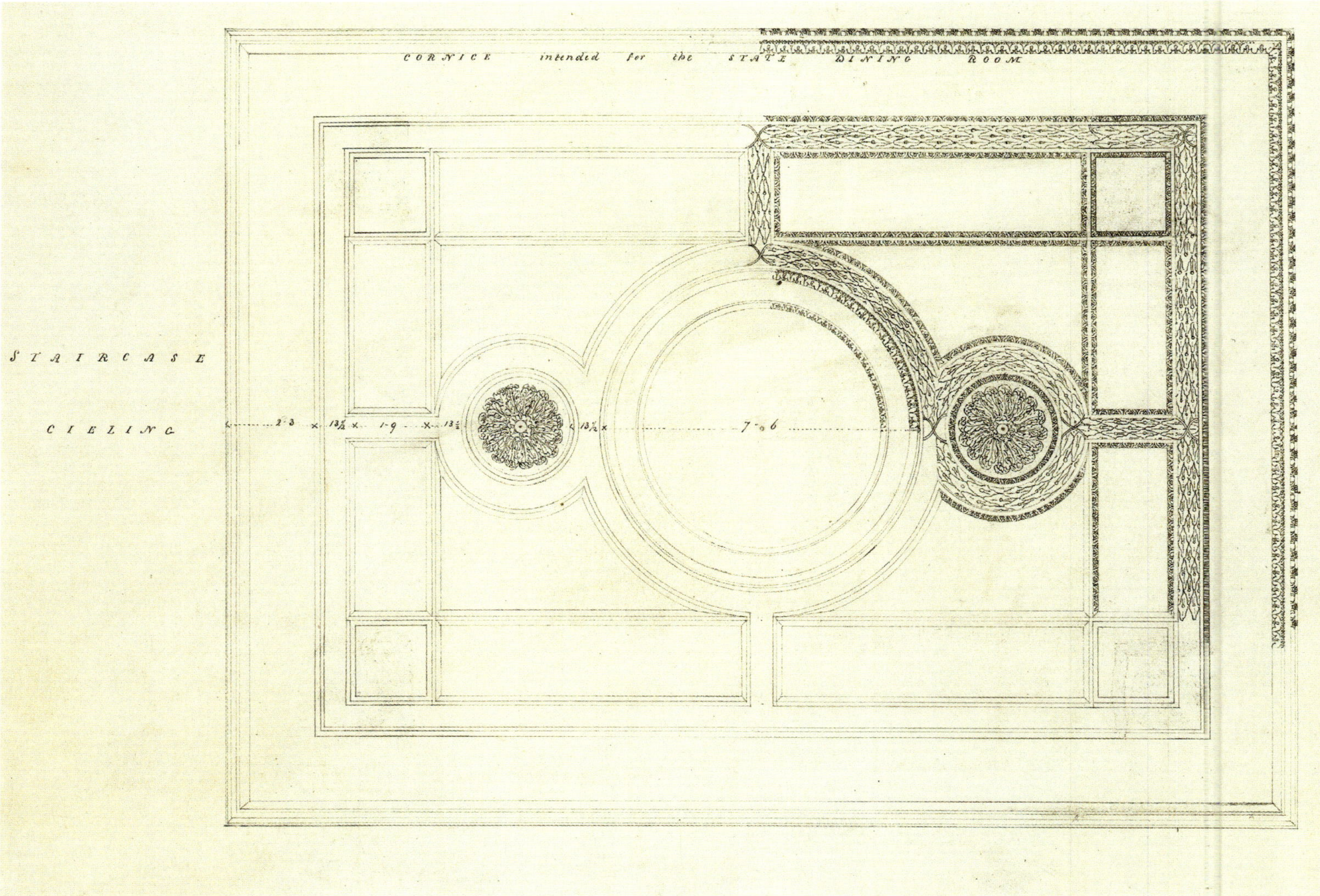

The final, executed design must have particularly pleased both client and architect since Ware made a point of dating a magnificent presentation drawing of its west elevation 'March 27, 1817' (Fig. 100). The outcome was a new ceremonial heart to the house: a monumental, technically advanced, modern staircase, the long, gently sloping, sixteen-tread central flight of which was supported on a pair of giant parabolic cast-iron arches weighing well over a ton each (Figs 101–103). The expense was prodigious: William Mears & Son's bill for the ironwork alone came to £576 6s. 8d. (equivalent to over £24,000 in 2005), almost the same as it cost to gild the new ball room (today's Reynolds Room).[81]

Ware's great staircase, which he probably began to design towards the middle of 1816, impacted directly on the design of the new north front since, to allow sufficient depth for the stairs to rise on a properly gradual incline, this now had to break forward more in the centre than in the wings. By now, Ware's earlier design for an Ionic palace front had been superseded by a more frankly 'modern' (i.e. Regency) interpretation of neo-Palladianism, largely composed of elements that he also

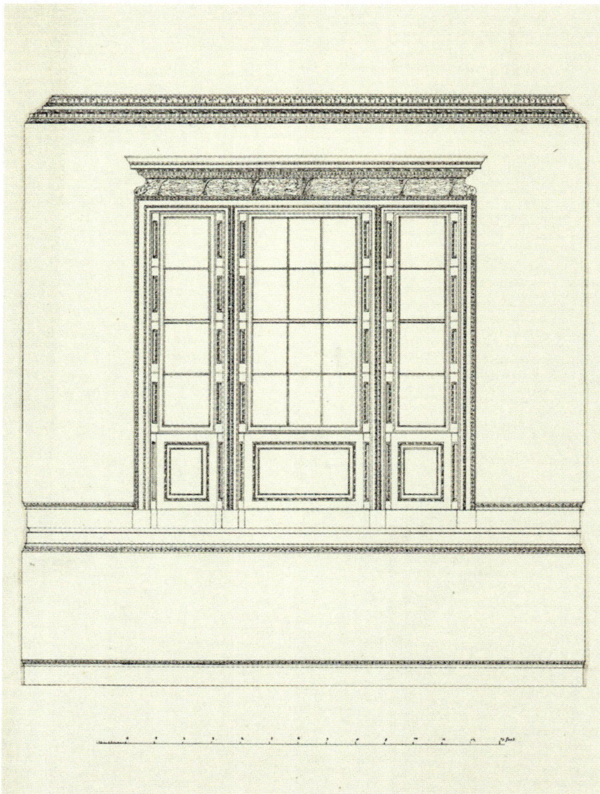

Fig. 101 (above)
Samuel Ware, Design, almost as executed, for the ceiling of the Great Staircase, *c.* 1816.
Royal Academy of Arts, London, 06/4534 (recto)

Fig. 102 (left)
Samuel Ware, Window on the Great Staircase: north-wall elevation, *c.* 1816.
Royal Academy of Arts, London, 06/4590

Fig. 103 (right)
John Wykeham Archer, *Staircase from the Hall, Burlington House*, 1855.
British Museum, London 1874,0314.324

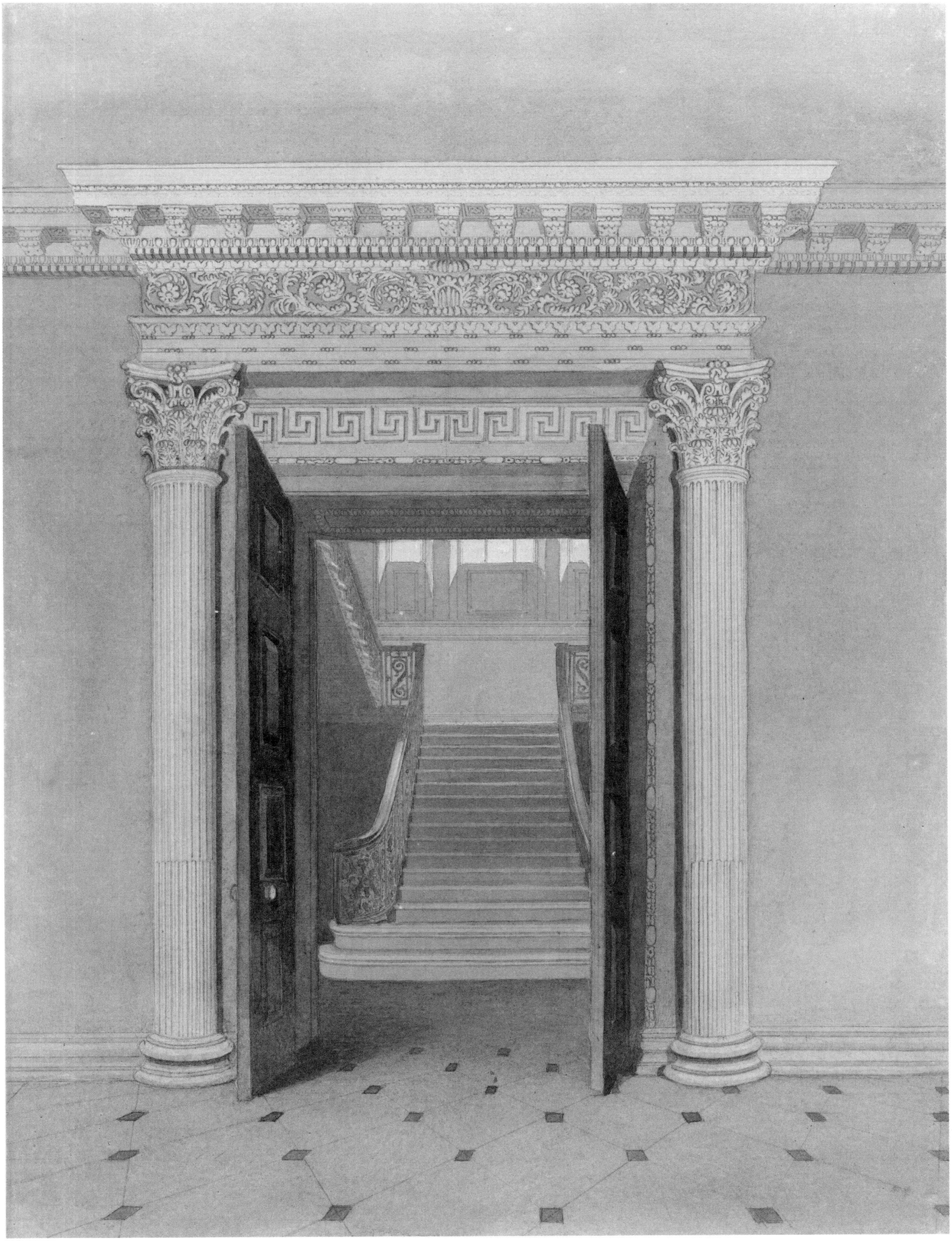

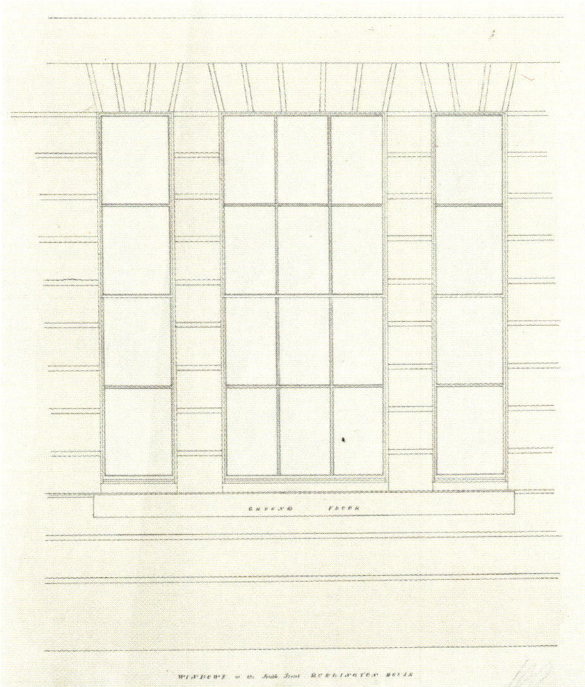

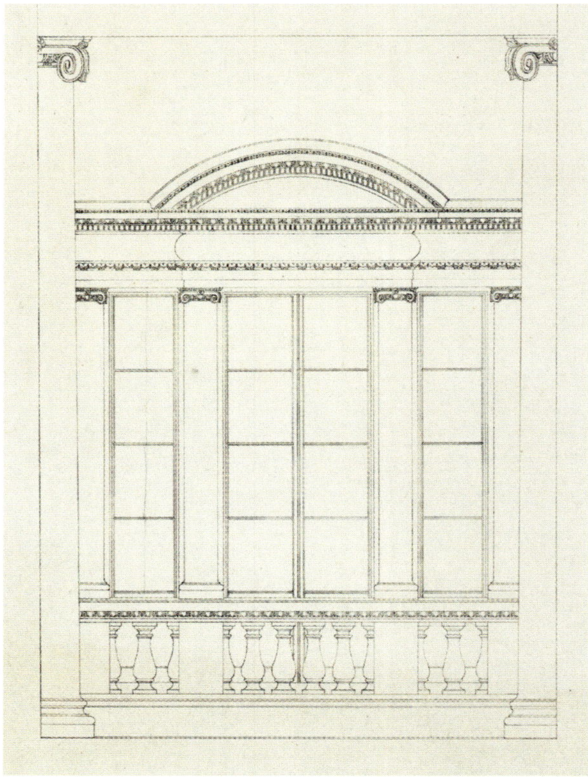

Fig. 104
Samuel Ware, Design for a ground-floor tripartite window, proposed for the south front but executed on the north front, *c.* 1816.
Royal Academy of Arts, London, 06/5071

Fig. 105
Samuel Ware, Design for first-floor tripartite window with segmental pedimented head, proposed for the south front but executed without enrichments on the north front, *c.* 1816.
Royal Academy of Arts, London, 06/4597

Fig. 106 (right)
Samuel Ware, North front of Burlington House as executed: elevation, *c.* 1816–20.
Royal Academy of Arts, London, 06/5835

proposed unsuccessfully for altering the south front (Figs 104, 105). As built, Ware's design echoed the bland seriality of Campbell's façade but not its austere harmony (Fig. 106). Although he was extremely wealthy, Lord George's purse was not bottomless, and it is probable, at least early on in the project, that Ware was under pressure to reduce projected costs. This would account for the major economy of facing the north front almost wholly in stucco (stone was used only for major horizontal external elements such as cornices and copings), and may well have been a factor in determining the comparatively plain detailing of the overall design as built (Figs 107, 108). Ware's use of stucco is a reminder also that for him 'restoration' did not mean avoiding new building materials or techniques if these were more economical or improved on those that had been used in the past. For instance, he eschewed James Parker's patent 'Roman' cement as producing in his opinion 'a very inferior stucco' and decided instead to follow a recipe for rough-casting that had recently been trialled on a warehouse at Troon in Ayrshire.[82] Similarly, he was quite happy to specify the insertion of two 14 × 12-inch girders to support the new floor in the 'Small' or 'South Drawing Room' (now the Richard Sharp Council Room) formed from the upper part of the former main staircase compartment.[83]

Evidence of some retrenchment as the project progressed is apparent also from the scaling-down of Ware's penultimate design for regularising Portland's ill-assorted annexes on the east and west sides of the house. Though enlarged at basement and ground-floor levels as Ware had proposed, and roofed with lead cisterns for the collection of rainwater, at first-floor level these extensions were reduced in size to no more than what was needed to accommodate service stairs up to the ball room on the east side of the house and, on the west, the successor to Portland's water-closet and similar stairs leading to Lord and Lady George's bedroom and the new State Dining Room (Fig. 109). While moving the west service staircase into the annexe could be justified at basement and ground-floor level by the need to create a self-contained three-room apartment for Lord George's daughters Anne and Caroline, it was not thought necessary to reroute the existing stairs from the first floor to the attic just for the sake of enlarging the lobby to the east of Lord and Lady George's bedroom.

Similar pragmatism lay behind Ware's painstaking stripping out of every room (apart from the Saloon and Slaughter Room to its west) and his careful storage of salvaged architectural fragments in the attic along with wooden bucks for casting new plaster ornament on site (Fig. 110).[84] Some of the Adam-style ornament that can also be glimpsed in Nattes's drawing of 1816 were no doubt destined for sale to builders' merchants; others may have been similar to the '12 Pieces of old Cleaned Moulding' that James Millbourne included in his bill for 'Carving 1030 Feet of Large Grass Leaf on Door and Window Architraves … at 6^{d} pr. ft.', presumably because he had incorporated these old sections in new work; and a few could have been important interior

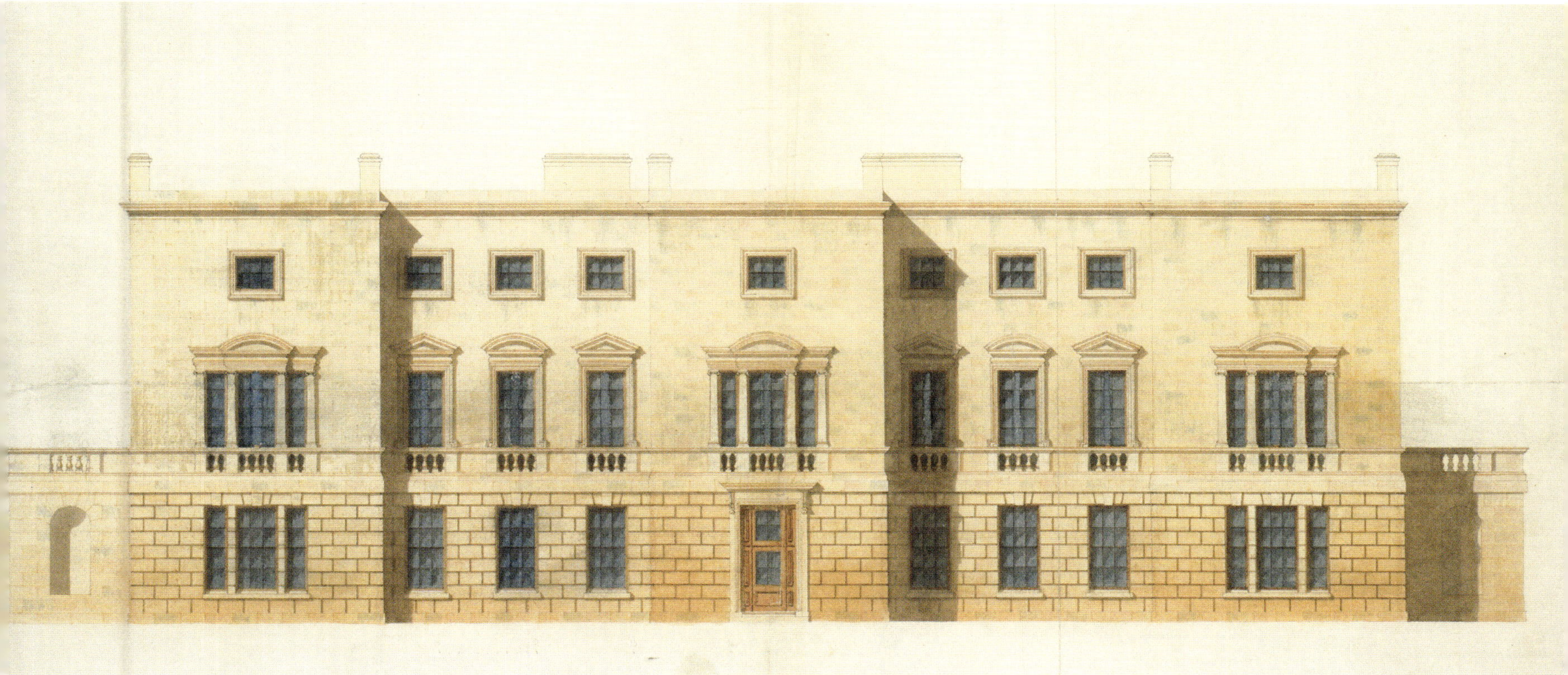

Fig. 107 (below left)
Samuel Ware, First-floor windows on the north front, as executed, *c.* 1815–18.
Royal Academy of Arts, London, 06/4007

Fig. 108 (below right)
Samuel Ware, Entablature to common windows on the north front: section, *c.* 1817.
Royal Academy of Arts, London, 06/5070

features for which new positions in the house might be found, such as the '4 Corinthian Columns Capitals & Bases for Marble Chimney pieces' and '2 Large Corinthian Capitals (Circular) and 6 Half D^o' that Millbourne charged £11 16s. to repair at some point during 1817.[85]

Apart from the removal of chimneypieces throughout and of the original glazing bars on the south front windows; the replacement of twin doorcases (the western one was a dummy) by a central doorway in the north wall of the State Dining Room (now the Academy's General Assembly Room) and the recent installation of two replica dummy doorcases in this room's west wall; the removal of a dummy door to the west of the fireplace in the south drawing room; the revelation of parts of the painted cove in the Saloon; and the incomplete (but otherwise accurate) detailing of the recent reinstatement of Lady Cavendish's drawing room in the north front (now the Tennant Gallery); apart from these relatively minor differences, the John Madejski Fine Rooms that

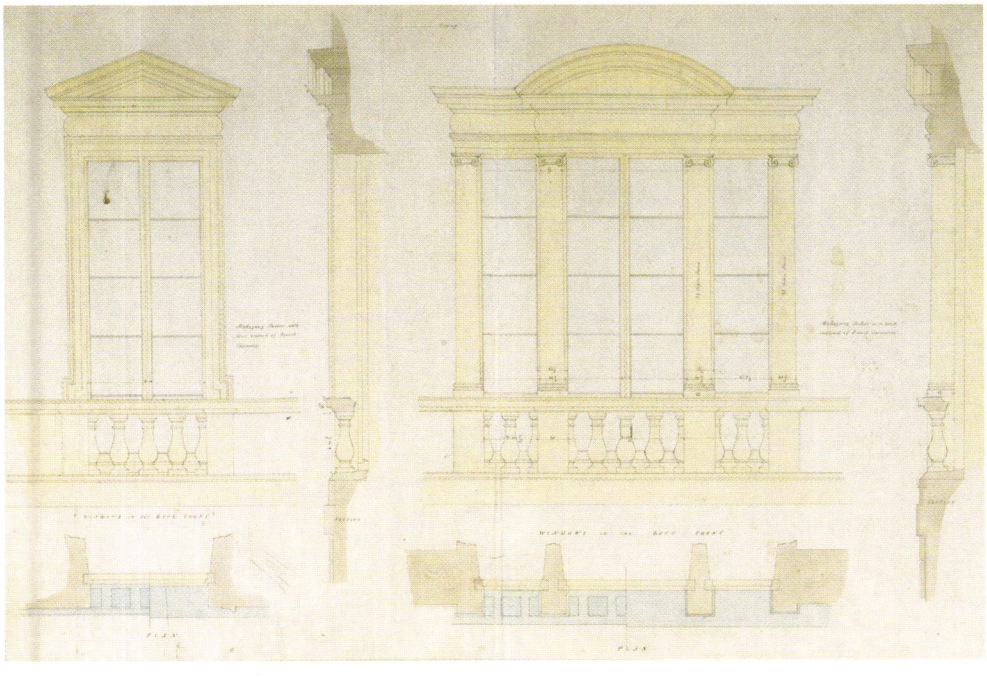

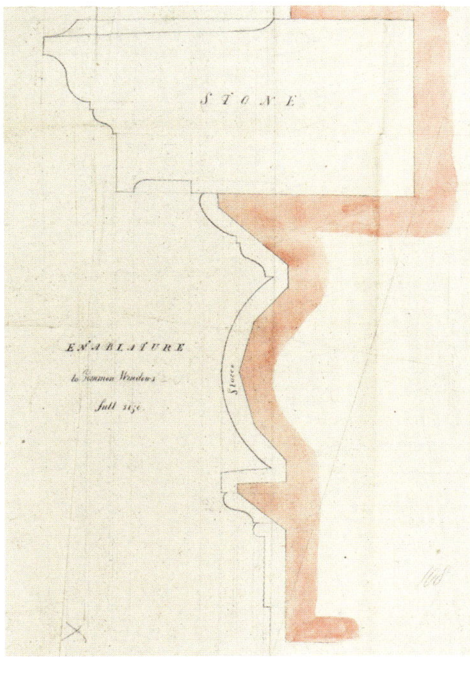

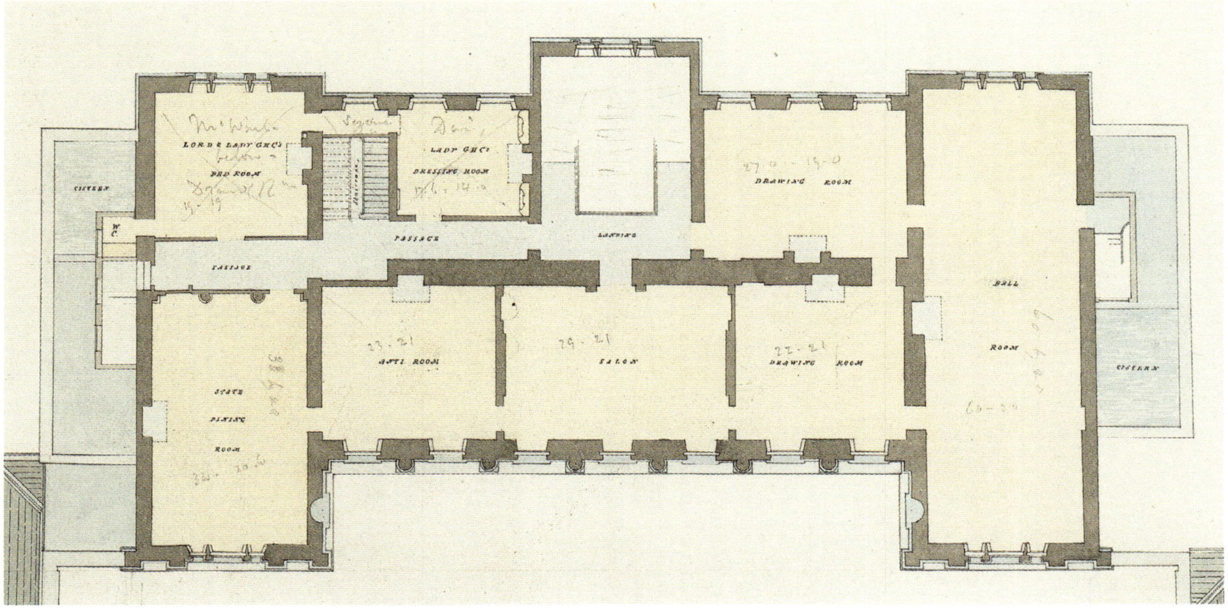

Fig. 109
Samuel Ware, Burlington House: first-floor plan showing the alterations as executed, *c.* 1820.
Royal Academy of Arts, London, 06/4955

we see today are how Samuel Ware handed them over to his client at the conclusion of the works in May 1819. Unlike Julian Harrap in 2004–05, whose restoration of these self-same rooms was founded on modern principles of architectural conservation, almost two hundred years earlier Ware had had to rely wholly on his own skill as a designer to recreate the out-dated style of interior associated with William Kent and the 3rd Earl of Burlington (Figs 111, 113).

One of the clearest demonstrations of Ware's approach is a pair of drawings he made for Lord George comparing the friezes and enriched mouldings of door-cases found in Burlington House with their equivalents in Devonshire House (see Fig. 111). The purpose of this comparison was to establish the appropriateness of three surviving friezes found in Burlington House as models for the new doorheads needed to replace modern interpolations. It is a measure of Lord George's confidence in his

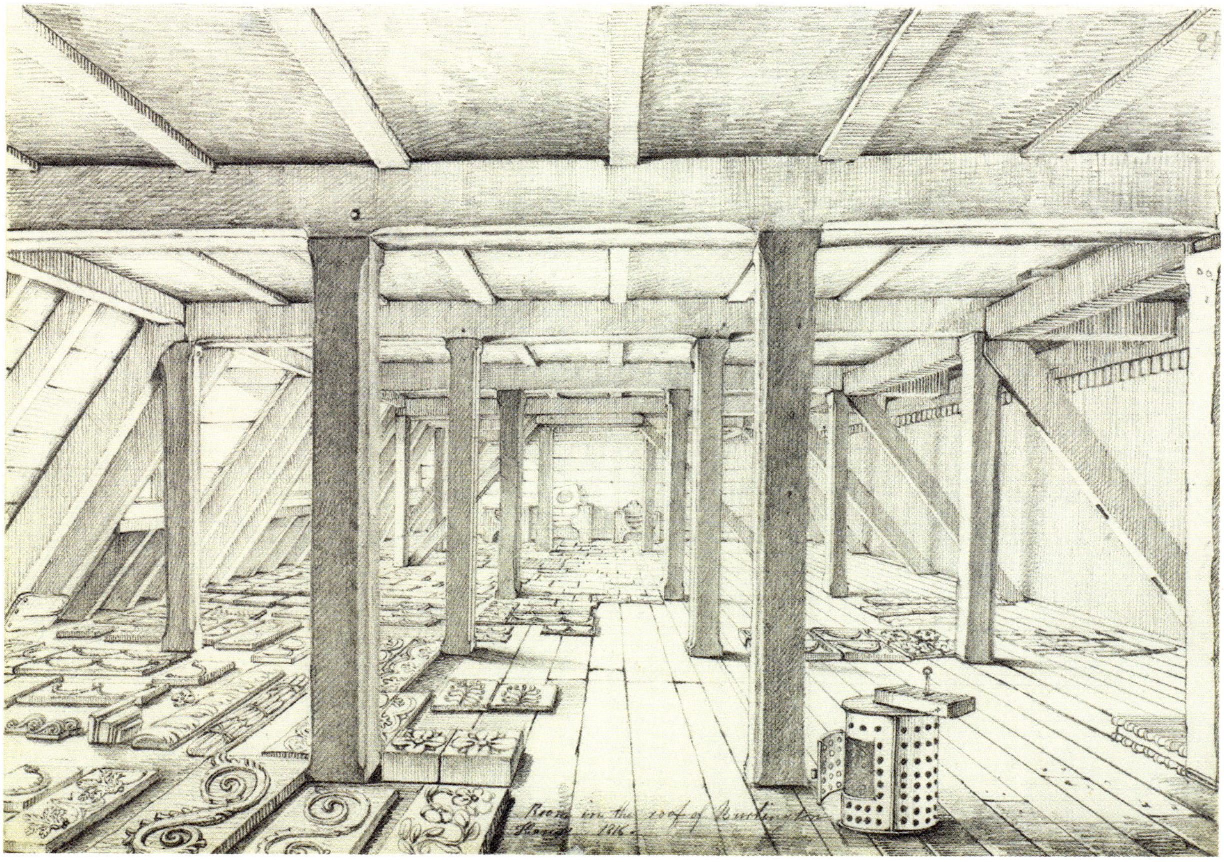

Fig. 110
J. C. Nattes (attrib.), Room in the roof of Burlington House, showing moulds for casting plaster ornament, 1816.
London Metropolitan Archives (City of London)

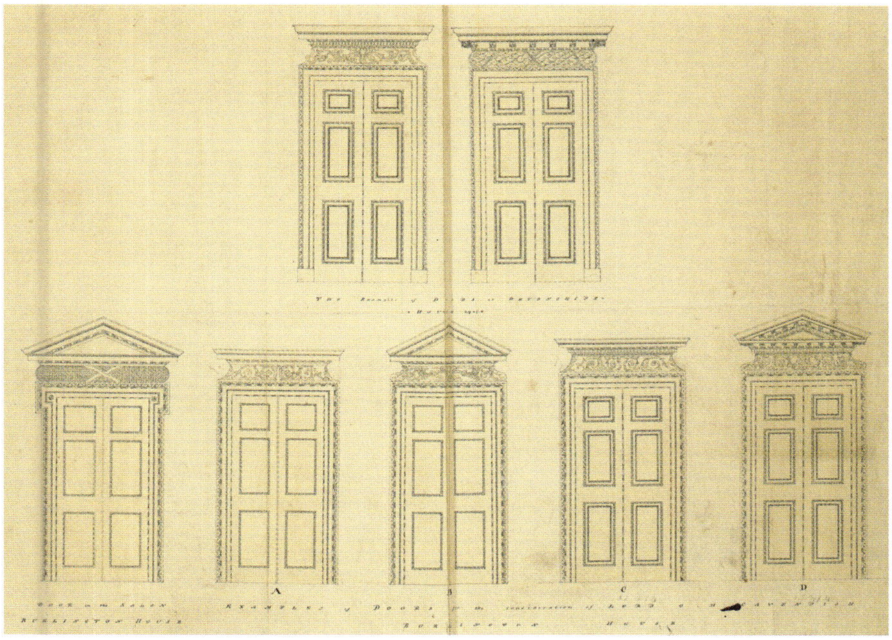

Fig. 111
Samuel Ware, Doors for Burlington House, examples for the consideration of Lord George Cavendish, *c.* 1817.
Royal Academy of Arts, London, 06/5054

architect's skill and knowledge as a designer that he turned down all three. Instead, he commissioned two entirely original designs for use throughout the house, a 'Corinthian' one that emanates west from the ball room into the south drawing room (i.e. the Richard Sharp Council Room; Fig. 116) and an 'Ionic' one that migrates east from the State Dining Room into the anti-room to its east (i.e. the Slaughter Room; Fig. 115). Ware's proposed economy of reducing the number of variant doorheads from three to two was, however, acted upon, to the extent that the intermediate doorcase in Lady Cavendish's drawing room (i.e. the Tennant Gallery), the need for which arose from its position between the Great Stairs and the ball room, was formed by replacing the highly enriched cornice of the 'Corinthian' doorhead with a plainer pediment.

Unlike a conservation-minded architect today, Ware was free to reuse historic fabric salvaged or copied from other parts of the house, and to introduce new work designed in an appropriate style as and where needed. Apart from doorheads, examples of the latter approach include, most obviously, the complex Kent-style ceilings (Figs 117, 118) and (probably) the convincingly period chimneypieces that Ware designed for the ball room, State Dining Room and elsewhere (Figs 119, 120).

Fig. 112
Samuel Ware, Angle leaf ornament for the State Dining Room and drawing room, *c.* 1817.
Royal Academy of Arts, London, 06/5124

Fig. 113
Samuel Ware, Ball Room, design for frieze, almost as executed, *c.* 1817.
Royal Academy of Arts, London, 06/5113

Fig. 114
Samuel Ware, State Dining Room, design for a frieze, as executed, *c.* 1817.
Royal Academy of Arts, London, 06/5118

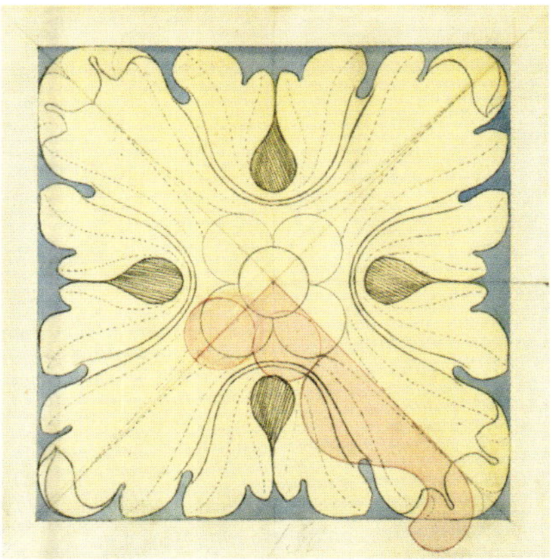

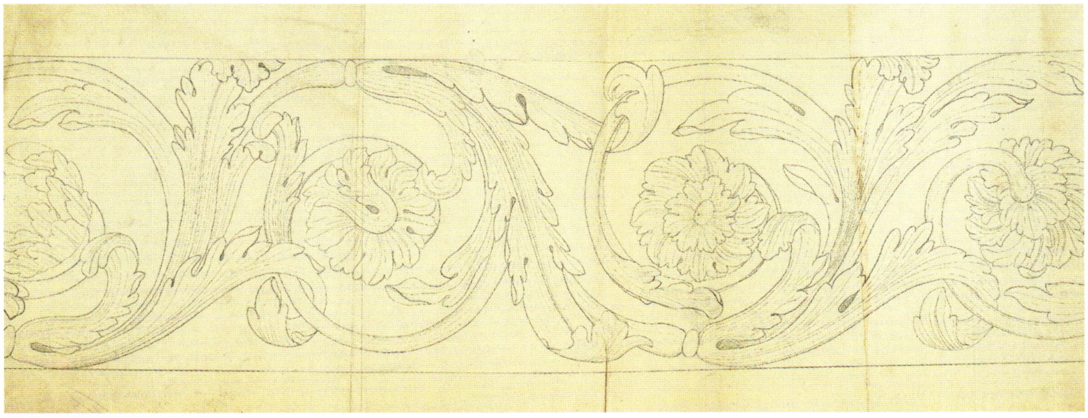

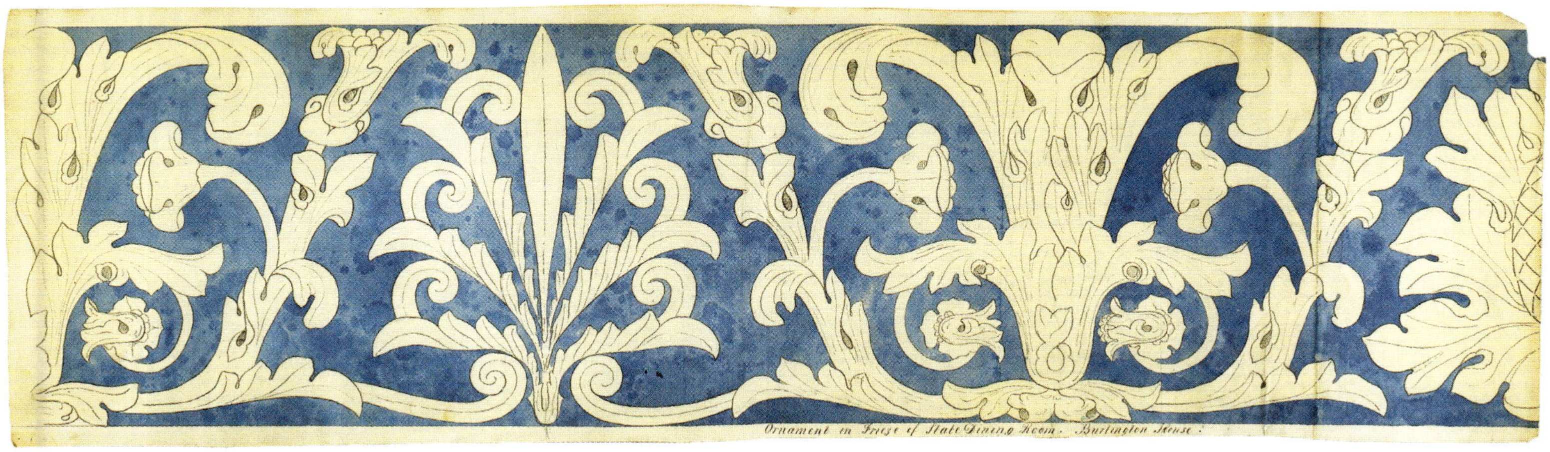

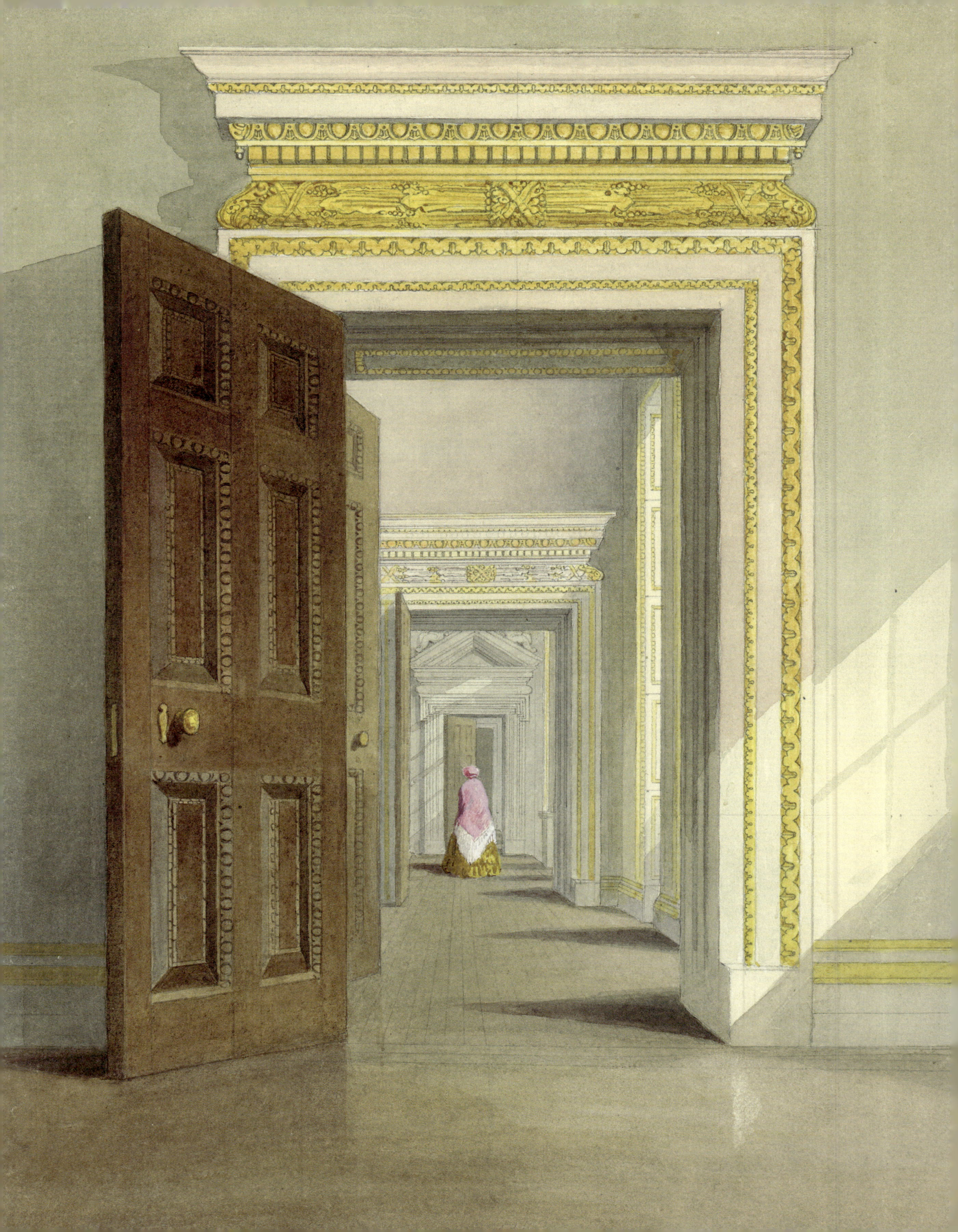

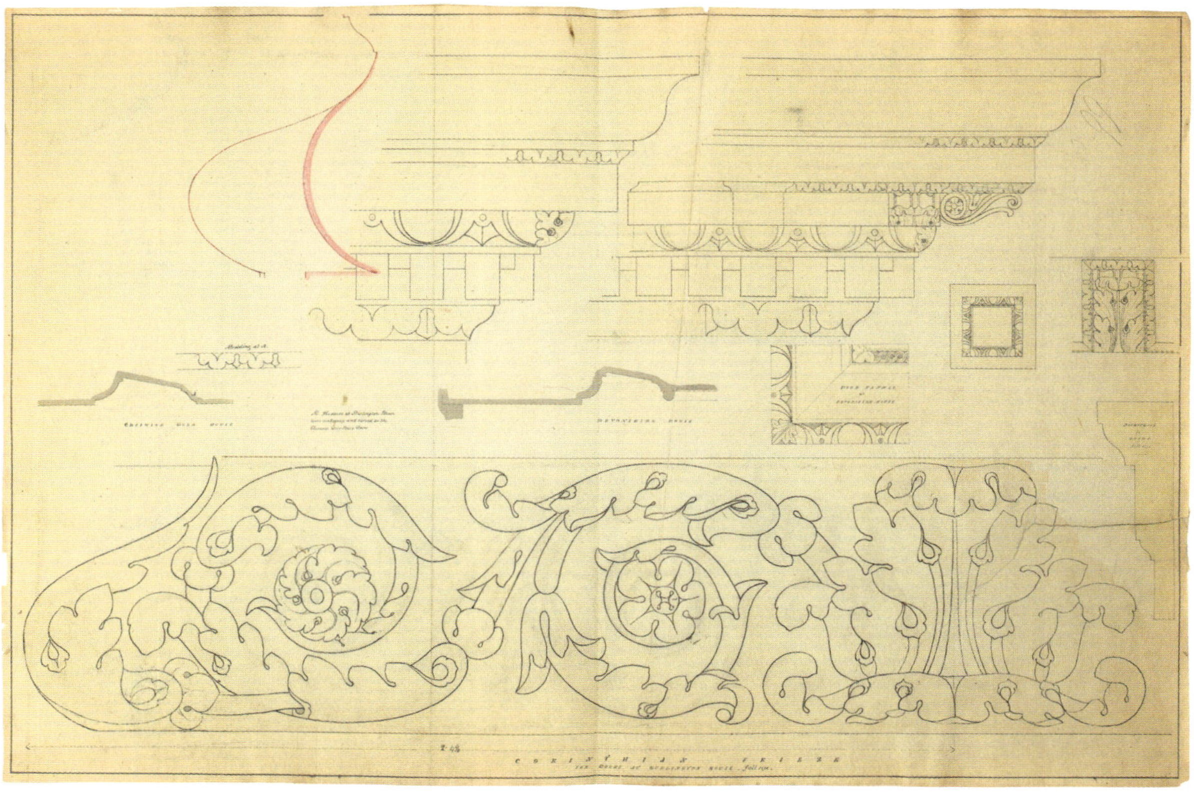

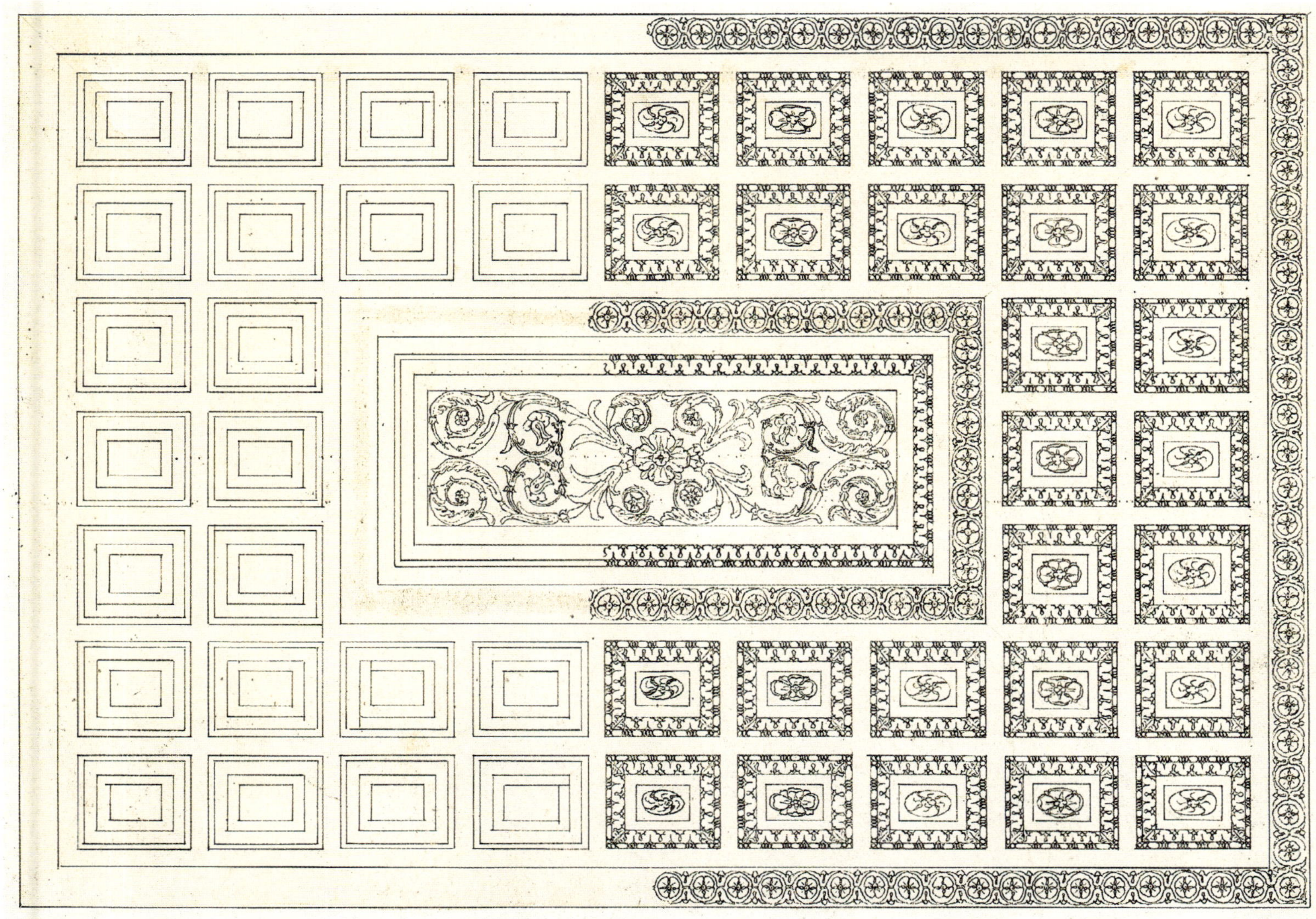

Fig. 115 (left)
John Wykeham Archer, *In Burlington House* (Ionic doorcase, State Dining Room and anti-room enfilade looking east), 1855.
British Museum, London 1874,0314.325

Fig. 116 (right)
Samuel Ware, Details of doors in Devonshire House and Chiswick Deer House, with full-size design for architrave and frieze of doors in the ball room of Burlington House as executed, *c.* 1817.
Royal Academy of Arts, London, 06/5059

Fig. 117 (below)
Samuel Ware, Unexecuted design for the State Dining Room ceiling, *c.* 1816.
Royal Academy of Arts, London, 06/4527

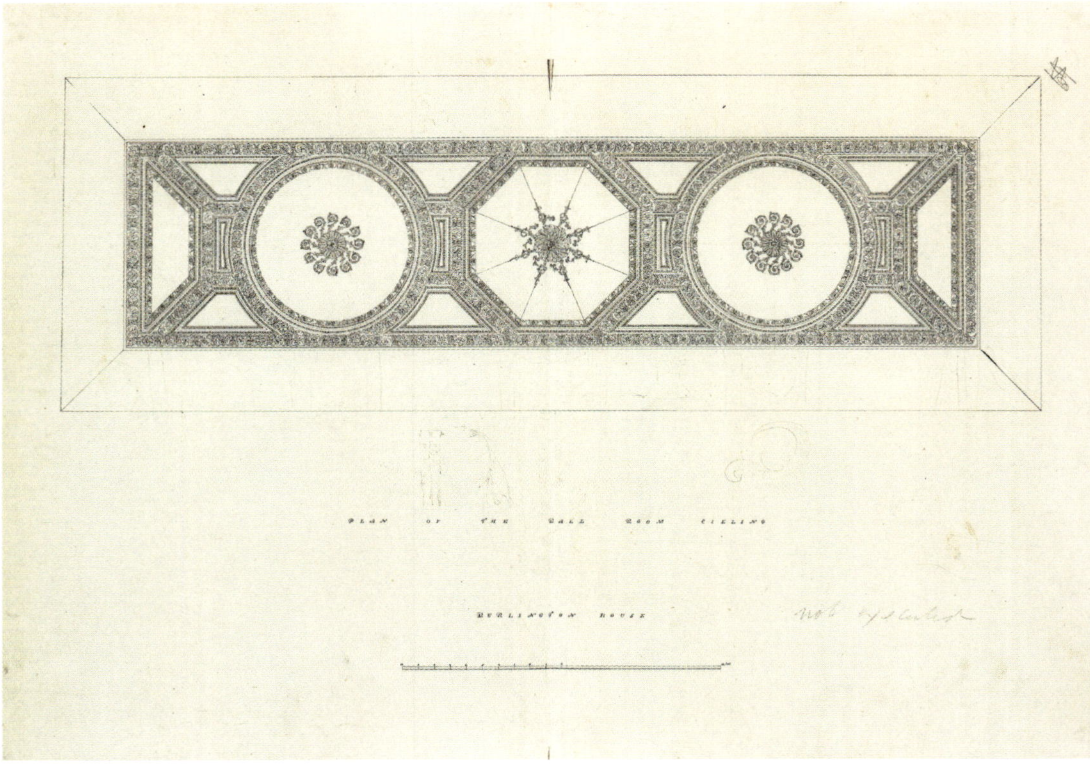

Fig. 118
Samuel Ware, Unexecuted design for the ball room ceiling, *c.* 1816.
Royal Academy of Arts, London, 06/4525

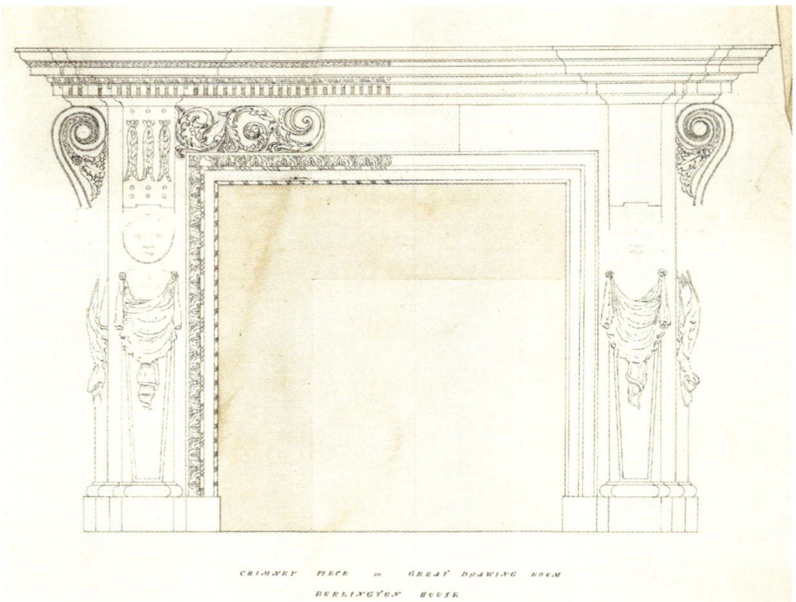

Fig. 119
Samuel Ware, Design for the ball room chimneypiece probably as executed: elevation and profiles, *c.* 1817.
Royal Academy of Arts, London, 06/5341

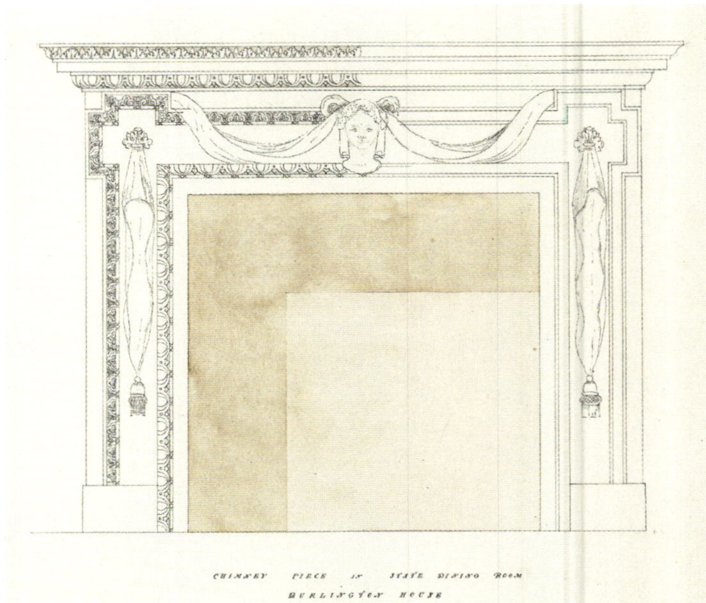

Fig. 120
Samuel Ware, Design for the State Dining Room chimneypiece probably as executed, *c.* 1817.
Royal Academy of Arts, London, 06/5342

Examples of the former are more difficult to identify, but probably include the engaged Ionic columns on the north wall of the State Dining Room (*in situ*, but modified to full columns; Fig. 122); the detached Corinthian columns placed against the south wall of the Common Dining Room (*in situ* as a free-standing screen until 1986; Fig. 121); and two large Corinthian doorcases with a Greek-key lintel panel, one framing the inside of the front door in the south wall of the entrance hall (*in situ*), the other the double door on the north wall leading to Ware's new staircase (see Fig. 103).[86] It is probably not coincidental that Ware made drawings of these three major architectural features to a similar scale and included on two of them careful measurements (Figs 123, 124). Screens were not originally planned for either the north wall of the State Dining Room or for the wall dividing the ground-floor rooms in the east wing, which suggests they might perhaps have been incorporated from elsewhere in the house. If so, it is not impossible that some parts of them at least were recycled from the Great Dining Parlour on the ground floor and the 'Pillar Bedroom' on the first floor.

Fig. 121
John Wykeham Archer, *Room in Burlington House* (Common Dining Room), 1855.
British Museum, London
1874,0314.321

Fig. 122
Samuel Ware, State Dining Room: north-wall elevation, *c.* 1820.
Royal Academy of Arts, London, 06/5767

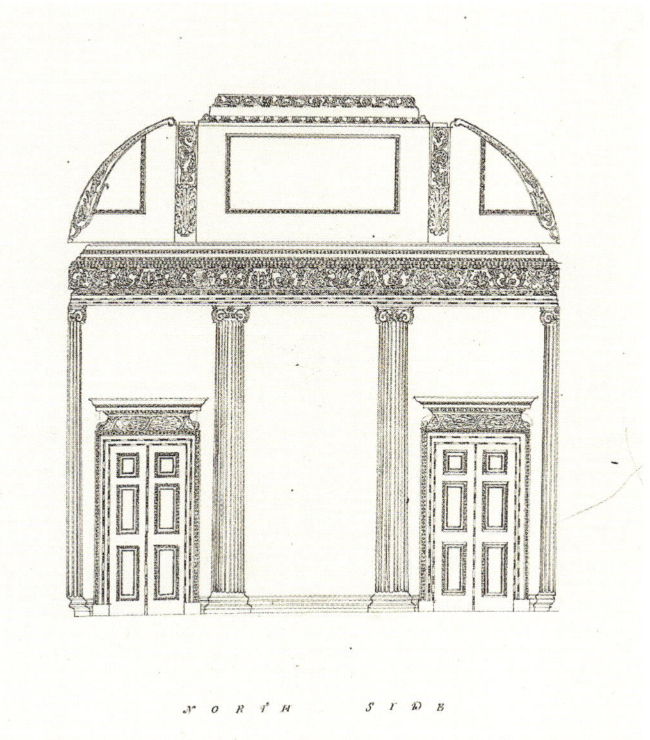

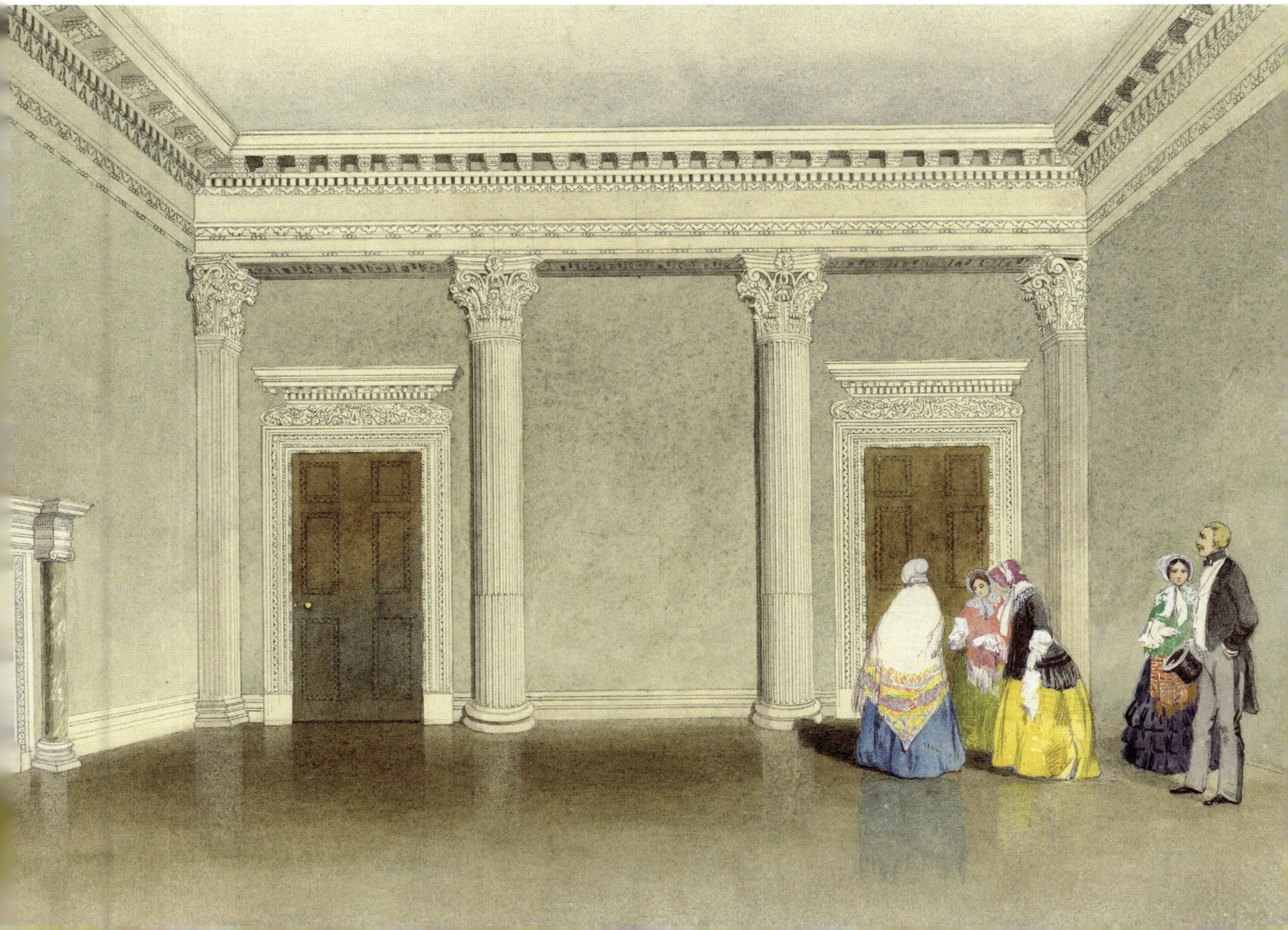

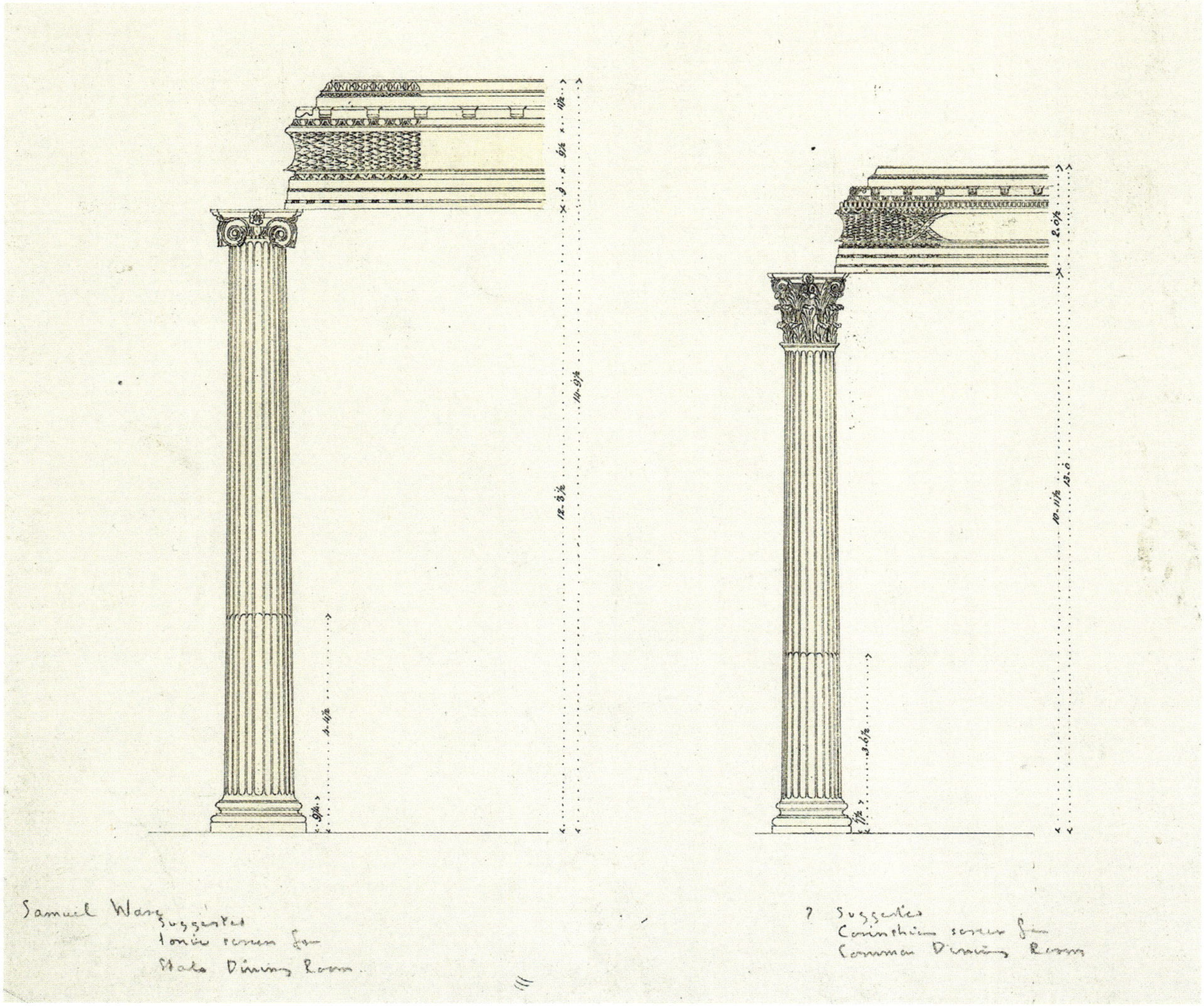

Fig. 123
Samuel Ware, Columns for the State Dining Room and Common Dining Room: elevations with measurements, *c.* 1816.
Royal Academy of Arts, London, 06/4489

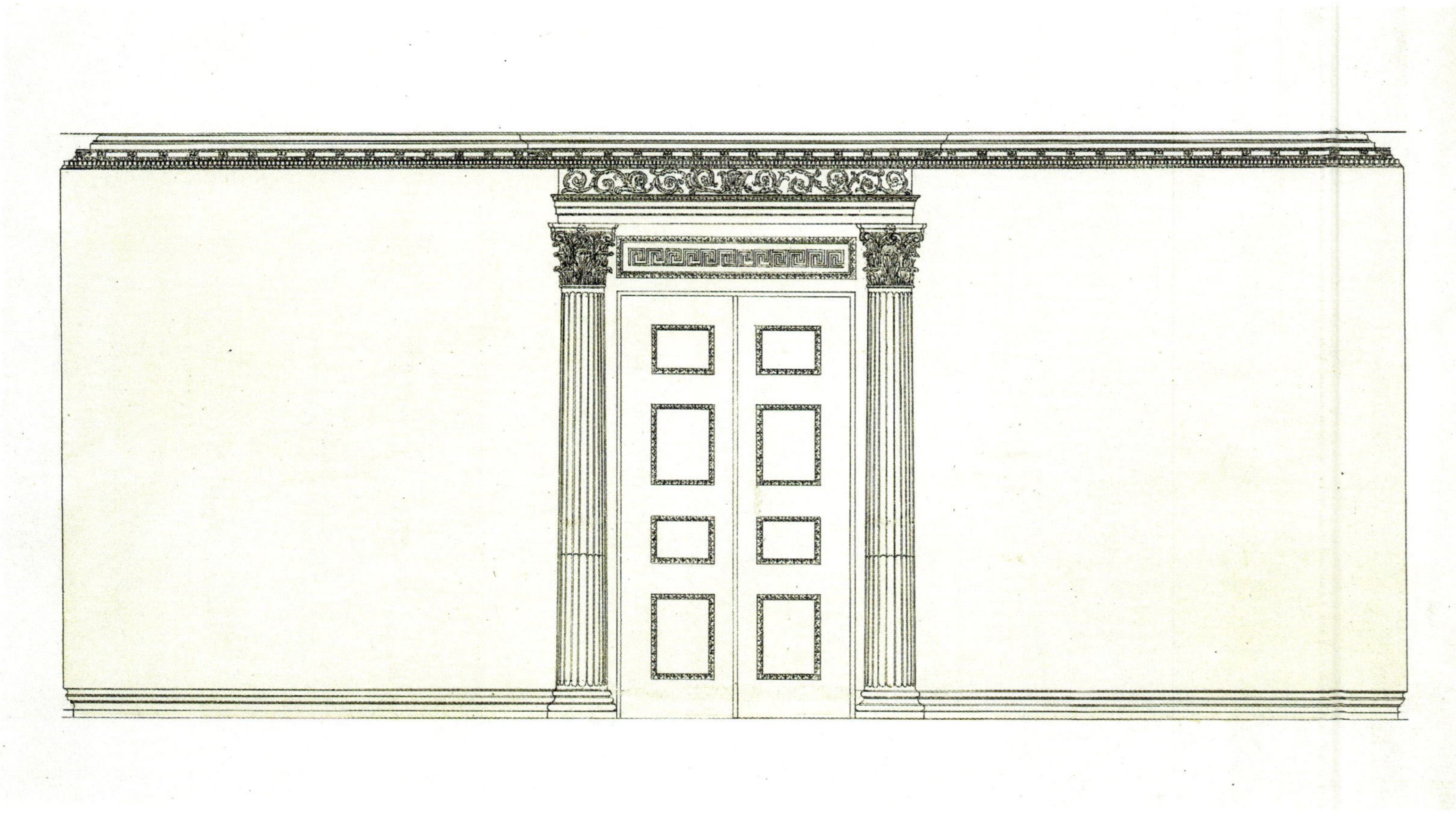

Fig. 124
Samuel Ware, Door to the Great Stairs on the north wall of the entrance hall, *c.* 1816.
Royal Academy of Arts, London, 06/4616

To judge from the surviving tradesmen's bills, only two incidents seemed to have disturbed the smooth progress of the works. The first occurred early on when, for a period of nine days in March 1816, up to ten police constables attended the site to prevent a breach of the peace.[87] A clue as to why they were needed is suggested by Ware's 'general statement' of 2 May 1818, in which he draws attention to the fact that 'These works have been carried on in a time of unexampled distress, when the greater part of the workmen in the metropolis & throughout the kingdom were unemployed and in great want.'[88] The second problem arose in August 1820 when, as an afterthought, Lord George began to build on the boundary with Albany an enormous arcaded screen wall, the piers of which were positioned to obstruct any view whatsoever of his garden. When an understandably irate delegation of Albany proprietors and trustees called round to object, Ware's response was exemplary. By the following day, he had not only defused the situation but succeeded in obtaining the trustees' permission to block out their view instead 'by stopping up the staircase windows, by carrying up the parapet walls to hide the dormer windows, and by partially building up the recesses in the external wall'.[89] At the same time, having no doubt impressed upon them how 'difficult' his client could be, he drafted, and got the trustees to sign there and then, a carefully worded conciliatory letter addressed to himself, in which they proffered this solution to the problem as if it was entirely their idea. It was a typically adroit move that only much later led to problems when it appeared to set a precedent for subsequent Albany residents' claims of rights to light. Thanks to Ware's quick thinking at the time, Lord George's eastern boundary did not have to compete in height with his neighbours' windows, and the latter were able to benefit from 39 low-level openings in his wall that encouraged the scent of mignonettes to percolate from his garden on warm summer evenings (Fig. 125).

Ware did, however, advise that these openings should be fitted with copper-wire mesh in order to 'prevent any thing being thrown from the lower windows'.[90] This precaution suggests there may be some truth in the urban myth that 'what first gave birth to the idea' of building the Burlington Arcade 'was the great annoyance to which the garden is subject from the inhabitants of a neighbouring street throwing oyster-shells, &c. over the walls'.[91] Be that as it may, just as important to Lord George was the fact that, as the *Gentleman's Magazine* wryly noted, 'the intended erections will … also block out their view of so delightful a place.' Unlike Lord George's absurd Albany screen, the idea of building a 'piazza' or 'covered passageway' of shops along the western boundary of Burlington House and its gardens was the culmination of many years' sustained thought on Ware's part on how best to derive a rental income from the site. Despite the Duke of Devonshire's lack of interest in pursuing the idea, and the new owner of the house's evident lack of need to do so, the businessman in Ware was clearly determined to find the best possible solution to the Burlington House 'problem' that Heaton has set him a decade earlier, even if in the end it was never built.

At some point Ware must have come to realise, as no-one had quite done before, that it would never be enough for a commercial development of the Burlington House site to be merely unobtrusive, it had to be totally invisible. Given the fine detail of the 'Report of the Rents and Advantages arising from the Erection of

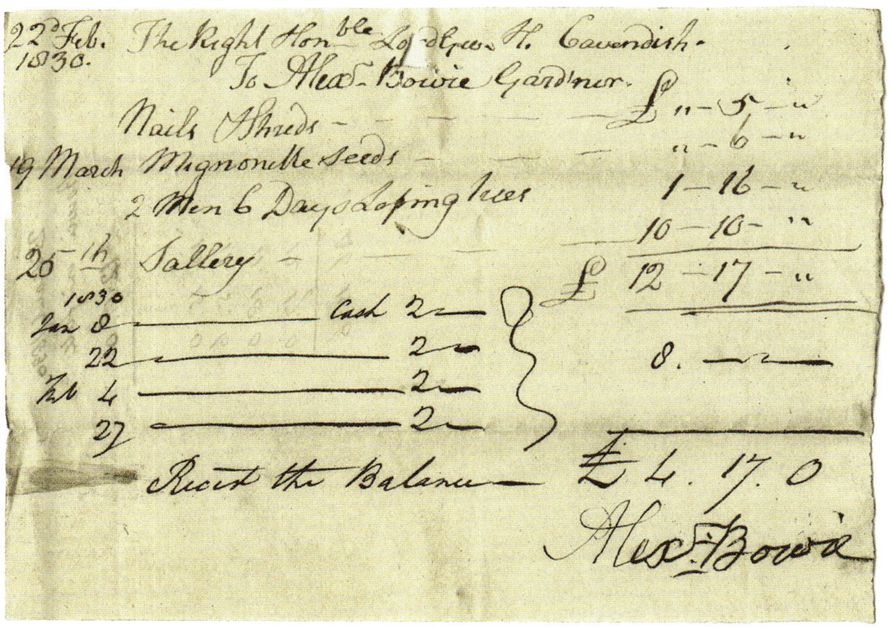
22d Feb. 1830. The Right Honble Lord Geo. H. Cavendish
To Alexr Bowie Gardner. £
Nails & Shreds — £ " 11 - 5 - "
19 March Mignonette Seeds — " - 6 - "
2 Men 6 Days Lopping Trees 1 - 16 - "
10 - 10 - "
25th Sallery — £ 12 - 17 - "
1830 Jan 8 — Cash 2 —
22 — 2 —
Feb 4 — 2 —
27 — 2 — 8. — "
Recd the Balance £ 4. 17. 0
Alexr Bowie

Fig. 125
Alexander Bowie's bill for garden work and seeds, from a bundle of bills settled by Pinder Simpson for Lord George Cavendish, 25 March 1830.
Chatsworth, Derbyshire, Devonshire MSS, AS 3101

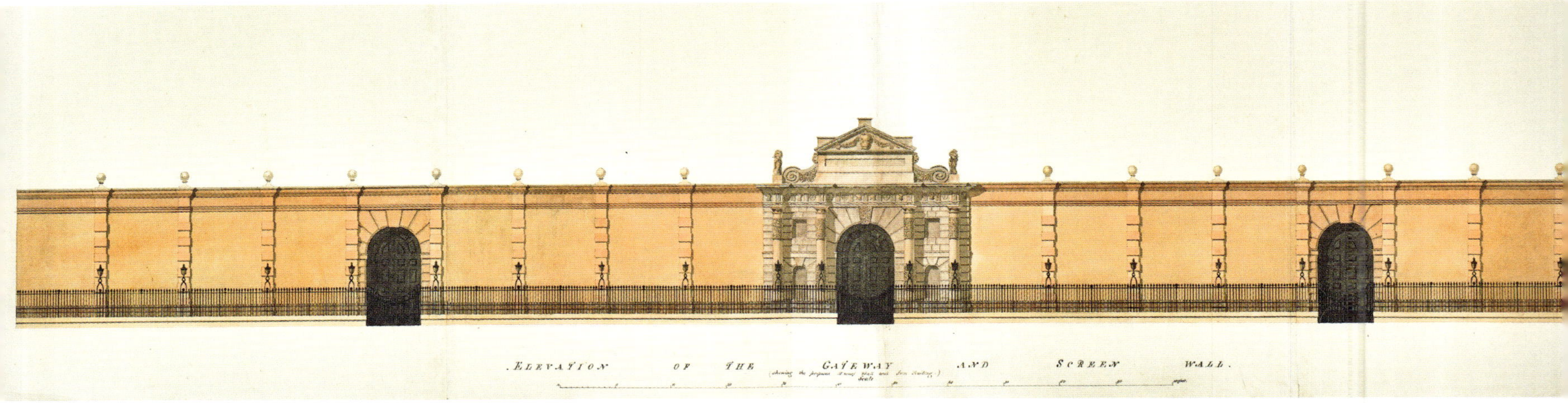

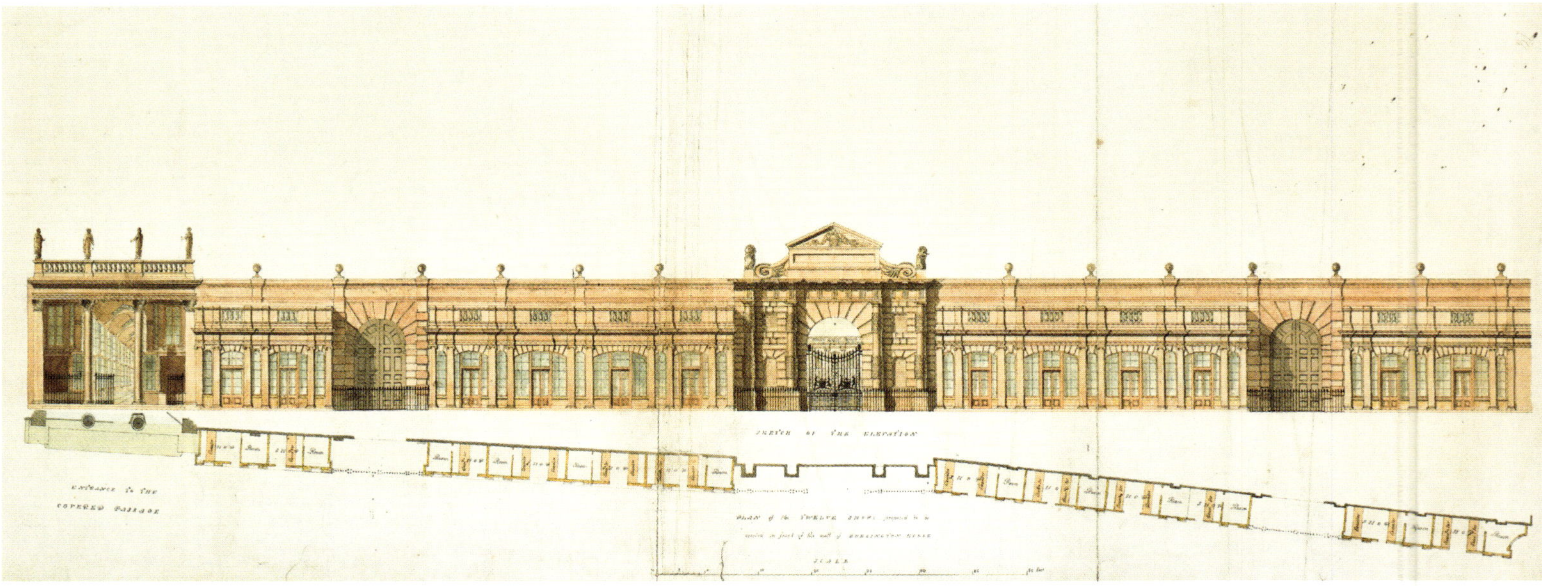

Fig. 126
Samuel Ware, Unexecuted design for railing and lamps on the Piccadilly frontage of Burlington House: elevation, c. 1811–15.
Royal Academy of Arts, London, 06/5716

Fig. 127
Samuel Ware, Unexecuted design for shops along the Piccadilly wall of Burlington House: plan, elevation and sketch elevation of shop, c. 1815.
Royal Academy of Arts, London, 06/5715

Two Entrance Facades and a Double Row of Shops … forming a covered Mall extending from Piccadilly through Burlington Garden to Vigo Lane' that he sent to Heaton on 5 May 1815, one might have assumed that his scheme had been under discussion for some time (Figs 129, 130).[92] However, Lord George's decision to proceed must have come after Ware had prepared his undated design for a dwarf wall with streetlamps and railings on Piccadilly, in which there is no sign of his proposed 'covered Mall' (Fig. 126).

Keen to maximise the projected financial return, Ware included as part of his original scheme a line of twelve Lilliputian shops projecting 8 feet in front of the Piccadilly screen wall, each with two counters, a tiny stock room, and customer area no larger than 6 × 4 feet (Fig. 127). No more than a row of diminutive kiosks, it was a clever but probably impracticable idea for obtaining income from passers-by in Piccadilly, rewarding them (at last) with a view of the house from the street, but still preserving the view from the house virtually unaltered. While Lord George evidently did not feel the need to pursue this aspect of Ware's proposal, he seems for a time at least to have been impressed by the idea of wrought-iron entrance gates decorated with the Cavendish family arms, since these reappear in Ware's largely executed design for a palisade of iron railings and sixteen street lamps in front of the Piccadilly screen wall.[93] In the end it was decided instead to install wrought-iron bracket gates in front of the original wooden Great Gate, the hinges and straps of which were repaired by Mears & Son in

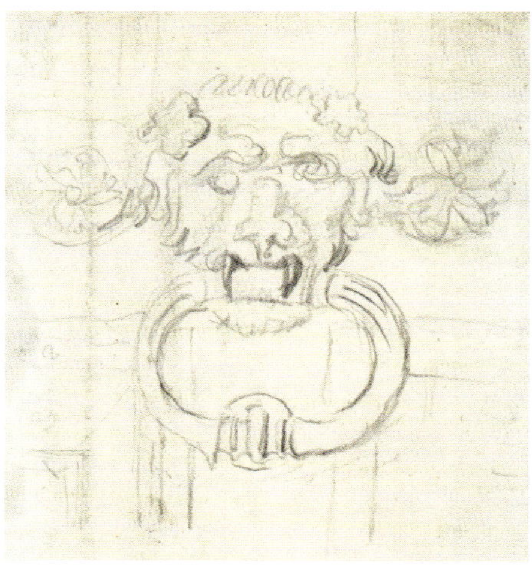

Fig. 128
John Carter, Sketch of a brass knocker on the Great Gate, 1815.
Royal Academy of Arts, London, 06/2153

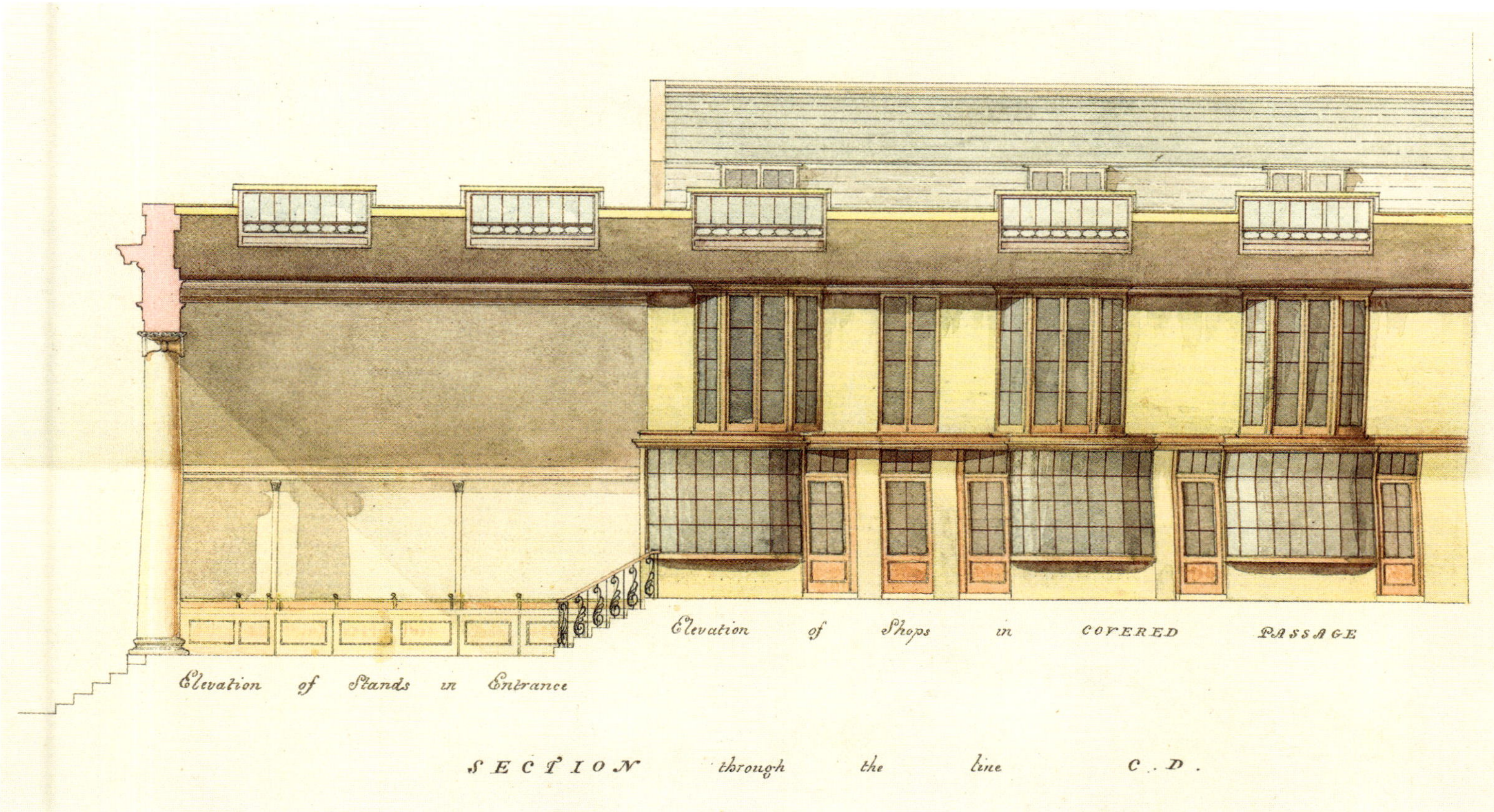

Fig. 129
Samuel Ware, Preliminary design of Burlington Arcade: section of the Piccadilly entrance and the first six shops with stands (detail), *c*. 1815.
Royal Academy of Arts, London, 06/5713

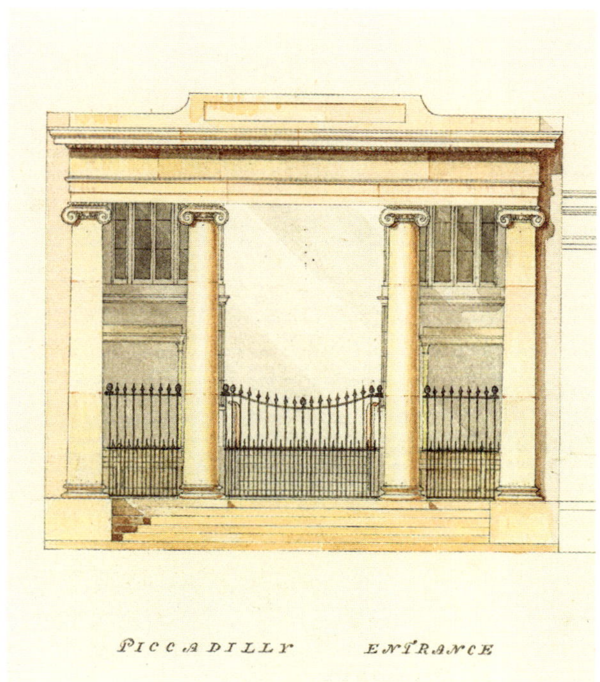

Fig. 130
Samuel Ware, Preliminary design of Burlington Arcade, the Piccadilly entrance: elevation (detail), *c*. 1815.
Royal Academy of Arts, London, 06/5713

November 1818.[94] In the same month, Mears also billed Lord George for 'Cleaning & repairing the large mask Knockers of great gates Burning off the paint Cleaning out the chased work [and supplying] New tooth to lion's head new bolts nuts &c' (Fig. 128).[95]

Christened the 'Burlington Arcade' when it first opened in January 1819, Ware's drawings and specifications refer to it only as a 'covered passageway' or 'piazza'. This suggests that, to begin with at least, there was no assumption that Lord George would necessarily wish to invest in the undertaking himself, or be associated with it after it had been built. Ware may also have been keen to avoid stirring up memories of the ill-fated 'Burlington Place' projects, all of which (apart from his own) had presumed to use the Burlington name to probably counterproductive effect. This would explain why, for instance, one of the first notices in the press of the impending arcade referred to it as 'The London Palais Royal' and stressed that 'The whole is a speculation quite unconnected with Lord GEORGE CAVENDISH's improvements' at Burlington House.[96] It might also explain why Ware could begin a letter to Lord George

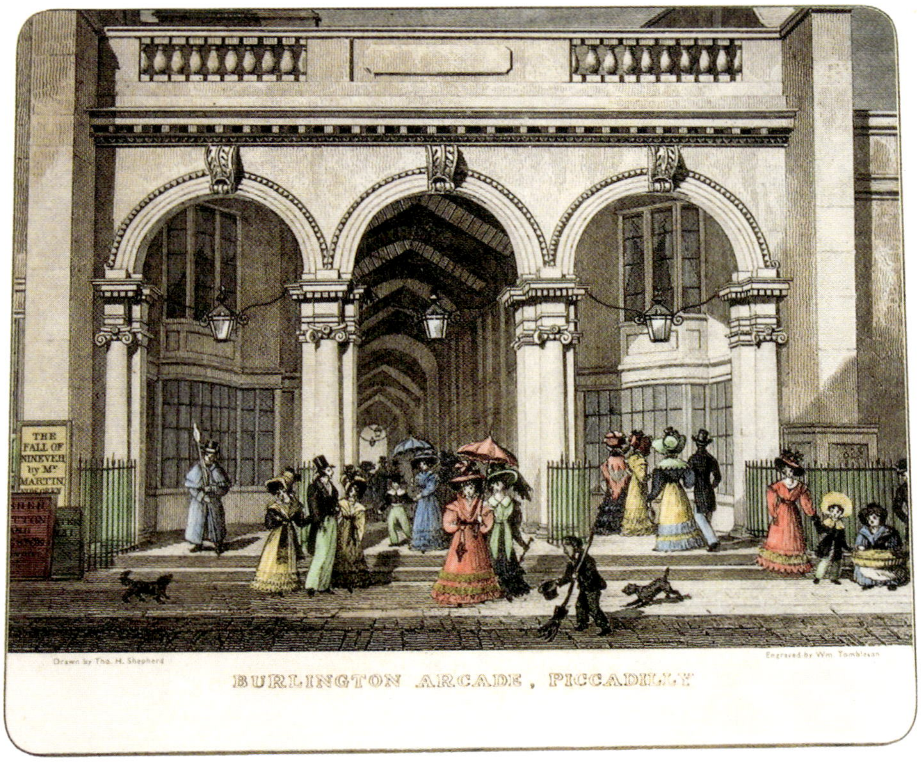

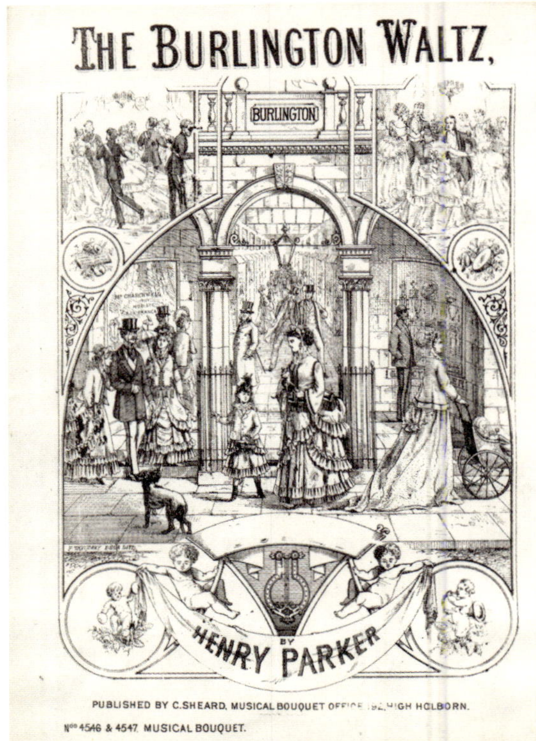

Fig. 131
William Tombleson, after Thomas Hosmer Shepherd, *Burlington Arcade, Piccadilly*, placemat from a set decorated with scenes of Georgian London, 1828.
National Trust, Scotney Castle

Fig. 132
Henry T. Parker and F. Travisany (engraving), *The Burlington Waltz*, sheet music published by C. Sheard, 1871.
John Johnson Collection, Bodleian Library

in July 1824 by declaring that he had 'often thought that Burlington House would be a more valuable property if it were detached from Burlington Arcade'.[97]

As the thin end of the wedge of the site's first and ultimately only commercial development, the 'Arcadians' (as the Lord Chancellor wittily dubbed the tenants of the arcade in their Chancery suit over unauthorised public access from a neighbouring bazaar) relied heavily on the social cachet of association with Burlington House to attract the *bon ton* of the town.[98] And because the arcade was the first permanently public use of any part of the site, what now passes as rather quaint special policing by beadles recruited from the 10th Hussars, and mildly eccentric regulations against singing, running, and carrying large parcels and open umbrellas, would set the tone for the admission of the public to Burlington House once it had passed out of private ownership. In the meantime, as the future habitat of 'Burlington Bertie' of music-hall fame, the arcade also generated a frisson of upper-class frivolity and dissoluteness not unlike that enjoyed by the fashionable loungers and *flâneurs* of previous generations at Vauxhall and Ranelagh Gardens, and which no doubt helped to ensure its immediate and continuing success as London's earliest double-sided shopping mall (Figs 131, 132).

While the purpose of the arcade was clear enough, less obvious was Lord George's intended use of 'Burlington's fair palace', which, by the time Ware presented his final accounts on 22 June 1819, had cost £47,397 10s. 10d. on top of its purchase price of £70,000 (in total equivalent to about £5 million in 2005).[99] There had been a moment during the course of its renovation when it looked as though Burlington House might become once again the headquarters of the Whig opposition that it had been in the Duke of Portland's time. A report to this effect even appeared in the press, reflecting Lord Brougham's view, first expressed in a letter to Earl Grey in January 1816, that 'In truth a house is more wanted than a leader, for half the contrarieties and misunderstandings among us arise from our never associating together.'[100] According to Brougham, even the Whig 'Mountain' (i.e. the independents led by Samuel Whitbread) would have accepted Lord George as the nominal leader of the party at that point had he been willing to make Burlington House available for political meetings and dinners. Like the *quid pro quo* that was talked of in January 1818 – 'Tierney is to lead, and Lord George Cavendish to feed the opposition' – the idea came to nothing, not merely because of the lack of ambition (and a greater devotion to the turf than to politics) that the latter's contemporaries accused him of, but also because of the social hypersensitivity that was so ingrained in his character.

The prominent social status that Burlington House conferred on its owner – the point that Ware had made in his July 1814 valuation by claiming 'that in some respects no Building in London can be compared with it, nor any one afford so characteristic an idea of the rank of the possessor of it' – was certainly one reason why, despite having started building work three weeks earlier, Lord and Lady George threw a spectacular ball on 5 May 1815. According to a report in the *Morning Post* a few days later, 'it was a new proof of what may be achieved, when liberality and taste are predominant. This entertainment', the *Post* continued,

> drew into its vortex all the fashion of the metropolis with very few exceptions; it was the very centre of pleasure about the 'twelfth hour'. Carriages innumerable poured into the spacious court-yard, with not less than two footmen behind each; all wore splendid liveries, and carried lighted flambeaux in their hands. The company were dressed in a style of grandeur unusual – the Ladies, mostly all, attired in gold or silver lama, with plumes of white ostrich feathers, towering in the full plenitude of beauty – the Gentlemen mostly in regimentals or court dresses. It may be asked – 'How came the invited to appear so gorgeously apparelled?' – They had previously attended a party given by the PRINCE REGENT, at Carlton House, at which was present the QUEEN and the PRINCESSES.[101]

It may reasonably be assumed that this timing was not coincidental, and also that the less sumptuous 'Grand Ball' held a few days earlier on 1 May, had been organised with less distinguished guests in mind. As the house was by now devoid of furniture, these parties were held in 'four drawing rooms' decorated 'with numerous festoons of artificial and natural flowers,' probably in a manner reminiscent of the garden 'fetes' of the year before.

Although the family was able to move out of Savile Row before the end of 1818,[102] it was not until 26 May 1820 that the ground-floor rooms of their new home were ready to be 'thrown open' for the first time for the admiration of a company of about two hundred 'other Fashionables' that included the Dukes of Wellington and Devonshire.[103] 'Rich' and 'massive' were the words that came most readily to mind in contemporary newspaper descriptions of the large quantities of Empire-style buhl furniture and 'superb articles in ormolu' that Lord George was reported to have spent 'upwards of thirty thousand pounds' in collecting 'on the Continent' in order to furnish the house in readiness for this occasion.[104] For the next five years (except possibly in 1823), Lady George's almost fortnightly routs, concerts and assemblies (*c.* 200–500 'fashionables') and Lord George's more intimate supper parties (up to one hundred 'friends') became a regular feature of the London season.[105] The main attraction of these events was undoubtedly the opportunity to promenade through the state rooms and admire the richness of their furnishings and the costliness of the numerous objects of decorative art on show. A detailed inventory and valuation of the contents of the house taken on 28 June 1834 (less than two months after Lord George's death) reveals, for instance, that the ball room was densely furnished with eight marble-topped 'ebony cabinets mounted in brass mouldings and brass ornaments'; a 'large circular rosewood table ... with marble top inlaid'; two 'large rosewood couches richly carved and gilt'; 27 chairs in various sizes; a 'grand pianoforte in mahogany case by Broadwood'; a 'large glass [i.e. mirror] with rich carved and gilt frame middlespoon plate 116 × 77' (valued at £176); three 'handsome 12 light chandeliers and Holland cases suspended from chains'; and four 'rich carved and gilt candelabra' in the four corners of the room.[106] The star attraction, however, was a 'large rich inlaid Italian marble top with massive gold framed stand underneath' valued at £210. This was almost certainly the colossal *pietra dura* circular table top inlaid with 101 varieties of agate, for which Ware made both a circular and a rectangular design, and which was reported as having attracted much interest when it first went on display in 1825 (Fig. 133).[107]

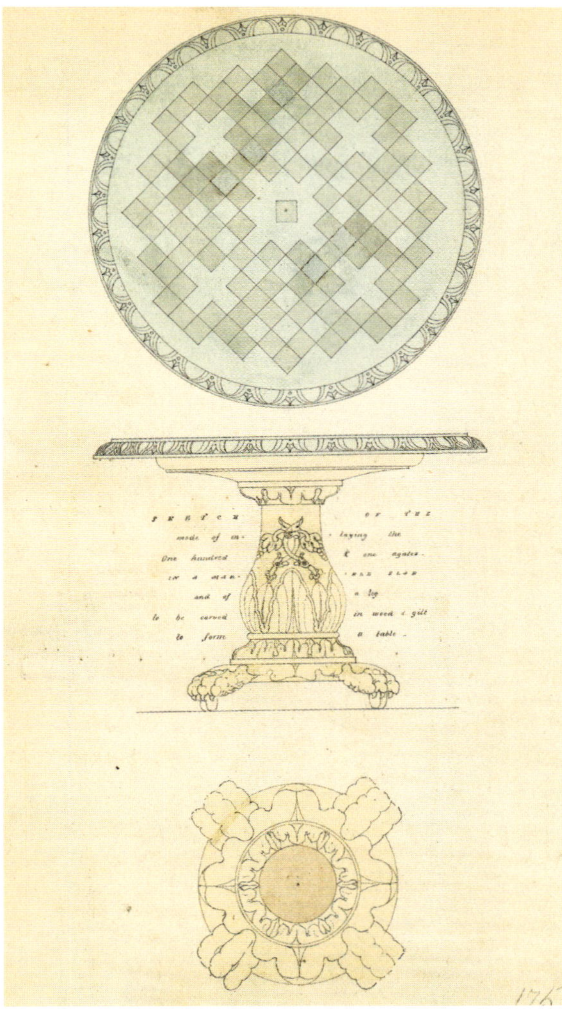

Fig. 133
Samuel Ware, Design for a round *pietra-dura* table top and gilt-metal stand, probably as executed, c. 1824.
Royal Academy of Arts, London, 06/5393

Fig. 134
John Hoppner, *Lord George Augustus Henry Cavendish*, c. 1800.
Given by Chesham branch of the Cavendish Family, 2015. Royal Academy of Arts, London, 16/1452

Fig. 135
John Gibson, *Sleeping Shepherd Boy*, 1818.
Royal Academy of Arts, London, 03/1919

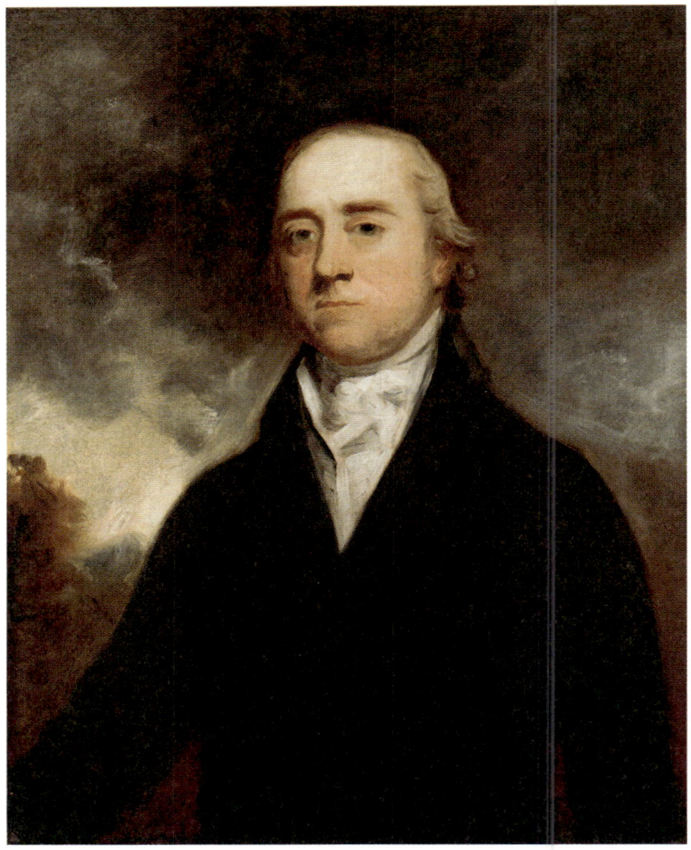

With one notable exception, there is little to suggest that Lord George showed more discernment in his selection of pictures and sculpture for the house. Although the painting by 'Sir Joshua Reynolds' recorded as hanging in the 'Ante Dining Room' may have been the fine whole-length of Lady Elizabeth Compton (now in the National Gallery of Art, Washington), there is no sign of John Hoppner's half-lengths of Lord and Lady George (both recently presented to the Royal Academy by the Chesham branch of the Cavendish family; Fig. 134), nor of Sir Thomas Lawrence's charming portrait of their three eldest children, George, Anne and William (see Fig. 79). In July 1834, the keeper of the National Gallery, William Seguier, valued a total of 106 mainly seventeenth-century Italian, Dutch and Flemish Old Master paintings hanging in six rooms (no pictures were recorded in the Saloon) at £4,020 but did not feel the need to distinguish any particular highlights in his list.[108] Seguier's valuation was of paintings only, so did not include the one identifiably important work of art in the house at the time – the marble of John Gibson's celebrated *Sleeping Shepherd Boy* which was by then on display in the Saloon. Lord George had commissioned this ten years earlier after seeing the original plaster model in the sculptor's studio in Rome (Fig. 135). Although this commission was of great importance in launching Gibson's career, in seeking out this particular artist on his trip to Rome in 1824 Lord George was following the example set by his nephew the Duke of Devonshire a good five years earlier.

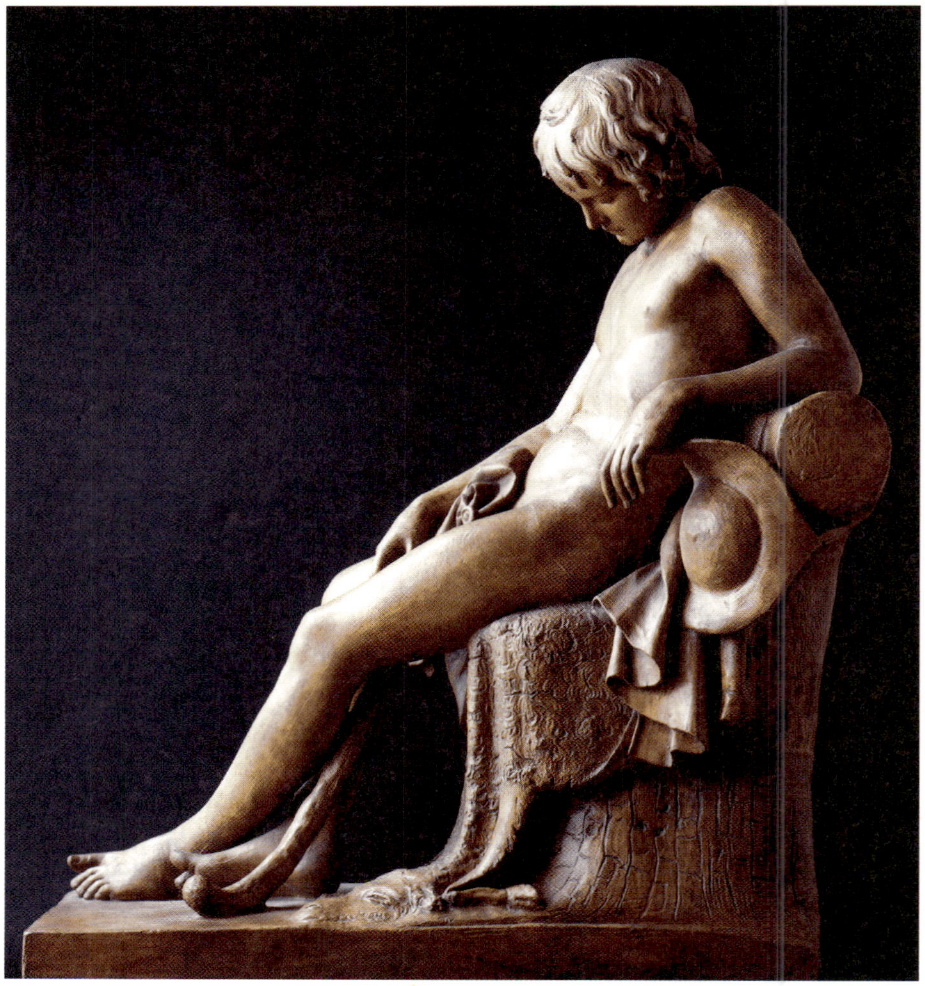

Ware concluded his 'general statement' of May 1818 by congratulating Lord George with typical tactfulness:

> In delivering this statement to your lordship, I should have been happy if the amount had not been so great; but I trust that your lordship will think that such works could not have been executed upon a better principle than that which has been adopted; & in relation to other works of the same character, that it will be found not a large sum; and to have expended it in such times among the labouring classes of society, and in preserving such a building will be a constant source of pleasing recollection to your lordship's mind and a cause of grateful feeling on the part of the public.

It is unlikely that Lord George Cavendish's elevation to the peerage in the coronation honours of 1831 as 1st Baron Cavendish of Keighley and 1st Earl of Burlington (2nd creation), would have been at all connected in the public's mind with his having restored 'the architectural beauties' of Soane's 'classical spot'; but there can be little doubt that it was in his own.

A FAIRYTALE ENDING to the story of the Cavendish family's custodianship of Burlington House would gloss its preservation for the nation as arising from public-spiritedness on the part of its last private owner and a moment of aberrant generosity on the part of the government. However, there is nothing in the surviving papers of the Hon. Charles Compton Cavendish, later 1st Baron Chesham, to suggest that he thought of preserving it for any reason other than his own comfort and pleasure in living there (Fig. 136). Cavendish had inherited a life tenancy largely because of the obduracy of his father's animosity towards his older brother Henry, and the fact that the Duke of Devonshire had turned down a six-month option to buy the property back for £200,000.[109] Not long after moving in from the east wing following his mother's death in April 1835, Cavendish commissioned C. N. Cumberlege, Ware's nephew and the successor to his architectural practice, to revive the latter's scheme from *c.* 1815 for a line of shops along the Piccadilly screen wall (see Fig. 127). Picking up from where this had left off, what is probably the earliest of Cumberlege's proposals – it is unsigned and undated – seems at first sight close enough to Ware's original idea to have been a variation made at the time.[110] There are, however, two key differences: firstly, instead of a row of single-storey shops in *front* of the existing screen wall, the proposal now is for the latter to be 'converted' into a glazed frontage for shops extending *behind* it, hence the absence of street entrances to the service areas behind the colonnade quadrants. And secondly, this design takes its cue from the entrance façade of the Burlington Arcade as executed, continuing its balustraded parapet at the same height and treating the Great Gate as an

Fig. 136
Thomas Barber the Elder, *Charles Compton Cavendish, 1st Lord Chesham*, c. 1815.
Hardwick Hall, Derbyshire, National Trust

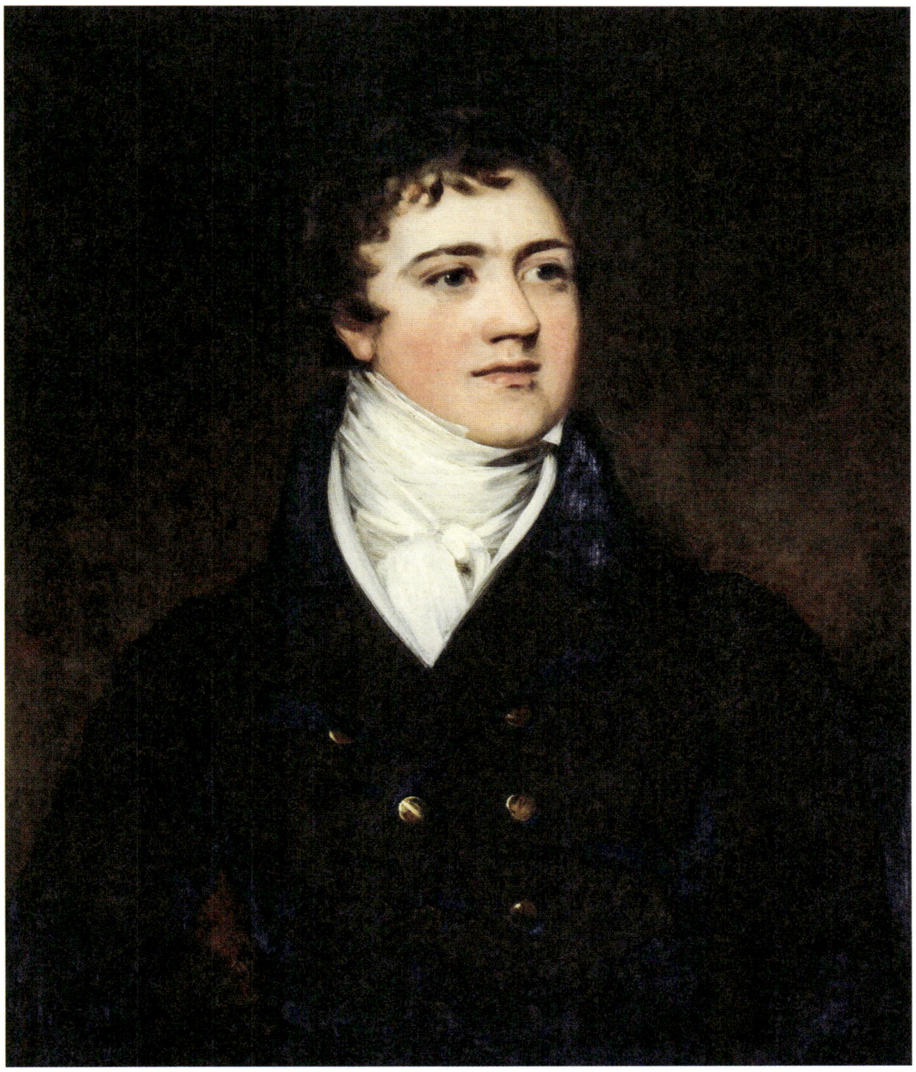

Fig. 137
Charles Nathaniel Cumberlege, Unexecuted design for shops, arcade and houses on Piccadilly: elevation with Burlington Arcade and two-storey shops, *c.* 1836.
Royal Academy of Arts, London, 07/715

Fig. 138
Charles Nathaniel Cumberlege, Unexecuted design for shops, arcade and houses on Piccadilly: elevation with Burlington Arcade, three-storey shops and Cavendish Arcade, *c.* 1836.
Royal Academy of Arts, London, 07/713

Fig. 139
Charles Nathaniel Cumberlege, Unexecuted design for shops, arcade and houses on Piccadilly, first scheme: ground plan retaining the colonnade, *c.* 1836.
Royal Academy of Arts, London, 07/710

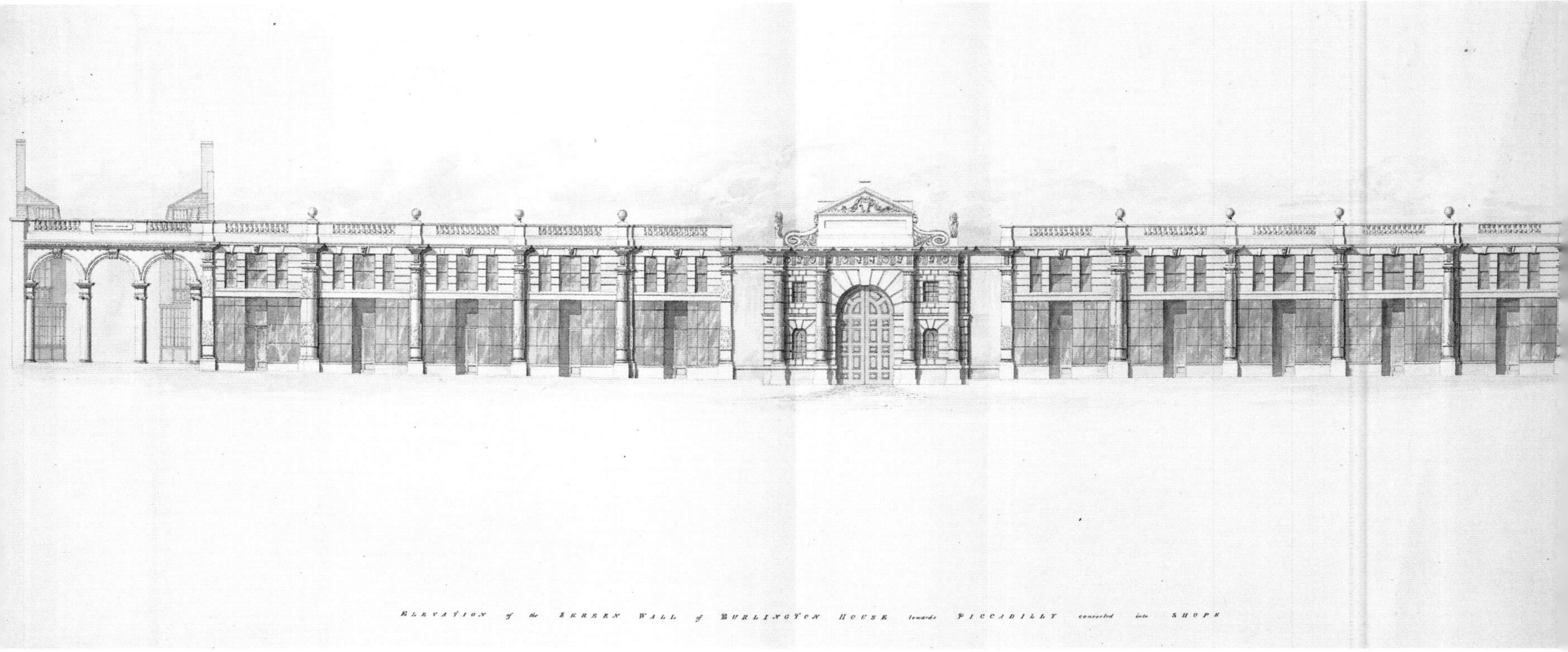

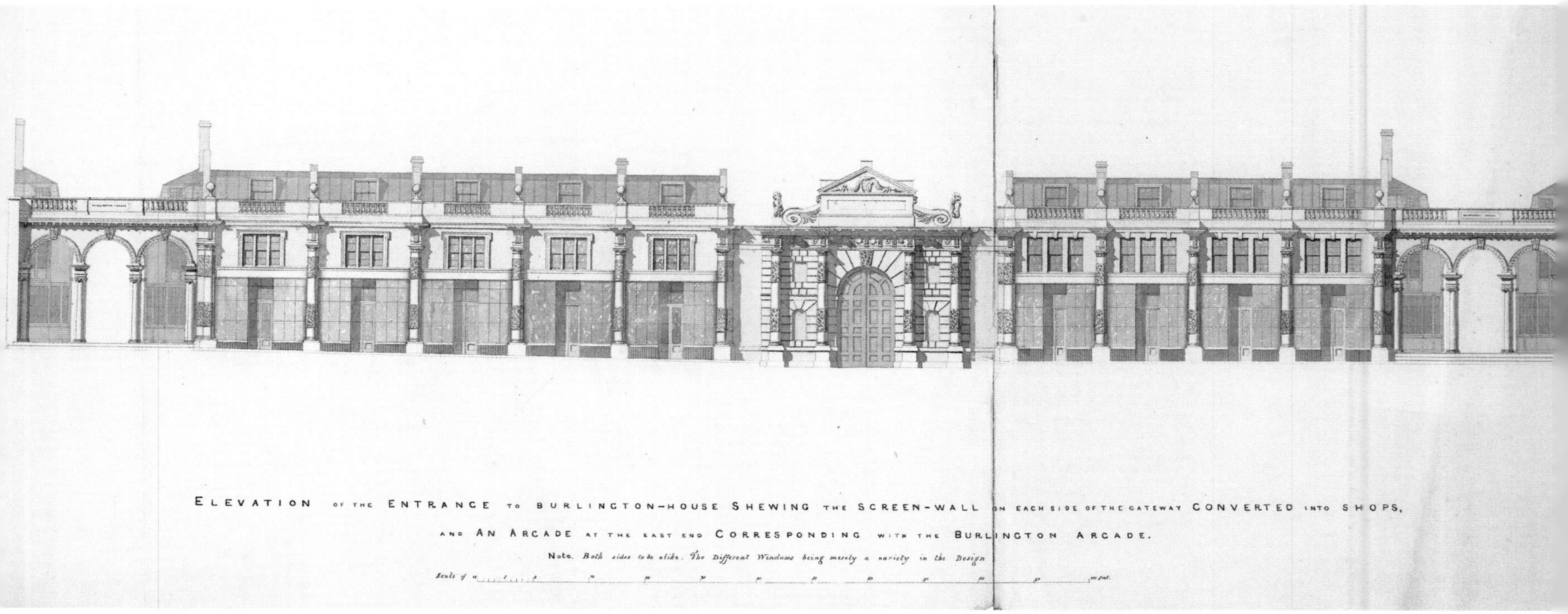

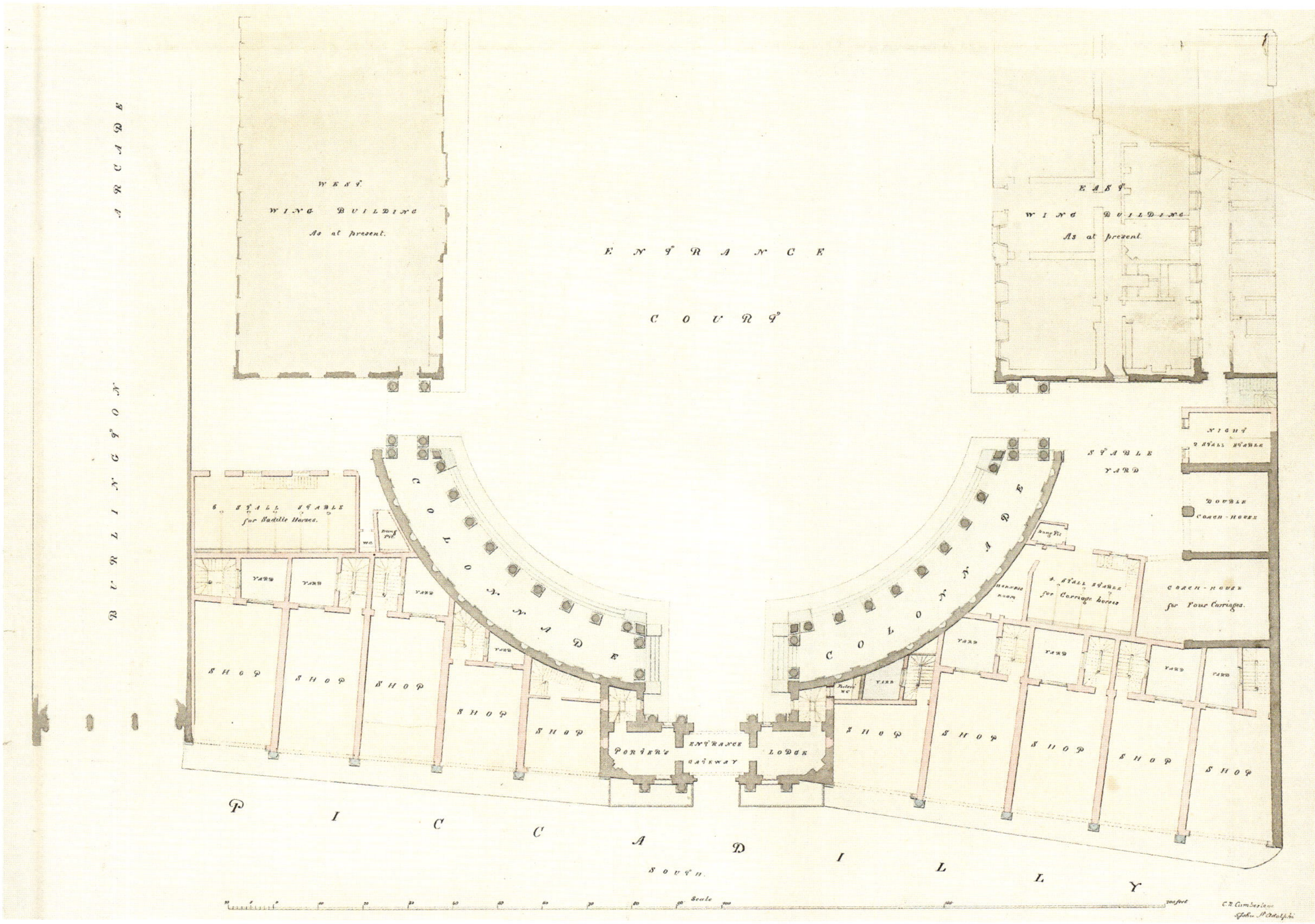

unrelated interruption in an otherwise uniform series of shop fronts. Cumberlege's alternative scheme – which is signed – shows this relationship reversed. Here the order of the Great Gate has become the keynote of the design and the Arcade entrance merely a coda (Figs 137, 139). There can be little doubt that this latter version was the starting point for Cumberlege's design for a corresponding 'Cavendish Arcade' at the eastern perimeter. By now, though, the so-called 'converted' screen that had been Campbell's wall has turned into a terrace of shops, the fronts of which can no longer be read as the boundary to the grounds of Burlington House (Fig. 138). The critical line crossed here is the raising of the shops' roofline to the height of the apex of the Great Gate's pediment in order to allow for an additional attic storey.

This airing of a long-shelved proposal to build shops along the Piccadilly front probably predates the fire that broke out on 26 March 1836 in the neighbouring Western Exchange bazaar, destroying the middle section of the Burlington Arcade. An earlier, pre-existing incentive to raise extra income from the Burlington House site at this time (the arcade was producing £3,214 annual rent in 1831)[111] is likely to have been the ongoing cost of rebuilding Latimers, Cavendish's Buckinghamshire seat, which had been gutted by fire in the early 1830s. It is clear also from a report prepared by Cumberlege in April 1836, that he saw his proposals for the Piccadilly frontage as part of an overall masterplan for 'appropriating to Building purposes certain portions of the ground belonging to Burlington House'.[112] This plan presented Cavendish with two options for the phased development not only of a second north–south arcade squeezed behind the east wing residence, but also for building a cul-de-sac of houses on the northern half of the garden, together with further shops on the Burlington Gardens frontage (Fig. 140). As Ware's nephew and successor, Cumberlege can hardly have been unaware of the irony of his recommendation that the proposed cul-de-sac should be centred on Burlington House so that, 'looking to the prospective appropriation of the entire site ... [it] may be continued hereafter to Piccadilly'.[113]

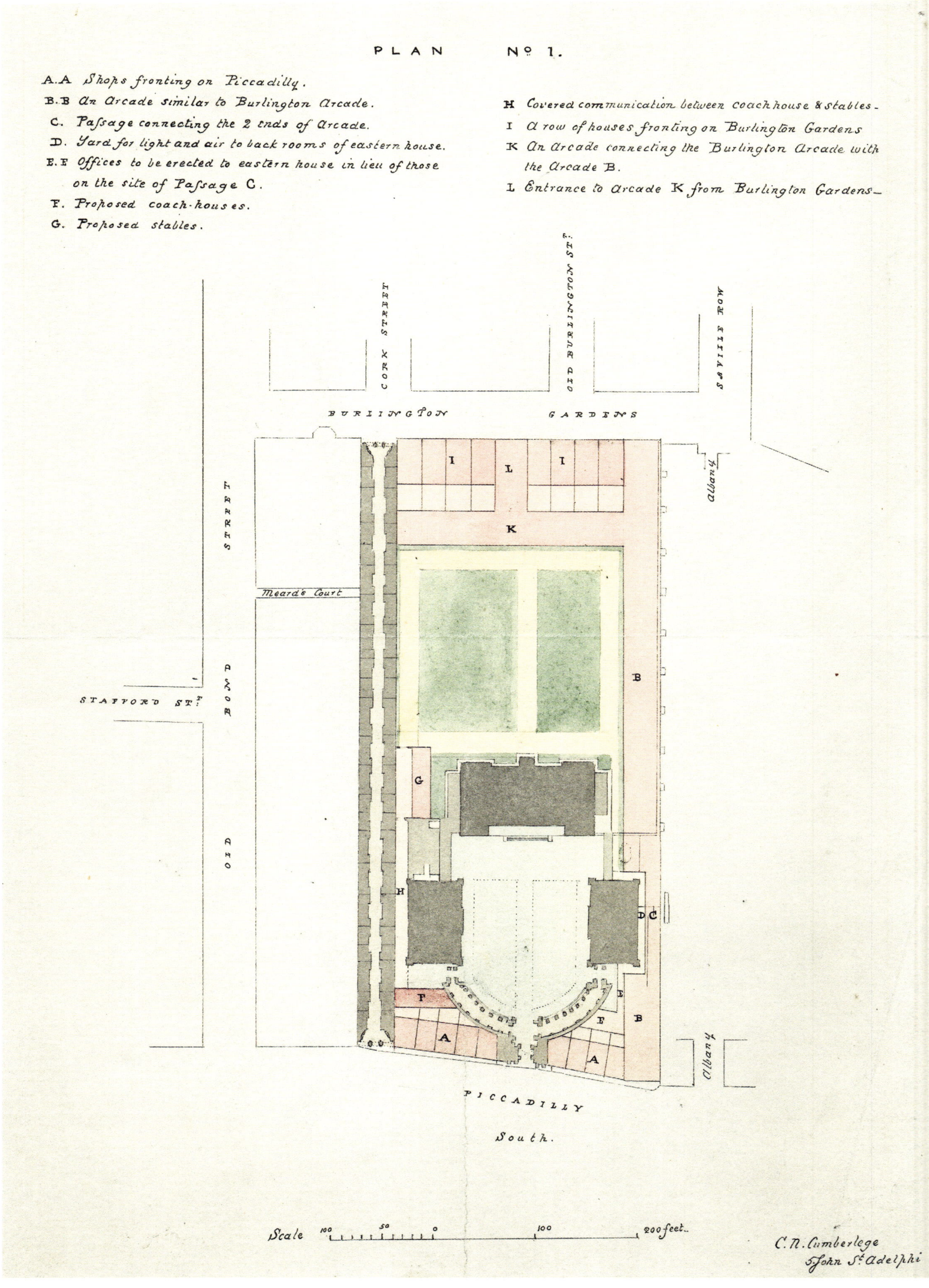
PLAN No. 1.
A.A Shops fronting on Piccadilly.
B.B An Arcade similar to Burlington Arcade.
C. Passage connecting the 2 ends of Arcade.
D. Yard for light and air to back rooms of eastern house.
E.E Offices to be erected to eastern house in lieu of those on the site of Passage C.
F. Proposed coach-houses.
G. Proposed stables.
H Covered communication between coach house & stables.
I A row of houses fronting on Burlington Gardens
K An Arcade connecting the Burlington Arcade with the Arcade B.
L Entrance to Arcade K from Burlington Gardens
CORK STREET
OLD BURLINGTON ST.
SAVILLE ROW
BURLINGTON GARDENS
OLD BOND STREET
STAFFORD ST.
Meard's Court
Albany
PICCADILLY
South.
Scale 100 50 0 100 200 feet.
C. R. Cumberlege
5 John St. Adelphi

Fig. 140
Charles Nathaniel Cumberlege, Unexecuted design for shops and houses on Piccadilly and Burlington Gardens and a second arcade, first scheme: block plan, c. 1836.
Royal Academy of Arts, London, 07/708

In May 1836 Cumberlege was also asked to design some slight alterations to the main house's ground-floor rooms facing the garden and, probably at around the same time, to the kitchen block in the west wing. The idea of switching the north drawing room from the east to the west side of house arose no doubt because by then Cavendish's elder sister Anne and her husband Lord Charles Fitzroy must have moved out of the main house into the east wing building, leaving her younger spinster sister Caroline a larger suite of private rooms than she needed. However, since there was no real need for such tinkering it is quite likely the proposed removal and insertion of partition walls was never carried out. The same was probably true of an undated proposal for a suspended gallery within the double-height main kitchen in the west wing, which seems to have been devised to stop the maidservants traipsing through the kitchen and annoying the cook. One suspects both these proposals gathered dust in Cumberlege's office, along with the time-bomb of his masterplan.[114]

Ten years later an unidentified surveyor sketched out a plan of the whole Burlington House site. This shows the areas behind the colonnade cleared of existing buildings (i.e. the stables, coach-houses and Evidence Room) and two-thirds of the garden cordoned off into a building plot divided down the centre by a road leading south off Burlington Gardens.[115] Probably associated with this site-plan is an undated ground-plan of the western colonnade area laid out into roughly equal building plots, as well as a diagrammatic block-plan dated January 1847 for laying out two cross streets off Burlington Gardens.[116] These three drawings are probably connected with a draft *aide-memoire* in Cavendish's hand querying what rent might be obtained 'if I added an additional Room to every shop in the Arcade on the B. H. side'; what he might 'get for letting for building on the Piccadilly front up to the end of the Wings'; and what the 'Garden [would] be worth for building, with strip taken off for the Arcade'. In the same note he identifies two major obstacles to his plans, namely whether he and his son William would be able to 'raise money on any of my estates to be disposed of for the improvement of the Estate' and whether 'the Trustees [would] be authorized to raise money on the Burlington House Estate in order to add to the Arcade …'.[117] Since Cavendish's title to Burlington House was that of a life tenant, any loans for its 'improvement' would have had to have been raised in the name of the trustees appointed under the terms of his father's will for the settlement of the estate.

Although Cavendish's trustees, the 5th Earl Fitzwilliam and 20th Baron Dacre, were to play an important part in the eventual sale of the house, it is not clear in the run-up to that decision how aware they may have been of his attempts to find a way of making it more profitable. Certainly, they do not seem to have objected when in 1849 he applied for and obtained a private Act of Parliament 'for removing doubts relative to the powers of granting building leases' contained in his father's will.[118] These 'doubts' had arisen over whether the specific power the will gave for granting and renewing leases in the Arcade was applicable to other parts of the Burlington House site; or whether, on the contrary, the testator's general exclusion of this power in relation to all 'Capital messuages or mansion houses … now used as Family residences' was intended to prevent any such application. As Ware had probably foreseen, it was a question that depended on whether or not the Arcade was still considered part of Burlington House. If it had been separately owned, it would have been less likely to have become grounds for an interpretation of Lord George's will that opened the door to similar commercial development of other parts of the site.

Probably on the strength of having obtained this Act, Cavendish commissioned an anonymous architect (probably Cumberlege) to design seven five-storey houses with shops on Piccadilly to the full height and depth of those already built to either side and opposite Burlington House (Fig. 141). The proposal presented the alternative of demolishing and rebuilding the colonnade and porters' lodges to provide plots of a uniform depth, or retaining the quadrants and lodges in their existing form and adjusting the size of the plots as necessary (Figs 143, 145). At the same time, the 1836 plan to build on the garden was similarly reactivated in the form of a design for twelve houses on three sides of a square opening off Burlington Gardens, and a further six with shops along the existing

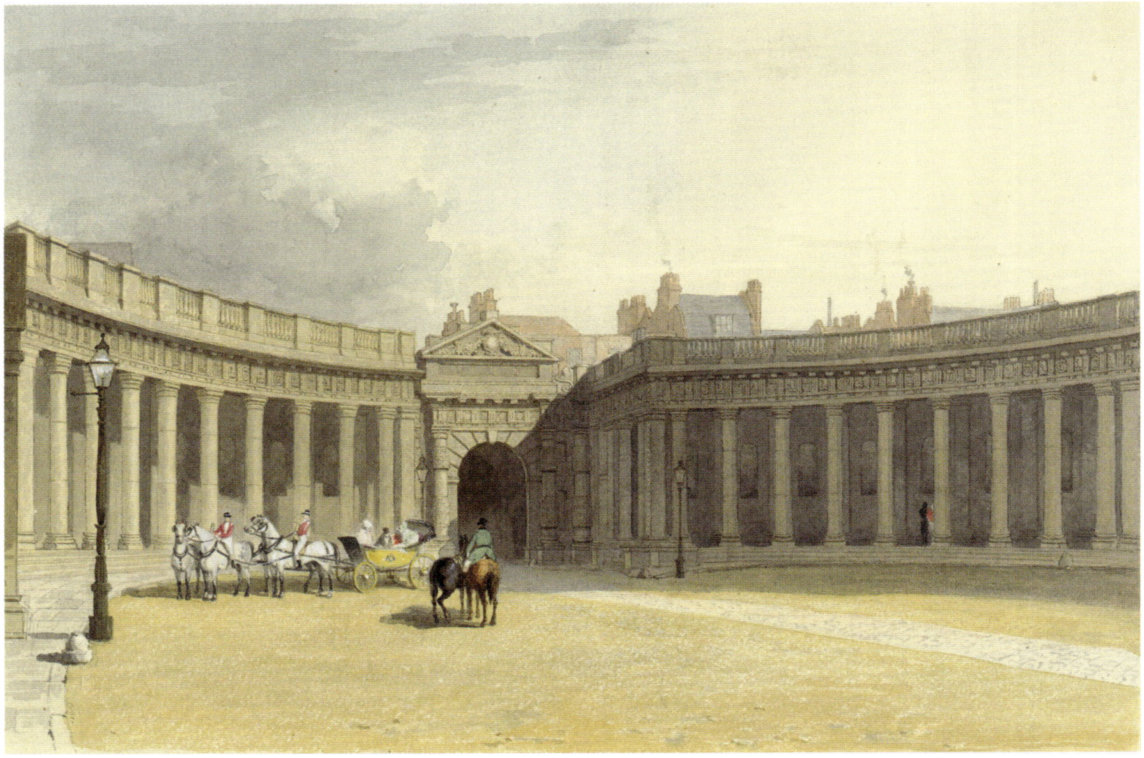

Fig. 141
John Wykeham Archer, *Colonnade, Burlington House, Piccadilly* (with the Great Gate, viewed from the terrace of Burlington House), 1850.
British Museum, London, 1874,0314.326

Fig. 142
Uxbridge House (Burlington Gardens frontage), 1850.
London Metropolitan Archives (City of London)

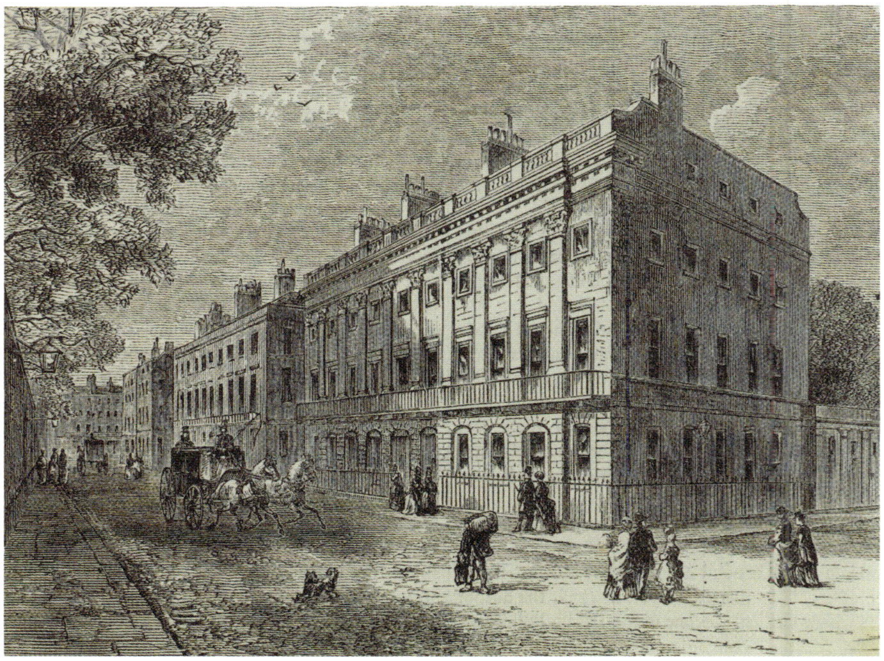

thoroughfare. As a conciliatory gesture in response to an idea suggested in June 1849 by Henry, his disgruntled elder brother (who felt Charles should have given up Burlington House long ago), the proposed square now included a garden directly opposite the latter's house at No. 34 Old Burlington Street.[119] Had this garden square been built, it might have saved some of the venerable trees leaning over the boundary wall of Burlington House that Henry could see from his drawing room window (Fig. 142).

To judge from the admittedly incomplete set of drawings that have survived relating to these schemes, Cavendish's only concern was to assess how much they would impinge upon his view from the windows of Burlington House (Fig. 143). In drawing 'No. 5' for instance, showing the elevation of the courtyard looking west, a gentleman in a frock coat stands on the balustrade of the central first-floor window of the south front. His line of sight is traced in blue dashes to just clear of a column representing the height of the parapet of a proposed additional two-storey extension at the rear of the shops on Piccadilly (Fig. 144). Seen from this perspective, Cavendish's proposed sacrifice of the colonnade and half his garden was that of a captain who has decided to go down with his ship.

It may well have been out of dismay at the threat of such a sacrifice that Charles Mayhew, the district surveyor of St James's parish, wrote to the editor of *The Builder* in April 1851:

> I have heard from good authority that the noble proprietors of Burlington-House, Piccadilly, would dispose of their property, in which, bye-the-bye, I am in no way interested; but I do not know a more eligible spot in the metropolis than that for a National Gallery, and the Government ought to be ashamed of itself, if it let the opportunity of purchasing slip: it has a frontage of 287 feet by a depth of 600 feet, and the present mansion might be applied for the accommodation of the Royal Academy, or any other purpose which the Government might choose to dedicate to art.[120]

Fig. 143
Charles Nathaniel Cumberlege (attrib.), Unexecuted design for houses with shops on Piccadilly: elevation looking south from Burlington House, *c.* 1850.
Royal Academy of Arts, London, 07/731

Fig. 144
Charles Nathaniel Cumberlege (attrib.), Unexecuted design for houses with shops on Piccadilly: elevation looking west (sightline from Burlington House), *c.* 1850.
Royal Academy of Arts, London, 07/732

As the architect-surveyor with legal authority for ensuring compliance with building regulations throughout the parish, Mayhew was fully aware both of the historical resonance of Burlington House as a potential new 'Home for the Arts and Sciences in the Metropolis' and of the threat of destruction it now faced:

> I am sure the noble Earl, the amateur architect and its founder, would right gladly bring this matter to bear if he could only rise from his grave and see how appropriate it would be for such a purpose, and how little appropriate it is now for a private residence, owing to the great alteration which has taken place in the surrounding property.

Mayhew concluded his letter with the hope that his ideas might 'rouse the British lion to plead for art'. Although the Royal Commission that was currently considering 'the question of a site for a new National Gallery' was to recommend a more bucolic location in Kensington Gardens, Mayhew's suggested survival plan for Burlington House was to prove extraordinarily prescient.[121]

At the same time, however, Mayhew's letter must have also encouraged prospective developers to beat a path to Cavendish's door, in the hope that he might prefer to strike a quick bargain rather than risk the delay and red-tape inevitable in any negotiations with the government. One such speculator was the builder George Tarlington, who in February 1853 offered £4,700 per annum for a 99-year lease, with an option 'to redeem any time within 3 years at 30 years' purchase' (i.e. £141,000).[122] On further investigation, Cavendish's agent John Simpson discovered that Tarlington was 'stuck fast in some buildings at Holborn' and had 'not money enough to go on with the building', so he was given short shrift.[123] Fortunately,

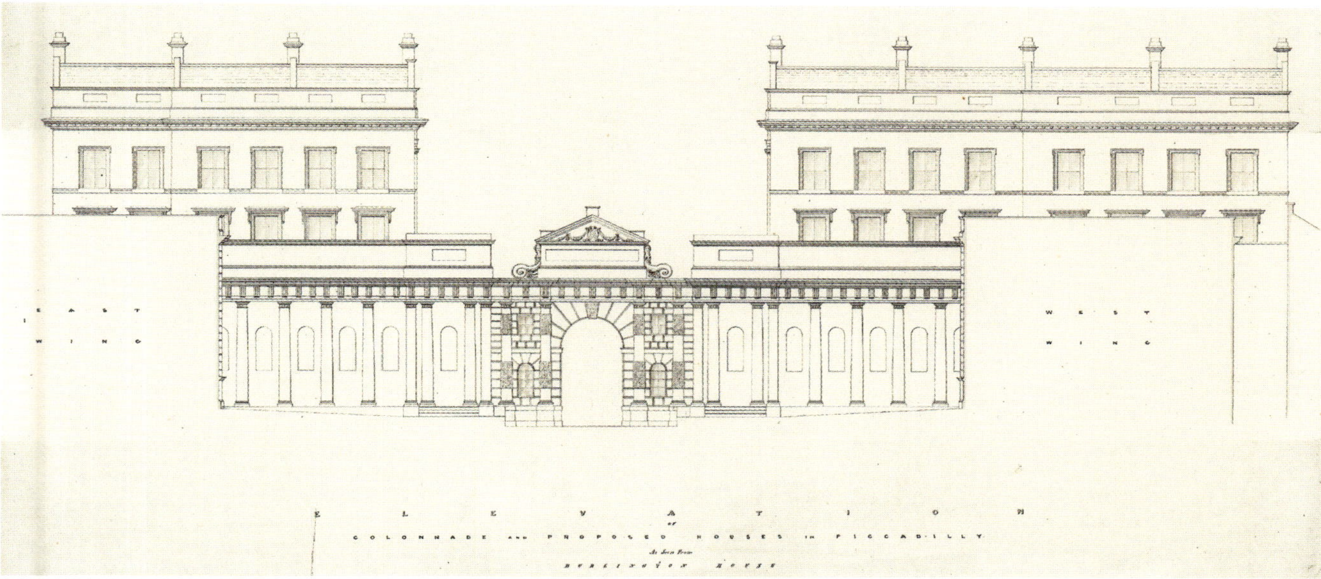

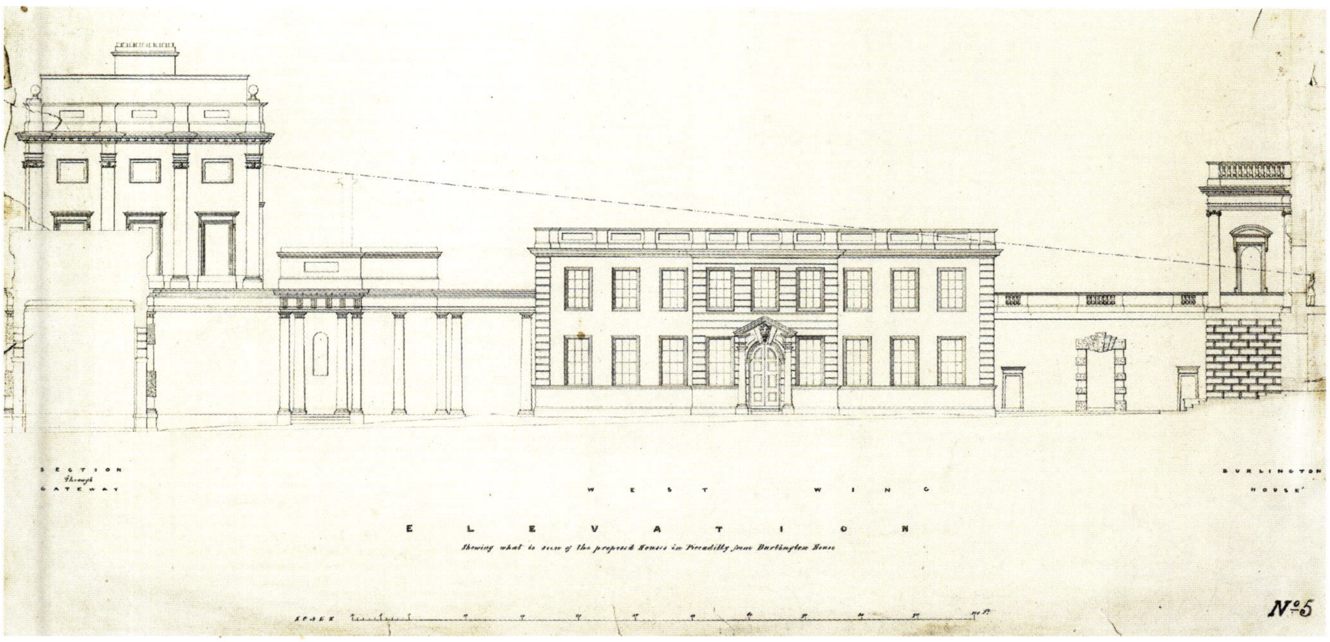

a more promising if somewhat mysterious approach had come earlier in 1852, via the highly respected architect Philip Hardwick. As Cavendish was later to recall, Hardwick told him 'quite in confidence, that his employers wanted the place, that if a fair price were put upon it an immediate offer wd be made but till that was done he could not stir'. Pressed to state what might be thought a 'fair price', Hardwick had 'in conversation intimated ... first that 150,000 would be given & subsequently 155,000 – but that no price was then put on the property.'[124]

In an attempt to establish what the property's full market value might be, in February or early March 1853 Cavendish commissioned two London-based architects, Charles Lee and C. J. Richardson, to lay out a theoretical Burlington House 'estate' in the most profitable manner possible. Lee came up with four variations of the standard formula of residential streets, shops on Piccadilly and Burlington Gardens, and the now obligatory second arcade (Fig. 146). Richardson, on the other hand, had the more original idea of a whole series of colonnaded shopping malls along the lines of the Galerie d'Orléans at the Palais Royal in Paris (Fig. 147). The valuation reports that would have accompanied these ideal scenarios have not been traced but they must have influenced Cavendish's fateful decision to turn down Hardwick's offer of £155,000 that summer. Instead he wrote to Simpson on 31 July 1853 instructing him 'to take preliminary steps for Auctioning', adding with characteristic prevarication, 'the later the better in my mind'.[125] Although he began his letter by claiming to 'have not entirely made up my mind' and ended it 'P.S. I have nearly made up my mind', for reasons no doubt connected with his current financial situation, a tipping point had been reached where in reality he had no choice but to consent 'to part with B. H.' He confessed to Simpson that 'a great obstacle' to making up his mind 'has been & still remains ... dread [of] having any further disturbance' with the 'General' – his brother Henry – who

Fig. 145
Charles Nathaniel Cumberlege (attrib.), Unexecuted design for houses with shops on Piccadilly: ground plan, *c.* 1850.
Royal Academy of Arts, London, 07/729

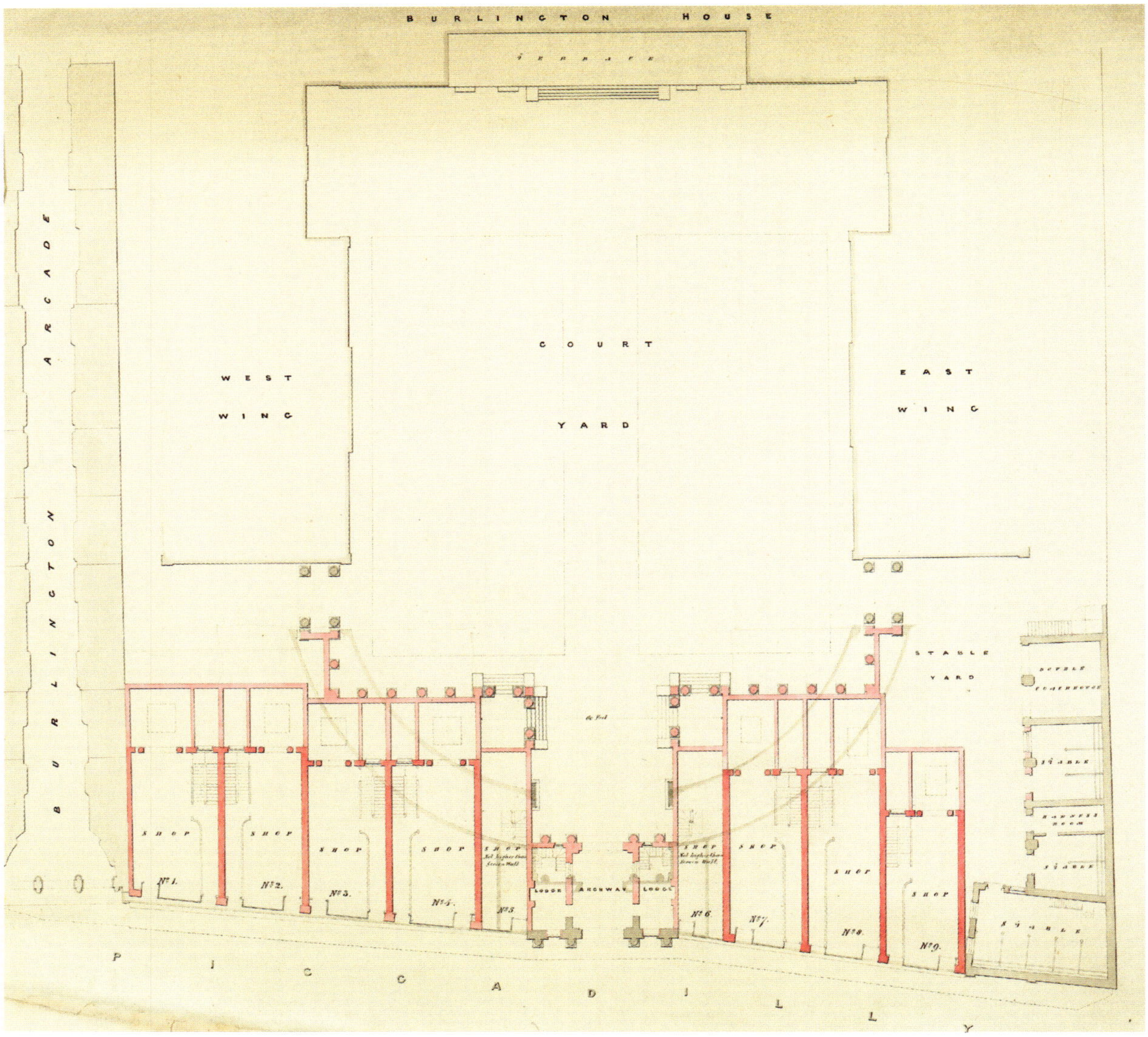

Fig. 146
Charles Lee, Block plan for developing the Burlington House Estate, fourth scheme, 17 March 1853.
Royal Academy of Arts, London, 07/836

had kicked up a fuss over what he believed would be the damaging effect of the sale of the Burlington House site on the market value of his own house in Old Burlington Street. A further obstacle in Cavendish's mind was

> the adoration I have for the comfort and beauty of the place, the Court is a great feature, but I care little for that in comparison with the real enjoyment & comfort of the House.

According to an editorial in the *Illustrated London News*, the announcement of the forthcoming sale of Burlington House 'during the next month or in the early part of the approaching year' (*The Times*, 9 November 1853), spelt its certain doom:

> The only attractive feature in Piccadilly is about to be removed. Who has not seen the advertisement announcing the sale of Burlington House? Yes – one of the finest buildings in London, is doomed to destruction. The temptation is too great – money is about to demolish the best example of the genius and munificence of the Earl to whom Pope addressed his noble epistle on 'Taste' ... As much, we hear, as £180,000 have been refused for Burlington House, and as much as £250,000 are asked. Several amphitheatre managers are looking longingly at the site, and with their hands in their pockets, but the sum is too large.[126]

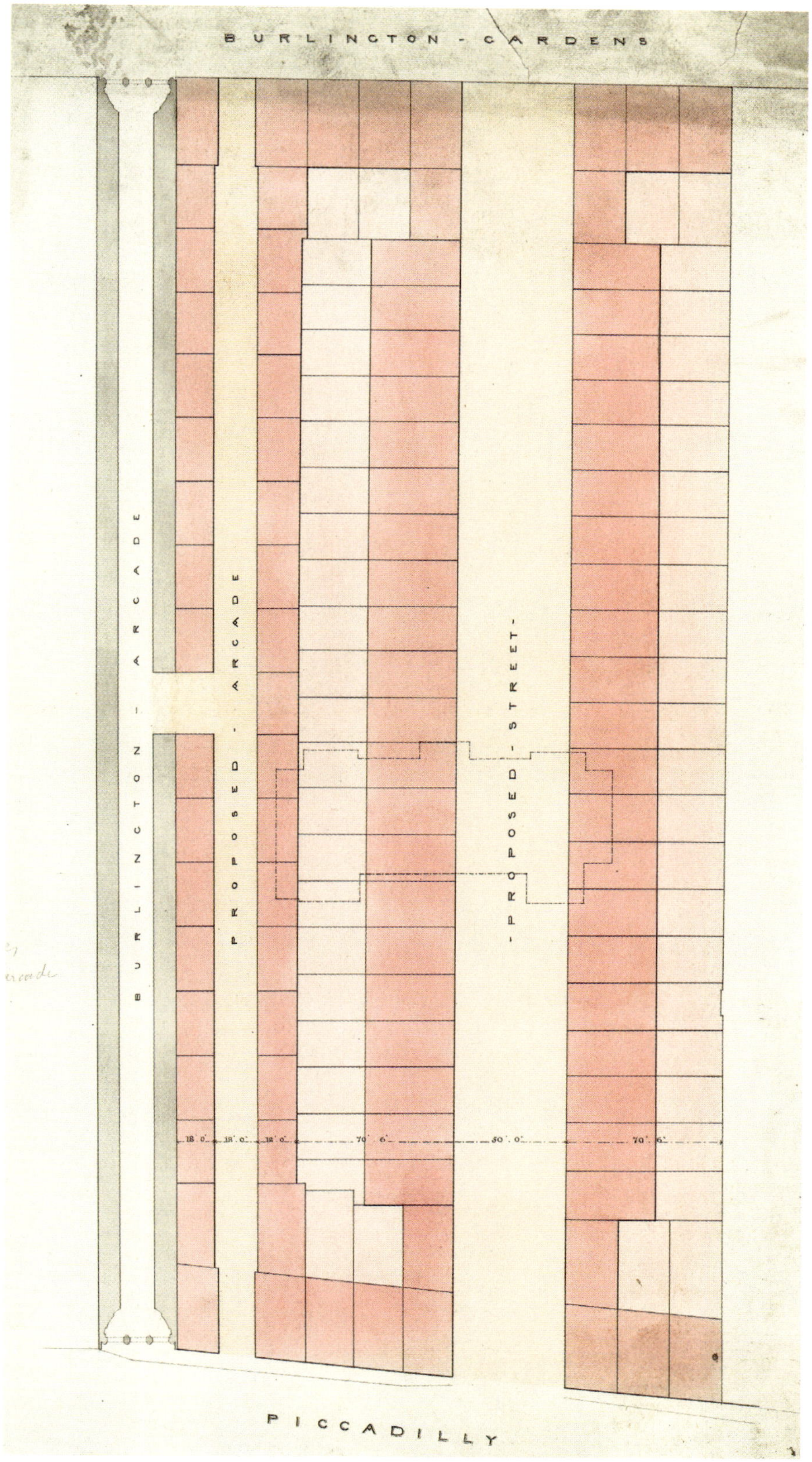

By 18 November, Simpson was able to report to Lord Dacre that there had been 'a great many enquiries here from Builders of great standing & character - & from Speculators – and from some of the most wealthy of our London Merchants'; and also, 'that H.M. Government entertain some idea of being possessed of the property.'[127] Keen to emphasise the exceptional commercial potential of the site, the auctioneers Farebrother, Clark & Lye hired Richardson to develop his 'Palais Royal' scheme for a pre-sale publicity 'brochure' that must rank among the most elaborate of its kind ever produced. A portfolio of eight imperial-sized lithographs, this contained not only a detailed site plan and elevations of the house and courtyard buildings in their present state, but Richardson's fully worked-up proposal ready for immediate execution, complete with a seductive bird's-eye view of the kind that gave mid-nineteenth-century architectural

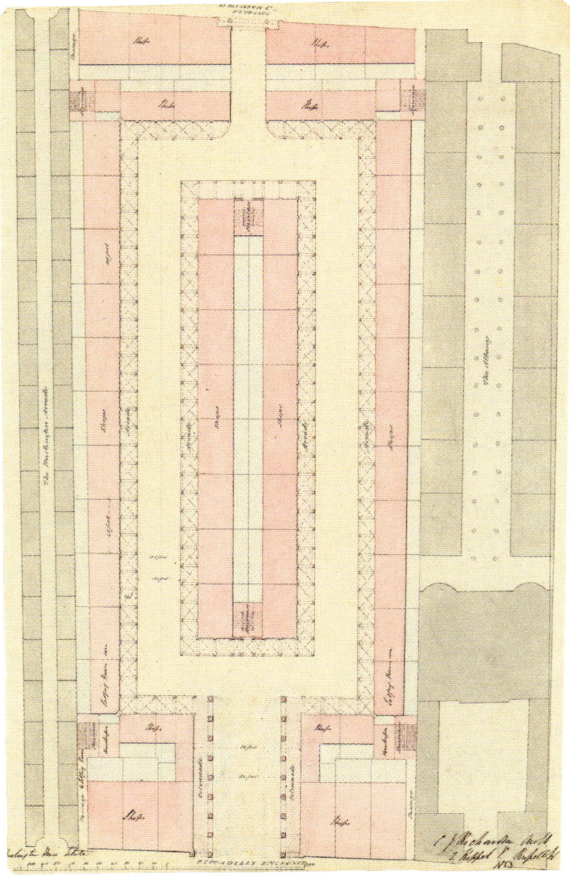

perspectives a bad name with leaders of the profession (Figs 148, 149). What Soane, Richardson's former master and mentor, would have thought of it one hardly dares to imagine.

Despite Lord Dacre's sanguine expectations of saleroom competition pushing the price to beyond £200,000, and Cavendish as a result now feeling 'it is almost a pity to delay the sale of B. H. to Feby', Simpson feared the danger of the house publicly failing to reach its reserve price and of potential future purchasers being put off.[128] By mid-December, with the Duke of Hamilton having turned down an option to purchase by private treaty for £160,000, Baron Lionel de Rothschild's reported interest having proved unfounded, and the government having offered only £140,000, Cavendish's other trustee, Earl Fitzwilliam, also got seriously cold feet over the risks of a public auction.[129] Bowing to this combined pressure and with Lord Dacre now sharing the same view, Cavendish cancelled the sale.[130] This left two offers on the table: Hardwick's £155,000 and the government's £140,000. So why did the lower offer win? Because unbeknownst to anyone, including Cavendish, Hardwick's mystery client was the Royal Academy of Arts.

Fig. 149
Charles James Richardson, Design for developing the Burlington House Estate: elevation and plans, 1853.
Royal Academy of Arts, London, 07/764

Fig. 147
Charles James Richardson, Block plan for developing the Burlington House Estate, 1853.
Royal Academy of Arts, London, 07/761

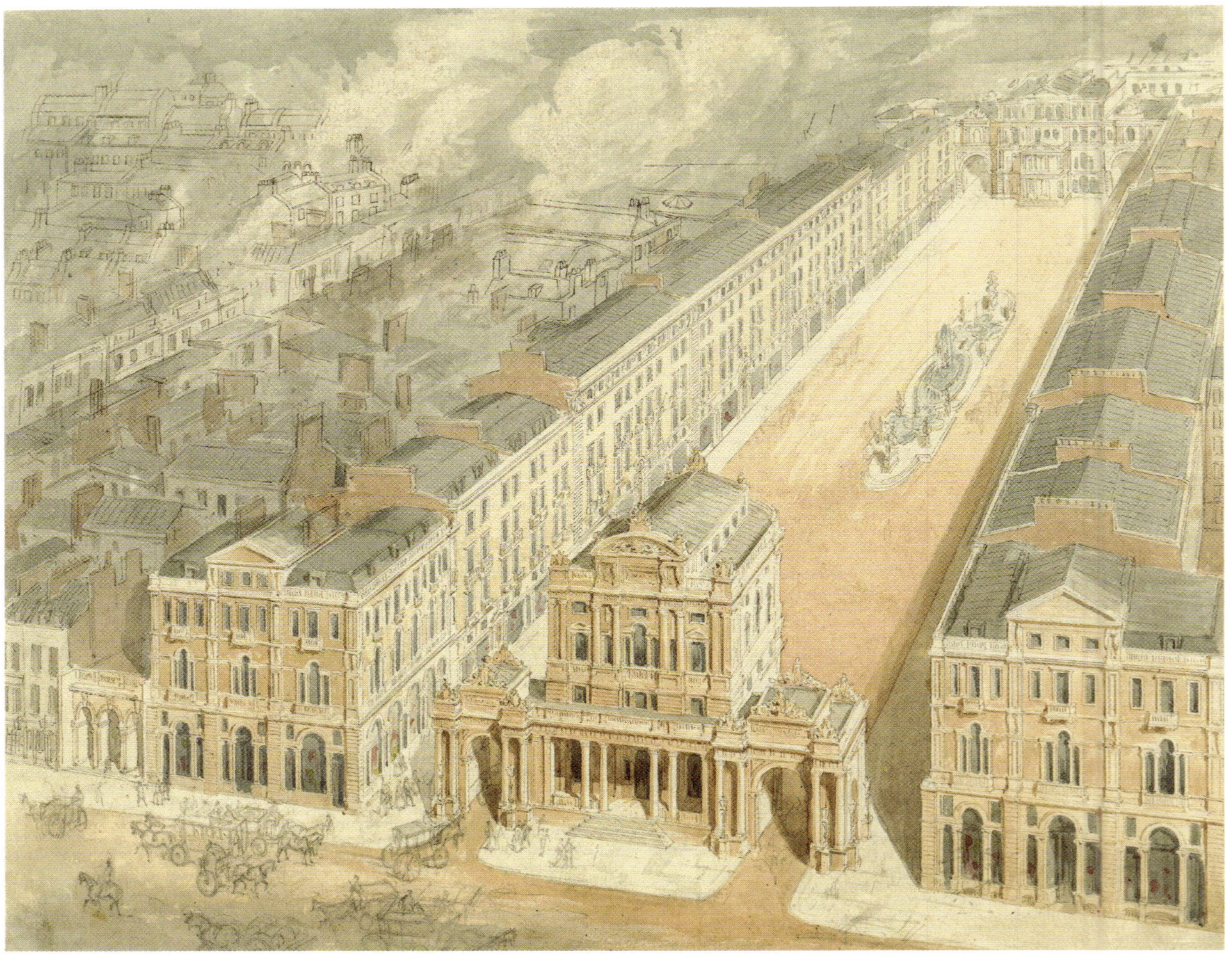

Fig. 148
Charles James Richardson, Design for developing the Burlington House Estate as London's 'Palais Royal': bird's-eye perspective, 1853.
Royal Academy of Arts, London, 07/766

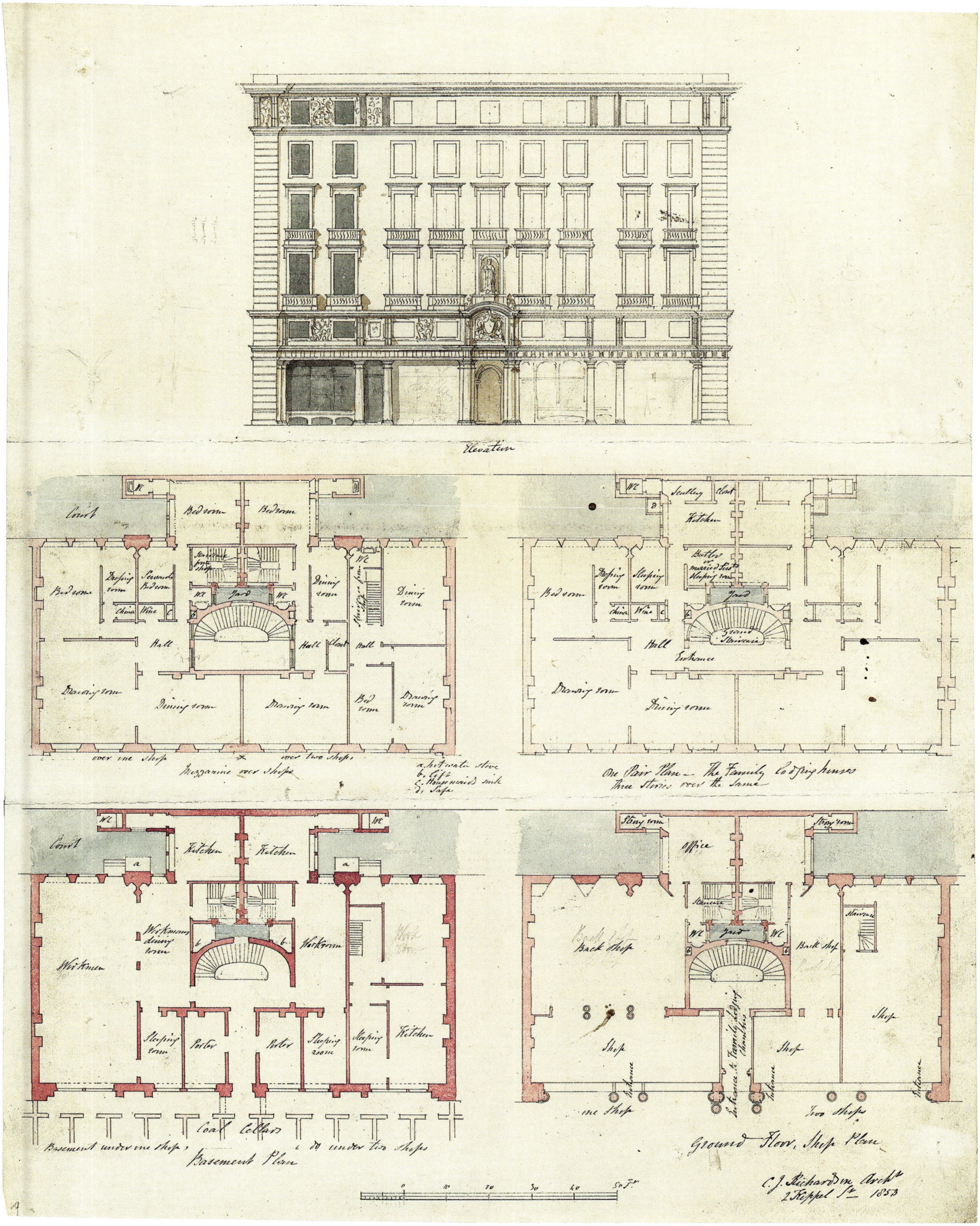
Elevation
Mezzanine over Shops
One Pair Plan – The Family Lodging houses
Three Stories over the Same
Basement Plan
Ground Floor, Shop Plan
C. J. Richardson Archt
2 Keppel St 1853

IV

HER MAJESTY'S OFFICE OF WORKS

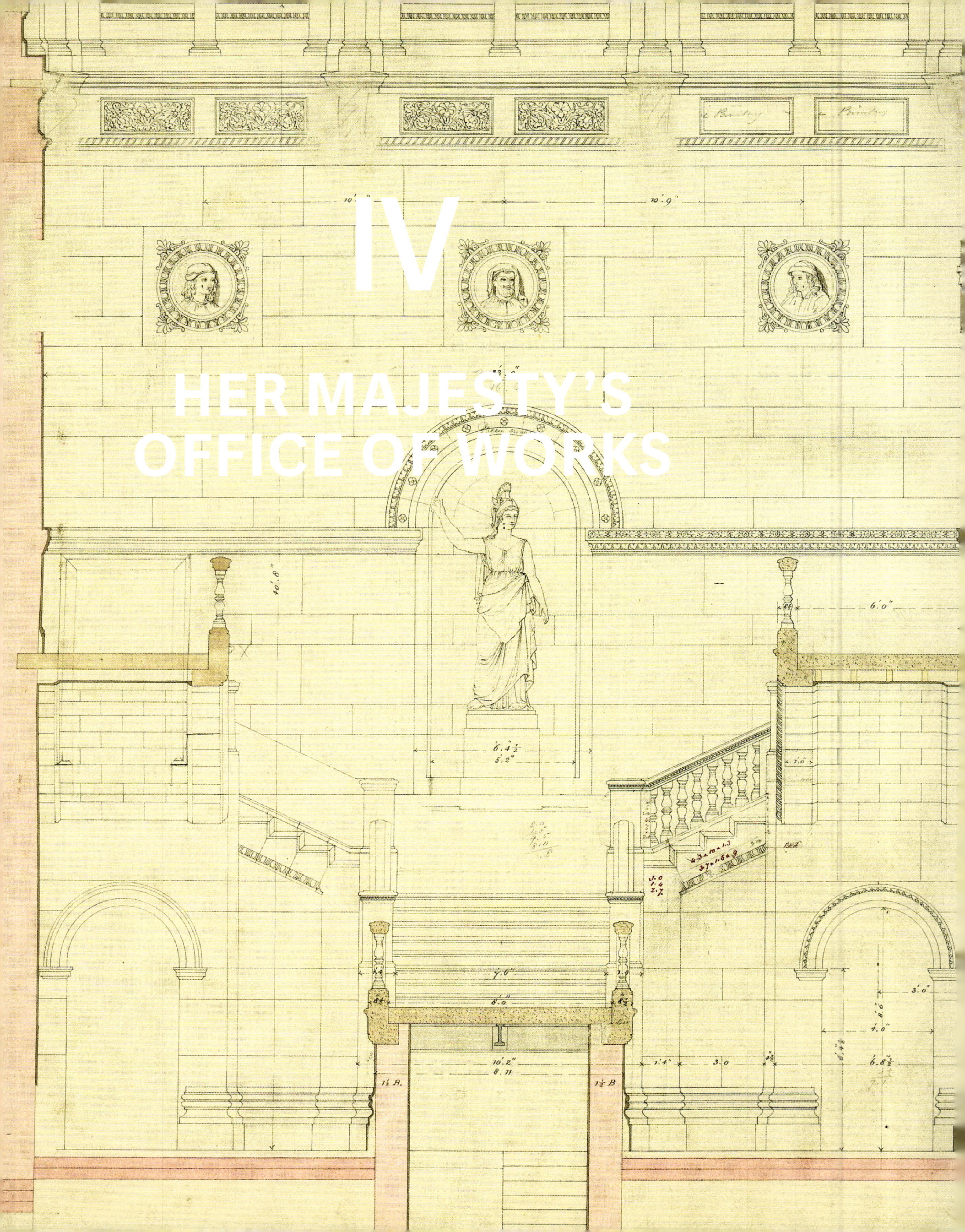

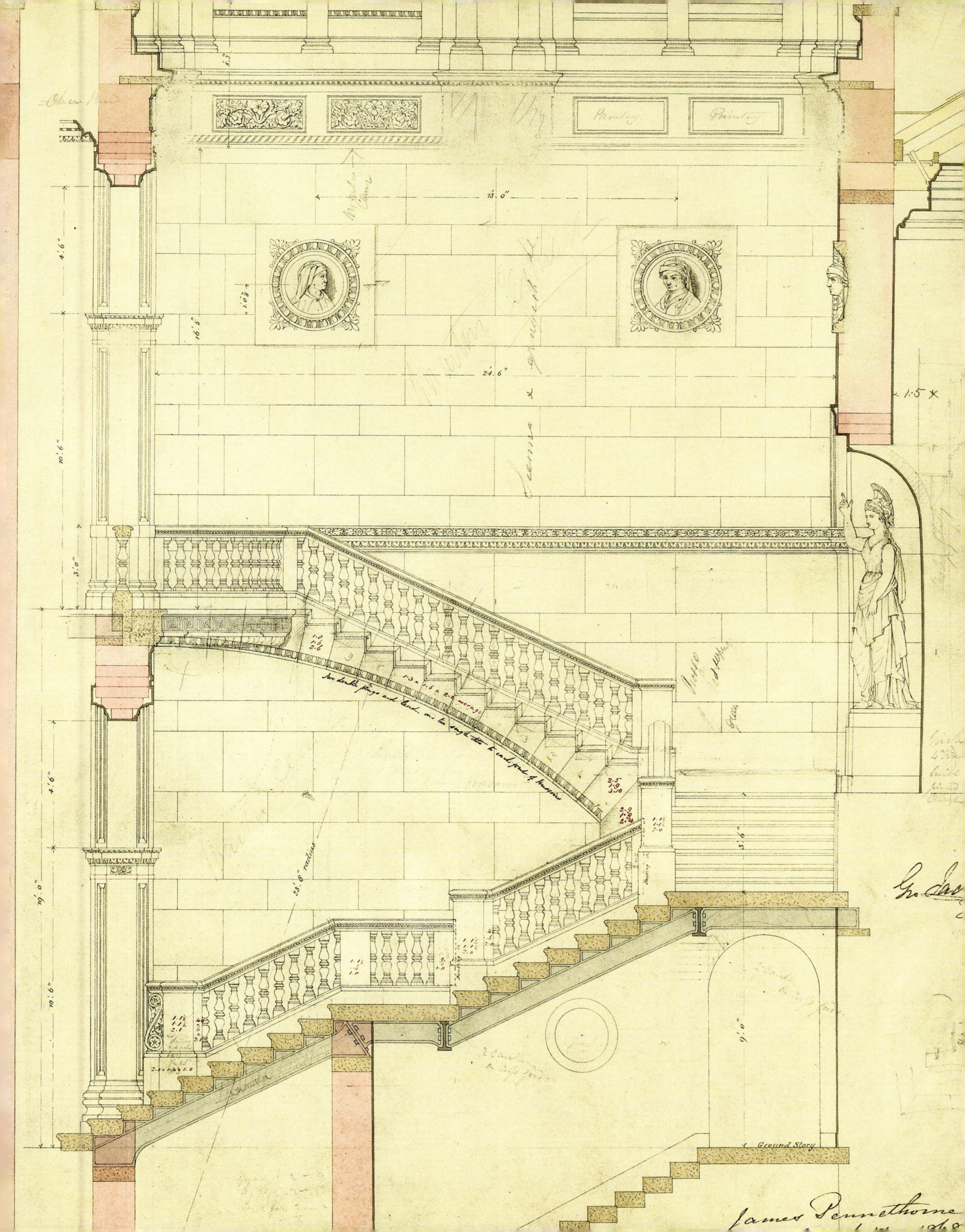

Painting
Painting
13.6"
24.6"
4.6"
10.6"
3.0"
4.6"
9.0"
10.6"
1.5
9.0"
Ground Story
James Pennethorne

'As to Burlington House . . . we could hardly go wrong in procuring such a site as this.'
W. E. GLADSTONE, 1 November 1853

FAR FROM GUARANTEEING ITS PRESERVATION, the government's purchase of Burlington House for the nation in March 1854 rendered its future more uncertain than ever. Less than a month after the sale was agreed *The Builder* commented, somewhat ungraciously, 'The misfortune is, that however good the purpose may be, government officials and commissioners always move so slowly that the present generation are not quite certain of benefiting by the acquisition' (Fig. 150).[1] Not even this cynic could have imagined that it would be twenty years before Burlington House was properly adapted to its new purpose; that its effective owner – the First Commissioner of Her Majesty's Office of Works – would change nine times during this period; and that what started out as an easy way to free up office space in another government building would become hopelessly entangled in two of the longest-running and most heated 'art questions' of the Victorian era, namely whether and where to resite the National Gallery. More than anything else it was the fallout from this intractable issue that was to frustrate successive governments' attempts to settle the future of Burlington House.

It was during his brilliant first term as Chancellor of the Exchequer in Lord Aberdeen's coalition government that William Ewart Gladstone took the lead in persuading his fellow ministers that 'we could hardly go wrong in procuring such a site' as Burlington House.[2] Writing to Lord John Russell in November 1853, he was prepared to accept that 'our course may in some degree depend on what the Cabinet may decide with respect to the National Gallery'. However, by the time the sale was agreed in the spring of the following year, he had no doubt that the house and grounds would be best used to meet a variety of small-scale accommodation needs rather than given over to a single space-hungry national institution.

Since this essentially pragmatic approach to the site was to characterise the government's attitude to its use over the next 150 years, it is worth going back to the Treasury Minute of 24 March 1854 where Gladstone's thoughts for its future were first embodied:

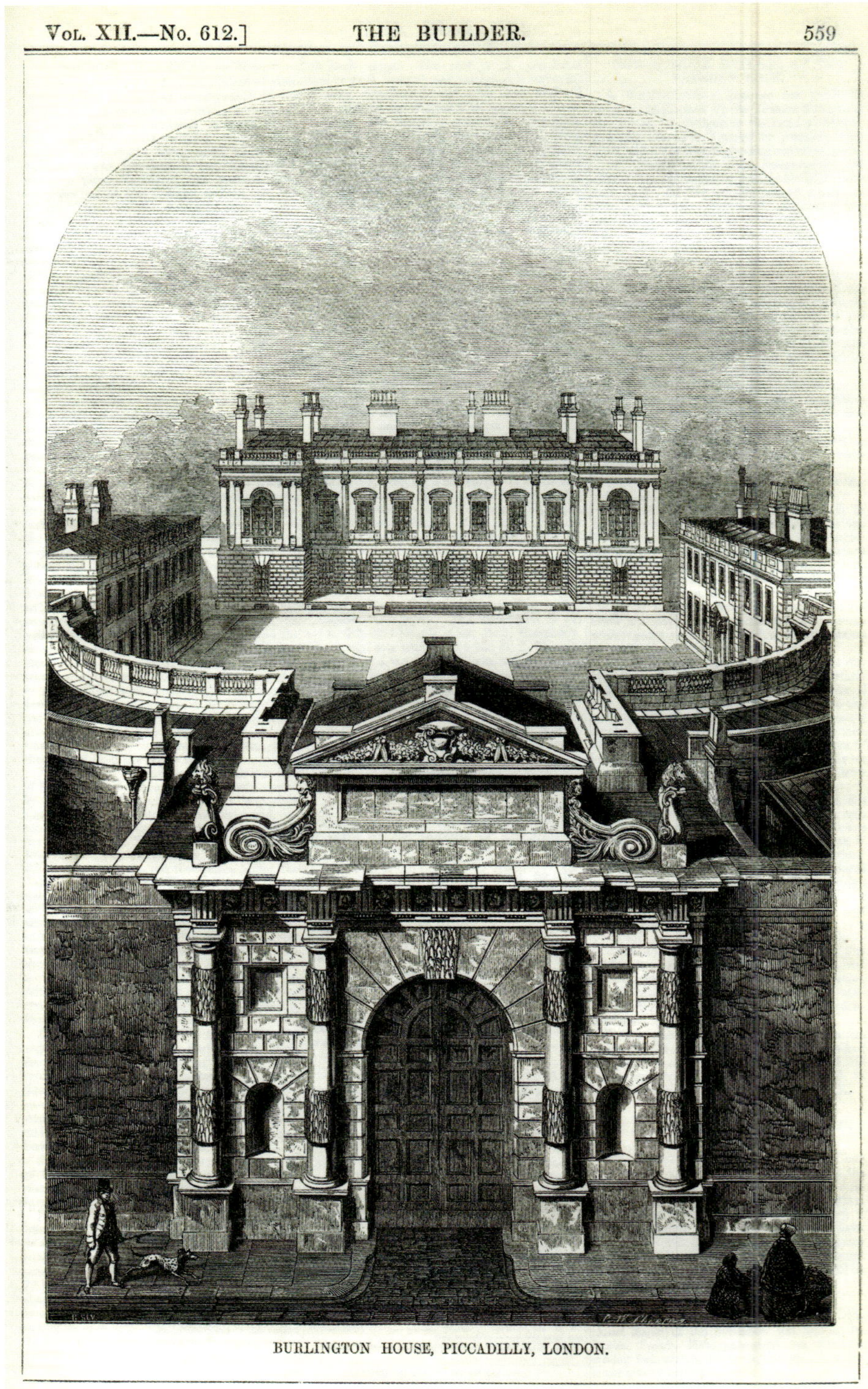
Vol. XII.—No. 612.] THE BUILDER. 559

BURLINGTON HOUSE, PICCADILLY, LONDON.

Fig. 150
Charles William Sheeres, after B. Sly, View into the courtyard of Burlington House from the house opposite, 1854, from *The Builder*, 28 October 1854, vol. 12, p. 559.
RIBA Collections

> The Ch. of the E. apprehends, that by a judicious use of the ground, exceeding 3 acres, which is included in this purchase, it may be made to yield a considerable clear income, besides affording a great amount of accommodation applicable to a variety of purposes, and serving in lieu, in many cases, of other accommodation at present provided at the public charge.
>
> One among these purposes would be to furnish offices for ordinary business, together with rooms for assemblies to meet the needs of various bodies connected with learning science & art. So far as rooms for assemblies are concerned it is plain that a very small number of such rooms of suitable dimensions, say two or at most three, may be made to serve the purposes of a very much larger number of Societies or Institutions.
>
> The accommodation however of this class, which is to be provided at Burlington House, should in the opinion of the C of the E. be designed in general for these purposes alone, and not for the purposes of accumulating or exhibiting the various stores or objects which may belong to these associations.
>
> But the site may also be made more directly conducive to the service of the State; and the First Comm.r of Works will himself be well able to consider whether there are any & what Public Offices or other Public B.gs or B.gs used as such, which may be given up, or, as the case may be, turned to profitable account so soon as the purposes to which they are devoted, shall be sufficiently provided for upon this large and important piece of property.
>
> For the present however, in the opinion of the C of the E it is not desirable to determine in detail upon the mode of applying the Ground, but it appears to him, that it would be of great advantage, that, with the probable general nature of the applications of it in his view, the First Comm.r of Works should proceed to consider of the best general method of laying out the Ground, taking for his guide the expectation that the ground floors with their frontages both external and internal will be available, speaking generally, for remunerative purposes, and that the site is not intended to carry buildings for great establishments but rather for a number of smaller ones; and endeavouring to combine in the utmost attainable degree what may be just in taste and not unattractive to the eye with the purposes of convenience and economy.
>
> It is possible that reasons may ultimately be found for placing some one or more depositories of objects of art, science or utility upon some part of this site, but before making the assumption that any public establishments, other than those of business properly so called, will be accommodated, it will be well in the opinion of the C of the E. that the First Comm.r should carefully consider, whether such accommodation might not more properly, because at the same time more liberally & more economically, be afforded on the Kensington Estate of the Comm.rs of the Exhibition of 1851.[3]

As in many government policy directives, what may seem at first broad-brushed was aimed in fact at a specific outcome. It is clear for instance that Gladstone envisaged from the start a new building on the site that would have combined government offices with rooms to accommodate learned societies, much as Somerset House had done since 1781. Apart from the fact that this building needed, in his view at least, to be no more than 'just in taste and not unattractive to the eye', the only difference was that in Piccadilly 'the ground floors with their frontages both external and internal will be available, speaking generally, for remunerative purposes'. It is also clear that his mention of 'various bodies connected with learning science and art' referred specifically, though perhaps not exclusively, to the Royal Society, the Society of Antiquaries of London, the Geological Society of London, and the Royal Astronomical Society, the four learned societies currently residing in the east wing of the Strand block of Somerset House; as well as to the Government School of Design (hence the reference to 'art') and the University of London (ditto 'learning'). Both of the latter institutions had occupied rooms vacated by the Royal Academy in the west wing since 1837 but had been recently evicted into temporary accommodation at Marlborough House in Pall Mall. And lastly, given Gladstone's crusade to streamline the administration of related government operations,

Fig. 151
John Wykeham Archer, *Gateway, Burlington House*, 1855.
British Museum, London, 1874,0314.450

such as concentrating revenue collection in one building, it is also more than likely that he would have been receptive to the thinking that underlay a landmark resolution adopted by the Council of the Royal Society in June 1852, *viz.*

> … that the general interests of Science would be materially benefited by bringing together the Societies cultivating the different branches of natural Knowledge, with such accommodation as each may require, in juxtaposition under one roof; leaving to each Society, as at present, its independent action and the independent conduct of its own affairs.[4]

This is presumably why the Chancellor was sure that 'two or at most three' meeting rooms 'may be made to serve the purposes of a very much larger number of Societies or Institutions.'

Therefore, when Gladstone moved for the necessary vote in the House of Commons on 26 July 1854, he was careful to quash any suggestion that the location of Burlington House in the West End of London might make it preferable to the suburb of Kensington Gore as a suitable site for national 'depositories of objects of art, science or utility'. More important, he thought, were the economic advantages of rehousing the learned societies so that vital government operations, currently reliant on disparate lodging rented at high commercial rates, could be brought together under one publicly owned roof. 'It would', he concluded,

> be impossible to retain the mansion as it stood; but the great bulk of the building erected in its place would be applicable to either one of the two great objects – the concentration of public offices, or the affording learned societies accommodation of which they were in need, and which it was clear should be given from the public resources.[5]

Gladstone had no difficulty in dismissing thoughts of retaining the existing buildings for aesthetic reasons. In the context of the economic impact of the Crimean War that had broken out only four months earlier, it was easy to skewer the contradictory logic of an hon. member who on the one hand objected to the vote as an unnecessary expense, but on the other was happy to withdraw his objection if the government pulled down that wretched wall on Piccadilly so that passers-by could admire the view.

The debate was adjourned to the following morning, but it was short and uncontroversial by the standards of the day and, although the committee did divide, the necessary vote of £140,000 was agreed by an overwhelming majority of 143 to 23. Unexpectedly perhaps, support for the purchase came from the opposition front bench when Gladstone's most implacable political adversary, Benjamin Disraeli, spoke eloquently of the importance of securing so valuable a site in central London for public use given how rarely such opportunities arose. Only one note of caution was sounded early on in the debate by Robert Vernon Smith, MP for Northampton, who pointed out a striking parallel with the Royal Academy's removal from Somerset House to Trafalgar Square eighteen years earlier. 'They all knew', he warned,

> what inconvenience had been experienced in the building of the National Gallery in consequence of a portion of it having been devoted to the Royal Academy, and they having thought proper to consider the occupation permanent.[6]

His advice – that the Chancellor of the Exchequer should 'be very careful how he admitted these bodies, and let it be distinctly understood that the accommodation was only temporary, and revocable at the pleasure of the Crown' – went largely unheeded at the time, but has echoed in the corridors of the Treasury down to the present day.

DESPITE GLADSTONE'S EMPHASIS on the benefits of releasing space at Somerset House, the first institution to gain a foothold inside Burlington House was not one of the learned societies overlooking the Strand but the Senate of the University of London who for the past two years had been dossing at Marlborough House in what they complained was 'a miserable garret'.[7] No doubt due to lobbying behind the scenes – by an odd coincidence the University's founding Chancellor was the 2nd Earl of Burlington, i.e. William Cavendish, Lord George

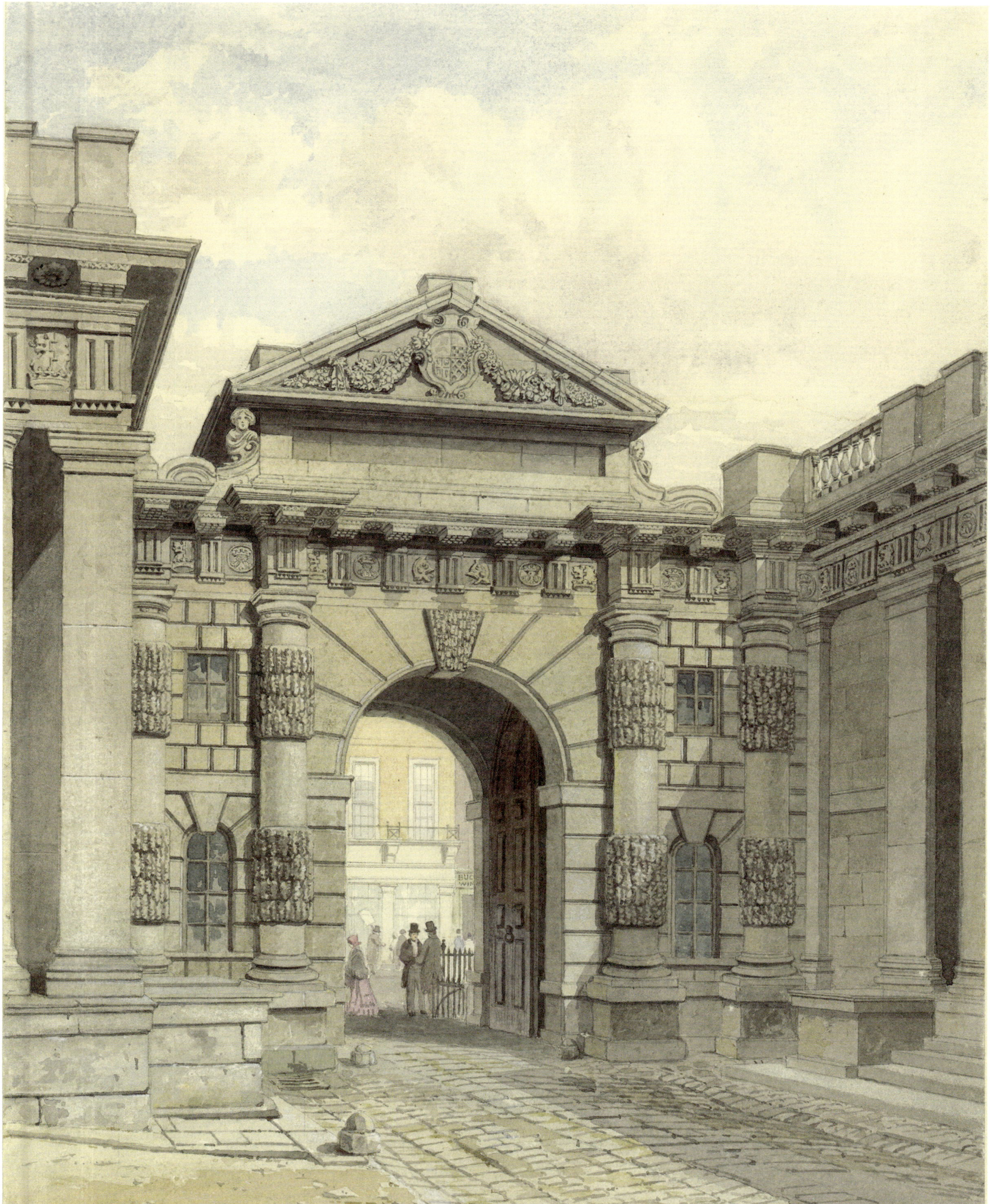

Cavendish's eldest grandson and later 7th Duke of Devonshire – towards the end of 1855 the Treasury gave permission for the University to 'occupy the Main Building [of Burlington House] subject to removal whenever the Building may be required for other purposes'.[8]

What these 'other purposes' would turn out to be became apparent on the morning of 14 January 1856 when three of the country's most eminent scientists, representing the Royal Society (Colonel, [later General] Edward Sabine), the Chemical Society (Sir Lyon Playfair) and the Geological Society (Sir Roderick Murchison), knocked at the Great Gate in Piccadilly expecting to be shown around the house (Fig. 151). Much to their consternation, and despite the fact they were accompanied by an employee of the Office of Works, they were turned away by the porter on the orders of the University's Registrar, the mild and retiring R. W. Rothman, who had not been informed in advance of this visitation and was not prepared to accept that the gentlemen in question had a right to enter simply on the grounds that Burlington House now 'belonged to the Crown'.[9] On the surface, this was no more than a bureaucratic mishap, but it took the personal intervention of the First Commissioner the next day to smooth ruffled feathers on both sides, and was a salutary warning of the diplomacy that the Office of Works would need to deploy when making arrangements for simultaneous use of the site by different institutions.

It was also an incident that signalled that there had been a significant shift in government policy. Following Lord Palmerston's appointment of Sir Benjamin Hall as First Commissioner in July 1855, the plans drawn up under the direction of his predecessor, Sir William Molesworth, for erecting a large public building of the kind that Gladstone had envisaged – for which an architect (or 'architectural assistant') by the name of Smith was paid a commission of £400 and 'drawing clerks' received £162 for their labours – were quietly dropped in favour of allowing temporary use of the building in its current state.[10] This decision may have been due in part to the success of a charity exhibition of contemporary paintings and drawings donated to the Royal Patriotic Fund in aid of the orphans and widows of soldiers killed in the Crimean War, which had been on public display in five rooms on the first floor of Burlington House since the beginning of May 1855 (Fig. 152). To all appearances abandoned since its sale, the house had suddenly come back to life that summer as, for the first time in its history, large crowds of exhibition visitors flocked through the entrance hall and climbed 'the noble staircase of the mansion appropriately decorated with trophies of the colours of the Allied armies' to see works of art created especially for the occasion by the Queen's five eldest children (Figs 153, 155).[11] It was to mark the opening of this great attraction that the *Illustrated London News* published an extended article on the history of the house (based largely on John Britton's account in *Illustrations of the Public Buildings of London*, 1825), while a leader in *The Times* on 29 June went so far as to claim that:

> Lately … Burlington-house has distinguished itself greatly in the eyes of the London public. The huge front gates have been hospitably thrown open, and the edifice on the further side of the courtyard has been visible even to the most heedless or rapid traveller. Flags denoting the alliance of the western Powers have been conspicuously displayed so as to appeal to the attention of the inert, and the ear has been saluted by military music performed within the precincts once as apparently silent as the interior of an Egyptian pyramid.[12]

The government's new willingness to allow temporary use of the house for good causes became apparent also when the recently formed Metropolitan Board of Works took over the long-deserted ball room on the first floor for six public meetings between 19 December 1855 and 18 January 1856 (Fig. 154). Obviously, the University could not expect to retain sole possession for much longer and whoever hoped to join them would need to move quickly.

It was probably no coincidence therefore, that on the same day the Royal Society's treasurer and vice-president tried unsuccessfully to gain entry to Burlington House, its president, Lord Wrottesley wrote to James Wilson, the secretary to the Lords Commissioners of the Treasury, requesting that he lay before their lordships a proposal submitted to the Prime Minister the previous summer:

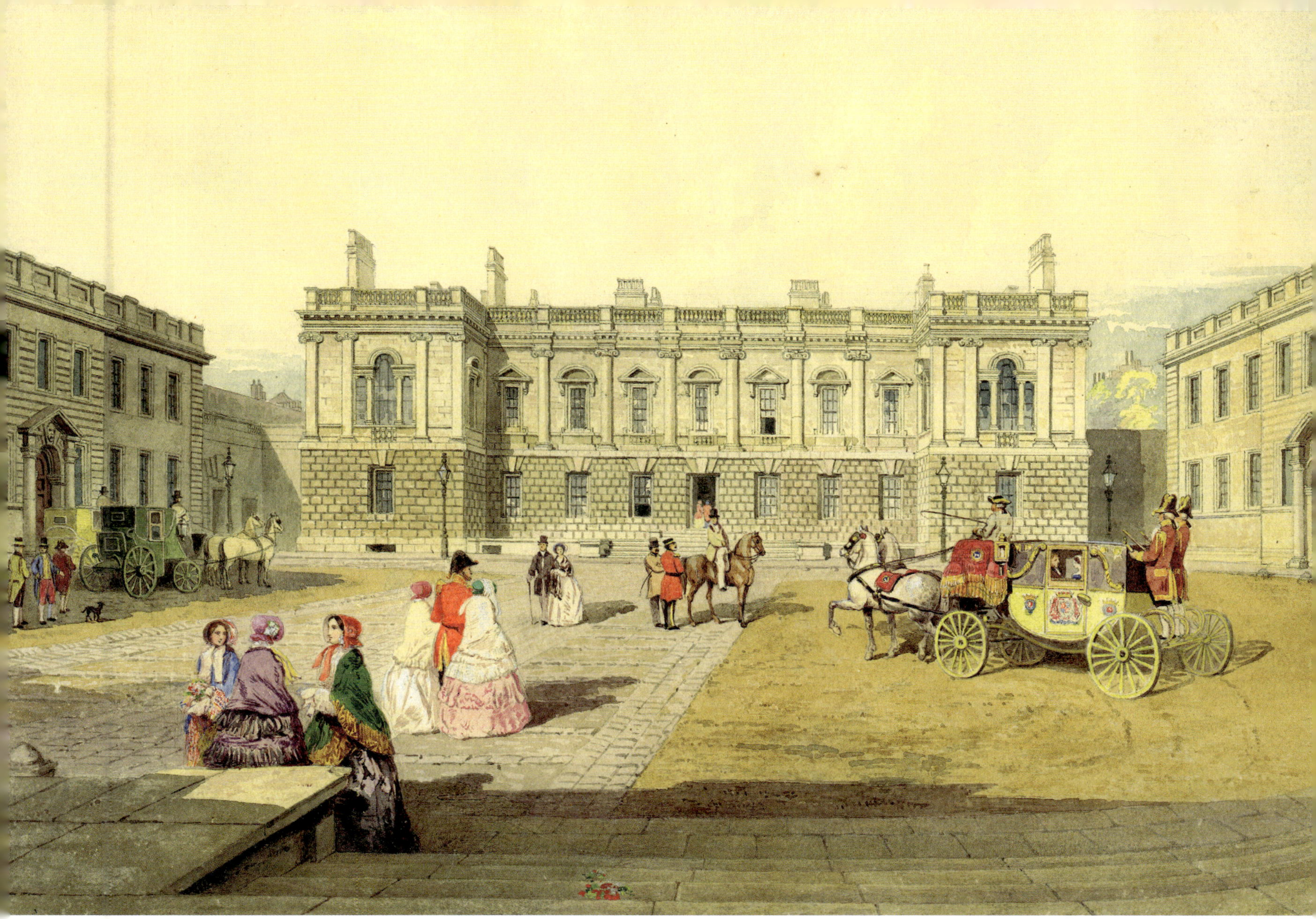

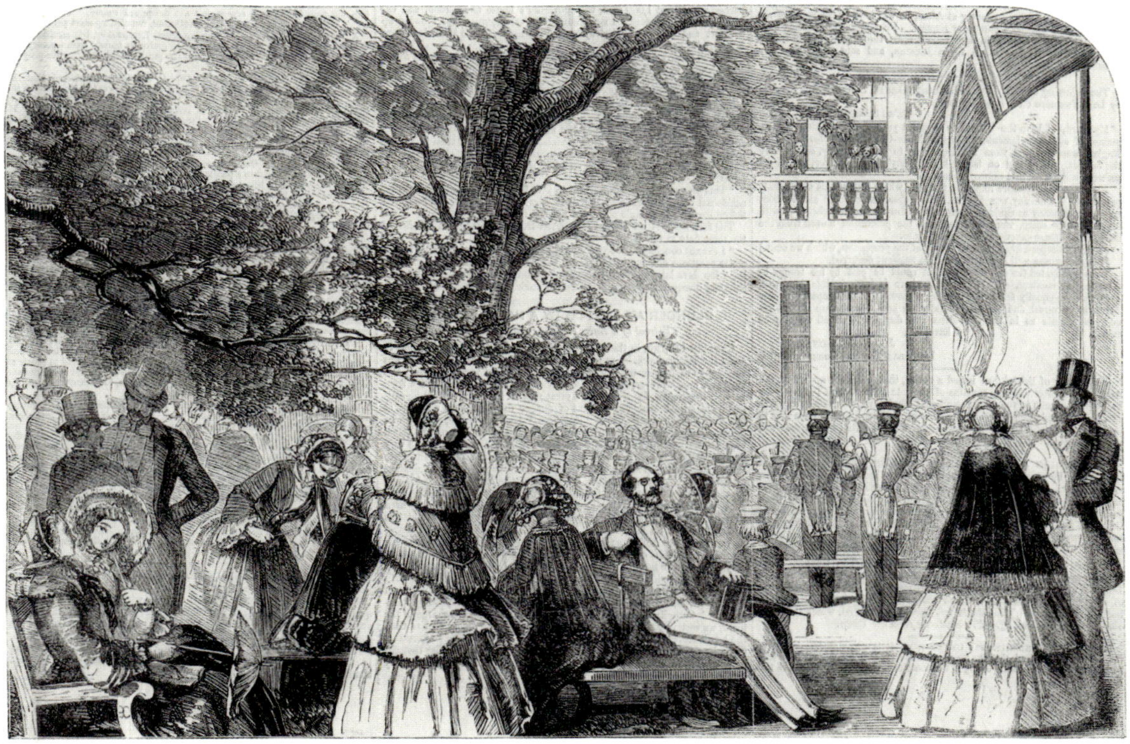

Fig. 152
John Wykeham Archer,
Burlington House, Front, 1855.
British Museum, London,
1874,0314.451

Fig. 153
'The Band of the Coldstream Guards playing at Burlington House in aid of the Patriotic Fund', from *Illustrated Times*, 21 July 1855.
Linnean Library, London

Sir,

As President of the Royal Society I was Chairman of a Deputation, which in June last had the honour of an interview with Lord Palmerston to represent to his Lordship the opinion very strongly entertained by a large proportion of the scientific men of this country, that, by placing the Royal Society in some more suitable & central locality than that which they now occupy, & in juxtaposition with the Linnean, Astronomical, Geological, & Chemical Societies (which are chartered Societies, & cultivate branches of that natural knowledge which the Royal Society was instituted to promote) – Science itself would be most materially advanced, & placed by the change in a position more corresponding to that which it ought to occupy in this Country.

The convenience of the juxtaposition, the value of bringing together the several libraries, which united would form one of the most important collections of scientific works in Europe, the economy which would result from having the Societies under one roof, enabling more of their funds to be devoted to the actual prosecution of scientific enquiries – were stated & explained; & Burlington House was pointed out as a very suitable situation for such an assemblage of the Societies, in which light it appeared to be viewed by Lord Palmerston; & the Deputation quitted his Lordship with the full impression that he was at least very favourably disposed towards the realization of the project by the assignment of Burlington House for that purpose.

I have since been informed that a part of that House has been occupied by the London University, but as I believe that large accommodation is only required by that body at two or three distinct periods of the year, I conceive that arrangements might be made by which the requirements of the University & those of such scientific societies as could be located in the present building might be provided for; while, as respects ulterior arrangements, the site purchased affords ample space for the extension of the boon to such other Societies as may be deemed worthy of national support.

I have the honour to request that this letter may be laid before the Lords of the Treasury, & that you will do me the favour to move their Lordships to oblige me with an early reply.[13]

This letter resulted in a meeting convened at Treasury Chambers on 29 April 1856 in which

... Deputations from the four societies now located at Somerset House attended Mr Wilson ... & on his addressing to them observations from which it might be inferred that the Gov^{nt} were willing to assign them apart^{mts} in Burlington House on certain conditions, without prejudice to the question of giving them increased accommodation, in case new buildings should be erected on the ground purchased, & of allocating other societies these in the same event – the Deputations from all the Societies except the Royal declined the offer of <u>temporary</u> accommodation; the Geological and Astronomical, however, professing

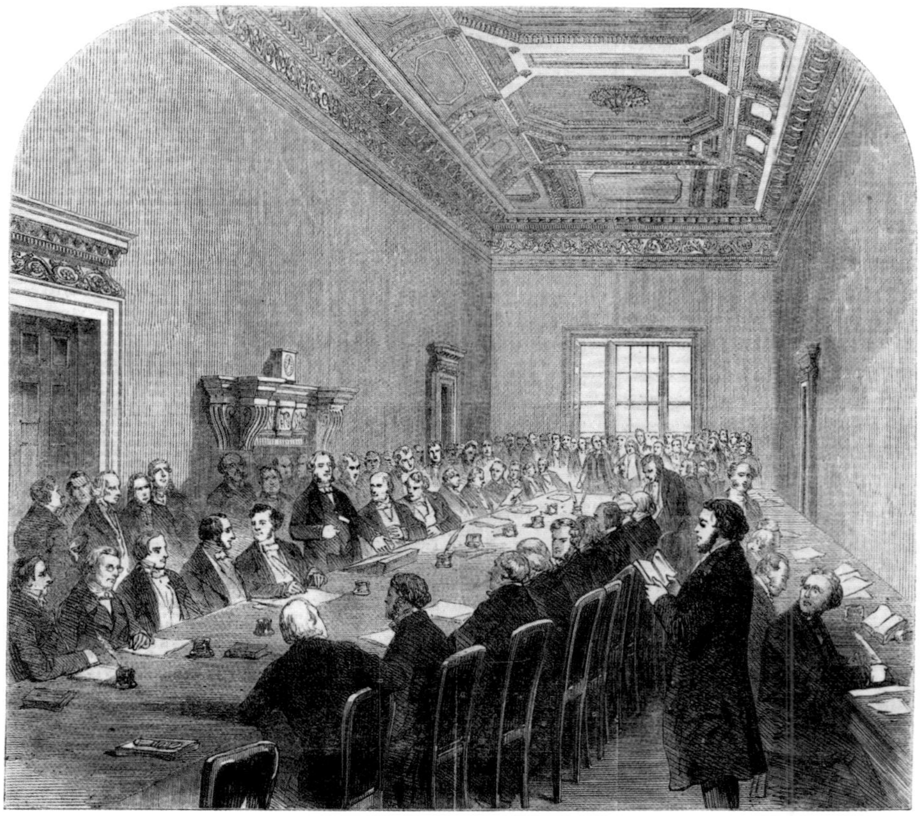

Fig. 154
'A Meeting of the Metropolitan Board of Works in Burlington House', from *Illustrated Times*, 19 January 1856.
Linnean Library, London

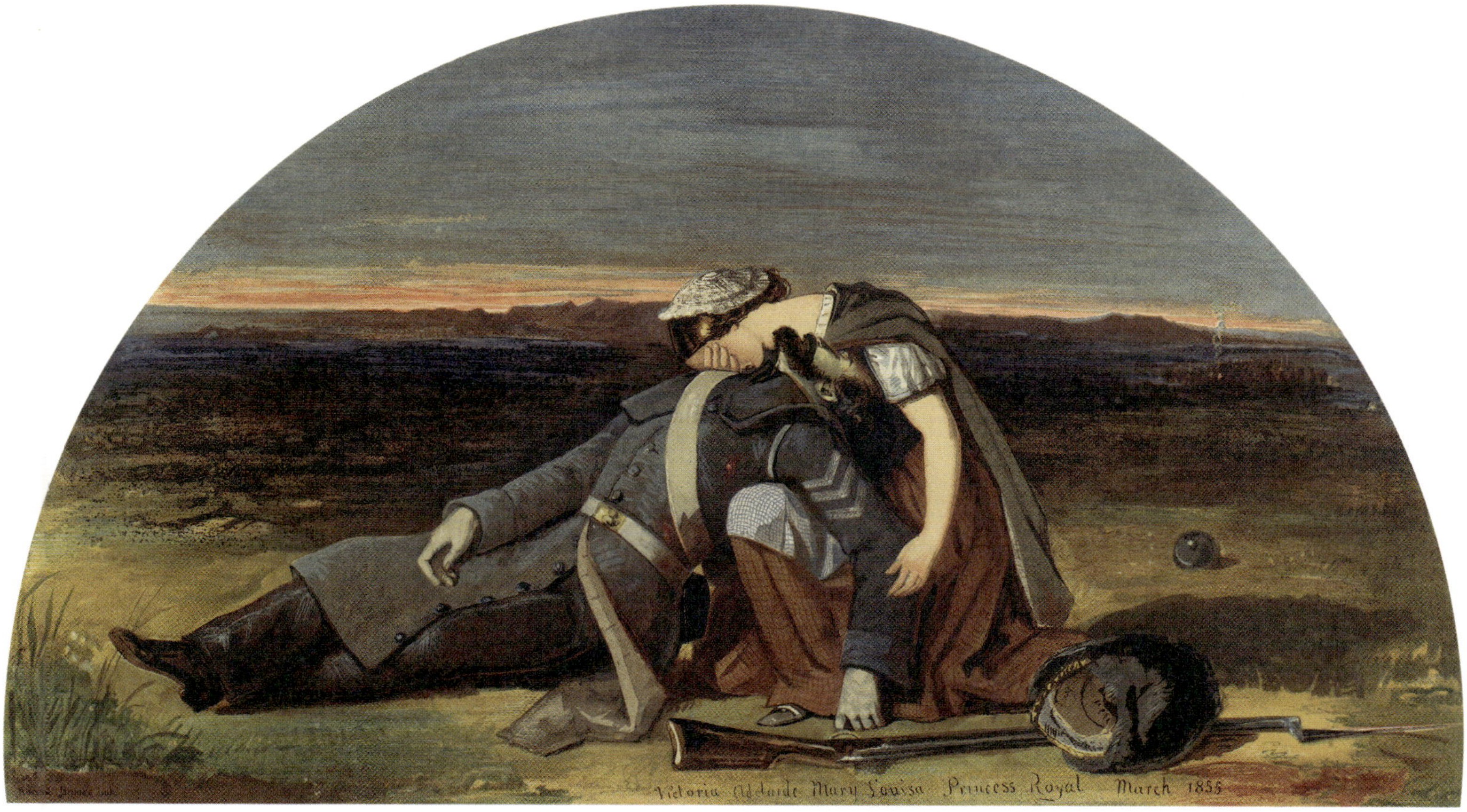

Fig. 155
Victoria Adelaide Mary Louisa, Princess Royal, later Empress Friedrich, consort of Friedrich III (emperor of Germany and king of Prussia), *The Field of Battle, March 1855*, exhibited in the Burlington House Royal Patriotic Fund Exhibition, 1855.
Royal Collection Trust, RCIN 981393

> their readiness to move when the Gov^{nt} sh^{d} consent to erect a building worthy of Science and the nation, in which the chief scientific societies might be placed in juxtaposition in a convenient & central locality.[14]

For those who declined the government's invitation to move there (i.e. the Antiquaries, the Geological and the Royal Astronomical societies), the problem with Burlington House was not only that it would not have provided them with sufficient space in its present state, but also that accepting temporary lodgings in lieu of their purpose-designed quarters at Somerset House risked letting the government off the hook of providing 'a building worthy of Science and the nation.' On the other hand, with the Royal Society as its sole occupant, not only did the problem of insufficient space no longer apply but the need for other societies to be allowed to join them in 'juxtaposition' became incontrovertible. It was probably this turn of events more than anything that led the government to make a crucial concession at this point, based no longer only on their own priority of freeing up space at Somerset House but rather on acceptance of the benefits juxtaposition would have for the learned societies themselves. Thus, although Wilson's cautious letter of 22 May 1856 began by stating 'that Her Majesty's Government are not at present in a position to enable them to state any definite views with respect to the project for the juxtaposition of the principal Scientific Societies', he was able to inform Lord Wrottesley

> … that their Lordships are however prepared so far to concede to the views advanced by your Lordship on behalf of a large number of persons connected with science, as to allow the temporary location of the Linnean and Chemical Societies, in conjunction with the Royal Society, in the present building of Burlington House on the following conditions vizt
>
> 1 That the removal of the Royal Society from Somerset House shall not prejudice the position of the other societies located in that building in regard to the terms on which they are permitted to occupy their present Apartments.
> 2 That the Royal Society shall be put in possession of the Main Building of Burlington House, on the understanding they will, in communication with the Linnean and Chemical Societies, assign suitable accommodation therein for those bodies.
> 3 A Common Library, to be formed for the use of the three Societies, on the understanding that suitable arrangements shall be made for the admission thereto, for the purposes of reference & study, of Men of Letters and Science, on orders given by fellows of the three Societies.
> 4 The Societies to be allowed the use of the Hall which it is proposed to construct in the West Wing

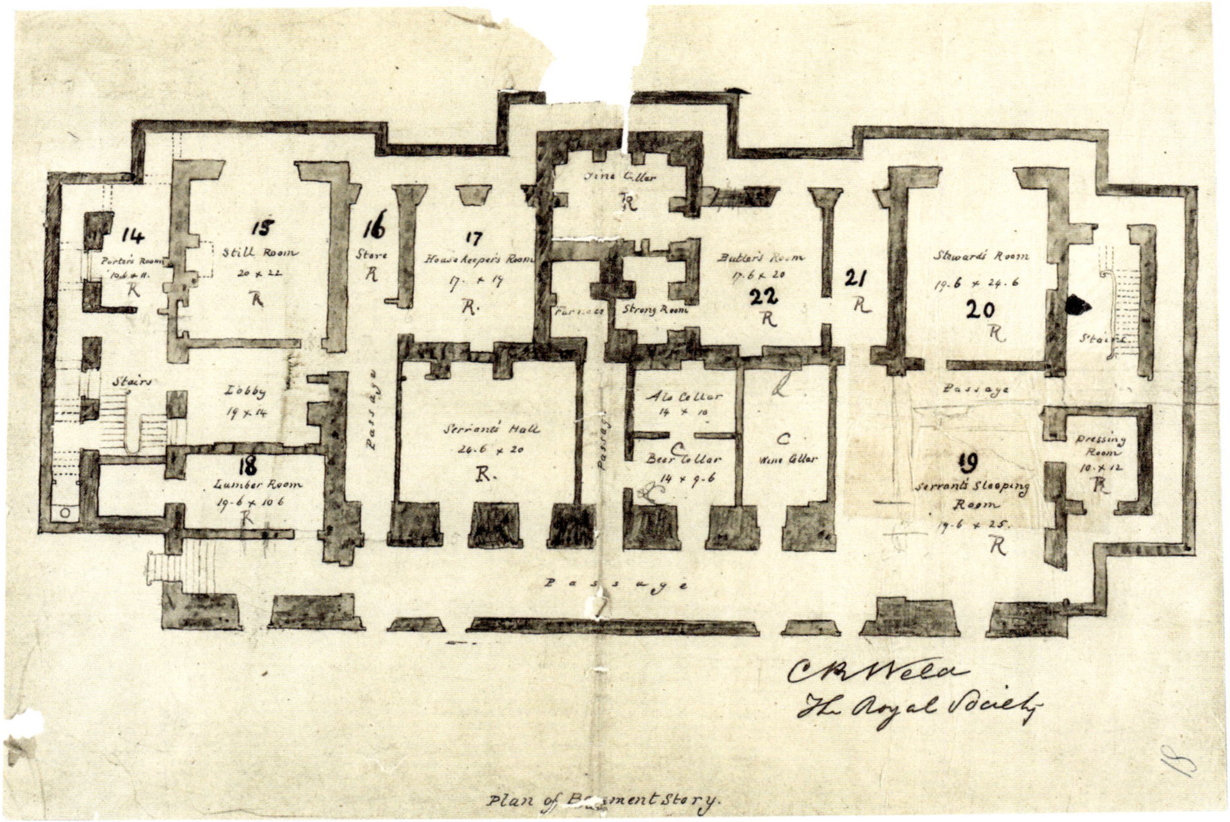

Fig. 156
C. R. Weld, Space allocation for the Learned Societies in the basement of Burlington House, 1857.
Royal Society Archives, MM/13/81

of Burlington House, at such times as it may not be required by the Senate of the University of London, it being distinctly understood that this permission is to be exercised as not in any way to interfere with the convenience of the University.

5 The Collection of Portraits belonging to the Royal Society to be hung on the Walls of the proposed Hall, and to be open to the inspection of the Public under such regulations as may be convenient and subject especially to the proviso in the preceding Clause.

6 That the adoption of this temporary arrangement shall not in any respect be held to weaken the claim of the Royal Society to permanent accommodation.[15]

While clauses 1 and 6 were clearly intended to address the Royal Society's concern that exchanging permanent apartments at Somerset House for temporary ones in Piccadilly might affect how the government interpreted their obligations in the future, clauses 3 and 5 reveal the government's concern that the new occupants of Burlington House should be seen to be providing a clear public benefit in the present. Similarly, while clause 4 established the priority of the University's proposed use of the West Wing as an examination hall, when Wilson wrote a few days later on 3 June to request the Senate's acceptance of the Royal Society's condition that the latter be given custody of this room, he hoped that the common public interest would prevail over any misunderstandings that might have arisen in the past:

> I have to observe that in the arrangement proposed by my Lords the interests of the Public have been considered independently of those of the Learned Societies by the stipulation that men of letters and science and others desirous to consult or study literary works shall be admitted to the common library on orders given by the fellows and that access shall be given to the public to the collection of portraits under such regulations as may be found convenient. The use of the Hall for this public object necessarily requires that the Royal Society should have some control over the building in which its property will be deposited. … I have to add that looking at the public objects to be obtained & considering that the substantial difficulties have been overcome their Lordships trust no obstacle of a minor description will be allowed to interfere with a final and satisfactory arrangement.[16]

The political reward for the government came three days later when, towards the end of a fractious debate in the House of Commons on a vote to meet the cost of constructing iron galleries at South Kensington (the so-called 'Brompton Boilers'), Wilson was able to parry a pointed question concerning the government's plans for Burlington House with an impressively detailed reply.[17]

Fig. 157
C. R. Weld, Space allocation for the Learned Societies on the ground floor of Burlington House, 1857.
Royal Society Archives, MM/13/83

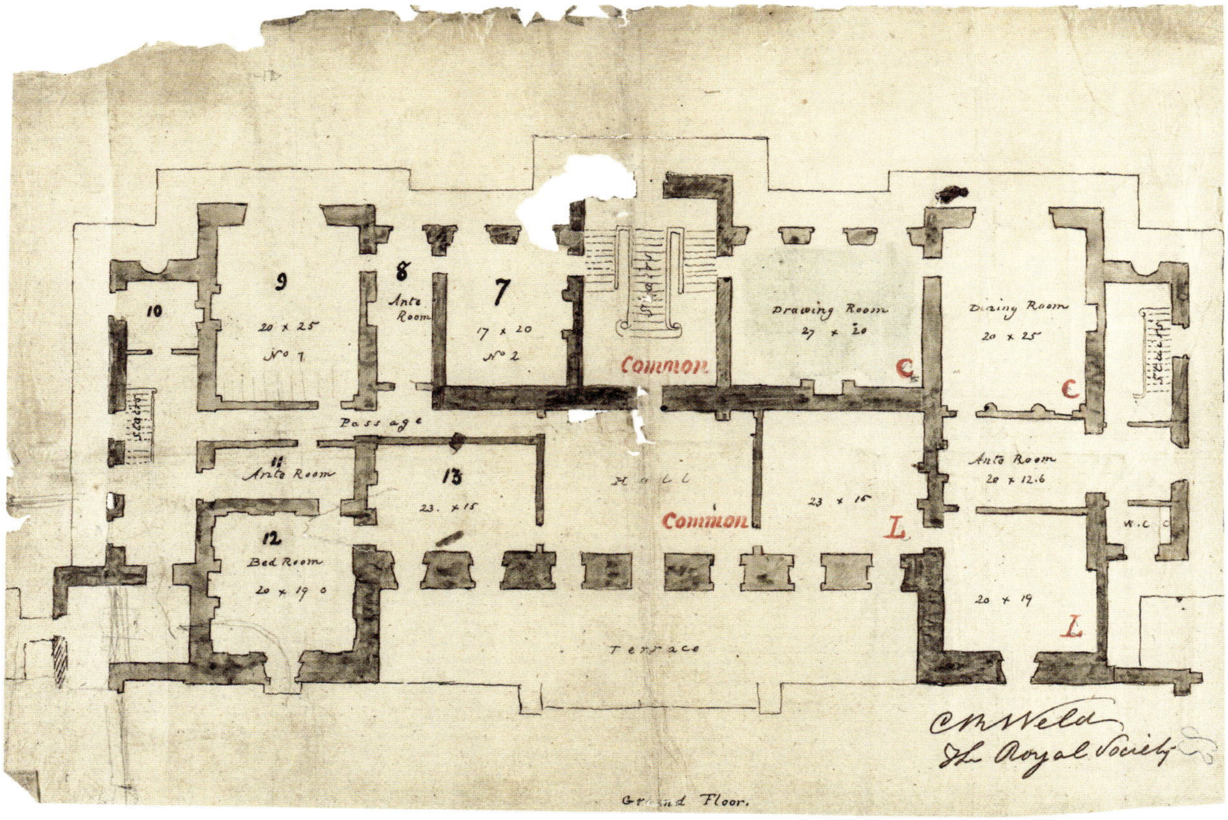

He was fortunate though that no-one spotted the error he made in the government's favour by stating that the Chemical Society would be releasing space at Somerset House for the Inland Revenue when in fact they were moving out of two rooms rented since April 1850 from the Polytechnic Institution at No. 5 Cavendish Square.[18]

AS THE OLDEST and most prestigious scientific body in the country, the Royal Society had naturally taken the lead in negotiating with the government for the possible transfer of other deserving societies to Burlington House apart from those already at Somerset House. However, whatever the strength of the argument they made for the 'general interests of Science' being 'materially benefited by bringing together the Societies cultivating the different branches of natural Knowledge', it was also the case that acute shortage of space for their rapidly overflowing library and back-stock of publications had made their own removal from Somerset House an increasingly attractive if not inescapable option. This is why, despite having advocated so strongly the benefits of their intended 'juxtaposition', Wrottesley concludes his letter to the Duke of Argyll on the day after the societies' meeting at the Treasury on 29 April, with the consoling thought that 'the question is now much simplified by the circumstance that there is only one Soc^{y} to treat with'. It is also why early in December 1856, when the University had moved out into its new administrative quarters in the East Wing and handed over the key of the main house to its new occupants, it was the Royal Society that took over by far the largest share of the building. Rather than insist on an equal division – they did after all in practice have the same need for a council room, library, administrative offices, assistant secretary's residence, servants' quarters and storage areas – the Linnean and Chemical societies were more than happy to be given rent-free space roughly equivalent to what they previously had to pay for (Figs 156–158). Thus, the Chemical's modest 'two back rooms with Ante-room on the Ground Floor in the east end of the building', 'Beer-Cellar in the basement for a coal-cellar' and use of 'the Linnean Society's eastern room on the Ground Floor as a Council Room', probably amounted more or less to what they had been accustomed to in Cavendish Square.[19] Sadly, despite the Linnean's much larger share of the house, namely the whole of 'the Attic story, the Ball Room and Room adjoining on the North Side of the house, the two front rooms on the Ground Floor in the east end of the building' and 'the Wine-Cellar in the basement for a coal-cellar', it seems there was no space to spare for their fine collection of zoological specimens, which was transferred instead to the British Museum and then dispersed in part to local natural-history museums in Hampshire and Suffolk.[20]

What would have struck a visitor to Burlington House in the early summer of 1857 was that almost every room

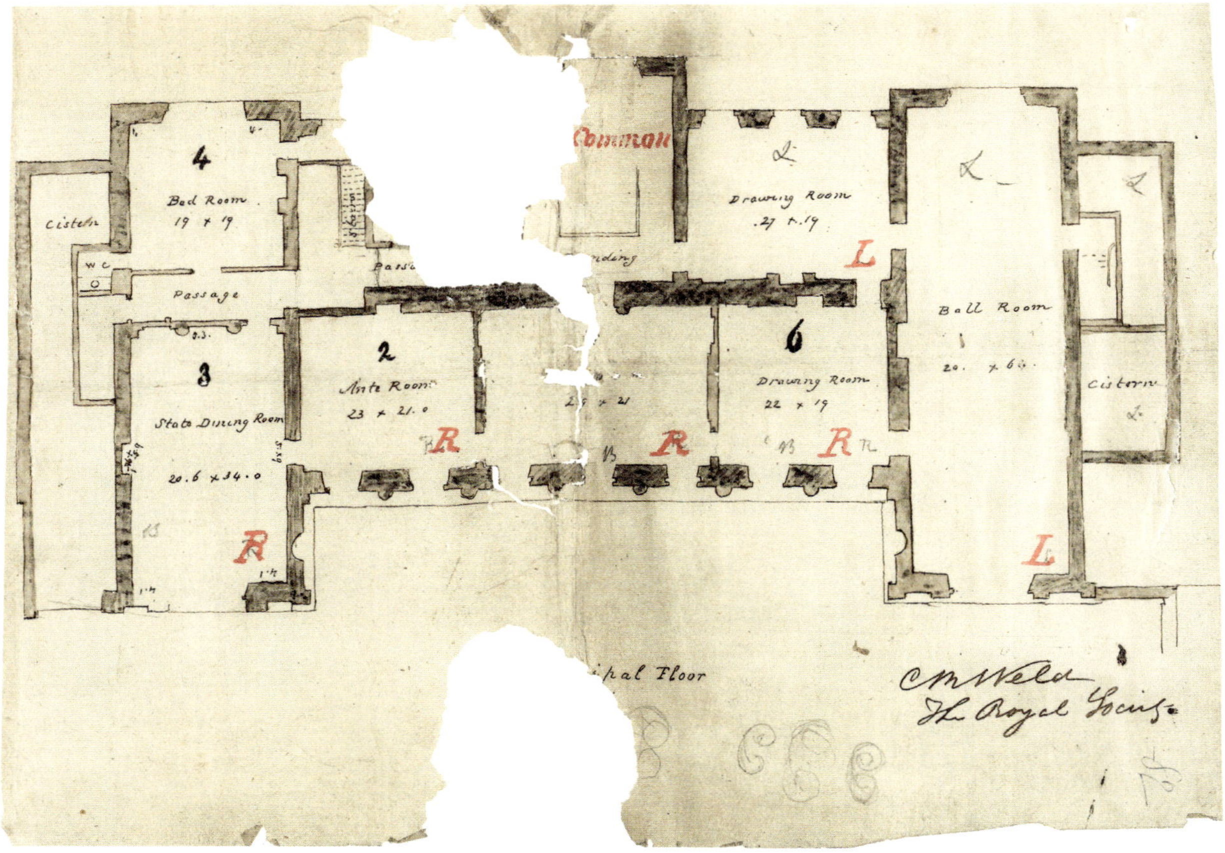

Fig. 158
C. R. Weld, Space allocation for the Learned Societies on the first floor of Burlington House, 1857.
Royal Society Archives, MM/13/82

on the first storey was now filled from floor to ceiling with books.[21] For although the societies had baulked at the idea of merging their libraries – and Wilson had wisely chosen to interpret the Treasury's stipulation of a 'common library' to mean nothing more radical than shared access, with borrowing rights still restricted to the fellows of a specific society – as Wrottesley had predicted, bringing their books under one roof did indeed create 'one of the most important collections of scientific works in Europe'. Not only were the Linnean's great botanical and zoological book and manuscript collections given a magnificently appropriate setting in the largest and most ornate room in the house, it was also able to display to full advantage its precious herbarium on the ground floor immediately adjacent to the entrance hall and its own Council Room. However, it was the Royal Society's historic library and archive that really dominated the building. Shelved in demountable 'open bookcases in mahogany (like those in the drawing-room of the Athenæum Club)', or in 'plain bookcases' recycled or copied from their old library in Somerset House, the Society's library, archive and historic relics spread through no less than ten rooms, including a newly formed ante-room – or 'Lower Library' as it was called – linking the 'Great Hall' or common meeting room in the West Wing with the ground-floor rooms in the main building allotted 'as household apartments to the Assistant Secretary'.[22] This great reordering of the Royal Society's library was undertaken not for show, but rather as integral to a concerted effort to improve intellectual access to the books. Not only was a new shelf arrangement by subject introduced to take advantage of a 50% increase in shelf space but a parallel project was also launched to compile a union 'Catalogue of Philosophical Memoirs' embracing all the sciences, beginning, naturally enough, with the Society's own particularly rich holdings of scientific journals.[23] The excitement felt by 'many persons connected with science' at this historic moment for the future of scientific endeavour in Britain is captured perfectly in Thomas Bell's inspiring conclusion to his 1857 presidential address to the Linnean Society:

> I cannot take leave of this subject [i.e. the removal of the Linnean Society to Burlington House] without expressing my sense of the sincerity and earnestness with which the authorities of the Royal Society have advocated our cause, and the anxious desire they have expressed to commence with us the practical development of the great principle of juxtaposition. To us the success of the present effort is all-important. The immunity from rent, the close association with our brethren in scientific pursuits, the approximation of our libraries and, let me add, the prestige attached to such a locality, must act as a powerful aid to our already growing prosperity, and enable us to carry out, unencumbered, our great mission – the advancement

> of natural science, with all its advantages, the amelioration of the condition of man, the elevation of his character, intellectual and moral, and especially the promotion of the glory of the Creator, by extending the knowledge of his works.[24]

However, despite the combined scientific knowledge of God's creation that the botanists and entomologists in the Linnean Society could now bring to bear on the problem, sadly it was too late to save the trees outside their meeting-room window. Following a letter to the Office of Works in March 1857, in which the resident assistant secretary of the Royal Society C. R. Weld had complained of the neglected state of the garden, in May the following year an inspection by the superintendent of Hyde and St James's Parks of the double row of venerable elms on the lawn behind the house revealed 'that they are all in a state of decay which nothing can prevent' (Fig. 159).[25]

At first sight, it would appear Gladstone's confidence in the purely practical benefit to be derived from 'the great principle of juxtaposition' had been vindicated, inasmuch as the three societies had agreed to share the Royal Society's 'Great Hall' and its adjoining 'Ante-room' in the West Wing, which were reported to be ready for painting in March 1857 (Fig. 160).[26] However, all the evidence points to the fact that the Linnean and Chemical societies did not use these spaces for their ordinary fortnightly meetings, but always preferred to meet in their own rooms in the main house. In fact, it must have been obvious that the idea of a shared meeting room was not going to work from the moment the Linnean and Chemical societies decided early in 1857 to change their ordinary meeting days to Thursdays to

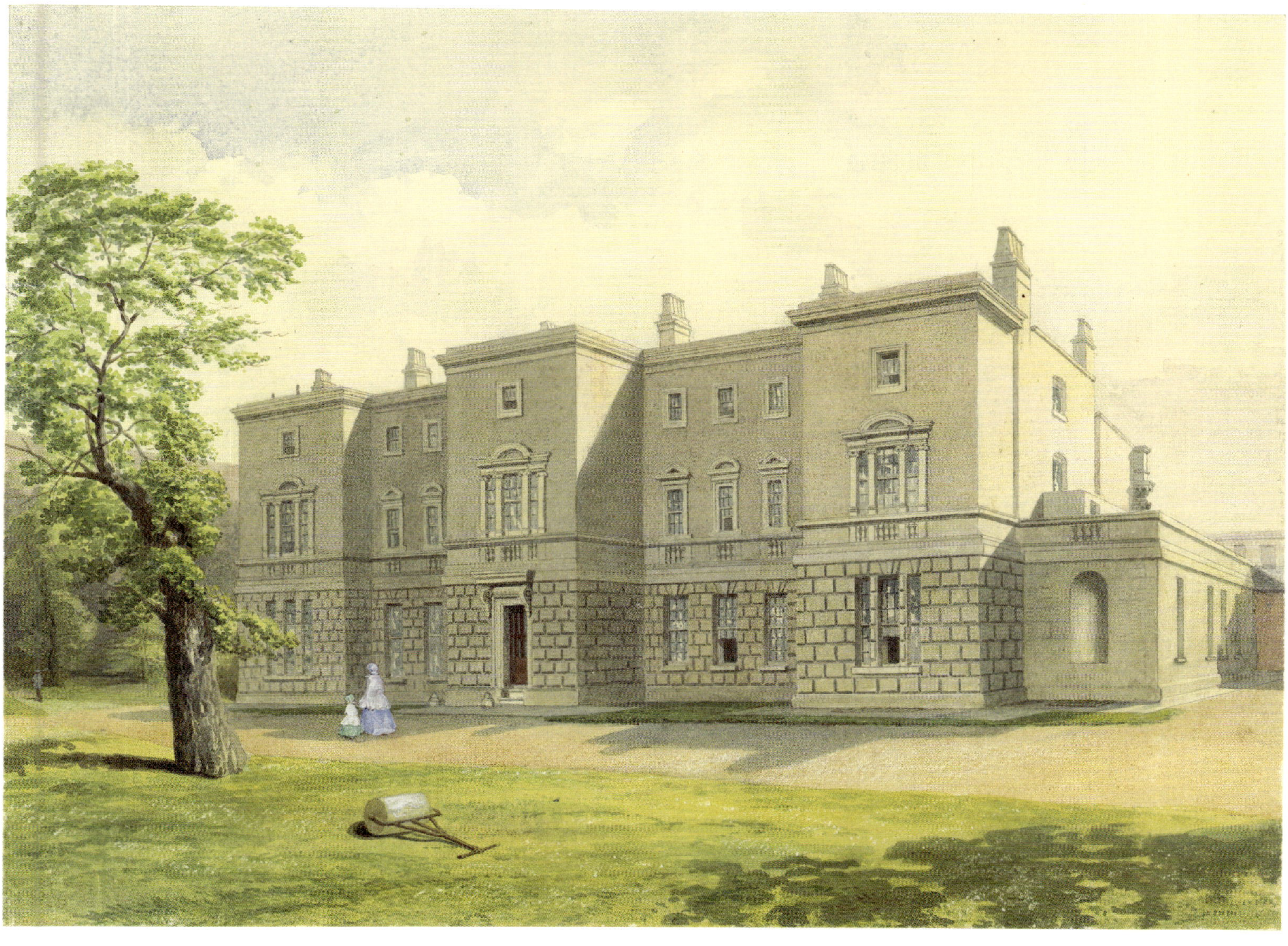

Fig. 159
John Wykeham Archer, *Burlington House, Back* (the north front), 1855.
British Museum, London, 1874,0314.323

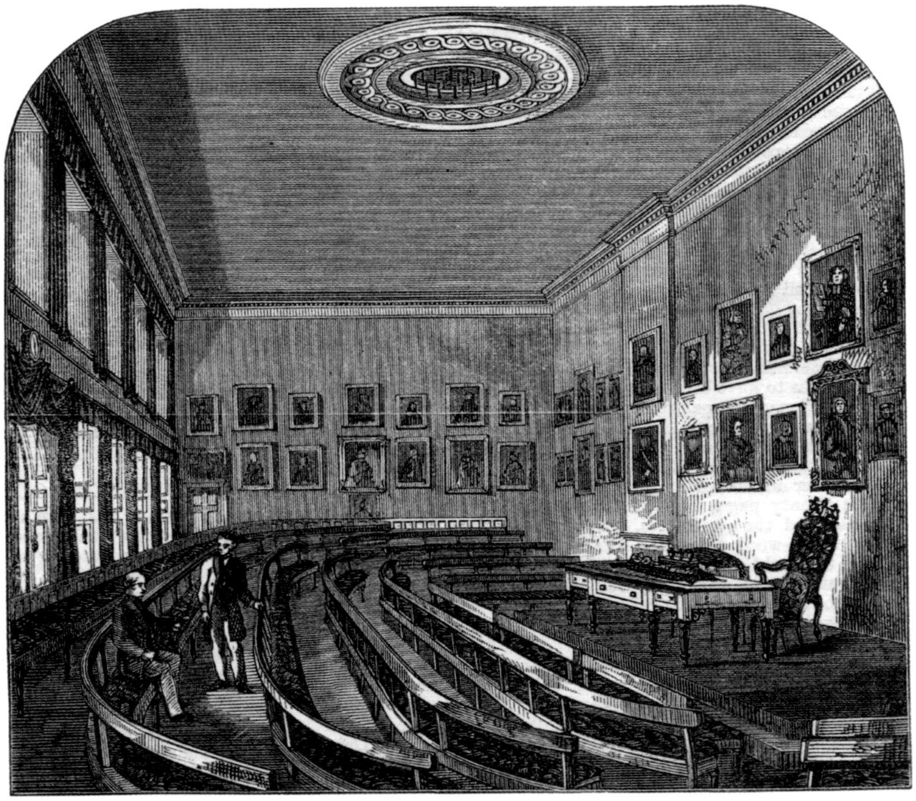

Fig. 160
'The present Meeting Room of the Royal Society in Burlington House', from *Illustrated London News*, 12 December 1863.
Illustrated London News archive

coincide with the Royal Society, it being 'considered desirable that the members of all three [societies] should have the opportunity of taking tea, and talk together after their respective meetings.'[27] When, therefore, on 16 November 1857 the Treasury forwarded the Ethnological Society's request to use either the Linnean or Chemical Society's rooms for their meetings, with a covering letter stating 'that my Lords will be glad if the wish expressed by Sir James Clark on the part of the Ethnological Society can be met, as it appears that the accommodation required cannot in any way interfere with the use of the rooms in question by the existing Societies', a fair degree of panic ensued.[28] The difficulty they faced was that, unlike the Royal Society, which had exchanged the tenure it had been granted by the Crown at Somerset House in 1781 for supposedly its exact equivalent at Burlington House in 1856, neither of the newcomer societies had been given any undertaking that secured exclusive use of the accommodation they now occupied. Only after a joint meeting of the presidents and officers of the three societies on 11 December 1857, at which it was agreed that each should have independent control over the spaces assigned to them, were they able to repel what was in effect an attempted invasion by another society.[29]

As had been demonstrated in November 1852, when to their horror the government had proposed that the Somerset House societies might like to be 'juxtaposed' on a new site at Kensington Gore, if they acted in unison learned and scientific bodies in Victorian Britain were a force to be reckoned with. On this occasion, however, they need not have worried, since it very soon became clear it was in the Treasury's interest for the societies to deal with external demands on their meeting rooms themselves. The advisability of this became particularly apparent in May 1858 when no less than twelve metropolitan societies asked to be 'allowed to use the smaller Hall and the Porter's Room on the opposite side of the Quadrangle, at such times as may be arranged for the convenience of all parties.'[30] None of these applications – which included second attempts by both the Ethnological Society and the Microscopical Society – were, it seems, any more successful than Henry Cole's, whose request on behalf of the 'Fine Arts Club' to use the 'Great Hall' was summarily rebuffed by the Royal Society's Council in May 1860, and again in December the same year when he tried to go over their heads by writing directly to the Treasury.[31]

Although only the University had an automatic right to use the 'Great Hall' and the 'Lower Library' meeting rooms in the West Wing for its exams, degree ceremonies and convocations, there seems from the start to have been an understanding with the government that these rooms would also be used for civil-service and army exams. This is probably why the whole cost of converting the old kitchen and laundry block and adjacent household offices in the West Wing was met by the Office of Works, while alterations and improvements in the main house, such as the construction of library bookshelves and installation of gaslighting, were paid for by the societies themselves. And it would also explain why, at their first meeting in

Burlington House on 23 April 1857, the Council of the Royal Society readily gave permission for the Royal Military Academy at Woolwich to hold officer-training exams in their new rooms in the courtyard. Similar permission was regularly granted in subsequent years, both to the RMA and to the Council of Military Education, which began to hold exams at Burlington House for direct commissions in the army in February 1858. As far as the army was concerned this followed a precedent set in the latter half of 1855 when the Office of Works had allowed an 'Examination of Candidates for the War Department' to be held in the main building.[32] Similarly, in a premonition of their permanent residence in 6 Burlington Gardens forty years later, regular use began to be made of the West Wing by the Civil Service Commission when, for 'three weeks or more' in July and August 1859, the 'Great Hall' was used for the first time for Indian civil-service exams.[33]

From 1859 especially, the Royal Society's *conversazioni* (or soirées) always drew a large and distinguished audience, but Burlington House probably became best known during this period as the regular meeting-place of an even higher profile society, reports of whose members' exploits could on occasion seize the nation's imagination like almost no other news. From as early as November 1857 the regular, usually fortnightly meetings of the Royal Geographical Society were staged in the 'Great Hall', where large audiences were frequently spellbound by travellers' tales, such as the discovery of 'practicable passes' in the Canadian Rockies (Captain Palliser and Dr Hector, 14 February 1859); evidence of tragedy in the Arctic (the search for traces of Sir John Franklin's doomed Northwest Passage expedition, 14 November 1859); and, most exciting of all, exploration of the 'Dark Continent' (letters from Livingstone, 22 May 1861; Speke and Burton's 'discovery' of the source of the Nile, 23 June 1863; the search for Livingstone's grave, 3 February 1868; Fig. 161).[34] As the RGS had been specifically named by Gladstone in his speech to the Commons in July 1854 as one of the 'other' societies that might be accommodated in a new building at Burlington House (they had recently been voted a grant of £500 per annum to hire a suitable meeting room and to make their map collection publicly accessible), it is likely that their use of the 'Great Hall', like the army's, was due more to government pressure than mere complaisance on the part of the Royal Society.

In contrast to the sensationalism of RGS meetings, on Thursday, 1 July 1858, the secretary of the Linnean Society, John Joseph Bennett, read extracts from Charles Darwin's unpublished book on the origin of species and Alfred Russel Wallace's paper 'On the Tendency of Varieties to

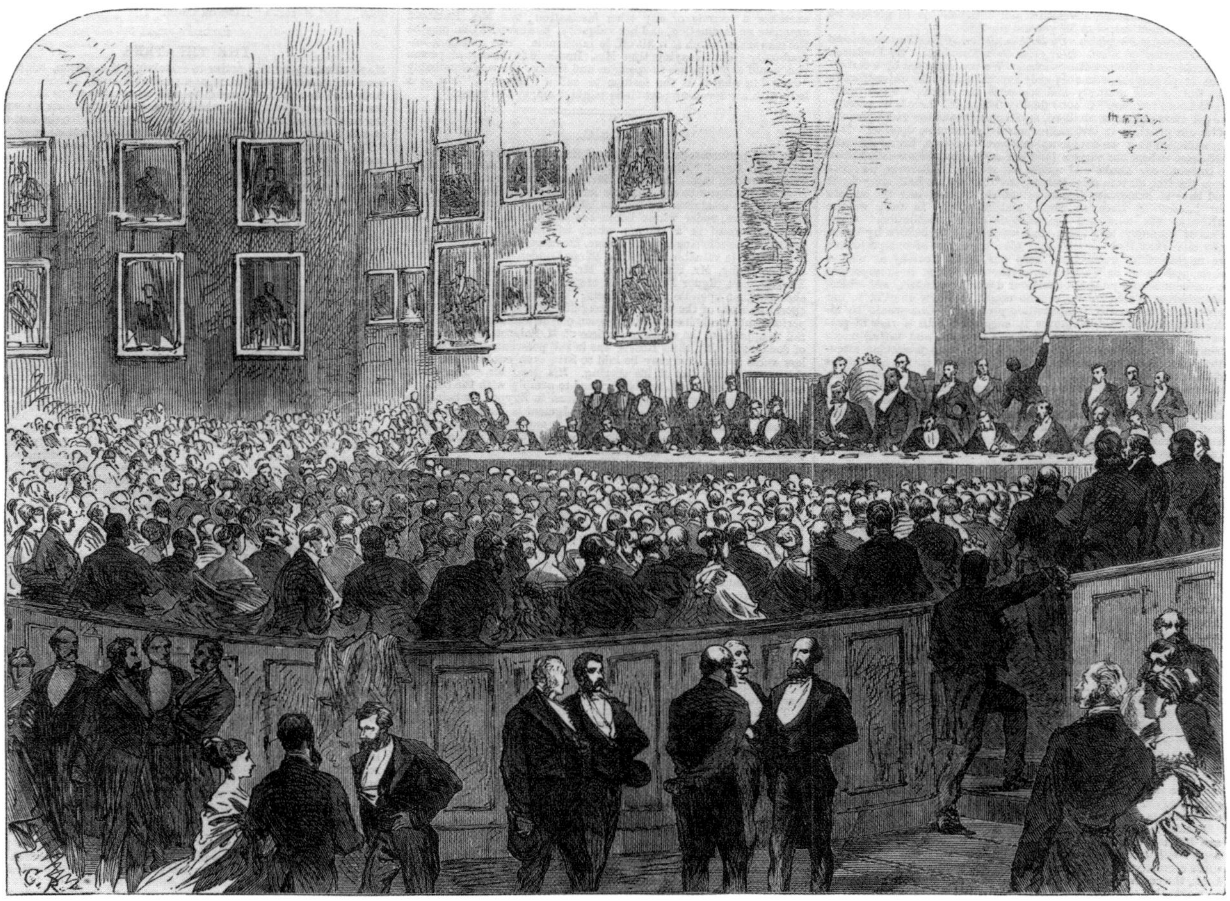

Fig. 161
'Mr Young describing his search for Dr Livingstone at the meeting of the Royal Geographical Society, Burlington House', from *Illustrated London News*, 8 February 1868.
Illustrated London News archive

depart indefinitely from the Original Type' in the Society's meeting room in Burlington House (now the Academy's Tennant Gallery) to an audience of fewer than thirty people, almost none of whom had an inkling of the revolutionary nature of what they were about to hear.[35]

Such was the popularity of Burlington House as a meeting place for scientists, on 22 April 1857, almost exactly a year to the day after it had decided not to move from Somerset House, the Geological Society resolved to petition the government to be allowed to join its former neighbour.[36] One of the main reasons for this change of heart was the fact that a scheme sketched out by the architect Philip Hardwick had demonstrated that it would be possible to meet all their requirements – including that of housing their indispensable and rapidly growing museum of geological specimens 'from distant lands throughout the world' – in a low, two-storey building on the east side of the courtyard, balancing that erected by the government for the Royal Society on the west.[37] After a considerable amount of stalling, the Treasury's eventual rejection of the Geologists' proposal in December 1857 – on the flimsy grounds that their apartments in Somerset House were not at that precise moment needed for the 'public service' – is a sign that the future of Burlington House was about to become enmeshed in wider political issues.[38]

AS IS OFTEN THE CASE IN POLITICS, this happened by association rather than direct cause and effect, inasmuch as a feeling that the public had gained nothing tangible from the purchase of Burlington House began to chime with longstanding dissatisfaction and distrust in the House of Commons over the government's repeated failure to resolve a scandalous shortage of space in both the National Gallery and the British Museum. Meanwhile, in what was seen an outrageous 'job', £180,000 had been spent in buying up apparently useless acres at Kensington Gore, for no other purpose it seemed than to suck up to the Prince Consort and encourage a toadying court faction to spirit away the nation's pictures from what Sir Robert Peel had called 'the finest site in Europe'.[39] As the artist Sir Edwin Landseer RA was to write in a letter to *The Times* some years later, 'Kensington had become a word depriving many people of their reason', and it is clear that the government's conspicuous inability to develop Burlington House and its valuable site for the benefit of the public was enough to draw down flak on whoever was using it, whether they were sparrows in the garden or gentlemen's clubs with a free roof over their heads.[40] A fractious, ill-informed debate in the Commons on 19 June 1857, triggered by the Treasury and Office of Works having omitted to obtain parliamentary sanction for the government's expenditure of £4,725 on converting the West Wing, elicited much John Bull mockery of the scientific pursuits of learned societies. As for 'declamations on the hustings about economy and retrenchment, [i]t was all stuff', declared the hon. member for Surrey Western, for as long as public money continued to be spent

> ... with respect to these societies – or, as they really are, clubs – one set of gentlemen, who were travellers, called themselves the Geographical Society; another set of gentlemen, who caught butterflies, called themselves the Linnæan Society. Those were the learned bodies which should be fostered and encouraged. Then there was a Geological Society: but what on earth was the use of a Geological Society? Could not the gentlemen who were fond of discussing questions of strata meet in their own houses? Why should the House go on year after year, providing out of the public taxes, for all these clubs, which they chose to dignify with the name of scientific societies?[41]

To give him his due, the Prime Minister jumped instantly to the societies' defence. However, it was enough to spark an inflammatory article in *Building News* the following week, in which the whole idea of public provision for learned societies at Burlington House, or anywhere else for that matter, was held up to high ridicule. Since this damaging piece was reprinted verbatim three days later in *The Standard*, the timing of the Geological Society's deputation to Downing Street that same week could have hardly been worse.[42]

The unexpected fall of Palmerston's ministry in February 1858 saw Lord John Manners reappointed by the new Prime Minister, Lord Derby, for a second stint as First Commissioner, with Disraeli as his Chancellor of the Exchequer. As leading figures in the 'Young England' movement both Manners and Disraeli were progressive Tories and evidently determined to find a once-and-for-all solution to the National Gallery's space problems, particularly since the 1857 Royal Commission on the site question had recommended that it would on balance be better for the Gallery to stay where it was in Trafalgar Square rather than move out to Kensington Gore. Disraeli's first step was to announce to the Commons on 4 June 1858 that it had been decided to accept the offer of the Commissioners of the 1851 Exhibition to buy back the half share of the Kensington Gore estate that the government had bought from them (somewhat ironically, at Disraeli's instigation) six years earlier. This popular decision had two immediate results: first, and most importantly in Disraeli's view, it meant

> there would be an end of all those jealousies which had so long prevailed, and all intention or power of placing the National Gallery at Kensington would, of course, be given up. If the House agreed to that arrangement, which it would soon be his duty to bring more formally under their notice, they would then have to consider the question of the National Gallery without reference to the site at Kensington-gore. Thus would terminate an old and painful controversy.[43]

And secondly, as Lord Elcho and William Coningham, two of the most experienced speakers on 'art questions' in the Commons were quick to point out, it meant ejecting the Royal Academy as soon as possible from Trafalgar Square.[44] Although he refused to be drawn into any definite statement in the debate on the National Gallery estimates the following month, in early February the next year Disraeli was able to make a dramatic announcement:

> The House will recollect that last Session, wearied by the continued unsettlement of the question, and having no confidence that any further inquiry by Select Committees or Royal Commissions would produce a very satisfactory result, there seemed to be a general feeling that the Government should attempt to cut the Gordian knot and bring the question to a final settlement. I undertook on the part of the Government, in deference to the feeling of the House, to obtain that result if possible, and I have the pleasure of informing the House that I have succeeded in accomplishing that which appeared to be the general wish of the country. The whole of the building in Trafalgar Square will speedily be entirely devoted to the National Gallery.[45]

Well aware of longstanding political sensitivity over the Academy's right to compensation for agreeing to quit 'their' half of the National Gallery building, Disraeli was keen to draw attention to the fact that they had 'announced their determination to raise [a] building for themselves' without accepting 'any public contribution' apart from the grant of a site. When asked whether he could name where site this was, for similar reasons he was careful not to go into what the consequences of allowing the Academy to erect its own building on the 'area around Burlington House' might be for its present occupants, stating only that it was to 'be connected with other public buildings', and that 'the interior will be left to the disposition of the Academy' and the exterior made 'subordinate to the design of the Government, if the Government insist upon that condition.' As Vernon Smith had reminded Gladstone five years earlier, the furore of criticism provoked in the press when the government had failed in its attempt to remove the Academy from Trafalgar Square in March 1850 – they had turned down Lord John Russell's proposed compensation (or, as some saw it, bribe) of £40,000 spread over two years – was not easily forgotten. This time the government prepared its ground more carefully, particularly in the House of Lords when, on 4 March 1859, Lord Lyndhurst, the former Lord Chancellor and son of the painter John Singleton Copley RA, delivered a long, impassioned and well-researched defence of the Academy's historic contribution to the fine arts in Britain.[46] Not only was this widely reported in the press (as was no doubt intended), but it also served as the perfect 'warm-up' for the Prime Minister's unveiling immediately afterwards of the government's latest plans for Burlington House.[47]

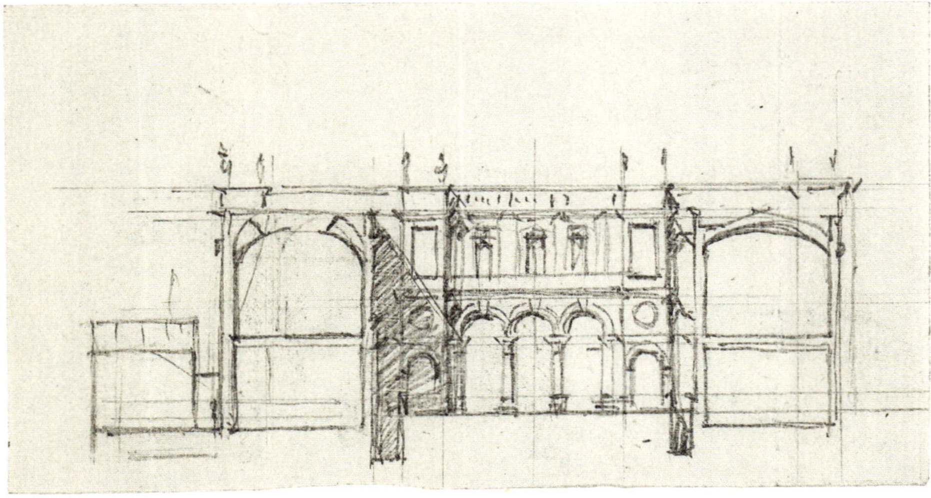

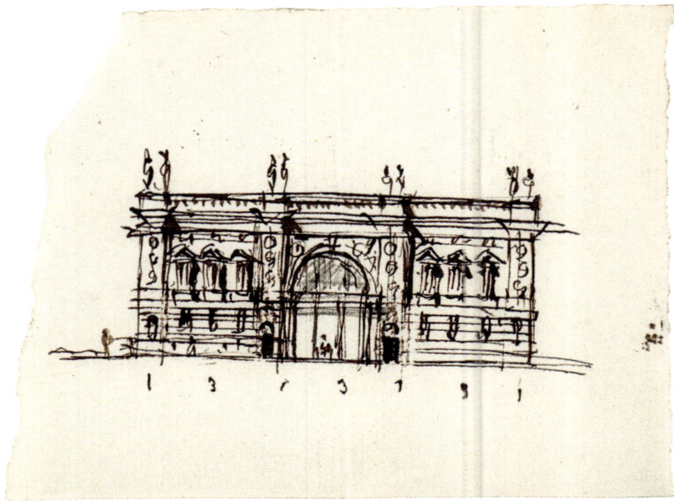

Fig. 162
Sir Charles Barry, Design for the Burlington House site, preliminary scheme for the Royal Academy building: section looking south, 1859.
Parliamentary Archives, BAR/31/6/8

Fig. 163
Sir Charles Barry, Design for the Burlington House site, preliminary scheme for the Royal Academy building: Piccadilly elevation, 1859.
Parliamentary Archives, BAR/31/6/9

An odd aspect of the government's approach to Burlington House at this point was its readiness to respond favourably to fresh applications for accommodation at the public's expense from other privately constituted institutions. This seems doubly strange in that it occurred at exactly the moment when it had been agreed that space would also have to be found to enable the Academy to build the larger galleries and art school that it claimed it needed to address acknowledged failings in the management of its exhibitions and the teaching it offered to its students. A clue to the thinking behind what seems a rather unusual level of government support for the promotion of art and science, either before or since, is to be found in a draft Treasury letter to the Board of Works dated 6 April 1859:

> Adverting to past correspondence, My Lords [Commissioners of H.M. Treasury] regard it as a settled point, that accommodation should be provided in the plans for –
>
> > The Royal & other learned Societies now enjoying the use of apartments in Burlington House & Somerset House, The University of London, The Patent Office, and the Royal Academy.
>
> The ulterior objects are –
>
> > 1stly the Association of other learned bodies with those who have obtained from sufferance or prescript claim to the grant of apartments, and 2ndly the extension of the facilities of public Exhibitions to other branches of the fine arts than those which are prominently represented by the Royal Academy.
>
> Of the first class, My Lords have before them applications from the Royal Geographical Society and the Royal Asiatic Society; and, of the second class, applications have been addressed to Her Majesty's Government for the grant of exhibition rooms, either freely or on such terms as may be agreed upon, from the two Societies of Water Colours, and the Photographic Society.[48]

Although they begin by stating categorically, 'With respect to the first [ulterior object], My Lords cannot admit that learned bodies, voluntarily associated, have any claim for accommodation at the public expense' – an easily misunderstood and misused statement when taken out of context – there was evidently good reason for the government to recognise such a claim *at that particular moment*, since their lordships immediately go on to state that

> … at the same time having regard to the number of these institutions which are already accommodated at the public expense, and to the great advantage which w^{d} accrue to science from the assemblage of learned associations in one locality, with a common Library, and hall for lectures and other purposes, My Lords would be willing if there be sufficient space available, to provide apartments for the societies that now seek admission, subject to arrangements to be framed in concert with the Royal & other societies now placed in Burlington House, for the use of the common Hall & Library.

The point to grasp here is that the wider the government cast its net in accepting these specific claims the more public in character a new building to house the resulting 'assemblage' could be made to appear, and the less risk there was of it becoming identified with one particular institution. This strategy becomes overt in the case of the 'second class' of applicants, where the government's proposed provision of separate exhibition galleries for both the 'Old' and 'New' watercolour societies and the

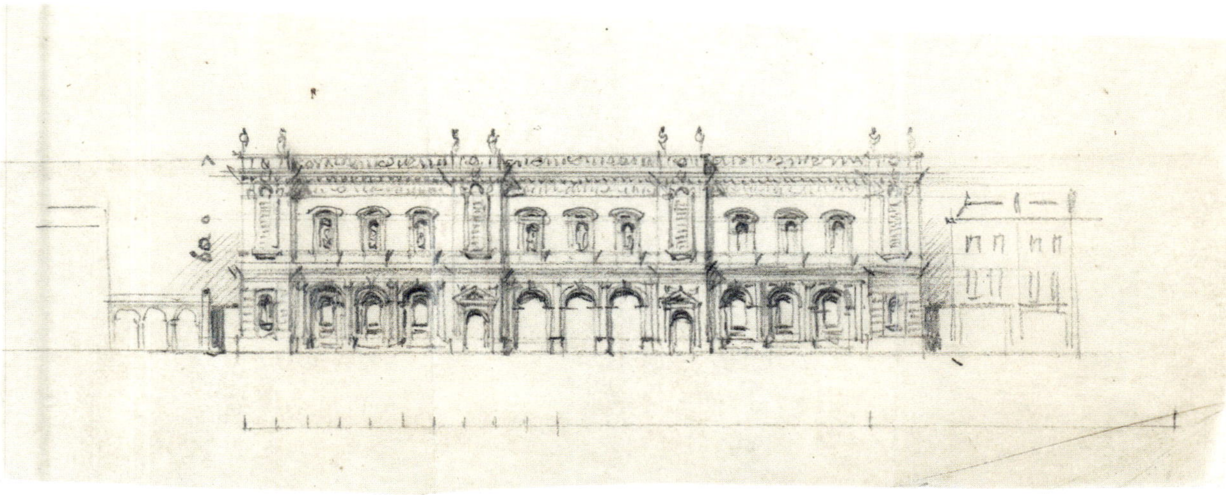

Fig. 164
Sir Charles Barry, Design for the Burlington House site, preliminary scheme for the Royal Academy building: Piccadilly elevation, 1859.
Parliamentary Archives, BAR/31/6/2

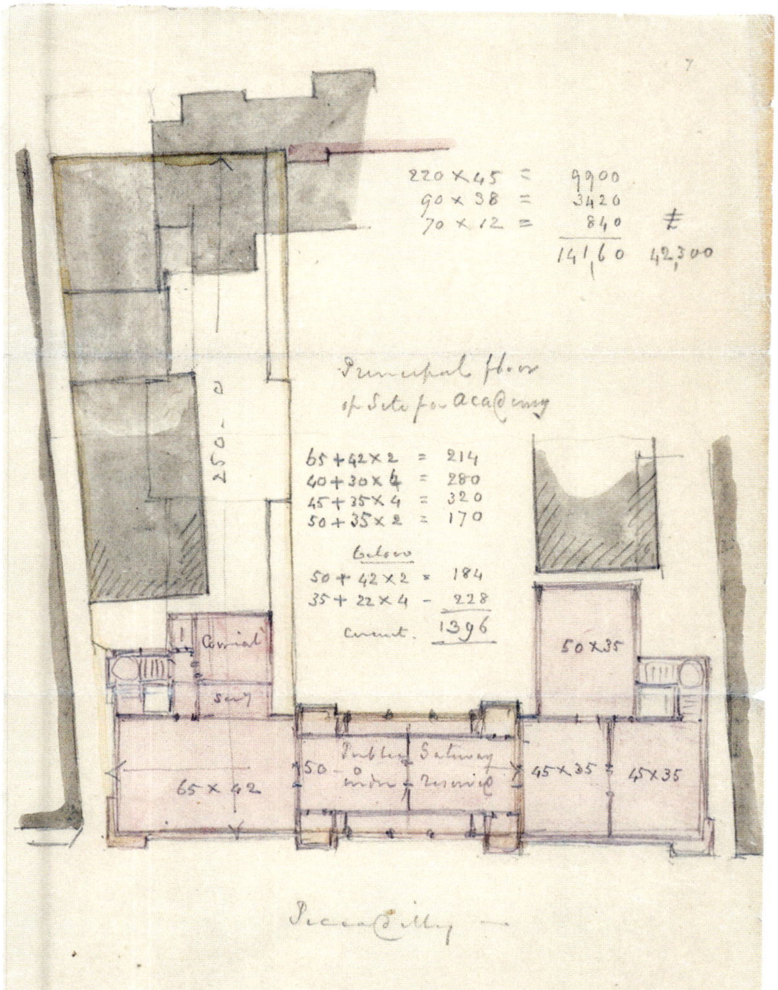

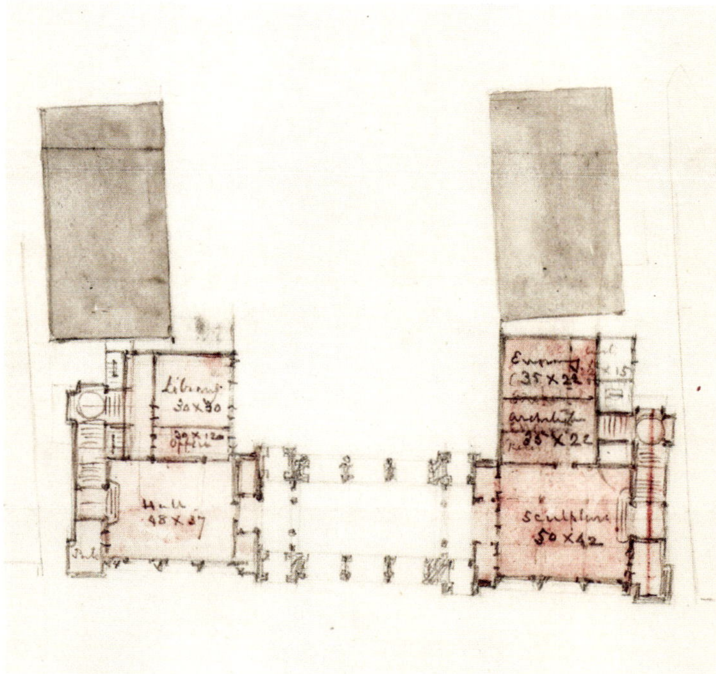

Fig. 165
Sir Charles Barry, Design for the Burlington House site, preliminary scheme for the Royal Academy building: plan of principal floor, 1859.
Parliamentary Archives, BAR/31/6/3

Fig. 166
Sir Charles Barry, Design for the Burlington House site, preliminary scheme for the Royal Academy building: ground-floor plan, 1859.
Parliamentary Archives, BAR/31/6/1

Photographic Society is an explicit attempt to prevent Burlington House from becoming synonymous with the Royal Academy. Realising, however, that the watercolour societies as presently constituted were more restrictive than the Academy in that they confined their exhibitions to the work of their respective members, the government went so far as to propose that it should retain 'the power of deciding on the terms and principles upon which the rooms, if erected, should be applied to the encouragement of this branch of the art' and 'not commit themselves at present to any understanding for granting the use of these to the Existing Societies either on payment of rent or otherwise, until their public position shall have been fully considered.'

An obvious difficulty in the way of ensuring that the Academy did not take up more space than it actually

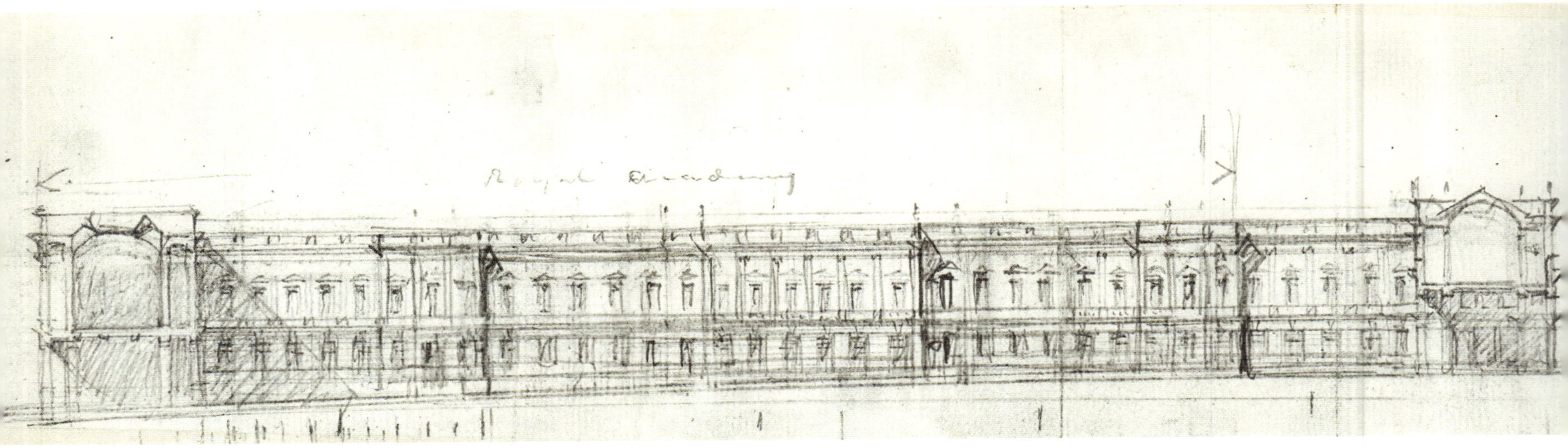

needed, and that its new building harmonised with how the government proposed to house other institutions on the site, was the fact that unlike the latter it was in a position to commission its own architect. Here the Office of Works had a stroke of luck: on 25 March 1859 the General Assembly of Royal Academicians elected Sir Charles Barry RA as the 'Architect for the new Royal Academy'. This choice was almost certainly made in the knowledge that Barry's former 'chief confidential assistant' Robert Richardson Banks and his eldest son Charles Barry junior had been or were about to be appointed as architects for the new building at Burlington House in compensation for the First Commissioner having passed over their 'Roman' Foreign Office competition design the previous November in favour of a Gothic design by George Gilbert Scott.

Although he started out by planning a separate building for the Academy on Piccadilly, Sir Charles's preliminary design clearly demonstrated that it would have been impossible to find room for the Academy's Schools within a building that was bisected by a public carriageway and pedestrian entrances (Figs 162–166). He had no alternative but to make the Academy's building integral with those proposed for the other institutions, which of course provided the perfect excuse (which he hardly needed) to collaborate directly with his son and former chief assistant in producing a design for a unified complex across the entire site. Known now only from a small group of exquisite preliminary plans and sketches drawn in his own hand, and from the recollections of Charles Barry junior published in his younger brother's biography of their father, this proposed rebuilding of

Fig. 167
Sir Charles Barry, Design for the Burlington House site, second scheme: section looking west, 1859.
Parliamentary Archives, BAR/31/6/20

Fig. 168
Sir Charles Barry, Design for the Burlington House site, second scheme: block plan with ground-floor plan of the Royal Academy building, 1859.
Parliamentary Archives, BAR/31/6/17

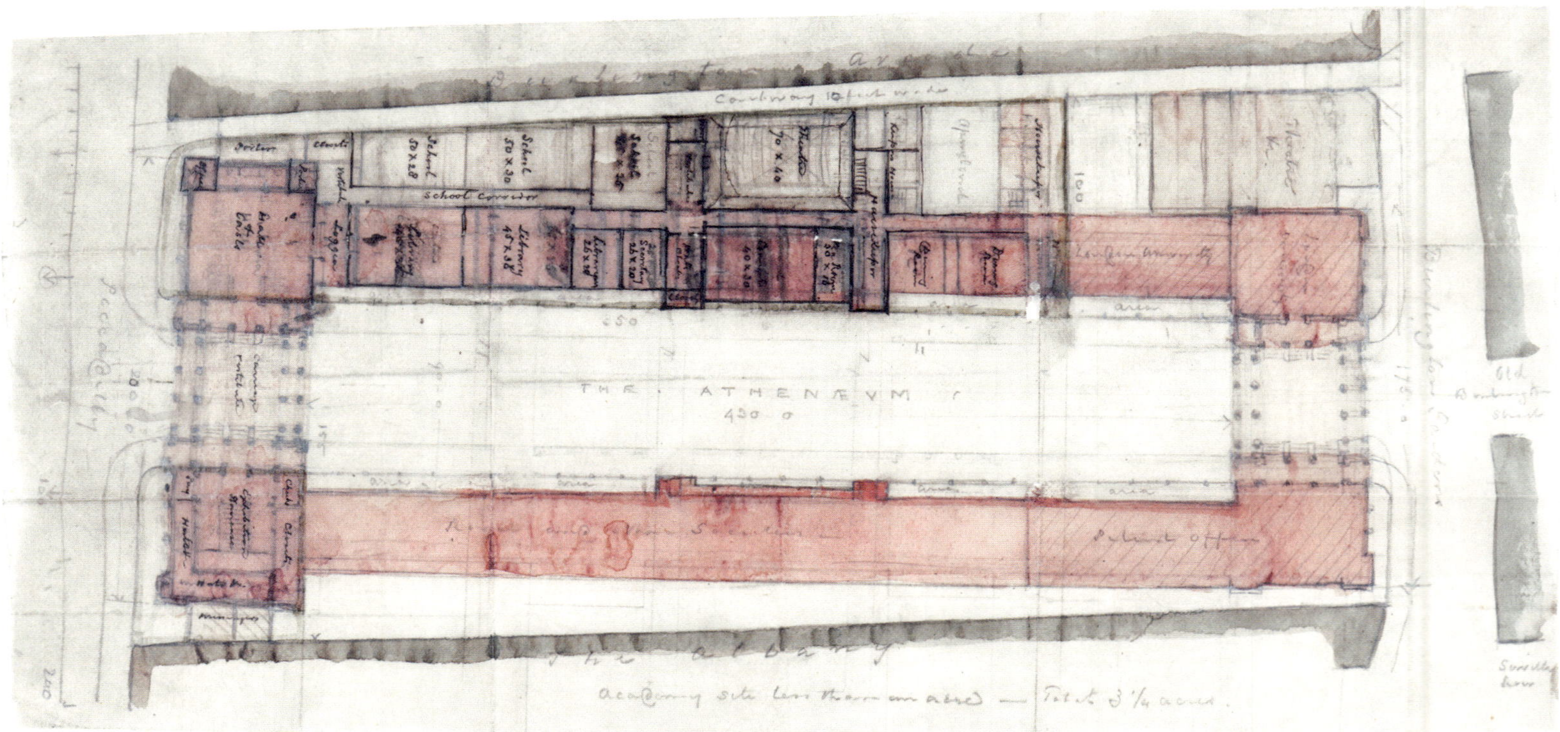

Burlington House as a great metropolitan centre for the arts, sciences, technology and academia was recognised at the time of his death the following year as 'among the last and finest of his designs'. Had it been built, it would have supplanted Trafalgar Square as London's grandest civic space.[49]

In what was probably the earlier of two variant schemes, Barry arranged all the institutions seamlessly around a single quadrangle, 430 feet long and 90 feet wide, to form what he termed 'The Athenæum' (Figs 167, 168). With matching triple-lane carriageways and flanking pedestrian entrances on the quadrangle's north and south sides, the University's offices and a large lecture theatre lay to the north-west with a frontage on Burlington Gardens; the Patent Office, with ample space for its museum and library, lay opposite the University on the north-east side; while an unspecified number of learned societies were grouped to the south-east facing the Academy on the south-west side. The latter took up not only the Piccadilly block but three-quarters of the entire western range as well, so it is hardly surprising Barry sought to lower raised eyebrows in the Office of Works by noting on his drawing 'Academy site less than an acre – Total 3¼ acres'. Bowing no doubt to pressure to reduce the Academy's requirements as a proportion of the available building area, Barry also produced a second, arguably finer variant design in which separate 'Academy' and 'University' courtyards were formed by a transverse range pierced by carriage and pedestrian thoroughfares matching those to the north and south (Figs 169–174). Reminiscent of John Webb's great unbuilt project for a new palace at Whitehall, this dividing range served to focus the whole composition not on the Piccadilly front (i.e. the Academy) but rather on the University's Hall, a 105-foot-long, 68-foot-wide and 50-foot-high basilica-like examination-cum-lecture theatre situated at the centre of the site and intended presumably to function in the same way as the 'Great Hall' in the old Burlington House courtyard had done.

On 14 July 1859, a little more than a month after Manners had vacated the post of First Commissioner for the second time in his career, Banks & Barry's report on their scheme for Burlington House, which they based on details of the space requirements provided by the institutions currently accommodated there and at Somerset House, landed on the desk of Palmerston's new appointee, Henry Fitzroy.[50] Although Gladstone's return as Chancellor of the Exchequer might have augured well (he had after all been largely responsible for the government's decision to buy Burlington House in the first place), there was now virtually no chance of Parliament agreeing to vote £300,000 for a building devoted mainly (or so some thought) to wealthy gentlemen's hobbies, when the country was in debt by £5 million and the Chancellor was about to raise income tax from 5d. to 9d. in the pound. It was hardly surprising that a Treasury note written for 'Mr Gladstone' on 18 October 1859 was aimed at scaling down the previous administration's commitments in relation to Banks & Barry's scheme and exploring as far as possible 'the chief points for consideration with a view to Economy', *viz*:

> 1 Frontage – whether any of this could be made available for shops
> 2 Height – whether any more could be added – they propose only a ground & first floor
> 3 Apportionment of site – whether the Royal Academy & Societies really need all they ask – Messrs Banks & Barry's plan probably gives them all they have asked for & certainly far more in many cases than they have at present. Can they not be made to do with less, & space be saved for the other Public Offices for which we now pay high Rents.[51]

A century later an old hand at the Treasury was to express similar scepticism in the same situation:

> As you know I do not think that the Ministry of Works' statements of the accommodation requirements of these societies are worth the paper they are written on. They are simply the result of a Ministry of Works official going round the societies and asking them for their bids. Having no public accountability whatsoever the size of the bid depends simply on the degree of effrontery possessed by the President and Secretary of the Learned Society concerned.[52]

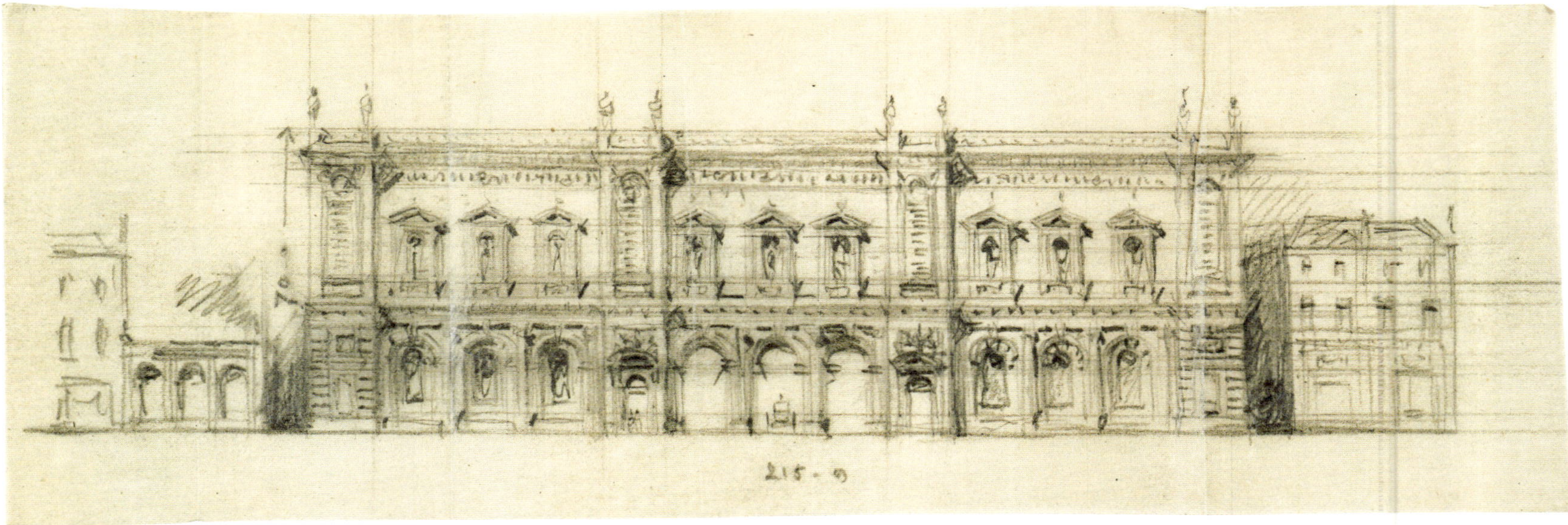

Fig. 169
Sir Charles Barry, Design for the Burlington House site: Piccadilly elevation, 1859.
Parliamentary Archives, BAR/31/6/6

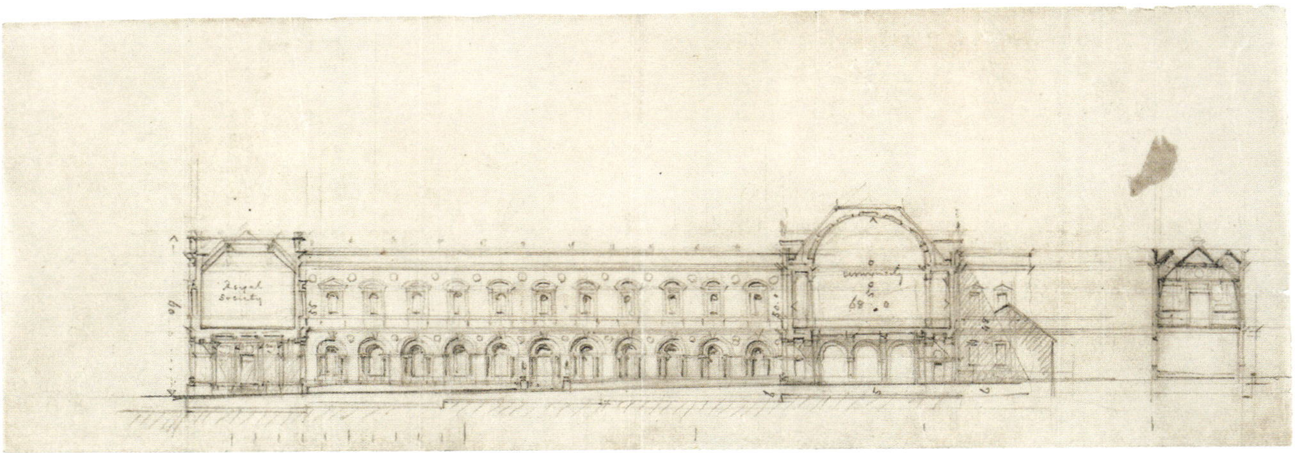

Fig. 170
Sir Charles Barry, Design for the Burlington House site, third scheme: part section looking west, 1859.
Parliamentary Archives, BAR/31/6/5

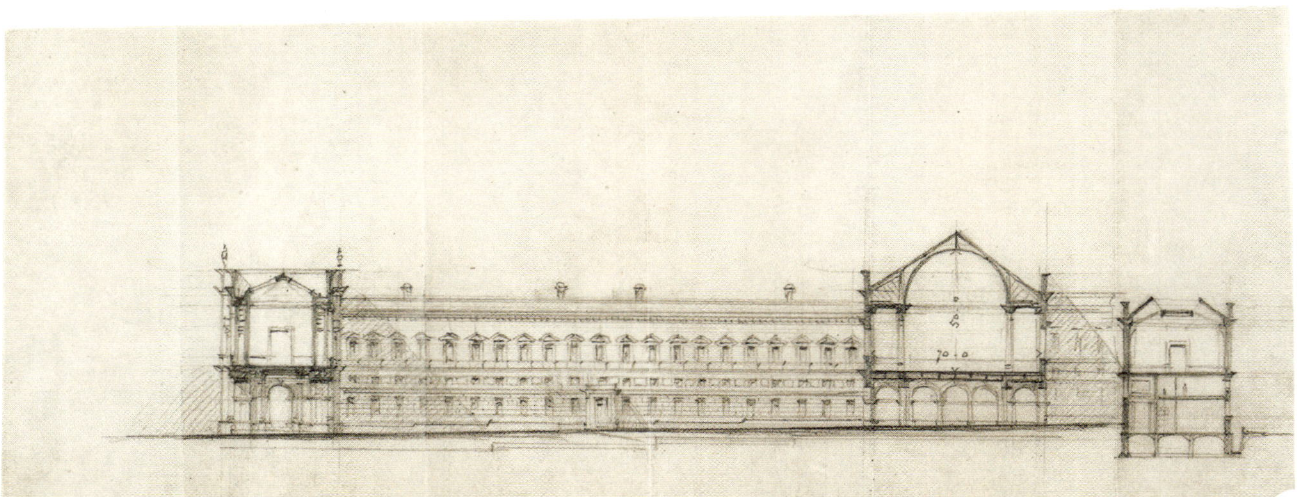

Fig. 171
Sir Charles Barry, Design for the Burlington House site, variant of third scheme with 21-bay courtyard elevation, and aisle and nave to University Hall: part section looking west, 1859.
Parliamentary Archives, BAR/31/6/4

Whether or not the Office of Works acted on the Treasury's recommendation that their in-house architect James Pennethorne 'might be employed with advantage, as soon as any general ideas are settled on the subject, to criticize Banks & Barry's Plans & show what could be done with a view to Economy', a further disincentive to proceed with Banks & Barry's project came into play on 21 January 1860 when the trustees of the British Museum voted to remove its natural-history collections from Bloomsbury. As a result, for a while at least, Burlington House was spoken of as a better option than Kensington as a site for rehousing what were then the British Museum's most popular exhibits somewhere where they could continue to be easily visited by most people.[53]

BY MAY 1860 it was common knowledge that the previous administration's ambitious plans for Burlington House had been set aside. Thus, on the 12th of that month – strangely, the day that Sir Charles Barry died – Leonard Horner, president of the Geological Society, wrote to Gladstone in the hope that Philip Hardwick's 1857 proposal might be reconsidered in the light of the fact that the previous government's 'proposed plan would not be carried into execution', and 'that it is considered by the [present] Government to be very undesirable that the existing Burlington House should be removed, or that its exterior should be altered'.[54] Like the Royal Society's 'Lower Library' on the west side of the courtyard, an equivalent building for the Geological Society on the east side could, he thought, be 'accomplished without in any degree affecting the external elevation' and at a cost well below the rentable value of the rooms they were currently occupying at Somerset House. Unfortunately, the Geologists were destined to be disappointed again on the grounds that 'Their Lordships … are not at present in a position to decide finally as to the application of the ground occupied by Burlington House.'[55]

Three months later, sensitivity over the government's inability to settle on a permanent use for Burlington House provoked one of Gladstone's famous outbursts in the Commons. Stung by a typically waspish jibe from Acton Smee Ayrton, MP for Tower Hamlets and a future

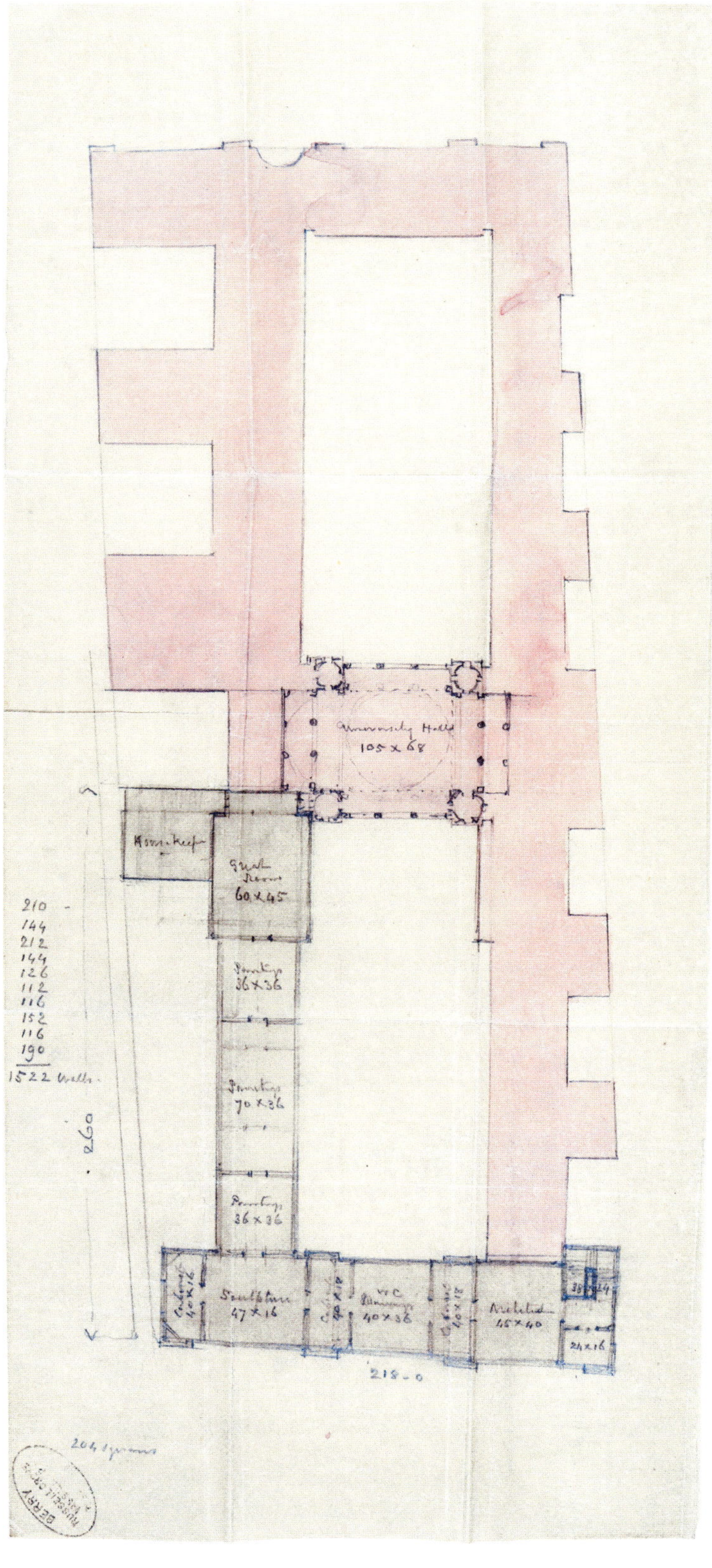

Fig. 172
Sir Charles Barry, Design for the Burlington House site, third scheme: block plan with first-floor plan of the Royal Academy building and University Hall, 1859.
Parliamentary Archives, BAR/31/6/19

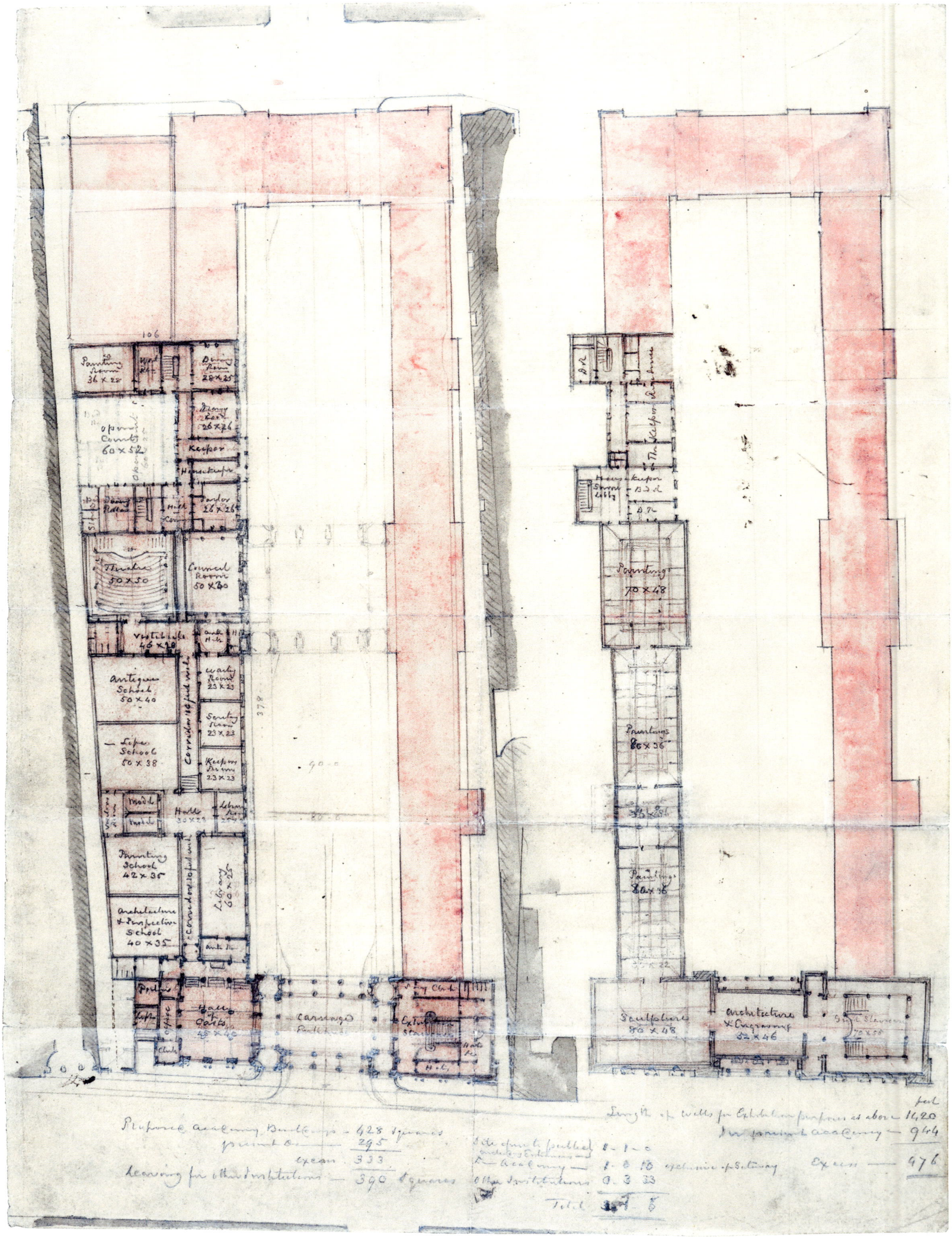
Painting Room 36 x 25
Drawing Room 28 x 25
Open Court 60 x 52
Keeper
Housekeeper
Parlor 26 x 26
Theatre 50 x 50
Council Room 50 x 30
Vestibule 45 x 20
Antique School 50 x 40
Life School 50 x 38
Painting School 42 x 35
Architecture & Perspective School 40 x 35
Library 60 x 25
Hall of Casts 45 x 40
Carriage
Painting 70 x 48
Paintings 86 x 36
Sculpture 80 x 48
Architecture & Engraving 55 x 46

Fig. 173
Sir Charles Barry, Design for the Burlington House site, second scheme: block plan with ground- and first-floor plans of the Royal Academy building, 1859.
Parliamentary Archives, BAR/31/6/13

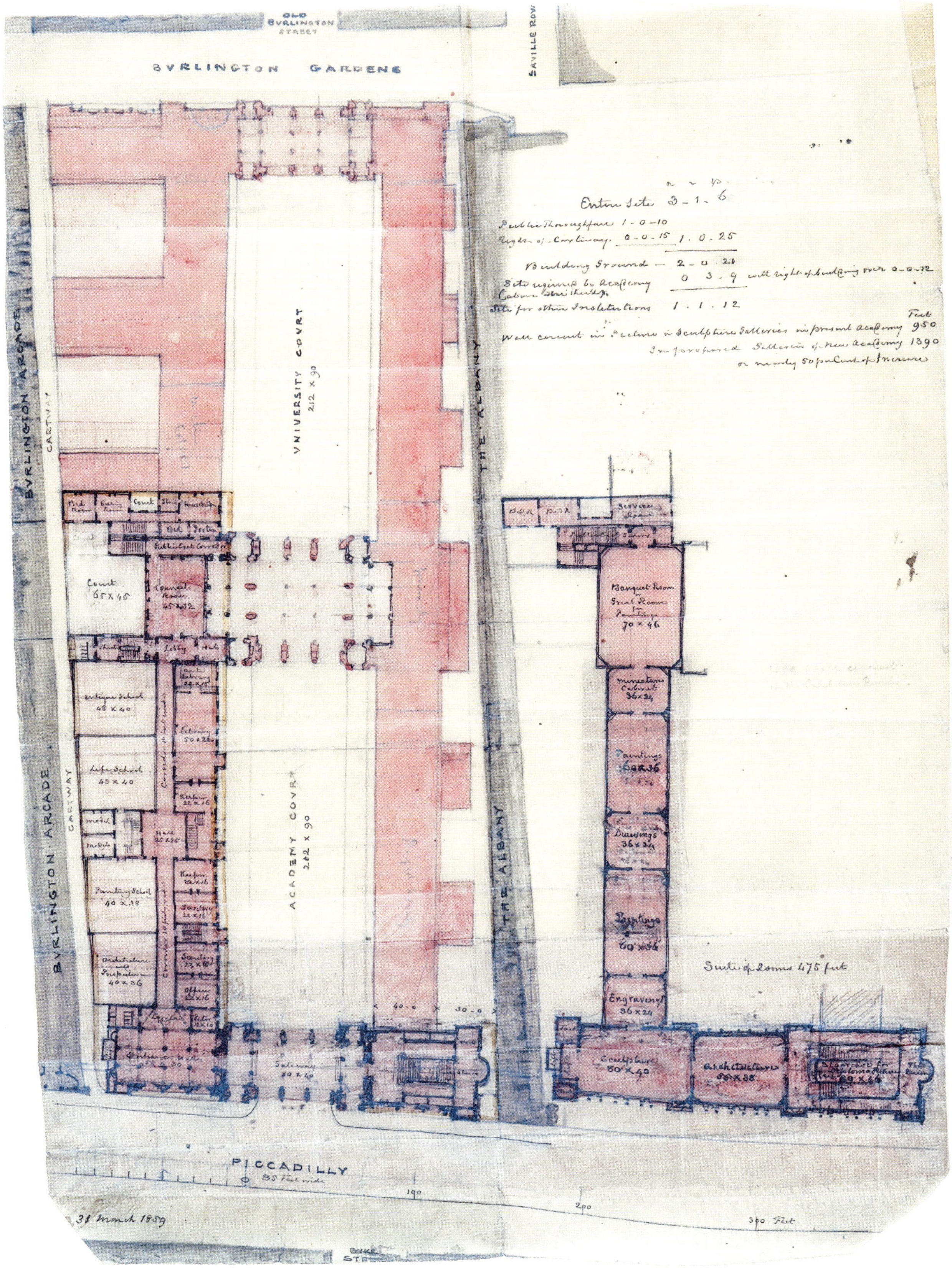

Fig. 174
Sir Charles Barry, Design for the Burlington House site, third scheme, block plan with ground- and first-floor plans of the Royal Academy building, 1859.
Parliamentary Archives, BAR/31/6/15

First Commissioner of Works, that Burlington House 'was unoccupied except by the London University that had almost no material existence, and by the Royal Society which might be considered as an effete body', Gladstone cast the blame everywhere except on himself. 'He regretted', he declared,

> as much as the hon. member for Tower Hamlets could do, that such long periods should elapse before any conclusion could be arrived at as to the disposal of buildings of that kind ... He had no hesitation in saying that this and other circumstances of a like kind were entirely owing to the lamentable and deplorable state of our whole arrangement with regard to the management of our public works. Vacillation, uncertainty, costliness, extravagance, meanness, and all the conflicting vices that could be enumerated were united in our present system ... When anything was to be done they had to go from department to department – from the Executive to the House of Commons, from the House of Commons to a Committee, from a Committee to a Commission, and from a Commission back to a Committee – so that years passed away, the public were disappointed, and the money of the country was wasted. He believed such were the evils of the system, that nothing short of a revolutionary reform would ever be sufficient to rectify it.[56]

It cannot have helped that Palmerston's stepson William Cowper, who succeeded as First Commissioner after a two-month interregnum following Fitzroy's death in December 1859, was well-known among his friends 'for his charming way of bowing in complaisance, if something was suggested to him that he did not mean to do'.[57] Tactical evasion seems to have come naturally to him since he was to deploy it frequently over the next four years whenever questions were asked in the Commons about the government's plans for Burlington House. Thus, to Austen Layard's prod on behalf of the RGS on 1 July 1861, 'Whether the Government were prepared to place plans before the House for the erection of suitable buildings on the site of Burlington House?', Cowper replied, 'No final decision had yet been come to by the Government on many plans before it for appropriating the site and garden of Burlington House; but he hoped in a short time that decision would be made'.[58] To a straight question from Lord John Manners on 16 July 1861, 'What was the state of the negotiations between the Government and the Royal Academy with reference to the transfer of the latter to Burlington House?', in Cowper's absence the Prime Minister flannelled that he 'was not aware of the exact state of the negotiations, but the Royal Academy was prepared to go to Burlington House when they were summoned to do so; but some alterations in the building would be required, and he believed the plans had not yet been prepared'.[59] To Lord Elcho's bombshell query on 14 February 1862, 'Whether there is any truth in the report that plans for a new National Gallery, to be erected on the Burlington House site, have been prepared, and that a vote for its erection is to be proposed to Parliament in the present Session', Cowper stuck firmly to the official line that, 'at present, the Government had not come to any decision in the matter'.[60] And to Alexander Baillie Cochrane's charge on 5 June 1863 that Burlington House was yet 'another glaring instance of money thrown away', all Cowper could muster in his defence was to assert, 'It was a most valuable possession for the country and that he hoped that before long the Government would be able to put before the House a scheme of appropriation for this site'.[61]

A fortnight later he was finally forced to admit, 'that a scheme had been for a considerable time under the consideration of the Government for erecting a new National Gallery at the rear of Burlington House, and for leaving the existing National Gallery entirely in the possession of the Royal Academy'.[62] When Cochrane renewed his attack on mismanagement in the Office of Works' three weeks later, he naturally began

> ... with Burlington House. It was purchased by the Government in 1852 for a sum of £160,000. In 1855, 1856, and 1857—in nearly every year since 1852—Her Majesty's Government had been asked by Members of that House what they intended to do with Burlington House. The same question was put to his right hon. Friend the First Commissioner of Works the other

day, and he made a very mild joke about it. He rather turned it off; and the other night the right hon. Gentleman the Chancellor of the Exchequer, when the same question was put to him, replied, 'Wait till you come to a decision about the building at South Kensington, and then I will tell you what we will do with Burlington House.' The grounds of Burlington House were now turned into a kind of practice ground for Volunteers, who threw up earthworks and carried on a kind of mimic warfare on a small scale. The house itself had been taken possession of by the Geological Society and some other societies, and the property was entirely lost to the country.

Apart from correcting some of Cochrane's factual errors, and committing several new ones of his own, Cowper's defence of the record of the Office of Works in its handling of Burlington House consisted mainly of the classic bureaucratic excuse that 'the action of the Department depended on other and wider considerations' (Fig. 175).[63] Another nine months were to pass before the First Commissioner was prepared to inform the Commons that 'he believed that he would soon be able to lay on the table an estimate for erecting a National Gallery in the Garden of Burlington House …'.[64] On the surface Cowper's procrastination seems merely a cover for indecision, and to amply justify Augustus De Morgan's prediction back in July 1854 that,

We [i.e. the Astronomical Society] shall not be stirred these ten years, I augur. You know the story of the birds in the nest listening to the farmer plotting how to cut the corn. Now Government is a man who cannot work for himself. He works through people who *report*. Deep calleth unto deep – that is, one office reports to another, and the other refers back, and they then consider, and red tape becomes grey before they have settled how to proceed. And if you give them six months start and set a snail at them, the snail beats them by a thousand lengths; and then there is a change of Ministry, and a new report to 'my lords', and my 'lords' make a minute, which in time means a year, and so *ad infinitum*.[65]

The political reality, however, was that, whatever good reasons there might have been for abandoning the previous Tory government's ambitious plans for Burlington House, the present Liberal government's change of course had merely served to increase the pressure to find a solution to the National Gallery's space problems that had a better chance of appearing to be definitive, economical, and 'worthy of the British people'.[66] Settlement of this thorny issue had become an even greater prize for Palmerston, Gladstone and Cowper than it had been when it slipped through the fingers of Derby, Disraeli and Manners.

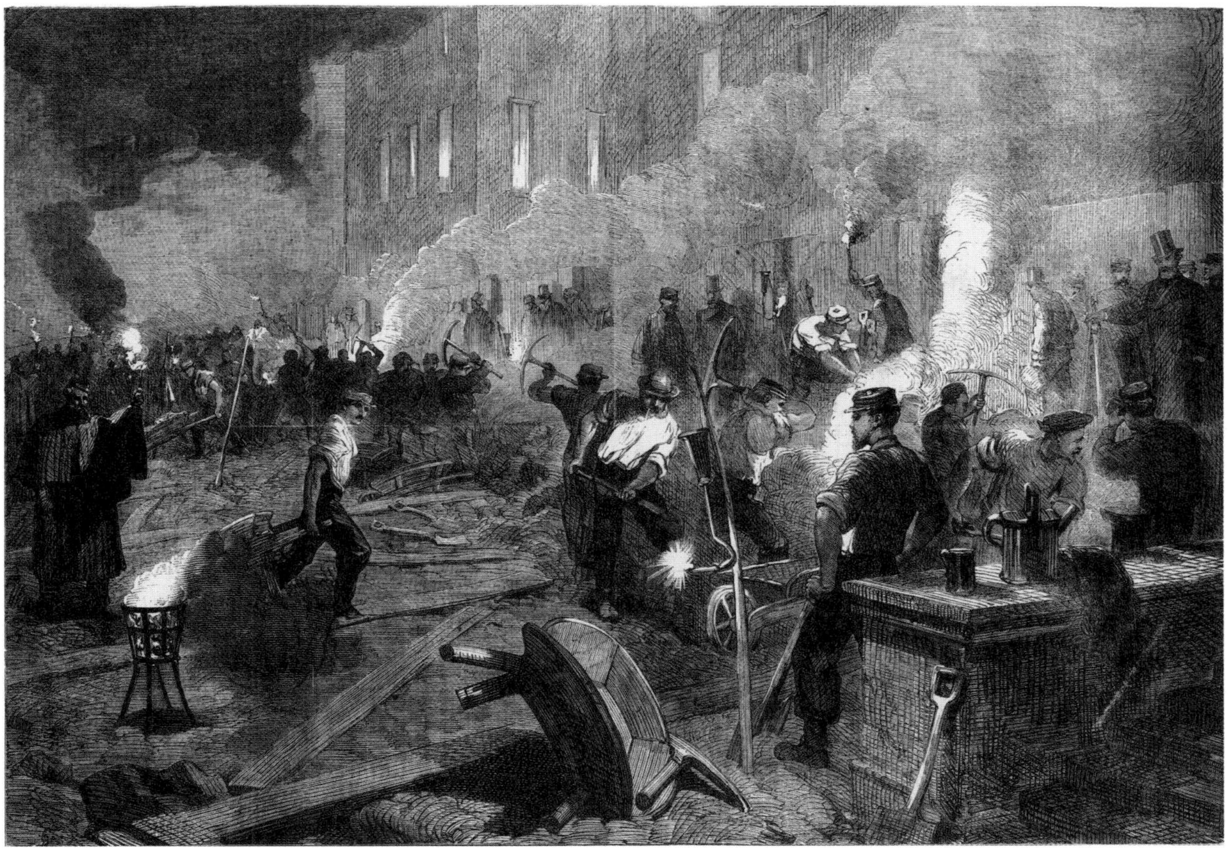

Fig. 175
'Members of the South Middlesex Rifle Volunteers at work by torchlight in the gardens of Burlington House clearing the ground for a drill-shed', from *Illustrated London News*, 18 January 1862, p. 77.
Illustrated London News Archive

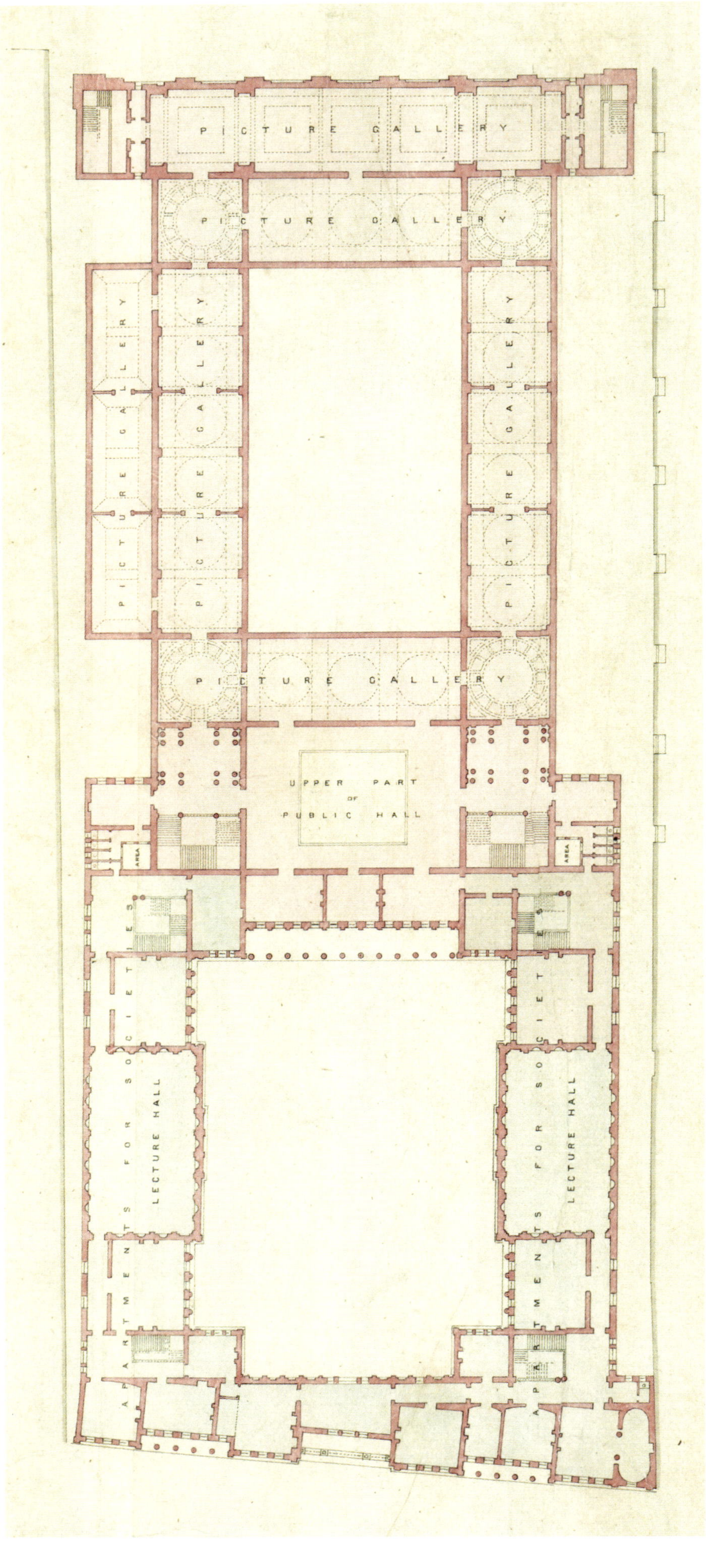

Fig. 176
Sir James Pennethorne, Design for a National Gallery on the Burlington House site: plan of the gallery floor, 23 November 1861.
The National Archives, Kew, WORK 30/529

Fig. 177
Sir James Pennethorne, Proposed National Gallery in Burlington Gardens, with existing buildings retained: ground plan, August 1861.
The National Archives, Kew, WORK 30/530

Palmerston's conversion to the idea of erecting a new National Gallery on the garden behind Burlington House rather than enlarging the Trafalgar Square building – a notion that he had dismissed as ridiculous in 1856 – may have stemmed originally from a recommendation in the report of the Select Committee on Public Institutions chaired by Lord Overstone early in 1860, where it was warmly endorsed both by the chairman and by Sir Charles Eastlake, the former director of the National Gallery and, as the president of the Royal Academy, one of the Gallery's most influential trustees.[67] Another factor that almost certainly affected the government's timing as well as Palmerston's change of mind was the fact that the report of the 1863 Royal Commission 'appointed to inquire into the present position of the Royal Academy in relation to the Fine Arts' had shown that it might well be preferable for the Academy to stay in Trafalgar Square and for the Gallery to move to Burlington House instead.[68] Thus, despite his earlier scorn, by 10 June 1863 Palmerston was writing to Gladstone that he took

> the general opinion about the National Gallery … to be that the best general arrangement would be to erect an unpretentious Building [for the Gallery] in Burlington Garden between the present House and Savile Row, with no ornament except towards Savile Row, and lighted from the Roof, while the Building in Trafalgar Square might be sold to the Royal Academy … who I believe could give us £70,000 for it which Sum would go a long way towards the Cost of a suitable Building in Burlington Garden.[69]

At some point previous to this letter, Cowper had written at length to Palmerston expressing a preference for enlarging the Trafalgar Square building rather than erecting a new National Gallery on the Burlington House site. The latter he had then envisaged as having 'an upper storey of picture galleries … combined with a lower storey occupied by the learned societies … arranged according to the suggestions of Messrs Banks and Barry with two inner quadrangles'.[70] This would appear to correspond to Pennethorne's design 'No. 4', which is signed and dated 23 November 1861 and evidently

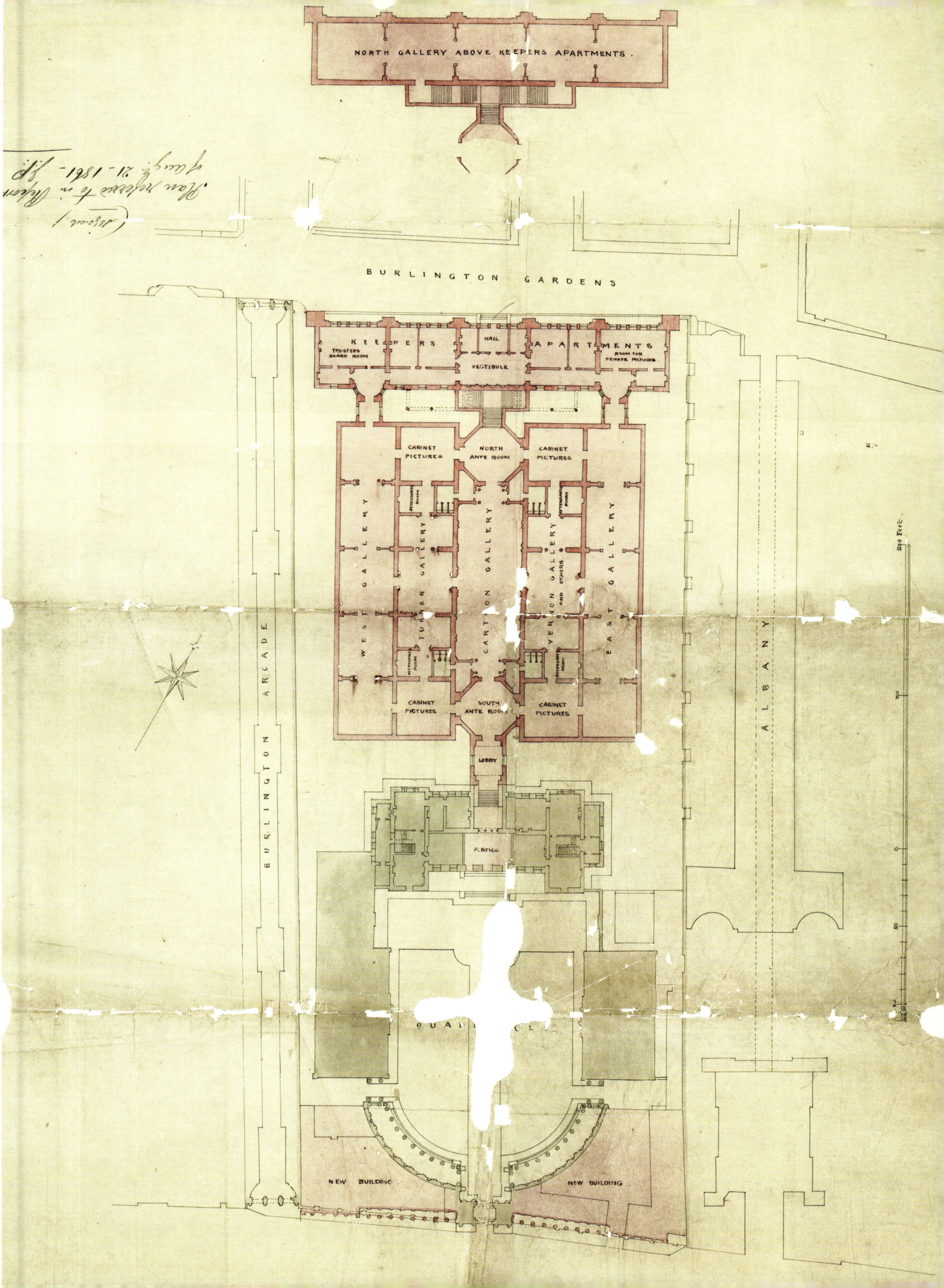
NORTH GALLERY ABOVE KEEPERS APARTMENTS.
BURLINGTON GARDENS
KEEPERS APARTMENTS
TRUSTEES BOARD ROOM
HALL
VESTIBULE
ROOM FOR PRIVATE PICTURES
CABINET PICTURES
NORTH ANTE ROOM
CABINET PICTURES
WEST GALLERY
TURNER GALLERY
CARTOON GALLERY
VERNON GALLERY AND OTHERS
EAST GALLERY
CABINET PICTURES
SOUTH ANTE ROOM
CABINET PICTURES
LOBBY
PORTICO
NEW BUILDING
NEW BUILDING
BURLINGTON ARCADE
ALBANY
200 Feet

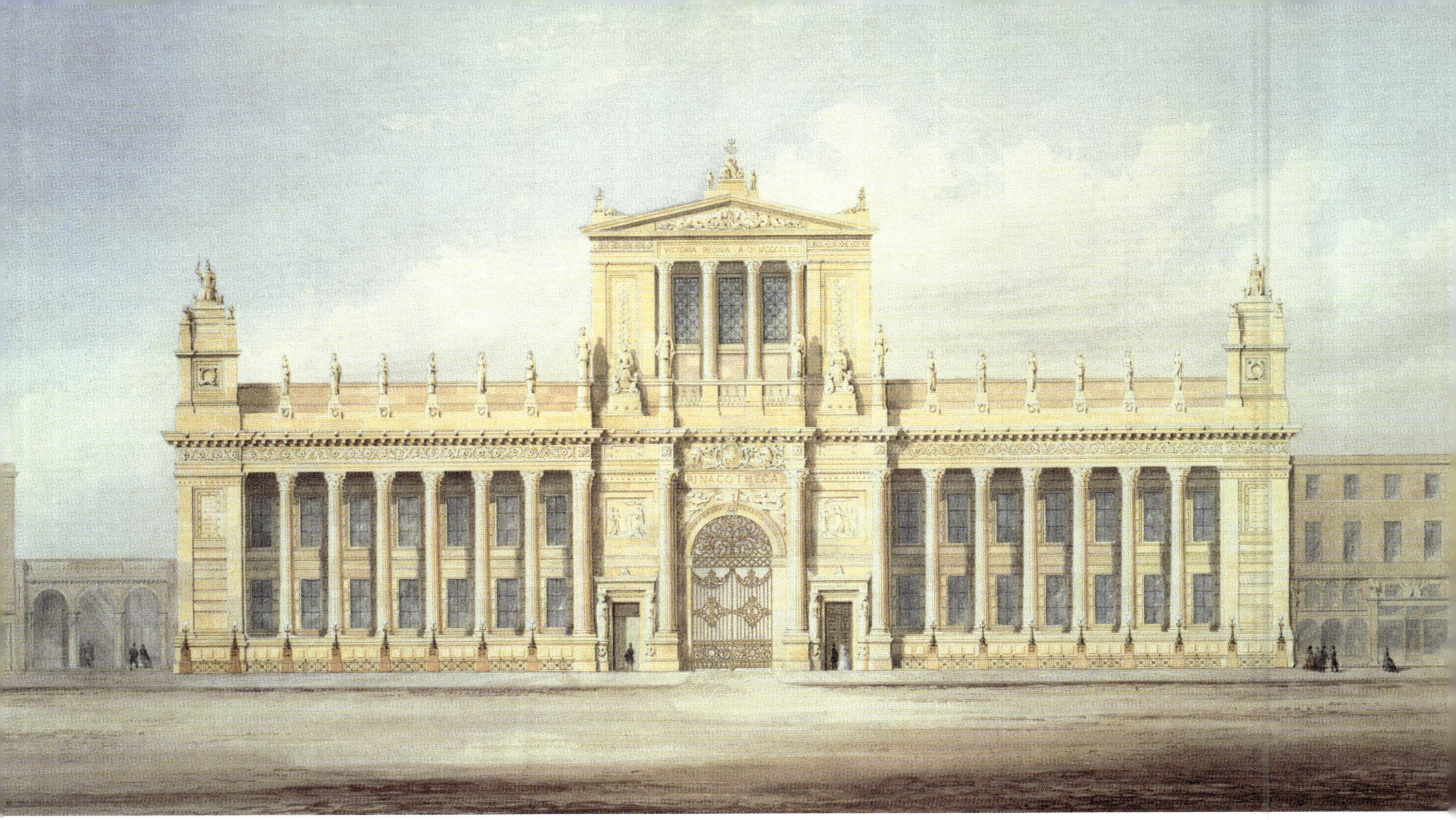

accompanied his letter to Cowper dated the same day (Fig. 176).[71] However, Palmerston's letter to Gladstone in June 1863 evidently refers to a proposal closer to Pennethorne's earlier, less costly design 'No. 2' dating from August 1861 (Fig. 177), in which a single-storey gallery extended over the whole garden and the learned societies were left where they were in the existing buildings. This suggests that Pennethorne's earlier option had become by then the government's preferred choice despite the architect's strenuous efforts to promote his later design with a spectacular presentation drawing of a monumental 'Pinacotheca' on Piccadilly reminiscent of Karl Friedrich Schinkel's Altes Museum in Berlin (Figs 178, 179).

The rumour of plans for a National Gallery at Burlington House that reached Lord Elcho's ears in February 1862 must have also been circulating by then in the architectural profession, prompting the architect Sydney Smirke RA, who had been appointed treasurer of the Royal Academy in March the previous year, to throw his hat into the ring with a fantasy of the Louvre transported to London's dingy West End (Fig. 180). Smirke's intervention was almost certainly not an attempt to pluck a prize plum from under Pennethorne's nose, but rather a way of signalling his (and by extension

Fig. 178
Sir James Pennethorne, Design for a National Gallery on the Burlington House site: Piccadilly elevation, *c.* 1862.
Private collection

Fig. 179
Sir James Pennethorne, Design for a National Gallery on the Burlington House site: perspective of the entrance including the Learned Societies' Rooms, *c.* 1862.
RIBA Collections, DR118/8

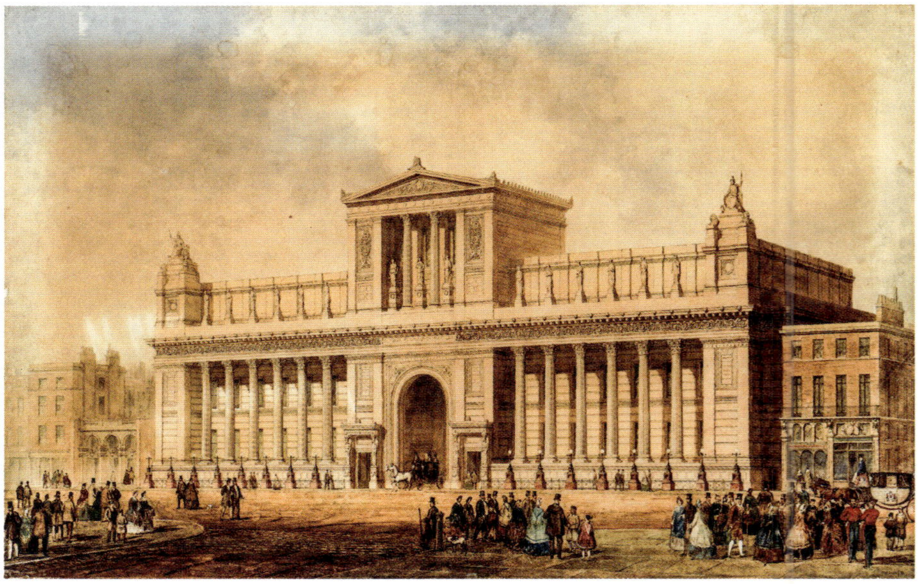

the Academy's) support for the whole idea of the National Gallery moving westwards. News of the government's plans for the site must have also reached the egregious C. J. Richardson who, undaunted by all his wasted work on the Palais Royal proposal eight years earlier, dashed off a pair of watercolours showing alternative designs for the Piccadilly entrance to the proposed new gallery (Figs 181, 182).

Fig. 180
Sydney Smirke, *Burlington House, Piccadilly* (design for a National Gallery), 1862.
RIBA Collections, SC95/18(11)

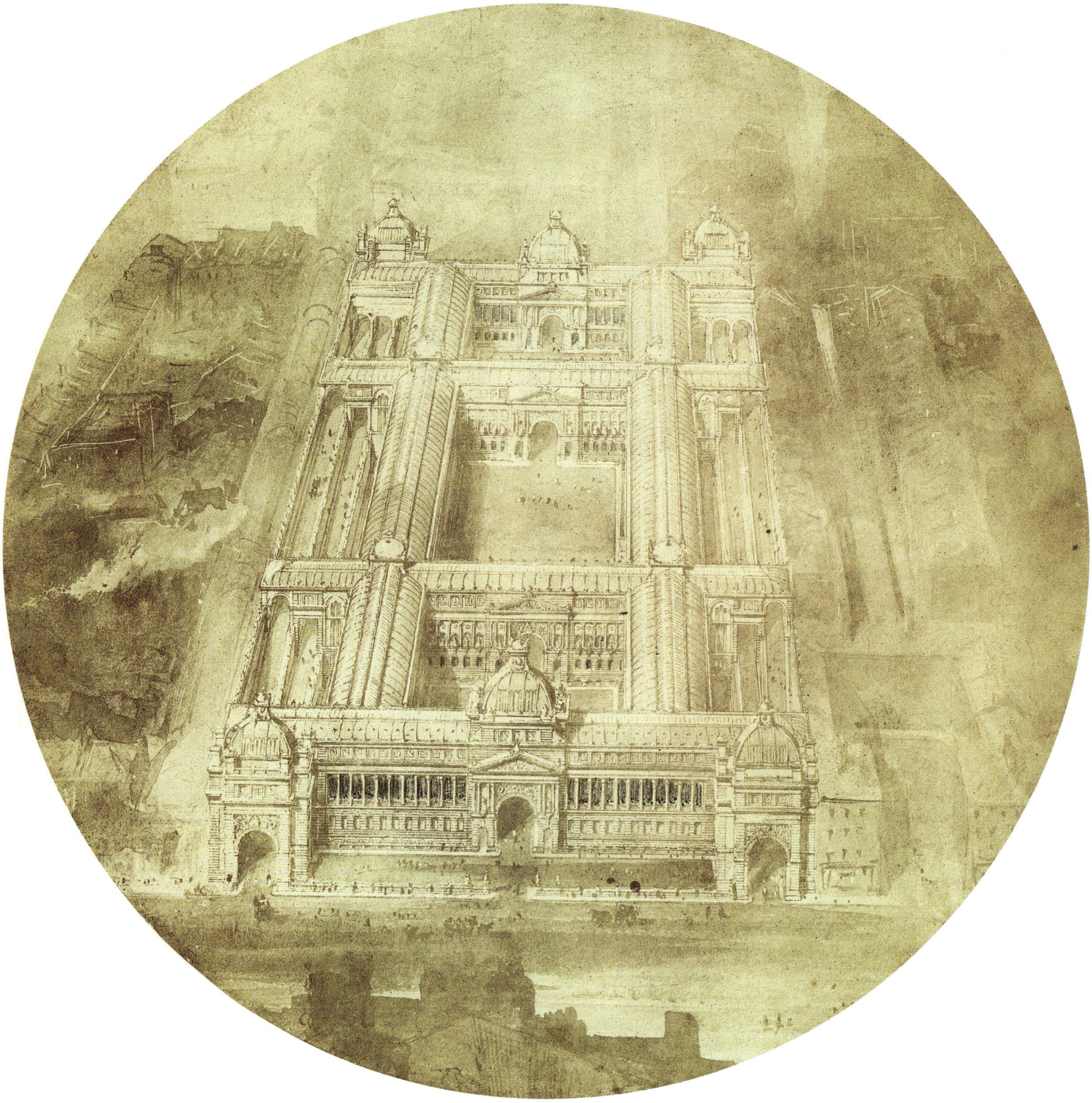

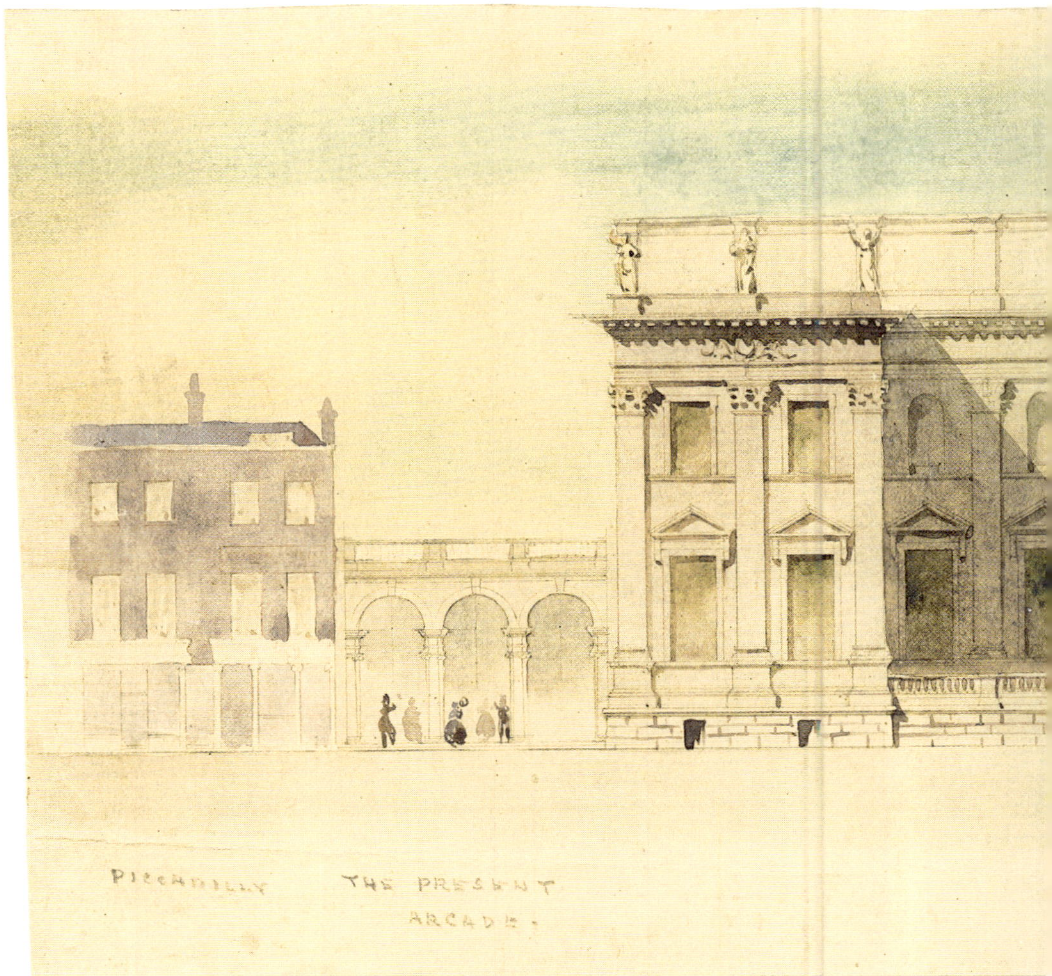

Fig. 181
Charles James Richardson (attrib.), Design for a National Gallery on the Burlington House site: Piccadilly elevation with triumphal-arch gateway, *c.* 1862.
Royal Academy of Arts, 07/922

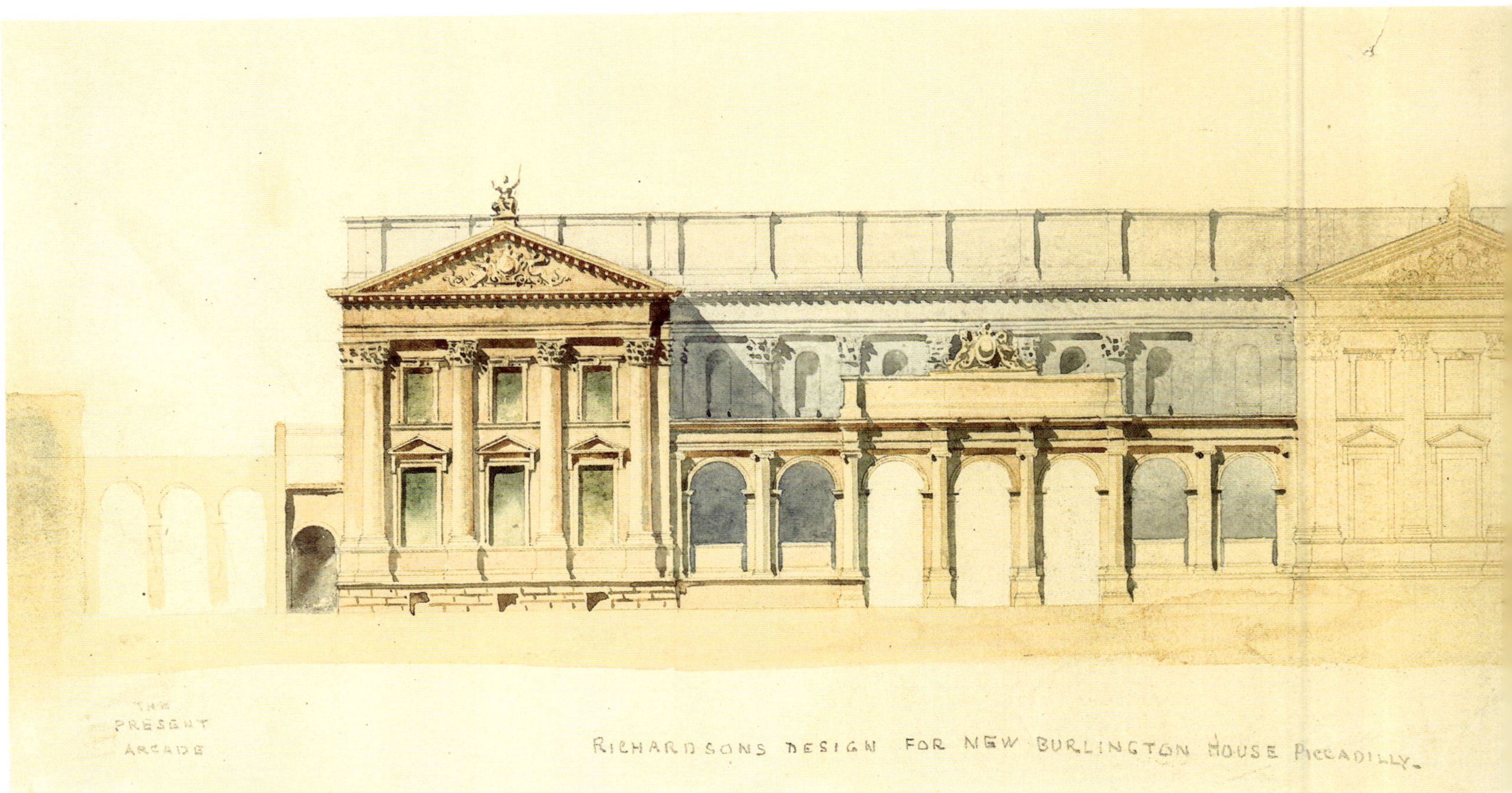

Fig. 182
Charles James Richardson (attrib.), Design for a National Gallery on the Burlington House site: Piccadilly elevation with screen, *c.* 1862.
Royal Academy of Arts, 07/921

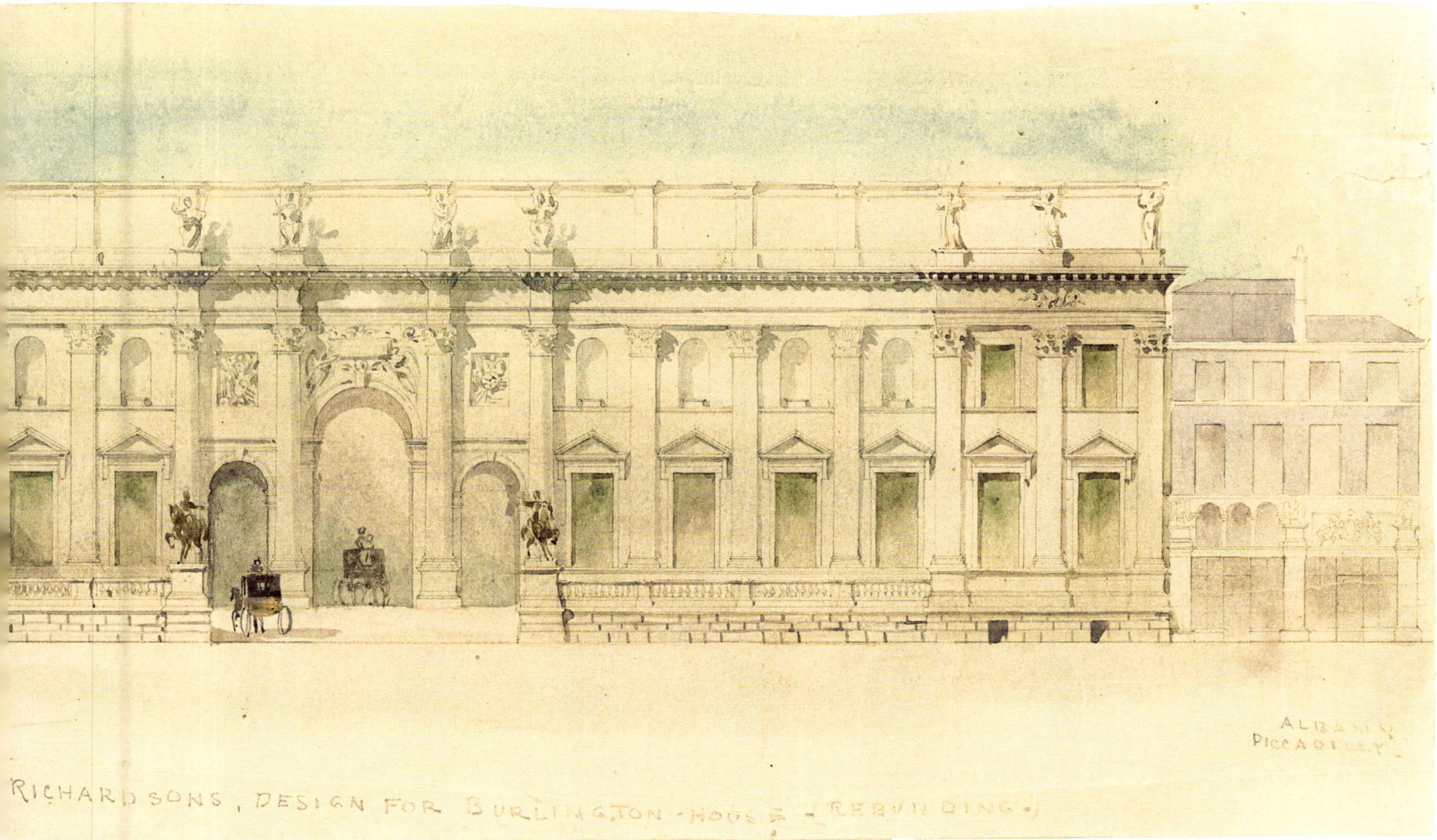
ALBANY
PICCADILLY
RICHARDSONS, DESIGN FOR BURLINGTON-HOUSE-(REBUILDING.)

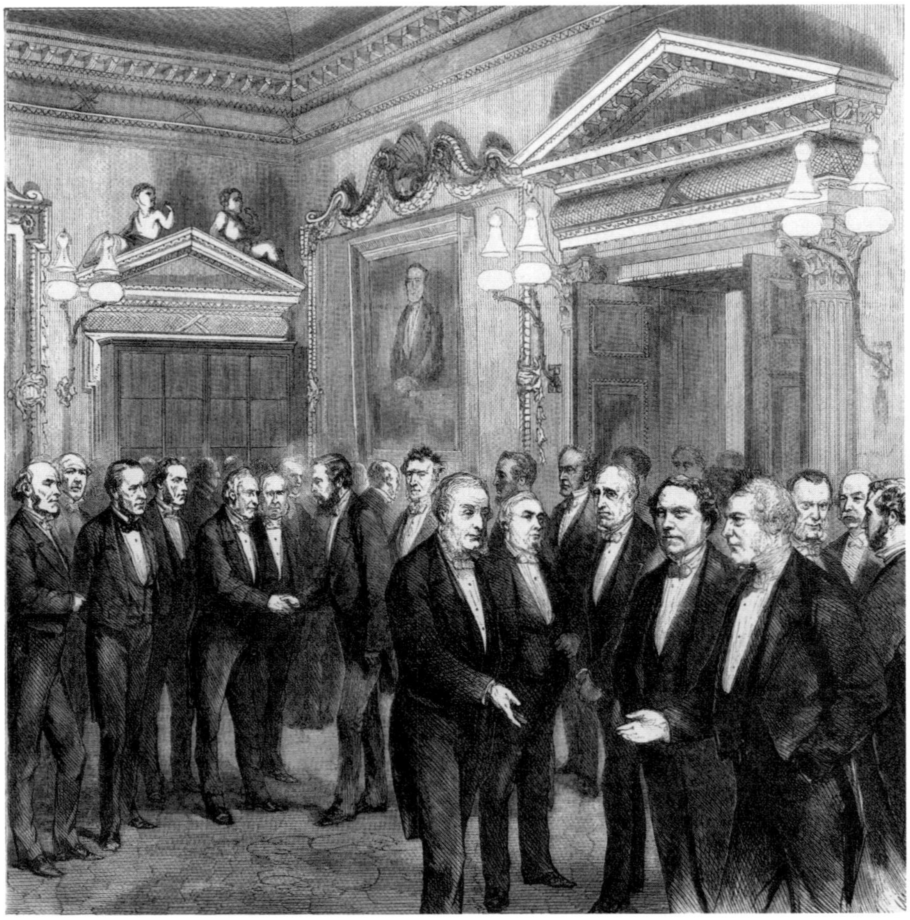

Fig. 183
'Soirée at the Royal Society' in the Saloon, Burlington House, from *The Graphic*, 30 April 1870, p. 508.
Mary Evans Archive

PERHAPS MORE THAN ANYTHING ELSE during these difficult years it was the Royal Society's soirées that sustained the dream of a greater 'juxtaposition' of the learned societies at Burlington House. From April 1859 onwards, and particularly during the presidencies of Sir Benjamin Brodie (1858–61) and General Sir Edward Sabine (1861–71), these became increasingly important social occasions that made the most of the decorative splendour of the first-floor rooms of the house with their recently installed gasoliers (Fig. 183). Here, over the course of a long evening, six hundred or so distinguished fellow scientists, inventors, artists, and patrons of science and learning could gather round newly improved scientific instruments and experimental apparatus; examine working models of mechanical inventions and engineering prototypes; scrutinise recently received geological, botanical, zoological and palaeontological specimens and ethnological and prehistoric artefacts; consult a wealth of maps, charts, diagrams, topographical drawings and photographs; and above all discuss with friends and colleagues the latest work being done within increasingly specialised branches of physics, chemistry, biology, geology, archaeology and astronomy.

It is of some significance in this context that Brodie's first soirée on 9 April 1859 was honoured by the presence of Prince Albert, for it was during his presidency of the British Association for the Advancement of Science in this same year that the prince explained publicly the grounds of his great belief in the importance of 'juxtaposition'.[72] Fearing that 'the tendency to push systematic investigation in every direction' may be detrimental to 'that consciousness of its unity which must pervade the whole of science if it is not to lose its last and highest point of sight', Prince Albert went on to stress, in a widely reported speech at that year's meeting of the Association in Aberdeen, that

> The only mode of supplying with any certainty this want is to be sought in the combination of men of science representing all the specialities, and working together for the common object of preserving that unity and presiding over that general direction.[73]

Three years later, the late prince's influence in having helped to persuade the government of the benefits of uniting the learned societies at Burlington House was sufficiently apparent for the architect William Bardwell to decide to site his design for the Albert Memorial there rather than in Kensington Gardens (Fig. 184). This legacy of the prince's past influence also sheds light on why, every year between 1864 and 1871, the Queen lent numerous original drawings by Leonardo, Michelangelo, Raphael, Poussin, Dürer and many other Old Masters, to

Fig. 184
Rigby Wason, after William Bardwell, Proposed design for the Albert Memorial on the Burlington House site, 1862.
London Metropolitan Archives (City of London)

no less than thirteen Royal Society soirées. On 30 April 1864, for instance, a selection of Hans Holbein the younger's portraits of members of Henry VIII's court was displayed in the 'Linnean Library' (i.e. the Reynolds Room) alongside such marvels as a 'Working Model of Joy's Double-acting and Self-acting Steam-Hammer'; 'Silver's Improved Voltaic Battery'; 'Specimens of Submarine Telegraph Cables' presented by C. W. Siemens; 'Tuning forks showing the composition of Sound'; microscopes manufactured by Smith and Beck; specimens of 'Insects in Amber and Gum animi'; and 'A Series of Implements and Ornaments in Stone, Bone and Reindeer-horn illustrative of the Industry of the early Cave-dwellers of Southern France' (Fig. 185).

In the long run-up to the government's final unveiling of its plans for Burlington House in April 1864, it is fair to say that the needs of its existing occupants were largely ignored. As for the possibility that the new building might enable other societies to move in from Somerset House or elsewhere, the Treasury's rebuff of the Geological Society's second application in 1860 was hardly encouraging. Indeed, it was probably due to uncertainty over the government's intentions that the Royal Society made a point of lending moral support to the Geologists' application for accommodation on the site by giving permission for them to hold 43 of their meetings in the 'Great Hall' at Burlington House between 2 May 1860 and 18 February 1863.[74] When it did eventually become public knowledge – in time for what *The Standard* vehemently attacked as 'Mr Cowper's Little Vote On Account For The "New" National Gallery' on 6 June 1864 – Banks & Barry's design must have

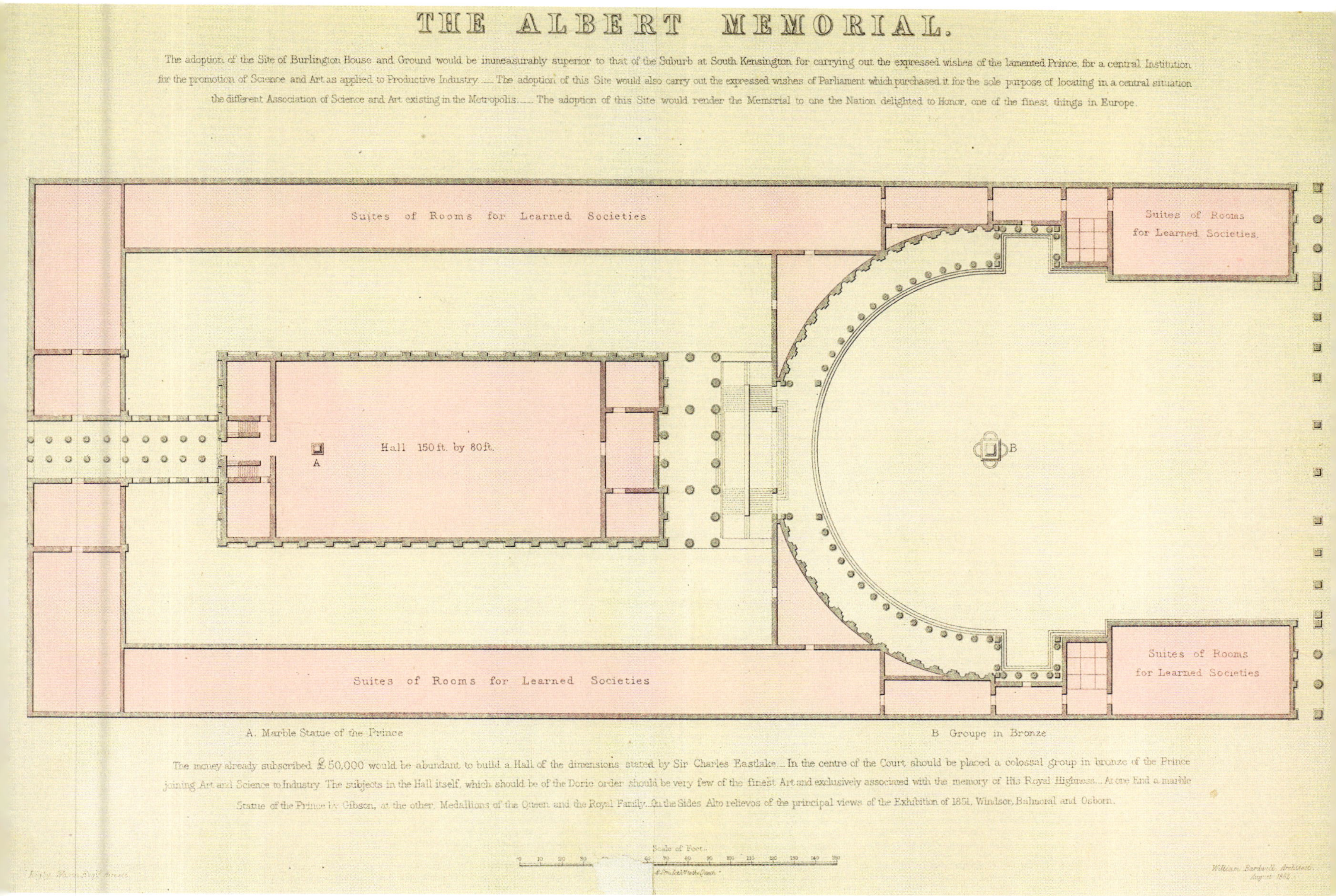

BURLINGTON HOUSE.

APRIL 30th, 1864.

Linnean Library.

Semaphore of the Patent Electric Signal Company; Morse's Apparatus.—Ragon's Bell.—Pneumatic Relay. } *Messrs. Silver and Co.*
Electroscope.—Various Telegraph Insulators, mounted.—Silver's Improved Voltaic Battery. } *Messrs. Silver and Co.*
Specimen of unmanufactured *Balata*, a newly-imported Gum: with Gutta Percha and India-rubber for comparison. } *Messrs. Silver and Co.*
Microscopes.—*Smith and Beck.* Ebonite Photographic Appliances.—*Mr. H. Lowcock.*
A Series of Implements and Ornaments in Stone, Bone, and Reindeer-horn illustrative of the Industry of the early Cave-dwellers of Southern France.—*Messrs. Lartet and Christy.*
Collection of Fossils from the Lias near Lyme Regis, and specimens of Emeralds and Opals.—*Mr. J. R. Gregory.*
Specimens of Insects in Amber and Gum animi.—*Mr. P. J. Butler.*
Original Drawings by Holbein.—Portraits of Royal and Illustrious Persons of the Court of Henry VIII., from the Royal Collection, *exhibited by permission of H. M. The Queen.*
Autographs and Letters of Eminent Persons, illustrated by Portraits.—*Mr. G. W. Manners.*
Tuning-forks showing the composition of Sound.—*Mr. Ladd.*
Specimens of Submarine Telegraph Cables, Magnetic Dial Instruments, and Differential Pressure Guage.—*C. W. Siemens, F.R.S.*
Working Model of Joy's Double-acting and Self-acting Steam-Hammer.—*Messrs. Tregelles and Taylor.*

Linnean Meeting Room.

The Kew Spectroscope, with eleven Bisulphide-of-carbon Prisms and twenty-two Prisms of Crown Glass. Invented and made by John Browning. } *J. P. Gassiot, F.R.S.*
The Group of Lines known as Fraunhofer's D in the Solar Spectrum, as shown by the above-described Instrument, drawn on a large scale. } *J. P. Gassiot, F.R.S.*
New Aneroid Barometer, without Springs or Chain, in which the Indication is multiplied by the reflexion of a Ray of Light. Invented by J. Browning. } *Mr. J. Browning.*
Pocket Spectroscope for showing Prof. Stokes's Absorption-Bands. } *Mr. J. Browning.*
Geissler's Vacuum Tubes, with Experiments.—*Mr. Ladd.*

Richards' Steam Indicator.—Prof. W. Thomson's New Electrometer.—Thermo-pile and Wave Machine.—*Messrs. Elliott, Brothers.*
Gas-burner for producing high temperatures: used for various heating purposes and to melt metals.—*Mr. G. Gore.*
Improved Mercurial open Scale Barometer, and Self-registering Maximum Thermometer.—*Invented and exhibited by Mr. J. Hicks.*
Series of Microscopic Specimens showing the successive stages of the development of the Pentacrinoid larva of the *Comatula* (Feather-star); full-sized specimens of the adult, and other Starfish preserved in Glycerine.—*Dr. Carpenter, F.R.S.*

Entrance Saloon.

Bust of H.R.H. The Prince of Wales, by Morton Edwards.—*Mr. Morton Edwards.*
Paintings: *The Görner Glacier,* from Zermatt; *Monte Rosa,* from Val d'Anzasca; *Burnham Beeches*; *Windsor Forest.*—*Mr. A. MacCallum.*
Bust of the late Sir B. C. Brodie, P.R.S., by W. Behnes.—*Mr. Morton Edwards.* Shakespeare Shield.—*Mr. J. Leighton.*
Model of Floating Dock, constructed for the Spanish Government at Cartagena.—Models of double-screw Gunboats—*Messrs. Rennie.*
A Frame, with Portrait of Shakespeare, carved from portions of Herne's Oak and an apple-tree from Anne Hathaway's Garden; Italian Standard; and Pendents.—*Carved and Exhibited by Messrs. Rogers.*
Manufactured Specimens of Parkesine, a new Flexible Waterproof Substance.—*Mr. Parkes.* Bronzes.—*E. W. Cooke, R.A., F.R.S.*
Adie's Transit Theodolite, with flush Vernier, and edge to edge reading applied to the Sloping Limb.—Adie's patent Levelling Theodolite.—Patent Level, and Improved Surveying Compass.—*Mr. P. Adie.*
Specimens of Gun-cotton, showing the modes of preparation for different uses.—*Mr. T. Prentice.*
Specimens of Cold Drawn Steel Tubes and Gun Barrels.—*Messrs. Harding and Hawksworth.*
Steel Blocks, showing the structure of the Metal, with printed impressions of the same.—*H. C. Sorby, F.R.S.*

All the Trees, Plants, and Flowers, throughout the Apartments, are lent by the Royal Botanic Society.

Experiment to determine whether the Earth's Motion affects the Refraction of Light.—Model of a Body moving similarly to a particle of a fluid medium which rotates the plane of polarized light.—Ophthalmoscope.—*Prof. J. Clerk Maxwell, F.R.S.*
Bust of C. Newton, Esq., of the British Museum.—Statuette of General Fox.—Portrait Statuettes of Mr. and Mrs. Daniel Home.—Portrait in Bronze of a Racehorse (Johnny Armstrong).—*Mr. J. E. Boehm.*
Microscopes.—*Powell and Lealand.*
Coloured Drawing of the Ice-Hummock formed at Niagara in the Winter of 1855–56.—*Mr. H. Christy.*
Original Coloured Drawings of Scenes and Incidents in Capt. Cook's Third Voyage (1777), by J. Webber, Artist to the Expedition.—*Exhibited by Capt. Richards, Hydrographer, with permission of the Lords of the Admiralty.*

Council Room.

Gisborne's Patent Apparatus for striking large Bells, whereby full Tones are produced without danger of cracking the Metal.—*Messrs. Silver & Co. and F. N. Gisborne.*
Sculptured Stones, Bronze Keys, Cranium and Horn-cores of *Bos longifrons,* found November 1863 at Wycombe, Gloucestershire, an ancient Roman Station.—*Mr. W. Lawrence.*
Photographs of Thorwaldsen's Bas-reliefs from the originals at Copenhagen.—Whole-length Portrait of The Queen, painted in Oils on a Photograph by the late Mr. Clifford, of Madrid.—*Messrs. Marion, Son, & Co.*
Collection of Gold and Silver Japanese Coins, and Silver Coins of China and Cochin China.—*Mr. S. W. Silver.*
Model in Plaster of the late W. M. Thackeray, and Bronze Statuettes, Boys at Play.—*J. Durham.*
New Statuettes illustrative of the Process of Photosculpture.—*A. Claudet, F.R.S.*

Apparatus for showing the Rotation of an Induction Spark in Vacuo when connected with an Electromagnet.—*Mr. Edward Atkinson.*

Lower Library and Meeting Room.

Gisborne's Patent Mechanical Signal Apparatus, for Naval use, as fitted on board H.M. Iron Frigate *Achilles.*—*Messrs. Silver and Co. and F. N. Gisborne.* Electric Safety Distance Signal; used on the London Chatham and Dover Railway.—*Mr. J. Imray.*
Model of Jointed Cast-Iron Bridge, lighter than the usual form of Wrought-Iron Girder; with Diagram showing the Strains. — *Mr. Fleeming Jenkin.*

Fig. 185
Poster for a Royal Society *conversazione* at Burlington House, 30 April 1864
Royal Society Archives

Fig. 187 (overleaf)
Robert Richardson Banks & Charles Barry Jr, Proposed design for the New National Gallery on the gardens of Burlington House: plan, 1864.
Royal Academy of Arts, London, 16/2552

confirmed the societies' and the University's worst fears. In response to Palmerston's wish for an 'unpretentious' single-storey top-lit building with no inner courts, their great cruciform gallery had none of the clarity of planning evident in Pennethorne's 'No. 2' design but, like him, they retained the existing courtyard buildings as a suitable approach from Piccadilly, replaced Campbell's gate and porter's lodges with a new, wider carriage entrance, and used the central staircase in the main house to form a bridge at half-landing level to the gallery beyond (Fig. 187).[75]

Leaving the present occupants of the house where they were not only went back on the previous government's assurances concerning a new building on the site, it also failed to address in any satisfactory way the difficulty the University was now having in finding enough room to hold its examinations. With an exponential increase in the number of candidates from 466 in 1858 to 1,018 in 1863, so urgent had this problem become by the latter year that prospective entrants to the University were sitting their exams in a large corrugated-iron shed erected in the garden behind Burlington House as a drill hall for the South Middlesex Volunteer Rifle Corps (Fig. 186).[76] No doubt as a result of the Senate having written to the First Commissioner in November 1863 stressing the urgent need for a more suitable place in which to conduct their exams, Banks & Barry designated an area of the garden on the east side of the courtyard (i.e. where the Geological Society had hoped for a building) as 'Space for Temporary Examination Hall'. However, there was nothing in their plan to suggest that this might be much of an improvement on the Volunteers' drill hall, and as for the idea that the adjacent French and Spanish School gallery might also be used as

Fig. 186
'Drill shed in Burlington Gardens, erected by the South Middlesex Rifle Volunteers', from *Illustrated London News*, 15 March 1862, p.275.
Illustrated London News archive

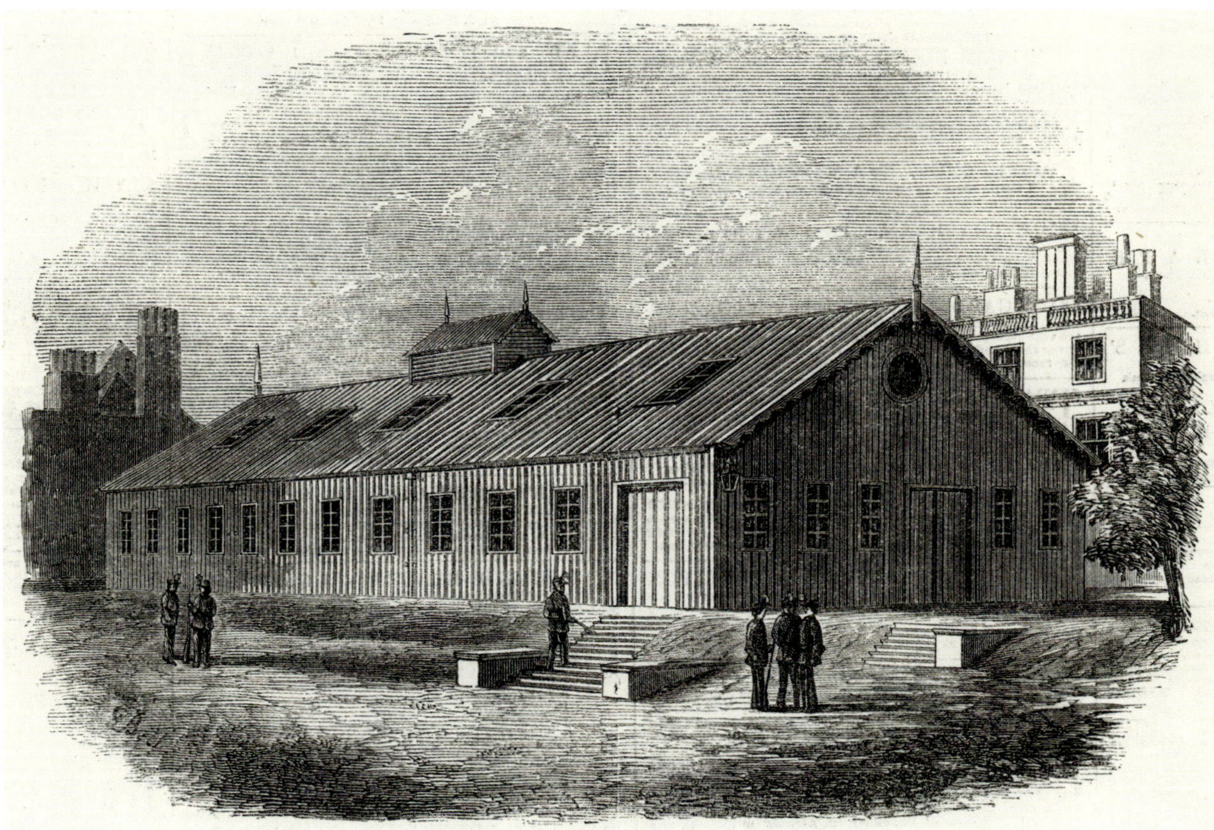

NEW NATIONA

PROPOSED TO BE ERECTED ON THE OPEN SPAC

AS APPROVED BY THE TRUSTEES OF THE NATIONAL
DESIGNED BY MESSRS BANKS AND

PLAN OF THE PRI

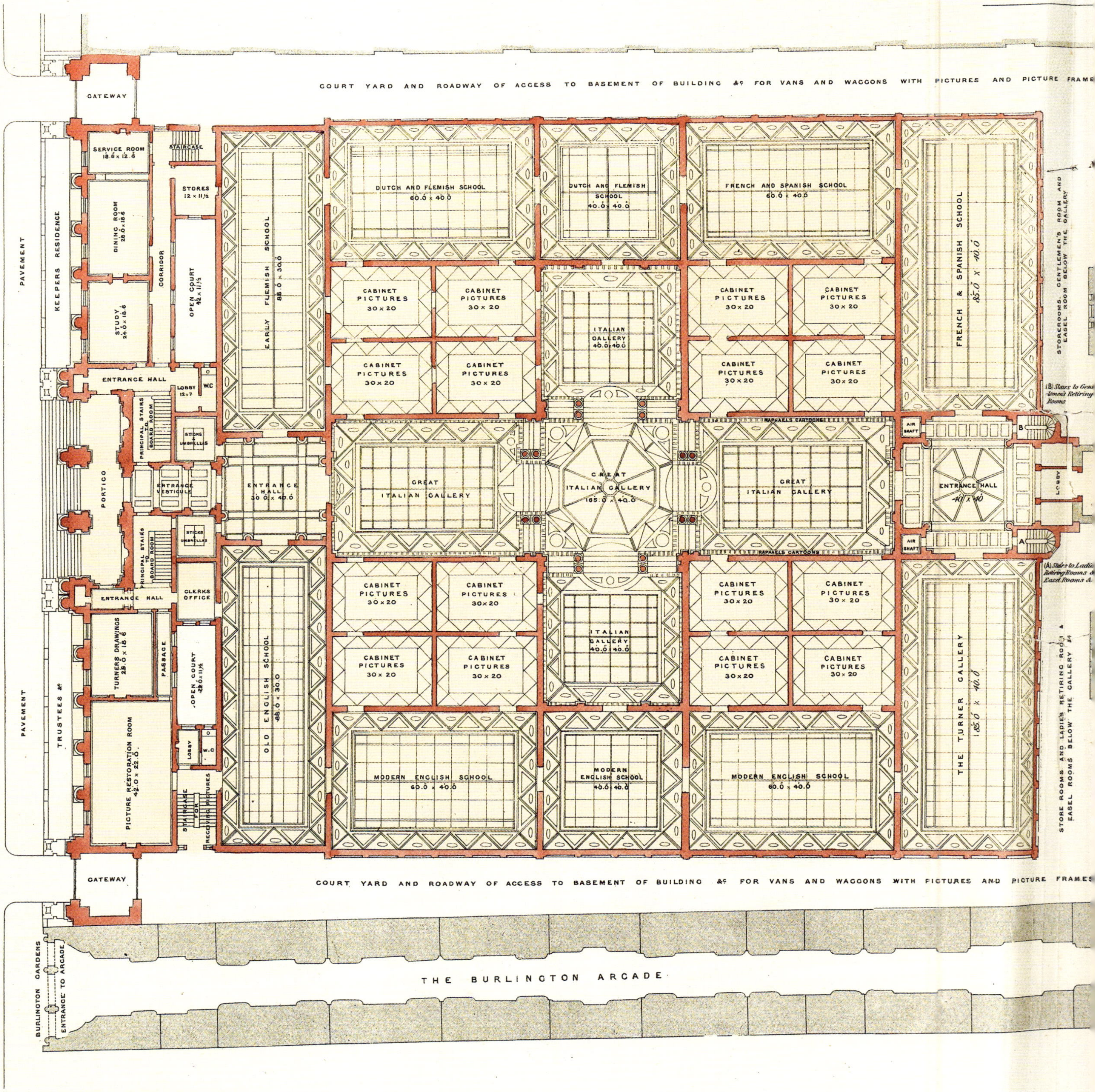

COMPARATIVE ACCOMMODATION PROVIDED IN ENGLISH AND FOREIGN PICTURE GALLERIES.

	Lineal Feet.		Lineal Feet.
The Old Louvre	1,300	The Old Pinnacotck, Munich	1,600
Picture Galleries, Berlin	1,116	National Gallery, Trafalgar Square 950 }	1,850
Ditto Dresden	2,220	South Kensington Gallery 900 }	
Ditto Vienna	1,700	New National Gallery, Burlington House	3,950

SCALE 20 FEET

10 5 0 10 20 30 40 50 60 70 80 90 100 110 120

GALLERY

THE GARDENS OF BURLINGTON HOUSE

D SUBMITTED TO PARLIAMENT IN 1864.
RCHITECTS.

AL FLOOR

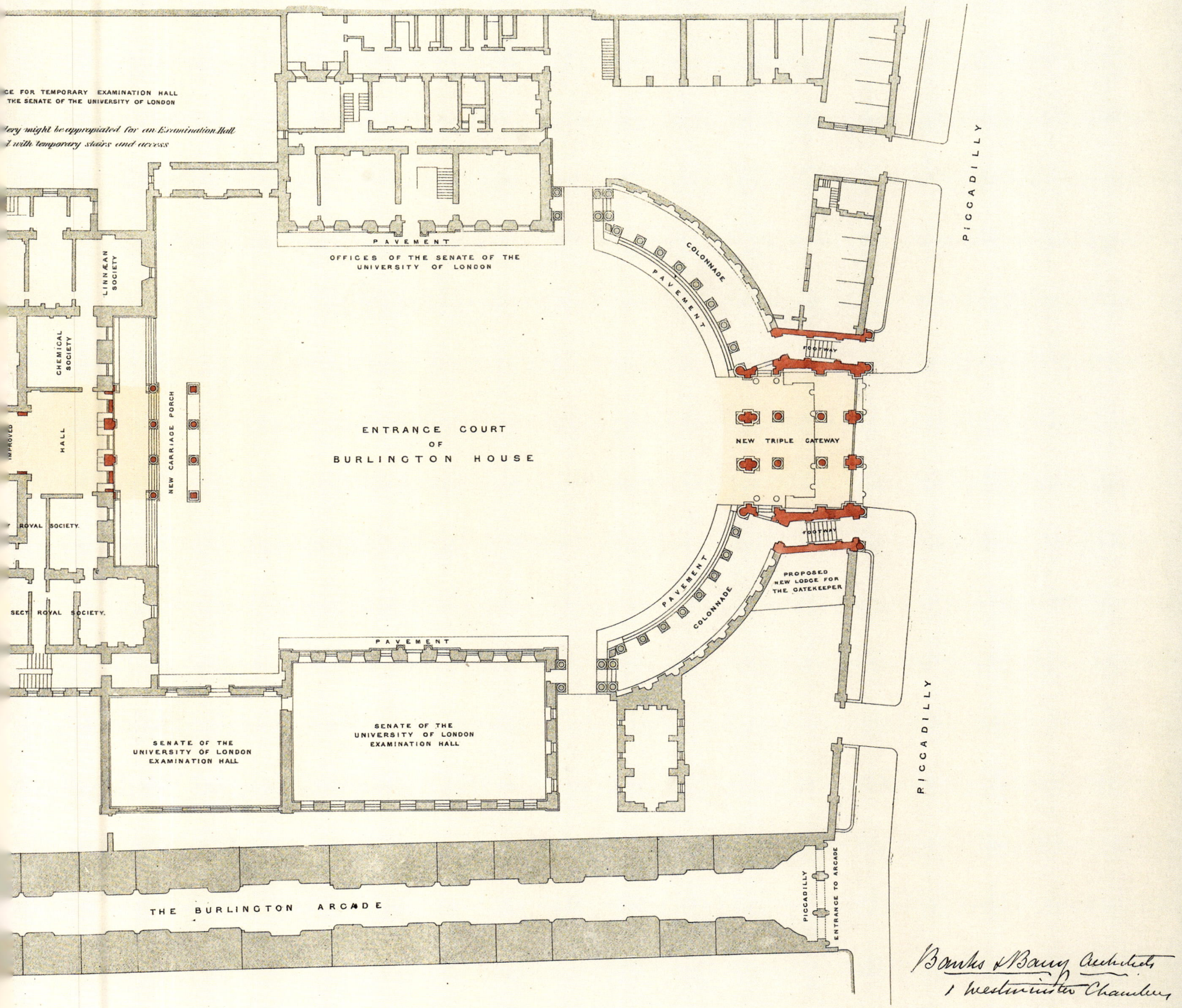

BURLINGTON HOUSE PROPERTY,

NEW NATIONAL GALLERY,

PROPOSED TO BE ERECTED ON THE GARDENS OF BURLINGTON HOUSE.

Entrance from Piccadilly by the Quadrangle and through the present buildings, also from New Facade in Burlington Gardens.

DESIGNED BY MESSRS. BANKS & BARRY, ARCHITECTS, IN 1864.

COMPARATIVE STATEMENT OF ACCOMMODATION.

	Present Building, Trafalgar Square.	Proposed Building, Burlington House.	
Surface of Floor	9,550	42,000	Superficial Feet.
Surface of Walls for Pictures	16,260	67,600	Superficial Feet.
Lineal Feet of Wall on Sight Line	950	3,950	Lineal Feet.

an examination hall, it is hard to imagine that both the National Gallery's keeper, R. N. Wornum, and the University's registrar, W. B. Carpenter, did not roll their eyes in disbelief.

As it happened, neither of them need have worried. For reasons that had nothing to do with the learned societies and the University, and everything to do with Parliament's extreme reluctance to hand over 'the finest site in Europe' to the Royal Academy, on 6 June 1864 a Committee of Supply of the House of Commons dealt the government's Burlington House project a resounding death blow. The immediate effect was to bring the Derby government's 1859 scheme back into play, which no doubt accounts for the fact that it was Manners who had made the most effective speech attacking the government's scheme.[77] A week later the humbled Cowper must have had a sense of déjà-vu as he confirmed, a full five years after Palmerston had originally done so, that the

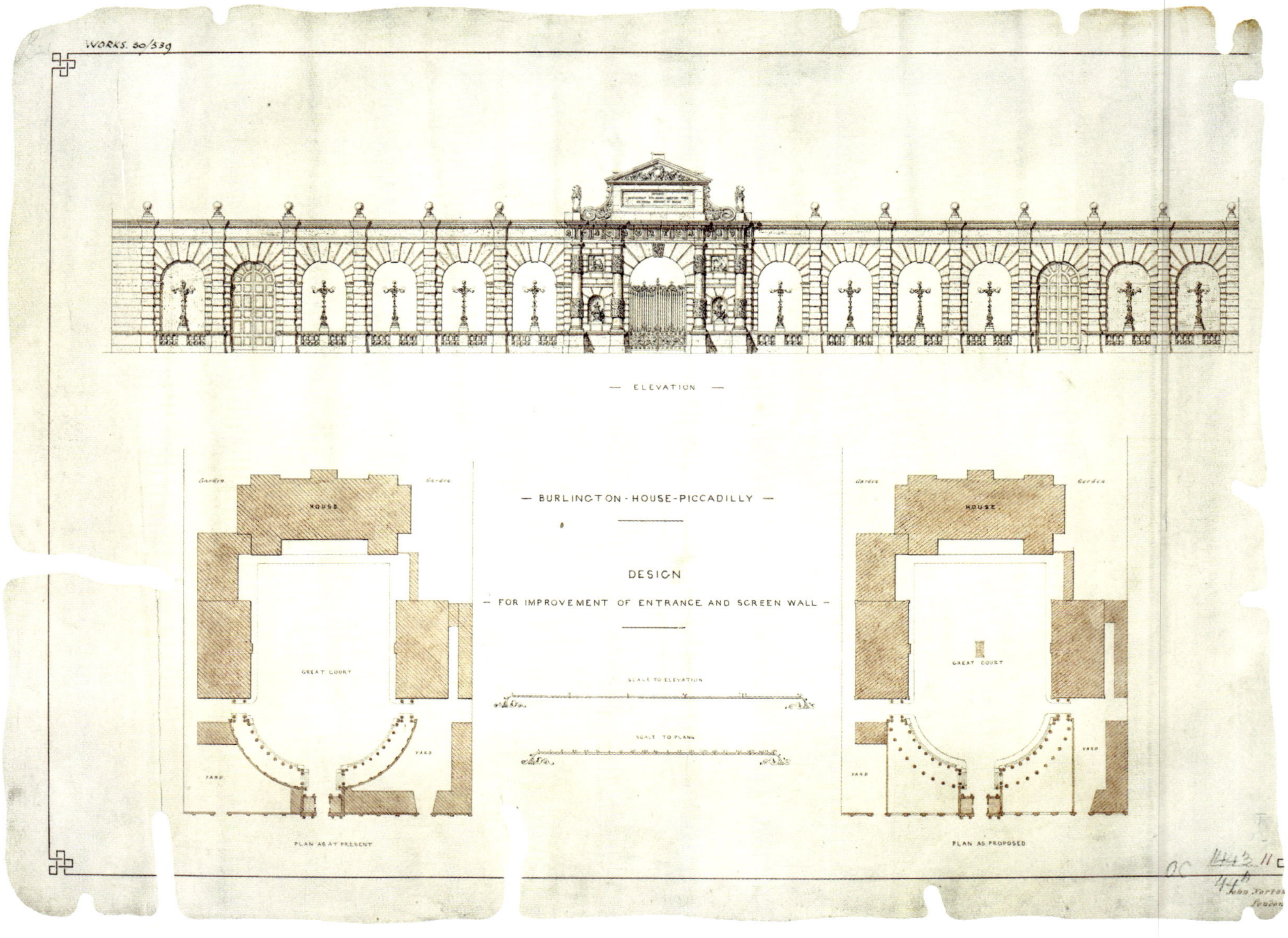

Fig. 188
John Norton, Design to improve the entrance and screen wall to the Great Court at Burlington House: block plans and elevation, *c.* 1866.
The National Archives, Kew, WORK 30/539

Academy was still prepared to spend its own capital on a new building at Burlington House, and that the government would be looking again at the comparative costs of enlarging or reconstructing the Trafalgar Square building for the National Gallery's sole use.[78]

Nor did the University lose any time in pressing their case. In this transformed scenario, however, the Senate did not merely write again to the First Commissioner pleading for more space, but immediately dispatched a deputation to wait on the Prime Minister with a proposal for a separate, purpose-designed building of their own on the northern third of the site facing Burlington Gardens.[79] Palmerston's acceptance and support of this idea in the immediate wake of the defeat of June 1864 was to prove a crucial step towards a definitive resolution of the future use of Burlington House and its grounds. The urgency of the University's need for better accommodation, the obvious threat to its rapid and self-evident success, the availability of a suitable nearby site already in government ownership, the shameful conditions in which students from all corners of the Empire were obliged to sit its exams, and the fact that it was a government department directly dependent on the Treasury and run by a Senate, three-quarters of whom were Crown appointees – all of these factors combined to make the University's case overwhelming. However, despite bowing in complaisant agreement with every point that Mountstuart Grant Duff raised in the Commons on the University's behalf in June 1865, and stiff letters of complaint sent by order of the Senate to Gladstone in April and to the new Prime Minister, the Earl Russell, in November that year, the First Commissioner of Works still contrived to let a year's worth of dust settle on the block plans and estimate that Pennethorne had prepared on his instructions the previous December.[80] Eventually in January 1866, when even Cowper had run out of excuses for further delay, the government agreed to introduce a Bill for a new building for the University on the Burlington Gardens site.[81] Pennethorne having been instructed to prepare the necessary plans and estimates, the die was finally cast on 30 April 1866 when the Commons granted a vote of £20,000 for the commencement of building work.[82]

As the first structural alteration to the site that the government intended to be permanent, this marked a moment of no return. Significantly only now, more than twelve years after the government's offer for Burlington House had been accepted, was the issue of preservation raised through the time-honoured medium of a letter to *The Times*.[83] Having heard in the Commons a few days earlier that the First Commissioner had given the Academy notice to quit Trafalgar Square and that they had accepted a plot on the Piccadilly frontage of Burlington House on which to build, Alexander Beresford Hope, MP, a well-known architectural pundit and currently president of the Royal Institute of British Architects, was the first person to make a case for saving Burlington House for the nation on the grounds of architectural merit. However, his plea that the ensemble of the courtyard needed protection from imminent vandalism at the hands of the Royal Academicians is not quite what it seems. Beresford Hope's concept of preservation, for example, quite happily encompassed exactly the alterations that the Academy was destined to make, namely heightening the house by another storey and creating the 'portal' to an exhibition gallery at its centre, both of which, a critic in *The Builder* felt sure, would cause Lord Burlington's spirit to hover 'over this monument of tasteful genius' and murmur 'in doleful apprehension, "Save me, oh! save me, from my friends."'[84] In fact, as the same writer pointed out with some glee, the resolution passed by the Council of the Royal Institute of British Architects on 28 May 1866, which Beresford Hope communicated to *The Times* the following day, *viz.* – 'The Council are of opinion that Burlington-House, with its colonnades, possesses considerable architectural merit, and that it would be a subject of regret if such a building should be wantonly interfered with, or needlessly destroyed'[85] – could have been designed to restrain their president's interference as much as that of anyone else.

The truth of the matter was a rumour had got about that the Royal Academy was on the point of rejecting the five-eighths of an acre offered by the government in front of Burlington House in favour of a rival offer by the 1851 Exhibition Commissioners of a no-strings-attached,

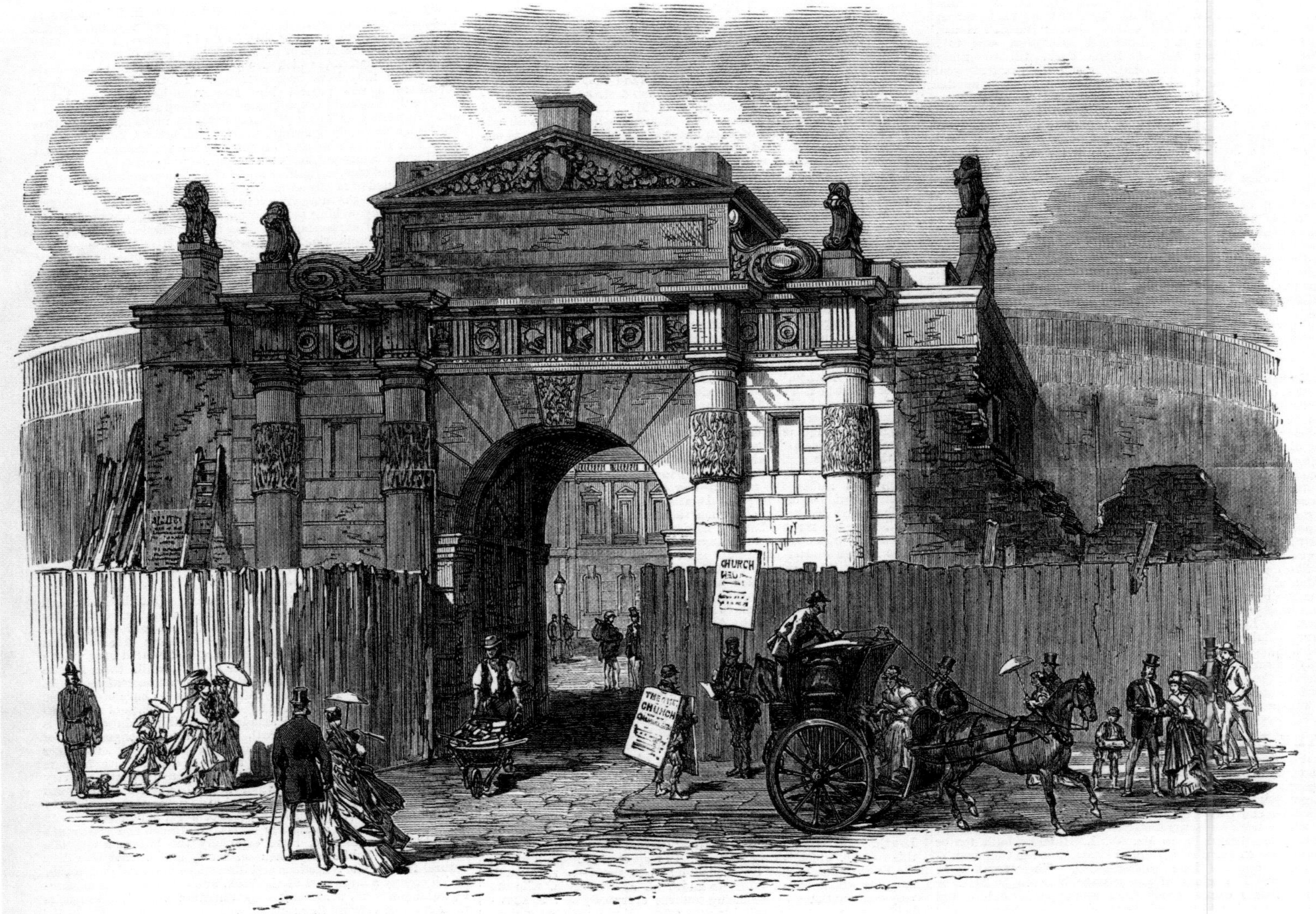

three-acre greenfield site next to the Royal Horticultural Gardens off Exhibition Road in Kensington. The immediate effect was to ignite a determined campaign to reverse the Commons decision of two years earlier not to move the National Gallery from Trafalgar Square. Launched by Lord Overstone in the House of Lords on the same day as Beresford Hope's letter appeared in *The Times*, and vigorously promoted in the Commons three weeks later by Lord Elcho, Austen Layard (who claimed to speak for the majority of the Gallery's trustees) and Beresford Hope himself, probably the main reason it looked for a while that this revived campaign had some chance of success was the new importance given by its promoters to the need to preserve Burlington House and its forecourt.[86] One of Cowper's largely unforced tactical errors at the time of the 1864 debate had been a failure to take advantage of the fact that Banks & Barry's design had at last created an opportunity for pedestrians on Piccadilly to appreciate what the government had bought in their name. More concerned to emphasise the extension of the gallery and the increase in accommodation for the learned societies that would be possible by later replacing the old house and forecourt with a new quadrangle, the First Commissioner had failed to realise the importance to his case of a proposal such as John Norton's remarkable design for replacing Campbell's notorious 'grimy' brick wall with an arcade based on repetition of the arch of the Great Gate, through which picturesque views of the house could have been created by making the courtyard colonnade open on both sides (Fig. 188).

By the time Beresford Hope's notice of a resolution 'to reverse the hasty and unfortunate decision of a Committee of Supply two years ago' came up for debate in the Commons on 23 July, the Russell administration had fallen and Lord John Manners was back at his old post in the Office of Works. Despite a leader in *The Times* on 11 June strongly in favour of moving the National Gallery to Burlington House, a letter in the same issue from Landseer also arguing that the Academy should stay in Trafalgar Square, and earnest speeches by Elcho and

Fig. 189
'Demolition of Burlington House, Piccadilly' (colonnade, wings and Great Gate), from *Illustrated London News*, 22 August 1868.
Illustrated London News Archive

Fig. 190
William Luker, 'Remains of Burlington House [the colonnade] removed to Battersea Park', from Percy Fitzgerald, *London City Suburbs*, London and New York, 1893, p. 222.
Private collection

Layard recapitulating the arguments of two years before, Manners had little difficulty in persuading the House to stick to its original decision.[87] In this he was helped by the failure of an attempt in the House of Lords to delay the second reading of the National Gallery Enlargement Bill and by the fact that he could argue that going back on the decision to erect a new building for the University on Burlington Gardens would be both needlessly expensive and a failure to honour his predecessor's undertaking to provide them with a building on that site.

It was also clear that Beresford Hope and his connoisseur friends had overestimated the strength of the preservation argument. When two years later he tried to embarrass Manners over a forthcoming auction of the dismantled colonnade and Great Gate as building materials, Manners jokingly offered to sell them instead to his hon. friend (Fig. 189).[88] And although a show was made of numbering the stones before they were dismantled, once out of sight they were dumped unceremoniously in Battersea Park, along with the oak doors from Campbell's Great Gate complete with their original lion-mask knocker (Fig. 190).[89] And there they stayed, despite well-meaning questions and proposals in Parliament and the press for their re-erection as late as 1893, the subject of colourful rumour as to their identity until they were pulverised for hardcore by the London County Council Works Department.[90] By October 1903 all that apparently survived of 'one of the finest pieces of architecture in Europe' was 'an angle stone from the corona course of a Roman (mutular) Doric Cornice … in a fairly good state of preservation, … a remnant of the colonnade which formerly stood in the Court of Burlington House.'[91] This last trace of Walpole's fairytale vision has not been seen since the 1920s.

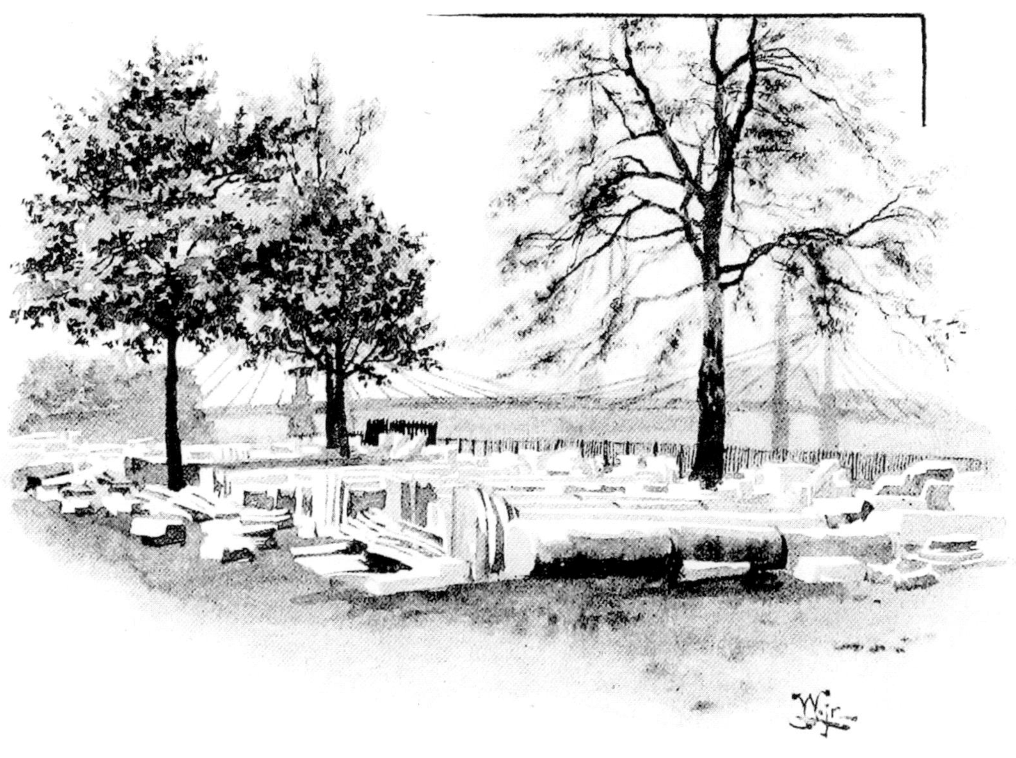

REMAINS OF BURLINGTON HOUSE, REMOVED TO BATTERSEA PARK

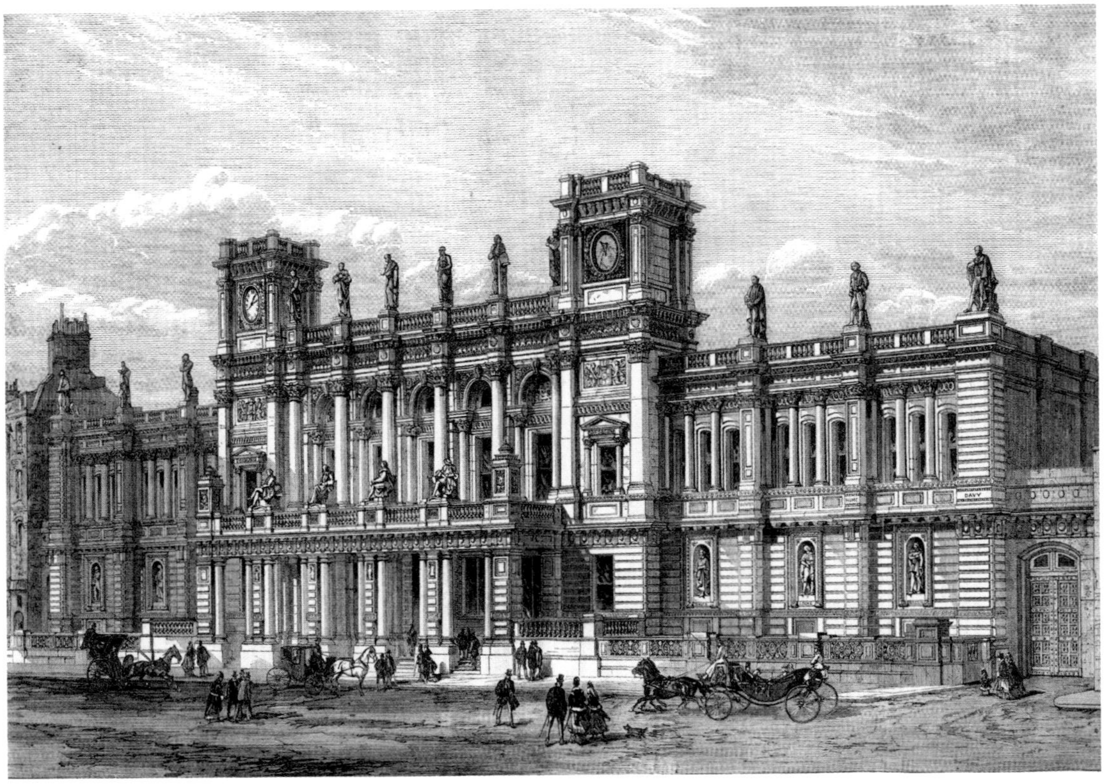

Fig. 191
'New buildings of the London University, Burlington Gardens, opened by the Queen on Wednesday', the north front, from *Illustrated London News*, 14 May 1870.
Illustrated London News archive

6 BURLINGTON GARDENS is a strange building. Not only does it not conform to an easily recognisable building type, there is also something odd about its most distinctive features. Why, for instance, are there so many statues – 22 no less – on a government-owned building erected at the tax-payers' expense? (Fig. 191).[92] And why was so much prominence given to a lecture theatre and a library in a building designed to house an institution that had at the time no pedagogic need for either (Figs 192, 193)? And, strangest of all, why had there been such disagreement about the style of architecture in which it should be built, so much so that its architect had been obliged to design its front elevation three times over, the third time in mid-construction? At the time the building's 'curious' history was thought to derive merely from the political vicissitudes of the day. Thus, waiting among the distinguished guests attending its ceremonious opening by the Queen on 11 May 1870 (Figs 194, 195), a reporter for the *Daily Telegraph* observed Lord John Manners sitting

> near Mr. Disraeli, wearing a scarlet gown, and looking handsome, thoughtful, and sad, as of yore. Was he mentally concocting, we wonder, a new rhyme to the effect that 'Laws and Learning, Arts and Commerce might die, but it is expedient to leave us still the London University'? Or was he musing over the odd revolutions of the whirligig of Time which brought him into this Palladian building, when he, years ago, as First Commissioner of Works had decreed that it should be a Gothic structure?[93]

However, there are grounds for seeing the building's peculiarities not merely as consequences of the vagaries of contemporary politics but rather as reflecting a critical moment in the evolution of the University of London from an obscure government department into probably the most progressive academic institution in the country.

Set up by Lord Melbourne's administration in 1836 with direct funding from the state, in 1870 the University of London was still a purely examining and degree-conferring body that undertook no teaching of any kind. What had begun in 1838 with less than two-dozen matriculants sitting their exams in one of the Royal Academy's old rooms in Somerset House had become by 1865 a logistical nightmare, with well over a thousand candidates descending on Burlington House every year from all corners of the British empire. Although in July 1864 both the Prime Minister, Lord Palmerston, and the First Commissioner of the Office of Works, William Cowper, had been sent copies of a detailed specification of the nature and extent of the rooms the University would need in a new building, nine months later its Vice-Chancellor, the eminent historian George Grote, was writing yet again to the Treasury to draw attention to how the government's prevarication

> ... has led to accumulated difficulties, and the adoption of expedients which, upon the most casual inspection on the spot, must be admitted to be exceptionally unsuitable, since they cannot even be made to meet the ordinary vicissitudes of weather.[94]

Fig. 192
'The lecture theatre, London University, Burlington Gardens', from *Illustrated London News*, 2 December 1871.
Illustrated London News archive

Fig. 193
'Room fitted for a practical examination in botany or zoology' (University of London Library), 1890s.
Photograph by Howard & Jones, London.
University of London Archives, RO 5/5/19

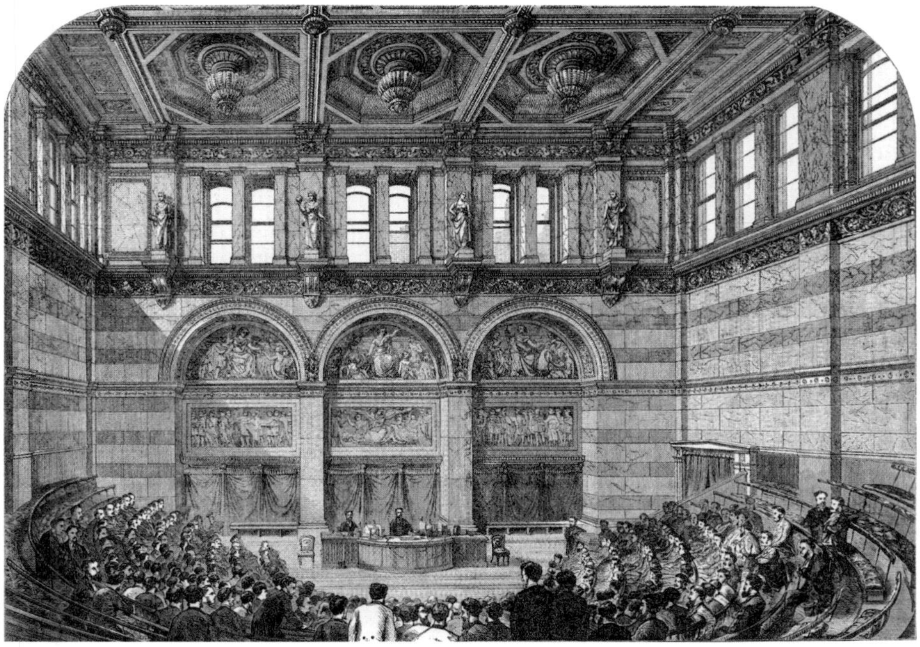

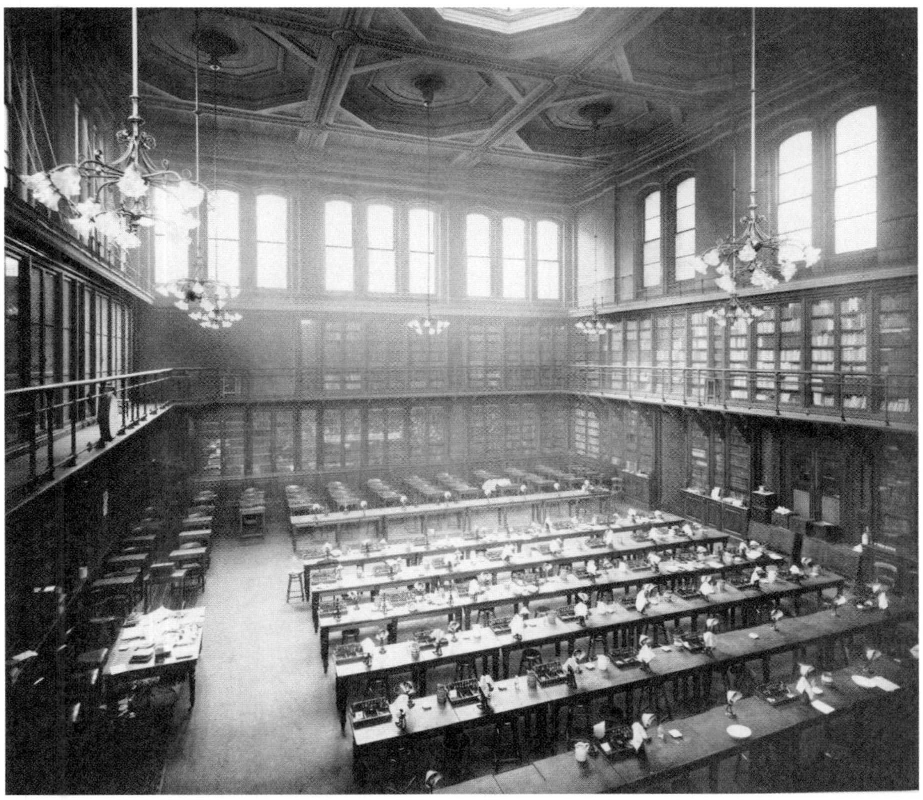

It was almost certainly a letter sent to Palmerston's successor, the Earl Russell, on 27 November 1865, that finally persuaded the government to come to a decision. This time Grote based the University's case not merely on a repetition of complaints about the 'discreditable' nature of such expedients as the use of the corrugated-iron drill shed in the garden of Burlington House, but instead 'ventured to represent that a Building is necessary to the University on other grounds. The University is', he wrote,

> not merely an Examining Board. It is the acknowledged Head of a great Educational System, having numerous Colleges and Schools in connexion with it under the provisions of a Royal Charter, in which studies are prosecuted in conformity with Curricula for Degrees prescribed by the Senate, and which Colleges and Schools, though not all grouped together in one town, but distributed through Great Britain and the Colonies, are not on that account the less interested in considering the University as their common centre.[95]

After pointing out that a suitable building was equally necessary to maintain 'ties of connexion, interest, and sympathy between the Graduates and the University', particularly since the incorporation of the University's Convocation by royal charter in 1858, Grote clinched his argument by stressing that the lack of visible evidence of the University's existence was hindering due recognition of its purpose and achievements:

> ... its progress has been cramped, and the public recognition of its position has been retarded, by its want of due prominence as a visible feature in the Metropolis. To not a few even instructed people in London, as well as in the provinces, its very existence is unknown; while many who possess some knowledge of it and interest in it identify it with University College.

What Grote was guarding against here was the risk that the government might want to fob them off with an additional building on the Burlington House site of the kind suggested in Banks & Barry's 1864 National Gallery

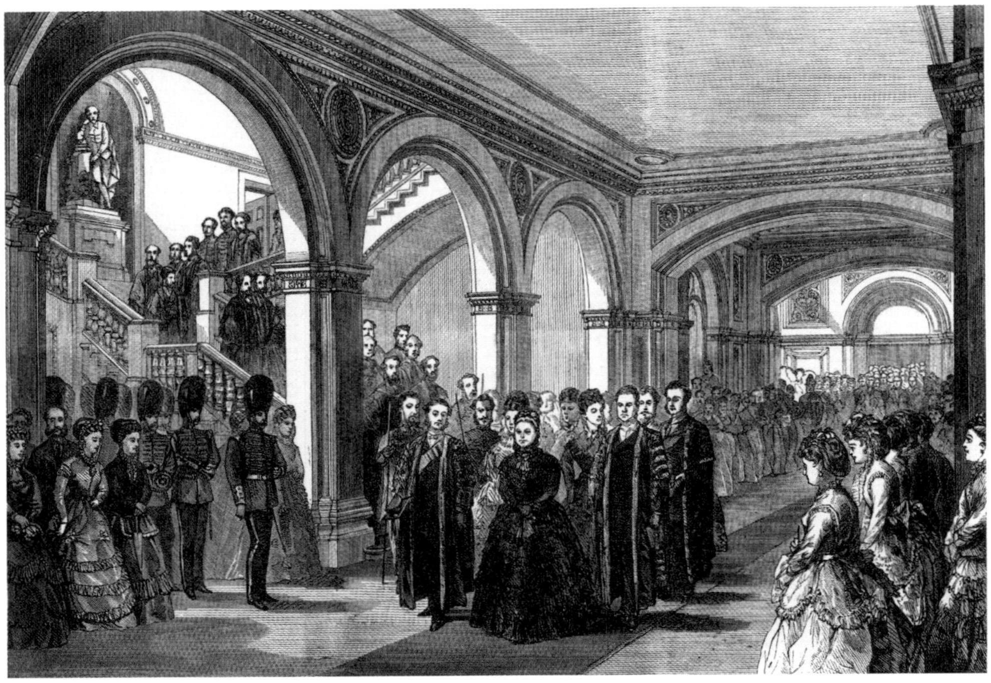

Fig. 194
'Lobby and staircase of the new building of London University', Queen Victoria's arrival for the opening ceremony, from *Illustrated London News*, 21 May 1870.
Illustrated London News archive

Fig. 195
'The Theatre of the new London University buildings – the opening ceremony', from *The Graphic*, 21 May 1870.
Mary Evans Archive

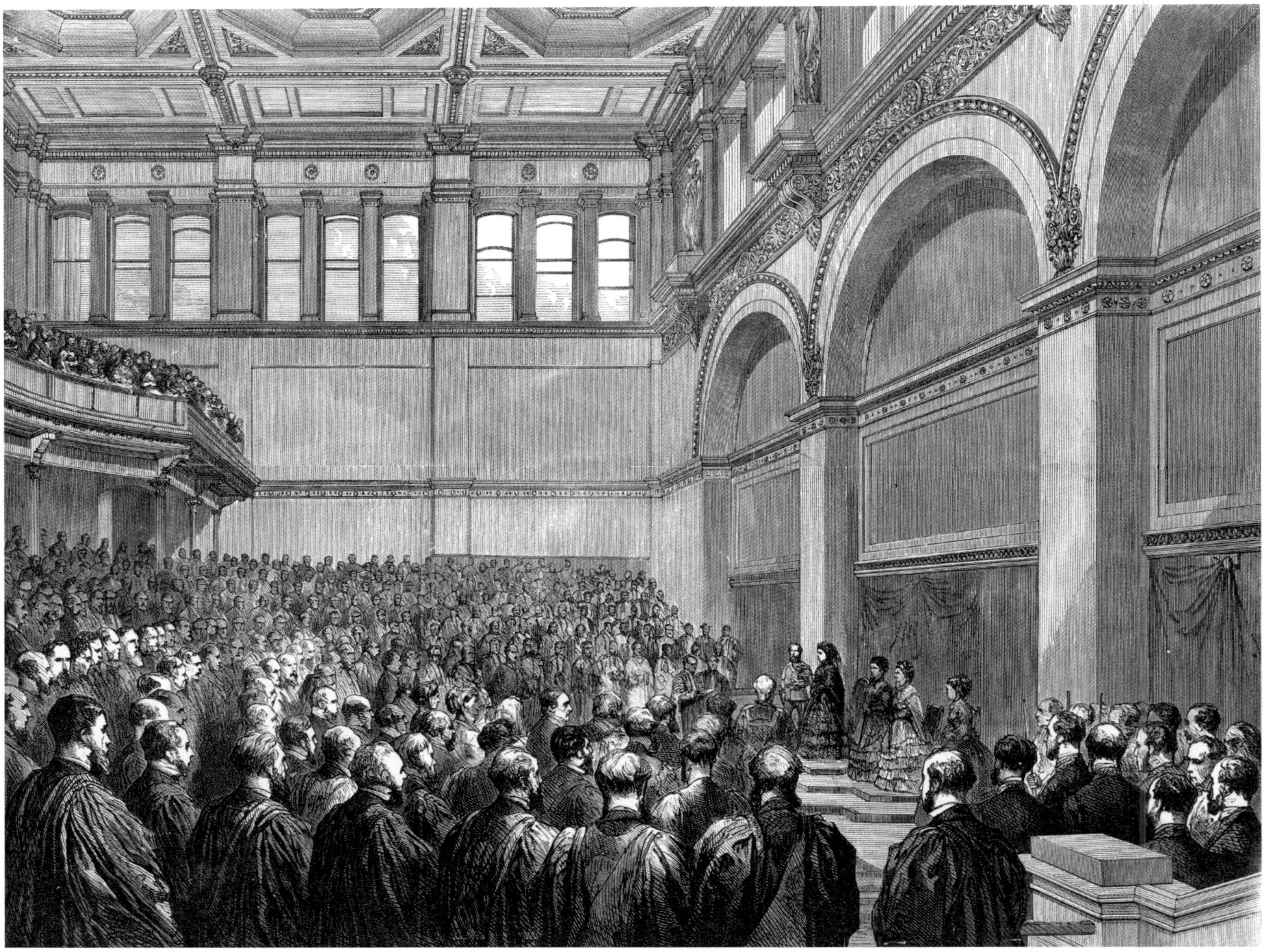

scheme (see above, Fig. 187). That this was the line currently favoured by the Office of Works was clear from the First Commissioner's response to Grant Duff's advocacy of the University's cause in the House of Commons on 2 June 1865. 'There were two ways', Cowper claimed,

> in which the accommodation might be provided .... On the one hand the University might remain in the apartments and halls and rooms which were at present appropriated to it, and such additions made to the premises as might be necessary for its work. It would not be difficult to add one or two examination halls and some other rooms to the present building. On the other hand, some of the friends of the University maintained that what was required was a new, distinct, and separate building, which might be known by all the world as a building to which the name 'The London University' was attached, and they thought such a building would make known to all passers-by that the London University was a tangible and visible institution. He [i.e. Cowper] thought there was considerable doubt whether the expenditure required for the erection of a really handsome, imposing, and dignified building, especially appropriate for the purposes of a University, would be commensurate with the advantages to be thereby attained, and whether, after all, the London University was not mainly known by its actual educational work in connection with educational institutions.[96]

Characteristically, Cowper did not divulge that six months earlier he had instructed Pennethorne to prepare a block plan for 'a new, distinct, and separate building' on the Burlington Gardens site. It was no doubt Pennethorne's estimate of £65,000 as the cost of such a building, which Cowper duly communicated to the Treasury on 31 December, that had given rise to the latter's opinion that 'at present, probably, the addition of one examination hall and a waiting room for candidates was all that was absolutely necessary', at a cost of between £6,000 and £7,000.[97]

In the Commons debate on 30 April 1866 to approve an initial tranche of £20,000 for the University's building, it was Gladstone, Russsell's Chancellor of the Exchequer, rather than Cowper, who was instrumental in deflecting calls from opposition MPs (including Manners, somewhat ironically) for further postponement, stressing that 'the case of the University was urgent in point of time', and 'on that account he should like the Committee to pass the Vote'. Gladstone went on to add that 'he accompanied that' (i.e. his recommendation),

> with this arrangement. His right hon. friend [i.e. Cowper] had already the ground plan prepared, and there would be no difficulty in immediately proceeding with the preparation of the designs, so as to give hon. gentlemen what opportunity for criticism they might desire before any step was taken in the erection of the buildings.

Cowper's acceptance of this 'arrangement' proved somewhat ambiguous:

> Mr Cowper, in explanation, said, the matter [of the University's building] had occupied a great deal of his attention, and that of his architectural advisor Mr Pennethorne; and, though he had not thought it necessary to mature the plans before the House sanctioned the principle that the London University was to have an adequate building, he could assure the House that the plans would be completed before any of the work was commenced, and he would promise to place them within reach of the hon. members, so as to show the portion that would be occupied by the Royal Academy on the southern side, that occupied by the London University at the northern end, and the intermediate space which would accommodate the learned societies. The plan might be executed at different times, but the whole would be settled before any part was commenced. The Royal Academy building would be designed by their own architect, subject to the approval of the Board of Works, and care would be taken that it harmonized in character and general arrangements with the University building. They need not be identical in style, but all the buildings that would cover the site would be viewed as one composition.[98]

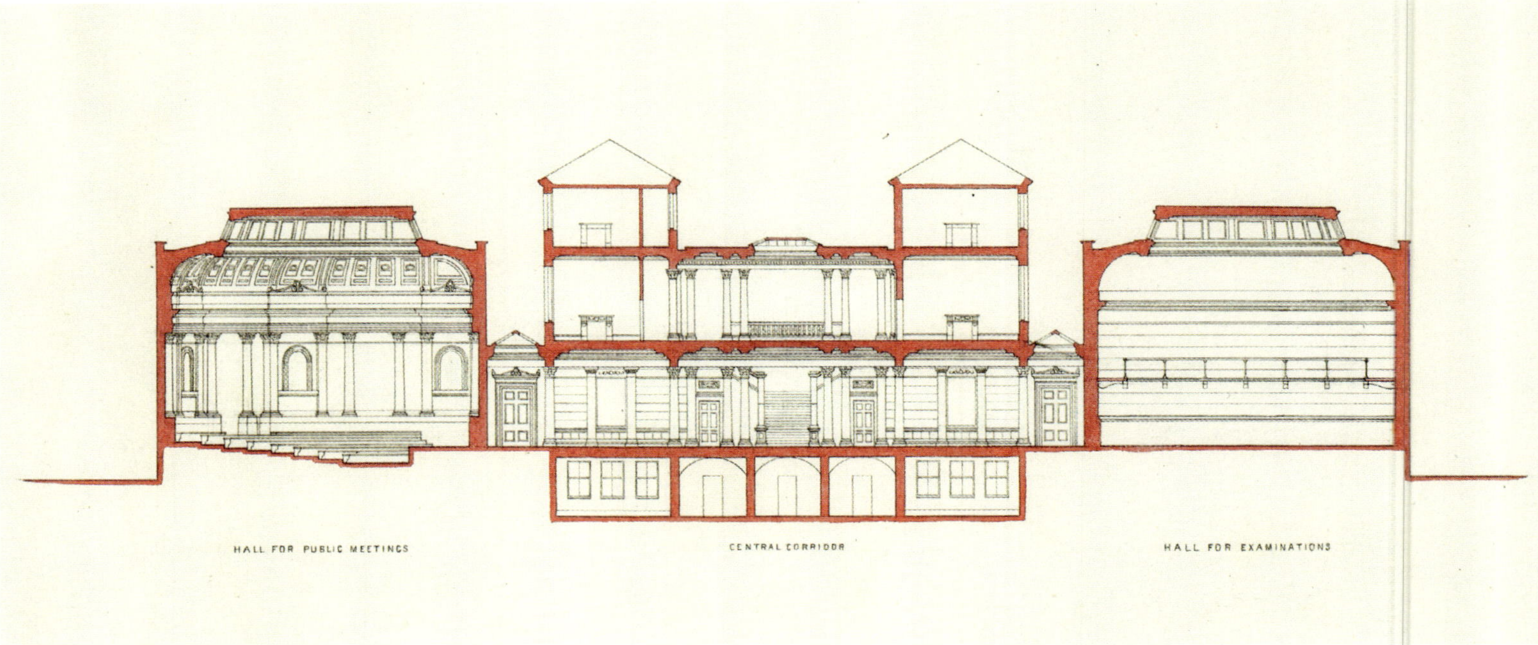

While there is little doubt Gladstone had expected Cowper to undertake to show Pennethorne's designs to the Commons before work started on the University's building, Manners may be forgiven for thinking that what his predecessor had actually promised was 'to place [plans] within reach of the hon. members' in order to show how 'all the buildings that would cover the site would be viewed as one composition.'

Despite Cowper's disclaimer that 'he had not thought it necessary to mature the plans', he had in fact instructed Pennethorne on 7 February 'to communicate with Dr. Carpenter, the Registrar of the University, respecting plans for the proposed new Building', and on 5 April Pennethorne had duly 'laid before the First Commissioner the plans prepared by him and approved by the Vice-Chancellor and Senate of the University'.[99] (These were presumably copies of or identical to the set of plans and sections of the so-called 'plain Classic' design signed and dated 15 March 1866 now in the National Archives, Kew.)[100] On 10 May, ten days after the vote in the Commons, Pennethorne was told 'to prepare Working Drawings and Specifications for the Foundations, but not to include therein any part of the Building that might be affected by the decision that must be made shortly as to the Elevation.'[101] Cowper's hesitation over the Burlington Gardens elevation was intended to allow time to establish what the Academy proposed to build on the south side of the site, so that, as he had promised in the Commons, the two buildings could be 'harmonized in character and general arrangements'.[102] Not surprisingly, Pennethorne found it impossible to prepare specifications and drawings for the foundations of the front wall without first considering 'the details of an Elevation', and reported as much when submitting these to the First Commissioner on 13 June. Presumably because of its purely theoretical status, Pennethorne did not show Cowper the front elevation 'of a plain Classic character' that he had had to consider for this purpose.[103]

On returning to his former post at the Office of Works on 6 July 1866, Manners was to adopt a more proactive approach to the University's new building than his predecessor, not because he wanted to reignite the worn-out 'Battle of the Styles' debate of the previous decade – as First Commissioner in Lord Derby's second administration he had been responsible for appointing George Gilbert Scott to design the new Foreign Office as a Gothic building – but because he was in a hurry. More pressing than any questions of architectural style was the danger that Derby's third administration would prove as short-lived as its predecessors, and that not enough progress might have been made in developing the site according to the current plan to avoid its cancellation by the next government. Thus on 6 August, exactly one month after taking office, Manners directed Pennethorne to obtain tenders for the foundations and at the same time 'to prepare and submit to him a Design for the Elevation of the front towards Burlington Gardens'. Three days later, Pennethorne submitted the 'plain Classic' elevation he had prepared but not shown to Cowper two months before.[104]

To judge from the sole surviving set of drawings relating to the 'plain Classic' scheme (the now missing front elevation of which was described by Pennethorne's obituarist Arthur Cates as 'Greek in character, dignified but somewhat plain'), Pennethorne's original intention was to evoke the atmosphere of an Athenian academy

Fig. 196
Sir James Pennethorne, University of London, his 'plain Classic' design for halls and apartments: longitudinal section, 1866.
The National Archives, Kew, 33/1745

(Fig. 196).[105] Its decidedly neo-Grecian as opposed to neo-Palladian character suggests that unlike Cowper, Pennethorne took the view that the new buildings on the north and south sides of the Burlington House site would not need to relate to one another stylistically. Although it was subsequently assumed by those who had not seen it that Pennethorne's 'plain Classic' design had been intended to harmonise with Burlington House, he appears in fact to have accepted from the start that this would be no longer necessary or desirable now that the site had been divided into three distinct plots. Both he and Manners would therefore have been in fundamental agreement with Beresford Hope's assessment of, if not his opinion on, the best that could be achieved under the circumstances:

> Under the old scheme [for the National Gallery] there would have been one grand harmonious palace erected on the ground, with a direct through communication and two façades saving withal Burlington House. ... But this had been given up, and the ground was to be cut up and frittered away partly between the Royal Academy and the London University. Each building would now have its own entrance front, and neither of them would have any intercommunication, nor back nor sides, but simple blank walls, except the façades. Moreover, there could not conceivably be two structures which it would be more impossible to comprehend in the same coup d'œil, except from a balloon, than the Royal Academy looking down upon Piccadilly, and the London University up Cork Street. Accordingly, the unity of structure which had to be maintained in the days when the National Gallery was to cover the whole space no longer existed. ...The good scheme that would cover Burlington Gardens with one building was passed and gone. It was to be covered with two buildings totally distinct in their objects. Let them be dealt with on their own merits. Let them forget that there was a Royal Academy to the south, and deal with the London University merely with a view to Burlington Gardens.[106]

According to the 'Memorandum' in which Pennethorne recalled the sequence of events leading up to his third and final design for the building's front elevation, when Manners had asked him to produce 'a fresh design' in mid-August 1866, Manners had suggested 'in very general terms the adoption of a character more Mediaeval or Renaissance ... but without fettering the Architect as regards style.'[107] As Manners was by then committed to rebuilding the forecourt of Burlington House for the learned societies, he might well have been expected to ask Pennethorne for a design that conformed architecturally with that building. The fact that the exact reverse happened was seized upon, both at the time by Manners's political opponents and in a report in *The Times* four years later, as *prime facie* evidence that he had forced Pennethorne 'to substitute a mediaeval elevation for the classical one'.[108] However, what Manners had actually asked for was no more than an alternative design in which, according to his own account, Pennethorne had been at liberty to adopt any style he chose, including if he so wished a different form of classical architecture (i.e. 'Renaissance'). The report in *The Times* also erred in stating that 'Mr. Pennethorne's original design ... [had] been approved by Mr. Cowper' and that 'all things were in train for its erection when Lord Derby came into power'; in fact, according to Pennethorne, Cowper had not even seen the 'plain Classic' elevation, let alone approved it.

Perpetuated by misinformation of this kind, the politically motivated 'Battle of the Styles' explanation for the building's 'curious' design history has tended to obscure the significance of the fact that Pennethorne was Manners's key source of information on a project that he was in more of a hurry to expedite than his predecessor. It is much more likely to have been owing to Pennethorne's long involvement in the project, dating back to November 1864, rather than to a determination to impose his own architectural opinions, that Manners asked him 'to reconsider the subject and to submit a fresh design.' Similarly, because Manners was adamant that the University should not expect to be able to demand design changes to its exterior after construction work had begun, it has been wrongly assumed that it must have been denied any influence over the latter right from the beginning.[109] In fact, given the high priority the University attached to having a building that expressed

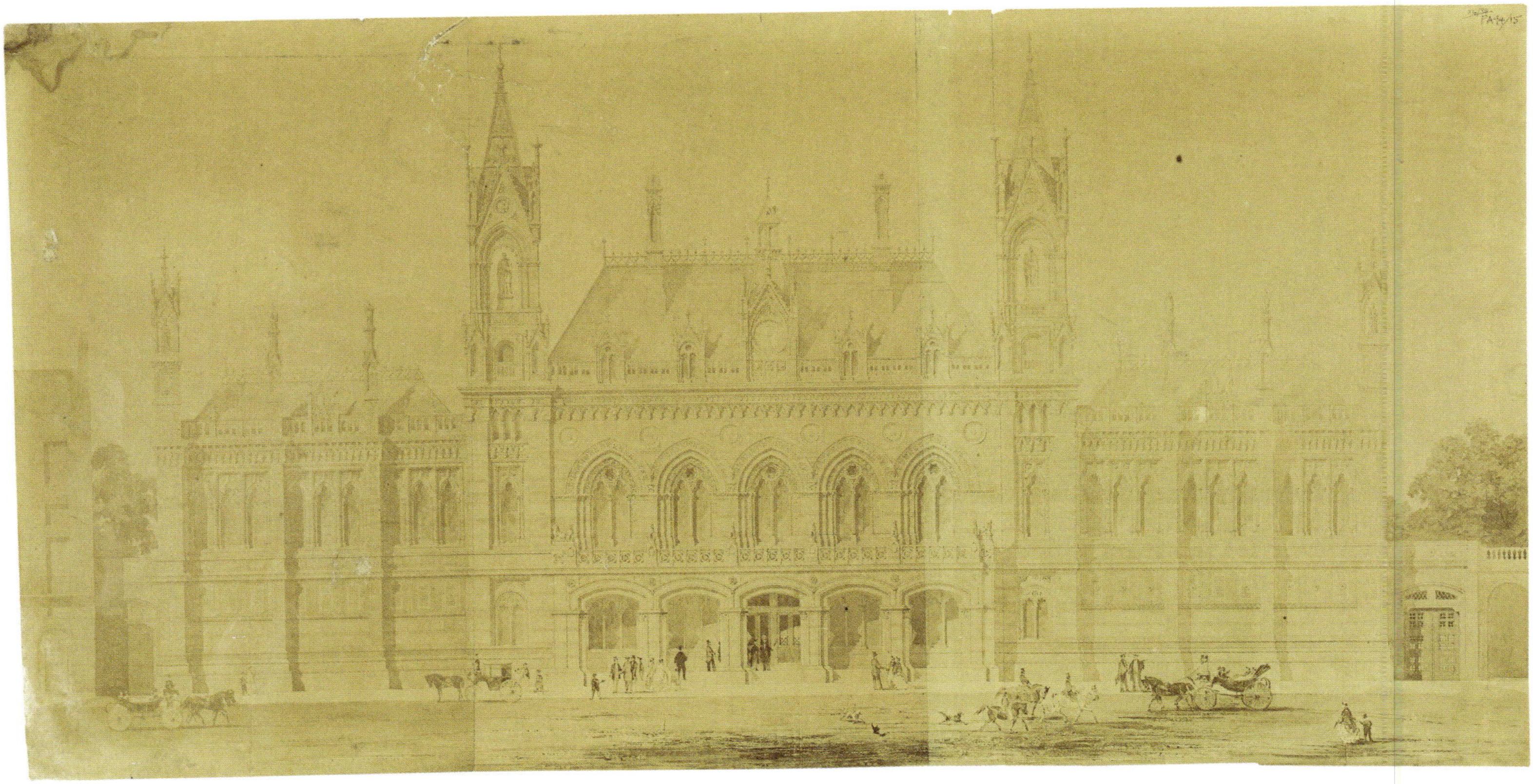

its purpose and character publicly, it is in fact hardly conceivable that Pennethorne would have been impervious to their expectations in this respect. And although the Office of Works as the commissioning client was the final arbiter of the building's architectural character, Pennethorne could hardly have been in the dark about the University's own views on a matter of such importance to it, even though these may well have been only informally communicated during his meetings with W. B. Carpenter, its registrar, to settle more practical questions about the design of its interior.

It was no doubt because Pennethorne was used to dealing with Carpenter that the latter's preference for the 'Italian-Gothic' design (Fig. 197) – expressed verbally at a meeting in Manners' office on 29 August 1866 and concurred with at the time by the architect himself – was assumed to represent the University's collective view. Carpenter himself, however, was to state categorically in May the following year that he had given this opinion 'while disclaiming any right to be speaking for the senate.'[110] It is indicative of a strong sense of urgency at this meeting – of which it appears no written record was made – that on the same day Manners 'returned the Design to the Architect, with instructions to prepare the Working Plans, &c. for the superstructure' of the building, 'accepted the tender of Messrs Jackson & Shaw for the construction of the foundations, and entered into a Contract for the same'.[111] In their haste it seems neither the First Commissioner nor his architect had heard what they did not want to hear.

It may have been for a similar reason that Manners now committed a major blunder in allowing three and half months to pass without giving the Senate an opportunity to see or comment on the design for their building's front elevation. The charitable explanation for this discourtesy is that there was a misunderstanding about who would ensure that the Senate was properly consulted. However, it is also possible that there was some complicity between the parties concerned, all of whom no doubt hoped to avoid time-consuming airing of conflicting opinions, particularly within the wider constituency of the University's Convocation. From this perspective, it may well have seemed preferable for the University not to be consulted any further over the elevation of its building as there was little chance of reaching wider agreement on what was purely a matter of taste and therefore best left to the First Commissioner's discretion.

If this was the case, and there was a tacit attempt to close down further discussion, it seriously backfired. Having finally been allowed sight of Pennethorne's 'Italian-Gothic' elevation on 14 December 1866, a sub-committee of the Senate and members of the Convocation's Annual Committee delivered a report on 22 February 1867 that was so deeply critical that it led the House of Commons to pass an amendment three months later ordering that design's total abandonment and the substitution of an entirely new one.[112] Quoted to devastating effect by Layard in the Commons on 5 April, this report was probably the source of the rumour that Pennethorne had redesigned his original 'plain Classic' elevation under duress:

Fig. 197
Sir James Pennethorne, University of London, his 'Italian-Gothic' design: perspective of the street front, 1866.
RIBA Collections, PA94/15

> They [i.e. the sub-committee] much regret that they cannot speak favourably of the elevation. They are, however, fully sensible of the disadvantage under which the architect has laboured in putting a Gothic casing upon an edifice planned for the adoption of an entirely different (and, indeed, antagonistic) style. Believing that ornament should be subservient to structural expression, they would gladly see the whole series of spires and pinnacles done away with. … They also cannot but regret that the principal range of windows should light a series of small or moderate sized apartments, and thus give a certain character of unreality to the design; but this has been in a great measure the result of adopting a Gothic elevation without recasting the plan of the building.[113]

To be fair, Manners had probably been unaware of this report when, just three days later on 25 February 1867, he signed a second contract with Jackson & Shaw 'for the erection of the building up to the level of the first floor', thinking no doubt that this would pre-empt any future interference in its design.[114] Of course, it ended up doing quite the opposite, in large part because Layard was able to portray the First Commissioner's apparent high-handedness in his dealings with the University as evidence that he had behaved with equal disrespect towards Parliament by ignoring his predecessor's pledge to obtain the approval of the House of Commons before beginning any building work. However, despite a further sub-committee's recommendation the following month that 'the Modern style of architecture would be preferable either to the Mediaeval or the Italian-Gothic' and the Senate's formal resolution on 27 March 'that a Building of which the style should be in harmony with that of Burlington House would be preferable' to either of Pennethorne's existing designs, Layard's triumph over his rival in the Commons put the University in even less of a position to choose the architectural style of their new building than they had been before.[115] And although halting building work for three months (between 6 April and 11 July 1867) might have seemed like a victory for those who thought the University should have had a say in the design of the exterior of its building, the effect of Layard's intervention was to constitute the House of Commons as a building committee that might well prove far harder to influence than either Manners or Pennethorne had been. Fortunately, however, the risk that the whole project might now become terminally mired in party politics helped to focus minds on the need for a more collaborative approach. Thus, when John Storrar, the chairman of the University's Convocation and a key member of the new building sub-committee appointed on 13 March, wrote to Carpenter on 11 June 'to represent strongly the opinion which has been arrived at … viz. that, the University should assert its right to be heard in the matter of the elevation', he went on nonetheless to add that

> Speaking for myself, I feel it would be very expedient were it possible to impress Lord John Manners with the assurance that the University is not under the influence of any opposition towards him, such as dictated by the line taken by Layard, that on the contrary it would be [only] too happy to be brought in as an *amicus curiae* to aid him in getting over his difficulties in the House of Commons.[116]

'Perhaps', he concluded somewhat ruefully, 'it is a misfortune to us that we have been unavoidably thrust into action with Layard, who cares nothing for us, except in so far as we may serve him in doing battle with the Minister.' However, although Manners had had no choice but to let the Commons decide the 'matter of the elevation', there was nothing to prevent Pennethorne from taking into account the sub-committee's strongly held opinion,

> that the Building should be so designed as to present the features of a separate and individual edifice – that it should be an University building and not an University in apartments, situate in the rear of a structure called Burlington House.[117]

For his part, Pennethorne was careful to stress that he had adopted 'the front of Burlington House as a foundation' of his new design because he knew that much of the hostility to the 'Italian-Gothic' elevation, both in the Commons and 'out of doors', had stemmed from the disappointed expectation (dating back to Cowper's

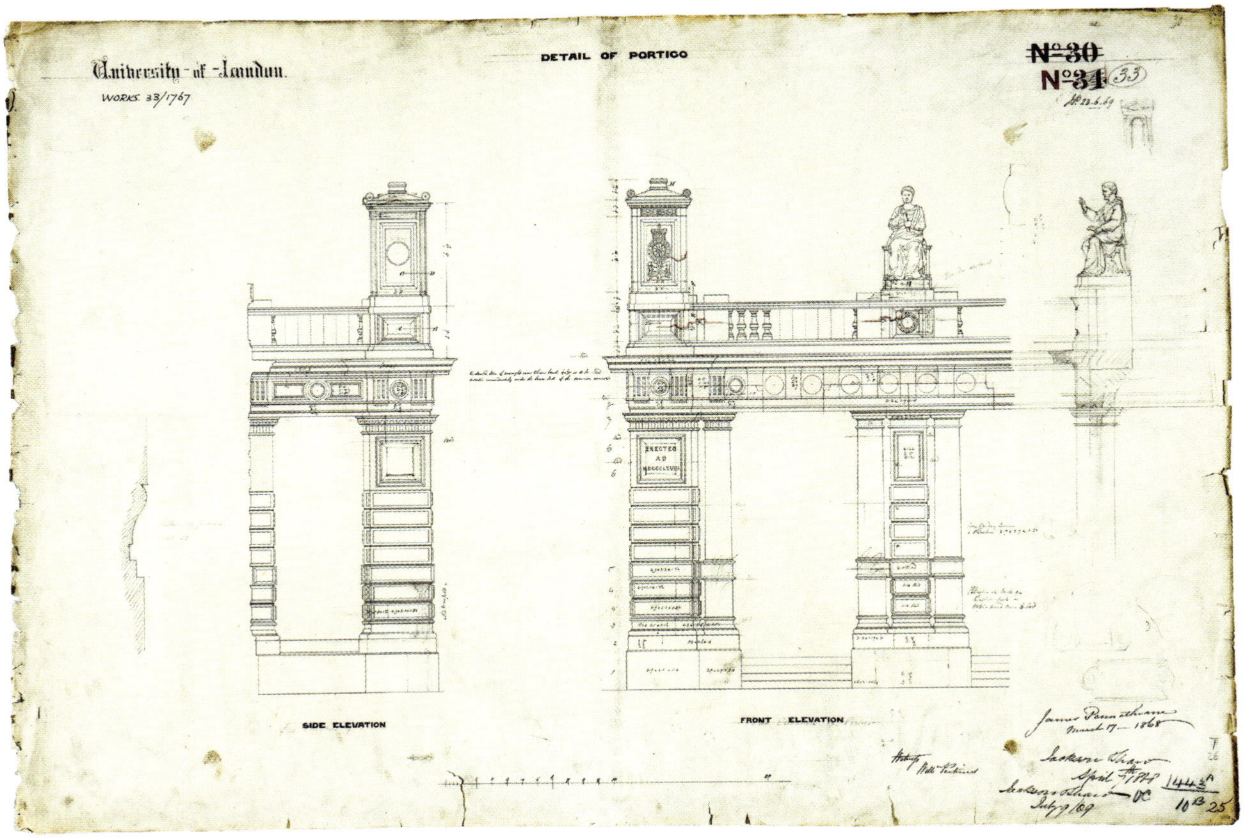

Fig. 198
Sir James Pennethorne, University of London: details of the side and front of the portico, north front, 1868.
The National Archives, Kew, WORK 33/1767

'pledge' to the House the year before) that all the buildings on the site should relate to one another stylistically.[118] That still left him with the problem of how to make the University's building express the purpose and character of the institution that occupied it. He and Manners had assumed, quite wrongly, that the University of London would welcome a building reminiscent of its venerable rivals on the Isis and the Cam. What they had failed to appreciate was that the inescapable association of Gothic architecture with medieval scholasticism might make a building in that style seem inappropriate for a modern university that prided itself on its progressive curriculum, its championing of the academic study of the natural sciences and modern languages, and the increasing opportunities it was creating for women to obtain university degrees on a par with men. They may therefore have been a bit surprised when the University's chancellor, Earl Granville, remarked in a degree-day presentation speech in May 1867 that he 'thought with some gentlemen around him that something more appropriate might be devised than a mediaeval design, with which that university had nothing in common.'[119]

What the University of London really needed was a modern building in a modern style of architecture, and this was precisely Pennethorne's difficulty, in that no such style could come to hand in the age of Victorian historicism. His solution was to convey the message of the building's purpose through sculpture rather than architecture, by personifying the goals of the University in a stone pantheon of famous learned men reminiscent of the Royal Society's portrait collection of great British scientists (Fig. 198). As there could be no difficulty in allowing the University to select and arrange this pantheon themselves, Pennethorne's solution gave Manners the perfect olive branch to make up for his failure to consult the Senate properly over the design of the building's façade and the resulting fiasco.[120] And as for his difficulties in Parliament, apart from, perhaps inevitably, some minor revision of its detailing suggested by the retired architect MP (Sir) William Tite, Pennethorne's new design gave rise to scarcely a comment when it was put on display in the House of Commons Library at the end of June 1867 (Figs 199, 200).[121]

IN PREPARING A BLOCK PLAN and estimate in November 1864 for a proposed building for the University on the Burlington Gardens site, Pennethorne had been able to work from the brief that the Senate had sent to the Treasury and First Commissioner that July.[122] As far as its administrative offices were concerned, the University's requirements were little different from those that had been met for the best part of a decade in the former home of Lady Charles Fitzroy (née Anne Cavendish) on the east side of the Burlington House forecourt. Rather surprisingly, it had found this domestic building 'extremely convenient', its only drawback being that

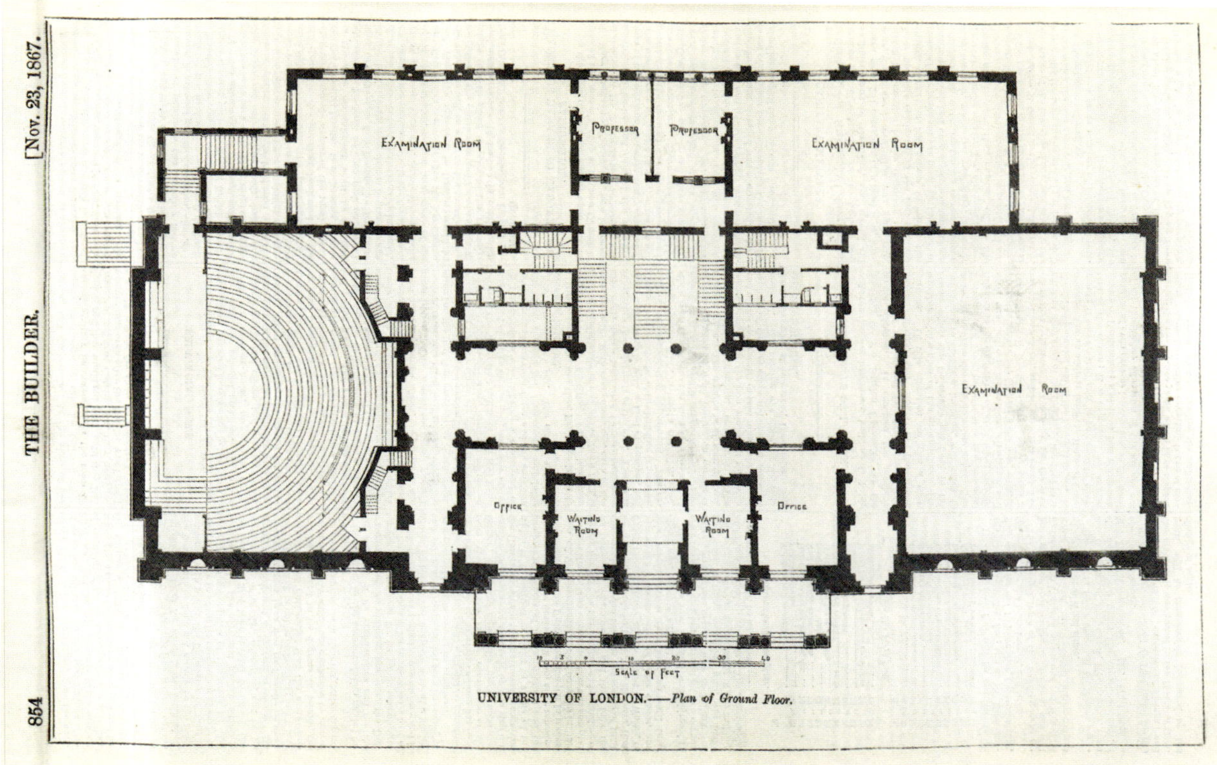

Fig. 199
University of London, ground-floor plan (Sir James Pennethorne's final design), from *The Builder*, vol. 25, 23 November 1867, p. 854.
RIBA Collections, Periodicals

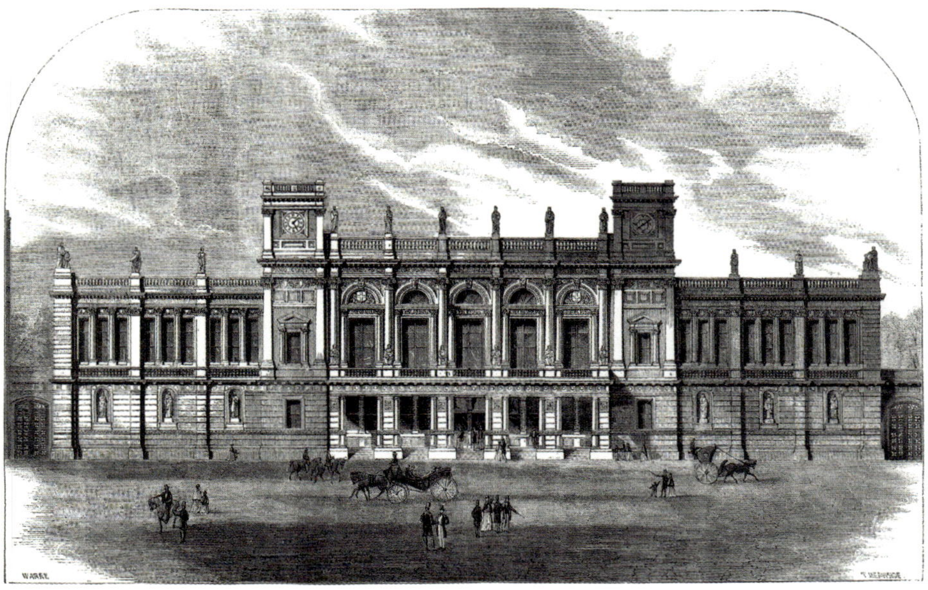

Fig. 200
T. Heaviside, after Daniel Robert Wary, University of London, from *The Builder*, vol. 25, 23 November 1867, p. 855.
RIBA Collections, Periodicals

the room the Senate used for its ordinary meetings (measuring 'about 35 feet by 20') was 'not … always sufficient' for its 38 members to sit in comfort. However, regarding suitable accommodation for conducting its examinations, degree presentations and bimonthly meetings of Convocation, the situation could hardly have been more different. Having for so long had 'recourse to temporary expedients of an almost humiliating character', the University claimed that it would need almost three times more space than it currently had for these purposes, *viz.*: two 'spacious' halls, each the size of the Royal Society's 'great room'; two rooms 'corresponding to the smaller hall in the west wing' (i.e. the Royal Society's Lower Library), one of which was to serve as the candidates' waiting room; and two more rooms of at least this size, preferably top-lit, for the University's practical examinations in anatomy and chemistry. They also asked for some new facilities, such as a 'reading room' of about 25 by 20 feet; two rooms for 'the lithographic presses &c. used in printing the examination papers'; two or more storerooms for 'stationery and voluminous papers' and the 'specimens and apparatus used in the University's practical examinations'; and a small fire-proof strong-room necessary for the preservation of the University's charter and registers. In planning the new building Pennethorne was able to follow these instructions remarkably closely, complying for instance with the requirement that the Senate's meeting room be adjoined by both a smaller 'Committee Room' and the Registrar's 'Official Room'; that the 'Clerk's Room' and a waiting room should be near the front entrance, alongside a small 'Messengers Room'; and that the 'Clerk of Convocation' needed a separate office. And the fact that the Senate's brief generally asked for rooms in pairs must have certainly aided in the composition of a plan that is perhaps chiefly remarkable for its almost perfect symmetry.

By the time the first 'plain Classic' design was completed in March 1866, the intended uses of the two 'spacious' examination halls originally specified had significantly amplified, reflecting the University's growing concern that its building needed to be worthy of an institution that was 'not merely an Examining Board ... [but]... the acknowledged Head of a great Educational System'. Thus, despite the fact that the 1864 brief makes no mention of the need for a library, Pennethorne's longitudinal section shows the proposed double-height examination hall in the west wing lined from floor-to-clerestory with bookshelves (see above, Fig. 196). And, in an even more dramatic transformation, what had been specified as a similar examination hall in the east wing suitable for occasional use on degree-presentation and Convocation days, is shown instead as a double-height amphitheatre with a permanent 620-seat west-facing auditorium. In May the following year, when Manners was under particular pressure to show that he was being responsive to the University's wishes, this space was set to become even more the showpiece of the building as a result of the acceptance by the Board of Works of the Senate's 'suggestions ... as to the theatre, which as now arranged, would accommodate 800.'[123] This was no minor alteration since it involved revising the plan of the entire east wing, sinking the lecturer's podium to basement level, turning the auditorium through 180° so that it faced east rather than west, and incorporating a 180-seat visitors' gallery supported on cast-iron columns (Figs 201–203).

Pennethorne's working drawings indicate that he intended public areas of the building to have a more sumptuous interior decoration than was carried out, not only in the lecture theatre but also in the Senate Room, on the main staircase and, to a certain extent, along the principal east–west corridors on the ground and first-floors (Fig. 204). Thus, faint pencil notes on drawings of the south and east elevations of the staircase compartment show that it was proposed at some point to line the walls below the string-course in contrasting green and red serpentine and rosso levanto marble, to include panels of painted ornament in the frieze and (possibly)

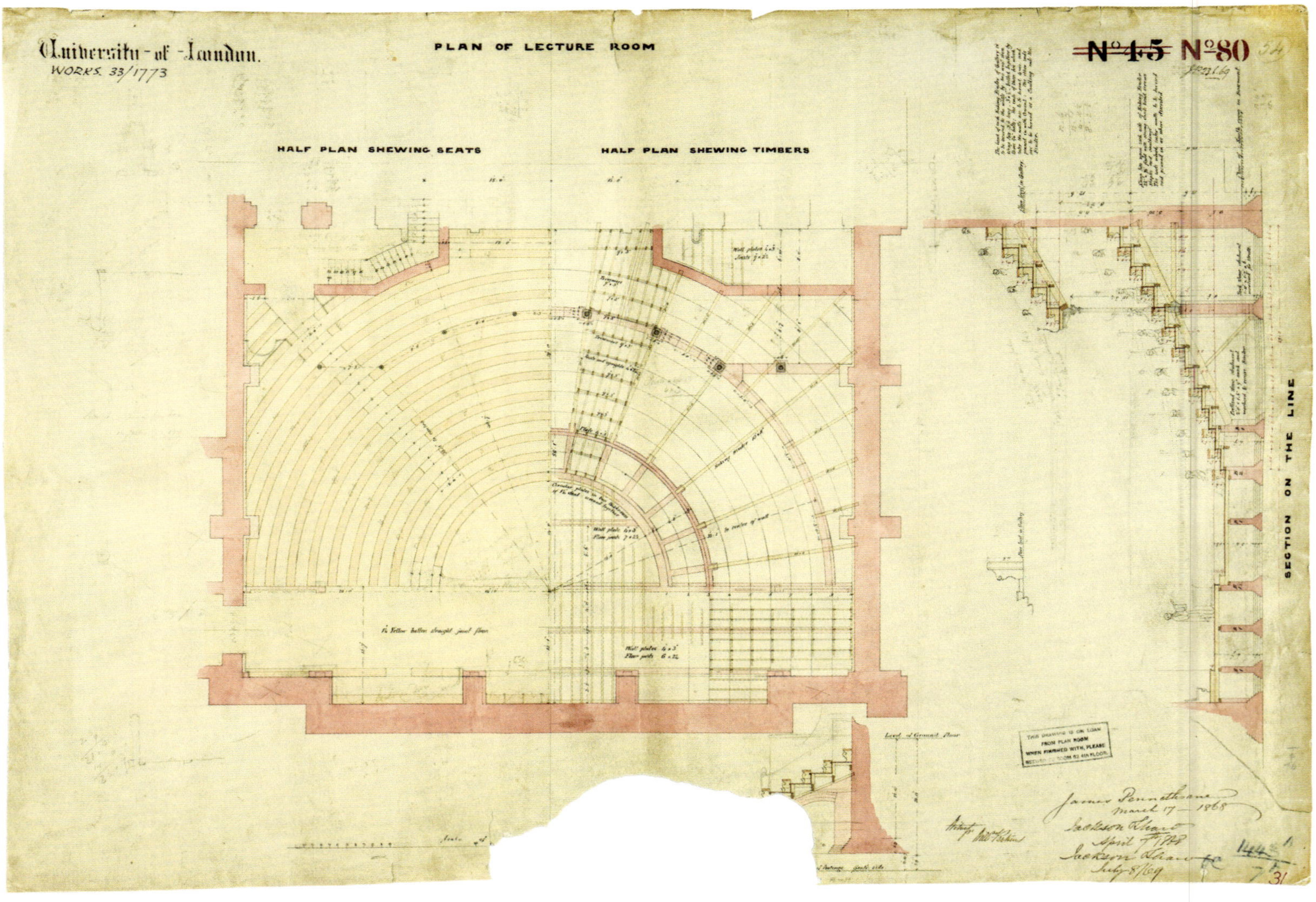

Fig. 201
Sir James Pennethorne, University of London: plan and section showing seats and timbers of the lecture theatre, 1868.
The National Archives, Kew, WORK 33/1773

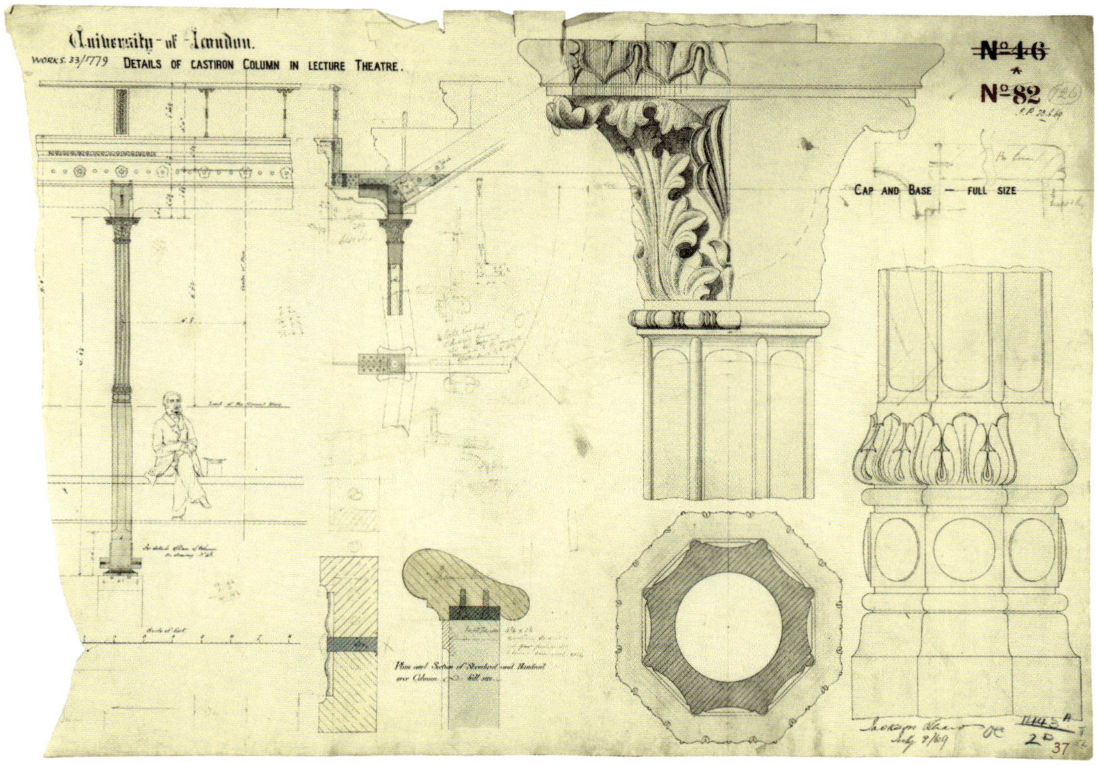

Fig. 202
Sir James Pennethorne, University of London: details of cast-iron columns in the lecture theatre, 1868.
The National Archives, Kew, WORK 33/1779

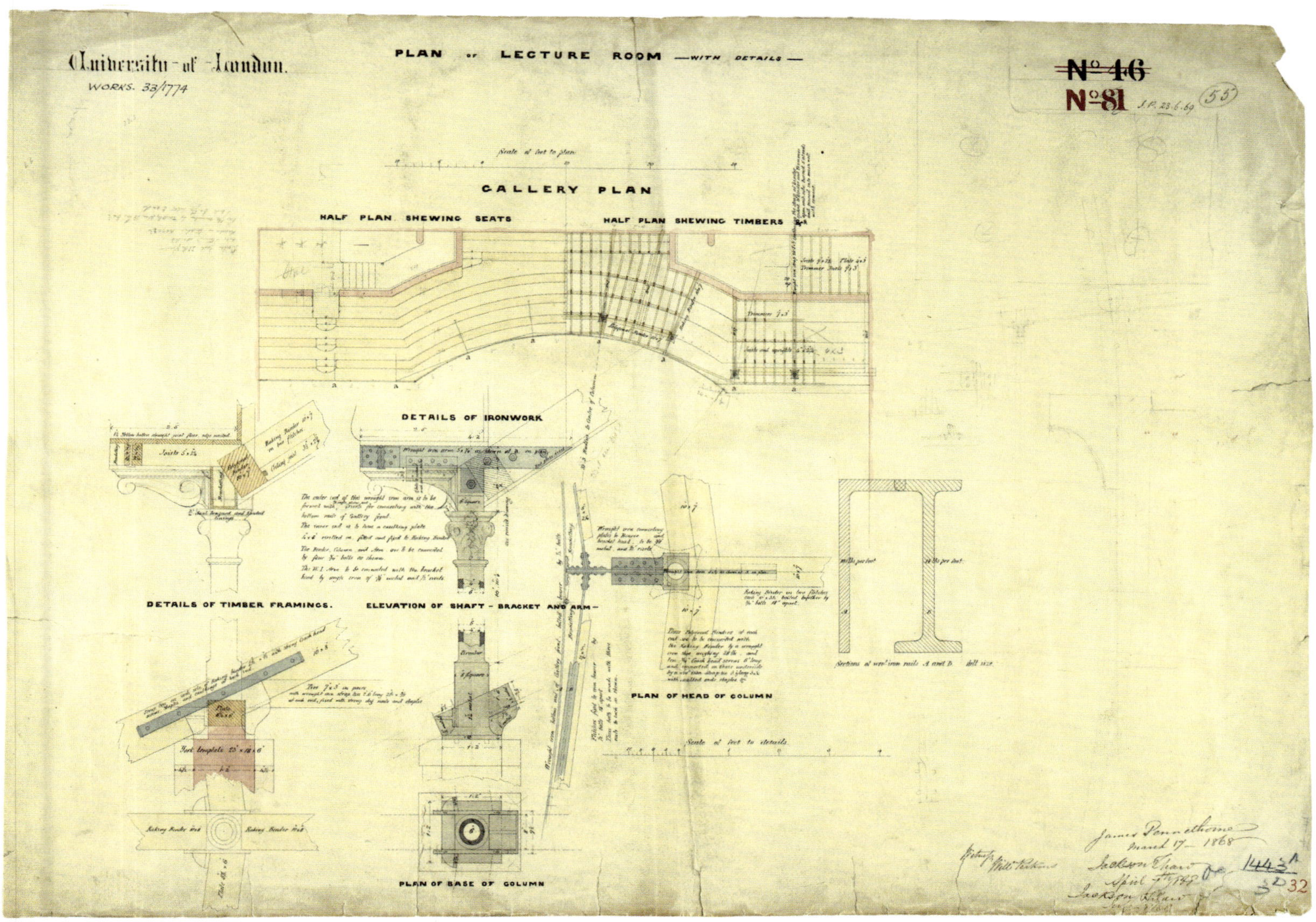

Fig. 203
Sir James Pennethorne, University of London: plan showing seats and timbers to the gallery of the lecture theatre, 1868.
The National Archives, Kew, WORK 33/1774

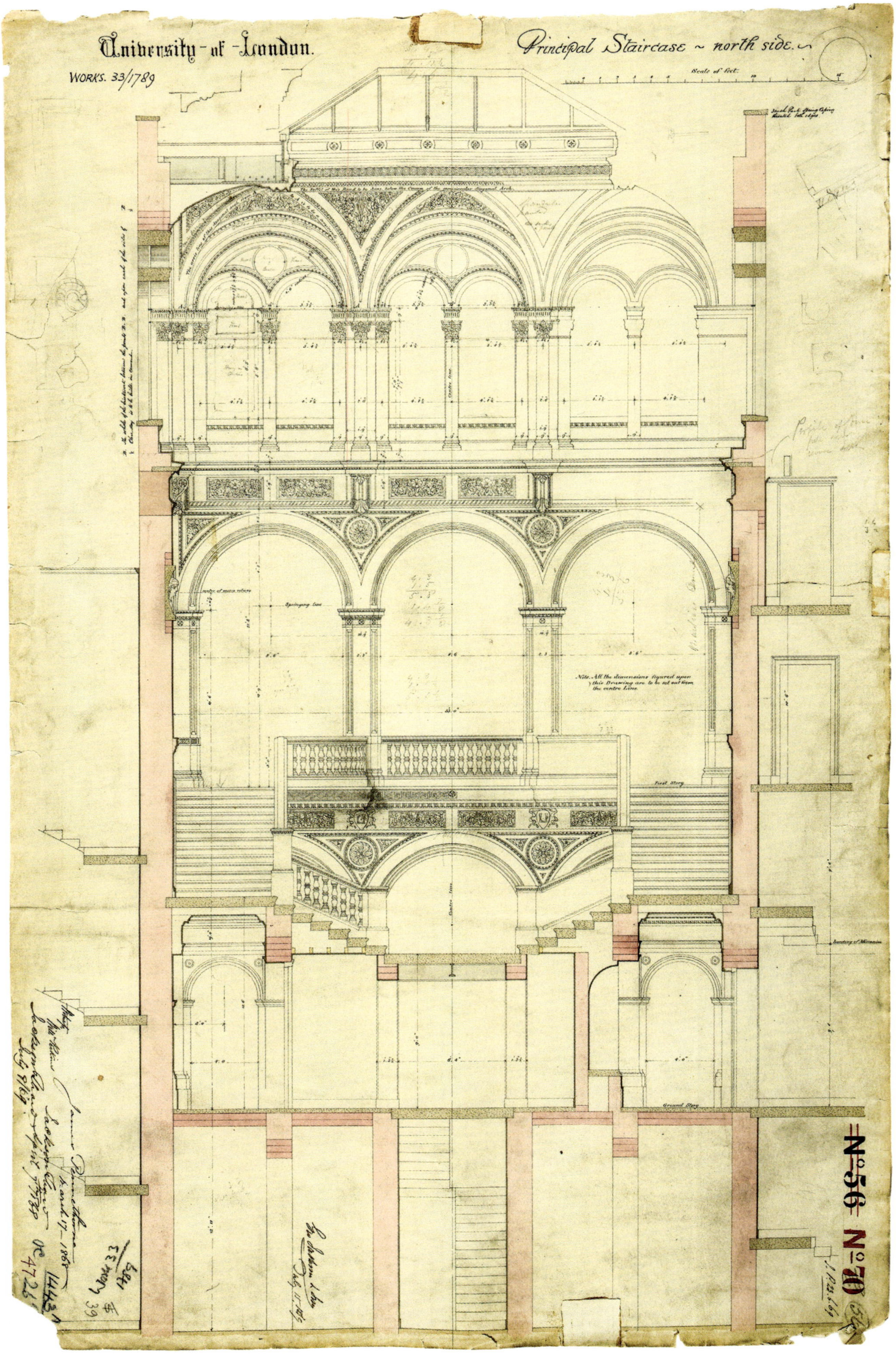
University-of-London.
Principal Staircase ~ north side.
WORKS. 33/1789
Scale of Feet.
Note. All the dimensions figured upon this Drawing are to be set out from the centre Line.
First Story
Ground Story
Centre line
No 56
No 70

Fig. 204
Sir James Pennethorne, University of London: section and elevation of the north side of the principal staircase, 1868.
The National Archives, Kew
WORK 33/1789

Fig. 205
Sir James Pennethorne, University of London: sections and elevations of the principal staircase, 1868.
The National Archives, Kew,
WORK 33/1790

inlaid sections of sienna and grey marble (Fig. 205). Similarly, a drawing of the elevation of the east wall of the lecture theatre indicates not only that this was to have been clad in decorative marble, including a Cosmati-style marble mosaic dado, but also that the triple blind arches of the *frons scenae* were intended to contain figurative roundels (Fig. 206).

Despite this promised opulence, newspaper accounts described the interior of the theatre at the time of its opening as 'ostentatiously plain', noting that all the internal walls of the building had 'a somewhat monotonous and dead appearance' (they had been whitewashed in preparation for the Queen's visit), and that it was all too apparent that 'permanent internal decoration is ... a matter for the future' (see above, Figs 194, 195).[124] *The Times* was confident that 'it is intended they [i.e. the walls] shall hereafter be enriched with all the glories of gold and colour', and trusted that 'Parliament will deal liberally, and will take care that the decoration shall be worthy of the building and its destined uses', since the University 'has five Cabinet Ministers among the Members of its Senate, and that they are all of them men ready to acknowledge the dignity of learning.' The *Daily Telegraph* on the other hand thought 'legislative parsimony may have had something to do with this poverty of adornment', and was puzzled to know

> why Mr. Pennethorne ... should have forgotten that in Vicenza ... there exists one of the most exquisite models of a classical theatre in the world [i.e. Palladio's Teatro Olimpico] but has chosen instead ... to give us a bare, common-place apartment that reminds the spectator equally of that lecture-hall at the Polytechnic Institution, where, in its scientific days, professors in spectacles used to hold forth on the representation of a flea five thousand times magnified, and of the dissecting-room of a district hospital in the State of Connecticut.[125]

With the possible exception of the Senate Room (Fig. 207), it is doubtful that any of the interiors of the University's building ever quite lived up to the promise of decorative splendour held out by the elaborate detailing

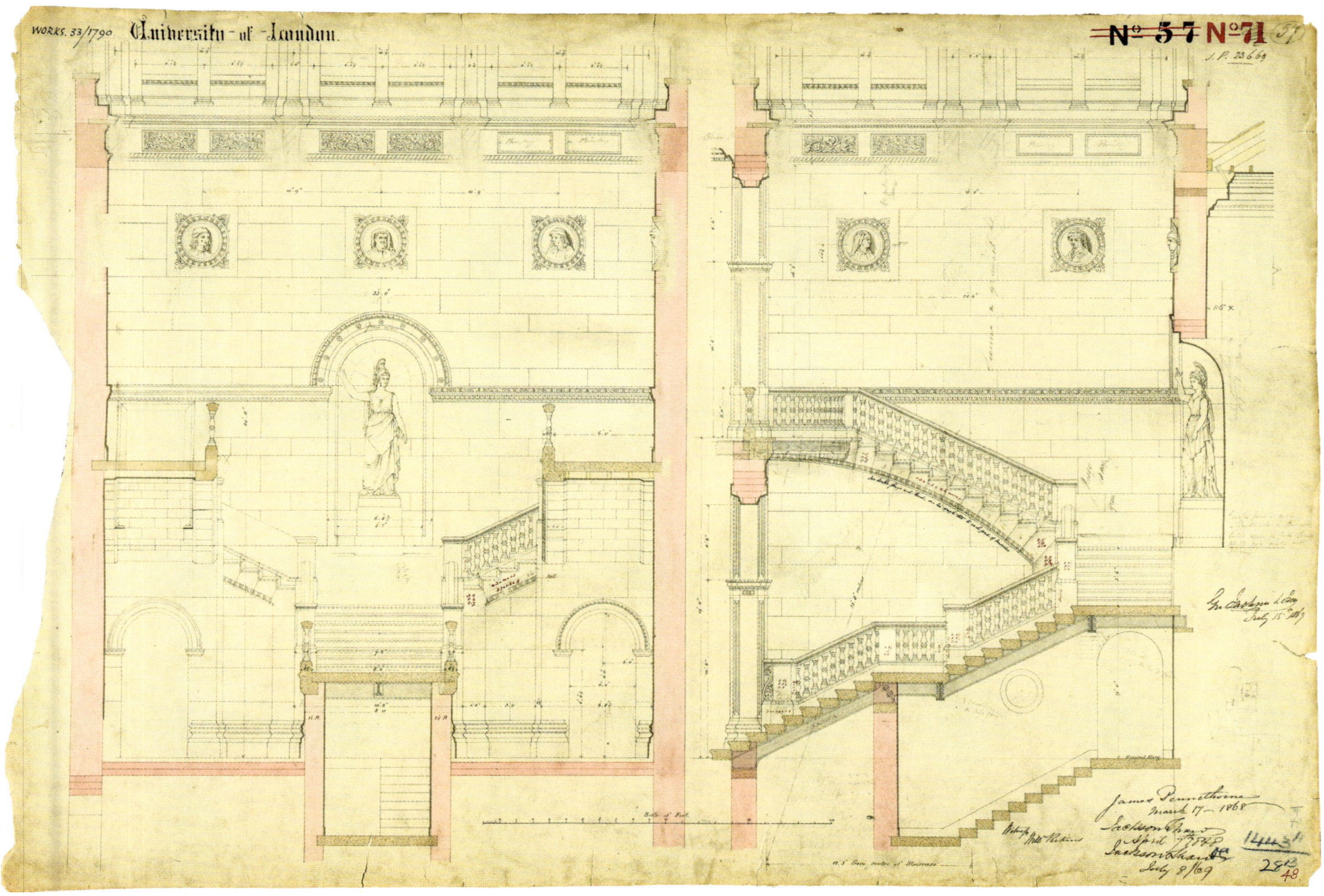

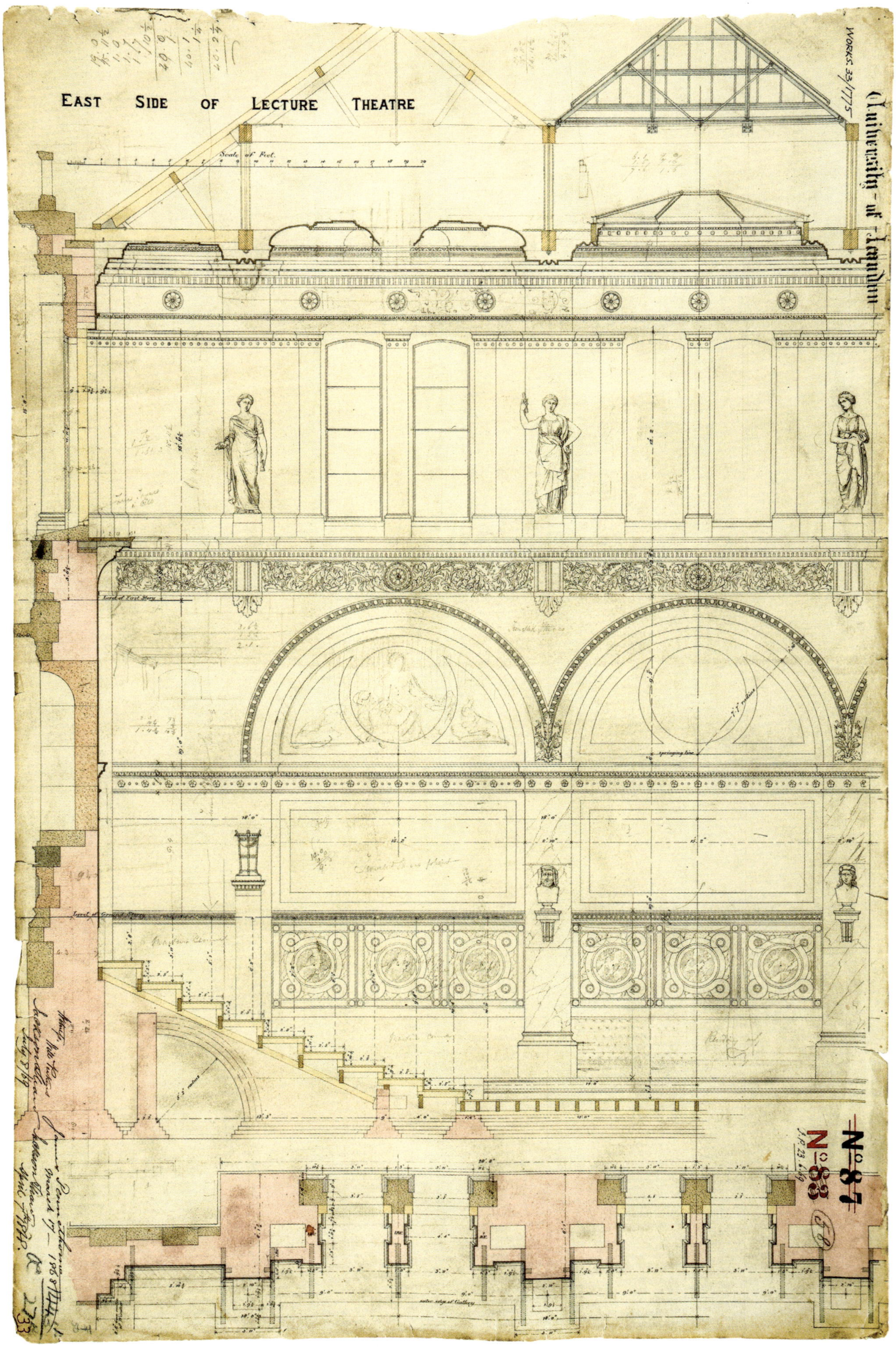

Fig. 206
Sir James Pennethorne, University of London: part plan and elevation of the east side of the lecture theatre, 1868.
The National Archives, Kew, WORK 33/1775

Fig. 207
Sir James Pennethorne, University of London: elevation of the south side and plan of the Senate Room ceiling, 1868.
The National Archives, Kew, WORK 33/1783

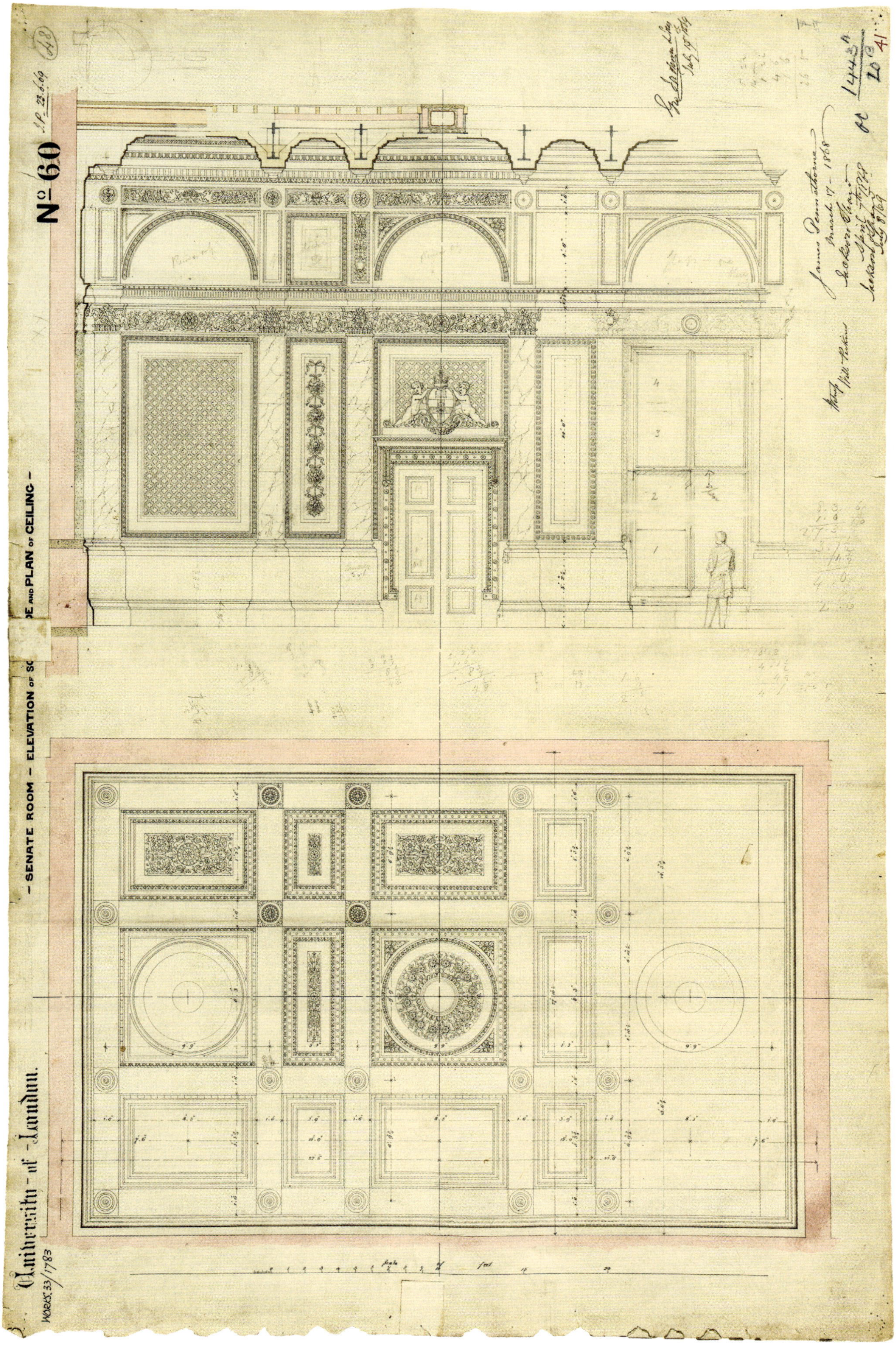

of its façade (see above, Fig. 191). While the latter was generally admired for its use of subtly polychromatic Portland, Mansfield and Hopton Wood stone and as 'an example of a refined or enriched style of Palladian or Italian architecture'[126], at least one critic complained that it was so 'cut and carved ... as scarcely to exhibit a plain stone surface anywhere' and 'executed in the most sovereign and contemptuous defiance of those simple principles of common sense on this subject which have been laid down so frequently.'[127] In the months following the Queen's visit it is clear that some effort was made to allay such a stark contrast between showy exterior and austere interior. Thus, the wood-engraving of the lecture theatre published in the *Illustrated London News* on 2 December 1871 gives an entirely different impression of its interior eighteen months later (see above, Fig. 192). In fact, it is likely that a good deal of interior finishing work – including for instance a separate contract for bookcases[128] – was carried out elsewhere in the building long after the official opening, accounting for the fact that between 8 April 1870 and 12 August 1871 the Commons voted a total of £24,762 'to complete the sum for the University of London Buildings'. Despite these additional votes, which brought the building's cost up to £66,762, the budget for finishing the interior was probably very tight, not only because of the £7,000 to £8,000 overspend that Manners estimated had been the cost of the building's mid-construction design change, but because Acton Smee Ayrton, who had succeeded Layard at the Office of Works on 26 October 1869, was a notorious penny pincher.[129] What look like stone or marble facings in the December 1871 wood-engraving of the lecture theatre were almost certainly painted imitations, and the figurative decorations on its east wall not bas-reliefs but mural paintings.

Paradoxically, now that it occupied a building it could be proud of, the University seemed to be even less master in its own house than it had been in its old forecourt lodgings. There at least the Vice-Chancellor and registrar had not had to battle with the Board of Works over the appropriate use and furnishing of each room, or, after a tour of inspection of their building, be given a dressing down by the First Commissioner over the 'inconvenience ... experienced in dealing with the Requisitions made of behalf of the University ... in consequence of the course that has been adopted by its Officers in requesting furniture for one purpose and then without the sanction of this Office applying it to another.'[130] The watchful control over the use of the building exercised by the Office of Works through the micro-management of the furniture and fittings permitted in each room was a constant reminder that the University's status as a minor government department had not altered one bit despite its grand Senate Room, well-appointed lecture theatre and spacious library. It was a point that Ayrton did not hesitate to rub in:

> The First Commissioner regrets that there should be any difficulty in dealing with the Furniture of the University, but it arises from the unfortunate circumstance that its business has to be transacted by the Officers of the Crown instead of its own Officers, in consequence of its funds being entirely administered by the Treasury. The First Commissioner would be very happy to be relieved of this service... .[131]

This lack of freedom to take responsibility for adapting or repurposing spaces within the building to meet changing needs and circumstances must have become steadily more irksome as the drive to reconstitute the University as a fully independent teaching institution gathered momentum over the next two decades, culminating in the watershed of the University of London Act of 1898. One of the most significant milestones on the road to this transformation – and one which is remembered to this day as the 'special glory' of the University – was the Senate's historic decision in 1877 to admit women to degrees in all faculties including medicine. However, while this put the University at the forefront of progressive higher education, it generated an increase in the demand for its honours that meant by the summer of 1888 it was having to find accommodation elsewhere for an overflow of 300 candidates and had obviously 'quite outgrown the resources of the present Building' (Figs 208, 209). Writing to the Office of Works on the Senate's behalf that autumn, 'to represent most strongly the necessity of immediately providing increased accommodation', the registrar Arthur Milman complained that

Fig. 208
University of London, room fitted for a practical examination in Physiology and Histology, *c.* 1890. Photograph by Howard & Jones.
University of London Archives, RO/5/5/5

Fig. 209
Sir James Pennethorne, University of London: detail of the roof and lights to the Laboratory and the Anatomical Room, December 1867.
The National Archives, Kew, WORK 33/1780

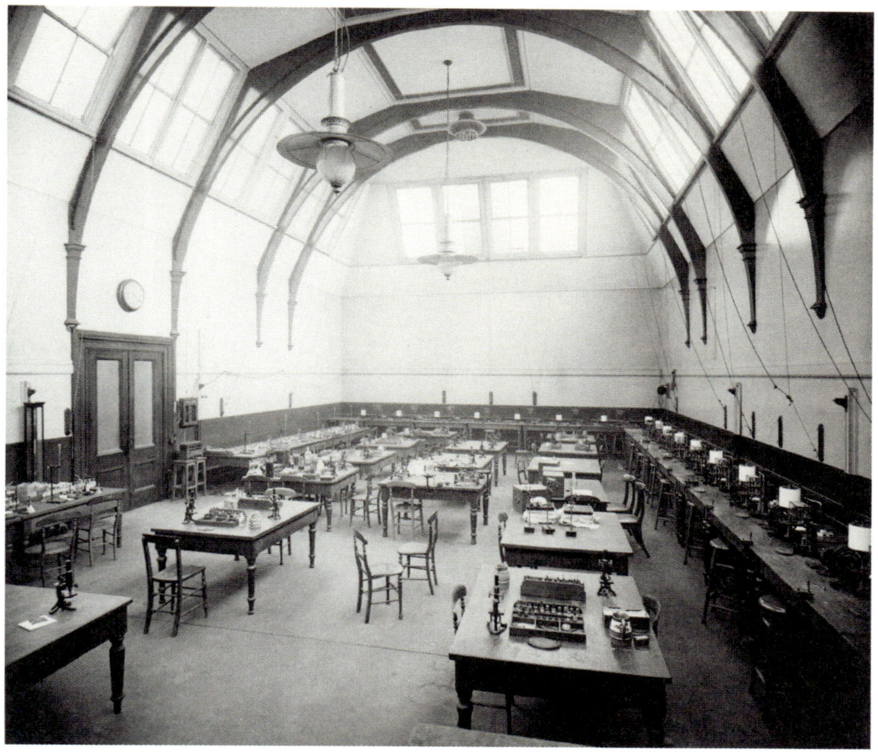

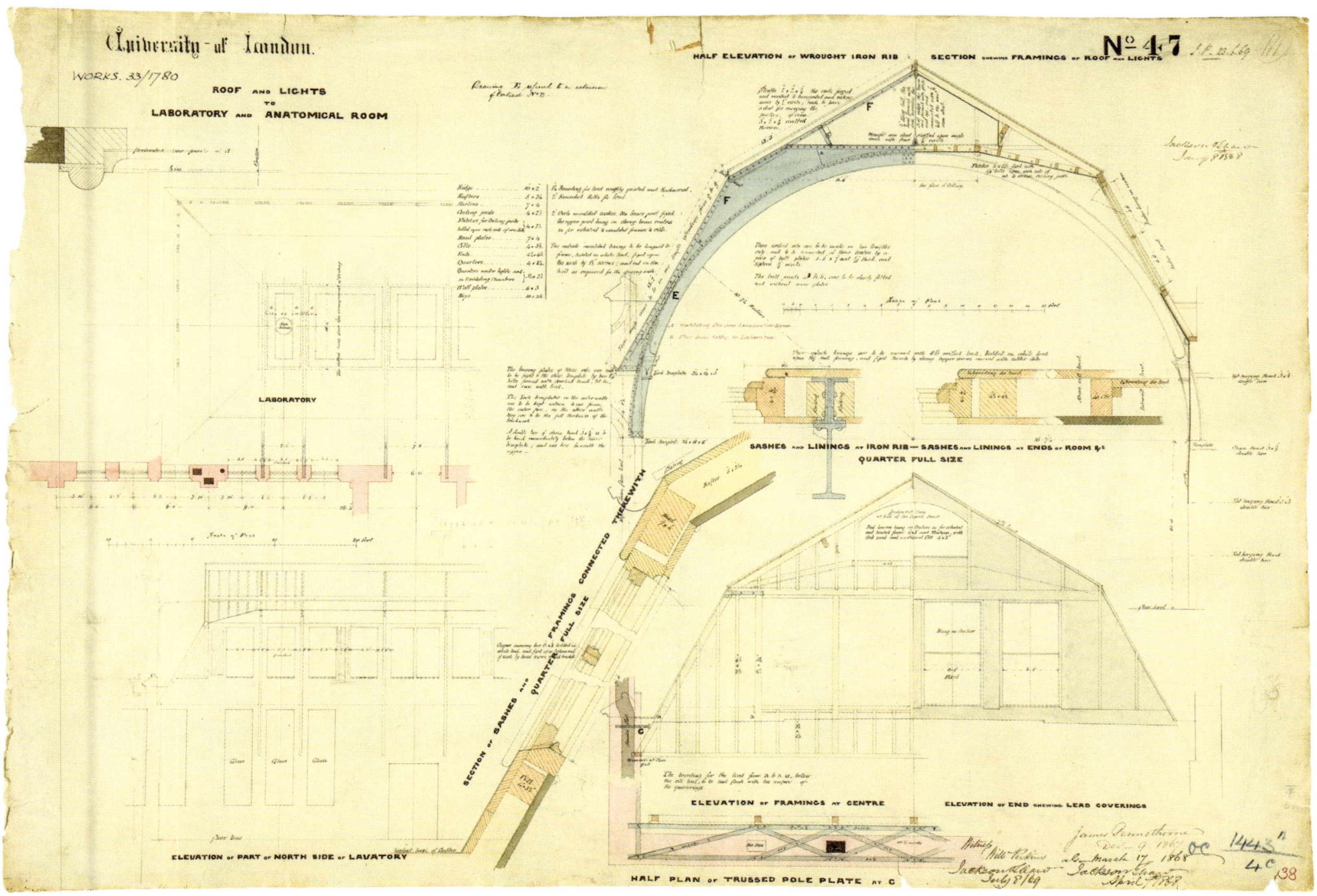

It is, however, with regard to the Practical Examinations in Science and in Medicine that the present arrangements are most lamentably deficient, and placing the University in a position of marked inferiority to all other Institutions of a similar character, render it impossible for the Senate any longer properly to discharge the duties with which it has been entrusted.[132]

Not surprisingly therefore, the proposal the Senate put forward then for 'raising the South Wing of the Present Building by a story and … laterally extending the Upper and Lower S.E. and S.W. Halls', had as its main objective the creation of a new suite of science laboratories, permanently equipped 'with all the necessary installations applicable exclusively for practical Examinations'. This would also, they hoped, free up the two former laboratories underneath 'for the ordinary written Examinations, including if possible a Ladies' Waiting-room'. The Treasury, which was by now receiving more than £12,000 a year in direct revenue from the University's exam fees, probably started to take some notice of its plight at this point since, two years later, the Office of Works gave serious consideration to a less ambitious but clearly cognate scheme to build an extension on the south-west flank of the building and to raise the centre of its southern range by sixteen or seventeen feet. On getting wind of this in November 1890, the Council of the Royal Academy wrote immediately to the First Commissioner 'pointing out the serious injury that would be inflicted on the Schools of the Academy, as the amount of sky-surface light of which the Schools would be deprived by such raising would render them practically useless', and 'that they felt bound to protest strongly against any raising of the London University buildings which would interfere with the lighting of the Schools.'[133] Perhaps realising (as Pennethorne had pointed out to Layard in 1869) that the restrictions that had been agreed with the Academy on the heights of both buildings were 'reciprocal', the following summer the secretary of the Board of Works made a 'confidential inquiry' via the Academy's president

as to whether the Academy's Schools 'must always remain at Burlington House, or whether their removal elsewhere is a possible contingency,' or if such a contingency was 'within a reasonable distance,' would the Council be 'disposed to enter upon a scheme of removal at once,' were the Treasury to agree to 'a substantial payment by way of compensation.'[134]

Although in their reply the Council were careful not to rule out such 'a possible contingency', they made it clear they had 'no intention … of taking any such step immediately, more especially as the question of removing the Schools from the main building, in addition to the expense involved, is one surrounded with many difficulties, requiring long and anxious consideration.'[135] The prospect of a prolonged wrangle with the Academy may well have influenced the decision by the Office of Works shortly afterwards to open negotiations instead with the University with a view to their relocation in another building. When it became known in the summer of 1899 that the University had finally agreed to move to the Imperial Institute in South Kensington, the Academy's alarm at the possible effect alteration of Pennethorne's building might have on the lighting of its Schools may have been one of the reasons it asked to be given first refusal should any part of the property become available. The fact that a year was to pass before Lord Esher, permanent secretary at the Office of Works, 'assured' the Academy's then president, Sir Edward Poynter, 'that the Government had no intention of giving up any part of the site, and required the whole of it for their own purposes', would seem to suggest there had been, and probably continued to be, a degree of departmental indecision over what to do with the building once the University had gone, particularly since it was not until early in 1902 that it was eventually handed over to the Civil Service Commission.[136]

In the two years between the University's departure in the spring of 1900 and the CSC's arrival, the Royal Geographical Society continued to use Pennethorne's lecture theatre for its large, well-attended evening meetings (Fig. 210), thereby maintaining a link with the

Fig. 210
A meeting of the Royal Geographical Society in the University of London lecture theatre, 28 April 1902.
Royal Geographical Society

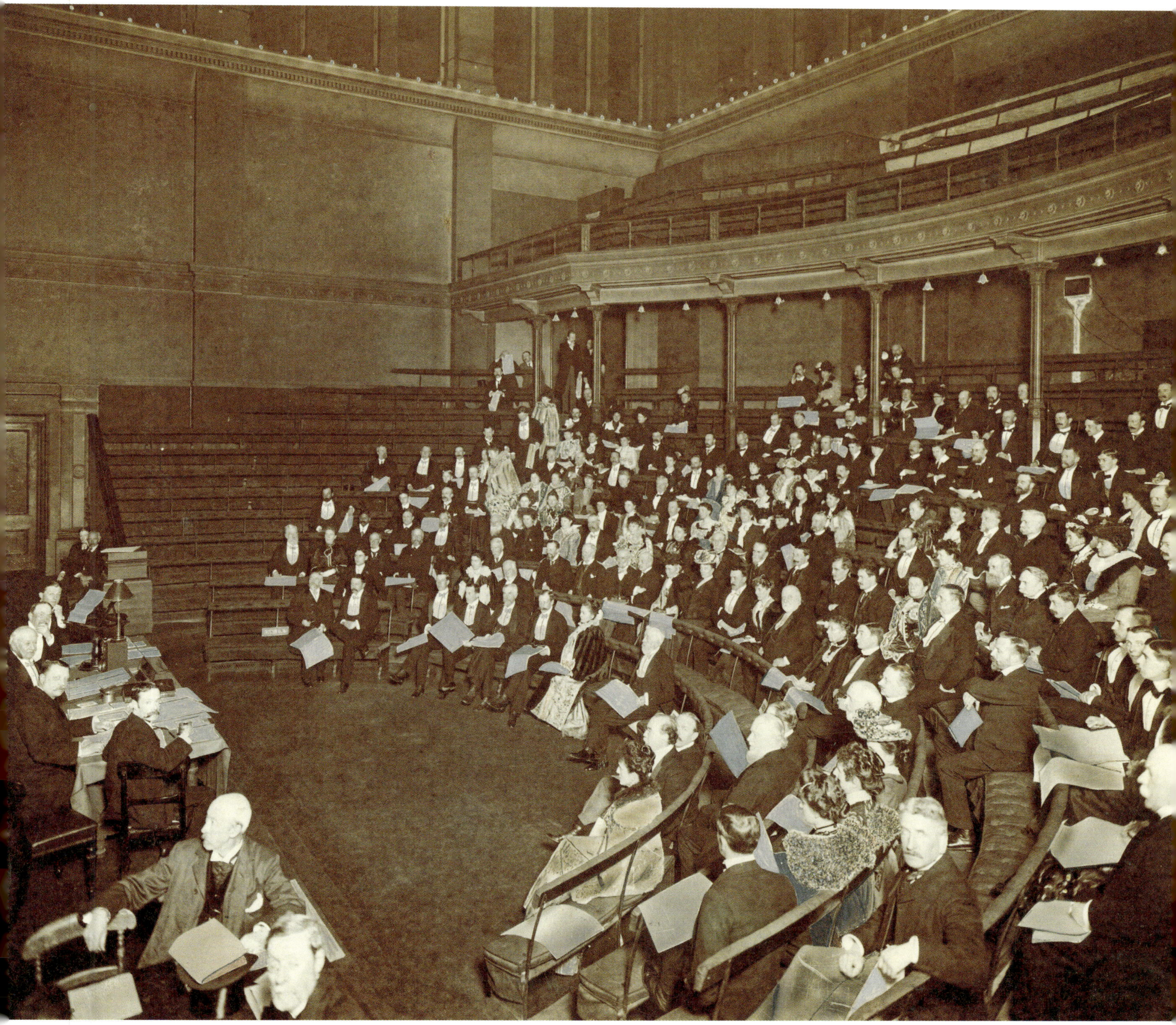

Burlington House site that had become particularly close thanks to the happy chance of its having moved to No. 1 Savile Row in the same year that the University had first opened its doors. It was no doubt partly on the strength of this long association that the president of the RGS, Sir Clements Markham, was able to persuade the government to allow 6 Burlington Gardens to be used as temporary headquarters for planning the National Antarctic Expedition in 1900–01; it was not only conveniently close to both the RGS and the Royal Society but also, perhaps more importantly, neutral territory for the sixteen representatives that each society fielded at the quarrelsome meetings of their Joint Antarctic Committee.[137] While these no doubt took place in the suitably grand setting of the Senate Room, the organisers of the expedition were probably also able to make use of a warren of adjacent offices recently inserted on a new floor in the west wing. Since the plans relating to this alteration are dated 16 December 1898 and January 1899, it seems to have been carried out speculatively on the grounds that whatever use was going to be made of the building in the future, it was certain to require more well-lit office space. Despite the proximity of the east wall of the Burlington Arcade, it is also possible that the new windows cut into the west wall provided more daylight than the library's lofty clerestory and single octagonal rooflight had ever done (see above, Fig. 193). Unfortunately, however, the new floor had to be supported on eight presumably second-hand cast-iron columns that raised it approximately fifteen inches higher than the level of the existing first-floor, thereby introducing a solecism that to this day speaks volumes for an attitude that was as disrespectful to the building as it was to the quality of the alteration being carried out.

It was probably the regular use of the lecture theatre for RGS meetings both before and after the arrival of the CSC that for a while at least deterred the Office of Works from converting it into office space in the same way as it had done to the library. Certainly, it seems more than a coincidence that in the same year that the RGS moved to its new home in Lowther Lodge, Kensington Gore, a proposal was put forward to the Treasury to insert new ground and first floors in the east wing. Although the project was postponed due to the outbreak of World War I, it was proposed again by the Office of Works in revised form in October 1919 and approved by the Treasury on 16 December that year at an estimated cost of £11,900.[138] The ground floor was to be divided partly into offices along the south and east sides where daylight could be obtained from new windows cut into the east wall, and partly into storerooms where no direct daylight was available. The first floor was similarly divided, two-thirds providing a new examination room and the remainder being given over to presumably grander and better-lit offices than those on the floor below. Under the ground floor was basement storage space with about eight feet of headroom, the southern portion of which was suitable for conversion into additional women's lavatories if required. Delayed by post-war shortages of steel and skilled labour, the project was not finally completed until July 1921, almost a year behind schedule and £6,420 over budget. The net gain was office space for 46 additional staff and an examination room large enough for 130 candidates.

Although described as still 'in fair demand for holding meetings in the evenings of learned societies, to whom it has long been the custom to lend it for this purpose', after the exigencies of war-time maintenance Pennethorne's 50-year-old theatre no doubt looked terribly forlorn.[139] In its heyday, however, with its spacious auditorium, perfect sightlines, elegantly profiled gallery and 2 feet 5 inches of clear legroom between each of its eleven tiers of seats, it had been much in demand as a venue for public events organised by a wide range of literary, scientific, artistic and educational bodies. These had included, for instance, the prize-giving days of the Female School of Art (1871, 1873, 1876, 1883) and the Burlington School (1896); important international conferences, such as the Geological Congress (1888) and the Hygienic Demography Congress (1891); public lectures delivered under the auspices of the Royal Society (March 1893, Croonian Lecture), the RGS (January 1902, Vaughan Cornish on 'Waves', for 'young persons'), the Anthropological Institute (November 1906 and 1911, Huxley Memorial Lectures), and the London Society for the Extension of University Teaching (June 1898, Herbert Beerbohm Tree on 'The Ideal Theatre'); the annual general meetings and *conversazioni* of professional and literary associations, such as the Royal College of Surgeons, the Modern Language Association and the Selborne Society; and last and not least, performances of William Poel's experimental staging of Shakespeare's *Richard II* (November 1899) and scenes from Schiller's plays and a dramatisation of Scott's *Marmion*, both enacted in costume for the Elizabethan Stage Society (December 1900).[140] Pennethorne's great amphitheatre had shown how the Burlington House site could still serve the wider public purpose envisaged by Manners and Disraeli in 1859.

Somewhat ironically in view of its remit to advise the government on artistic matters, one of the first beneficiaries of the sacrifice of the Burlington Gardens lecture theatre was the newly appointed Royal Fine Art Commission which set up a permanent office on the ground floor in May 1924. Over the next four years the RFAC's presence in the building lent weight to a proposal by the Royal Institute of British Architects to oust the CSC and take over some or all the building as their headquarters. The Institute's proposal drew attention to the 'fact' that Pennethorne's building was 'designed … as an integral part of the Burlington House group which was built by the Government for the purpose of housing the Royal Academy and other chartered bodies.' A building of such importance on such a valuable site, the RIBA argued,

> … is not a really appropriate place for such work as is carried on by the Civil Service Commission, and … a less valuable site further from the centre of London might well be devoted to this purpose, leaving Pennethorne's building free to be restored to its original character and turned into an appropriate home for the Royal and Chartered body which controls the greatest of the Arts and is the centre of the architectural education system of the Empire.[141]

What made the RIBA's proposal worthy of further consideration from the point of view of the Office of Works was the fact that the Land Valuation Office had put an open-market value of £325,000 on the site (equivalent to £17.33 million in 2018). As Sir Arthur Durrant, Director of Lands and Accommodation, lost no time in pointing out, since this figure equated to an annual cost of £16,250 at 5%, 'the Govt are suffering the annual loss of a sum running into thousands of pounds by the present occupation.'[142] The viability of any deal depended therefore on the money that could be saved by rehousing the CSC more cheaply elsewhere and the ability (and willingness) of the RIBA to pay a full commercial rent. However, despite four years of on-off negotiation, the financial attraction of the proposal evaporated after it turned out that it would cost an estimated £7,500 per annum to rehouse the CSC and the most the RIBA was prepared to pay for a 99-year lease was either £4,000 a year or a one-off payment of £50,000.[143] The chances of this unrealistic offer succeeding were further reduced by the fierce resistance put up by the CSC, both to the idea of moving to a less grand building and to any proposal that required a separation of examination rooms from administrative offices. Furthermore, as a result of the Office of Work's investigation of the viability of the RIBA's bid, it became increasingly apparent that the Commission's needs were being met extremely well at 6 Burlington Gardens and that this was in fact a highly appropriate and effective use of the building.[144]

Another factor that reduced the chances of a successful outcome from the RIBA's point of view was the government's decision in May 1927 to accommodate the British Academy in the building free of charge. The problem was not so much that this lessened the available space (though the British Academy ended taking up much more of the building than originally envisaged) but rather that this was seen as setting a dangerous precedent. As one of Earle's staff pointed out in a departmental minute dated 29 July 1927,

> In considering this question [of the CSC's removal] the recent grant of quarters in the building to the British Academy free of rent should, I think, be borne in mind. There may be other bodies which have, or may consider they have, claims on the Government for special consideration (not excluding the R.I.B.A. itself). The removal of the Civil Service Commission in whole or part from the building may be the occasion of the submission of such claims and acceptance of

them may result in the transfer of the Commission to other accommodation being attended by a loss instead of a gain.[145]

Realising that the RIBA's failure to offer a realistic rent meant there would now be strong pressure from the Treasury to dispose of the site, Earle took the bull by the horns. Writing to Sir Russell Scott, his opposite number at the Treasury, he frankly acknowledged that although 'Burlington Gardens serves the purpose of the Civil Service Commission extremely well',

> There is ... the primary question whether the value attaching to the site for commercial development is not sufficiently high to warrant the Department taking, if necessary, exceptional steps to rehouse the Civil Service Commission elsewhere with a view to realising a capital asset of considerable value.[146]

This was a purely tactical stance, since Earle was quite clear in his own mind that 6 Burlington Gardens should be preserved if at all possible, and consistently defended its retention in the face of opposition within his own department, particularly from W. Leitch, the assistant secretary, who felt that

> We should also consider on its merits the question of the disposal of the property – the site has a potential development value far in excess of the value of the present building and I question very much whether we are justified in assuming out of hand that the present building must be retained. It may be that its architectural merits & associations will outweigh the financial considerations but they should be weighed in the scales with full knowledge of the facts.[147]

It is noticeable that in his letter to Scott, Earle did not express the opinions he had made clear in his response to Leitch's minute on this occasion, namely that he did 'not think we can contemplate the demolition of the building', and that

> If we are to consider the potential site value we should consider equally the sale and development of Burlington House courtyard and buildings. But they are far too important to demolish.[148]

Despite his apparent display of objectivity in now seeking the Treasury's opinion, it is clear from Scott's reply that Earle had been careful to prepare the ground by making his own views known beforehand:

> ... I am inclined to think that all things considered it would be better to leave the Civil Service Commission where they now are for the time being at any rate. ... I also think there would be a loud outcry if the Burlington Gardens site was sold with a view to commercial development, and failing a transaction on this basis it seems doubtful whether the re-housing of the Civil Service Commission would really be a paying proposition. Perhaps the best plan would be to continue to look out for premises that might be expected satisfactorily to serve the purposes of the Commission and the two other bodies now housed at Burlington Gardens. If and when the chance offered of securing such premises we could consider the whole question in the light of a concrete scheme.[149]

Armed with this stay of execution, Earle was able to persuade the First Commissioner, Viscount Peel, 'to put the problem of the value of the Pennethorne building at Burlington House, from an architectural point of view, up to the Royal Fine Art Commission.'[150] The RFAC's brief report, written jointly by Sir Edwin Lutyens RA and S. D. Adshead, professor of town planning at University College London, emphasised the originality of the building, especially when compared with Pennethorne's west wing of Somerset House and Duchy of Cornwall Office at Buckingham Gate, and pronounced it as 'perhaps [his] most important work', that 'can well be compared with the best contemporary works of its period.'[151] Although omitted from the final version of the report, the most perceptive comment on the architectural quality of the building was almost certainly contributed by Lutyens:

> From the point of view of its intrinsic interest, it is a very original Palladian classic composition and combines all the qualities of a distinctly monumental building with a freedom of grouping that is almost Gothic in its tendency. This is more particularly seen in the picturesqueness of its skyline.[152]

In the end, however, it was the importance of the site as a source of civic amenity that was felt to be the building's strongest card:

> Finally, it should be remembered that this building has a value not only on account of the use to which it is put, nor merely as a fine example of mid-Victorian monumental architecture, but also as a source of amenity giving a feeling of dignity and spaciousness to the neighbourhood. ... It would not perhaps be until this building were replaced by a commercial building, hotel or apartment block, that we should feel the actual loss that had been sustained.[153]

As far as possible alterations were concerned, while the authors of the report thought 'some effort should be made to retain at least the front block and the grand staircase', they laid greater emphasis on the potential to create 'much more accommodation by re-planning in the rear,' particularly in the light of the pressing space problems currently faced by the Royal Academy and the courtyard societies.

Earle was jubilant, not least because Sir Reginald Blomfield, the Academy's former Professor of Architecture, had told him that 'he personally dislikes the Pennethorne building, and attaches no importance to it.'[154] In a covering letter to the First Commissioner on 27 April, Earle now revealed his true colours:

> I have always felt that this building ought to be reserved for giving extra facilities to some of the varied learned societies housed in Burlington House, who I know are sadly lacking in space, but if this view is supported by the Government, it means of course a loss to the Exchequer, as they are not in a position to pay economic rents, if any.[155]

Later that summer, Peel took a rather less encouraging view of the building's future, although in the circumstances it was probably the best that Earle could hope for:

> The First Commissioner has since paid a visit to No. 6 Burlington Gardens accompanied by Mr. Leitch, and while he does not think we should go out of our way to seek a purchaser for this site, he would be quite prepared, if a tempting offer is forthcoming, to give it careful consideration. In short, he does not regard the arguments in the letter from the Fine Art Commission as weighty enough to justify us turning down any proposal without consideration.[156]

Almost certainly as a consequence of Lutyens's involvement in the RFAC report, the secretary of the Royal Academy, Walter Lamb, wrote to Earle the following summer to test the waters:

> The President and Council of the Royal Academy understand that the question of the disposal of the building No. 6 Burlington Gardens is being considered by His Majesty's Government, and they would like to know whether there is any possibility of an arrangement by which the Royal Academy could have the usership of that building, or some part of it, for much needed extensions of the Royal Academy Schools, which are seriously cramped for space, and of the Galleries, which at present allow insufficient room for the Exhibition of Sculpture and Architecture.[157]

According to Lamb, Lutyens had already 'prepared preliminary plans for the purpose of the extensions desired', but 'before considering them in any definite way', the president and Council wanted 'to know whether and on what terms the Government could offer to the Royal Academy this opportunity of carrying out more effectively the main objects of its foundation.' Earle's reply six days later was so discouraging that it was not until two years later, when it became publicly known that the Howard Frank Report on Government Properties had recommended the disposal of 6 Burlington Gardens, that the Academy applied again to the Office of Works in connection with a 'semi-official' proposal designed by Reginald Blomfield for an extension of Gallery VI northwards by 24 feet.[158] This time however, the Academy was not interested in acquiring or using any part of the Burlington Gardens building, but wanted instead to trade on the reciprocity of the 45° angle height restriction which was believed to have been agreed by Smirke and Pennethorne, but which if the Burlington Gardens site was to be redeveloped it would obviously be in the

Fig. 211
The ground-floor east corridor of the Museum of Mankind, with Hoa Haka Nana Ia, an Easter Island statue, on the right, 1979.
Photograph by Saul Peckham.
British Museum, London, BM EU,A8.29

interests of the Office of Works to waive as long as the Academy was prepared to do likewise. Although a subsequent scheme designed by Lutyens in October 1932 came close to being accepted – it included in addition an 115-foot-long extension of the Academy's Main Galleries over the 'West Yard' service lane that would have been subject to separate agreements with the Burlington Arcade landlord and tenants – in the end it became apparent that the expense of rehousing the CSC meant there was little chance of the Treasury adopting the Frank Report's recommendation within the foreseeable future.[159] As a result, a year passed and both the Academy and the Office of Works let the matter drop.

A further deterrent to the sale of the building was the increasingly incongruous but firmly ensconced presence of the British Academy and its subtenant, the Bibliographical Society, whose library it housed. Although until it was granted a formal tenancy in January 1956, the BA had no greater security of tenure than the courtyard societies. Thanks to a donation by Sir Charles Wakefield it had been able, before it arrived in July 1928, to fit out at its own expense a small and large lecture room and a luxurious council chamber in the space that, somewhat ironically, only seven years earlier had been the new ground floor inserted into Pennethorne's original lecture theatre. It was for this reason no doubt, as much as out of sentiment, that when the BA finally managed to escape what its president described in a letter to the Prime Minister as 'a poor recommendation for a third-rate warehousing firm', its secretary had tried to persuade the Ministry of Works to reinstall its mahogany-panelled council chamber in one of the rooms it was about to take over from the Royal Society.[160]

Virtually empty after the CSC's departure in May 1963 and deliberately run down thereafter by the Ministry of Works, it was a miracle 6 Burlington Gardens survived the decade. With hindsight it is clear that, in the teeth of fierce opposition from the Treasury, Pennethorne's building was saved in the nick of time for its centenary by being transformed into exhibition space for the British Museum's Department of Ethnography, and that this was achieved almost entirely thanks to the equally fierce determination of Harold Wilson's Minister for the Arts, Jennie Lee. When it came to the crunch in September 1967, Lee was supported by Harold Lever, the newly appointed Financial Secretary to the Treasury, who was brave enough to defy a chorus of civil servants advising him that the building needed to remain available for disposal to a private developer at short notice. An important consideration influencing Lever's decision, which naturally had nothing to do with architectural preservation, was the need to lessen the political fall-out from an imminent announcement of the government's decision to scrap Sir Leslie Martin's scheme for an extension to the British Museum on its Bloomsbury site. This was potentially a highly embarrassing *volte-face*, firstly because the government would need shortly to embark on 'difficult negotiations' with the Museum over the future of its library, and secondly, because Jennie Lee's genuine shock at the plight of its ethnographic collections had been given a great deal of press coverage.[161]

Since £80,000 of the £150,000 available to adapt 6 Burlington Gardens to its new purpose was earmarked for deferred maintenance, curators had no choice but to use the existing building as best they could. As a result, between 1970 and 1997 the British Museum's Ethnography Department mounted a celebrated series of innovative 'as-if-you-were-really-there' temporary exhibitions and educational programmes in what became known as the Museum of Mankind. All of these depended on creating an immersive effect that removed any awareness of the surrounding building. As visitors came and went they were observed not by the busts of humanist philosophers and famous scientists that Pennethorne had expected would populate his wall niches, but by glowering Easter Island *moai* (Fig. 211). The incongruity worked both ways by making the building seem equally strange.

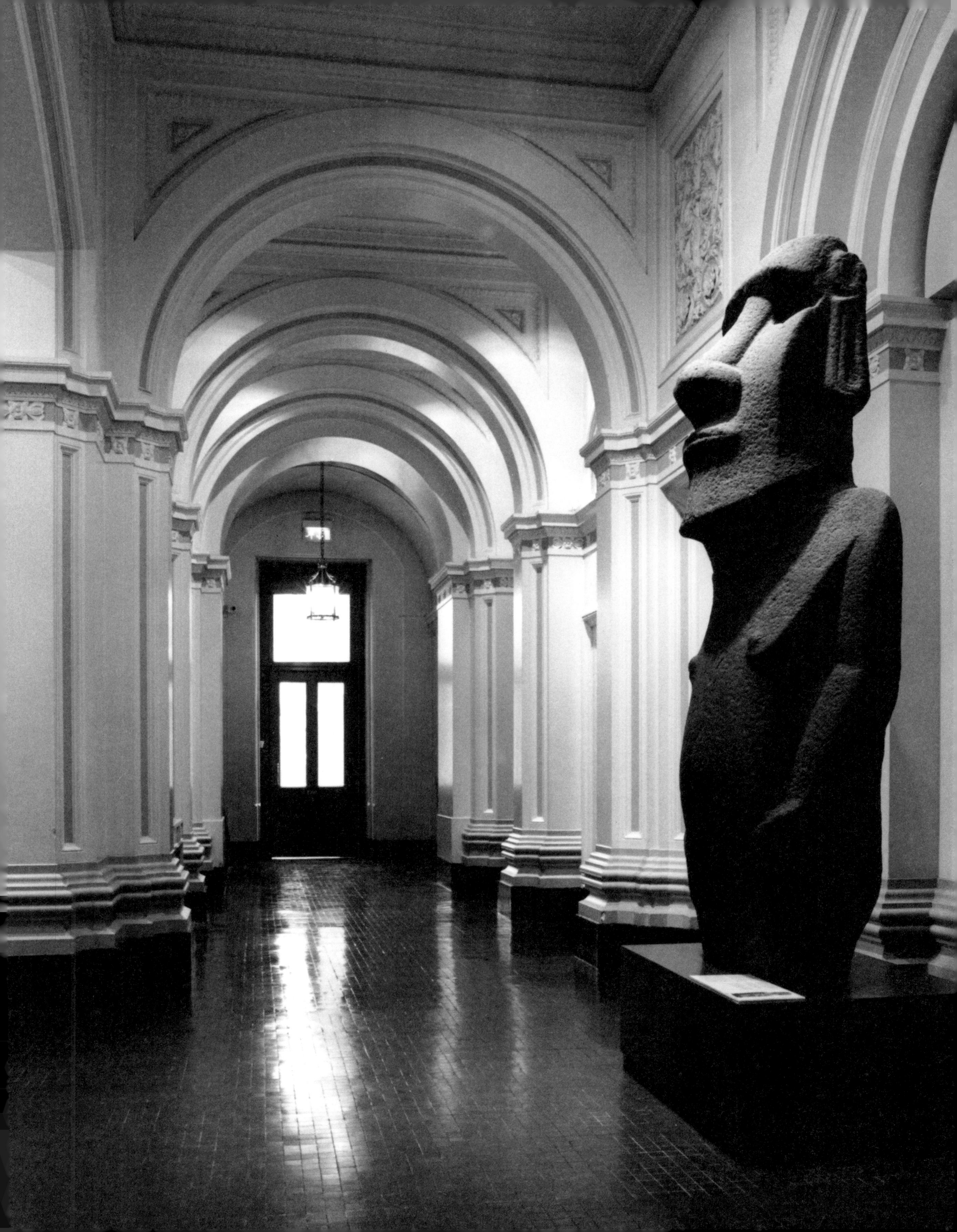

V

THE ROYAL ACADEMY OF ARTS

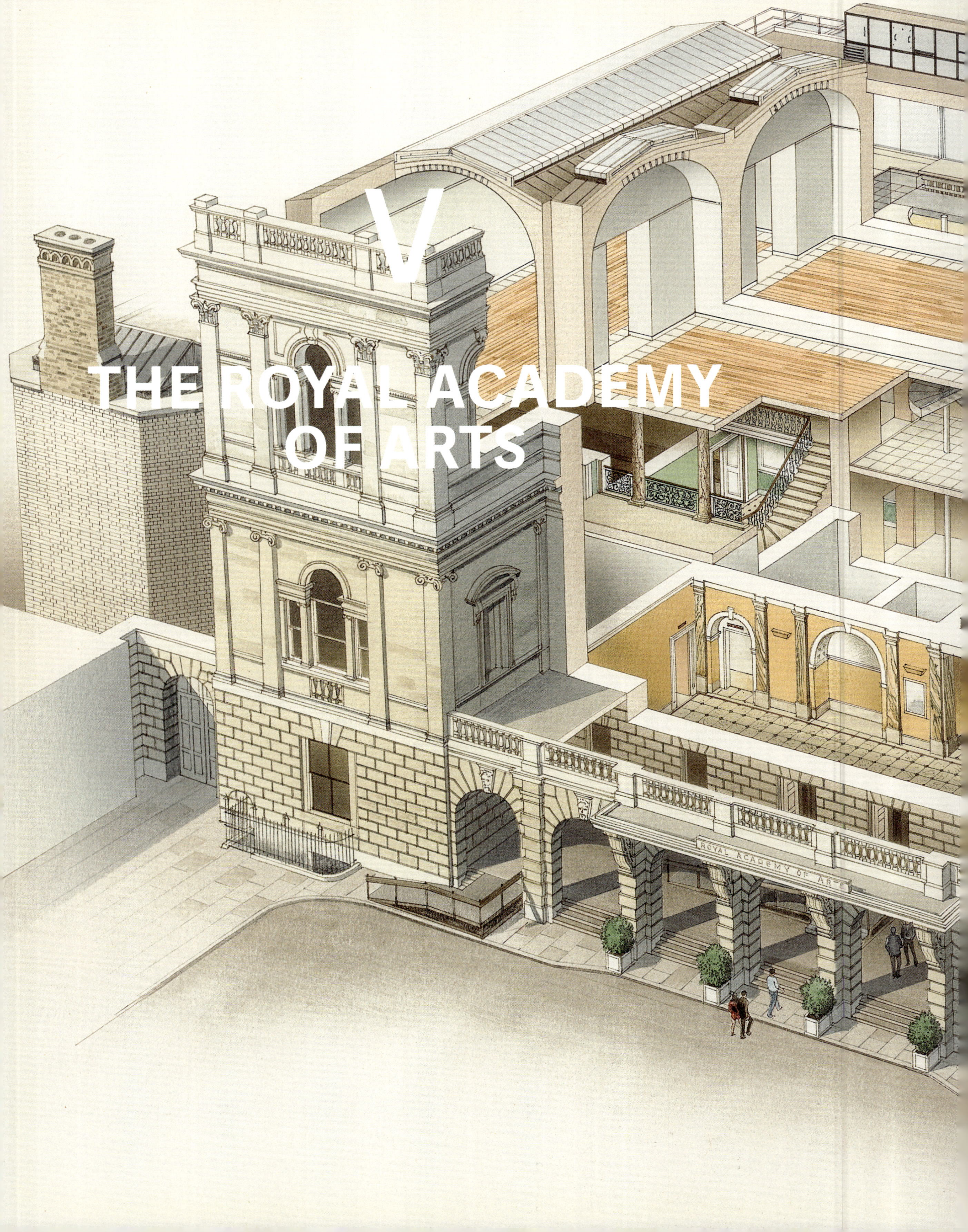

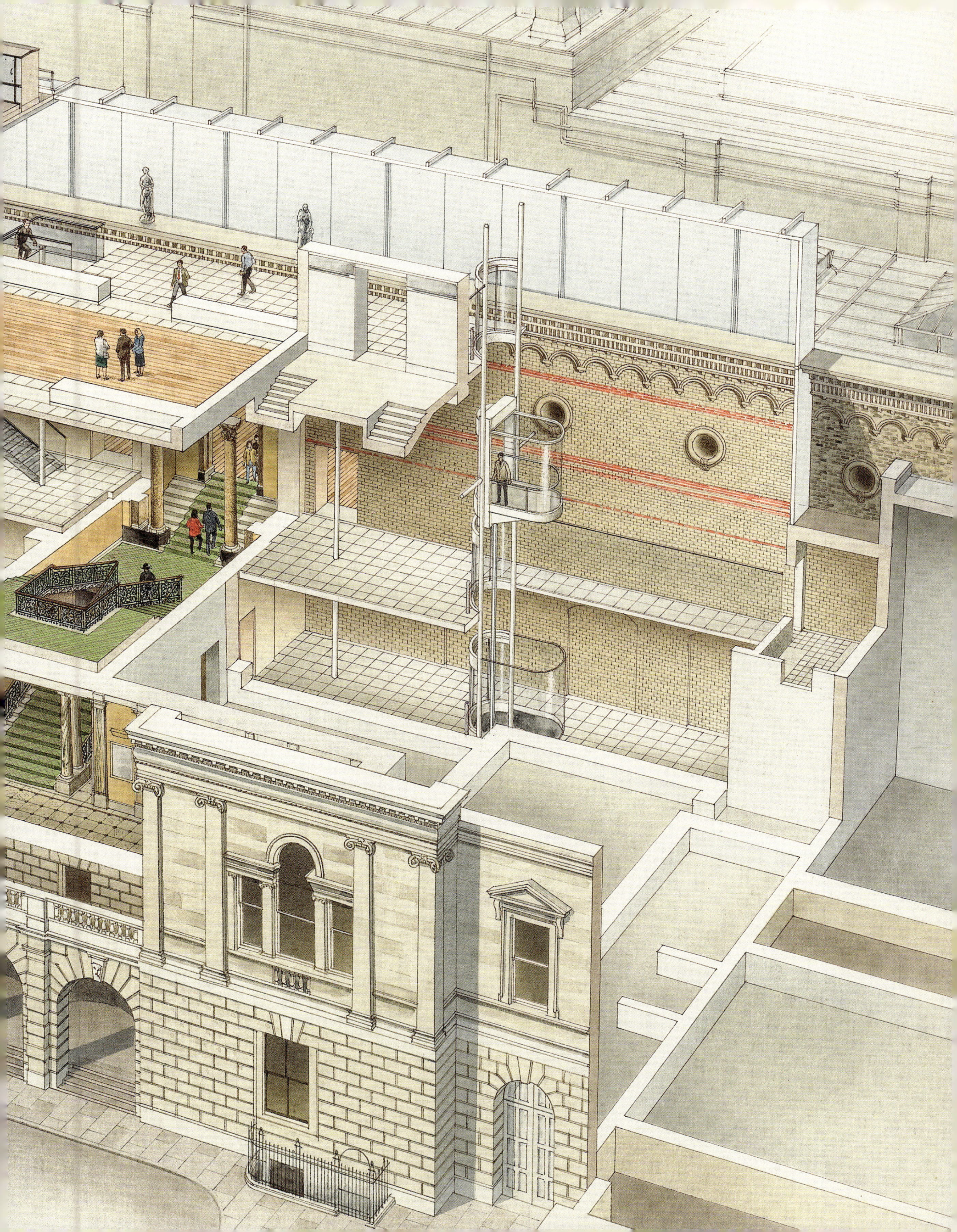

'Burlington House can of course be only a dream.'
SIR ROBERT SMIRKE, RA treasurer, 10 April 1850

ONE SUMMER'S DAY IN 1866, AS HE WAS WALKING around the garden behind Burlington House, the treasurer of the Royal Academy had a bright idea. It was an idea that would resolve more than a decade of uncertainty, not only for the Academy but for everyone whose destiny lay on the site of Lord Burlington's former home. Like all really good ideas, it swept aside any doubt about what needed to be done. No-one in the Office of Works or the Treasury, no-one in Parliament or the press and, despite their hopes that the Academy might have moved instead to South Kensington, not even the Prime Minister or the Queen could fail to see that it made complete sense. Indeed, so compelling was this idea that another architect, who had thought of it first for a different purpose, had to admit that it was 'highly worthy of consideration'.[1]

Sir Francis Grant, the self-taught portrait painter who succeeded Eastlake as the seventh president of the Royal Academy in February 1866, is often credited with having secured Burlington House as the Academy's first permanent home, helped it is said by social connections with politicians in high places and the advantage of being related to Lord John Manners through marriage.[2] In addition, Grant's style of leadership – adroit flattery of his superiors, constant badgering of everyone else – served the Academy well at a critical point in its history. However, more than anything else it was the simplicity of Sydney Smirke's idea that was to carry all before it, as he saw for the first time with an architect's eye the space between the back of Burlington House and the plot at the northern end of the garden cordoned off for the University of London, because it showed at last how the whole site could be turned to the public's benefit.

Austen Henry 'Nineveh' Layard, who succeeded Manners at the Office of Works in December 1868 and never forgave him for having twice sabotaged an opportunity to move the National Gallery to Piccadilly, once asserted in a Commons debate that

> ... of all the architectural blunders which had ever been committed in this country that connected with Burlington House was the most considerable.[3]

Layard's point – echoed in the twentieth century by Pevsner's description of Burlington House's alteration as an act of 'High Victorian cruelty'[4] – was that it would have been better to have demolished it altogether than to disfigure it with a third storey and entrance portico, which he considered 'a ridiculous and absurd thing' to do 'after so great a sacrifice had been made to keep the building as an architectural monument'. Heavy price as this may have been, it was Manners's determination to salvage what he could from the lost opportunity of 1859 that finally secured Burlington House's future as a public building.

That this was likely to prove a tortuous process had long been apparent when William Cowper, the predecessor of Manners at the Office of Works, received a letter from the president of the Royal Academy on 23 June 1866, 'respectfully declining' the site on Piccadilly that the government had offered it exactly a year earlier.[5] None of the problems that Grant gave as reasons for the Academy's sudden change of mind – the plot was insufficient for their needs, a carriage entrance through the middle of the building meant there would be a staircase of 70 steps to reach their exhibition rooms, and anyway they couldn't afford the £135,000 needed to erect a suitable building in such a conspicuous situation – none of these obstacles had been thought insurmountable until now. In fact, just two months before Grant's letter the solicitor to the Board of Works had written to Cowper to say that everything was in place to draft a lease. By then it had been agreed, for instance, that the Academy would have possession of the whole of the east side of the courtyard and not just the Piccadilly frontage that had been at first proposed (Fig. 212). And, critically for the Academy's future, the Treasury had also agreed that the term of its lease should be extended from 99 to 999 years, subject to a peppercorn rent of £1 per annum and the normal covenants to erect certain buildings within a specified period, to use them solely for the purposes described in the lease, and to insure and keep them in repair.[6] For its part the Academy had, among other things, agreed that the number of its associate members (ARAS) should be set in future at a minimum, rather than limited to a maximum of twenty and, more

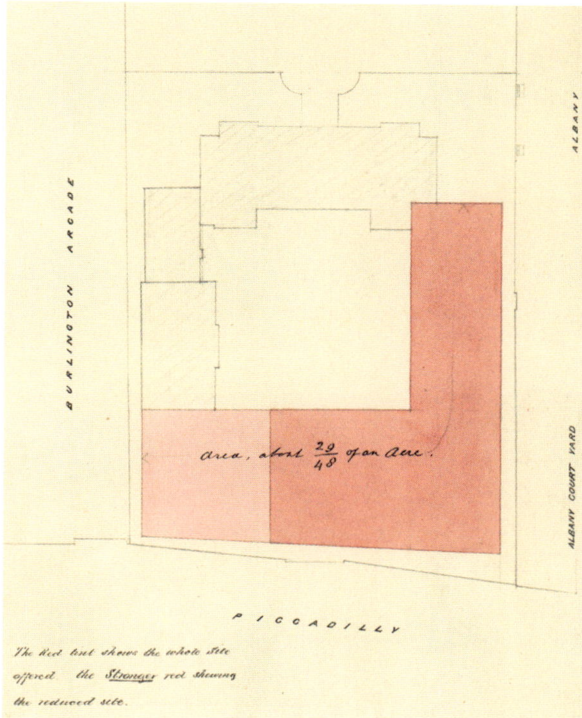

Fig. 212
Sydney Smirke, Block plan of the site offered to the Royal Academy by the government, May 1866.
Royal Academy of Arts, London, 06/1244

Fig. 213
Sydney Smirke, Block plans of proposed South Kensington and Burlington House sites offered to the Royal Academy, July 1866.
Royal Academy of Arts, London, 06/1246

importantly, that they would be allowed to vote in the election of all new members and Royal Academicians.[7] Grant had managed to steer this major constitutional reform through the minefield of the Academy's General Assembly by convincing them that they had already agreed to it three years earlier.[8] Crucially this avoided any appearance of bowing to external pressure for the 'enlargement of the constituency of the Royal Academy' (an equivalent in miniature to the 1867 Reform Act) that the government had insisted was the *sine qua non* of their grant of the Burlington House site.[9]

What Grant did not mention, although it was by then common knowledge, was the fact that just the month before the Commissioners of the 1851 Exhibition had offered the Academy a rent-free three-acre plot next to the Royal Horticultural Society's garden in South Kensington (Fig. 213).[10] Had the Commissioners made their offer much earlier, the assurance given by their president Lord Derby that it was 'against the wish of the Commissioners to interfere in any way with the entire

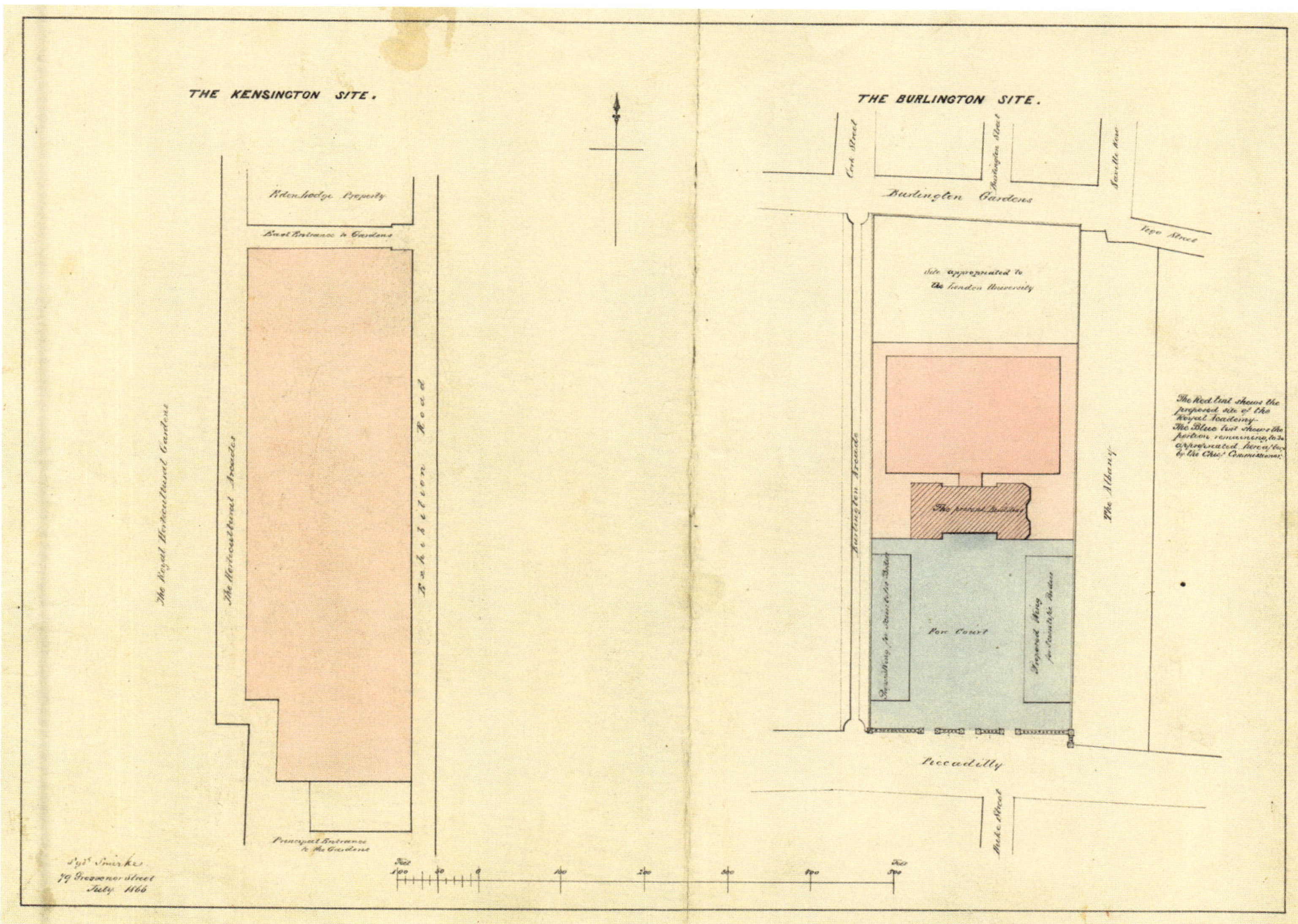

independence of the Academy', might have been enough to outweigh the prejudices of its old guard against South Kensington.[11] Typical of the latter was the opinion of the retired keeper, librarian and former deputy president George Jones, who was convinced that Henry Cole's Museum of Ornamental Art and the teaching methods of the Department of Art and Science had simply 'made more workmen to diffuse bad taste'.[12] As it turned out the Commissioners' offer came too late for the Academy to backpedal on its commitment to reforms that Grant had formally communicated to the government on 26 March. In addition, although Smirke had estimated that building on the more open South Kensington site might cost up to £55,000 less than in Piccadilly, he also predicted a serious drop in exhibition revenue if the Academy were to move to such an inaccessible suburb.[13]

At this critical juncture, it was typical of Grant to realise that the fall of the Russell government just four days after he had written to Cowper was the ideal moment to seize the initiative. It was clear that if the Commons decided to keep the National Gallery in Trafalgar Square, the Academy should press for a better site at Burlington House rather than accept *faute de mieux* what Lord Derby – now, rather awkwardly for the Academy, the Prime Minister – had offered them at South Kensington. Apparently taking no-one apart from Smirke into his confidence, Grant's first move was to write to the Queen to warn her 'of the possibility of an offer being made on the part of the new Government which the Academy might feel it their duty to accept in preference to South Kensington.'[14] Then, as soon as the decision of the Commons was known, he bearded Manners in his office 'to put it to him if he would give us a site on the Burlington Estate which we could accept', as well as to propose 'one or two plans' of his own which were found to be 'open to some objections.'[15] As he was to recount to a jubilant General Assembly of the Academy on 29 August, it was as a result of this otherwise fruitless meeting that he and Smirke went the next day and 'examined the ground' at Burlington House, and that the latter then 'suggested the Plan which is now before you' (Fig. 213).

It is clear from the Assembly's instantaneous approval (Smirke was elected architect for the project on the spot) that the Academicians were unanimous in recognising that Burlington House would be an ideal home both for themselves and the institution. Some of their enthusiasm was no doubt due to the fact that Smirke had estimated it would cost no more than £40–45,000 to build their galleries and schools there, which was only half as much

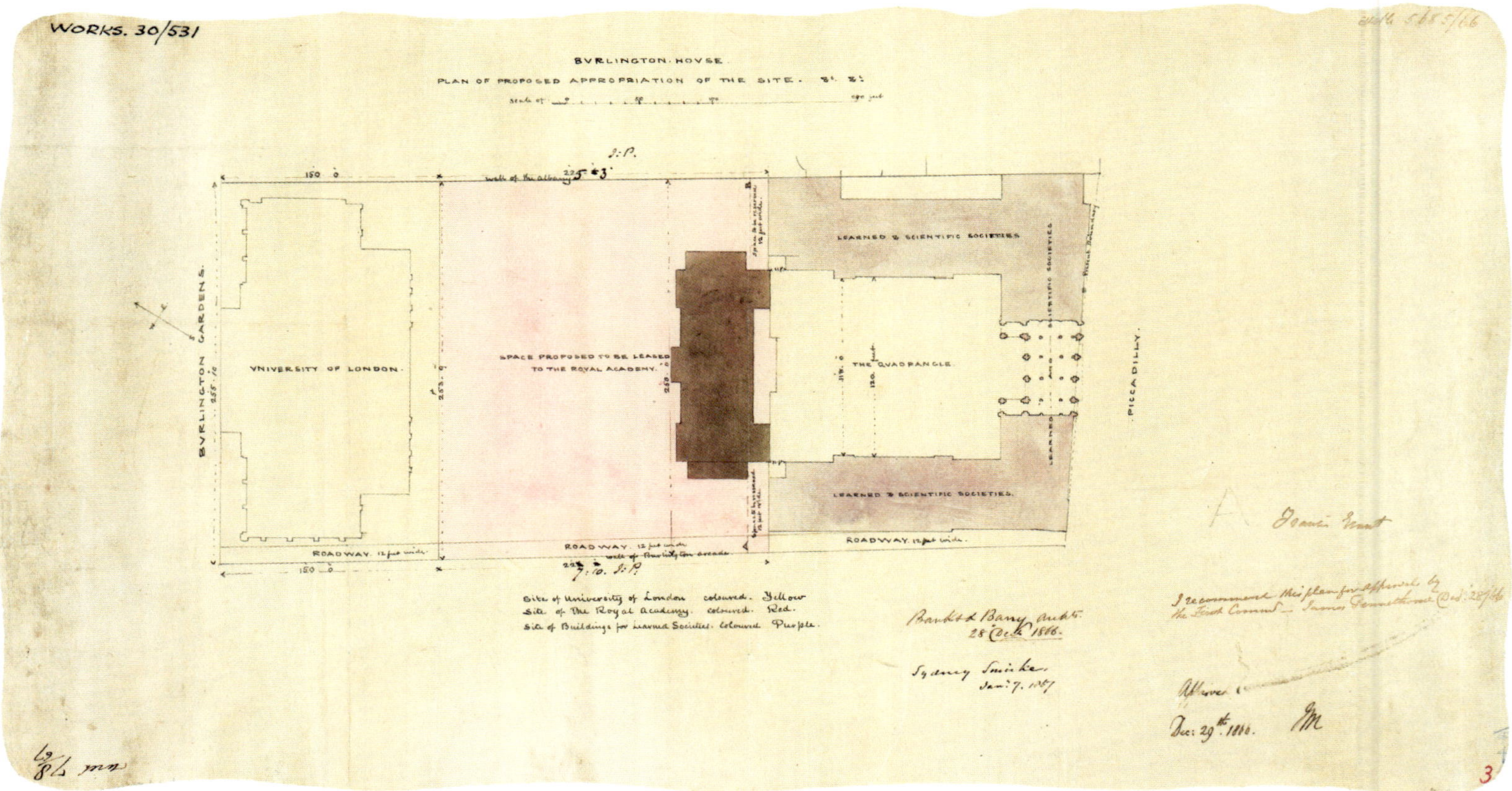

Fig. 214
Robert Richardson Banks & Charles Barry Jr, Sir James Pennethorne and Sydney Smirke, Block plan showing proposed appropriation of the Burlington House site by the Learned Societies, the University of London and the Royal Academy, December 1866.
The National Archives, Kew, TNA WORK 30/531

as at South Kensington and came comfortably within the £65,000 limit that he thought the Academy could prudently spend on a new building. An equally important attraction, however, was the prospect of exchanging cramped temporary lodgings in a borrowed building generally contemned as an architectural disgrace to the nation, for permanent and spacious accommodation in what their president confidently described as 'certainly one of the most faultless and beautiful buildings in London.'[16]

In fact, to older members in particular, it must have seemed the Academy was predestined to move to Burlington House. Some may even have remembered hearing of a momentous meeting at 10 Downing Street in March 1850, when George Jones as acting president had suggested to the then Prime Minister, Lord John Russell, that Burlington House might be acquired by the government on the Academy's behalf. Faced with imminent eviction from Trafalgar Square, and the tempting offer of £40,000 in compensation, the Academy had had two pressing concerns at that meeting: firstly, to avoid parliamentary interference as the price for receiving public funds; and secondly, as Jones put it, the great difficulty of 'finding … a good site, for our respectability, and the continuation of our means.'[17] At the time, the venerable architect Sir Robert Smirke, the Academy's treasurer of 30 years standing ('little Syd', as he called Sydney, was his younger brother by eighteen years), had thought that 'Burlington House can of course be only a dream'.[18] However, of all the sites that were then considered – Chandos House in Pall Mall, a part of the grounds of Marlborough House at the west end of Carlton Gardens, John Nash's former house on the east side of Regent Street, a vacant plot on the east side of Leicester Square, and even the centre of Leicester Square itself – of all these possibilities, only Burlington House came close to becoming a reality. In fact, had Charles Cavendish accepted the offer that the Academy's treasurer Philip Hardwick had attempted to broker in 1852, when the political pressure for the Academy to move out of the National Gallery to make room for the Vernon collection was at its height, there is no doubt Burlington House would have been the Academy's preferred destination.

As it was, by the following year the scandal over what seemed to be the alarming deterioration of the nation's pictures in the polluted atmosphere of Trafalgar Square had made the removal of the Academy from Wilkins's building seem much less urgent than the removal of the paintings. Consequently, it was not until Disraeli decided in June 1858 to abandon all thought of transferring the National Gallery to South Kensington that public indignation at the Academy's continuing presence in Trafalgar Square fully rekindled.

As treasurer of the Academy in the 1850s, Philip Hardwick had been well placed to keep his fellow members in touch with developments at Burlington House. Not only had he been responsible in May 1857 for designing an abortive proposal to build a home for the Geological Society on the north-east side of the courtyard, but the year before had served on the Royal Society's 'Burlington House Removal Committee' and supervised the fitting out of their apartments in the main building. When asked by Manners in spring 1859 whom the Academy might choose to design their building on the Burlington House site, Eastlake had replied that 'Mr Hardwick' their treasurer was considered 'by his office … most entitled to be selected' and it was only 'on account of the state of his health' that he had 'distinctly declined to be put in nomination'.[19] Despite chronic back pain Hardwick continued to serve as the Academy's treasurer for another two years, and remained an active member of the institution until his final retirement on 18 March 1869.

Having witnessed many past attempts to adapt Burlington House more fully to public use, Hardwick must have relished the opening of the Academy's new galleries just six weeks after his retirement and seeing how 'little Syd' had turned dream into reality. However, had he himself undertaken that same challenge ten years earlier, he would doubtless have agreed with Eastlake in dismissing any idea of hiding the Academy behind Burlington House as unthinkable. Since the audience for an exhibition depended to a large degree on where it was held, when asked by a Select Committee of the House of Lords in 1861 what he thought would be the effect of building the Academy behind Burlington House, Eastlake had no doubt that it 'would be tantamount to the extinction of the institution'.[20] Speaking simultaneously as president of the Academy and director of the National Gallery, Eastlake had in fact tied himself into a knot on that occasion by trying to claim that the tranquillity of the Burlington House forecourt would enable visitors to approach the Old Masters in a suitably contemplative frame of mind, whereas the hurly burly of Trafalgar Square he thought, somewhat disparagingly to his fellow artists, a more suitable setting for the Academy's transient 'shows' of contemporary art. Three years later, Manners was to have a field day in the Commons quoting Eastlake's evidence against Cowper who had fallen into a similar trap by claiming that the removal of the National Gallery to Burlington House would make it less liable to be visited for frivolous purposes. What Manners could trade on here for the purposes of his argument to retain the National Gallery in Trafalgar Square, was the common assumption that a former citadel of aristocratic taste would always be more conducive to the proper appreciation of the fine arts by the leisured classes than the working population. It is telling therefore that during Grant's presidency there was never a shadow of doubt that Burlington House provided the Royal Academicians – sometimes dubbed the 'Knights of the Brush'[21] – with the exactly the setting *they* needed. It was partly for this reason that the problem of how to adapt the building to other needs did not begin to be fully addressed until after Grant's death in October 1878.

On being informed privately by the Prime Minister on 11 August 1866 that the government had accepted the Academy's proposal to lease Burlington House 'and a portion of the grounds at the back not allocated to the London University or other purpose', Grant almost immediately leaked the good news to friendly journalists at *The Times* and *Illustrated London News*.[22] As a result, both papers covered the story in great detail before the secretary of the Board of Works had time to notify the current occupants of the Academy's impending appropriation of their building.[23] It was not a good start.

WHEN LORD JOHN MANNERS took up the post of First Commissioner for the third time in summer 1866 it was as a consequence of the return to power of a Tory administration led once again by Lord Derby and Benjamin Disraeli. This augured well for finally sorting out the problem of Burlington House in that the three of them had been responsible for the ambitious plan in 1858–59 to create a campus there for a variety of government-sponsored artistic, scientific, technological and educational institutions. A new obstacle, however, was that pressure from the Queen for the Royal Academy to move to South Kensington might leave the Prime Minister with little choice but to oppose any plan to move them elsewhere. Although this did not prove the case, it was partly why on 6 August 1866, just four days before he was due to confer with the Prime Minister and Chancellor of the Exchequer over whether or not to accept the Academy's proposal, Manners pre-empted the decision as far as he could by instructing Pennethorne to obtain tenders for laying the foundations of the University of London's new building.[24] Not only did this emphasise that the use of this part of the site had been settled, it also drew attention to the importance the Academy's proposal now had for the remainder. Ignoring Pennethorne's 'musical chairs' suggestion – whereby the Academy might agree to make do with the rooms in Burlington House currently occupied by the Royal Society were the latter willing to move into the east forecourt building after the University had moved out – Manners saw immediately that Smirke's suggested rebuilding of the forecourt to rehouse the learned societies was a chance to revive, if only in modest form, Banks & Barry's great abandoned scheme of 1859,[25] and only this would do justice to the government's original purpose in buying the site, by providing 'accommodation … for the Royal Academy and for the different learned societies, and the new building for the London University'.[26]

If in his eagerness to seize the day Manners made some mistakes – the most notorious being his failure to consult either Parliament or the University properly over the design of the exterior of the latter's new building – these were not, as Layard was to maintain, the consequence of an arrogant misuse of his power. Rather this was a man who, just four days after he had been accused of egregious blundering at Burlington House, wrote a personal letter to the president of the Royal Society appealing for their co-operation with the Academy ahead of an impending tsunami of building in the courtyard, pointing out that, 'in a complicated work of this kind, carried out on a limited area, it is only by mutual concessions that the desired end can be obtained'.[27] By the same token, ensuring that three different architects answerable to nine different clients were able to work simultaneously on the same site would also require considerable powers of diplomacy on his part.

Since the Academy had undertaken to pay for building its own galleries and for altering Burlington House as needed, it could influence the external appearance of the new forecourt in a way denied to the latter's intended occupants. This influence was an ingredient in the project from the moment the Treasury authorised Manners on 13 September 1866 to commission Banks & Barry to design accommodation 'in new buildings suggested to occupy a part of the space between Burlington House and Piccadilly' for the three learned societies that would be displaced by the arrival of the Academy alongside the three still at Somerset House.[28] Thus, while it was relatively easy for Banks & Barry to pick up the threads of their 1859 scheme – for instance by updating the space requirements that had been agreed to by most of the societies – as far as the area they could build on was concerned, they had to start again.

Their first problem was what to do about Campbell's dead brick wall on Piccadilly. Like many a pedestrian in the past depressed by its gloomy shadow – it was, a neighbour complained, 'more suited to a gaol, or a madhouse, or a nunnery, than to a public building'[29] – Smirke had thought that in its place 'a handsome open Palisade next Piccadilly might complete the Quadrangle', and had suggested as much in the proposal that Grant had forwarded to Manners on 27 July (see Fig. 213). Attractive as the idea of an open screen on Piccadilly may have been, it presented Banks & Barry with an almost impossible problem. One way they might have shoehorned all six societies into two sides of a quadrangle would have been to colonise some of the garden east and west of the main house. However, quite understandably, as soon as Smirke got wind of this he warned his fellow architects in no uncertain terms: 'You must not expect me to agree to any encroachment on the Frontage of old Burlington House.'[30] While they could put pressure on the Royal Astronomical Society to reduce the over-optimistic bid they had made in 1859, and they warned the Geologists that 'our limits are very confined & we may not be quite able to give you all', the only real way of saving space was the one suggested by Gladstone long ago, namely to persuade the societies to share meeting rooms.[31] Although the Geological and Astronomical societies had privately accepted this as a possibility in 1859, only the former seems to have been prepared to consider the idea again in 1866.[32] The Geologists no doubt thought it wise to be amenable because of the extra space they needed for their museum. More typical was the response of the Royal Society who, having shared Burlington House with the Chemical and Linnean societies since 1856, had long deemed it

> … essential for the convenient and undisturbed transaction of the business of the … Society, that whatever apartments may in future be assigned to them should be appropriated wholly to their own use, and be so placed in any common building, as to form a division by themselves distinct from any other establishment.[33]

So strongly were the Royal Society's Council of this opinion that they twice rejected the Chemical Society's proposal in June and July 1868 that 'a convenient intercommunication' might be made between their rooms in the new building.[34]

Of the three societies still at Somerset House, the Antiquaries were the least likely to agree to an arrangement that reduced in any way the space or autonomy to which they were accustomed. As their president, Earl Stanhope, had emphasised in the House of Lords on 4 March 1859, they had no wish to relinquish the apartments that had been specially designed for their use in Somerset House and which, uniquely, they had occupied without interruption since their grant by command of George III in 1781. As a result, when Barry attended a

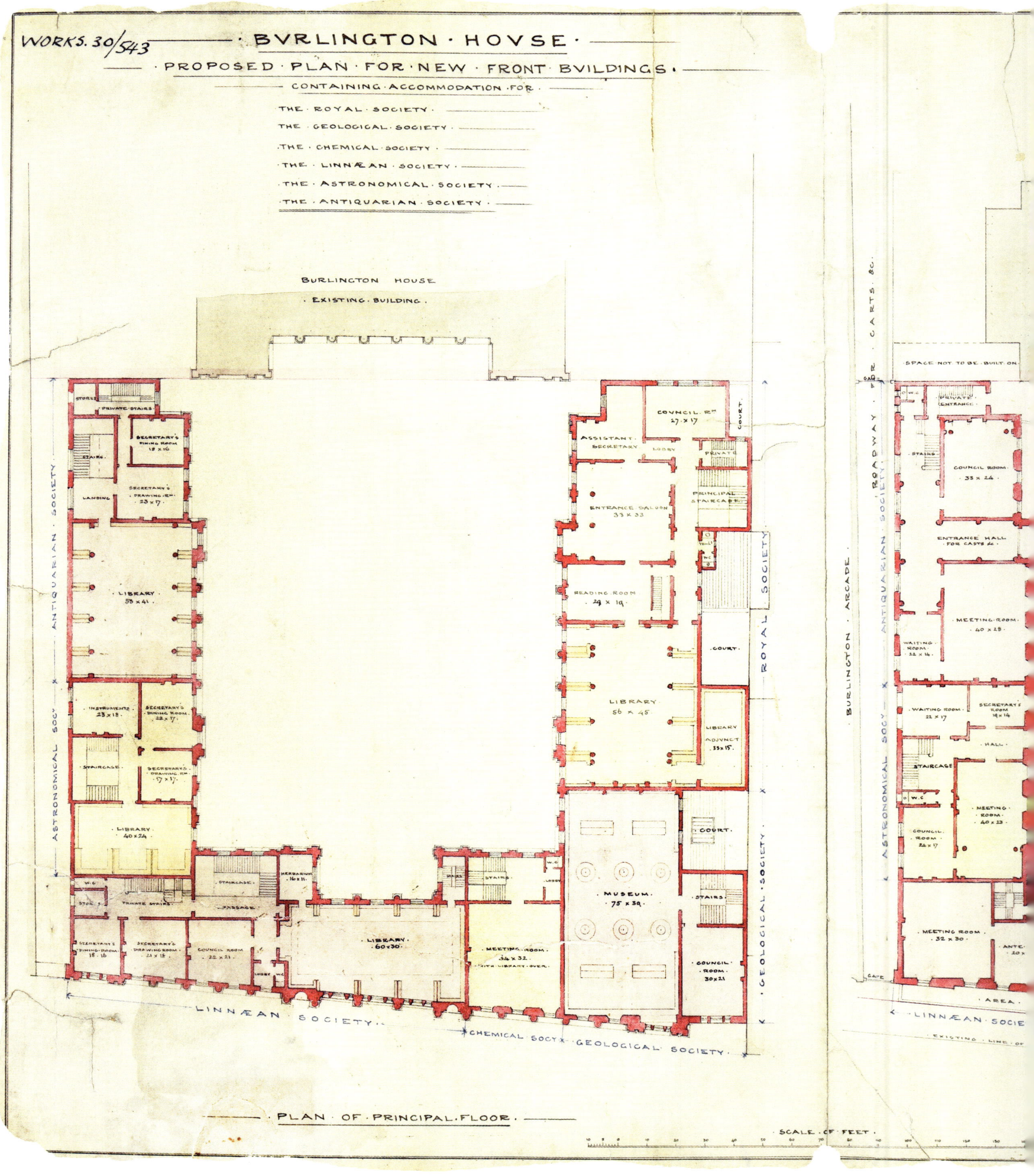
WORKS. 30/543
· BURLINGTON · HOUSE ·
· PROPOSED · PLAN · FOR · NEW · FRONT · BUILDINGS ·
CONTAINING · ACCOMMODATION · FOR ·
THE · ROYAL · SOCIETY ·
THE · GEOLOGICAL · SOCIETY ·
THE · CHEMICAL · SOCIETY ·
THE · LINNÆAN · SOCIETY ·
THE · ASTRONOMICAL · SOCIETY ·
THE · ANTIQUARIAN · SOCIETY ·
BURLINGTON HOUSE
· EXISTING · BUILDING ·
ANTIQUARIAN · SOCIETY
ASTRONOMICAL · SOCY
LINNÆAN · SOCIETY
CHEMICAL · SOCY
GEOLOGICAL · SOCIETY
ROYAL · SOCIETY
BURLINGTON · ARCADE
ROADWAY · FOR · CARTS · &c.
SPACE · NOT · TO · BE · BUILT · ON
LIBRARY 53 x 41
LIBRARY 40 x 24
LIBRARY 60 x 30
LIBRARY 56 x 45
ENTRANCE SALOON 33 x 33
READING ROOM 29 x 19
COUNCIL Rm 27 x 17
MUSEUM 75 x 39
MEETING ROOM 34 x 32
COUNCIL ROOM 30 x 21
COUNCIL ROOM 33 x 24
MEETING ROOM 40 x 29
MEETING ROOM 32 x 30
PRINCIPAL STAIRCASE
COURT
· PLAN · OF · PRINCIPAL · FLOOR ·
SCALE · OF · FEET ·

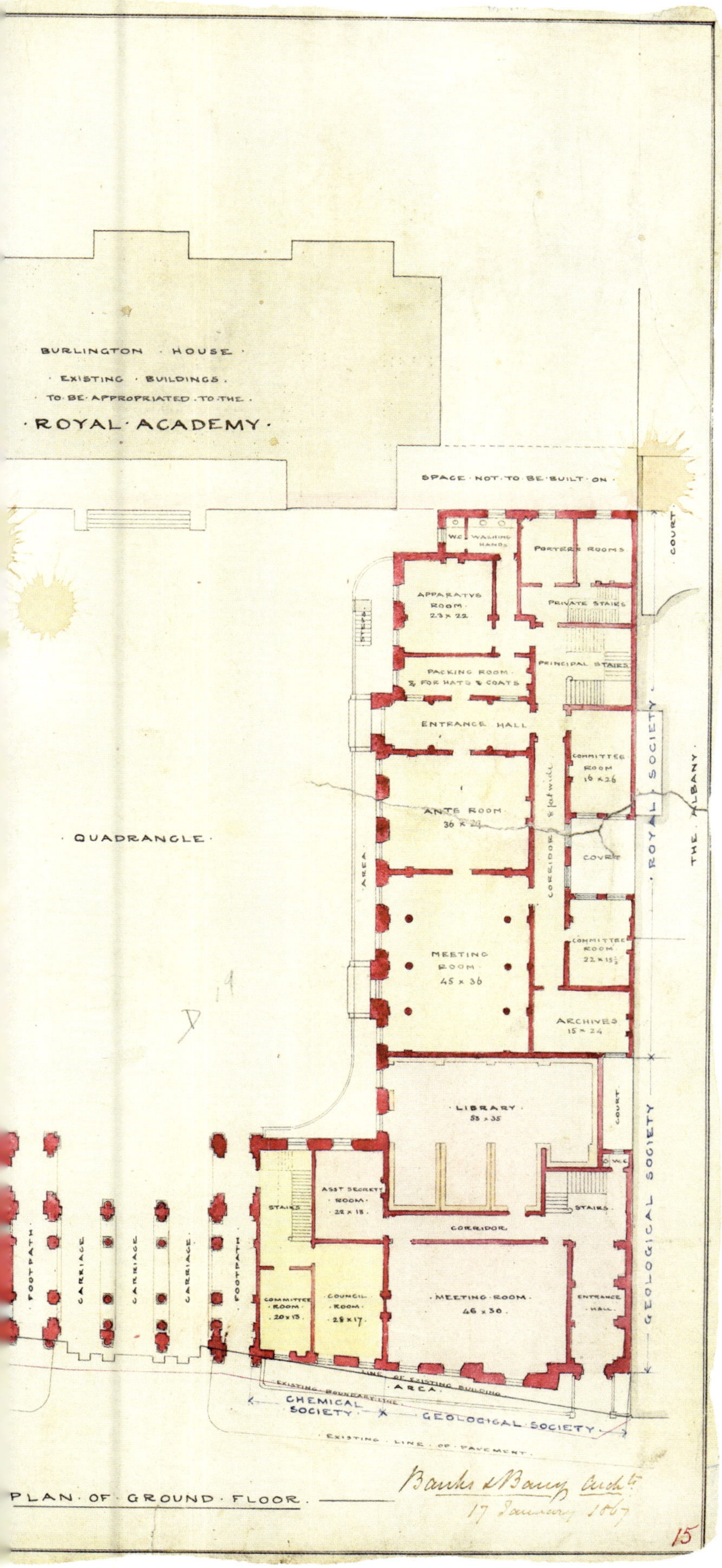

Fig. 215
Robert Richardson Banks & Charles Barry Jr, Burlington House, proposed ground-floor plan for new buildings containing accommodation for the Learned Societies (Royal Society, Geological Society, Chemical Society, Linnaean Society, Astronomical Society and Society of Antiquaries), early design, 17 January 1867.
The National Archives, Kew, TNA WORK 30/543

Council meeting of the Society of Antiquaries on 6 November 1866 to present a comparison of what had been proposed for their accommodation in 1859 with the smaller and fewer rooms he could now offer them, their agreement to move to Burlington House was by no means a foregone conclusion. The Council's decision – apparently reached only after long discussion as Barry waited outside the door – took the form of an elaborate 250-word 'resolution', which, after a long preamble, came to the reluctant conclusion that

> … they would … be prepared to accept this exchange of Apartments provided that the amount of accommodation contemplated in these plans be not in any manner curtailed or impaired, and provided also that the expense of the fittings be borne by Her Majesty's Government.[35]

Much to the annoyance of the Treasury, the tacit acceptance of these conditions by the Office of Works enabled the Antiquaries to drive a harder bargain than the other societies when it came to defining the nature and extent of the interior fittings the government was obliged to pay for.

At around this time, if not somewhat earlier, Banks & Barry did what all architects do when faced with an impossible brief. Alongside the flawed design that adhered to it, they started to work on a patently better one that didn't. The obvious solution was to return to the 1859 concept of a quadrangle enclosed by a full-height building on the Piccadilly front. Thus, it was probably at their meeting in Pennethorne's office during the week of 12 November, 'to settle a plan for submission to the Chief Commissioner', that they hatched a plot with Smirke to obtain the Academy's approval of a revised scheme, without which it had no chance of acceptance by the Office of Works.[36] In case it should appear that the latter had already agreed to alter the brief without consulting the Academy, it was a situation in which Smirke's role as Banks & Barry's intermediary became critical, hence the conspiratorial tone of his letter to them on 6 December:

> In order to prevent the possibility of error I write to remind you that the arrangement between us was that your Plans for the building in Piccadilly should be sent to me, here [i.e. 80, Grosvenor Street], in

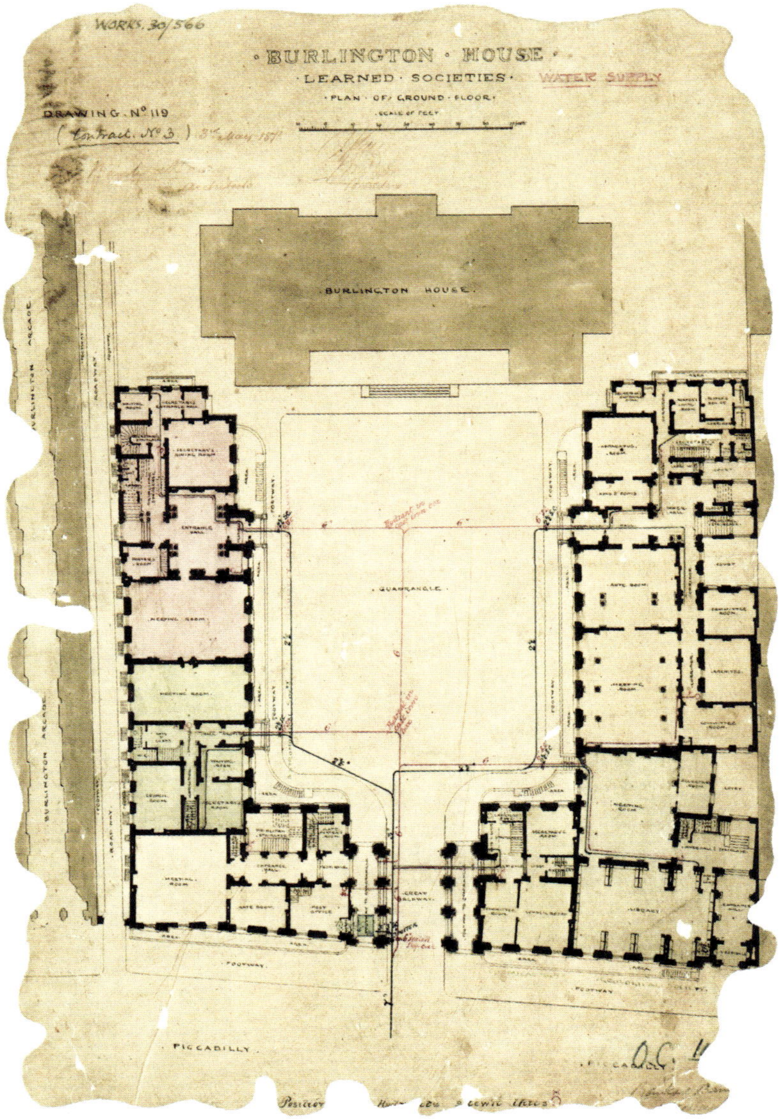

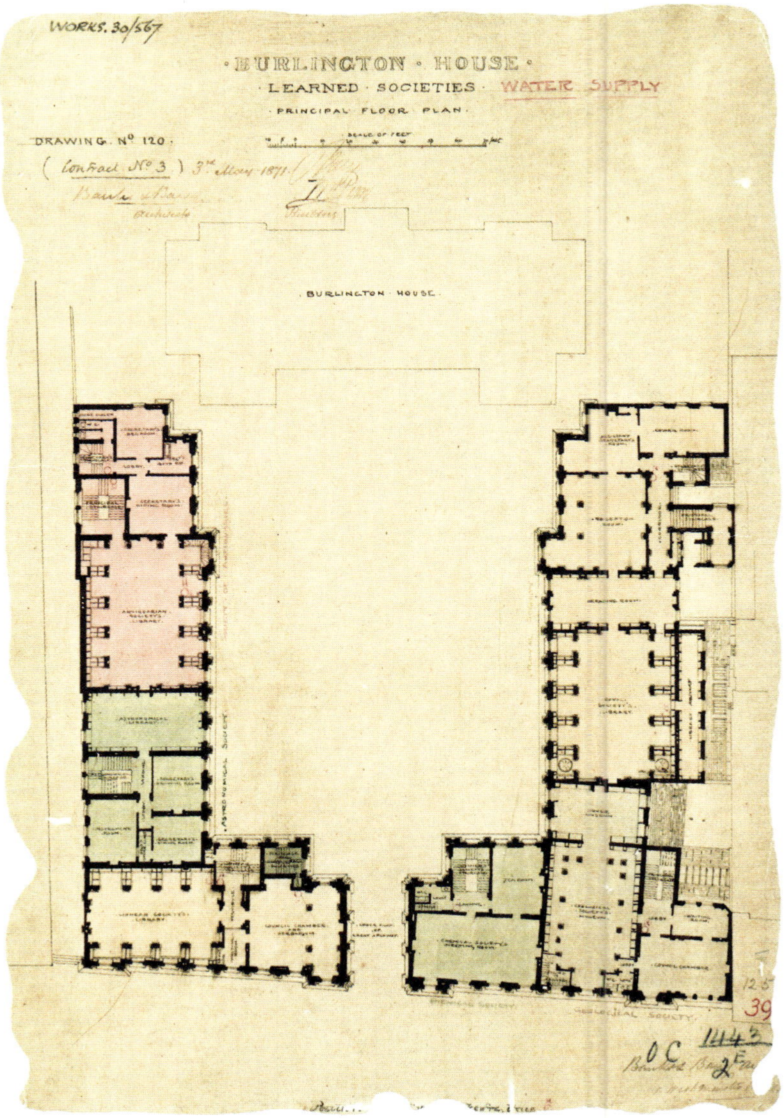

Fig. 216
Robert Richardson Banks & Charles Barry Jr, Burlington House, ground-floor plan showing accommodation for the Learned Societies as executed, 1871.
The National Archives, Kew, WORK 30/566

Fig. 217
Robert Richardson Banks & Charles Barry Jr, Burlington House, first-floor plan showing accommodation for the Learned Societies as executed, 1871.
The National Archives, Kew, WORK 30/567

> the early part of the day tomorrow (Friday) to be submitted to the Building Committee of the RA in the afternoon, when I have no doubt whatever your plan will be fully approved.
>
> I believe it was arranged that you would be in the way late in the afternoon at the RA in case the Building Committee should wish to have an interview with you.[37]

Unfortunately, no records of the meetings of the Academy's Building Committee are known to have survived. However, there can be little doubt that on this occasion Smirke impressed upon its members that it was in the Academy's interests to resolve the difficulties that were preventing Banks & Barry from finalising the block plan of their forecourt building, the lack of which was causing a delay that might prove disastrous if there was a change of government before the Academy's lease could be signed. Unaware that Grant had already informed Manners privately of the Building Committee's decision 'not to press their views on the subject of the proposed open arcade opposite Burlington House in preference to the continuous Façade facing Piccadilly'[38] – a decision not in fact taken until the Committee's subsequent meeting on 10 December – Banks & Barry wrote to him a week later to explain the reason for their long delay in submitting plans:

> … the Plans so carefully prepared are wasted and we are with all speed preparing another set which we hope to place in your Lordship's hands in a week or 10 days and which will we believe be satisfactory to the Royal Academy to Mr Pennethorne and to ourselves. We write these few lines to explain the seeming delay which has entirely arisen from the rather protracted negotiations with the Royal Academy.[39]

True to their word, Banks & Barry had a new set of plans ready for submission to Manners on 11 January 1867 and on the 17th of that month signed and dated a detailed ground- and first-floor plan of their revised scheme that, in terms of the overall distribution of space, is remarkably close to the executed building (Figs 215–217). In fact, although a legal dispute over the Albany residents' rights to light was to delay the start of building work in the forecourt for another eighteen months, Banks & Barry were to make only one significant alteration to these plans before preparing contract drawings in May–June 1868.[40]

On the same day that the Academy's Building Committee was due to decide on the question of the Piccadilly frontage, its secretary C. W. Cope RA wrote privately to Barry with a suggestion:

> Will you forgive me for venturing to offer a suggestion which occurs to me, which if possible, might harmonize any differences in the view taken of matters at Burlington House.
>
> I confess sympathy with you for the continuous façade to the South, with the exception of the deep tunnel-like entrance in the centre archways, either 60 or 30 feet deep. Now would it be possible to have one noble high arch in the centre? To be subdivided possibly below for ingress & egress of carriages. It will preserve the continuous front in Piccadilly & yet give a good peep into the court yard beyond, & also give you more room for the learned societies in the building.
>
> It is merely my own thought but an architect tells me that it would be very possible. I merely throw it out as a suggestion.[41]

In his letter thanking the Building Committee two days later for 'the public spirit which has prompted' their decision, Manners expressed his 'hope that the interests of the Royal Academy will in no respect suffer from the character of the Buildings which may be erected facing Piccadilly.'[42] In these circumstances neither the Office of Works nor Banks & Barry had much choice but to go along with Cope's suggestion, despite the fact that, contrary to his claim, it clearly gave less rather than more room to the learned societies, and was certain to add considerably to the final cost of the building.

The importance the Royal Academy attached to 'a good peep' from Piccadilly of the 'perfect architectural front' of Burlington House, and to giving visitors arriving by carriage a pleasant surprise as they swung into the courtyard from the street, is evident from the series of 'private' (as opposed to official) letters that Grant wrote to Banks & Barry in late February and March 1867 urging them to make their arch 'a grand thing per se' (Fig. 218). Illustrating his idea in hasty sketches, what Grant wanted in effect was a triumphal arch:

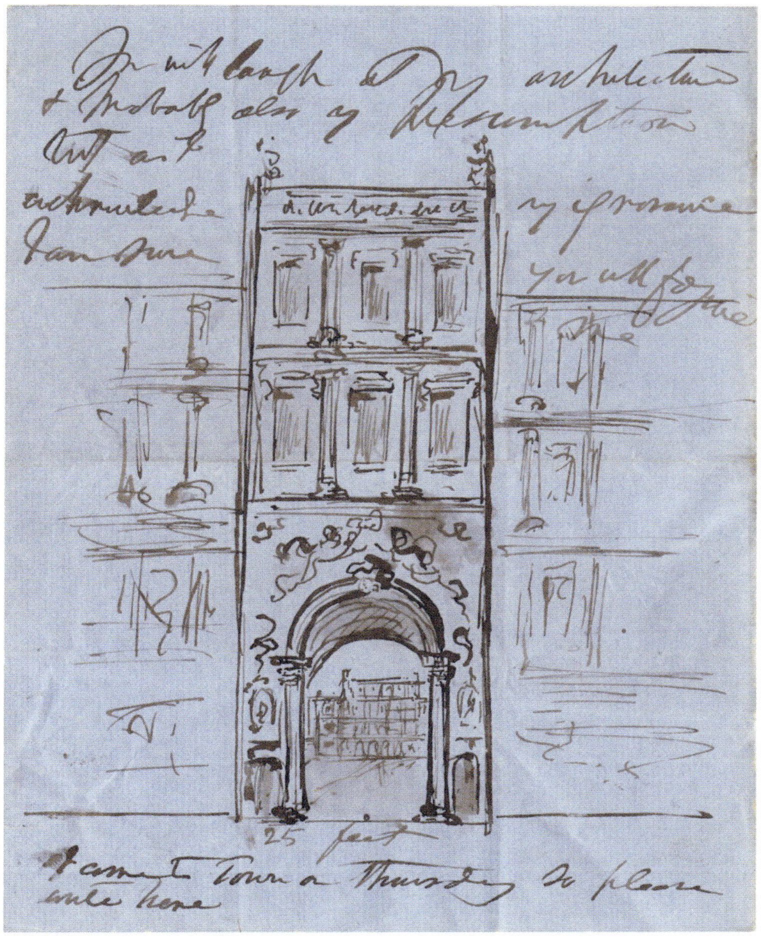

Fig. 218
Suggested design for an entrance arch to the courtyard of Burlington House, from a letter from Sir Francis Grant to Banks & Barry, 11 March 1867.
Royal Academy of Arts, London, MIS/GR/6

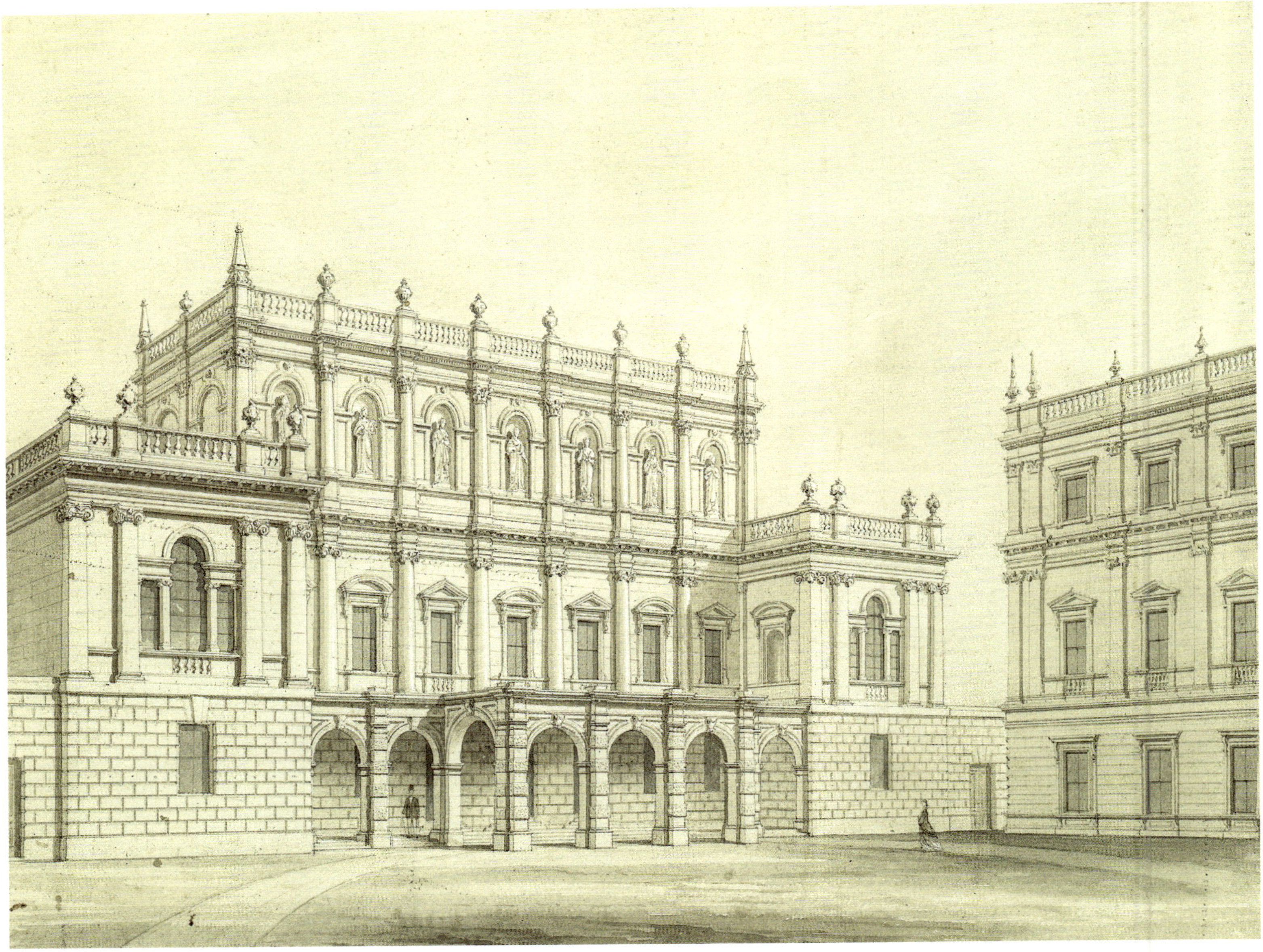

> The whole of the central front shoud be auxiliary to the archway – you may by adopting this arrangement produce one of the most striking & original things in this or any other Capital – of course it will involve no end of trouble – but only on paper. But you will cover yourselves with glory if you succeed ... What I feel is that the portion of the building tinted red shoud be one grand idea, in harmony with a very wide arch & shoud be quite independent of the continuation on either side.[43]

While Banks & Barry wisely ignored the idea of building first and second storeys over the archway at different levels from those of 'the continuation on either side', the pressure on them to widen the arch was another matter. Having expressed his own view, 'merely as an artist & no architect,' that 'the narrowness of the archway only 18 feet is inadmissible' since such 'a very narrow entrance ... woud make ladies & old gentlemen very nervous', Grant was able a few days later to pass on the unanimous opinion of four of the country's leading architects:

> I had the pleasure of receiving your obliging letter & reading it to the Building Committee, to whom I submitted your plan for the one lofty archway. You are right in anticipating the cordial approval that it met with from the whole committee so far as its architectural effect was concerned.
>
> But as I expected there was an unanimous feeling expressed as to the insufficiency of the width of the archway to meet the demands which will occasionally be required (not only for the Royal Academy but for the other societies) for a string of carriages going in & coming out at the same time.
>
> There were present four Architects who were for nearly an hour busily occupied in examining & measuring it with compasses. The result was that Mr. G. Gilbert Scott moved the enclosed resolution which I send to you exactly as he wrote it out.[44]

Grant's vigorous campaign for a triumphal arch on Piccadilly that would form the starting point of a processional route leading through the centre of Burlington

Fig. 219 (left)
Sydney Smirke, Proposed alterations to the entrance front of Burlington House, February 1867.
RIBA Collections, SC95/18(5)

House and on up into its exhibition galleries behind, was only one of the several ways he busied himself over Banks & Barry's designs in the run-up to the crucial supply vote in the Commons on 31 May 1867 (Fig. 220). Throughout this period he was constantly borrowing their drawings: to pin up alongside Smirke's at an Academy General Assembly on 27 March; to hawk round to Gladstone, Layard, Beresford Hope, William Gregory, and other opposition MPs 'who are supposed to have weight in matters of taste'; to show to the editor of *The Times*, J. T. Delane and 'one of his staff' E. S. Dallas, so that they could write 'an article commendatory of Lord John Manners' whole scheme'; and, most importantly, to lay before the Queen, whose signature approving Smirke's design for the front of the new Royal Academy would, he felt, 'be useful in the House of Commons' (Fig. 219).[45] At the same time, he had photographs taken of Banks & Barry's designs to be 'put in a handsome portfolio' alongside Smirke's and 'left with the Queen not to be returned'; urged that they make more up-to-date drawings for reproduction in the press, as this would 'more readily dispose the Members of the House to understand & to approve as the plans at present exist'; and gave a good deal of unsolicited advice on which drawings it would be best to display in the library of the House of Commons before the debate:

> The more I look at [the] painted large drawing [of the] archway, with the lady in the green petticoat, the less I like it – I advise you not to send it to the H^{c} of Commons – it will turn the whole thing into ridicule – and I woud equally advise you to have a drawing plainly tinted in sepia to correspond with the other drawings – The original drawing which I now have, is beautiful but as regards the RA is imperfect – I wish it could be repeated, correctly making the colonade on the lower story arched as it is on Smirke's drawing which in spite of your high authority, I think looks far more picturesque than your square ⊓ – Smirke's ∩∩∩ looks better.[46]

In fact, Grant was so worried about the 'lady in the green petticoat' that when he returned the offending drawing to Banks & Barry, he admitted that he had 'toned down the green petticoat, & the pink petticoat, & the green parasol, also subdued the white blinds, & the jet black windows, & with a little water made the shadows on B House more tender – which now keeps its place', offering by way of justification, that 'the drawing looks now sufficiently respectable.'[47]

The 'no end of trouble, but only on paper' involved in widening the archway on Piccadilly seems to have led Banks & Barry to revisit one of the major problems of

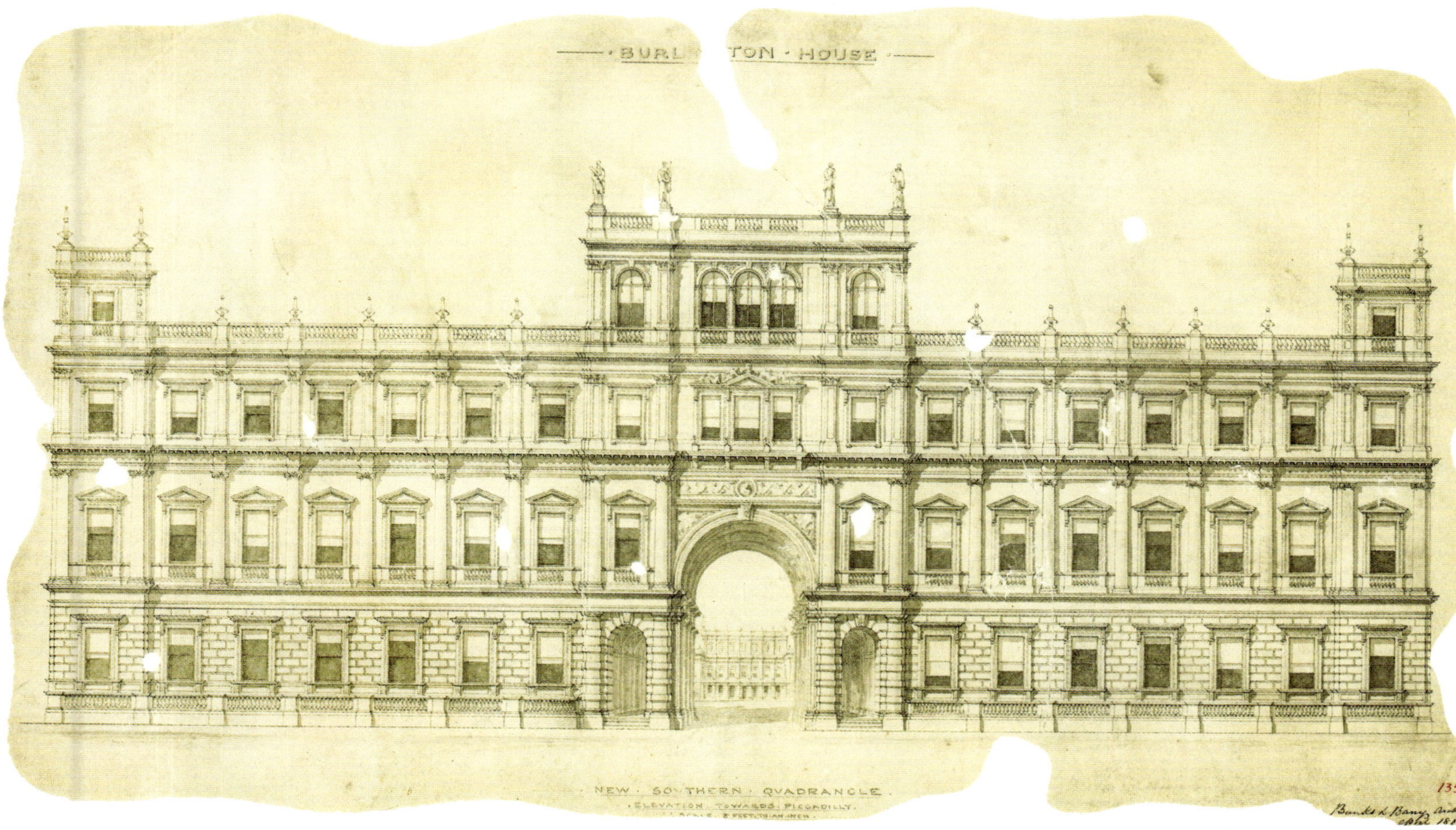

Fig. 220 (below)
Robert Richardson Banks & Charles Barry Jr, Burlington House, new southern quadrangle with accommodation for the Learned Societies: elevation towards Piccadilly, April 1867.
The National Archives, Kew, WORK 30/662

the site, namely the obliqueness of its southern boundary relative to the necessarily orthogonal alignment of the new forecourt with the old house. This slanting southern boundary, which was what the famous colonnade had been designed to conceal and why the Great Gate was set at an angle to the Piccadilly wall, presented a particular problem insofar as it was necessary to make the north and south faces of any new entranceway as far as possible parallel. In the single-storey triple carriageway that they had originally proposed (and which was probably modelled in part on the Strand entrance to Somerset House), this could have been done by adjusting the thickness and position of the dividing piers of each lane, and Banks & Barry certainly did this in their executed design in order to mask the difference in the length of the east and west pedestrian passageways. In a single barrel-vaulted archway, however, there was much less opportunity to disguise obliquity through such visual correction. And it was probably awareness of this problem as much as anything that led Banks & Barry to alter the building line they had proposed in their drawing of 17 January 1867. Thus, by tilting the orientation of the Geological Society's rooms nearer to the street on the east side of the site they made it easier to align the face of the arch on the Piccadilly front with the façade as a whole, while at the same time keeping it parallel to the

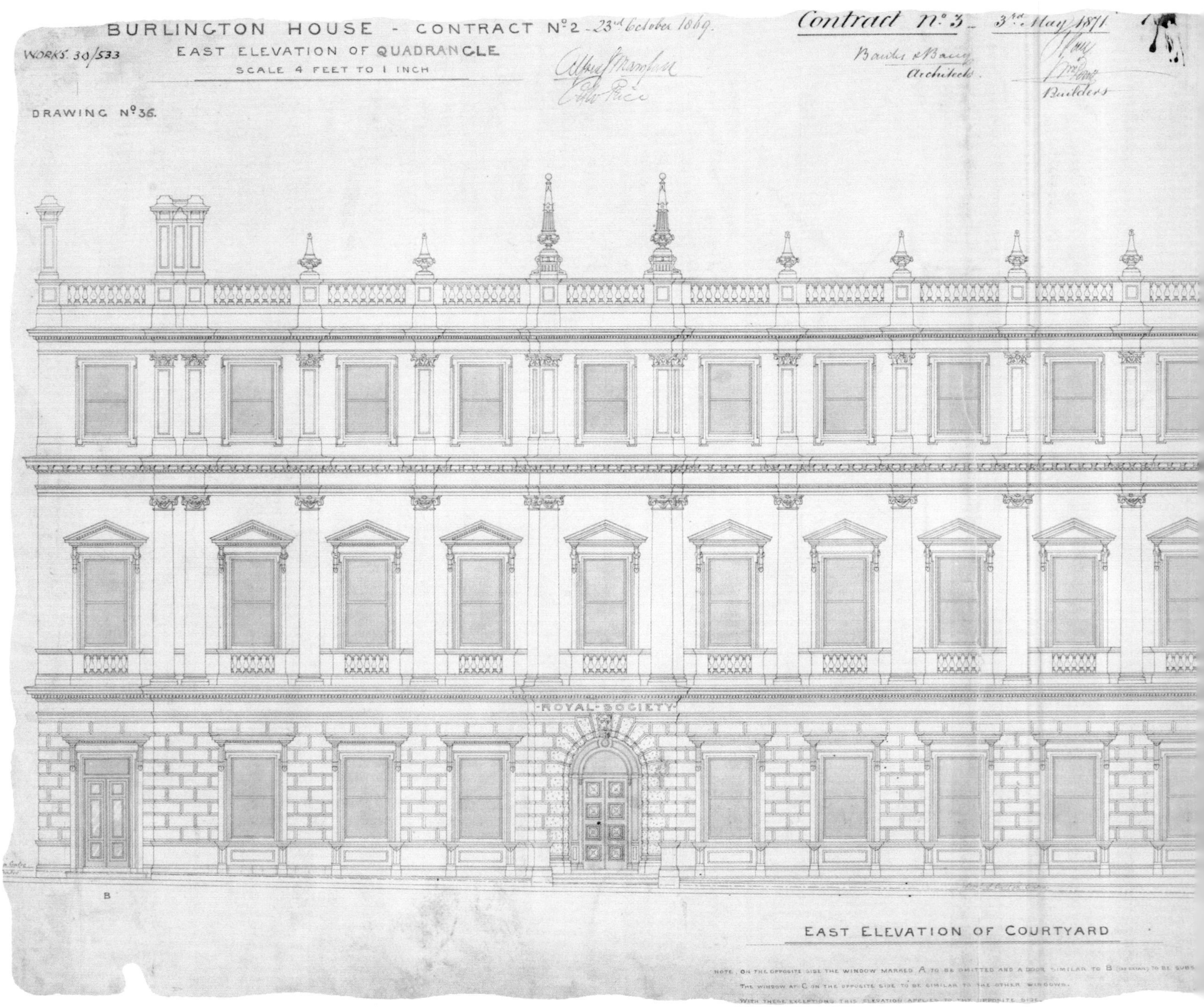

face of the arch on the courtyard front. It is small wonder that the stereotomy involved in the construction of the new 'Great Entrance' to Burlington House required separate large-scale plans to be drawn for each of the twelve courses of interlocking blocks of Portland stone that form the piers supporting its massive weight; or that by March 1871, the builders for the superstructure, Messrs Alfred Mansfield & R. W. Price, found that they were unable to complete a contract that included the complication of so many tapering party walls and rhomboid room shapes in the Piccadilly range of the new building (see Figs 216, 217).[48]

As the propylaeum to a temple of art, science and learning, Banks & Barry's 'new noble archway' on Piccadilly can affect even a familiar visitor as he or she passes under it to exchange the tumult of one of the busiest shopping streets in the capital for the urban equivalent of an academic grove (Figs 221, 222). The form of this sanctuary is not, however, the result of architectural choice but was determined solely by the position of Burlington House in relation to Piccadilly. Consequently, although Banks & Barry's revised design did in the end provide almost exactly the amount of room the societies asked for, there was not one square metre to spare for growth. Those societies, such as the Antiquaries, Royal and Linnean, that had applied for and been given more generous domestic arrangements, were in a position to mitigate the effects of their constriction by converting these spaces as and when needed into administrative offices, library annexes and additional storerooms. Despite having an ample cushion in this respect, the Royal Society was so short of space by the close of the nineteenth century that they asked to be given room in 6 Burlington Gardens when the University of London departed for South Kensington in spring 1900.[49]

Of all the societies the Chemical Society was the most severely handicapped in this respect, for not only had it been provided with the least space on the basis of its current needs, but its membership was destined to become larger than that of all the other societies combined. In 1968, when they finally moved from their original home on the east side of the Piccadilly archway into the Royal Society's former quarters, the Chemists were able to repay a longstanding debt, for among the rooms they could then pass over to the Geological Society was one which the latter had relinquished in the interests of neighbourly relations exactly a century earlier. Suggesting in a tactfully worded letter of 15 June 1868 that the Geologists might consider giving up a room on the ground floor that had been promised for the use of their secretary, Banks & Barry had pointed out that this was 'the only case where we have not arranged for a continuous party wall between each Society, from bottom to top of the building.'[50]

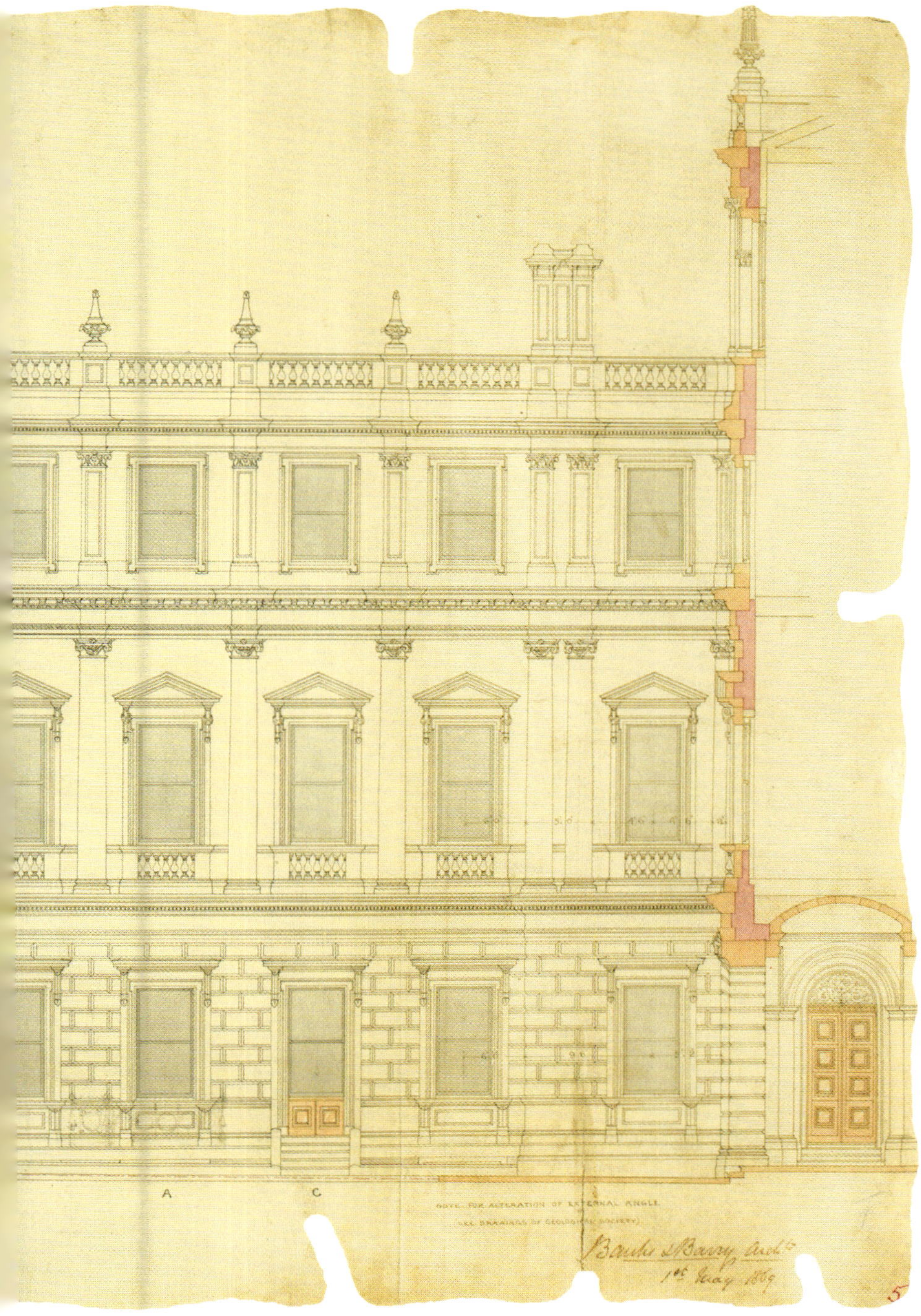

Fig. 221
Robert Richardson Banks & Charles Barry Jr, Burlington House: east elevation from within the quadrangle, 1869.
The National Archives, Kew, WORK 30/533

Fig. 222 (overleaf)
Robert Richardson Banks & Charles Barry Jr, Burlington House: elevation facing Piccadilly (Learned Societies), 1869.
The National Archives, Kew, WORK 30/535

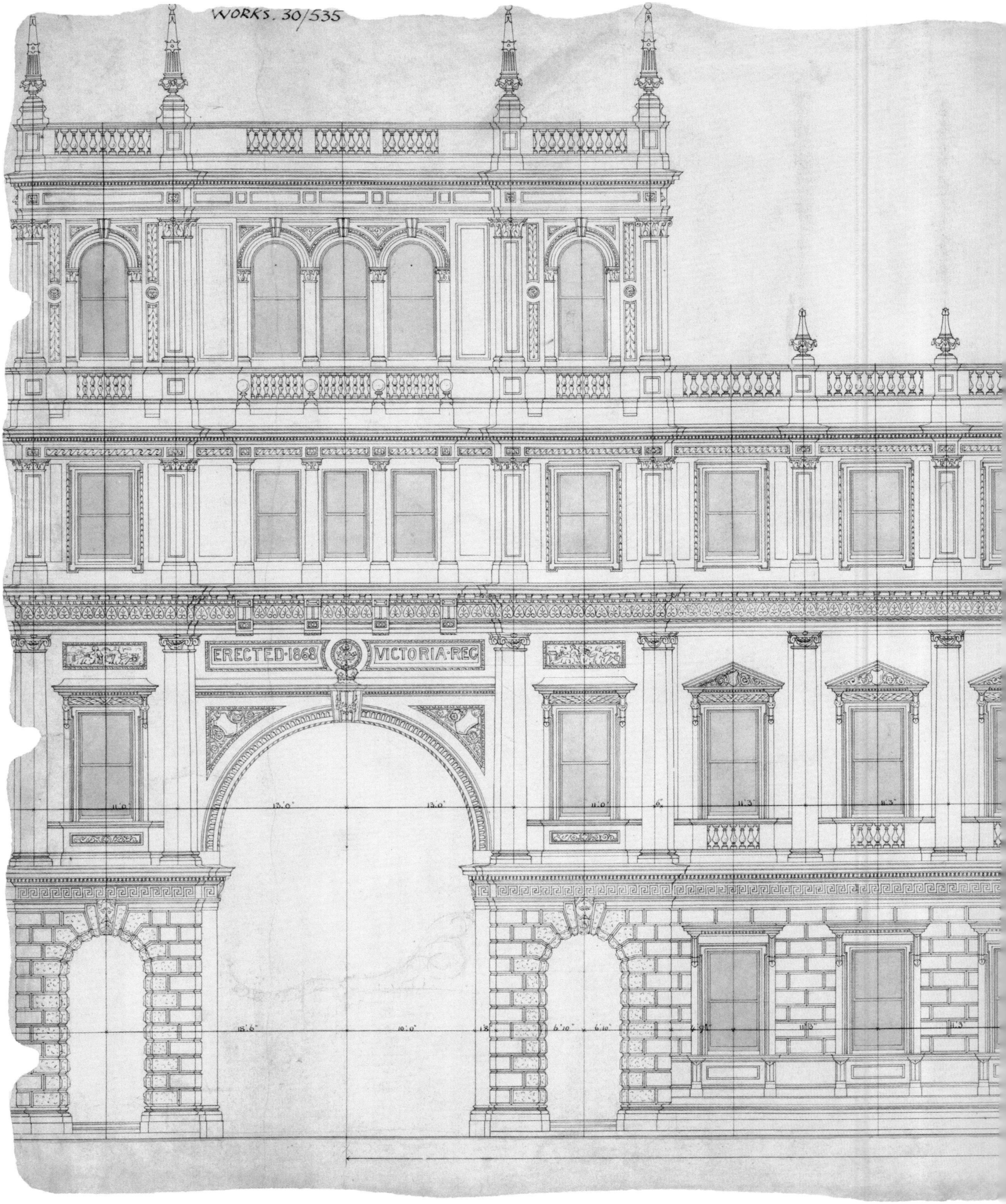
WORKS. 30/535
ERECTED·1868
VICTORIA·REG

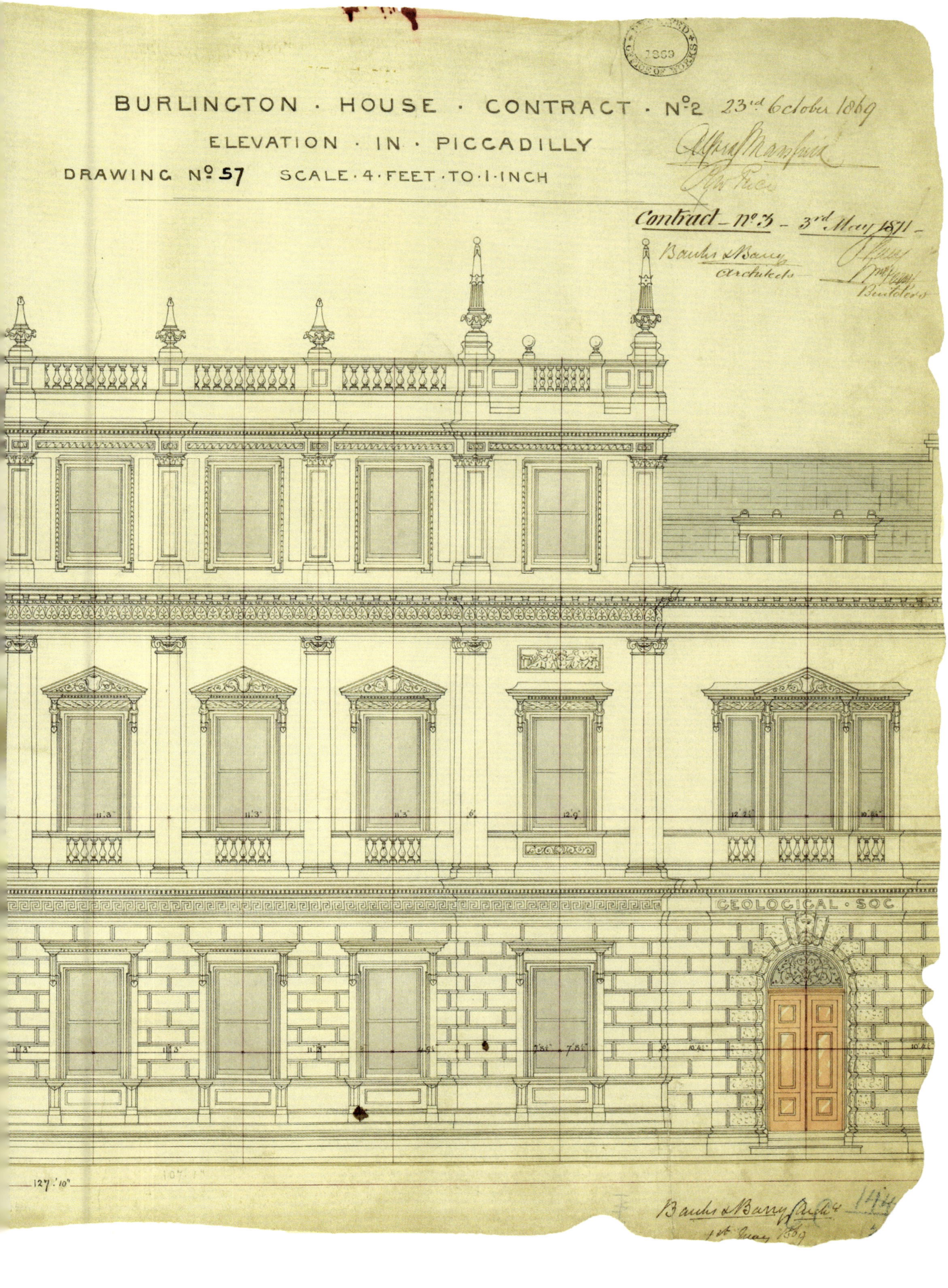
BURLINGTON · HOUSE · CONTRACT · No 2
23rd October 1869
ELEVATION · IN · PICCADILLY
DRAWING No 57 SCALE · 4 · FEET · TO · 1 · INCH
Contract – No 3 – 3rd May 1871 –
Architects
Builders
GEOLOGICAL · SOC
127 . 10"

Because of the varying amounts of space allocated to the six societies, it was only thanks to such careful interior planning that Banks & Barry had been able to provide all but one with their own main entrance inside the courtyard, along with tradesmen's entrances to porters' and housekeepers' living quarters in the basement and, in the case of the Society of Antiquaries and the Royal Society, separate front doors and staircases for their resident officers. Only the Geologists had to make do with a front door and (still in-situ) coal-hole directly on Piccadilly, leading to an entrance hall that corresponds in position to the service lane on the western side of the Piccadilly block leading to Burlington Gardens. Although the exception made in their case might seem connected to the presence nearby of the Museum of Practical Geology (demolished in 1935), it was more probably a consequence of the fact that it would have been impossible for Banks & Barry to position the Geologists' main entrance opposite that of the Astronomers on the other side of the courtyard without moving a party wall at least one bay either way, thereby disturbing the carefully calibrated allocation of space between the societies. Therefore, when the Geologists asked in April 1867 for an entrance to be provided from the courtyard directly to their meeting room, Banks & Barry's solution was to convert a window into a door as unobtrusively as possible so as not to draw attention to this slight flaw in what is otherwise a masterpiece of interior planning.[51]

Although the Antiquaries, whose apartments on the west side of the quadrangle were the last to be completed, did not move in until January 1875, enough of the scaffolding on the east side and on the Piccadilly block had been taken down by the beginning of May 1872 to provoke Edward Welby Pugin, eldest son of A. W. N. Pugin, to write a letter to *The Times* that must rank as one of the most intemperate attacks ever made on a fellow architect's work:

> But what is to be said of the present flaunting pinafore of vulgarity which now masks the ancient structure, and what will be thought of the Academy of Arts, which, without real knowledge of its lofty purpose and without the faintest approach to originality, presents to the world a building devoid of principle and beauty. …
>
> Let me add that this building, while overladen with crude and metallic ornamentations, is devoid of two most essential qualities – light and shadow.
>
> … The more one examines this work, the more insipid, inconsistent, and ridiculous does it appear; what is not the reproduction of types which have been stereotyped for years, and which it is most fatiguing to meet with again, would disgrace a rococo toy cabinet, glued together by the hundred, and sold in Venice for the delectation of English and American tourists.[52]

The following day *The Times* published a short, dignified reply by Sydney Smirke, pointing out that the Academy was 'no more answerable for the architecture' of a building 'erected by Her Majesty's government' than 'Mr Pugin himself', which was not entirely true given the influence of the Academy's Building Committee. Apart from questioning 'whether it would not have been more becoming, when writing on the works of a brother architect, to have adopted a kinder and more forbearing style of criticism', it is noticeable that Smirke says not a word in *his* brother architect's defence. In fact, as grossly biased and uncharitable a critic as Pugin undoubtedly was, Smirke might have had a sneaking feeling that he had put his finger rather well on why the final effect of the detailing of Banks & Barry's building is disappointing. Did he know perhaps that its 'flaunting pinafore of vulgarity' was carved by Samuel Sansom of Lambeth, an architectural sculptor who had worked in the 1850s as a designer for the Nottingham lace manufacturer Josiah Handford?[53]

TO JUDGE FROM A LETTER Grant wrote on 1 August 1866 to General Sir Charles Grey, the Queen's private secretary, describing how the Academy intended to use Burlington House, it was proposed originally to convert the State Dining Room, the Saloon and the two rooms to its east and west into top-lit galleries in order to display the Royal Academicians' diploma works and other important paintings and sculpture in the Academy's possession.[54] Startling as such an alteration of the original fabric of the old house now seems, it could have been done quite easily, and without great detriment to its architectural integrity, simply by glazing the roof of the building and replacing the Ricci and Kent ceiling paintings with lay lights. More surprising in its way was Grant's proposal to put the Academy's collection on permanent public display. While a few people may have noticed that in 1857 the Academy had lent 68 works to the 'Art Treasures of the United Kingdom' exhibition in Manchester, complaints that it had 'jealously concealed' the art treasures in its possession, or awareness even that it had a collection at all, rarely featured in the torrent of press criticism of its manifold institutional failings in the 1850s and '60s.[55] And while it was true that the Council had had to do something about the poor condition of many of the diploma works at the time of the Manchester exhibition, it could hardly be claimed that the Academicians had ever shown great interest in making them better known. It is rather surprising therefore to find Grant assuring Manners on 4 August 1866 that

> The Council of the Royal Academy highly approve of the plan I mentioned, of making the upper story of Burlington House available for the benefit of the public, by placing there the collection of diploma pictures and other valuable works of art belonging to the Academy among which I may mention there are four fine pictures by Sir Joshua, a beautiful & very valuable fresco by Paul Veronese recently bequeathed to the Academy, an undoubted group of the Holy family in basso relievo by Michel Angelo, & groups in marble by Nollekens Banks & other eminent sculptors. In the wing woud be placed our library to which every accommodation woud be given to the public, to enable them to consult the valuable & extensive works on art contained in the library.[56]

There is an echo here not only of a conversation the two men have just had, but also more faintly of the government's stipulation ten years earlier that the Royal Society would undertake to make its collection of historic portraits accessible to the public, and that 'men of letters and science and others desirous to consult or study literary works ... [would] be admitted to the common library' proposed to be formed by the three societies intending to occupy Burlington House. Grant likewise took the trouble to sketch out a plan of a 'Diploma Gallery' in his letter to General Grey, almost certainly because the Academy's memorial to the Queen in July 1851 concerning its current lack of space had drawn attention to the fact that

> The Pictures, Models and drawings required by the Rules of the Academy to be deposited by Members on receiving their Diplomas as Royal Academicians, form now, from their number, an important and interesting Gallery of British Art, and if a proper room could be appropriated to them, they might be exhibited to the Public, instead of which they are necessarily covered over during the time of the Exhibition.[57]

Perhaps because it could not serve as a lever for its proposed appropriation of Burlington House, Grant omitted to mention in either of his letters the Academy's concurrent legal obligation to provide, 'in any new Building which may be erected', a public gallery for the display of the sculpture bequeathed by John Gibson RA in December 1864, along with a useful £32,000.[58]

Smirke's letter to Banks & Barry on 10 November 1866, apologising for not being able to 'furnish you with any plan of the new R.A. as none has been settled yet',[59] suggests that thoughts on how to use the rest of the house had not progressed much beyond Grant's somewhat over-optimistic idea that the old ball room in the east wing (now known as the 'Reynolds Room' but used then to house the Linnean library) could serve simultaneously as the Academy's library and council room, and his vague belief that 'the lower story [i.e. ground floor] would afford ample accommodation for Secretary's offices and residence of the Keeper and Registrar and servants of the Institution.'[60] As late as mid-December 1866 Grant was still referring to 'alterations in the interior and roof of Burlington House ... viz[t]. for a Gallery to contain the Diploma and other works of art belonging to the Academy,'[61] and it was not until Banks & Barry produced their long-awaited design for the learned societies the following month that it became clear, as Pennethorne

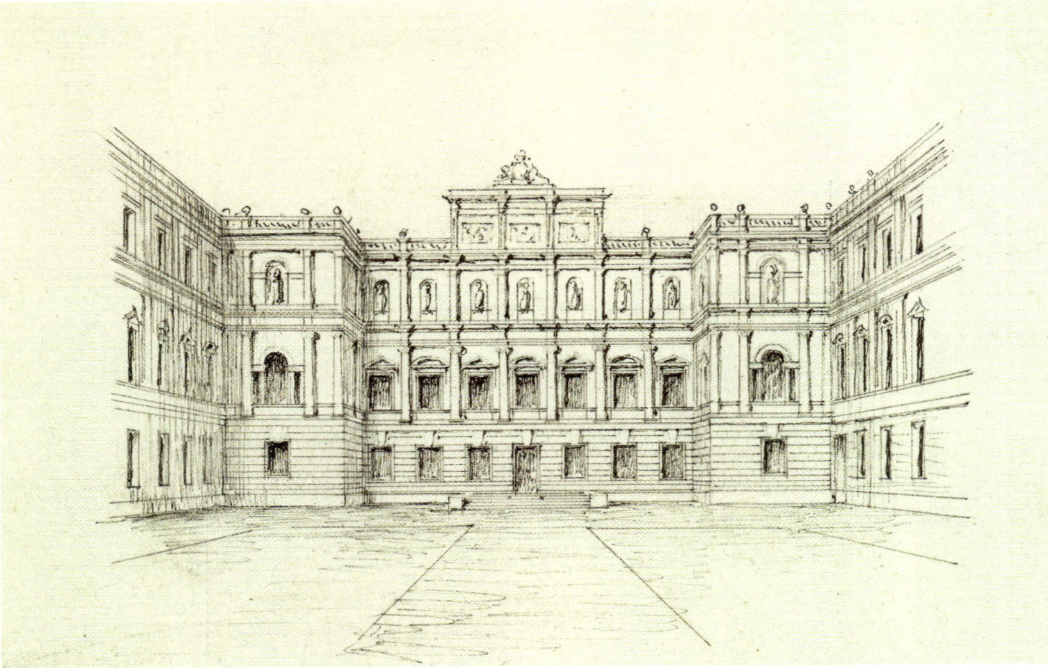

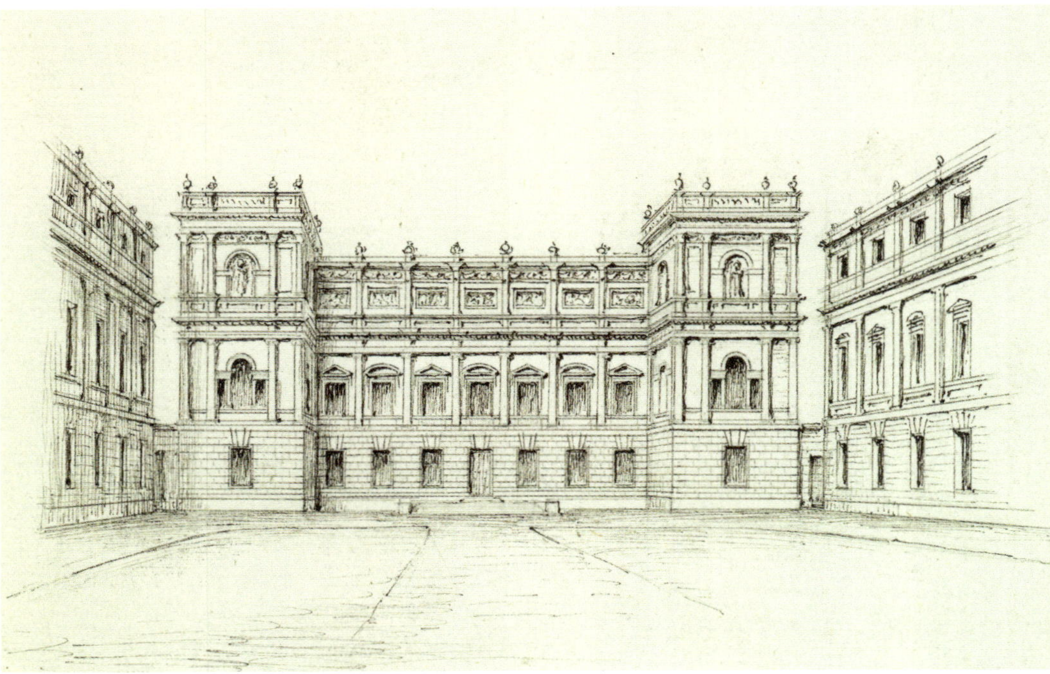

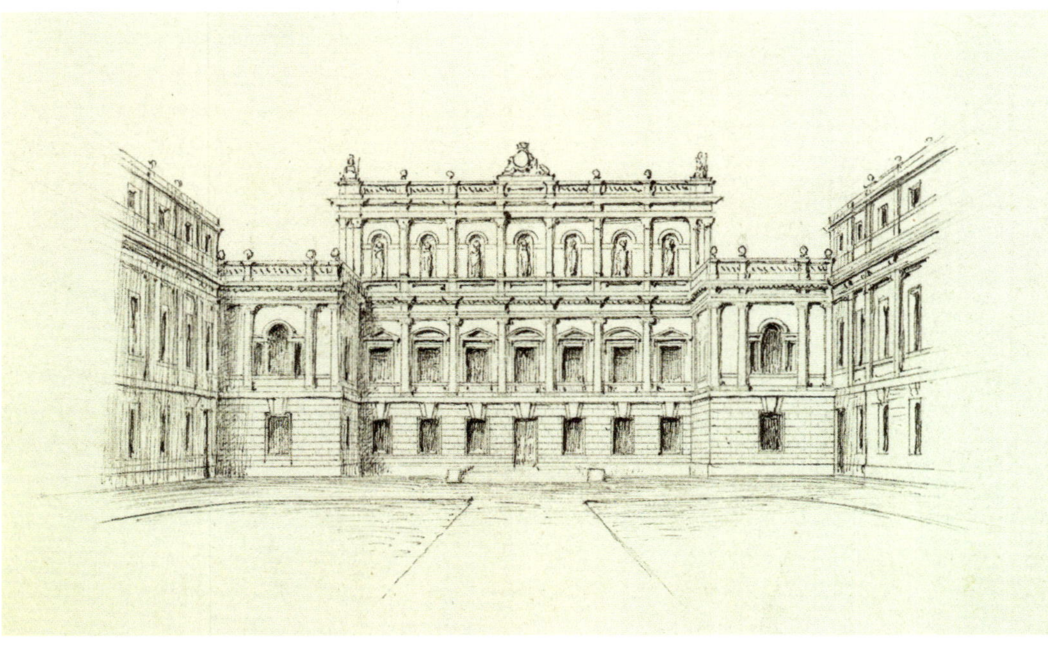

Fig. 223
Sydney Smirke, Preliminary design for proposed alterations to the south front of Burlington House, 1867.
RIBA Collections: SC95/18(1)

Fig. 224
Sydney Smirke, Preliminary design for proposed alterations to the south front of Burlington House, 1867.
RIBA Collections: SC95/18(3)

Fig. 225
Sydney Smirke, Preliminary design for proposed alterations to the south front of Burlington House, 1867.
RIBA Collections: SC95/18(2)

had predicted the previous summer, that it would be necessary to add another storey to the house.[62] Sensing that this defeated the point of preserving the house in the first place, Layard rounded on Manners in the Commons on 5 April 1867, accusing him of having not only destroyed the best hope of ever building a National Gallery worthy of the nation ('For the interests of Art no more disastrous Vote ever passed the House'), but of now also destroying Lord Burlington's celebrated forecourt in order to raise 'new and lofty buildings round about it', which he likened to 'marrying a little short man to a very stout woman who would be smothered in her embraces.'[63]

Notwithstanding this opening salvo, Layard's real target on this occasion was the fact that for the past seven months the Office of Works had been erecting a large building on Burlington Gardens to an 'Italian-Gothic' design of which the University of London, its intended occupants, had publicly disapproved and of which, despite a clear undertaking by Manners's predecessor, Parliament had so far been denied all sight. Since Grant had reported to Banks & Barry only a few days before that Layard and Beresford Hope 'admire [your plans] extremely & have promised their support', it seems likely that Layard's backing was at least partly due to the way their neo-Palladian design for the new quadrangle highlighted the discordancy of Pennethorne's 'unauthorised' design for the University at the other end of the site.[64] This explains why Layard's choice of battleground in the Commons debate on 31 May 1867 was not in fact the learned societies – the £15,000 estimate for which passed unopposed – but the University's building which, in spite of the fact that at least some of its walls were by then nineteen feet high, was stopped in its tracks by his amendment rejecting not only Pennethorne's Italian-Gothic design thus far executed but also the 'plain Classic' alternative that Manners himself had rejected the previous July (see above, Figs 196, 197).

Despite the due deference Banks & Barry paid to Burlington House in terms of architectural detailing, supplying the fourth side of their quadrangle posed an impossible problem for Smirke. Undated design sketches in the RIBA Drawings Collection show him trying to give his new storey sufficient height for the house to escape the smothering 'embrace' of the adjacent buildings while at the same time not crushing Campbell's existing façade under a disproportionate mass (Figs 223–225). To judge from a perspective drawing dated February 1867, his preferred solution at that time, i.e. when Banks & Barry were preparing their presentation drawings for the House of Commons, was to leave Campbell's wings untouched and to heighten only the body of the house so that this appeared to be set farther away from their quadrangle buildings than it actually was (see above, Fig. 219). This distancing effect, reinforced by a triple-arched *porte-cochère* jutting into the forecourt, certainly helped to give Smirke's proposed façade room to breathe. However, his insertion of a seven-bay entrance arcade to shelter the Academy's visitors interrupted the continuity of Campbell's façade at ground-floor level, visually detaching the original wings from the towering central block of the house to such an extent that these now seemed remnants of a quite different building. A variant of this design, also dated February 1867, reduces this unfortunate effect by dispensing with the *porte-cochère*, restricting the entrance portico to three central bays so that it corresponded with the balustraded first-floor windows above, and retaining the original lintels of the front door and converted window/doors either side. In yet another version however, dated the following month (Fig. 226), these modifications are reversed, and the ground-floor windows in the wings enlarged in the way Samuel Ware had proposed in 1815, all no doubt in response to comments and suggestions by the Academy's Building Committee.

According to Grant's letter dated 'Tuesday 30' [January 1872] to Acton Smee Ayrton, who had succeeded Layard as First Commissioner on 26 October 1869, the decision to adopt in the end a somewhat different design (Fig. 227) was not Smirke's but

> made in consequence of a conversation I had with you in the Park last summer. I had heard one or two Members express an opinion that it would be better to carry the wings up – and you were so good as to express a similar opinion. I got the sanction of the

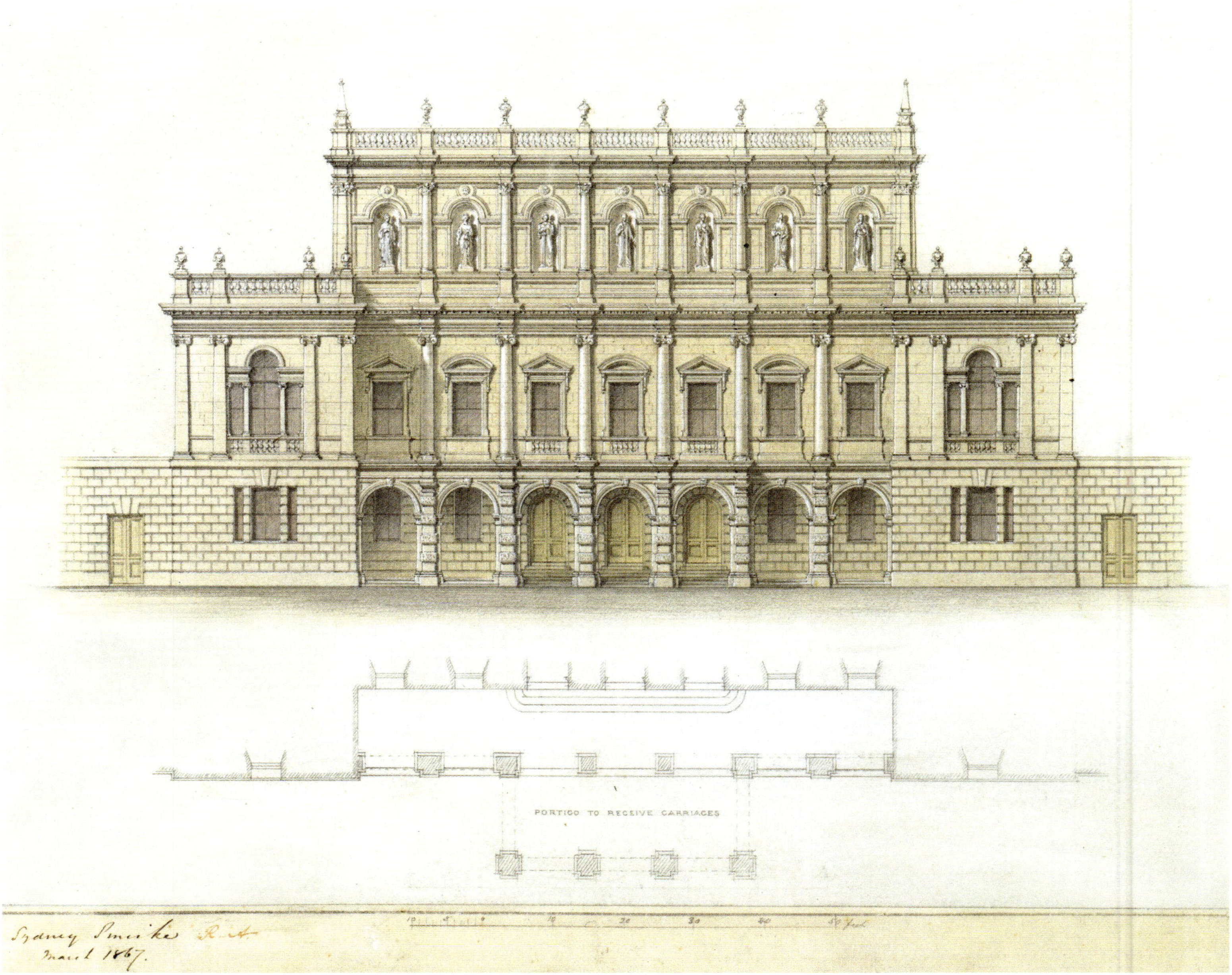

> building committee, & Mr Smirke was authorized to carry it out.[65]

Although Banks & Barry did not send Ayrton their own proposal for altering the south front of Burlington House until 28 February 1872 – the Academy had submitted Smirke's revised design for the First Commissioner's approval four days earlier – their accompanying letter suggests that they may have influenced, at least verbally, the opinion the latter had expressed the previous summer:

> When you asked us a long time since to think over the best means of uniting our building with the new Façade of the Royal Academy it inevitably led us into considering a design for the Academy façade. We made a drawing in case you further asked us about it & which has lain in our slides ever since. We send it now in case it may be useful to you.
>
> The statues we have drawn would be fully 7 to 7½ feet high which is quite enough.
>
> We had maintained a level cornice & parapet throughout & fearing to overload in effect the small order of columns to 1st floor of Old Building, & trusted to the different planes of the old façade giving enough variety of skyline even without actually raising the wings above the general level.
>
> Kindly return us the drawing when you have quite done with it.[66]

Ayrton was sufficiently impressed to forward Banks & Barry's design to Grant the next day, adding, however, that 'it rests with your Academy to adhere to the plan you sent me or make any alteration of it they think proper'.[67] There was of course no possibility now of supplanting Smirke's adopted design but Banks & Barry's preference for straight lintels (which Grant had

Fig. 226
Sydney Smirke, Proposed alterations and additions to Burlington House, with ground plan of the loggia and *porte-cochère* and elevation of the south front, March 1867.
Royal Academy of Arts, London, 05/2111

thought less 'picturesque' than Smirke's arches), did perhaps influence the only significant change that was made to the finally approved version that Ayrton signed off on 12 June 1872, in that it was decided after all to retain the original straight lintels on the ground floor of the house rather than reshape them into arches to match those of new portico (compare Fig. 227).

While it had always been apparent that statuary would be needed to animate what would have otherwise been an unacceptably blank wall, it was not until 17 December 1872 that Grant 'directed the consideration of the Council to the matter of the Seven statues which it is proposed should occupy the seven niches in the front of the upper story now building at Burlington House'. Apparent confusion over how many statues were needed probably arose as a result of referring only to Smirke's elevation drawing, in which of course only the seven forward-facing niches are represented. It also strongly suggests that the subject had only now become urgent because Grant had taken the Council on a tour of inspection of the works on 29 November, during which Smirke had no doubt brought up the subject as a matter of some urgency. Aware that time was now short, it made sense to accept the offer of the two sculptor members on Council, Henry Weekes and William Calder Marshall, 'to undertake such statues at the ordinary terms of 200 Guineas each'.[68] Early in the new year, Weekes, the painter C. W. Cope and the architect G. E. Street were appointed a 'Committee to take into consideration the question of the statues', which a fortnight later recommended to a packed Council meeting 'the following illustrious names as representing the Fine Arts generally – Giotto – Leonardo da Vinci – Wm. of Wykham – Flaxman – Michel Angelo – Raphaelle – Titian – Reynolds – and Wren.'[69] The inclusion of the founder of Winchester College and New College, Oxford in a pantheon of great artists may seem a bit surprising, but there can be no doubt William of Wykeham was chosen by the ardent Gothic revivalist George Edmund Street to represent the glorious achievements of English medieval architecture in counterpoint to those of the great scion of English classical architecture, Christopher Wren. At this point, however, a drawback of the enlargement of the Council from eight to twelve members in November 1870 became evident when a rival faction, probably led by the engraver-academician Lumb Stocks, succeeded by one vote in carrying an amendment to the effect that the statues 'should be made representative of British art exclusively'. A ballot was then held, as a result of which it was proposed to replace the old masters with William Hogarth, Thomas Gainsborough, David Wilkie, J. M. W. Turner and, rather oddly, one of the Academy's bitterest enemies, the Orkney-born line-engraver Sir Robert Strange.

At the following Council meeting on 11 February it was clear that the choice of statues was threatening to become a divisive issue and that the best answer was to refer the whole matter to a forthcoming General Assembly on 25 February. The resolutions passed at the latter meeting to substitute Phidias for Giotto and to revert to the statue committee's original list, were almost certainly carried thanks to the intervention of Richard Redgrave who was serving on the Council at the time and had therefore been party to the previous discussion. He had found a particularly neat solution to the problem of the order in which the statues should be arranged. In what is surely a deliberate echo of the tutelary bust that had guarded the doorway to the Academy's rooms at Somerset House, the key to Redgrave's arrangement was to place 'Michael Angelo as Painter, Sculptor & Architect in the centre' of the façade, where he is 'supported' (i.e. flanked) by Raphael and Titian, the great masters respectively of beauty of form and colour. These in turn support, in a different sense of the word, Flaxman and Reynolds, who represent between them the European-wide fame won by English sculptors and painters in the century since the founding of the Academy. To their left and right are then placed Leonardo and Wren, two of the greatest polymaths in the history of Western art and architecture, while facing each other across the Academy's threshold stand Phidias and Wykeham, holding in equilibrium the highest artistic achievements of ancient Greece and medieval England.

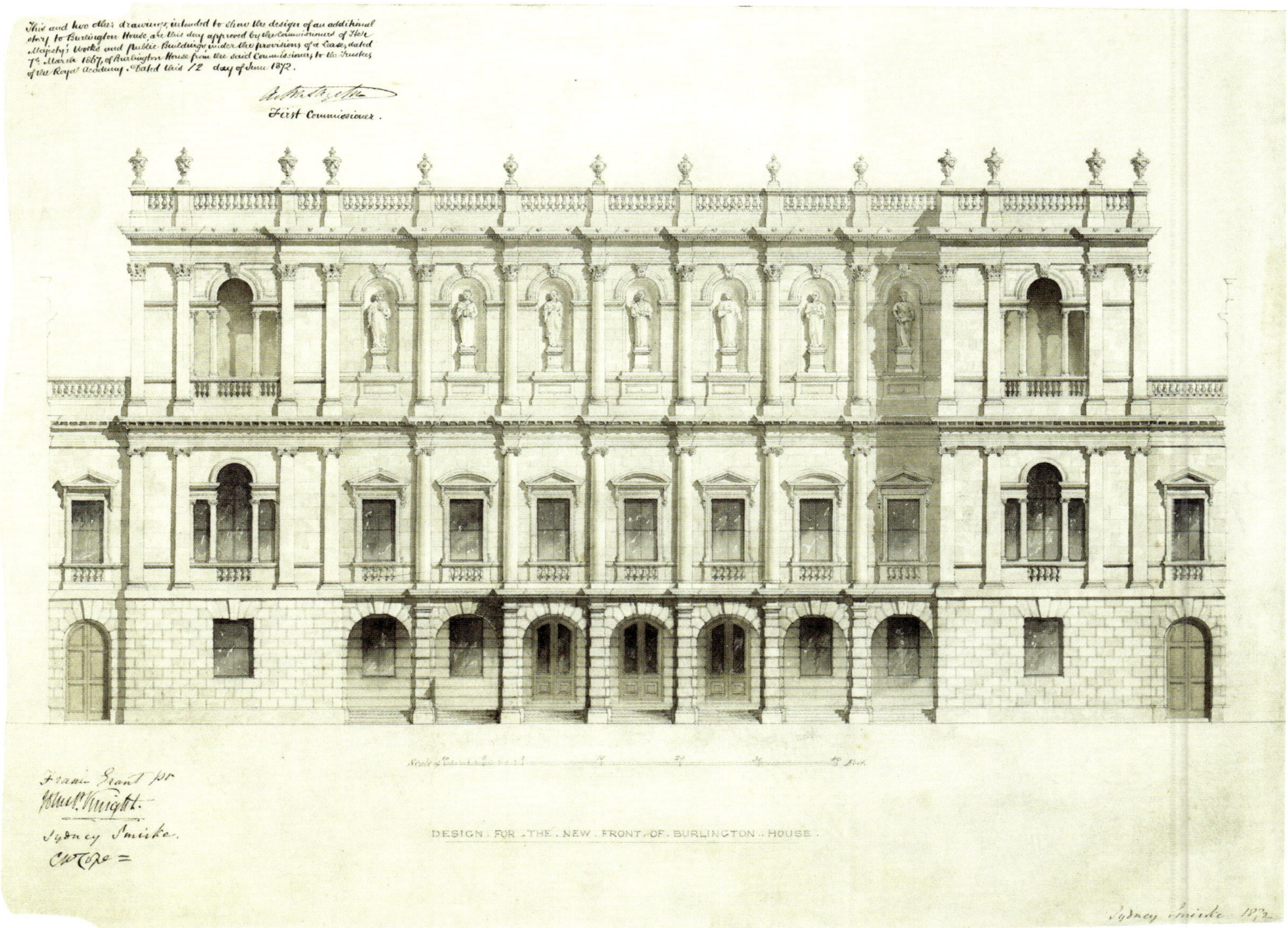

THE STARTING PISTOL in the race to build the Academy's new exhibition galleries and schools was fired at a Council meeting on 20 March 1867, when the secretary 'laid on the table the Lease of Burlington House and grounds attached', and 'It was ordered that Mr. Smirke the Architect, commence operations without delay.'[70] Speed was of the essence: not only did the lease stipulate that the Academy's new building had to be built within two years, but the long delay in drawing it up meant that at least a month of the current year's building season had been lost. In view of this urgency, Grant arranged for a General Assembly the following week to rubberstamp Smirke's designs, and the Building Committee authorised him to award the contract for the foundations to the prominent London building contractors Jackson & Shaw without going through the normal tendering process. Not only did this obviously save time, it also took advantage of the fact that Jackson & Shaw had been engaged since the previous September in laying the foundations of the University of London's building at the other end of the garden and, less than a month before, had been awarded the contract for its construction to first-floor level. Since working on neighbouring sites reduced Jackson & Shaw's overheads, it is not surprising that, of the seven contractors invited to tender for the construction of the superstructure of the Academy's building on 29 June 1867, their quotation came in the lowest at £42,596 (not including foundations and fittings), and that they were prepared to take on the challenge of completing the contract 'under a penalty ... by Michaelmas 1868'.[71]

According to Smirke's annual updates to the General Assembly on the progress of the works in 1867 and 1868, the 'South-West Gallery' had been 'roofed in, and so far finished internally as to enable a safe judgment to be formed of the mode of lighting and of the general proportions of the apartment' in time for the inspection of the Building Committee on 29 January 1868. On the

Fig. 227
Sydney Smirke, Front elevation of the Royal Academy, showing the additional storey, entrance loggia and screen wall, almost as executed, 1872.
The National Archives, Kew, WORK 30/537

latter 'being fully approved', Smirke assured the Council that 'the roofing of the whole building is now being proceeded upon with all proper speed.'[72] It was a nervous time though, as money poured out of the Academy's bank account at Drummonds (by 24 January 1868 £14,000 had been paid to the contractors on architect's certificates and by 7 January the following year £50,000), and a stirring address, probably composed by the secretary J. P. Knight, marked the Academy's centenary year by raising expectations that their new building would deliver a promised land:

> ... we have now arrived at the summit of our arduous ascent, and a new century has been inaugurated by the possession of a permanent home built at the sole cost of the Institution, on a noble site, liberally granted by the Government as the promised equivalent for the advantages originally relinquished by the Academy at Somerset House. A home well calculated to stimulate the Arts of the country, and to satisfy the friends and well-wishers of the Institution; a home which, while it assures permanence, will also facilitate such improvements in its action as well as enable it to give a higher education to the student, and a larger field of display to the accomplished artist.[73]

Fortunately, the gods were smiling, for early in 1869 Smirke was able to report that

> The dryness of the summer of 1868 was very favourable to our proceedings, and to that is mainly due the absence of any of those evils which so often arise from the hurried execution of a building. The fineness of the season so favoured the rapid progress of the work, that by the commencement of the present year all doubt and anxiety ceased as to the proper completion of the building in time for the Exhibition at the usual period.

Furthermore, he had the satisfaction of being able to add 'that although over 200 workmen have been constantly engaged on this work, but one accident has occurred during the year.'[74]

The Academy's 'Main Galleries' are by far the best preserved of the various additions and alterations Smirke designed for the adaptation of Burlington House to the needs of the Academy between March 1867 and June 1875. That they were purpose-built can only be part of the reason for this, since the same was true of the Keeper's House and the Diploma and Gibson Galleries (1872–74), and the vaults and artists' studios in the basement, all of which have been or are about to be altered in some way to enable radical changes in their use. Unlike the Round Reading Room at the British Museum, for which he is probably best remembered, Smirke's galleries at Burlington House have continued to fulfil their original purpose without interruption for 150 years. They are of course quintessentially of their time but unlike many other Victorian art galleries built somewhat later for the display of permanent collections around the country, they manage to impart a quality of timelessness. Paradoxically, one of the reasons for this was the speed with which they were designed and built, since this meant that architect, builder and client had no choice but to concentrate on essentials. As a result, from the moment they opened to the general public at 8 a.m. on Monday, 3 May 1869, Smirke's galleries have remained, for visitors and exhibitors alike, the architectural space that most powerfully represents the Academy as a national institution (Fig. 228). By the standards of the day there was nothing overly grand about them in spite of the gilded splendour of Gallery III, the 'soberly elegant' decorations by L. W. Collman (with whom Smirke had worked on the entrance hall to the British Museum twenty years earlier), the fine marble, oak and walnut door-casings by W. H. Burke & Co. and S. J. Ruddock (Fig. 230), the 'quiet-coloured, reddish, diaper paper' with which the walls were first lined, and the generous provision of Messrs Holland & Co.'s 'well-stuffed sofas' for lounging in the central Octagon (Fig. 229). Nor did Smirke set out to make any grand architectural statement for its own sake, but stuck instead to the sound principles of axial planning and top-lighting perfected in the great continental galleries of Dresden, Berlin, Munich and Paris (Fig. 232). In short, his galleries have all the fitness for purpose associated with the great traditions of Victorian civil engineering (Fig. 231).[75]

While many of the contract drawings for building the Main Galleries have survived in the Academy's collection,

Fig. 228
Henry Jamyn Brooks, *Private View of the 'Old Masters Exhibition', Royal Academy, 1888*, 1889.
National Portrait Gallery, London, 1833

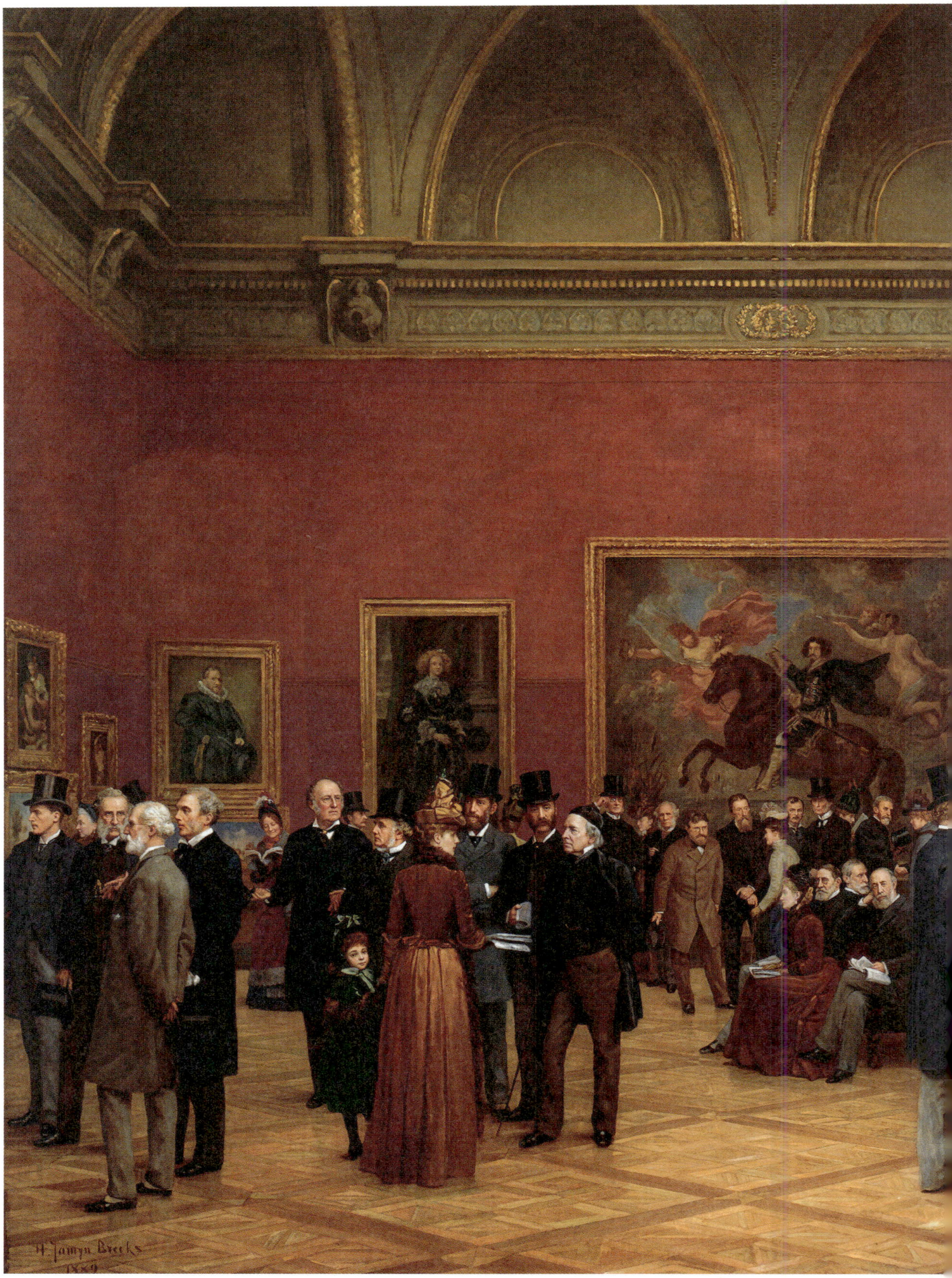

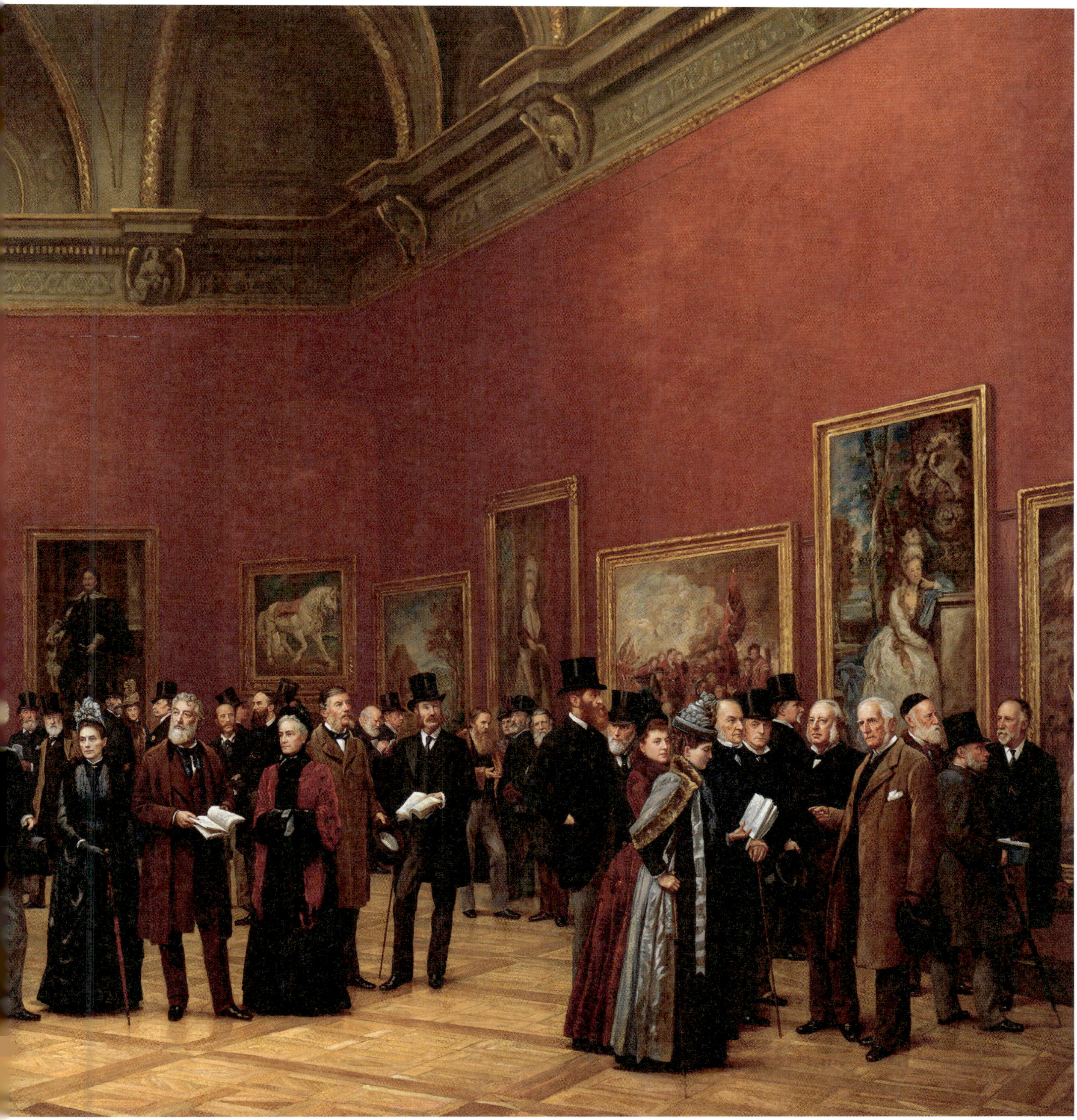

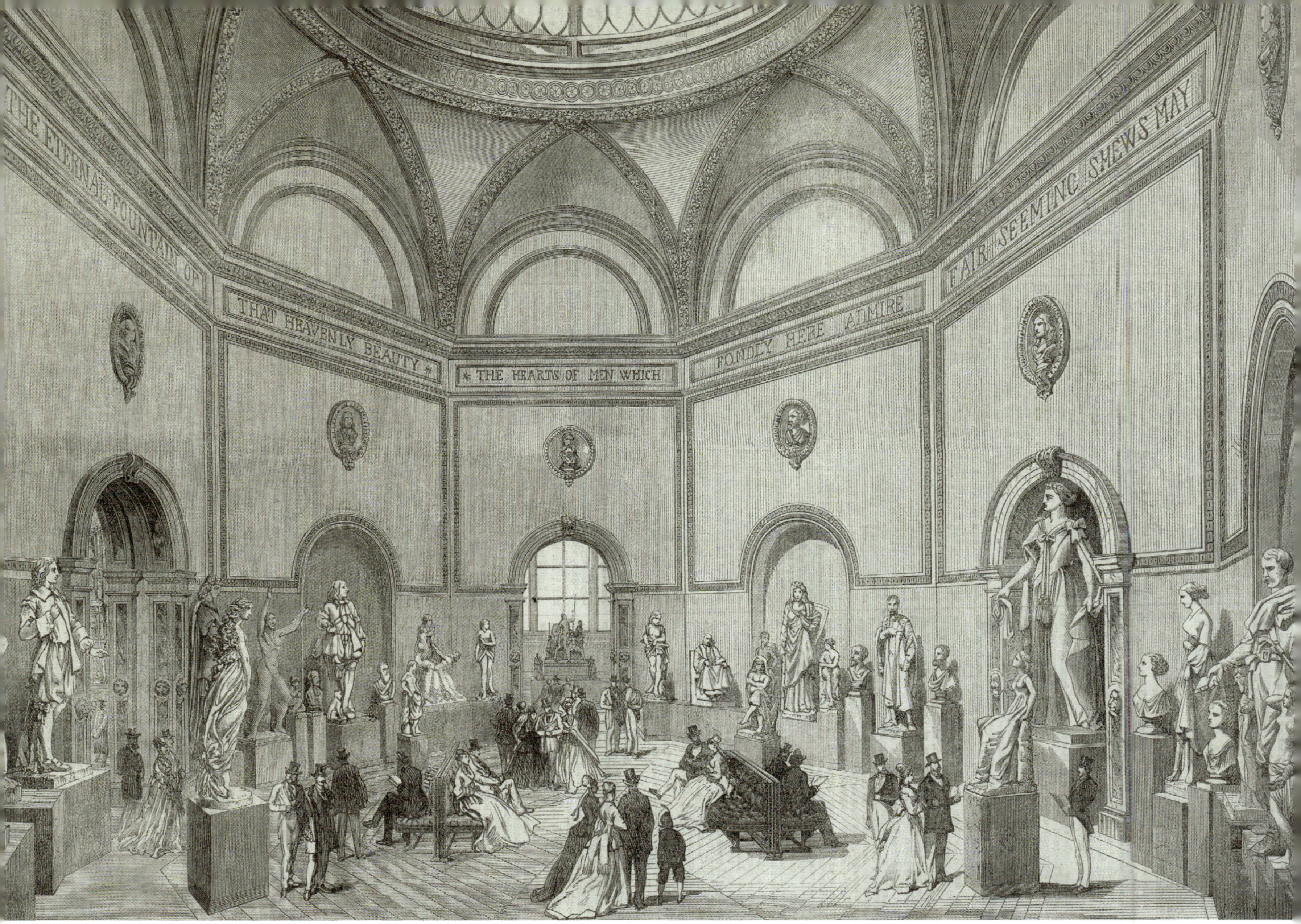

Fig. 229
The Central Hall of the Royal Academy (the Octagon), from *Illustrated London News*, 10 July 1869
Royal Academy of Arts, London, 06/4000

Fig. 230
Sydney Smirke, Royal Academy exhibition galleries and schools: design for the eight minor doorways, 1868.
Royal Academy of Arts, London, 07/1276

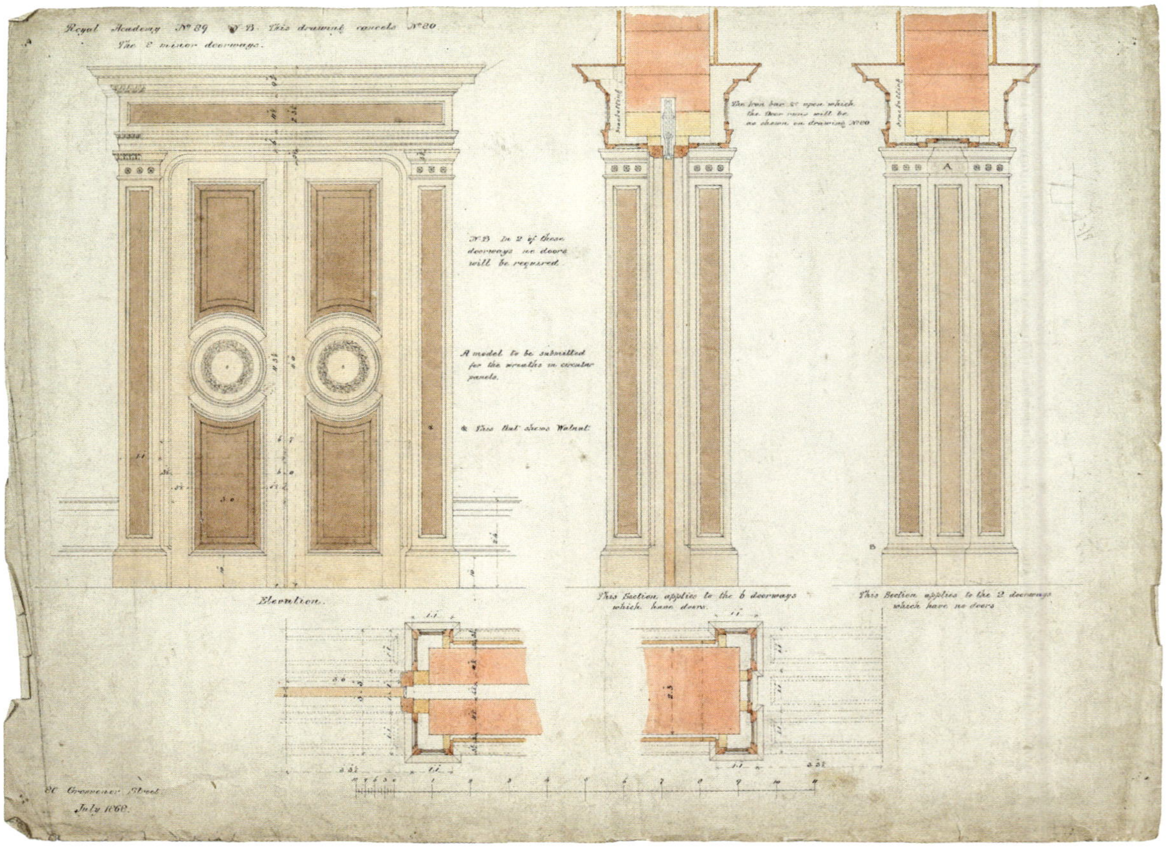

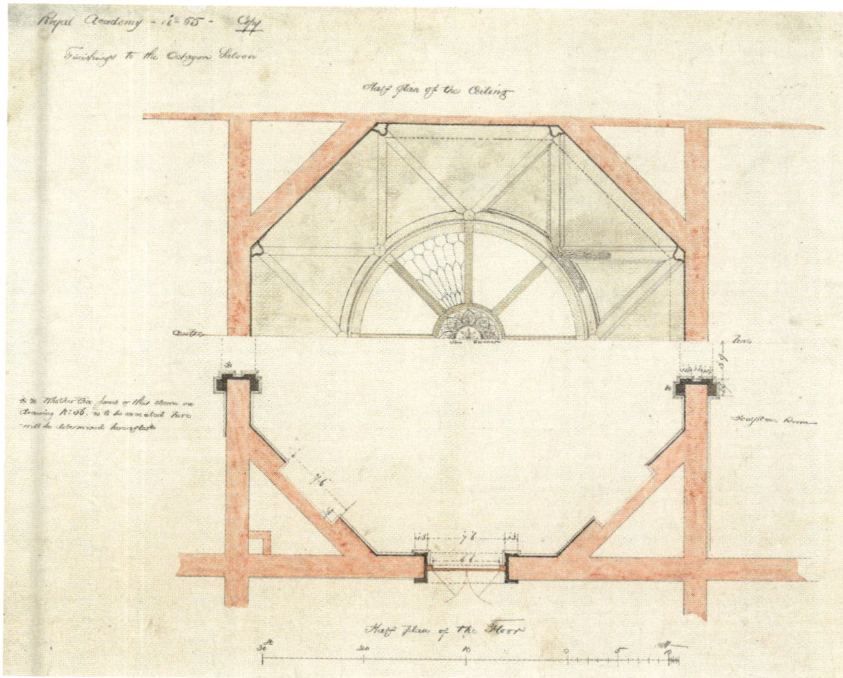

the only surviving clues to how Smirke arrived at his design is a plan and section dated July 1867 comparing 'the net width of lighting surface' in the Academy's North Room at Trafalgar Square with that of the Sheepshanks Gallery at South Kensington; some preliminary design sketches proposing alternative seating arrangements for the 'Lecture Room' to the east of the Octagon; and an undated watercolour perspective of Gallery III that may perhaps have been among the presentation drawings that Grant pinned up for the approval of the General Assembly on 27 March 1867 (Fig. 233).[76] The last shows that the introduction of half-length angel corbels in an otherwise classical cornice (Fig. 234) – no doubt part of the carved and modelled work for which Ruddock was paid £700 between 28 July 1868 and 23 March 1869[77] – probably arose out a structural need to strengthen the ceiling cross-beams, which in turn made it necessary for

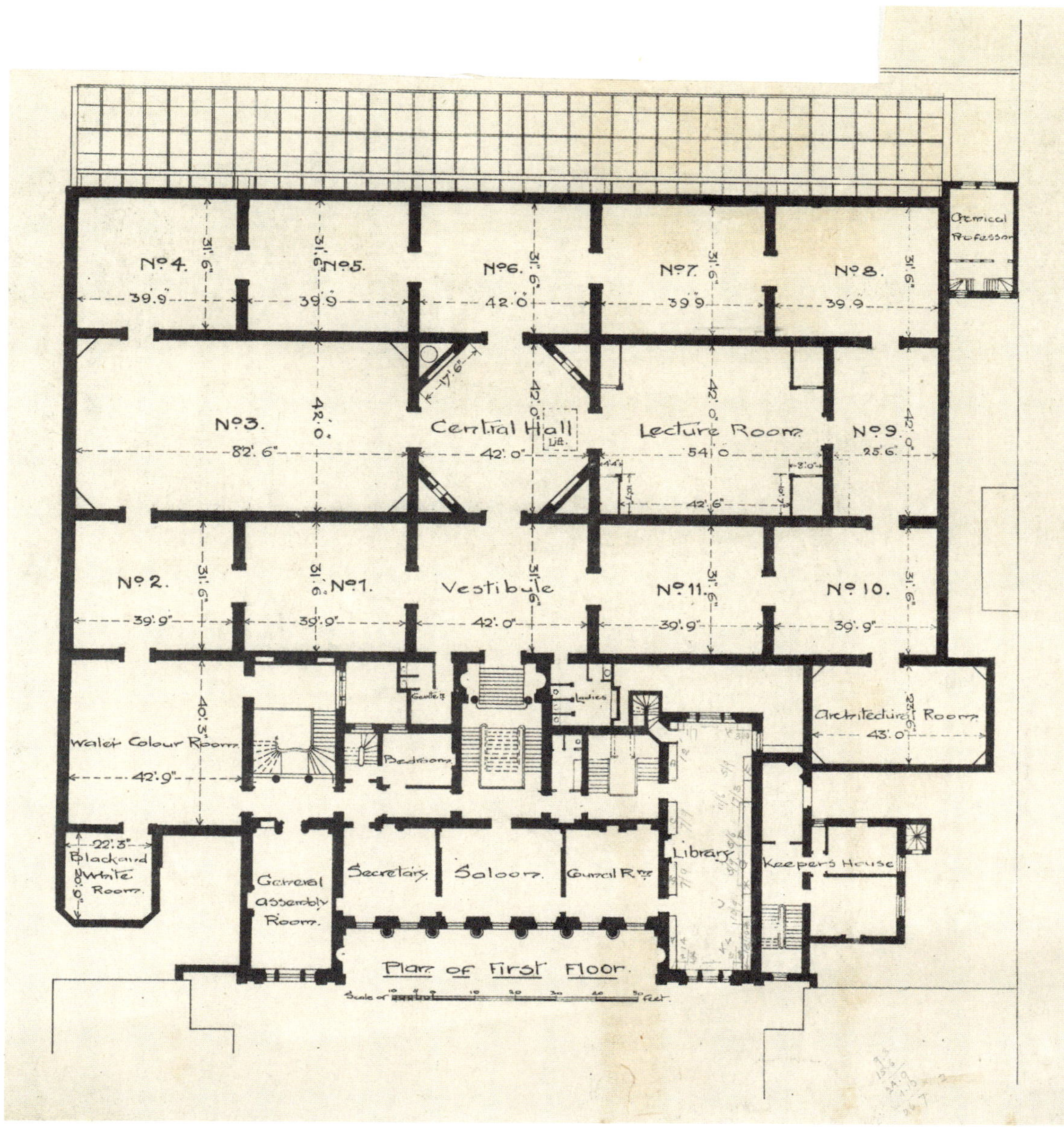

Fig. 231
Sydney Smirke, Royal Academy exhibition galleries and schools: half-plans of ceiling and floor of the Octagon, *c.* 1867.
Royal Academy of Arts, London, 07/1153

Fig. 232
Richard Phené Spiers (attrib.), Burlington House: first-floor plan, *c.* 1890.
Royal Academy of Arts, London, 16/2559

Fig. 233
Sydney Smirke, Perspective of Gallery III looking east, *c.* 1866–67.
Royal Academy of Arts, London, 05/2123

Fig. 234
Corbel in Gallery III, probably designed by S. J. Ruddock in 1868–69.
Photograph by Paul Highnam, 2010.
Royal Academy of Arts, London, 10/4576

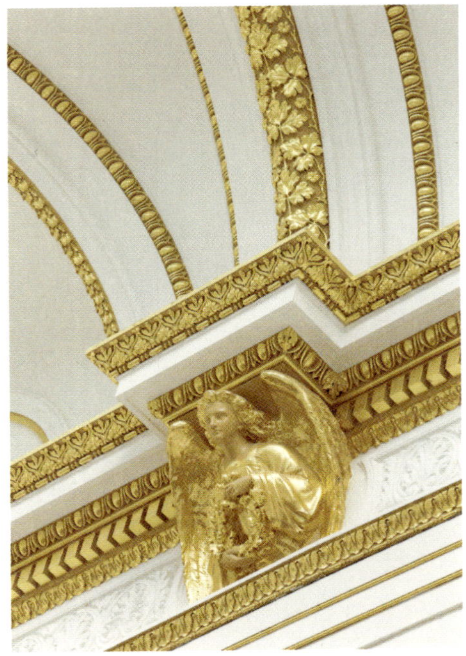

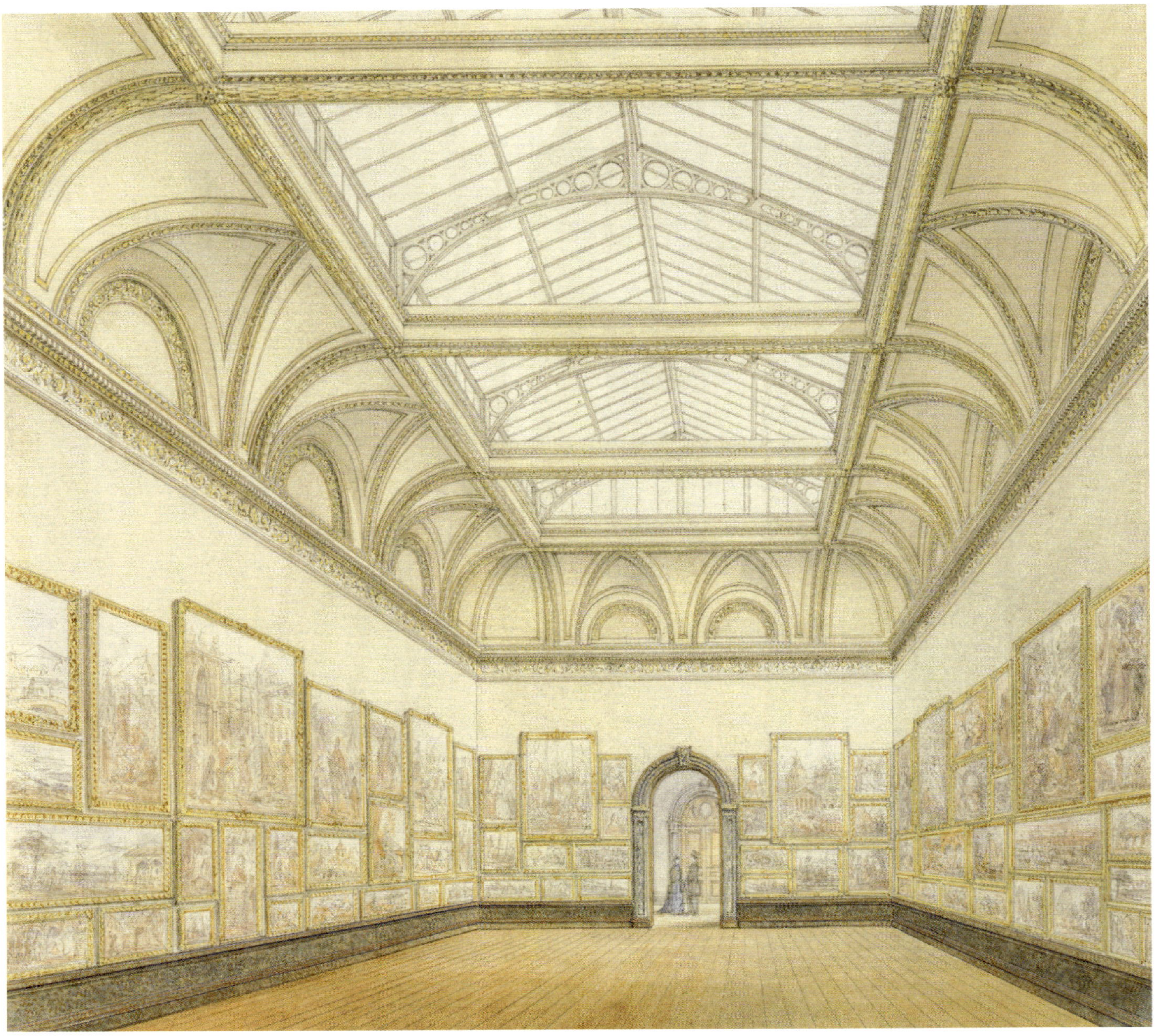

Fig. 235
'The Great Room at the Royal Academy' (Gallery III), from *Illustrated London News*, 3 July 1869.
Royal Academy of Arts, London, 06/4071

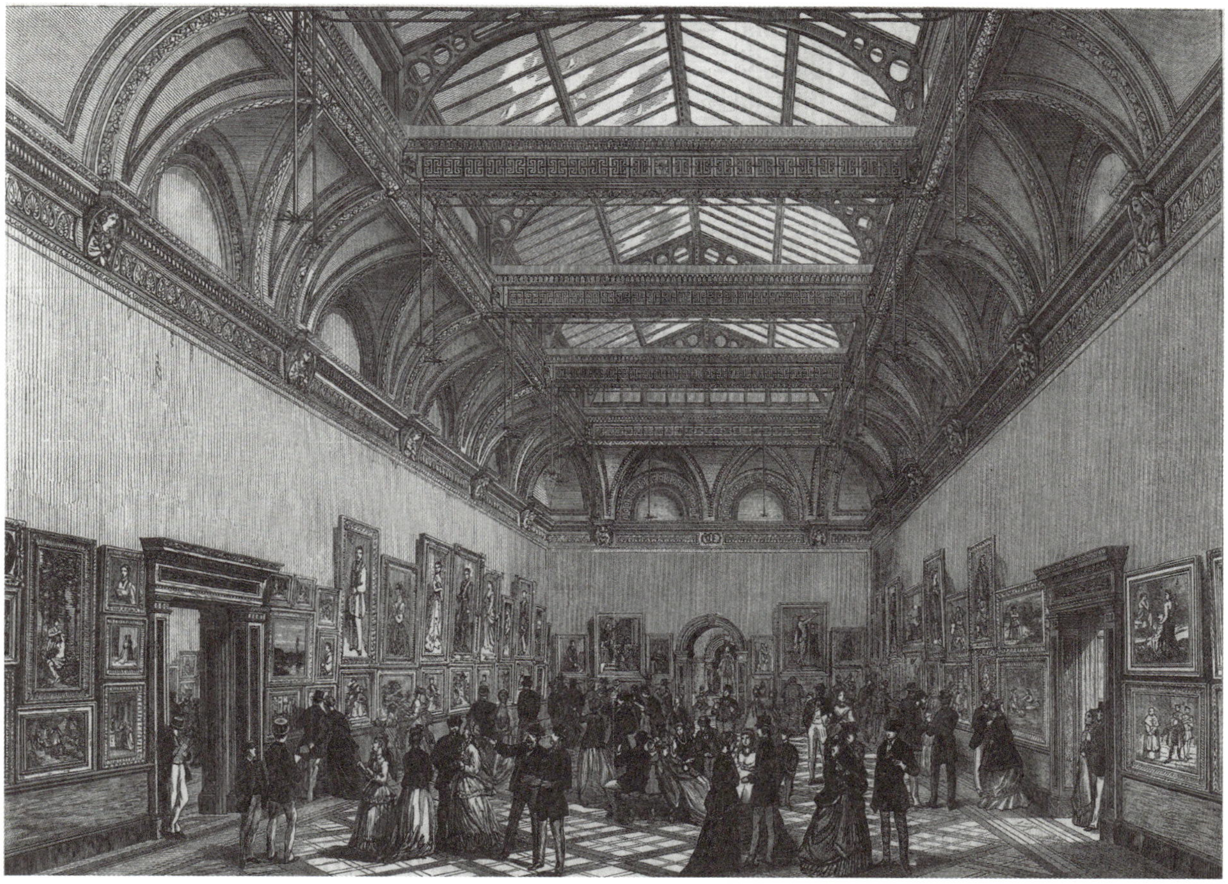

Fig. 236
Ludwig Gruner (after drawings by Federigo Lose), Church of Sta Euphemia at Pavia, from *The Terra-cotta Architecture of North Italy (XIIth–XVth centuries)*, 1867, pl. 1.
RIBA Collections, Library

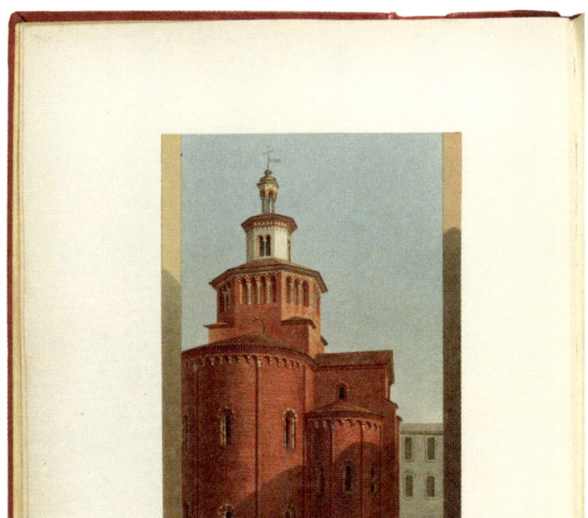

the cornice to break forward where it meets the resultant wider mouldings running down the cove from the corners of the rooflight (Fig. 235). To this somewhat meagre evidence of how Smirke's design evolved may be added the possibility that the Lombardic detailing of the exterior brickwork of Smirke's galleries (Figs 237–239) may have been inspired in part by the illustration and description of the 'Church of Sta Eufemia at Pavia' in Ludwig Gruner's *The Terra-cotta Architecture of North Italy* (1867), a copy of which was purchased for the Academy's library 'on the recommendation of Mr. Smirke' at a Council meeting on 5 August 1867 (Fig. 236).

The only embellishment of the new galleries by a Royal Academician was undertaken by Sir Edwin Landseer, who made, probably at his own suggestion (or possibly that of Grant who was a particular friend), 'a model of a Lions Head to be executed in bronze for the decoration of the door way in the Central Hall'. At least sixteen of these were cast – almost certainly by J. A. Hatfield who was paid £73 10s. on 17 June 1869 for 'Lions Heads'[78] – and inset in the roundels of the door jambs of the Octagon. Although no trace of them is evident today and none is known to have survived, they are visible in the wood-engraving published in the *Illustrated London News* on 10 July 1869 (see above, Fig. 229) and were still *in*

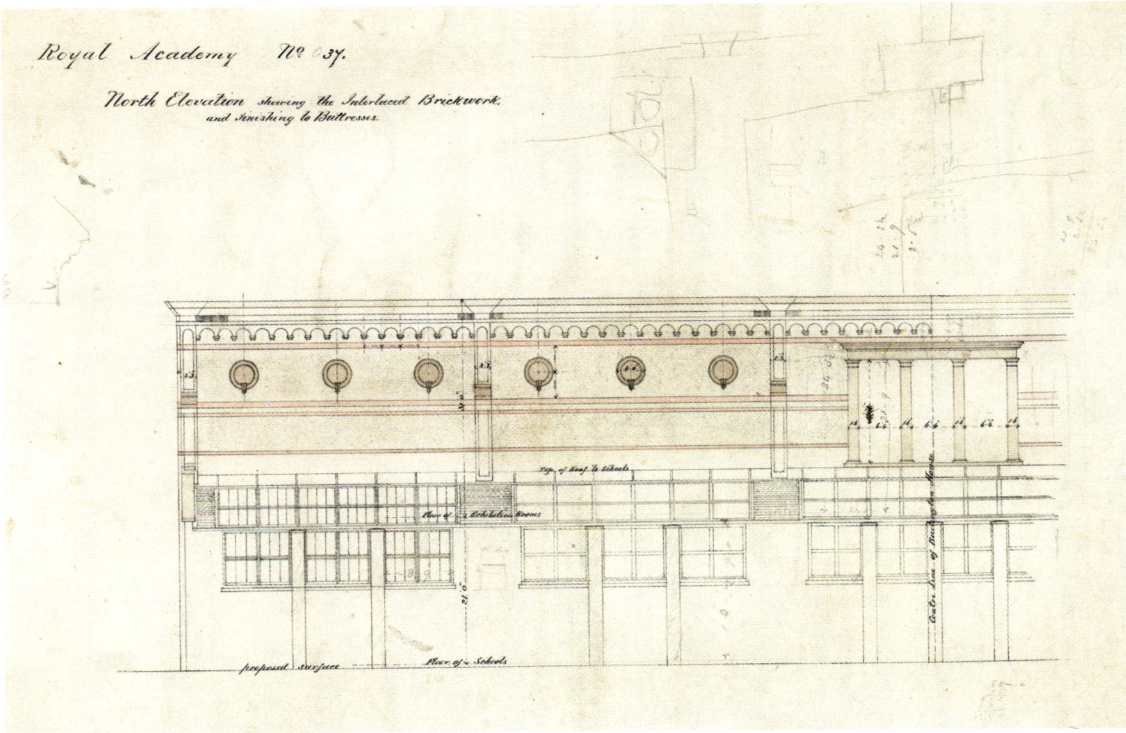

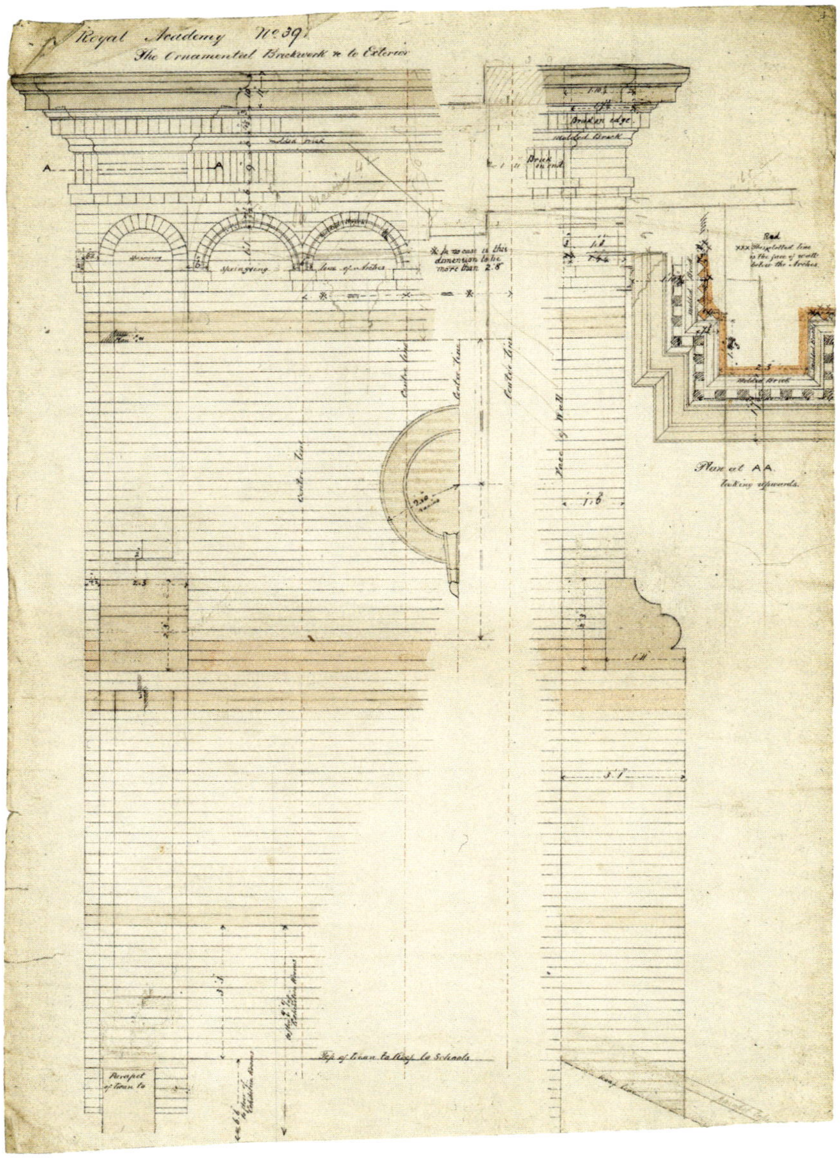

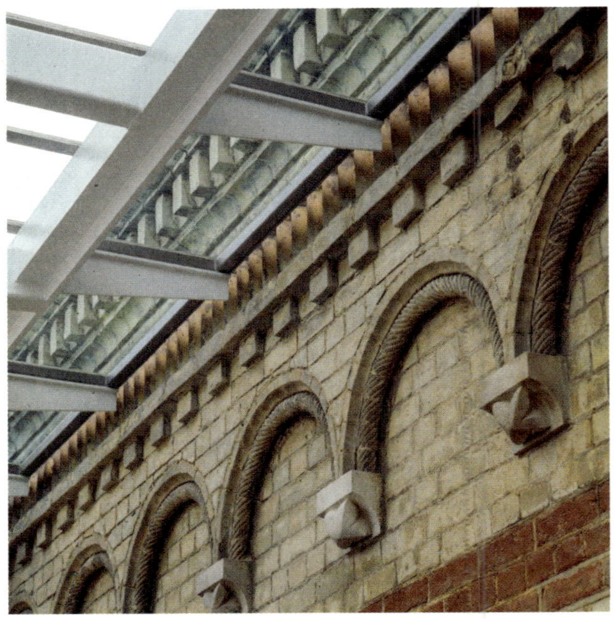

Fig. 237
Sydney Smirke, Royal Academy exhibition galleries and schools: north elevation showing the interlaced brickwork and finishings to buttresses, 1867.
Royal Academy of Arts, London, 07/1145

Fig. 238
Sydney Smirke, Royal Academy exhibition galleries and schools: part-plan, part-elevation and detail of ornamental brickwork and roundel to exterior, 1868.
Royal Academy of Arts, London, 07/1148

Fig. 239
Royal Academy exhibition galleries: cornice of south elevation showing the junction with the Sackler Landing floor, designed by Foster Associates and Julian Harrap, 1991. Photograph by Richard Davies.
Foster + Partners, London

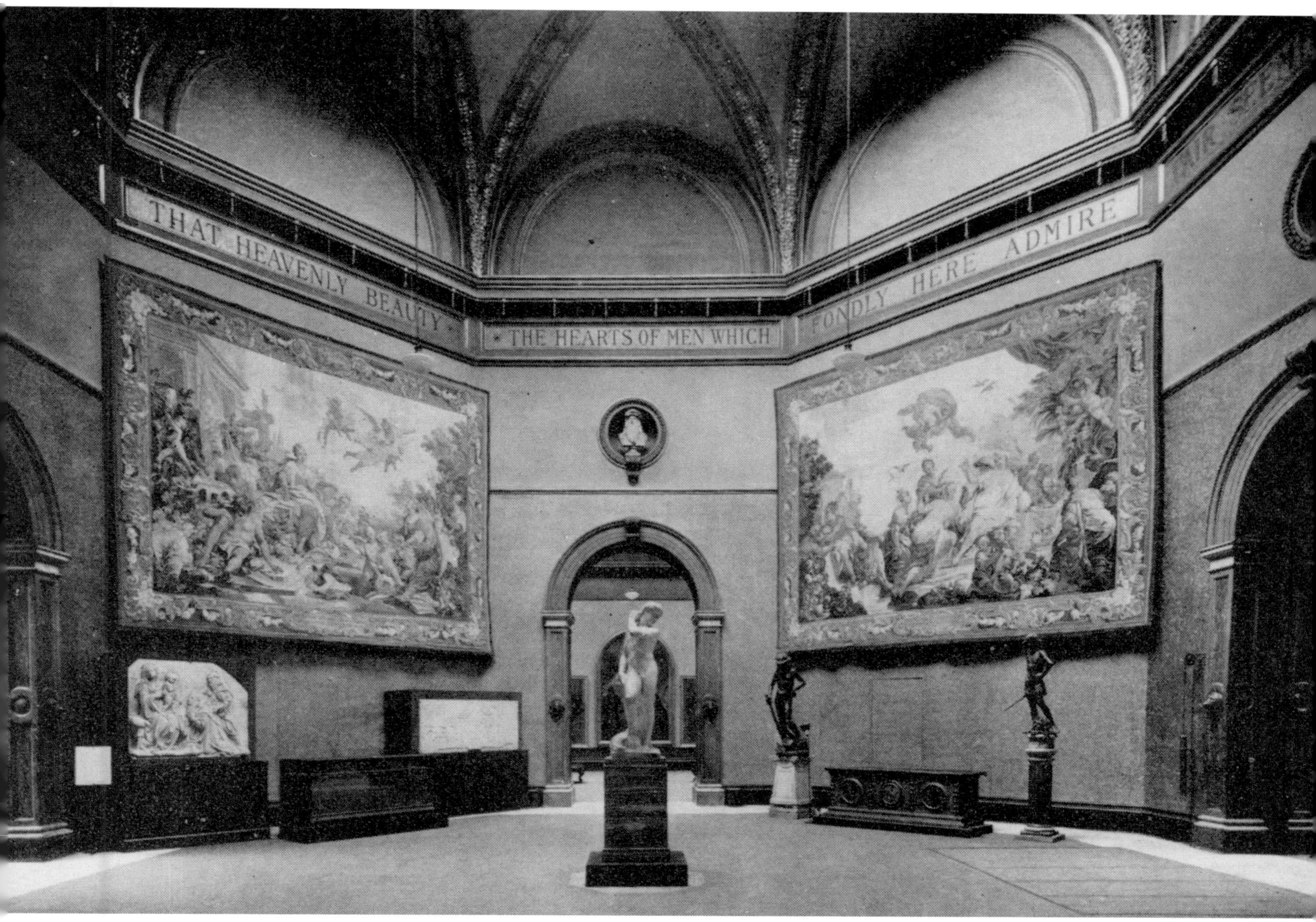

Fig. 240
'Exhibition of Italian Art 1200–1900'. installation in the Octagon, 1930.
Royal Academy of Arts, London, 12/305

situ at the time of the 1930 'Exhibition of Italian Art 1200–1900' (Fig. 240). Criticised by a reviewer in the *Illustrated London News* as 'not one of the artist's happiest efforts, the character seems to partake something of the canine type',[79] they had nonetheless a particular resonance, not only because they alluded to the already famous 'Landseer Lions' that had, after much tribulation, been installed at the foot of Nelson's Column in Trafalgar Square just two years before, but also because of the attention they drew to the way sculpture had been given pride of place in the exhibition. Thus, in sharp contrast to the notorious 'dungeon' into which it had been long banished in the Trafalgar Square building, sculpture was now arrayed along the entire central axis of the exhibition. While one critic in the *Illustrated London News* complained that the vertical light from the dome in the 'Central Hall' (i.e. Octagon) gave 'To the living subject ... a ghastly hollow-eyed aspect' and was therefore an 'inexplicable' mistake, others in general approved of the fact that the visitor was greeted by 'some of the best of the busts' in the Vestibule, and that a large triple window in the centre of the north wall of the new building allowed the optimum 45° angle of light to penetrate an exclusively designated 'Sculpture Gallery' (later Gallery VI).[80]

To judge from early plans published in *The Builder* in February 1869 (Fig. 241), it was originally intended to reserve Galleries IX and X for watercolours and architectural drawings respectively, to meet longstanding criticism of the poor representation of these genres in the exhibition. The Academy's laudable intentions were soon frustrated by what now seems an anomaly, in that the second largest of Smirke's 'noble suite of rooms' was not a gallery at all. Lying to the east of the Octagon and thus corresponding to Gallery III (i.e. the new 'Great

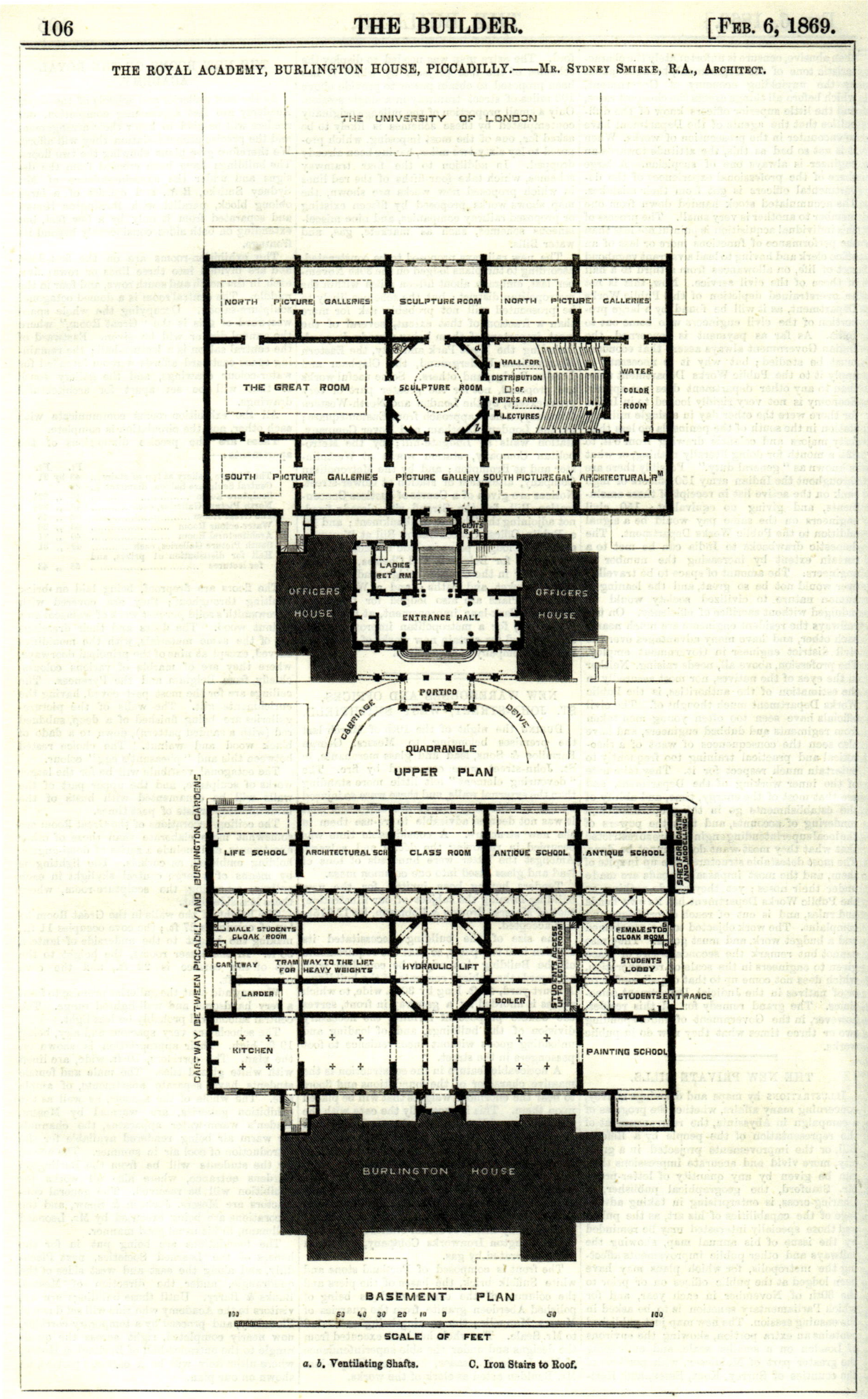

Fig. 241
Royal Academy exhibition galleries and schools, designed by Sydney Smirke: plans of the principal and basement floors, from *The Builder*, 6 February 1869, vol. 27, p. 106.
RIBA Collections, Periodicals

Room') in the central range, the Academy's first ever permanent lecture theatre could hardly have been given a more prominent position in the building. According to the published plan just referred to (which would have been based on information supplied by the architect), it was to have been accessible by the public either from the Octagon or from one of two doorways in the 'Watercolour Room' (i.e. Gallery IX), while a small door in the south wall, intended but perhaps never executed, would have provided private access to the lecturer's podium from the 'South Picture Gallery' (i.e. Gallery XI, now the RA Bookshop).[81] To preserve decorum on public occasions as much as for the sake of convenience, the Academy students had their own entrance via a spiral staircase in the basement that came up through a trapdoor in the floor, thereby avoiding any danger of disorderly mingling with the Academicians' guests. All in all, there can be little doubt that the Academy's 'Lecture Room' (as it was known) was intended from the outset to be a formal public space not dissimilar in purpose from the permanent lecture theatre opened by the Queen in 6 Burlington Gardens a year later.

Today's Summer Exhibition Hanging Committee benefits from 150 years of inherited wisdom about how the Academy's galleries work. Not surprisingly therefore, the 'Committee of Arrangement' for the first exhibition in the new building found it 'impossible to calculate the available space relatively to the works to be placed.'[82] Its task was made doubly difficult by a new policy 'that every picture should be more or less separated by intervening wall space, and that no picture should be hung with its base line higher than 12 feet from the ground.' A further problem was that a place had to be found for every 'accepted' work, unlike in previous years when it was common for well over a hundred in this category to be returned to the artist unhung due to lack of space. Despite intense pressure from critics in the press and Parliament, the Academicians had always resisted the demand that they reduce the number of works they were entitled to exhibit in order to make room for accepted works by non-members, on the grounds that this was a problem that would go away once they had more exhibition space in a new building. By the time Galleries I to IV had been hung, however, any idea of leaving inches of wall space around each picture had to be abandoned, and the hangers were faced with no choice but to commandeer the Lecture Room despite the fact that much of it was taken up by a 'graduated floor'. Here the exhibition concluded, in much the same way as it had done at Trafalgar Square, with a gallimaufry of paintings, miniatures, architectural drawings, engravings, etchings, and 'oddities' impossible to place elsewhere, such as no less than 50 Egyptian travel sketches by the Royal Academician Frederick Goodall.

Initial press reaction to Smirke's galleries was overwhelmingly positive, leading one reviewer in *The Times* to declare that 'No European capital can now boast a more commodious and noble suite of rooms for its yearly display of painting and sculpture than London now possesses',[83] and another in the *Daily News* to aver that

> As one of our national public buildings, the Academy promises to be one of the most ornamental and best proportioned in the metropolis, and of its fitness it may be said that the unanimous opinion by all who visited the exhibition, and walked through the magnificent galleries, was that they far surpassed all the picture galleries in existence.[84]

Smirke's satisfaction on reading the latter notice would have been somewhat spoilt once he realised its author had been fooled into thinking the University of London's new building belonged to the Academy. And unfortunately, whatever credit he and the Academy had gained on account of the new building was to vanish overnight when the story got around that in spite of an estimated three times more space and a record number of submissions, the exhibition included 'upwards of one hundred' fewer oil paintings by non-member artists than in the previous year, while those by Academicians and associates had increased by 47.[85] Worse still, if one took into account the fact that there were 60 more paintings by foreign artists than in the previous year and assuming an equivalent proportion of accepted works as then, the number of pictures by non-member British artists had fallen by as much as 400. This was nothing less than a public-relations disaster, especially since Grant had proclaimed at the Annual Dinner just days before that 'we [the Academicians] recognise with infinite satisfaction the vast amount of talent among those who are commonly, though I think improperly, spoken of as outside the Academy' and that 'No artist should consider themselves outside this institution.'[86]

Not surprisingly as soon as the exhibition closed, Smirke was instructed by the General Assembly to replace the 'graduated floor' of the Lecture Room and to

> render the space afforded by the walls ... available for the purposes of the Annual Exhibition – by means of which a vista will be opened up from the 3rd Gallery into the Water Colour Gallery – and also for the conversion of the Class Room into the purposes of a Lecture Room.[87]

Finding room in which to hold lectures in the newly opened Schools would not be easy, since just six weeks before this instruction Frederic Leighton, currently serving his first term as a member of the Council, had drawn the latter's attention to a serious problem in the Painting School, which he claimed was already so overcrowded that only half the students in the class could work from the same model. A month after the General Assembly's decision to dismantle the Lecture Room, Smirke wrote to Pennethorne, admitting rather forlornly that 'we (the RA) are sadly in want of more room' and asking whether they could agree to relax a condition in the lease restricting the height of an extension he proposed to make to the Schools within twelve feet of the Academy's boundary with the University.[88] Pennethorne however was in no mood to budge, pointing out to Layard somewhat sanctimoniously:

> It should be remembered that the condition is reciprocal, and that when the University was built, the President & Architect of the Academy interfered to prevent even the slightest encroachment being made – therefore the Academy have no right to any special consideration ...[89]

Although the most dramatic increase in Academy student numbers did not occur until the mid-1870s – between 1873 and 1877 the annual attendance of students in the Painting School rose from 2,806 to 4,160 – the roots of this expansion stemmed from the determination of more progressive members – which, despite his conservative instincts as an artist, included the president – that the long-deferred reform of the Schools could and should coincide with their move to Burlington House. When therefore, thanks to the concerted efforts of Leighton, Redgrave, Street and Cope, the General Assembly approved on 3 January 1870 the most radical extension of the teaching curriculum in the Academy's history, providing for the first time instruction in the technical aspects of oil painting, modelling and architectural composition, as well as new incentives for the practise of mural painting, it was clear that the success of these initiatives depended first and foremost on sufficient space in the new building. As a result, not long after 'the new Laws relating to the preliminary class' came into effect on 1 January 1871, the Council resolved 'that the room designed and set apart as the Lecture Room according to the Architect's plans approved by General Assembly, be furnished as the Academy Lecture Hall as originally intended', and on 17 July adopted the School Committee's recommendation that 'for the purpose of providing a remedy for the present inadequate accommodation in the painting schools ... the Lectures be in future delivered in the room originally destined for that purpose.'[90] However, the following February Redgrave's motion proposing that 'the present lecture room, be continued as a lecture theatre, and not used for hanging part of the modern exhibition', failed to carry.[91]

IF THE ADJACENCY OF Jackson & Shaw's two sites at the back of Burlington House between 1866 and 1869 aided the rapid build of the Academy's galleries, quite the reverse was true at the front of the house where what one journalist aptly described as 'masonic chaos' reigned supreme, from the arrival of Mansfield & Price's demolition crew in July 1868 through to the installation of the Midland Iron Company's great gates in the Piccadilly archway in December 1873. Until the courtyard was finally paved and macadamed, probably in the autumn of that year, the only authorised pedestrian route in or out of Burlington House was along a fourteen-foot-wide glass-roofed 'covered way' which ran down the centre of the courtyard to the front door of the house (Fig. 243). Somewhat superior to an ordinary building-site board-walk – it had a gabled portico on Piccadilly, waxed floorboards, coconut matting and had even been used by the Queen when she paid a private visit to the exhibition in its second week (Fig. 242) – it was nonetheless lampooned in the *Daily Telegraph* as resembling 'nothing half so much as a corridor in a county gaol'.[92] Like all such temporary structures, it parodied what it was a substitute for, i.e. the processional route that Grant hankered after. That it must have deterred visitors in the meantime is apparent from the fact that the Academy's attendance figures shot up in 1874, the first year that it was possible to avoid slipping on awkward steps and be certain of entering Burlington House with 'cleaner shoes'.

Apart from converting two windows on the south front into doors, slightly widening the doorway from the entrance hall into the existing staircase lobby (Fig. 244), and extending the main staircase on through the central window of the north front to connect with the Academy's new building, Smirke could not touch the interior of Burlington House until the societies' new building was ready to receive them. Although under the terms of its lease the Academy's right to occupy Burlington House had been deferred for a maximum of three years to allow for this to happen, by the time work eventually started in the courtyard some fourteen months behind schedule it was obvious that there was virtually no chance of the societies moving out in that time. Keen to hasten progress in any way possible, Grant made an offer to General Sir Edward Sabine, the current president of the Royal Society, which, had it been accepted, would have much pleased Gladstone:

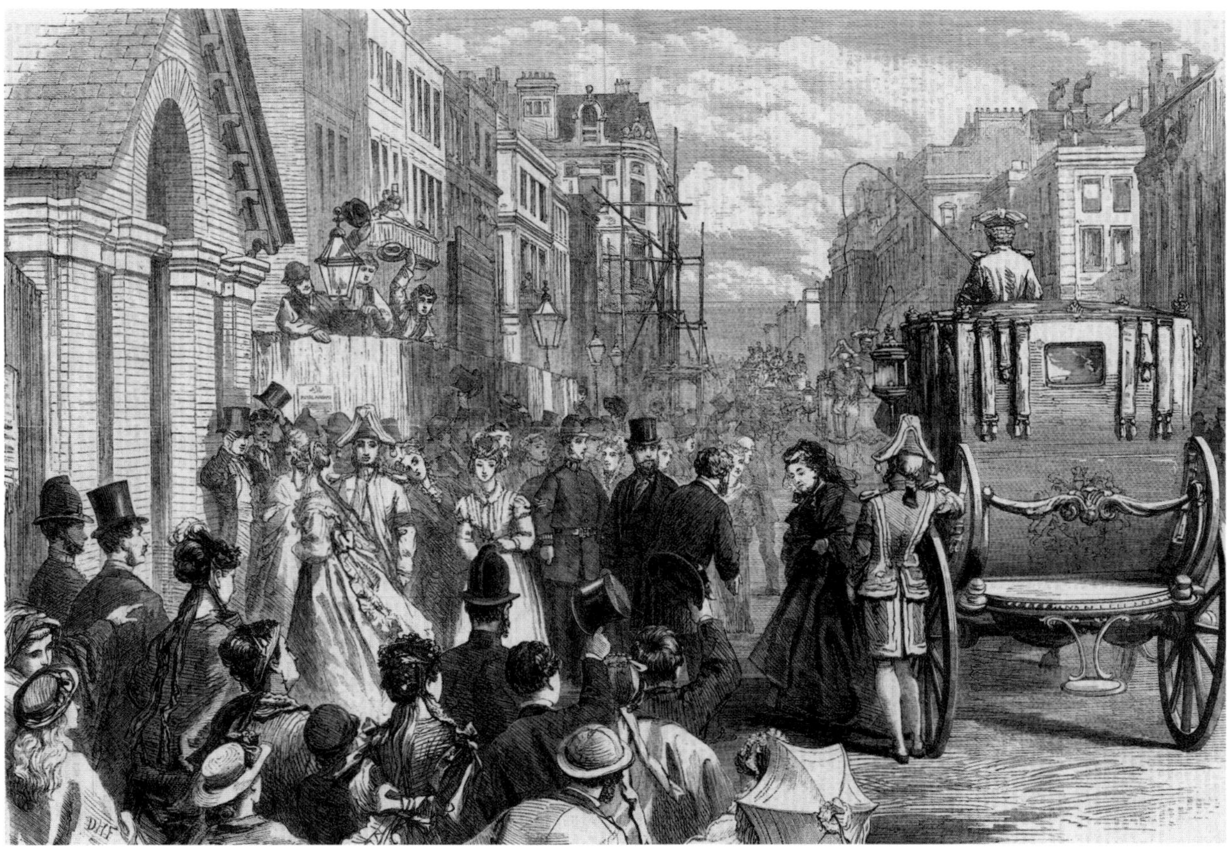

Fig. 242
'The Queen's arrival at Burlington House to inspect the Royal Academy exhibition', from *Illustrated Times*, 22 May 1869, p. 329.
Linnean Library, London

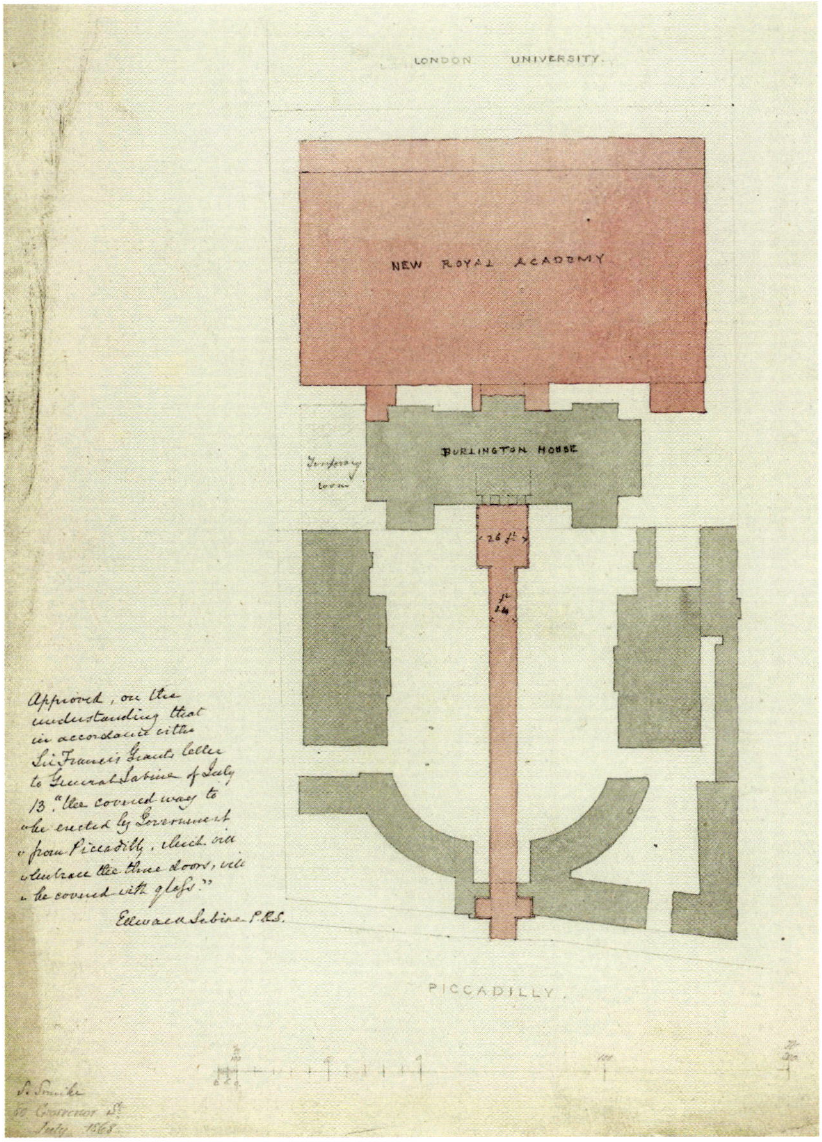

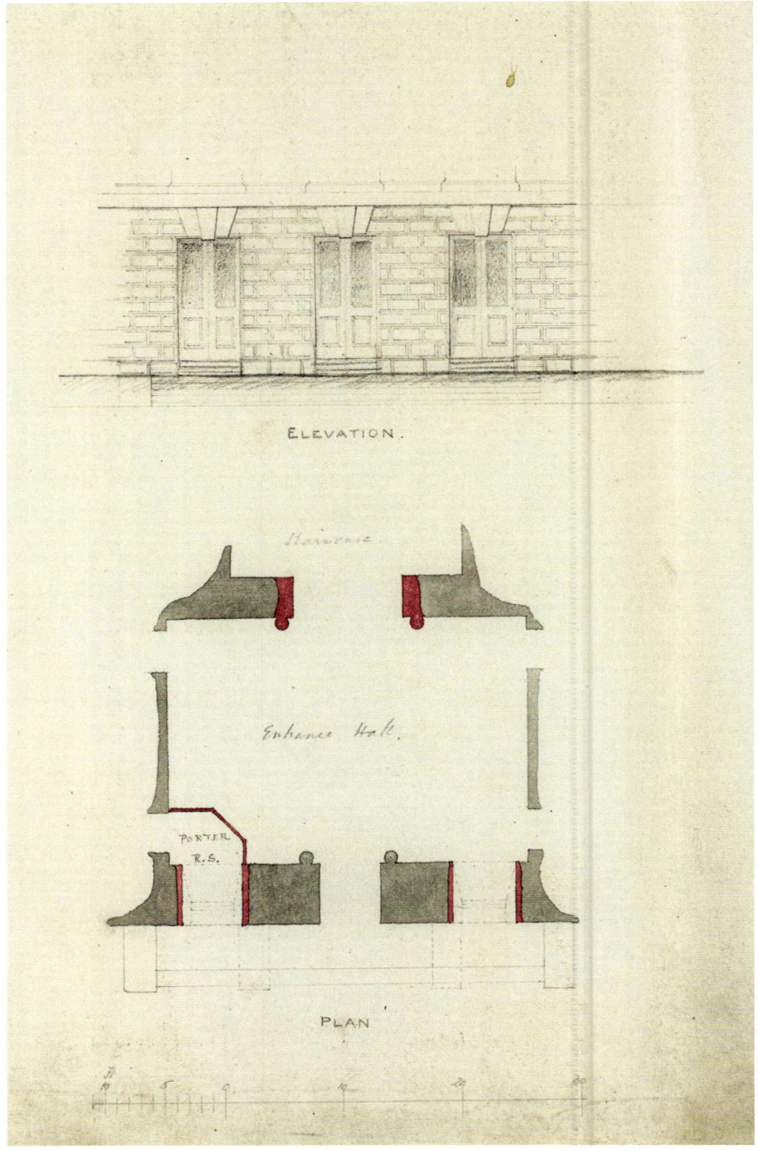

There is one point which makes us [?] a little unhappy and that is the necessity of maintaining the meeting room & lower library of the Royal Society undisturbed until the Society is accommodated in their new house.

This will make it 5 or 6 years before the whole group is completed. This will be really as great a source of discomfort to the Royal Society as to the Royal Academy & the other learned societies.

If you had the advantage of a large room to meet in on certain occasions, could not the books in the lower library find accommodation elsewhere?

If so I think I have a way of escape from the difficulty. The Royal Academy in their new Galleries intend to devote a very large room in the centre of the building to be a permanent Lecture Room, & I feel sure the academy would be only too happy, during the next three years, to allow the Royal Society, & also the Geographical & Civil Engineers the use of that room, on occasions of their great gatherings.

I merely throw this out as a suggestion for your consideration, for I have not yet mentioned the idea to the Council of the Royal Academy.[93]

Grant's suggestion was probably as impracticable as Gladstone's idea of shared meeting rooms had been in 1854, not least because, as General Sabine pointed out, apart from the president's soirées (i.e. the 'great gatherings' with which Grant would have been familiar as a guest), 'our meetings prescribed by Charter are weekly from Nov. to June, with receptions of one week each at Christmas, Easter & Whitsuntide'.[94] However, it does suggest that for a while there was a possibility that the Academy's 'permanent Lecture Room' might have assumed the mantle of the Royal Society's large meeting room in the west wing. As it turned out, the Academy gave permission instead for the Office of Works to erect for the Society's use, 'a temporary room in the vacant space adjoining the west side of Burlington House' (see Fig. 243) which, Banks & Barry assured them, 'shall

Fig. 243
Sydney Smirke, Block plan of a proposed temporary covered way across the courtyard, July 1868.
RIBA Drawings Collection SC95/18(7)

Fig. 244
Sydney Smirke, Design for partitioning the entrance hall to form separate doorways for the Royal Society and the Royal Academy, July 1868.
RIBA Drawings Collection SC95/18(8)

be at least equal to that of the present lower library, or meeting room, and around the sides of which can be ranged the present bookcases with their contents.'[95]

For a time, it looked as though the University might need a similar building for their autumn exams. Although this did not prove the case – Pennethorne was able to assure them in early July 1868 that at least four rooms in their new building would have 'an efficient means of Warming and Lighting' by the last week of October[96] – when Grant wrote to Barry on 20 June 1868 he had been worried that a temporary building for the University on the east side of Burlington House would interfere with the Academy's intention to 'erect a laboratory' nearby.[97] His concern stemmed from the fact that the General Assembly had resolved on 24 March 1866 to accept the 1863 Royal Commission's recommendation 'that there should be a Chymist and a Laboratory attached to the Academy to submit colors and vehicles to practical tests, ... the question of space alone preventing its adoption'. The failure to provide for this in the new building had become even more embarrassing in the light of Lady Eastlake's gift in January 1867 of 'a collection of pigments and varnishes &c. formed by the late Sir Charles Eastlake, with a view to chemical examination, ... which she conceived might form the nucleus for the Chemical laboratory proposed to be instituted in the Royal Academy.'[98]

On New Year's Day 1870, Smirke summed up what remained to be done with some carefully chosen words:

> The arrangements are, I believe, now as complete as they can be made, until the Royal Academy comes into possession of the old mansion, when no doubt very important improvements can be made, both for increasing the public accommodation, for extending the Schools, and for enlarging the Exhibition.[99]

It is striking that the focus of these 'very important improvements' is unrelated to, and extends well beyond, the Academy's existing commitment to add another storey to the house, build a chemical laboratory, and provide living quarters for the keeper of the Schools. What Smirke does not reveal, for obvious reasons, is the fact that he had withdrawn from the Academy's Building Committee in March 1869 because of disagreement over the nature and extent of the work that remained to be done.[100] Nothing is known in any detail of Smirke's envisaged 'improvements' apart from what can be gathered from a cross-section and perspective sketch in the RIBA Drawings Collection and two fragmentary drawings on tracing paper in the Academy's collection. However, taken together these are enough to indicate that what he had in mind amounted to the most radical alteration to the 'old mansion' since Campbell and Kent's work for Lord Burlington.

Probably the earliest of Smirke's proposals was for a monumental top-lit staircase, the most remarkable feature of which was the way it would have served the galleries only, giving no access to the first floor of the house and indeed suppressing all evidence of the latter's existence (Fig. 245). The effect aimed for seems to have been an amalgam of Pennethorne's 1861 staircase to the Academy's exhibition rooms in Trafalgar Square with the entrance-hall staircase that Smirke had designed (and L. W. Collman decorated) for the British Museum a quarter of a century earlier. Taking as a starting point the fact that the return flights of the existing staircase were currently screened off to preserve the privacy of the learned societies,[101] Smirke's new staircase was clearly intended to be the finale of the processional route announced by Banks & Barry's triumphal arch on Piccadilly. By October 1871, however, rather than cut the house in half, he was proposing to replace Ware's *démodé*, domestic-scaled imperial staircase with a top-lit, modern club-house equivalent in marble that would probably have been not dissimilar from the one that Pennethorne had recently designed for the University of London in 6 Burlington Gardens (Fig. 246, and see above, Fig. 205). To reflect more appropriately the Academy's new use of Burlington House, Smirke suggested that two of its own full-size copies of Raphael's Hampton Court tapestry cartoons might be hung in place of the Ricci canvases.

It was almost certainly this later design, or something close to it, that Grant referred to as 'a handsome architectural entrance lighted from above' during the course of a long letter in December 1872 to Douglas Galton,

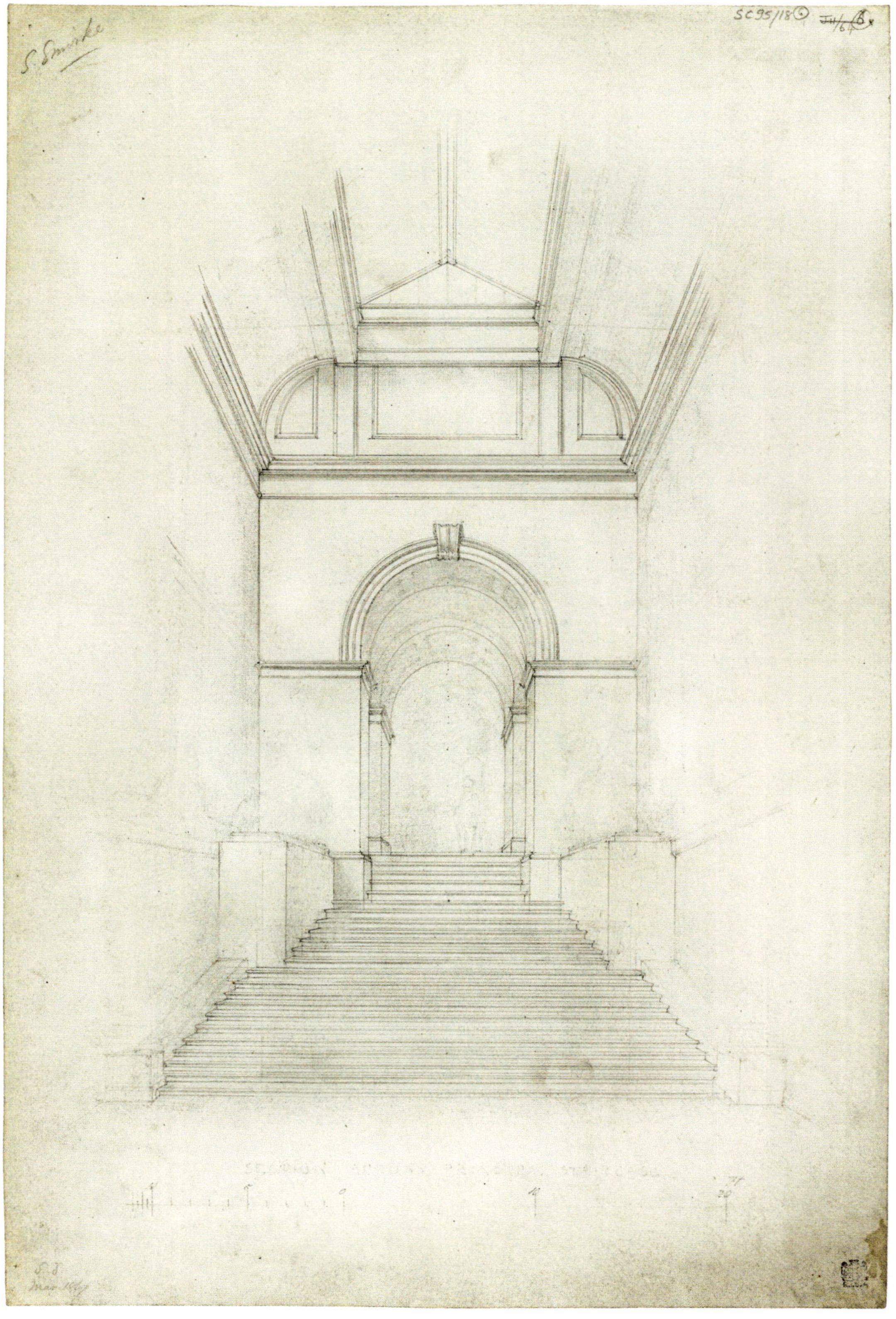

Fig. 245
Sydney Smirke, Preliminary design for the new main staircase, probably 1869: perspective sketch
RIBA Drawings Collection
SC 95/18(6)

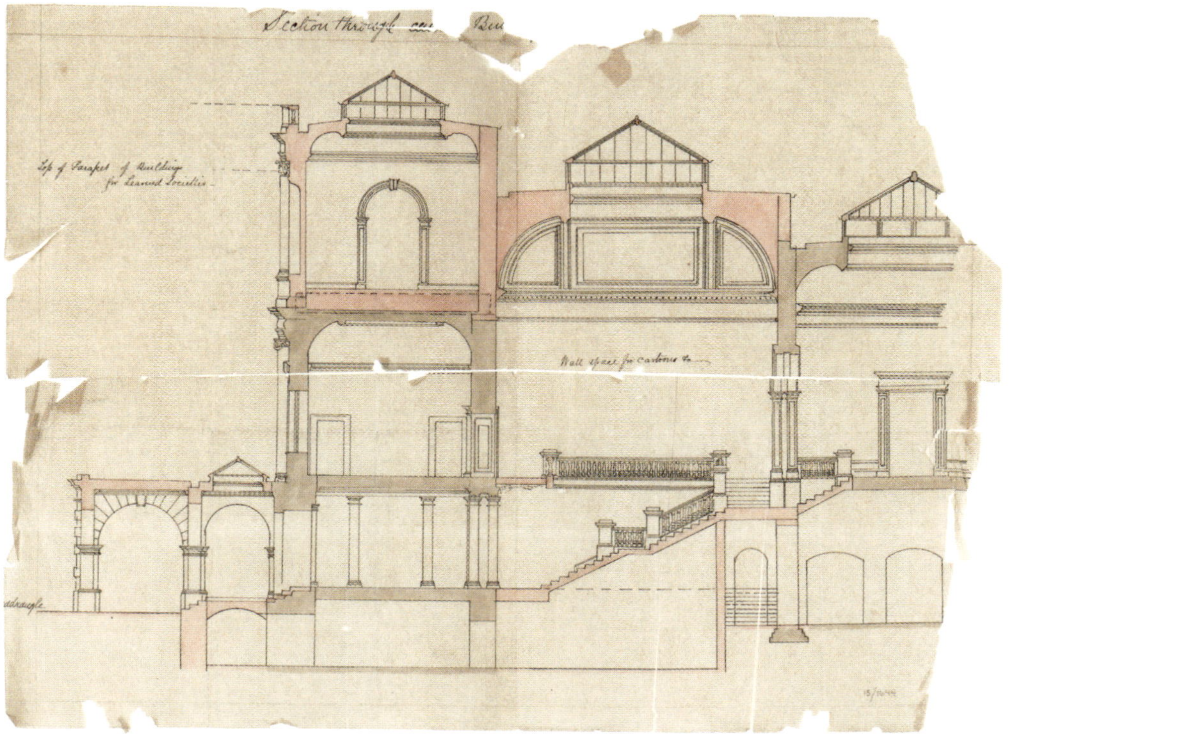

Fig. 246
Sydney Smirke, Alterations and additions to Burlington House (unexecuted design for *porte-cochère* and new main staircase): section looking west, 1871.
Royal Academy of Arts, London, 15/1644

Director of Works and Public Buildings under Ayrton, complaining most bitterly of continuing mayhem in the courtyard:

> I have been with our architect Mr Smirke all the forenoon at Burlington House and he has quite explained to me all his wants which are very simple. He requires one quarter of the quadrangle abutting Burlington House – on the day after it is cleared he is prepared to commence building the arcade entrance. He would have been glad to have done this two months since if it had not been for the confusion ... which Messrs Banks and Barry have created in the Quadrangle. This will require the removal of their office and some sheds in which some people of theirs dwell in, constantly burning fires with two iron chimneys immediately adjoining the inflammable temporary passage ...
>
> ... I cannot help protesting earnestly on the part of the Academy against Messrs Banks and Barry's conduct in for 6 or 7 months occupying the Quadrangle and rendering a chaos and confusion to enable them to carry on other works having nothing to do with the buildings of the Learned Societies, but which I understand are for a circus for a Mr Cook who organises tourist expeditions whilst they have been most remiss in carrying on the internal work, an opinion in which I am happy to find you entirely agreed with me.
>
> ... He [i.e. Smirke] writes to me: 'Shall you or I ever live to see all this chaos ever come to an end? You will, I have no doubt, but that I shall see the end of it is very doubtful indeed.' I am equally despondent.[102]

In spite of these sombre reflections on *ars longa, vita brevis,* neither Grant nor Smirke could have foreseen that less than a fortnight later, Barry's business partner, Robert Richardson Banks, would precede both of them to the grave.

The building of Smirke's portico or 'arcade entrance', to which Grant refers in the above letter – it included a projecting central canopy (now removed) supported by masonry brackets decorated with bas-reliefs carved by John Birnie Philip[103] (Fig. 247) – formed the third and final phase of the works that Jackson & Shaw undertook for the Academy working solely from outside the house. This meant that the long-suffering occupants of the building were surrounded above, below, and on all sides by continuous building work from at least 1 April 1872, when Thomas Farrar was appointed clerk of the works for 'the erection of the New Story upon Burlington House', to the symbolic moment on 24 October 1873, when 'the keys of the apartments occupied by the Royal Society ... were ... delivered to Mr. Taylor of the Board of Works and by him transferred to the keeper of the Royal Academy'.[104] In fact, to judge from a letter that Smirke wrote to the Royal Society on 30 December 1871 to explain how it was proposed to construct the new storey over their heads, enabling works must have already begun by January 1872:

> It is proposed to erect early next Spring the Upper Story designed to be added to Burlington House. In carrying out this work the first step will be to lay a temporary wooden platform over the lead roof of the whole building. A Lift placed at the North West

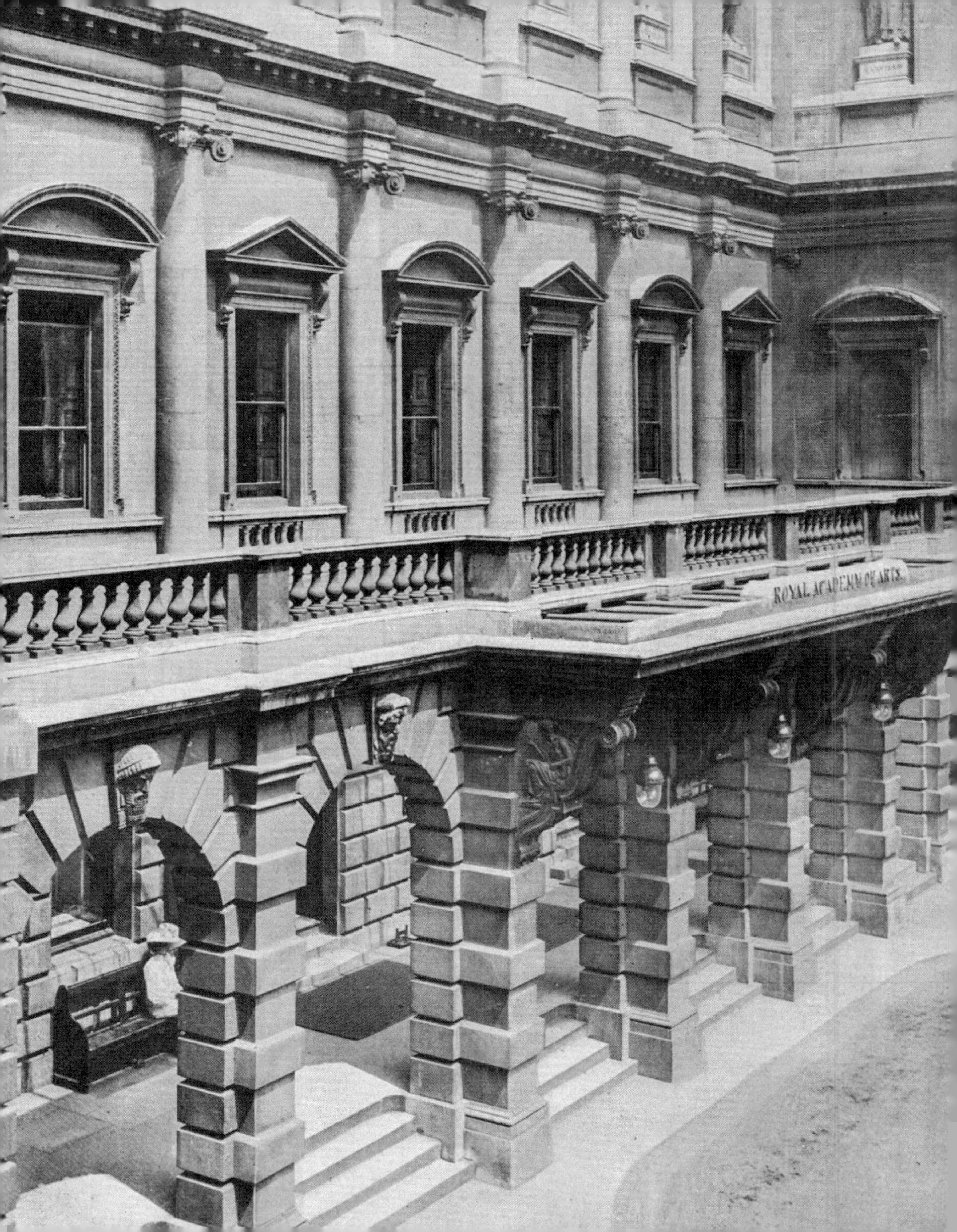
ROYAL ACADEMY OF ARTS

Fig. 247
Entrance portico including canopy (reliefs designed by John Birnie Philip), from *Architectural Review*, October 1904. Photograph by Henry Irving.
Royal Academy of Arts, London, 13/1932

Fig. 248
Sydney Smirke, East screen wall window: elevation, 1872.
Royal Academy of Arts, London, 06/1314

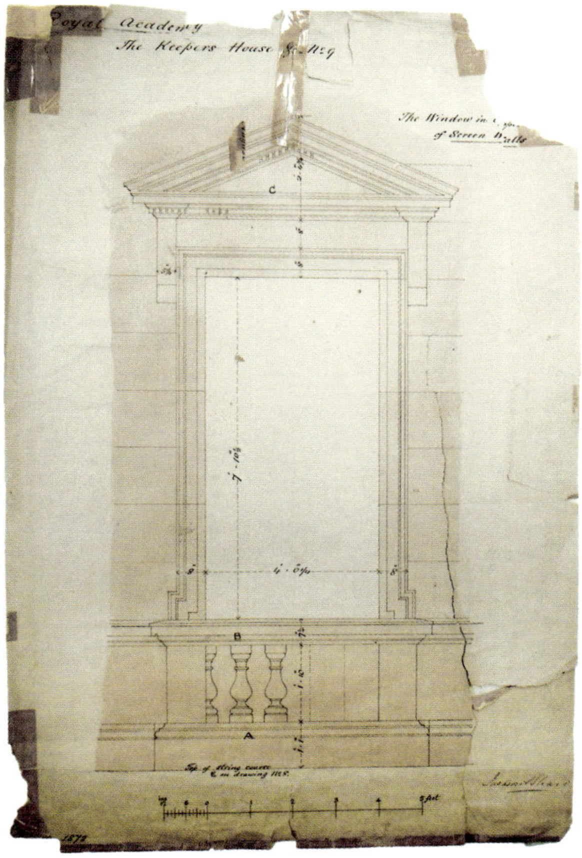

> angle of the Premises would be formed for raising the building materials & workmen up to the highest level of the new Story.
>
> ... According to the mode of proceeding intended to be adopted no stonework will be executed on the spot, but all will be prepared at the Contractors works in Westminster, & brought in waggons to the Lift, & then, at once raised & set. The workmen's access will be solely from Burlington Gardens, so that no confusion nor inconvenience of any kind need be apprehended from them.
>
> The erection of the Lift & of portions of the platform will be commenced immediately, but the building of the new walls would not be commenced until the month of March & the whole would be externally finished about the following August.[105]

Smirke calculated that 'fully one twelvemonth or more' would be saved by starting work on the house now, 'thereby hastening to that extent the period when the whole Quadrangle would be relieved from all encumbrance & confusion.'

Meanwhile, it was reported at a meeting of the Academy's Council on 21 February 1872 that the secretary had received a letter from the Treasury stating 'that the only arrangement their Lordships can consider satisfactory in regard to the safety of the National Gallery from fire, is the removal of all persons residing on the premises.' The imminent eviction of the Academy Schools' then keeper, Charles Landseer, would have certainly drawn attention to the question of where to site his proposed residence at Burlington House, especially since at the time Grant wrote to Ayrton on 29 February in reply to the latter's objection to sham windows in the screen walls to the east and west of Smirke's new façade (Fig. 248), it had not yet been decided to build it in either of these positions:

> With regard to the windows in the connecting walls, I believe it is not intended that they should be sham windows, but the windows of two small rooms, to be built which will be useful additions, but are contemplated cheifly [*sic*] with the view of avoiding the architectural heresy of sham windows – I will direct Mr Smirke to mark out these proposed rooms in the plan which will be again submitted to you very shortly.[106]

By August 1872, however, Smirke had prepared working drawings for the construction of 'The Keeper's House' behind the east screen wall adjoining Ware's service-stair annexe (Fig. 249), and between 16 September and 9 November Thomas Farrar's duties were described as 'superintendence of the works in erecting the new Upper Story and of the Keeper's House'.[107] The point was to push on and do as much as possible without waiting until the learned societies had moved out, which is why what was destined to be the door connecting the Keeper's House to Ware's annexe is still shown as an internal window in Smirke's ground plan (Fig. 250).

With the backing no doubt of the new 'Building Committee' appointed by the Council at his request on 7 August 1871, it is not surprising that Smirke felt justified in retaining Jackson & Shaw as contractors for all these works. Furthermore, despite his earlier pessimism, he was now able to see his way clear to completing the whole project in time for the 1874 Summer Exhibition, provided the Royal Society's new building was ready by the end of August 1873, as Barry had promised him it would be, and the Academy was prepared to forego holding a winter exhibition that year. Smirke's 'Statement' to this effect dated 11 February 1873 summarised what he thought remained to be done as follows:

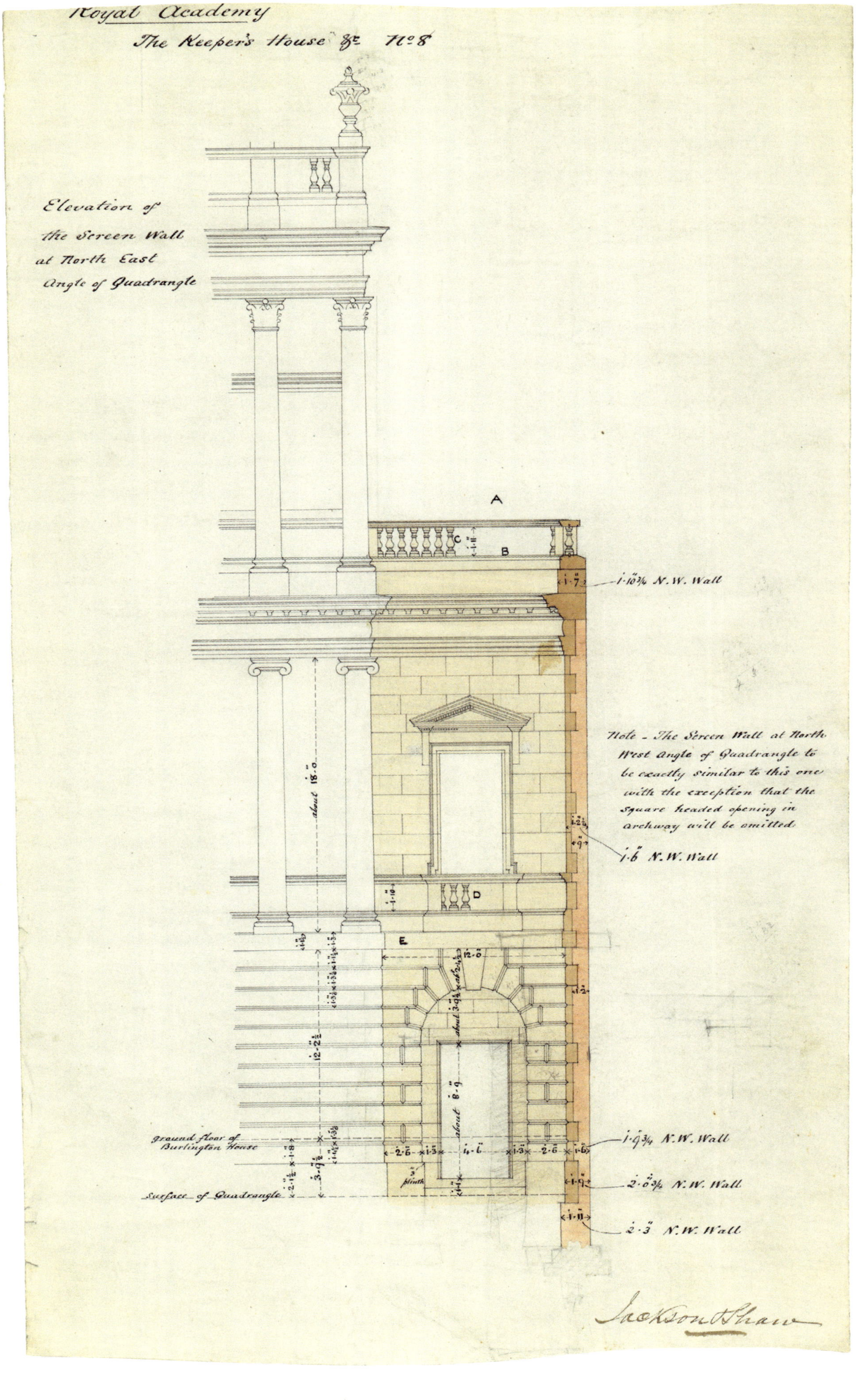

Fig. 249
Sydney Smirke, Keeper's House: elevation of the screen wall with entrance, south front façade and east end, *c.* 1872.
Royal Academy of Arts, London, 11/3178

... we shall be enabled to take down the temporary meeting room of the R.S. & build on its site our intended Refreshment Room; build the two new Public Staircases; complete the Keeper's House; alter the entrance Hall, build the new dwellings for the Registrar & Housekeeper, & carry out all the other, minor works necessary to fit the old building to our uses ... [108]

However, continuation of the works 'by an elastic schedule of prices' rather than 'under definite contracts authorized by the Council', was about to land Smirke and the remainder of the project in serious trouble with the Academy's auditors.[109]

Partly as a consequence of 'the Council not feeling themselves competent to deal with the details of the subject [of the expenditure on the New Buildings]', and more generally as part of a growing recognition within the institution of the need for 'changes ... in regard to the Officers and their duties corresponding to the present enlarged sphere of the Royal Academy, & for the sake of greater efficiency', the remit of a newly constituted 'Committee of Auditors' had been expanded in November 1870 to include responsibility for examining 'all bills before being submitted to the Council for order of payment, with power to inquire into any item or items that may appear to them objectionable'.[110] Not surprisingly, the large sums still being paid to Jackson & Shaw on the authority of architect's certificates issued by Smirke – already amounting to £14,000 by mid-April 1873 – were of particular concern, not only because of the open-endedness of their contract but also because of the conflict of interest inherent in Smirke's position as both treasurer and architect to the Academy. While it had been perfectly acceptable a century earlier for the Academy's first treasurer, Sir William Chambers, to act simultaneously as the guardian of its financial assets and the architect of its new apartments at Somerset House,

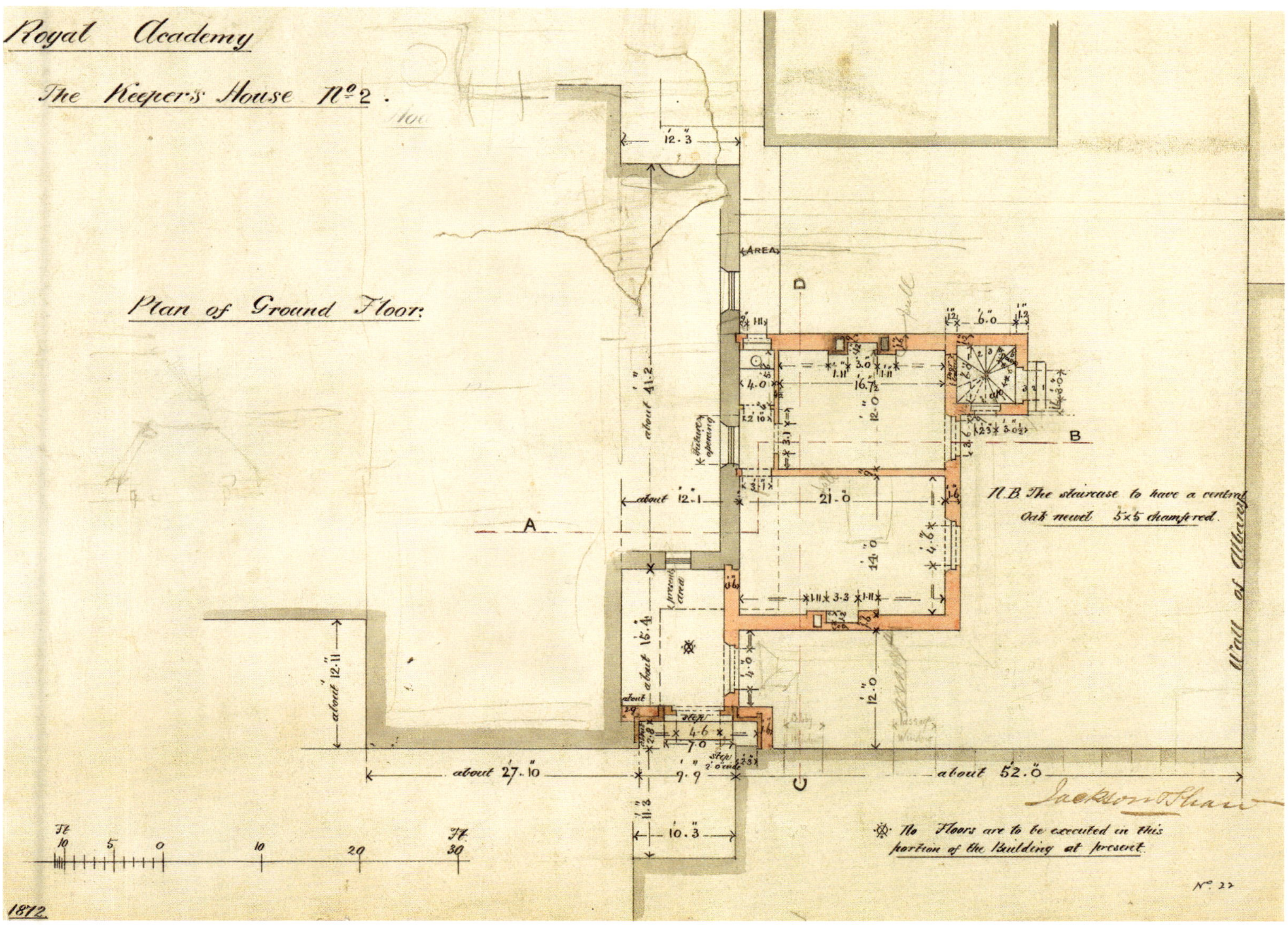

Fig. 250
Sydney Smirke, Keeper's House: ground-floor plan, 1872.
Royal Academy of Arts, London, 06/1313

Fig. 251
Sydney Smirke, Unexecuted design for new main staircase, refreshment room, and internal alterations to Burlington House: first-floor plan, *c.* 1872–73.
Royal Academy of Arts, London, 15/1645

and for subsequent treasurers, as architect-members personally appointed by the sovereign, to take responsibility for the repair and maintenance of the fabric of the Academy's premises, the fact that Smirke charged the normal architect's commission of 5% on the cost of work he was himself commissioning, exposed him to the insinuation that he might have been acting in his own interests by making or advocating unnecessarily expensive alterations and additions to the house.

Matters came to a head at a Council meeting on 8 June 1873, when 'it was … moved by Mr Street and seconded by Mr Redgrave & resolved',

> That the Architect of the New Buildings be requested to lay before the Council at their next meeting the whole of the plans for the additions now in progress, or recommended by him to be undertaken. And that he also be requested to submit at the same time a clear statement of the cost of the proposed works shewing the amount of the Builders contract for the works already in progress, and the amount of their tender for works (such as the new Refreshment Room) which are not yet commenced or in anyway sanctioned by the Council. And that he be also requested to lay upon the table the Contract under which these works are being carried on.

As one of the Academy's auditors and a member of a special committee recently appointed by the Council to 'act in the matter' of Redgrave's 'proposal to employ an Accountant and Actuary to examine the Accounts of the Academy and to report on the Capital, Income, and Expenditure &c.', Street was uniquely well-qualified to take on responsibility for investigating the Academy's financial commitments in connection with the building work at Burlington House.[111] Clearly what he found – or more probably failed to find – must have caused him considerable concern, for over the next six months he and Redgrave mounted a concerted campaign to curtail as much as possible any further expenditure on alterations or additions to the house. This was partly a drive to reassert the authority of the Council to approve or reject the architect's plans and the power of the Committee of Auditors to pass bills for payment (the respective responsibilities of the treasurer and the Building Committee appointed in 1871 were ambiguous in both these respects), but it was also partly the result of wider alarm that the Academy had overstretched itself financially, particularly in view of the fact that income from the Summer Exhibition had fallen from £17,642 in 1871 to £16,412 in 1872, and was to fall yet again in 1873 to £15,069.

It was this alarm that came to the fore at a bruising meeting of the General Assembly on 8 August 1873, at which news of dismal exhibition figures was followed by an auditors' quarterly report that 'drew especial attention to the State of the Funds of the R.A., the expenditure on the New Buildings, & the advisability of separating the offices of Treasurer & Architect'. The minute of the ensuing discussion is unusually revealing, possibly because this was the first General Assembly attended by the newly appointed lay (i.e. non-member) secretary, Frederick A. Eaton:

> The Treasurer replied to the Auditors' statements, & expressed his intention of resigning the office of Treasurer. A general discussion then took place upon the financial position of the Academy, in the course of which Mr. Wells, Mr. Street, Mr. Redgrave & Mr. Horsley urged the necessity for more economical expenditure of the Funds, especially in connection with the new Buildings at Burlington House. Mr. Cope, however, said that economy was not the only thing to be considered in the matter of new buildings, but also beauty & convenience. Mr. Street read his report already laid before the Council [on 31 July], on the new Buildings (see Book of Reports). The suggestions contained in it were accepted by Mr. Smirke, who said he should lay the revised estimates for the alterations & additions yet remaining to be made before the Council that evening … On the motion of the President, seconded by Mr. Horsley, & carried nem. con. a vote of thanks was accorded to Mr. Street for his exertions in regard to the new Buildings. The President also expressed his opinion that great credit was due to Mr. Smirke for all he had done as Architect of the new Buildings.

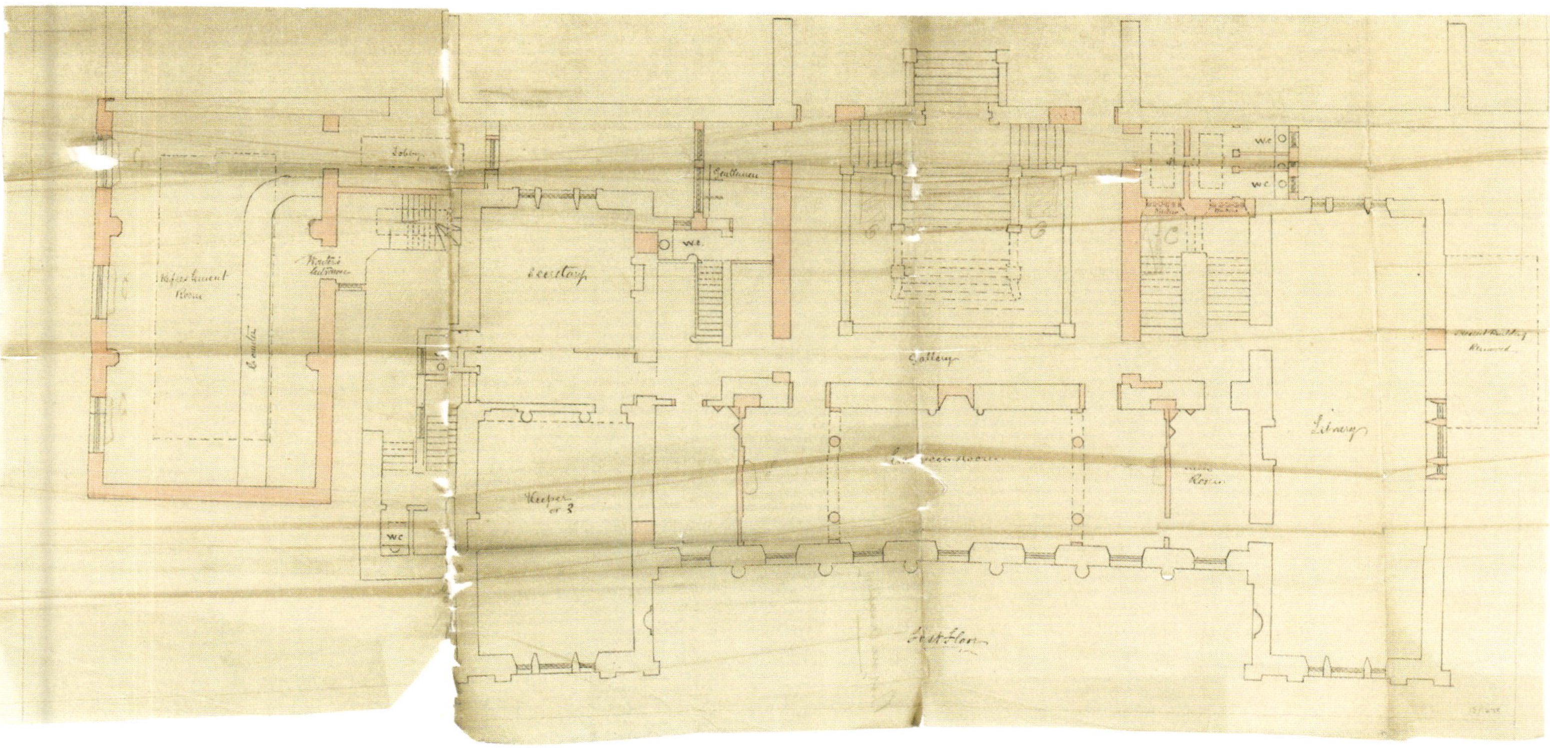

Unfortunately, Eaton's 'Book of Reports' does not appear to have survived in the Academy's archives. It is clear, however, from a sole surviving first-floor plan of Smirke's proposed adaptation of the house to the Academy's needs, and from the account in the RA Council's *Annual Report* for 1873 of the economising effect of Street's 'suggestions', that he had intended to go considerably further than replacing and widening Ware's staircase (Fig. 251). Perhaps most alarming was his plan to enlarge the Saloon by blocking up its central door, extending it one bay to east and west, and opening up new doors behind columnar screens at either end. Although Kent's cartouches may perhaps have been reinstated, there is a nice irony in the fact that it was Street, the arch 'Goth', who saved the only original neo-Palladian interiors remaining in the house.

The largest savings in terms of cost came from dropping the whole idea of adding a two-storey extension at the south-west corner of the new building that would have provided living accommodation for the Academy's registrar and housekeeper on the ground floor and a new Refreshment Room above communicating with and on the same level as Gallery II. As far as the registrar was concerned, it was decided that it would not be necessary after all for Henry Eyre to live on the premises, while Ware's north-facing attic rooms (all of which could be retained if there was no need to insert a rooflight over the main staircase) would, it was thought, be quite sufficient to accommodate both the resident housekeeper, Mrs Charlotte Wise, and her niece.[112] On the other hand, the need for a fully functioning and attractive visitors' restaurant and bar – those essential amenities and sources of income for any museum today – had become incontrovertible. Indeed, the sale for the first time in the Academy of 'refreshments' for exhibition visitors had been one of the most noticeable improvements made possible by its new building, and the subject of some waggish humour in the *Sunday Times* two months before the 1869 exhibition had opened:

> There is no impropriety in mingling ham sandwiches with high art, neither need any one be horrified at the association of champagne and *chiaroscuro*. There is no reason why Grant and gingerbread, Ward and wine-and-water, Poole and pork pies, Knight and noyeau, Calderon and Clicquot, Leighton and lemonade, Millais and *meringues* should not go well together, and form a pleasant banquet equally beneficial to the mind and the stomach.[113]

At the opening of the new building the caterers Messrs Spiers & Pond had been praised in the *Standard* for having made the 'new refreshment department', despite its inconvenient location in the south-west vault (subsequently the boiler house) under Gallery II,

> one of the attractive corners of the Academy. It will be found leading out of No. 2 room and no visitor will be disappointed with the red and white drapery which hides the bare walls, or the comfortable accommodation afforded in a room that will, it is to be supposed, be superseded next year by an apartment of easier access.[114]

Rather than erect a new building solely for this purpose, however, Street's solution was to construct a lobby bridging the fourteen-foot gap between Gallery II and Lord George Cavendish's former bedroom, and to remove the partition walls (but apparently not the columnar screen) between the latter and the former State Dining Room to form a large, readily accessible 'Refreshment Gallery' with waiters' access down the existing west service stairs to a kitchen in the north-west corner of the basement of the main house (the former Cavendish housekeeper's room). It was with such economising 'improvements' in mind therefore that the Council paid a site visit to Burlington House on 20 November 1873 and, sitting for the first time in what is now the Richard Sharp Council Room, made the following decisions:

1 That the room opening out of the Library be used as the Council Room; & that the walls be covered with a lining paper distempered; the woodwork washed; the gilding cleaned; the floor washed, & the sides, if of oak, polished, if of deal, stained & varnished ['sides' presumably refers to the ends of bookcases and fittings left behind by the Royal Society].
2 That the room E. of the Refreshment Room be the Secretary's Room; & that it be treated in the same way as described above for the Council Room.
3 That the window at the N. end of the Library be moved as previously suggested [by Street at a Council meeting on 10 October 1873].
4 That an estimate be obtained for altering the book-shelves & laid before the Council at its next meeting.
5 That the fittings offered by the Royal & Linnaean Societies be taken at the price named by them.
6 That the General Assembly room [i.e. the Saloon] be left to be cleaned as per contract.
7 That the ladies W.C. be enlarged at a cost estimated by Mr. Smirke at about £80.
8 That the chimney piece now in the Council Room at Trafalgar Square be removed to the Council Room at Burlington House [this refers to Joseph Wilton's marble mantlepiece of *c.* 1780–86, still *in situ*]; the destination of that now in said room at Burlington House to be decided hereafter [granted at the keeper's request on 16 December 'for his principal apartment', and still *in situ* in the Sir Hugh Casson Friends' Room].
9 That the adaptation of the two ceilings at Trafalgar Square to rooms at Burlington House be left to Mr. Smirke.
10 That the Secretary obtain an estimate for the furnishing of his room at Burlington House, & submit it to the next meeting of Council.[115]

What is most remarkable about this list is how little the Academicians felt they needed to do to make themselves at home. All the front rooms were no doubt filthy from the years of building work in the courtyard, and those on the first floor probably looked sad and shabby, denuded of the great scientific libraries that had lined their walls for almost twenty years, until the day that is, in September 1873, when the last of the Royal Society's treasures had been transported by means of an aerial tramway rigged up by the contractors between the first-floor windows of old and new Burlington House.[116] At a subsequent Council meeting it was decided 'on the recommendation of the architect' [i.e. Smirke], to leave Ware's window at the north end of the 'Library' untouched, and that instead 'a new window of small dimensions as per plan … be opened in the East side', the problem being, of course, that the new galleries had taken away most of the light from the northern end of the room.[117]

What the Council authorised Smirke to carry out from October 1873 'under a contract with Messrs Jackson & Shaw for £6890' is less clear than what they had prevented him from doing.[118] To judge from the payments Jackson & Shaw continued to receive – a total of £13,200 between 26 November 1873 and 20 August 1874 – their later contract did not relate to the completion of the Keeper's House in April, the Diploma and Gibson Galleries in June, or the entrance portico in March, all of which they presumably carried out under an earlier agreement. The new contract would therefore have related only to additional work, such as the alterations necessary for forming the Refreshment Room in the west wing of the old house; probably some modification of the attic rooms for the housekeeper and her niece; and almost certainly the opening up of the entrance hall to its present width by the removal of all partition walls. It would have been at this time also that Ware's black and white stone-paved floor was replaced with 'common red and black tiles' that may well have resembled the quarry tiles then being laid in the Diploma and Gibson Galleries (these can still be seen in the latter gallery, now the Academy's library). Work on altering the entrance hall seems to have been postponed until autumn 1874 (in early November the Council rejected Smirke's suggestion that 'before the last coats of paint were put on something should be done to improve its appearance', deciding instead that 'any embellishment [was] to be a subject for future consideration').[119] The new Refreshment Room on the other hand was certainly ready in time for what proved to be the most popular exhibition so far in the Academy's history, with a total attendance of 332,365 people over thirteen weeks and one day.

As they thronged the front hall and crowded round the bar in the splendid new 'Refreshment Gallery' leading directly off Gallery II, the more seasoned visitors would have registered that the Academy was now truly in residence at Burlington House, as they glimpsed ceiling paintings by Reynolds, West and Kauffman transferred from Trafalgar Square, and on their way home caught sight of a public notice board under the handsome new archway on Piccadilly advertising the 'Exhibitions, Lectures, Meetings, &c.' held by the Royal Academy and (it is to be hoped) its neighbours in the courtyard.[120] As for the Academicians themselves, the feeling that destiny had played a part in bringing them to this 'classic spot' was well caught in Richard Redgrave's diary entry for 31 December 1873:

> I finished the old year at the Royal Academy dining with the old and the incoming Council, as our usual practice is. This dinner was so far unusual in that we this day took living possession of Burlington House and dined in one of the suites of rooms in which the Royal Society gave their *soireés*, and where, before them, the noble proprietor and architect used to hold his pomp and state. It is hard to tell how the rest of the household lived, especially where the servants 'pigged in,' unless it was under the table of the servants' hall, or the pantry.
>
> After dinner, the President's health was proposed, and in replying he told us a curious fact. 'In this very room,' said he, 'forty-two years ago, I commenced my professional practice as a London portrait painter. The old Lady Burlington desired me to paint her grand-daughter (or niece), Lady Elizabeth Cavendish, and while my easel was placed in yonder window, she sat, as nearly as possible, where I now sit as your chairman. I had painted one portrait before in Edinburgh, but this was my first in London. It was less than life, head and bust, and I had thirty-five guineas for the work. Little chance seemed there then that I should take my place as your President at the first dinner of the Academy Council in the same chamber!'[121]

As he enjoyed his after-dinner reminiscence Grant probably did not realise that his treasurer, who more than anyone else had been responsible for what his old friend Edwin Landseer had described excitedly in May 1869 as 'the birth of our new House ... !!',[122] had almost certainly decided by then to resign his post. Smirke was far too seasoned an architect to lose sleep over the Academy's rejection of a scheme that would have achieved a better integration of old Burlington House with the new buildings around and behind it. However, as Grant wrote in a letter to General Sabine in June 1868, he was 'a discreet, quiet man of sound judgement',[123] who must have felt that he had no choice but to resign when, on 16 December 1873, the Council endorsed a thoroughly pessimistic report on the future of the Academy's finances prepared for them by a Mr Finlaison, Actuary to the Commissioners for the National Debt. It was probably not mere chance therefore, that six days later he brought along to the last Council meeting he was to attend as treasurer, 'a model of the façade of the building at Burlington House.'[124] Ostensibly his purpose was to obtain the Council's sanction for 'the balustrade as proposed by him', but it was also, surely, a pointed reminder of the exceptional service he had given to the Academy as the architect of its new home.

UNLIKE THE PRESIDENT, who was and still is elected annually by the General Assembly, at the time of Smirke's resignation the treasurer of the Academy was appointed by and continued in office 'during His Majesty's pleasure'.[125] In addition, as Grant was to write to the Queen's private secretary Sir Thomas Biddulph on 11 February 1874 naming E. M. Barry and G. E. Street as the two equally eligible and 'eminently qualified' candidates (George Gilbert Scott having declined nomination), it had 'always been the custom that the appointment shall be held by an architect.'[126] Although the Queen left the choice between Barry and Street up to the Academy, probably because of the complications attendant upon any question concerning the royal prerogative, Redgrave decided not to pursue at that point his sensible proposal that tenure of the office be brought into line with that of the keeper and limited to five years.[127] As a result, and most regrettably in the light of subsequent events, the Academy failed to grasp the nettle that H. T. Wells RA (already a zealous student of the Academy's laws) gave clear warning of when Barry was elected treasurer on the president's casting vote at a General Assembly on 26 February 1874:

> Mr. Wells asked whether the Treasurer would be entitled to fees for building work done for the Academy. The President replied in the negative: it would be the duty of the Treasurer to attend to all necessary repairs in the existing buildings, but in the case of any new buildings being needed some other architect would be employed.

What Grant failed to make clear at the time was that this was merely his opinion, based on no resolution passed by either the Council or the General Assembly, and in fact contrary to all precedent.

The issue could be safely ignored for the time being since, despite having resigned as treasurer, Smirke was still of course the architect in charge of the remaining works in Burlington House, for which he was paid a commission of £800 on account in June 1874 and the final balance of £975 16s. a year later.[128] By early 1875, however, virtually all this work was finished, the Diploma Gallery being sufficiently complete for the Council to order on 9 February that 'the Circular Bas-relief by M. Angelo formerly in the Council Room at Trafalgar Square ... be placed at the S. end of the W. Diploma Gallery between the Reynolds Portraits of George iii and Queen Caroline'. In what was perhaps his last act as the Academy's architect, and to mark the completion of his commission almost exactly eight years to the day building work had begun, on 16 March 1875 Smirke presented the Council with a silk-lined plan he had 'prepared with great care ... of the drains, water & gas services, Hydrants &c. throughout the premises of the Royal Academy'. By now the requests of the Academy's energetic librarian Solomon A. Hart RA for more bookshelves and 'a proper press for containing the fine engravings of large size presented by different members'[129] were being directed to Barry's attention rather than to Smirke's and on 25 March, for instance, it was Barry rather than Smirke who reported that he had 'instructed Messrs. Jackson & Shaw to construct an enclosed serving lobby at one end of the Kitchen, & to carry out some air flues for ventilation.'[130]

Thus, almost without anyone noticing, Barry took over responsibility for any further alteration to Burlington House as part of the treasurer's duties, in spite of Grant's assurance to the General Assembly on 26 February 1874 that he would be concerned only with 'necessary repairs in the existing buildings'. When therefore, as a consequence of 'two or three accidents having happened during the Exhibition from persons tumbling down the stairs leading from the Entrance Hall', Barry presented at a Council meeting on 14 December 1875, 'a plan ... for altering & completing the Staircase, explaining at the same time that it was necessary to do something, as the existing stairs were partly wood, and consequently not in accordance with the requirements of the Building Act', his proposal was not only approved (apparently without any mention of costs), but he was also 'desired to devise some means of decorating the entrance generally.'[131] No doubt keen to secure the current Council's approval before the end of the year, he lost no time in submitting nine days later at least two different 'plans for the proposed improvement & decoration of the Entrance archway', as a result of which he was 'authorised to carry out a plan at an outlay of not more than £300.'[132] However, having had insufficient time to look at the structural implications of the chosen design, Barry was obliged to report at the following Council meeting in the new year that

> on further examination of the entrance archway over the staircase he found that the arches required to be of a sufficiently substantial material to support a considerable super-incumbent weight, & that consequently they could not be made of lath & plaster.[133]

On a motion of George Richmond (a staunch ally), and seconded by Leighton, the Council thereupon resolved 'that the columns be of marble instead of lath & plaster, & that the sum authorised to be increased to between £500 & £600.' Although no specifications or drawings of Barry's alteration of the main staircase and entrance hall are known to have survived, there is little doubt that he was responsible not only for introducing the existing Doric marble-columned entrance arch and matching pilasters on the north wall, but also for a complete reconstruction of the staircase leading to the galleries. This must have entailed quite considerable structural work since it included the replacement of Smirke's 'temporary' wooden extension of Ware's original first flight of stairs, the division of the latter into two flights in order to provide a less steep overall incline, and the provision of wider and more open curtail steps to both flights. In what is probably the earliest sign of a concern on the Academy's part to retain the original character of this important public part of the house, the Council decided not to modernise in any way the appearance of what was practically a new staircase, resolving instead 'that the decorations on the staircase be made to accord with those of the rest of the building, & that an estimate be obtained from Mr. Merritt for the cleaning &c. of the large pictures at the side.'[134] Since Ware's banister panels were of cast iron, they could be readily replicated from a new mould. It was probably at this time that a pair of these panels were installed on the first-floor landing as gates to deter unauthorised entry to the Academicians' 'Private Rooms'.

Carried out in the interval between the Summer and Winter exhibitions of 1876, Barry's 'decoration and improvement' of the front hall and reconstruction of the main staircase to the galleries could not have been more conspicuous, both while the work was underway and once it was complete. In fact, the project had hardly begun before the Committee of Auditors in their August quarterly report 'especially drew attention to Messrs. Jackson & Shaw's bill for the alteration of the staircase as being apparently beyond the amount authorized by the Council.'[135] While Barry was able to show at the next Council meeting that his expenditure had been approved, this was not the end of the matter as far as the auditors were concerned since, in February the following year, they went on to question the Council's authority to initiate expenditure on any building work, stating that:

> They object to the sum of £1597. 17. 8., the cost for the new staircase as having only been authorized by the Council, although the General Assembly on Aug. 8 1873 decided that the staircase should not be altered & that they consider it their duty to report on this irregularity in order that it may be brought to the notice of the General Assembly before which in their opinion this Report has to be laid.[136]

Despite it having been pointed that the latter was not 'usual' practice and moreover that the Council was 'not aware of any irregularity in respect of the alterations recently made in the staircase', when the report of the Committee of Auditors was read out at a General Assembly on 21 March 1877, Redgrave promptly gave notice of a motion 'that no new building works (other than current repairs) be undertaken without the consent of the General Assembly being first obtained, the estimated expense being at the same time laid before the meeting'.[137] Carried by the General Assembly on 24 November 1877 and confirmed ten days later against Grant's vehement protest that it 'was contrary to the spirit and intention of the original laws of the institution', this resolution reopened an ancient fault line in the Academy's governance, namely whether the General Assembly had any power to make changes to the laws without these having been first proposed and approved by the Council.

Worse from Barry's point of view was the fact that this row also drew attention to the issue that had been hanging over him ever since he became treasurer. His hopes of it being settled in his favour had not looked promising when he had been informed by the secretary on 13 December 1876

> that the Council after long & careful deliberation on the subject are of opinion 'that the Treasurer being an architect, & therefore the person best qualified to give information and advice to the Academy on the subject of any new works to be built by it, & to watch over the expenses incurred in the building of such works is not himself at liberty to be employed professionally upon them.'[138]

One might think this could not have been plainer but, as can often be the case in institutions, less than a month later the new Council overruled its predecessor, resolving that since 'no motion was made, seconded or voted upon' at the General Assembly on 26 February 1874 'as to the question of the freedom of the Academy to appoint whomsoever it would as its architect, [they] are of opinion that this liberty has not been relinquished.'[139] This was a far cry from declaring that the Academy's treasurer could or should be employed as its architect, but it did defuse the situation sufficiently for Barry to write and thank the Council for a resolution that went some way towards redressing 'the unfairness of ... a decision' to automatically disqualify him from working as such, and 'the slur that [this] cast upon an honourable office'.[140] Barry's adamant refusal to accept an architect's fee was no doubt intended to avoid any imputation of a conflict of interest. However, like his wishful thinking that 'the duties of the Treasurer ... do not include advising the Academy on new building works nor exercising any control over expenditure upon such works',[141] it served merely to prolong a dangerous anachronism that the reformers in the institution, such as Redgrave, Cope, Wells and Leighton, saw as preventing the Academy from addressing the serious problems caused by shortage of space in its rapidly expanding Schools and making good its undertaking to provide the means of achieving a better representation of the work of non-members in the Summer Exhibition.

It is hardly surprising therefore that less than three weeks after Leighton's election on 13 November 1878 as the Academy's eighth president with an overwhelming mandate for reform, Wells gave notice in General Assembly of an amendment to a notice of motion that had been hanging fire since 10 July:

> To call attention to the architect's work carried out by the Treasurer in the building of Burlington House since its completion by Mr. Smirke, and to the fact that the Treasurer has given his services because the Academy is without a properly appointed architect, and to move: That Mr. Barry be remunerated for those services in the usual way and that the Council be requested to lay before the General Assembly a plan for the appointment of an architect.[142]

Although the final clause was omitted in the resolution as carried in General Assembly on 5 December, the new president 'undertook to bring the question of the relations of the Architect & the Treasurer before the Council who should report to the General Assembly.' Thanks to Leighton's determined handling of the issue, two resolutions passed by the new Council on 21 January and subsequently carried by a large majority in the General Assembly on 7 March 1879 succeeded in laying the necessary foundations for the future adaptation of Burlington House to the Academy's needs. While the first of these finally carried into effect the recommendation of the audit committee's report of July 1873 by categorically stating 'that the holder of the office of Treasurer shall not receive professional fees for architectural work connected with the buildings of the Royal Academy', the second broke new ground by deciding

> to appoint an officer to be entitled 'Surveyor to the Royal Academy' whose duty shall be to examine the buildings with a view to alterations and repairs, and to report on the same to the Treasurer, and when these or other similar works have been ordered by the Council, to superintend their execution and supervise the expenditure.[143]

Needless to say, Barry was devastated. Not only debarred from undertaking new architectural work for the Academy, now he was not even to have an ordinary surveyor's responsibility for the fabric of the building. Worse still, an amendment moved by his ally George Richmond and seconded by J. E. Millais, 'that in the interests of peace any further consideration of this subject be postponed until the office of treasurer become again vacant' had been defeated by a margin of eight to seventeen, and his own ill-judged attempt to canvass members by circulating a printed 'Memorandum' before the meeting had backfired to the extent that 'an expression of regret' that he had done so 'was ordered to be entered on the Minutes'. What hurt most was that such a slur on his reputation should have been cast not by penny-pinching government officials but by his brother artists. In a letter to thank Richmond for his support the day after the meeting, Barry emphasised that this was 'the most unpleasant business I have ever encountered in a not untroubled professional career',[144] and saddest of all, wrote again a few days later,

> I have not had long to wait for a taste of what is before me. It was said last night in the smoking room at the Athenaeum. 'I hear the Royal Academy have dismissed its architect because they find they cannot trust a comrade.' These were the exact words which will soon be said everywhere. I could not have believed it possible that a body of English gentlemen would have placed a brother artist in such a position. God knows what I have done to provoke so much ill will! It makes me very unhappy though my conscience is clear, and I can safely say that I have done all I could to serve the Academy while I have taken nothing from it not even a word of thanks.[145]

Although some words of thanks did come later, from the Council on 15 July and the General Assembly on 8 August – and as a result Leighton was able to dissuade his treasurer from resigning – however Barry's 'comrades' may have eased their consciences, those who happened to be seated around the Council table on 27 January 1880 were in for a shock:

> The Treasurer, enclosing the Report of the Surveyor on the Lighting and Ventilation of Gallery III, & the Warming of all the Galleries. During a discussion which arose before the Report was read, the Treasurer (Mr. E. M. Barry) was suddenly seized with an apoplectic fit, & expired in less than five minutes before medical aid which was instantly summoned could arrive. The business of the meeting was immediately suspended.[146]

As he lay dying in the arms of the Academy's keeper Frederick Pickersgill, an old and dear friend, Barry's last words are said to have been, 'Who is it?'[147]

AT THE FIRST MEETING of the new year's Council on 13 January 1880 just two weeks before 'this sad and terrible event', it had been resolved

> that a Committee be formed to inspect the vacant ground belonging to the R.A. on the W. side, & prepare a scheme for submission to the Council as the best means of utilising it for Galleries, Schools, &c. The following were chosen to contribute to the Committee: Messrs. Horsley, Frith, Calder Marshall, Street, Shaw.

The decision to appoint this new Building Committee, which in the past would have automatically included the treasurer, arose out of an informal discussion that had begun in November the previous year when the historical genre painter W. F. Yeames came up with a number of suggestions for 'the re-arrangement of the Galleries'.[148] One of his ideas – to convert the Sculpture Gallery into 'a Gallery with skylights similar to the other Galleries' – the Council had adopted for immediate recommendation to the General Assembly. At the same time, Norman Shaw – currently serving his first term as a Council member and about to join the painter J. C. Horsley on the Audit Committee – had also submitted 'a plan for altering the Vestibule and Octagon', which, although it had led to a decision 'not to alter the existing structural arrangement of these galleries', had clearly opened up the whole subject of how to obtain more exhibition space for oil paintings.[149]

As an Academy Gold Medal winner and Travelling Student in the 1850s, an assistant in Street's office between 1859 and 1863, and now a highly successful architect in his own right (whose first important domestic work had been an addition to Horsley's house Willesley at Cranbrook in Kent), Shaw must have played a key role on the new committee from the start, since it led seamlessly to his election on 25 June 1880 as architect for both the conversion of the Sculpture Gallery into 'Gallery VI' and the redecoration of the Vestibule for use 'as an Entrance Hall' rather than exhibition gallery. Not fully completed until spring 1882, these two minor jobs proved more complicated than expected, giving Shaw valuable experience in how to handle the Academy as a client as well as an understanding of the building and the constraints imposed by the seasonal cycle of Summer and Winter exhibitions and the work of the Schools. His report to the Council on 13 June 1882 that the two projects had come in at £131 6s. 5d. under the contract price of £2499 2s., was perfectly timed to justify the General Assembly's confirmation of his appointment the following day as architect for an enlargement of the Academy's galleries and Schools that would prove to have a more far-reaching architectural impact on Burlington House than any other since.

It may have been partly due to the severe breakdown in Shaw's health at the beginning of 1881, necessitating a prolonged recuperation on the French Riviera under doctor's orders, that the new Building Committee failed to report to the General Assembly until 20 July 1881. Their principal proposal was that the 'vacant ground' on the west side of the old house should be used to build three new exhibition galleries devoted respectively to (1) watercolour drawings, (2) engravings, etchings and miniatures, and (3) architectural drawings; and that beneath these new galleries, and publicly accessible solely from them, there should be a 2,100-square-foot Refreshment Room served by a new staircase in the north-west corner of the old house. To compensate for the loss of the two original rooms of the old house that the latter entailed, the present Refreshment Room was to be restored 'to its old shape' (i.e. that of Ware's State Dining Room) for use 'as a Council Room (the present one being given up to the library)', and the corridor from the main stairs running past the secretary's bedroom (now the president's office) was to be 'enlarged' (Fig. 252). It was further proposed that the visitors' lavatories should be moved from their current 'very objectionable' position off the Vestibule, the gents' to the foot, and the ladies' to an 'entresol' on the half landing of the new Refreshment Room staircase (Fig. 253). In their place it was intended to create on the east side a top-lit two-storey laboratory for the Professor of Chemistry (then Sir Arthur H. Church) and on the west an office for the treasurer (Street), who as a result of the reform of the post after Barry's death was required for the first time to work 'within the building'. Although not part of their original brief, the Committee also proposed that an additional Diploma Gallery should be constructed above the housekeeper's attic rooms on the north front (Fig. 254) and that the former Watercolour Gallery (i.e. Gallery IX) be extended eastwards to create an exhibition space for oil paintings second in size and importance to Gallery III and to provide a proper students' staircase from the Schools in place of their current trapdoor access (Fig. 255). Of these remarkably ambitious proposals only the last-mentioned – and the relocation of the lavatories – failed to materialise in some form over the next four years.

The favourable response given to the Building Committee's report at the General Assembly meetings on 3 August and 24 November 1881 must have been much helped by the fact that the Council had been able to point out that

> during the last ten years, whilst a sum of upwards of £52,000 has been spent on the building, the vested funds of the Academy have been increased by £35,000, after deducting £8060 recently transferred to the Turner Fund. With an annual income which, on average, exceeds the expenditure by £10,000, the Council feel it cannot be deemed a rash or an unwise thing to advise an expenditure of £27,000 when they are able to say the result will be of enormous advantage to the Academy in every respect. There will be an addition of no less than 2290 feet area in

Fig. 252
Norman Shaw, Proposal for extension of the galleries, first scheme: plan, 1881.
Royal Academy of Arts, Archives, RAA SEC/22/6 Exh Notices

Fig. 253
Norman Shaw, Proposal for Refreshment Room and visitors' lavatories: basement and entresol plans, 1881.
Royal Academy of Arts, Archives, RAA SEC/22/6 Exh Notices

Fig. 254
Norman Shaw, Proposal for North Diploma Gallery, first scheme: plan, 1881.
Royal Academy of Arts, Archives, RAA SEC/22/6 Exh Notices

Fig. 255
Norman Shaw, Unexecuted proposal for extension to Gallery VIII (later IX) and students' staircase: plan, 1881.
Royal Academy of Arts, Archives, RAA SEC/22/6 Exh Notices

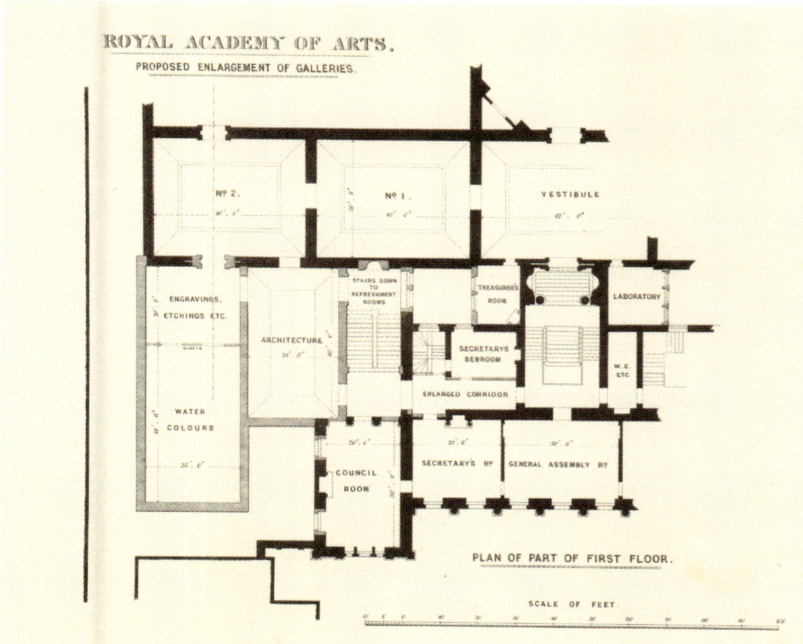

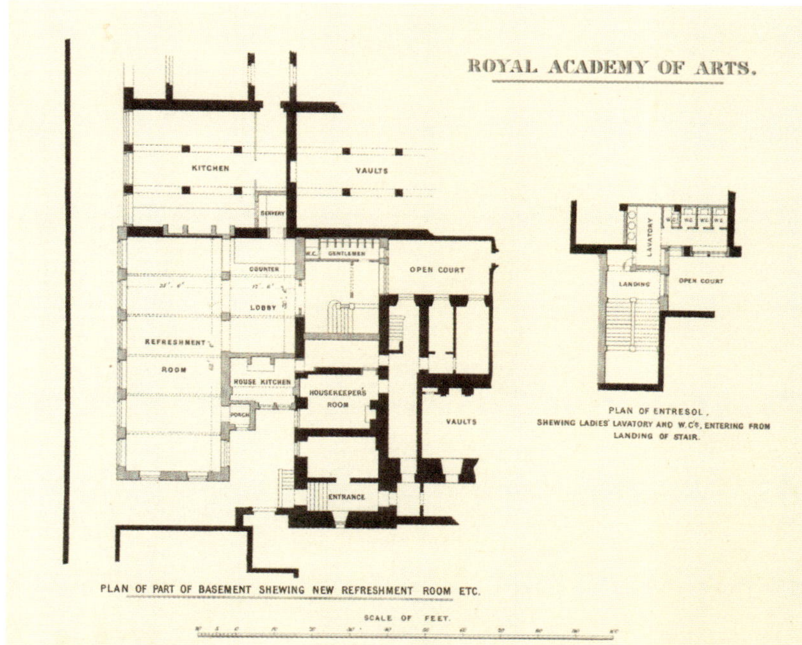

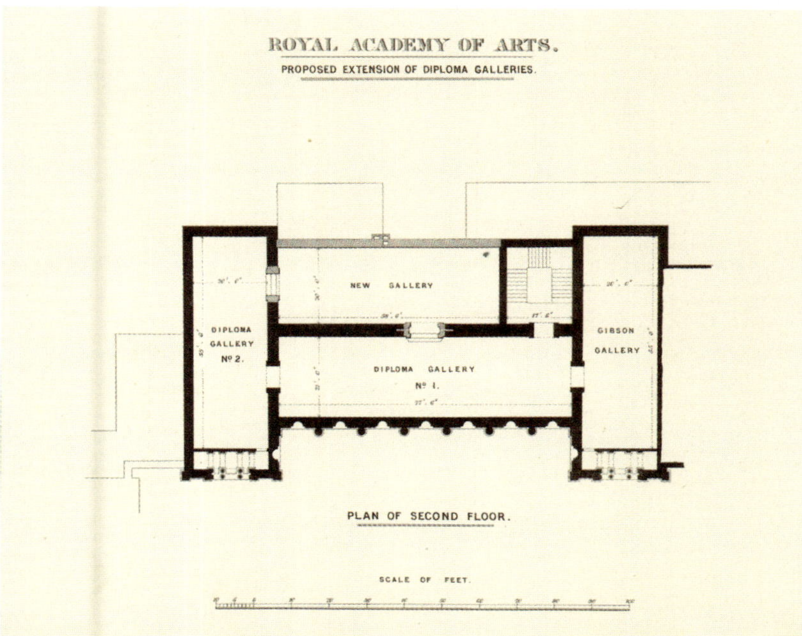

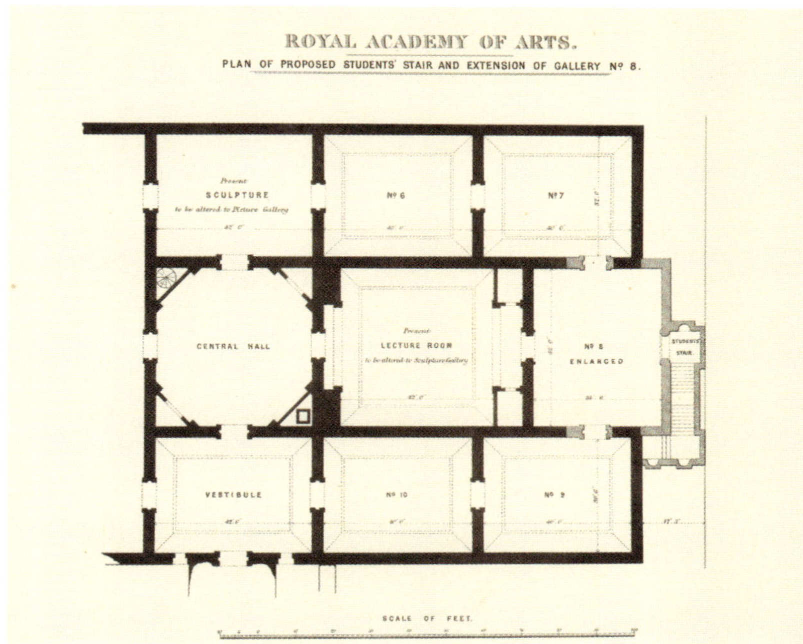

> Galleries exclusively devoted to oil paintings; the Oil Galleries will be continuous throughout; the rooms for Water-Colour Drawings, for Engravings, and for Architecture, will all be distinct, and the advantages thus offered to Exhibitors will be so great as to justify the proposed expenditure.[150]

Any lingering doubts some members may have had about the need for new galleries and better 'visitor services' would have been dispelled on August Bank Holiday 1881 when 8,290 people streamed through the doors of the Academy – the largest daily attendance thus far recorded in its history.[151]

Although he was clearly pushing at an open door, it was typical of Shaw that he went to the trouble of ensuring that easily understandable floor plans of the Committee's proposals were lithographed and distributed to every member of the Academy, along with printed copies of its report. One drawback of this lengthy canvassing process was that it prolonged the development of the brief to two and a half years as new ideas and suggestions ping-ponged back and forth between the Council, the General Assembly and the Building Committee. It did mean, however, that a project that was initially limited to enlarging the Academy's exhibition space progressively expanded to encompass a whole gamut of improvements,

Fig. 256
Norman Shaw, Proposal for extension of the galleries, etc., revised scheme: plans and section, March 1883.
Royal Academy of Arts, Archives, RAA SEC/22/6

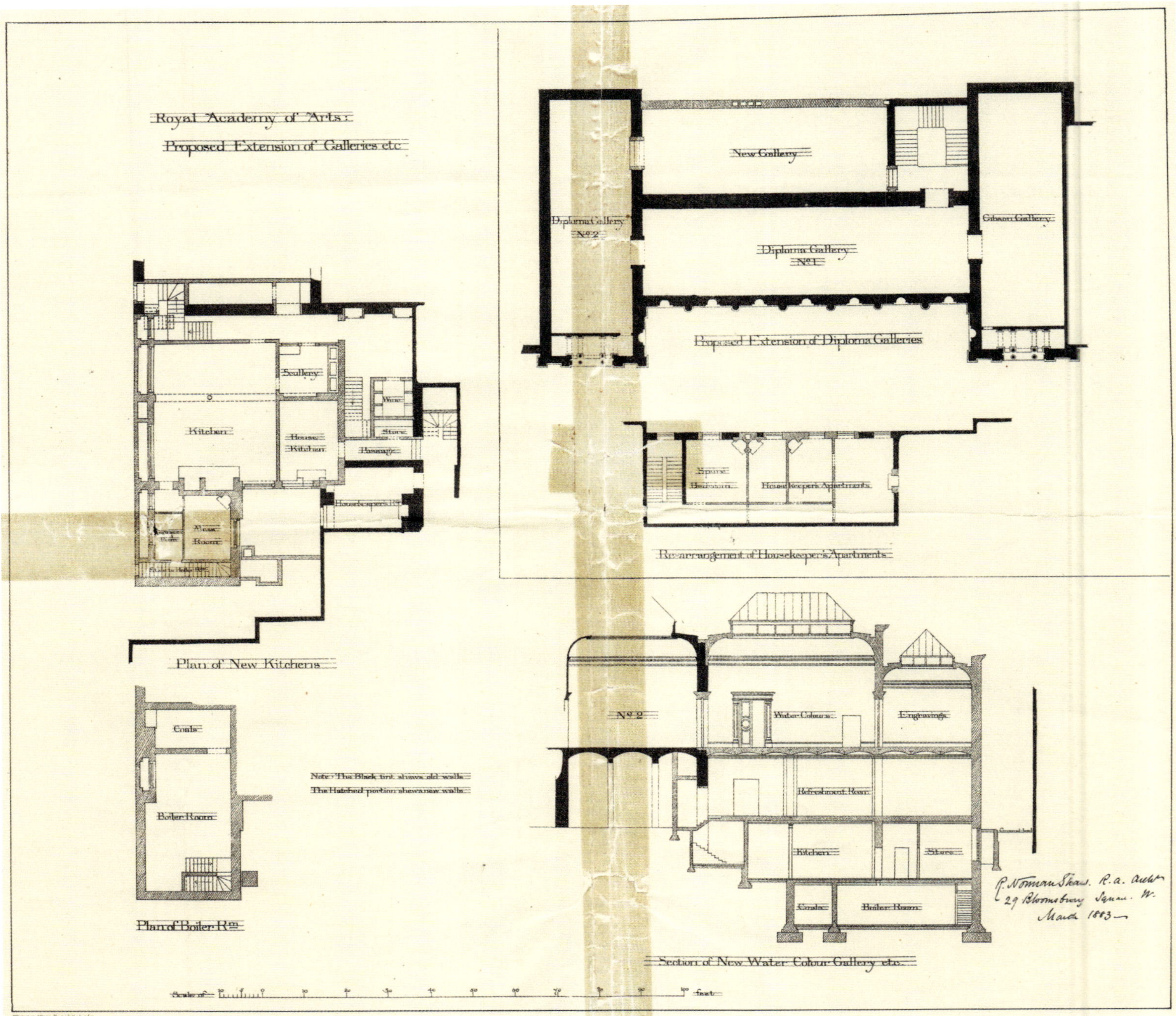

additions, alterations and reconstructions affecting the Schools, the administrative offices, the officers' and servants' quarters, the kitchens, sculleries, storerooms, drains and boiler house. In fact, by the time Shaw was appointed executant architect on 14 June 1882, the Building Committee could claim with some justice that his work would indeed prove to be 'of enormous advantage to the Academy in every respect',[152] inasmuch as it stood to benefit every constituency: the public, the exhibitors, the students, the staff, and the members themselves.

Despite the time he had spent on it, Shaw came close at one point to having to hand over the Academy's commission to a different architect. Street's sudden collapse and early death through overwork in December 1881 put Shaw immediately in line for election as the Academy's new treasurer, which duly took place at a General Assembly on 8 March 1882. While one of the reasons he gave for handing in his resignation ten days later – that he had been 'out of health' – was perfectly true, it is hard to believe that he genuinely 'felt himself in many respects unfitted for the post', particularly when Leighton and many of his fellow Academicians clearly thought otherwise.[153] It is equally unlikely that he turned the post down to avoid a loss of income since he was already overstretched and there was certainly no pressing financial need to retain the Academy's commission. It is difficult not to conclude that at least one of the reasons for Shaw's decision was that Burlington House had assumed more importance for him than simply a routine job (Fig. 256).

Given that Shaw's interventions at Burlington House resulted in the complete loss of two rooms in the north-west wing, it might be thought that his treatment of the building was scarcely less cavalier than Smirke's, and that his evocation of Campbell's *serlianas* in the Refreshment Room windows was little more than adventitious (see above, Fig. 253). However, as Andrew Saint, author of the definitive biography, has pointed out, Shaw's work at Burlington House coincided with a major shift in his attitude to classical architecture, in which 'getting the technicalities of structure, heating, lighting and ventilation right' went hand in hand with a deepening respect for eighteenth-century architectural traditions. It was precisely during this period that Shaw was altering, adding to and restoring a whole series of Queen Anne and Georgian country houses, culminating in Moor Place, Much Hadham (1886–87), by which time 'Every year was turning him into more of a devotee of Georgian architecture'.[154] Probably the clearest evidence of Shaw's sympathetic approach to the original house comes in a letter he wrote from Bordighera in Italy on 9 April 1881 to his office assistant Arthur Keen back in London:

> My dear Keen,
>
> As you are manager in general of the RA drawings, I send you the enclosed ones. I want you to make as soon as convenient two plans … showing the whole of the old building, part of the galleries, and a rearrangement of the new proposed addition containing the engravings, water colours and architecture, and shewing the closets turned into Treasurers Room and Laboratory. …
>
> The other drawing is to shew more particularly the alterations in existing old house, and these we want to be as few and unimportant as possible. I should like to keep all the rooms exactly as they are, only making the 'Enlarged Corridor' a really good approach to General Assembly and Council Room. At present it is so dreadfully back passagish. I don't like the recess on side of council room, but many of them thought this wd be the thing to do. It destroys the fireplace which would have to be under the window at x_____x. However, draw it in as I have shewn, make a neat drawing of this, put in bases round the columns &c and make it look as tidy as possible.[155]

It is clear from a description of the preliminary sketch plans for the new galleries that he sent to the Council on 1 July 1880, that Shaw had at first proposed to retain what had been Lord George Cavendish's bedroom

> for the accommodation of the Architectural drawings, [since] for these a roof-light is not by any means necessary, and a very good room might be formed out of a portion of the present refreshment Room with ample light, the front portion of this room being used for a Secretary's room.[156]

Fig. 257
Royal Academy Refreshment Room staircase (Norman Shaw Staircase), 1883–85. Digital image by Martin Charles, 2009.
RIBA Collections

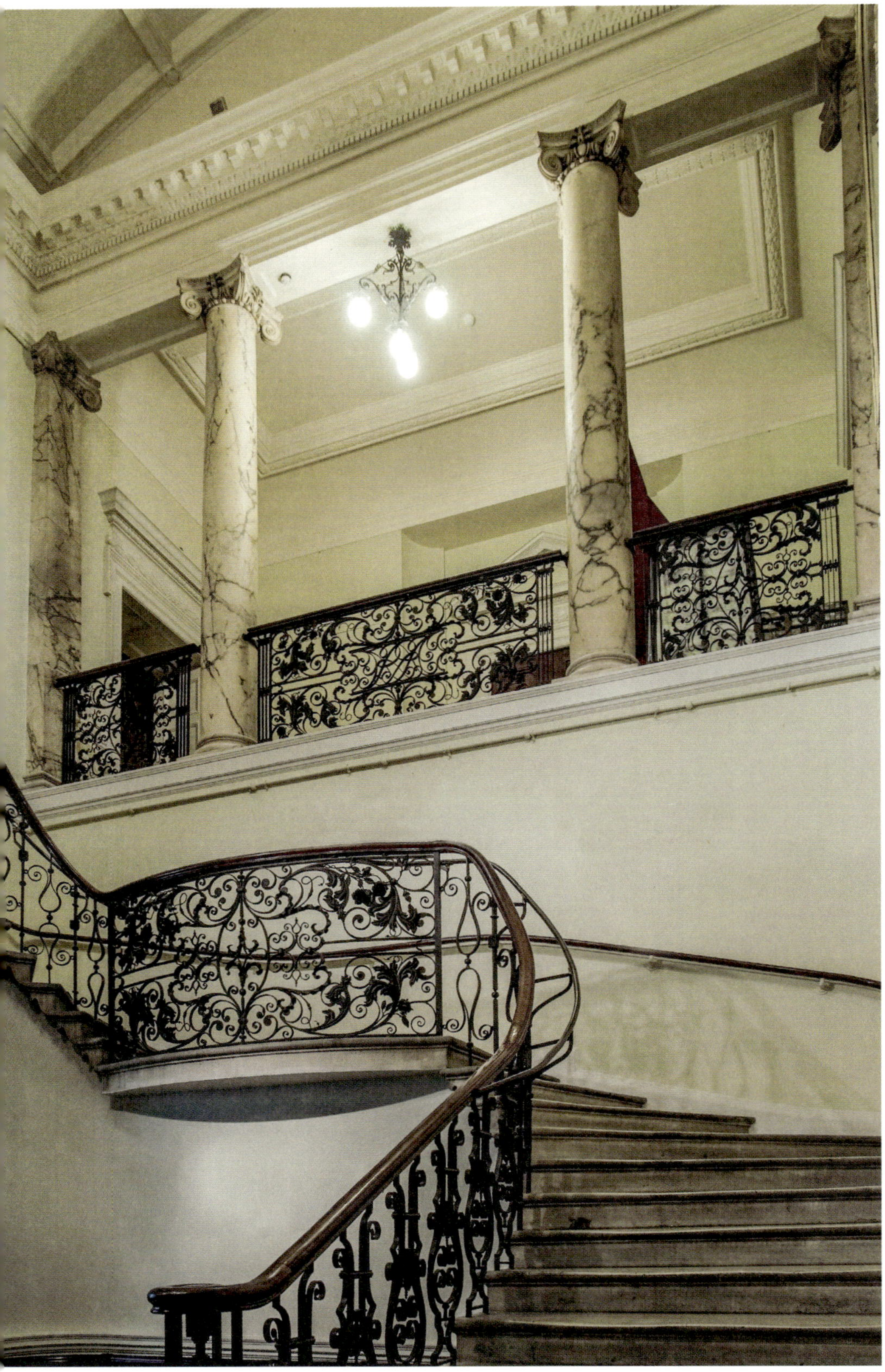

This option was not pursued, almost certainly because it would not have sufficiently separated the public space of the galleries from that used by the Academicians in the old house. It was to achieve precisely this separation that Shaw went on to design and execute what Andrew Saint has rightly described as 'a noble staircase in a discreet yet robust Georgian taste' (Figs 257, 258).[157] Known now as the 'Norman Shaw Staircase', it does precisely the opposite to what staircases are meant to do, in that it promises communication only to deny it, just as the proscenium in a theatre separates the real world of the audience from the fictional world of the actors on the stage. To appreciate the playful wit of this separation it has to be remembered that Shaw's staircase not only led only to the Refreshment Room, but that it was also the only way there until, probably in 1962–63, it was rendered superfluous by a dog-legged corridor through to the entrance hall, a dreadful 'back passage' of the kind that would have mortified Shaw and was fortunately superseded thirty years later by the restaurant ramp designed by Foster Associates.

As Shaw had feared, moving the visitors' lavatories proved a more difficult challenge, so much so that in the end, despite their 'very objectionable' position leading off the Vestibule, they remained where Smirke had originally put them. Shaw's first idea had been to locate the 'retiring places for Ladies ... in the upper part of one of the large Vaults (under No. 1 Gallery)' (see above, Fig. 253), where they could have been reached from 'off the half landing of the stair down to the Refreshment Room', making the interesting point that

> Visitors will often hang about the top landing of stair waiting for friends to go down to lunch, and for similar reasons they will often wait about the foot of stairs, but the half landing itself might often be free for a few minutes at a time.[158]

Since this solution depended on building at the same level as the kitchen in the basement, it had to be abandoned when it was decided instead

> that in order to lessen the distance between the Galleries and the new Refreshment Room, the floor of the latter be raised, & a kitchen built underneath, the present kitchen being converted into an additional store-room, which is much wanted.[159]

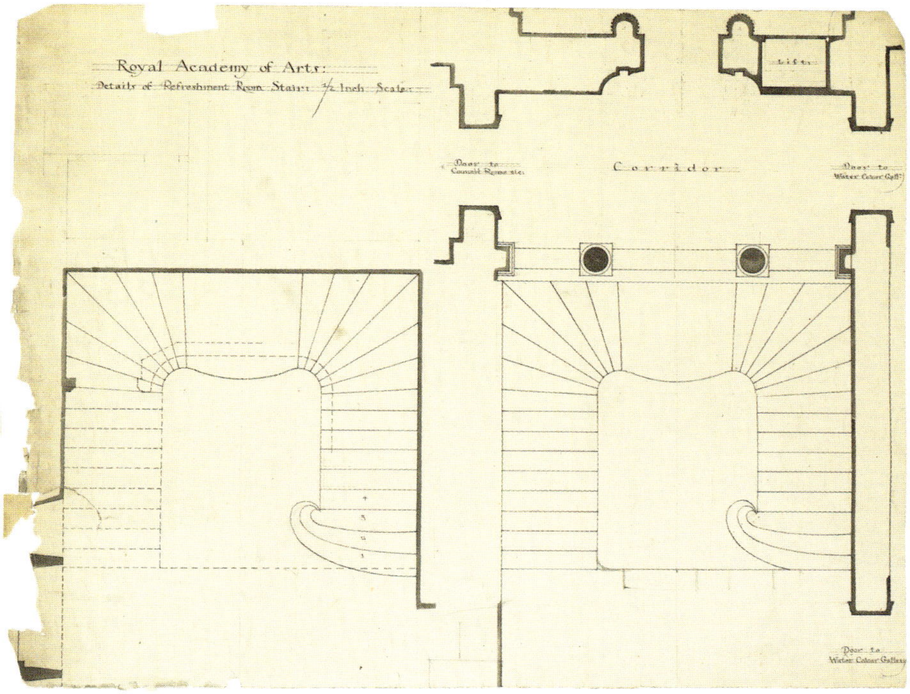

Fig. 258
Norman Shaw, Design for the Refreshment Room staircase and General Assembly Room landing, as executed: plans, *c.* 1884.
Royal Academy of Arts, London, 06/1757

Although a proposal for putting both the ladies' and gentlemen's lavatories at the foot of the new stairs is shown in a later set of lithographed plans dated March 1883 (Fig. 259), this was not carried out either, possibly because they would have been ventilated solely from roof-lights. It also proved impossible to construct a new boiler house beneath the kitchens, due to 'the nature of the soil which, though composed of solid gravel for a depth of thirteen feet, proved below that to be sand with running water.'[160] As with the 'quite inadequate' drain to Piccadilly (that naturally had to be replaced), it was probably Shaw who insisted that 'it was ... impossible for various reasons to leave [the boiler house] in its present position in the centre of the building'. As a result, four new boilers were duly installed in an externally accessed room constructed at the same level as the new kitchen 'on that portion of the old kitchen which remained un-encroached upon by the Refreshment Room', thereby ensuring the exclusion from the basement of 'all the dirt and dust inseparable from a boiler-house'.[161]

More minor changes of plan included the installation of a dumbwaiter lift in the west bay of the reapplied Corinthian screen on the restored north wall of Ware's State Dining Room, reflecting a decision to use this room rather than the Saloon for general assemblies and the Council lunches and dinners, and thereby fortuitously returning it to its original domestic use. According to the March 1883 lithographed plan it had been intended that a pair of dumbwaiters would serve the top landing of the Refreshment Room stairs, presumably with the needs of the Annual Dinner in mind. However, as one of the few surviving drawings of his work for the Academy indicates, Shaw subsequently proposed a built-in alcove seat at the top of the stairs to provide for those 'waiting for friends to go down to lunch' (Fig. 260). In another last-minute change, arising out of the need for uninterrupted hanging space sufficient to accommodate very large pictures such as Giampietrino's full-size copy of Leonardo da Vinci's *The Last Supper* and Daniel Maclise's 45-foot-long cartoon of *The Meeting of Wellington and Blücher after the Battle of Waterloo*, the Building Committee had decided in February 1882 that there should be 'no Door between the present large Diploma Gallery & the proposed new Gallery'.[162] Fortunately, common sense prevailed when the latter came to be built, since the doorways proposed originally at the centre of its west and south walls were in the end both suppressed in favour of entrances tucked as close as possible into its south-east and south-west corners.

The most significant expansion of the scope of Shaw's improvements to the building dates from May 1882 when, in response to a request by the General Assembly in March that year 'that there should be some provision made if possible for a new Life School', John Loughborough Pearson RA (who had replaced Street on the reconvened Building Committee) made 'some suggestions for obtaining the desired additional school space by building over the annex'.[163] Prior to this broadening of scope to include the Schools, the Committee had recommended that 'the proposed Water Colour Gallery be enlarged to include the space devoted to Engravings, &c.' and that the latter 'be placed in another Gallery to be constructed over the roadway between the existing Galleries & the Burlington Arcade.'[164] However, although the idea of constructing a permanent western extension to the Main Galleries over the service lane connecting Piccadilly and Burlington Gardens was to resurface at least twice over the next fifty years, this was never really likely to happen because of the separate agreements that it would have required with the Office of Works, the owners of the Burlington Arcade freehold and all the shopkeepers on its east side affected by the proposal.[165] In view of the problem of overcrowding in the Schools, it made more sense to build instead a separate gallery for the exhibition of architecture adjacent to and leading off Gallery X on the south-east corner of Smirke's building since, fittingly, this could also provide a much-needed extension of the Architectural School below (Figs 261–263).[166]

Admittedly, the net gain of 2,232 square feet in the Schools achieved by incorporating Smirke's 'Annex' and enlarging the Architectural School was not huge. However, more important for improving working conditions in the Schools than a mere gain in aggregate floor area was the opportunity this gave to increase the number of classrooms from six to nine, providing for the first time a 1,767-square-foot Preliminary Painting School, separate Men's and Ladies' Upper Painting Schools, two Life Rooms, two rooms for Drawing from the Antique, separate Schools of Modelling from the Life and the Antique (both conveniently close to a Casting Shed), and an Architectural School with room for up to 75% more drafting tables. As the account of Shaw's planned alterations printed in the Academy's *Annual*

Fig. 259
Norman Shaw, Proposed extension of Royal Academy Galleries and Schools: ground-floor plan, 1883.
Royal Academy of Arts, London, 10/1585

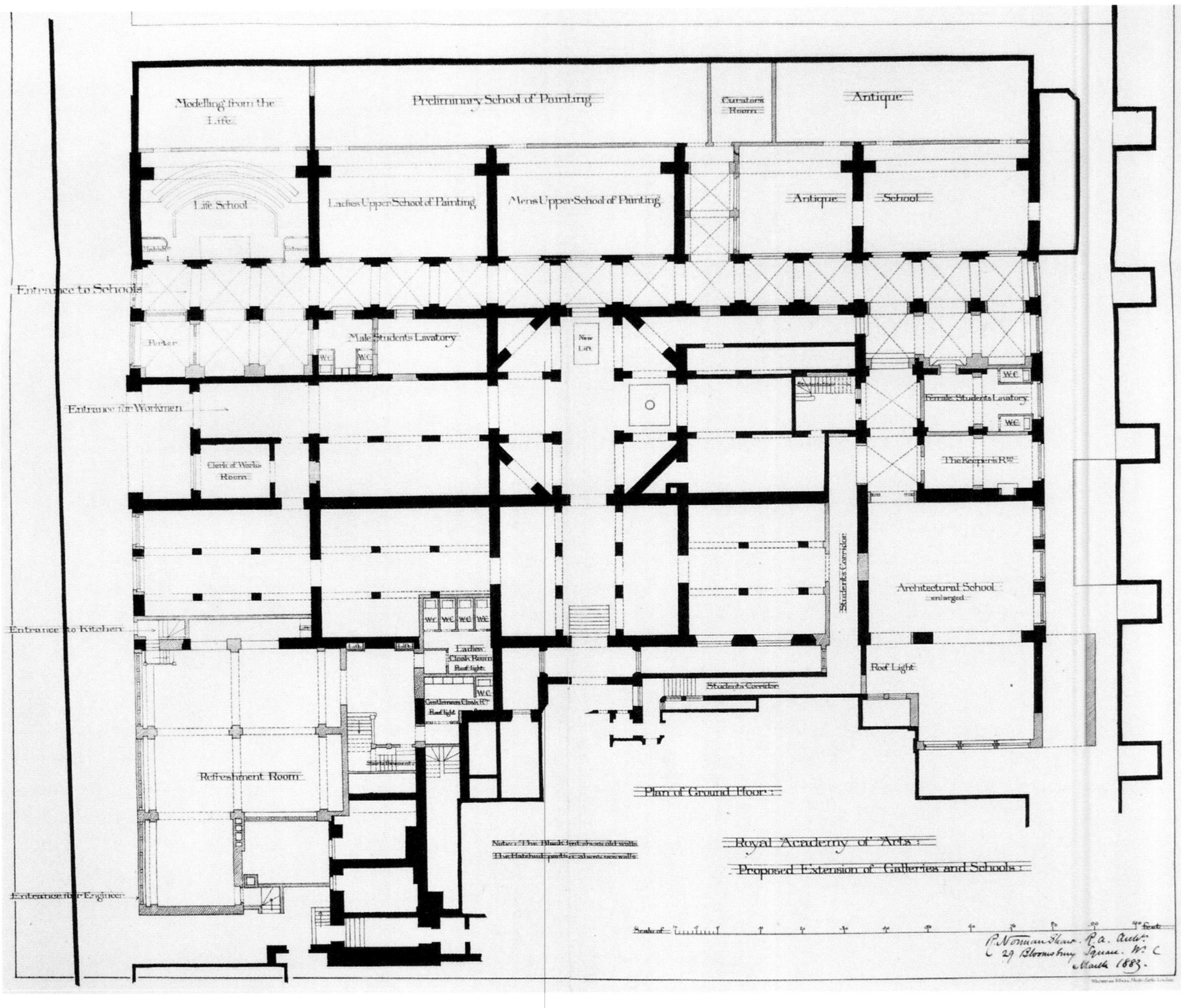

Fig. 260
Norman Shaw, Design for Refreshment Room: staircase, well, niche and wall elevations, c. 1884.
Royal Academy of Arts, London, 06/1758

Fig. 261
Norman Shaw, Proposal for extension of the galleries, etc., almost as executed: plan, March 1883.
Royal Academy of Arts, Archives, RAA SEC/22/6

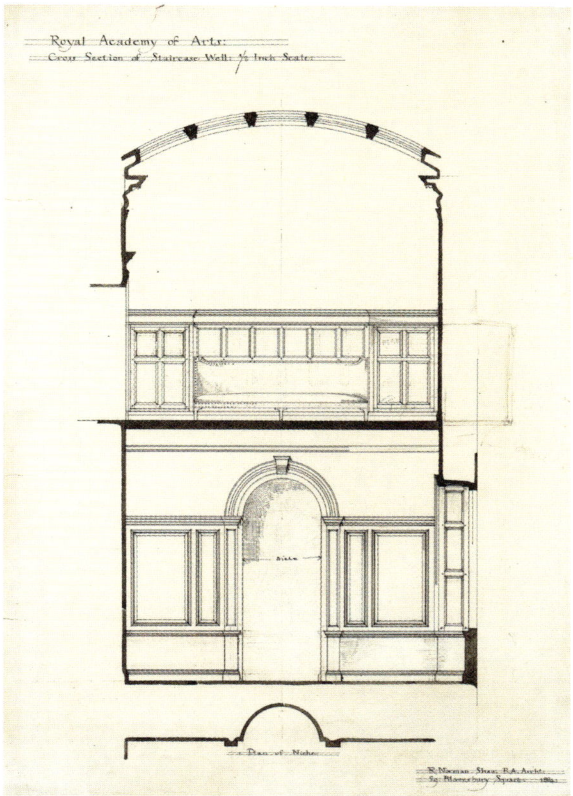

Report for 1883 makes clear, however, his most radical proposal was for a redesign of the roof, both in the existing Schools and the range of classrooms formed from the 'Annex' along the north wall:

> The present Schools are lit partly by vertical windows, and principally by a very flat roof. The former give very little light, and the lower edge of the latter is 19 feet from the floor level. It is proposed to do away with the vertical windows, and to make the roof light much steeper, so as to bring the lower edge within 9 feet of the floor. At present no light of any use reaches the back of the Schools, so that for all practical purposes there is 10 or 11 feet on the side next the Corridor absolutely useless; if better lit this space would become available for working purposes thus materially enlarging the capacity of the Schools.[167]

So critical was Shaw's design of this new roof, it was decided to delay carrying out any work on enlarging the Schools until a properly constructed prototype had been tested for a year in the Life Room (Fig. 264). Consequently, by the time alterations in the Schools

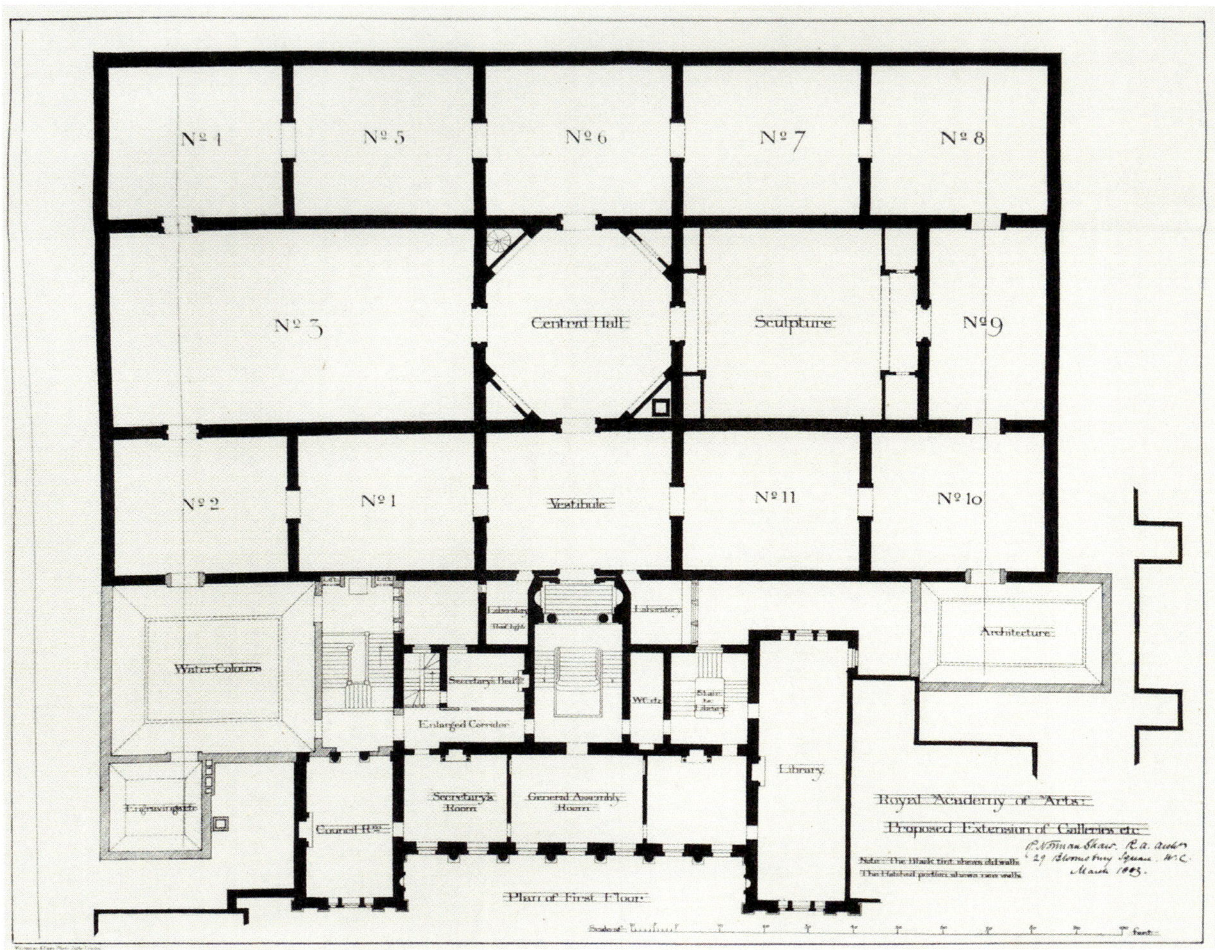

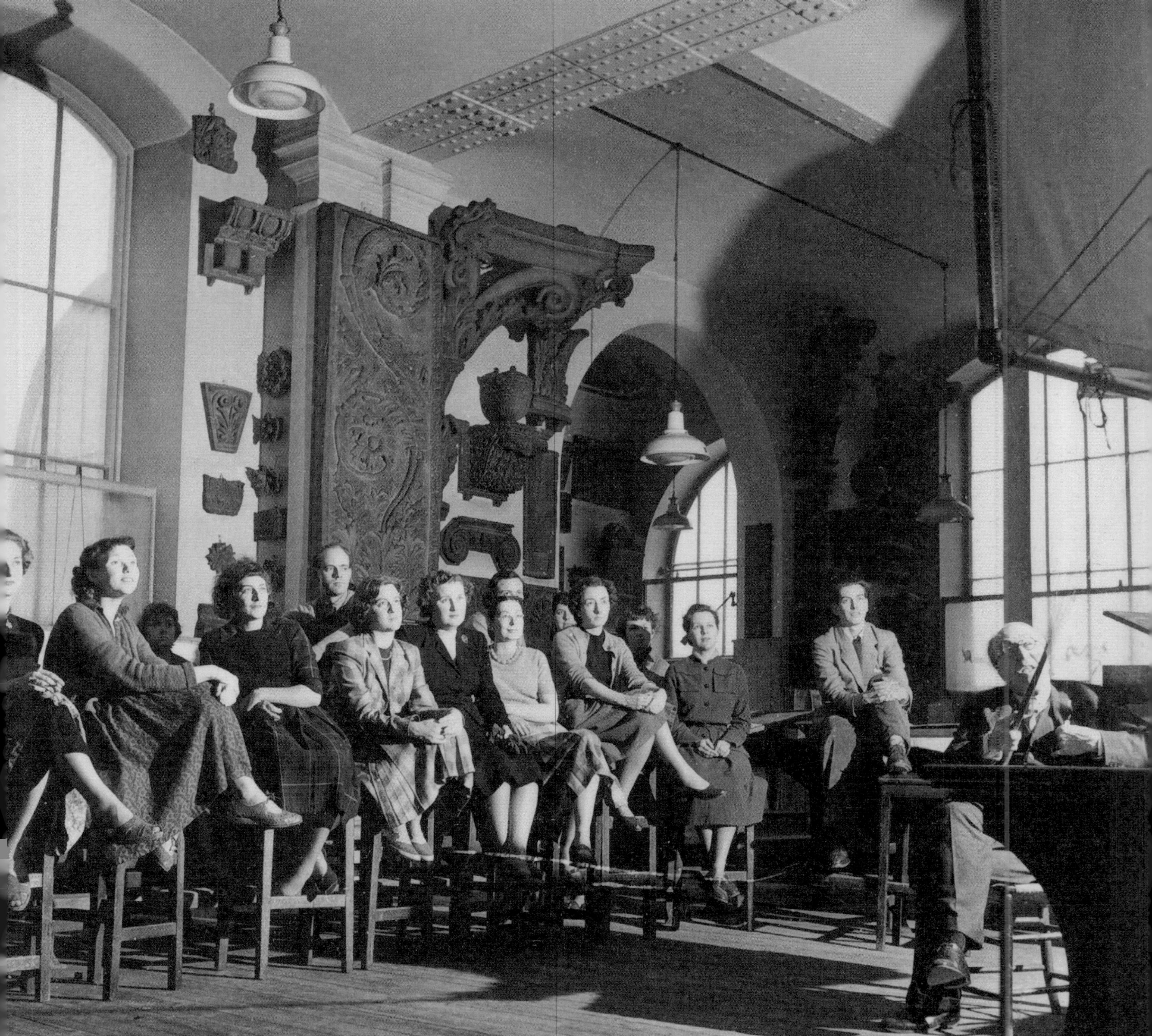

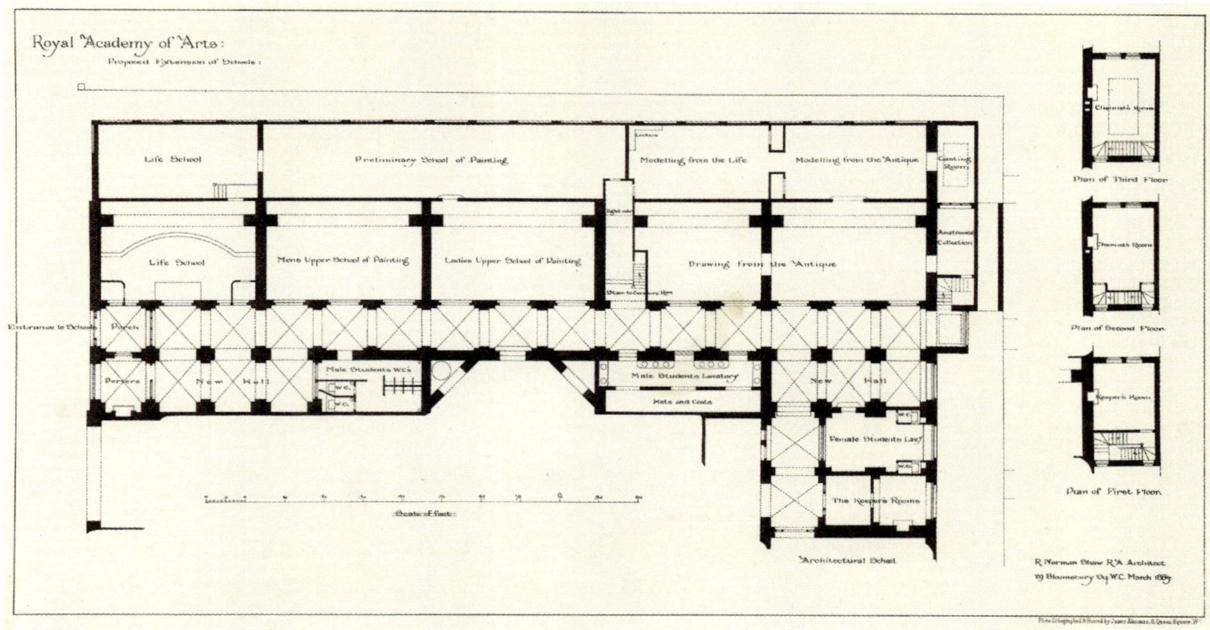

Fig. 262
Norman Shaw, Proposal for extension of Royal Academy Schools: plan of revised scheme as executed, dated March 1883 (but later).
Royal Academy of Arts, Archives, RAA SEC/22/6 (05)

Fig. 263
Sir Albert Richardson lecturing to art and architecture students in the Royal Academy Architectural School (as altered by Norman Shaw, 1883–85), March 1953. Photograph by Russell Westwood.
Royal Academy of Arts, London, 10/3406

finally began in 1885, an amended plan and flyer had to be printed for circulation to the members explaining a number of changes to the proposals they had approved two years earlier. Chief among these was the addition of

> A small building at the east end of the Schools, to contain on the ground floor, a room for the Collection of the Professor of Anatomy; on the first floor, a Store-room for the use of the Keeper; and on the two upper floors, rooms for the Professor of Chemistry, the upper one having a top light.[168]

Known subsequently as the 'Cottage', this four-storey eyrie at the north-east corner of Smirke's building not only solved the problem at last of where to put the Professor of Chemistry's laboratory, it also provided a location for the Academy's first anatomical museum, the need for which had been pointed out by the current Professor of Anatomy John Marshall in a well-timed letter to the Council in 1883, 'suggesting the advisability of forming an Art Anatomy Collection for the use of the Students'.[169]

Despite, or perhaps because of the long prehistory of Norman Shaw's work for the Academy, it took just two years – from the first payment of William Oldrieve's monthly salary as clerk of the works on 4 October 1884 to the last on 4 September 1886 – to complete everything that Smirke had hoped to achieve fifteen years earlier.[170] Despite an ominous warning from the Audit Committee in 1885 that its running expenses had begun to outstrip its income, so prosperous had the Academy grown since it moved to Burlington House, scarcely a murmur was heard about the wisdom of having spent some 85% more on a building project than had been originally agreed.[171]

THE DAY THE GIBSON GALLERY finally opened to the public on 27 November 1876 – from 11 a.m. to 4 p.m. every weekday all the year round and free of charge – the Council panicked, resolving unanimously that

> In view of the inconvenience likely to arise from visitors to the Gibson Gallery & Diploma Galleries going through the hall at the time of the arrangement of the Exhibitions, the Treasurer [be] instructed to turn the extreme east window in the hall into a door & cut off a passage from the hall to lead direct from this door to the Gibson & Diploma Galleries.[172]

There is no physical or documentary evidence to suggest that Barry ever carried out this instruction, although it was dutifully recorded both in the minutes of the meeting and in the Academy's *Annual Report* for 1876. The auditors' recent criticism may have made him wary of rushing into any further expenditure on the front hall. Furthermore, it must have soon been obvious that the Council had wildly over-estimated the likely nuisance arising from visitors making a special trip to the Academy to view its new public galleries. Edmund Gosse's reaction in 1883 was probably not that untypical:

> The least known public collection of art in London is certainly the Diploma Gallery of the Royal Academy. In vain is it 'open free from 11 a.m. till 4 p.m.;' there is no-one to respond to the mute appeal. The determined visitor who makes his way to the entrance of it – within the precincts of Burlington House, but a good deal to the right of the entrance to the Royal Academy – feels like Juan Fernandez arriving in an unknown island. Vainly does he twirl the handle of the door towards which the public notices incline;

Fig. 264
Royal Academy Schools Life Room in 2017. Photograph by Maciej Urbanek.

> that is plainly not the way in, though it might be styled the entrance. If he is strong in purpose and hammers on the panels with the knob of his umbrella, pale faces presently peer at him through the dusky glass, and after a solemn pause a voice far away up the façade invites him to explain what it can be that he wants. At last his wish being slowly comprehended, he is led through winding musty ways and shown up a staircase with all the courteous circumstance that attends angels' visits. Surprise and meek elation welcome the unhoped-for stranger, and at last he finds himself shown into a triple gallery, or suite of three rooms, which he finds to be badly lighted, and crowded with works of art of a very miscellaneous description.[173]

Although no-one realised it at the time, the opening of the Gibson and Diploma galleries sowed the seed of a new phase in the Academy's relationship with the public, one that would be no longer tied to the rhythm of its Summer and Winter exhibitions, the semesters of its Schools, or the observance of its rituals. That this seed lay dormant for the best part of the twentieth century as the Academy turned inwards to cling to old ways in the face of its loss of financial muscle and artistic authority, was in large measure made possible by its occupancy of Burlington House as private property rather than a public building.

Today there are only two places where the Academy is identified by name on the fabric of Burlington House and both are easy to miss. When Smirke erected a small, stone tablet lettered ROYAL ACADEMY OF ARTS above his new entrance porch in March 1874 (see above, Fig. 247), he wrote to the Council 'with regard to the desirability of gilding the letters of the Inscription … to render them more legible.'[174] The Council's opinion at that time, which may have been influenced by the newly gilded lettering that had probably appeared by then over the front doors of the learned societies, was 'that it would be better to cut the letters deeper & square.' Even more understated is the 'RA' gracefully entwined in the wrought-iron foliage on Shaw's balcony outside the General Assembly Room (see above, Fig. 257). When therefore the Council decided to ask John Dibblee Crace's advice on how to redecorate the Saloon in 1891 'in accordance with the intentions of Kent, the architect of Burlington House, who, as shown by a number of published drawings to which they were referred by Mr. J. D. Crace, had himself designed the panelling and woodwork of the room', it was rather extraordinary that they ended up commissioning him to design instead a painted cove to celebrate the most illustrious names in the history of the Academy since its foundation.[175] Although there may be no direct causal connection, it is striking that it was only after the shock of its first annual deficit for more than a century in 1885 and the catastrophic drop in Summer Exhibition visitor figures the following year that the Academy started to seek solace in its glorious past. Certainly, it can hardly have been coincidental that at the time of the Crace commission, its secretary F. A. Eaton and its current librarian J. E. Hodgson RA were already hard at work on what would become the first of no less than three semi-official histories of the institution to appear within the first six decades of the twentieth century.[176]

Painted over in white emulsion little more than thirty years later, and now only fragmentarily revealed beside a small section of the original fresco by William Kent lying many paint layers beneath it, Crace's scheme consisted of a roll-call of seven presidents of the Academy (including Leighton but omitting the architect James Wyatt) depicted in a series of cameo portraits arranged clockwise around the room within Kentian guilloche-bordered lunettes dividing the east (× 2), south (× 3) and west (× 2) coves (Fig. 265). Inside the four inner spandrels formed by these lunettes were ornamental plaques naming the four most illustrious members of the Academy in successive eras of its history: on the east wall, Thomas Gainsborough between Reynolds and Benjamin West; on the south wall, John Flaxman and David Wilkie between Thomas Lawrence, Martin Archer Shee and Charles Eastlake; and on the west wall, J. M. W. Turner between Grant and Leighton. The cove of the north wall – visible only from inside the room – honoured George III and Queen Victoria as the Academy's founding patron and its current protector, whose portraits were flanked by plaques naming the two eminent Academicians who

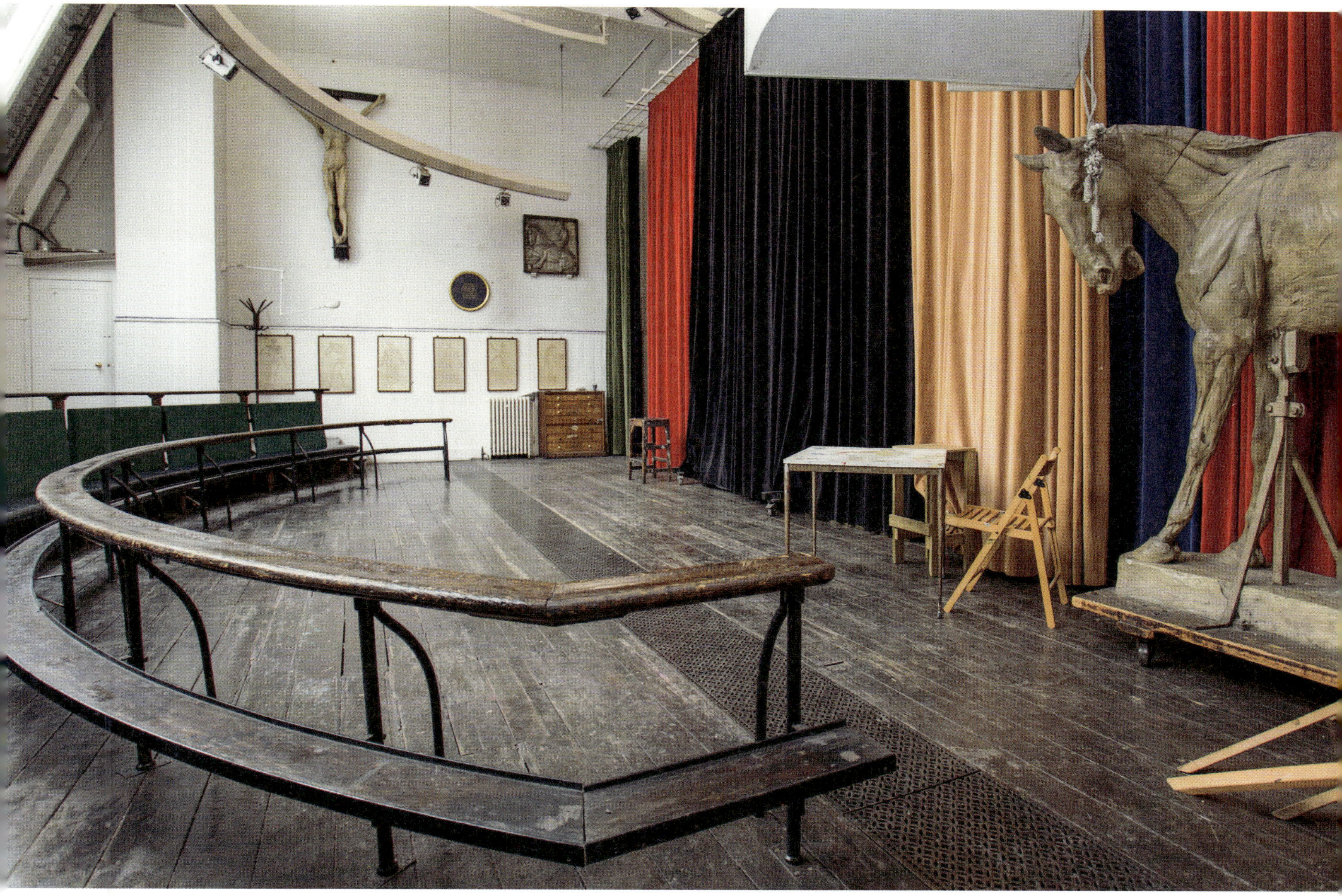

had served them as tutors, William Chambers and Edwin Landseer, thereby neatly alluding to the pedagogic responsibilities of every Academician.

One probable reason why a project to redecorate the Saloon – which included incidentally the first permanent installation of electric lighting anywhere in the building – was susceptible to becoming a celebration of the Academy's history was the room's obviously eighteenth-century character. Another was the fact that, despite its central position and high status in the original house, once it had been decided to use Shaw's newly formed dining room in the west wing for General Assemblies and Council lunches and dinners, it had ended up serving no obvious practical purpose. This in turn made it more suitable for symbolic use as a place of honour in the building where the Academy could celebrate its heroes in a display of memorabilia.

The sudden and unexpected death of Lord Leighton on 25 January 1896 dealt such a severe blow to the Academy it is not surprising that his close friend George Aitchison RA, who over the course of three decades had designed and enlarged Leighton's celebrated house and studio in Holland Park Road, Kensington, was moved to show in that year's Summer Exhibition two suggested designs for replacing the floor in the Entrance Hall of Burlington House (Fig. 266). In view of the interest Leighton took in the embellishment of public buildings, had either of these spectacular marble floors been executed it might well have formed a lasting memorial in Burlington House to the most universally admired of all presidents after Reynolds. However, Aitchison's designs did not chime in the least with the eighteenth-century heritage that the Academy had begun to identify with in its decorative 'appropriation' of the Saloon five years earlier. When therefore, towards the end of 1898, the Council decided that something needed to be done about the 'very bad condition' of Smirke's black and red terracotta floor tiles in the Entrance Hall, it was almost

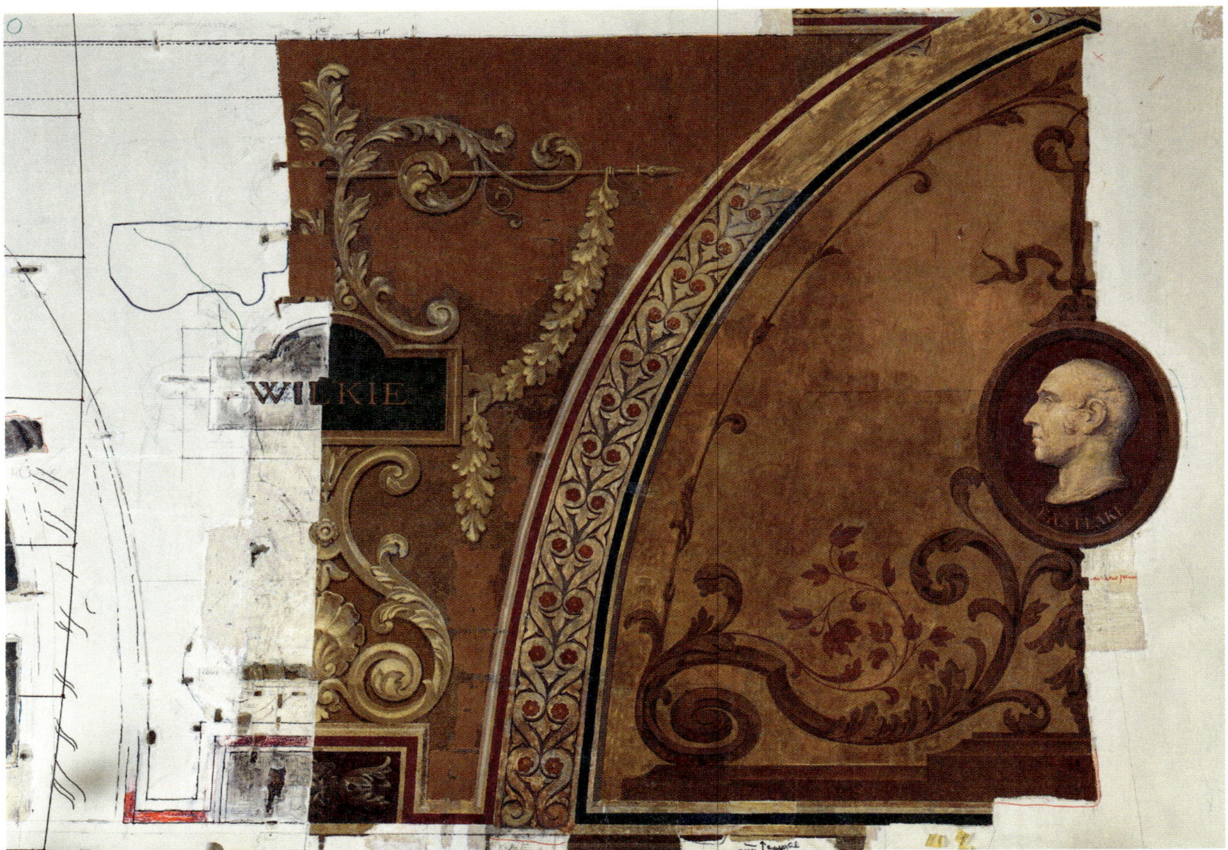

Fig. 265
J. D. Crace, Decoration of the Saloon cove, Burlington House, 1891.
Royal Academy of Arts, London, L12624

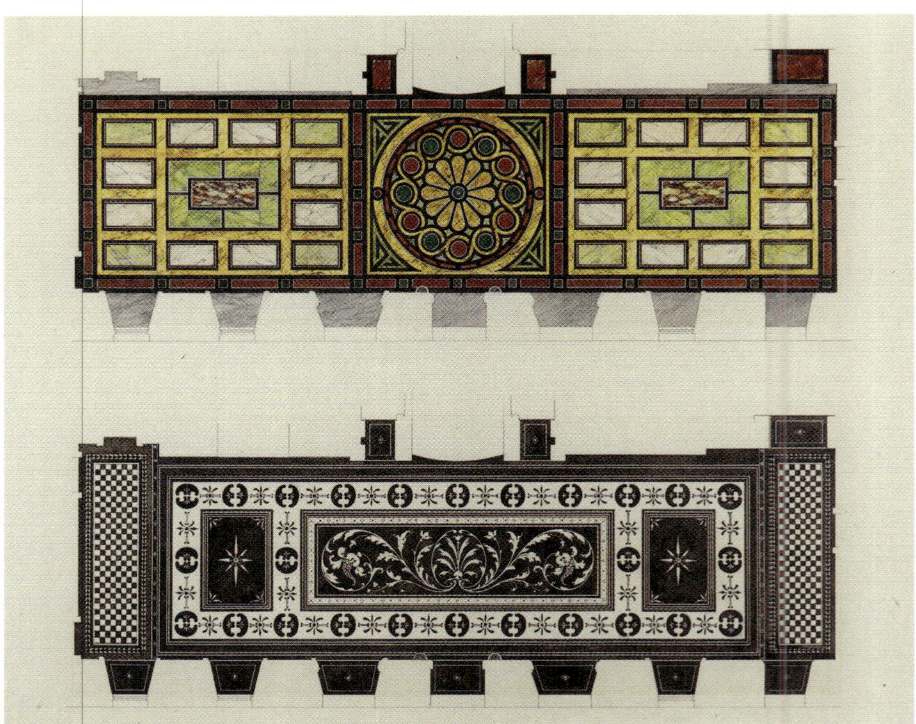

Fig. 266
George Aitchison, Unexecuted designs for repaving the entrance hall of Burlington House, 2 April 1896.
RIBA Collections, SB94/1(5)

inevitable that they would opt 'to repave it with black and white marble slabs after the pattern of the old pavement in the Hall of Burlington House, as can be seen in the entrance passage of the Keeper's House.'[177] Similarly, when early in 1899 their attention was drawn 'to some paintings by Angelica Kauffman RA [and Benjamin West PRA] which formerly decorated the ceiling of the Council Room at Somerset House, and subsequently at Trafalgar Square, but which, since the removal of the Academy to Burlington House, had lain neglected in the basement', it was hardly surprising that they asked 'Mr. Jackson … to make a design for having them put up in the Entrance Hall ceiling … to be carried out in the autumn at the same time as the repaving of the Hall.'[178] Although described in the *Survey of London* as typical of his trademark 'Anglo-Jackson' style, the overall effect of Sir Thomas Graham Jackson's new ceiling for the Academy's front hall was undoubtedly intended to evoke that of the Council Room at Somerset House, as well as to complement the presumed 'eighteenth-century' (i.e. Ware's) paved hall floor.[179] Asked at the same time to improve 'the somewhat mean aspect of the Hall', Jackson applied a high dado of oak panelling to all four walls; positioned a pair of temple-fronted glazed porters' kiosks alongside the two side entrances on the south wall; designed bespoke brass door-furniture, manufactured and supplied by Hart Son, Peard & Co. for £37 6s. 6d. (Figs 267–269);[180] and (possibly) formed the pair of arched openings in the north wall over the cloakroom and 'money-taking' counters.[181] Carried out by the building contractors Farmer & Brindley between 18 October 1899 and 21 April 1900 at a total cost of £3,562 7s. 7d., Jackson's Entrance Hall was to remain reassuringly unaltered for more than sixty years (Fig. 270).[182]

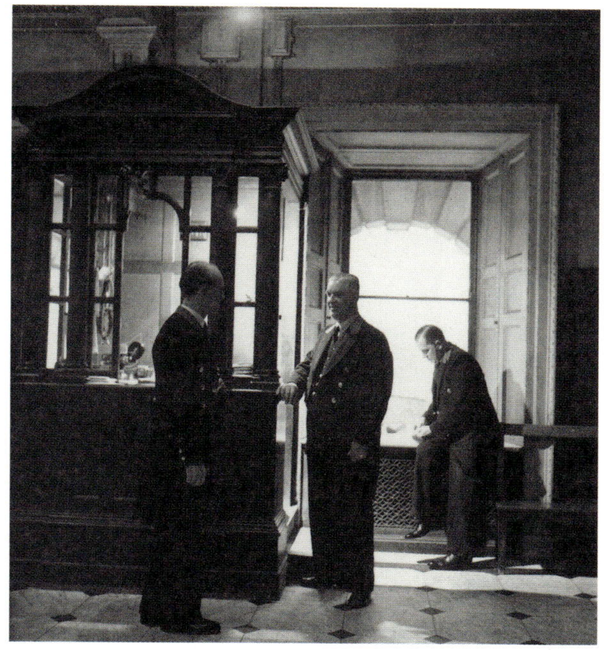

Fig. 267
Porters in the entrance hall of Burlington House (kiosks designed by Sir T. G. Jackson), March 1953. Photograph by Russell Westwood.
Royal Academy of Arts, London, 10/3398

Jackson's slightly earlier improvements to the interior of the Keeper's House, carried out by D. Charteris & Co. at a total cost of £1,808 8s. following the death of the incumbent keeper P. H. Calderon RA in April 1898 and completed by the end of December that year, are not identifiable today since no drawings or specifications for this work have been traced. Apart from the treasurer's summary accounts (which reveal that Calderon's successor Ernest Crofts RA – or perhaps his German wife Elizabeth – chose paper hangings manufactured by Wylie & Lochhead Ltd, Arthur Sanderson & Sons, Essex & Co. and Jeffrey & Co.), the only clue to the nature of Jackson's alterations occurs in a list of (now mostly missing) drawings compiled by the Academy's first surveyor Richard Phené Spiers. This list mentions a design for a 'New arch between Study and Drawing Room' and a 'Cross section through passage to Schools and Picture Store', which if executed were probably both altered by William Curtis Green in 1927. There was, however, one feature that Jackson introduced that can be readily identified since the Council asked him to provide the same for Burlington House:

> One of the improvements included in the alterations of the Keeper's house was the making an area in the front to give access to servants and tradesmen, and the Council thought it a good opportunity for making a corresponding area on the other side of the building, so as to provide a means of approach from the front for servants and tradesmen to the Academy's premises.[183]

Because the Burlington House courtyard is government land, the Academy had to apply to the Office of Works for permission to alter any part of the area in front of Burlington House not included in its lease. Only after this permission had been granted in February 1899 did it occur to the Office of Works to consult either the Society of Antiquaries or the Royal Society over the Academy's plans. Since these involved sinking spiral staircases extremely close to their residential front doors, not surprisingly both societies lodged vigorous protests with the Treasury and the First Commissioner. Although the

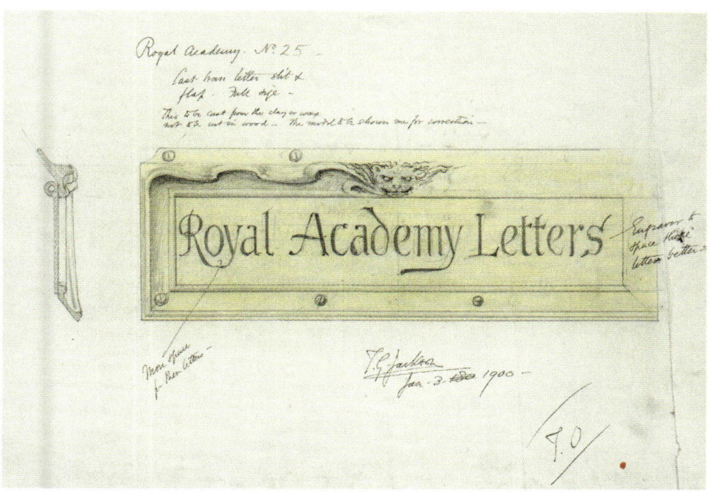

Fig. 268
Sir T. G. Jackson, Cast-brass letter slit and flap for the entrance hall of Burlington House: elevation and profile, 11 December 1899.
Royal Academy of Arts, London, 08/4295 (verso)

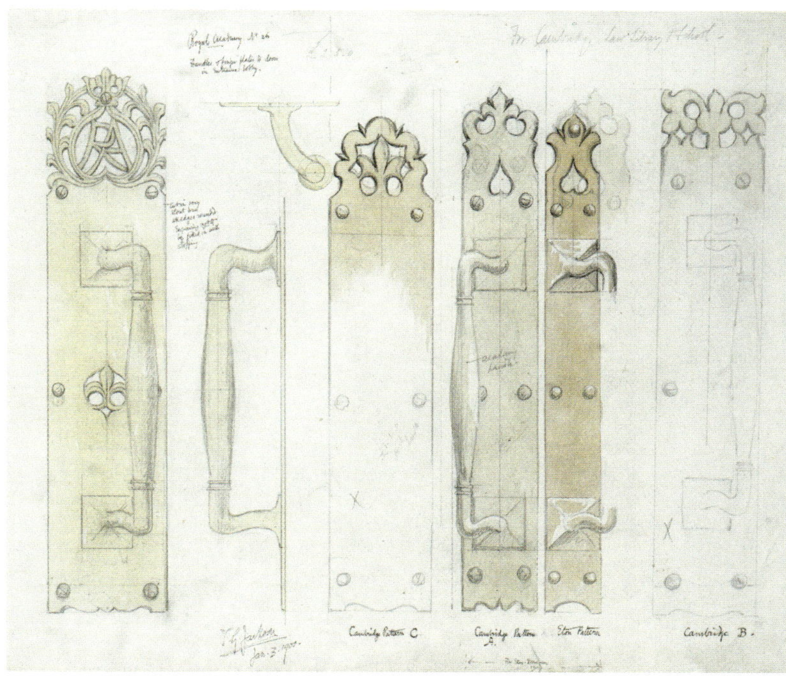

Fig. 269
Sir T. G. Jackson, Entrance hall, alternative designs for brass door-handles and finger-plates: full-size elevation, plan and profile, 3 January 1900.
Royal Academy of Arts, London, 08/4293

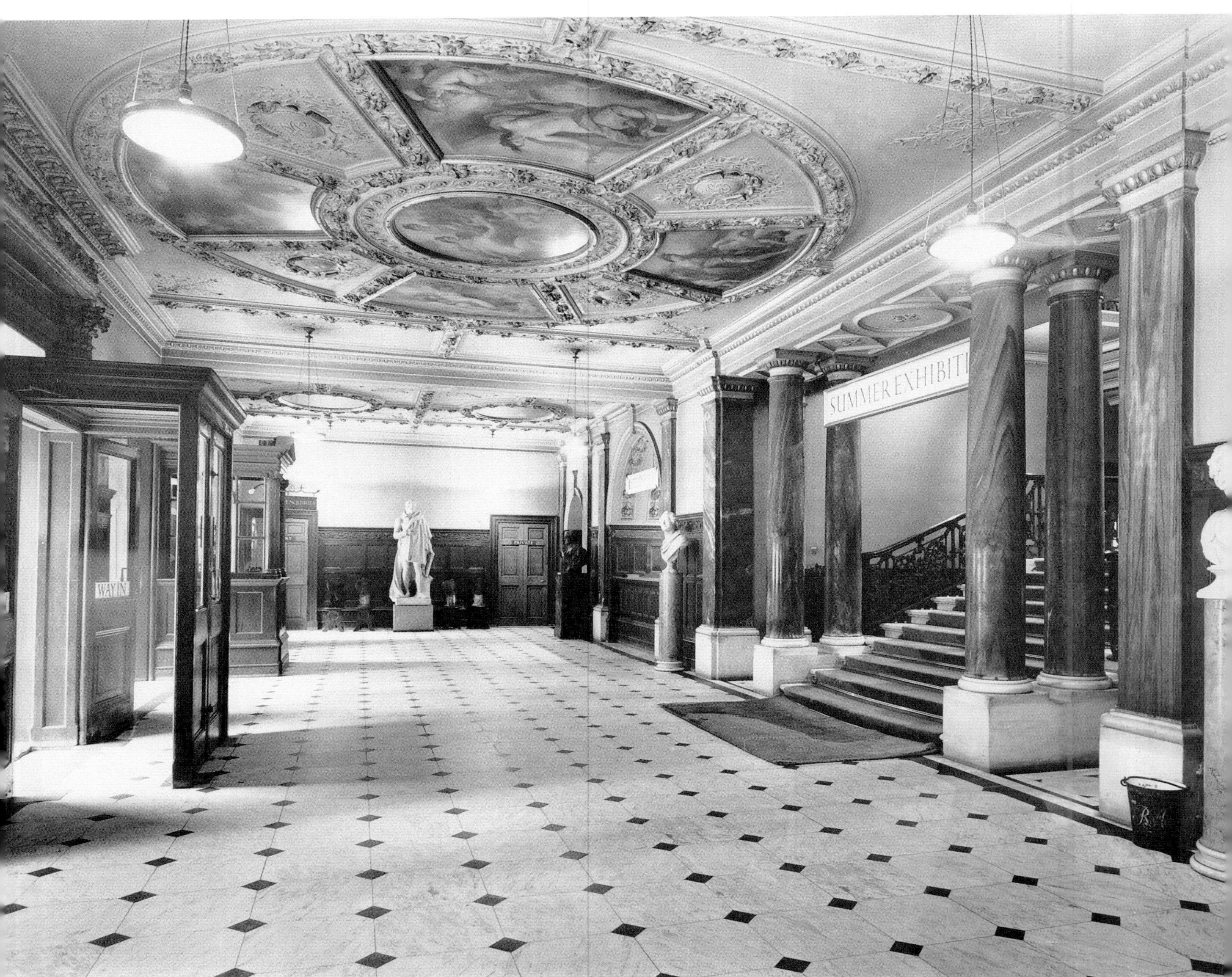

Fig. 270
Burlington House, entrance hall (designed by Sir T. G. Jackson in 1899–1900) looking west, 1962.
London Metropolitan Archives (LCC Photograph Library), SC/PHL/01/508/62/2578

Fig. 271
Sir T. G. Jackson, Wrought-iron railings, gate and stairs to the tradesmen's entrance in basement of the Keeper's House, showing alteration to the courtyard as agreed with H.M. Board of Works, 21 July 1899.
Royal Academy of Arts, London, 11/3176

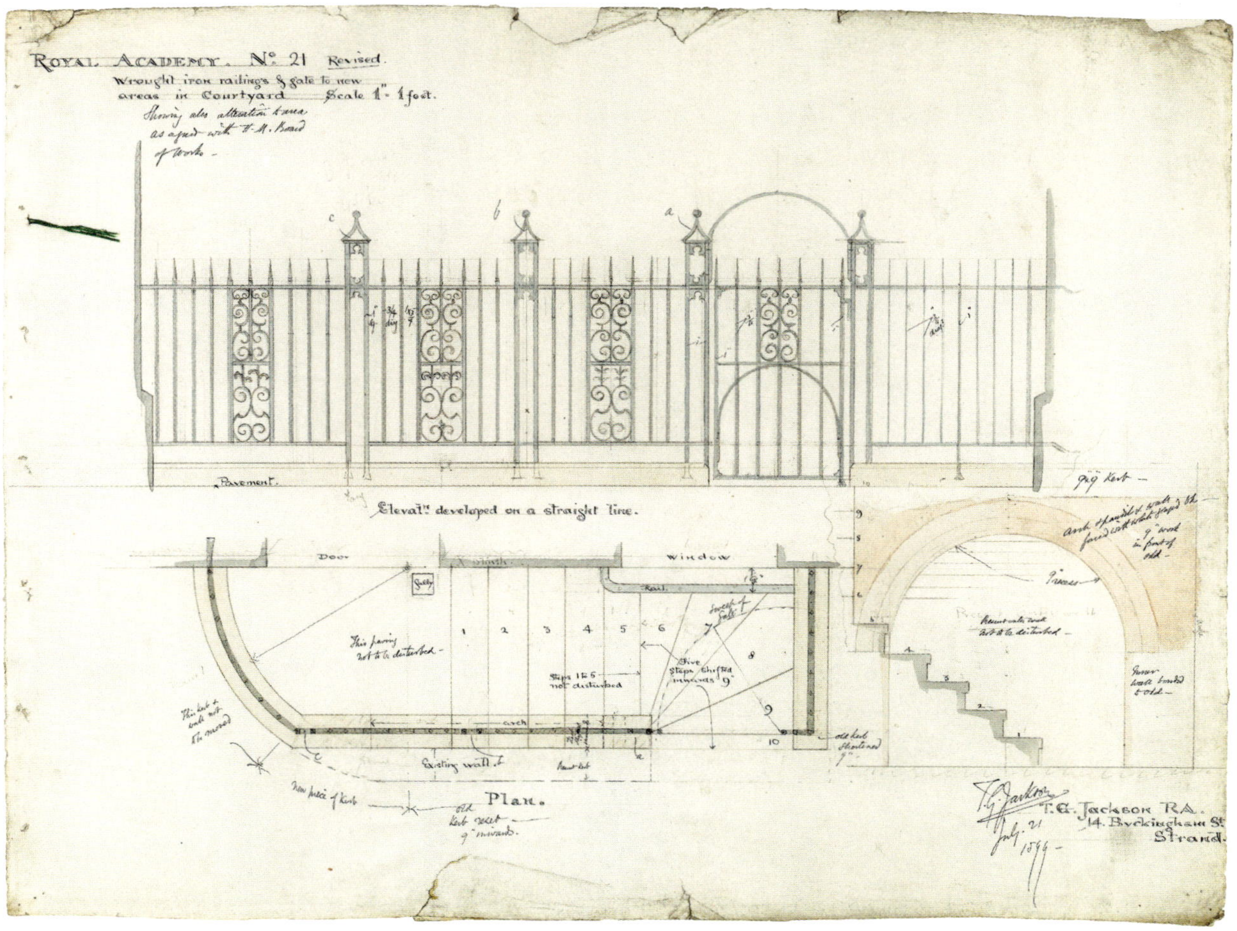

Academy's *Annual Report* for 1899 maintained that it had held its ground in the face of 'frivolous objections' from the neighbours, it is apparent from Jackson's revised drawing of 21 July 1899 'showing … alterations as agreed with H.M. Board of Works', that a compromise had in fact been reached requiring less intrusive flights of steps parallel to the façade of the house as originally suggested by the Board's consultant architect Sir John Taylor (Fig. 271). As far as the Academy was concerned it was simply asking to be allowed to provide for itself what Banks & Barry had provided for the learned societies. In hindsight however, there could hardly be a more telling sign that it had begun to model itself on a gentlemen's club.

When the Academy's General Assembly decided in June 1927 that Charles Sims RA's successor as keeper did not need to reside permanently on the premises, it led to the first significant change in the use of Burlington House for forty years. As had happened considerably earlier in the case of the learned societies, it enabled residential space to be converted to relieve pressure on other areas of activity. Unusually, in the Academy's case the demand for more space did not come from its library, for the simple reason that this had stopped acquiring books since the budgetary retrenchments of 1911. The pressure to move the library came instead from the members' desire for a grand reception room in which to host large meetings and social gatherings. It is not surprising therefore that the Council supported a suggestion made in April 1927 by Sir Reginald Blomfield RA, the Academy's former Professor of Architecture, 'that the existing Library might be moved elsewhere' and the 'very fine Gallery' that it now occupied ('the finest room in the building') be 'restored to the general use of the Academy.'[184]

The library acquired no additional shelf space therefore when in the autumn of 1927 William Curtis Green RA refitted its existing bookcases in a new room immediately below formed from an amalgamation of the keeper's former drawing room, anteroom and study (now the Sir Hugh Casson Friends' Room; Fig. 272). It did benefit from one significant gain the following year, since the opening of the Aston Webb Print Room (so named in recognition of a donation of £1,000 by the architect Sir Aston Webb PPRA) marked the first time in the Academy's history that it could claim to have made proper provision for the care of its print collection.[185] Similarly, Curtis Green's reinstatement of Lord George Cavendish's former ball room as a large reception room – it was named the Reynolds Room because it was hung at first with the Academy's collection of paintings by its first president – may have started life as a congenial venue for the Academy's Dining Club, but by the late 1980s was serving, if increasingly inadequately and despite formidable acoustical challenges, as a crucial resource for its fledgling educational programme.

Inasmuch as the library had been obliged to move down one floor to make room for social gatherings in 1927, history was to repeat itself almost 60 years later when it moved again in 1986 to give the Friends of the Academy more space on the ground floor of the building (Fig. 273). This time it went up two floors to an elegantly modernist reinterpretation of a traditional galleried library designed by the Academy's then Professor of Architecture, H. T. (Jim) Cadbury-Brown, and handsomely funded by the Wolfson Foundation (Fig. 274). Cantilevered off the walls of a rehabilitated, reroofed, and climate-controlled Gibson Gallery – which since the outbreak of World War II had been pressed into service as a storeroom for the dismantled contents of the Diploma Galleries – Cadbury-Brown's splendid new library had only three drawbacks. The first of these – the loss of the direct access that the students in the Schools had previously enjoyed via stairs connecting with Barry's covered passageway in the basement – seemed to the librarian at the time the most serious. When the library had moved to the ground floor Curtis Green had been particularly careful to preserve this student access by means of a short oak stair leading down to the basement at the north end of the library. The equivalent to this on the first floor had been a small, tightly turned back stair built in 1888 at the north-west corner of the room, which Curtis Green retained in 1927 as a service stair (concealed behind a jib door) for receptions in the Reynolds Room. First recorded in a survey plan of about 1890 (see above, Fig. 232) and long since disused when recorded in an equivalent survey by Denis Serjeant in 1981, this obscure back stair seems to have survived until, like everything else clogging up the gap between the north front of Burlington House and the south front of Smirke's galleries, it was swept away by the Sackler Gallery scheme of Foster Associates.[186]

Fig. 272
The Royal Academy library (designed by William Curtis Green in 1927) *c.* 1965.
Royal Academy of Arts, London, 12/1355

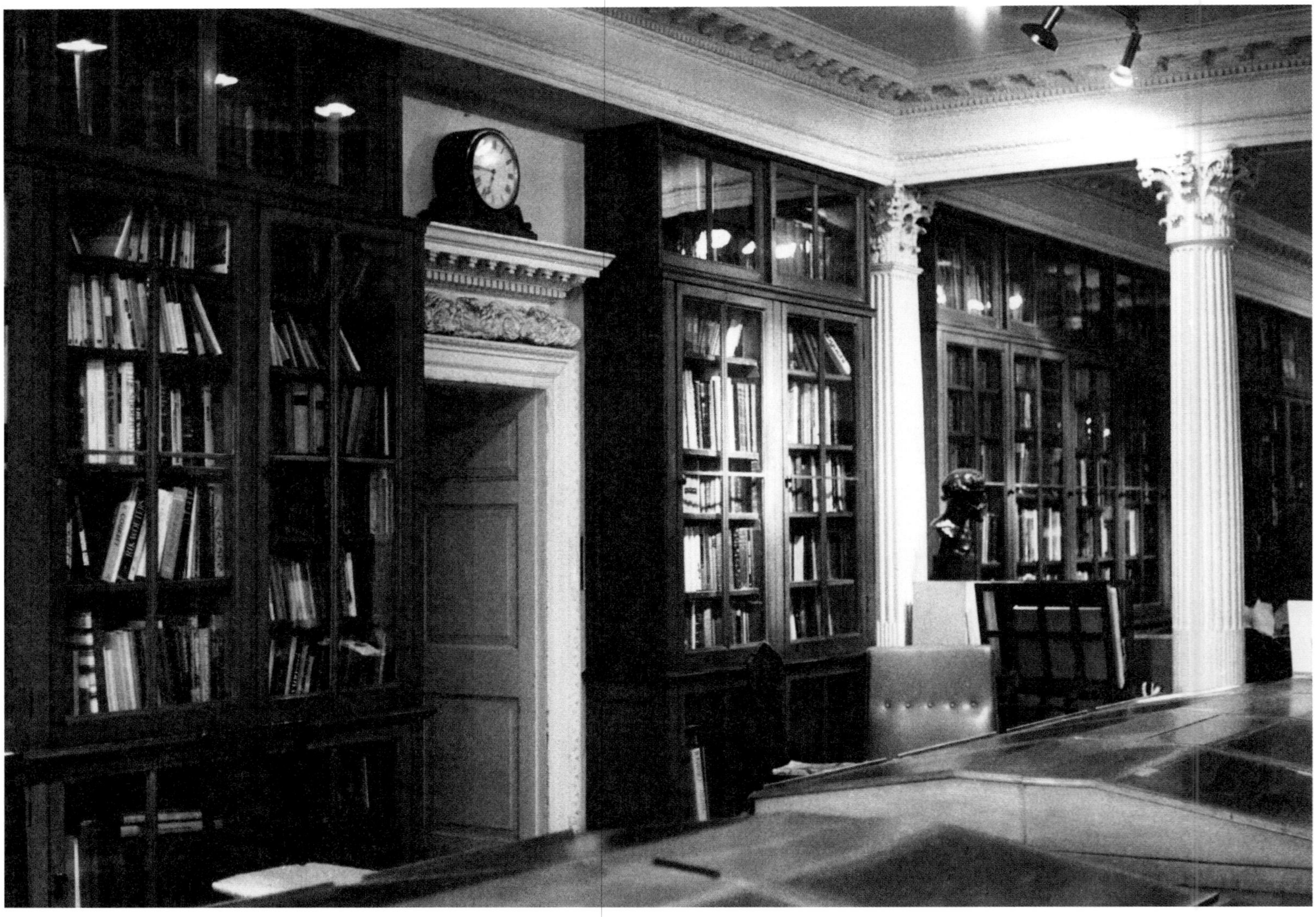

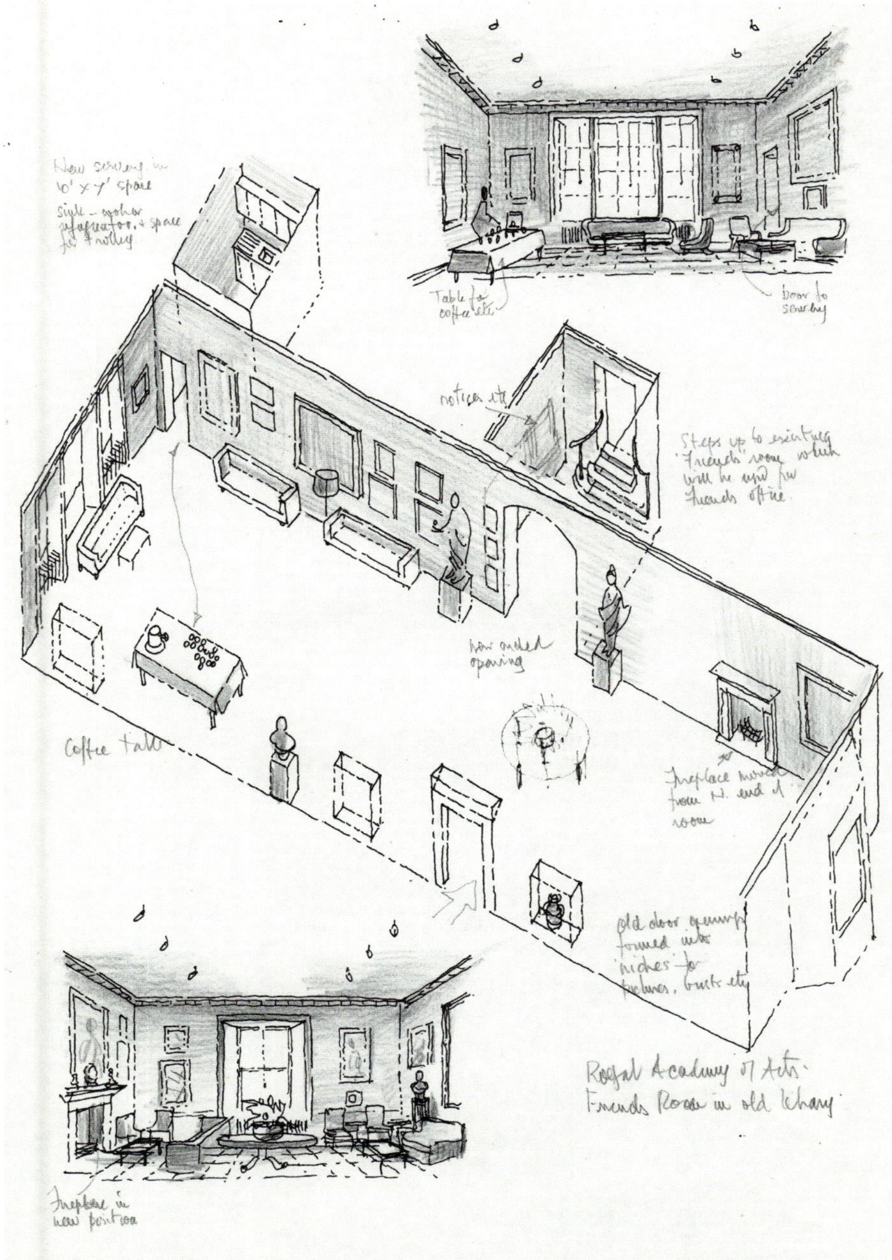

Fig. 273
H. T. Cadbury-Brown, Design for the Royal Academy Friends' Room in the former library: axonometric sketch with perspectives looking north and south, 1986.
Royal Academy of Arts, London, 09/3262

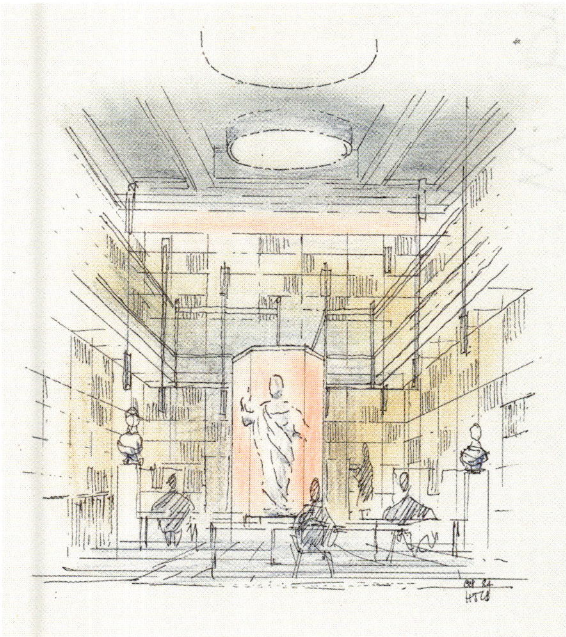

Fig. 274
H. T. Cadbury-Brown, Sketch design for the new library in the former Gibson Gallery, Burlington House: perspective looking north, October 1984.
Royal Academy of Arts, London, 09/3238

The second drawback of Cadbury-Brown's library was that it was no larger in floor area than either Curtis Green's or Smirke's had been, the Academy's policy of substituting an equivalent space with no allowance for growth being similar to that favoured by the Office of Works in relation to the learned societies. Fortunately, the solution both to this problem and to that of student access was close at hand, in that it proved possible to establish a small but serviceable satellite 'Schools' Library' in the disused passageway to the former library. Similar good fortune was to supply the third deficiency of the new library, namely the lack of space for the storage of prints and drawings. Since the only way to reconcile the existing floor level of the Cadbury-Brown library with that of Foster's new Sackler Gallery (whose floor had to be built about five feet higher to accommodate air-handling plant) was to hive off a so-called 'Long Gallery' at its east end, it made sense to treat the latter as an adjunct to the library rather than as part of the Sackler Gallery itself. Consequently, Cadbury-Brown and his wife, the American-trained Elizabeth Elwyn, designed a casket-like interior reminiscent of the work of the Viennese father of modernism Adolf Loos, for the storage, study and display of the Academy's large collection of works on paper (Fig. 275). Turning every cubic centimetre to practical advantage, this exceptionally elegant space provided not only a well-equipped modern replacement for the long-dismantled Aston Webb Print Room (now the Belle Shenkman Room) but also a temporary haven for the Academy's entire historic archive that had been consigned for many years, along with much else besides, to perilous nooks and crannies throughout the basement. This in turn helped to generate the wider awareness of the richness of the Academy's documentary heritage that led to the building in 2004 of the Dame Jillian Sackler Archive over part of the roof of the Keeper's House. Designed by Alex Dobbs under the supervision of the Academy's surveyor Peter Schmitt, this climate-controlled, purpose-designed 'muniment room' not only serves the storage and retrieval needs of one the busiest specialist research archives in the country, but is also the symbolic descendant of the Saloon, in that it is where the Academy's

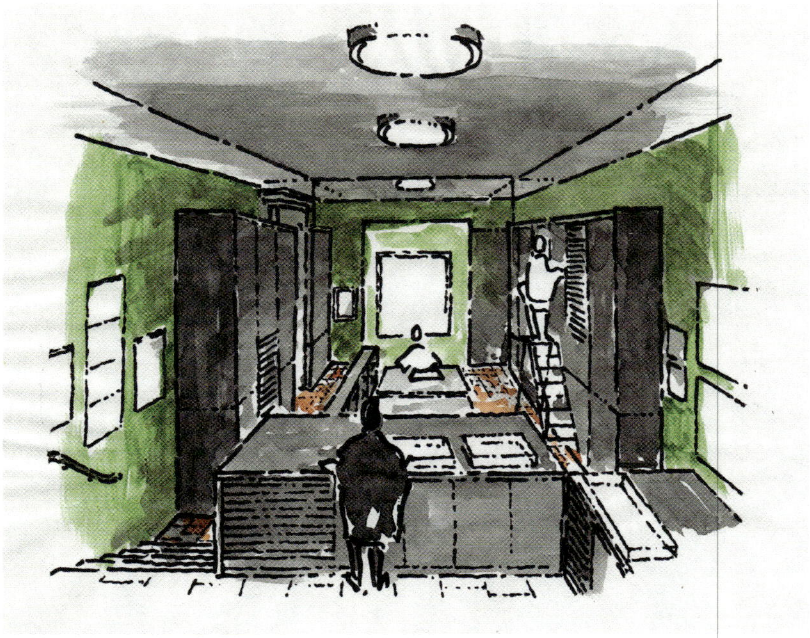

Fig. 275
H. T. Cadbury-Brown,
Preliminary sketch design for the library print room in part of the former Diploma Gallery, Burlington House: perspective looking south, *c.* 1990.
Royal Academy of Arts, London, 09/3253

sense of its own history is now most effectively preserved for all-comers (Fig. 276).

In the aftermath of the intensely hostile press generated by the Academy's sale of Leonardo da Vinci's cartoon of *The Virgin and Child with St Anne and St John the Baptist* in summer 1962, the redecoration of the entrance hall and main staircase of Burlington House at the end of that year was the first sign in more than half a century that it saw the need to present a less stuffy image to its visitors. As a perceptive disciple of the principles of Palladian architecture, Raymond Erith RA must have relished this chance to work on the former home of his great eighteenth-century forerunner. Although the Academy was no longer quite as broke as it had been, Erith achieved a remarkable visual transformation at very little cost by stripping out Jackson's dingy oak panelling; erasing the fussier elements of his ceiling, in particular the pseudo-rococo shields bearing the letters 'RA'; painting the newly exposed walls in his favourite buff yellow; relighting the room with wall-mounted uplighters

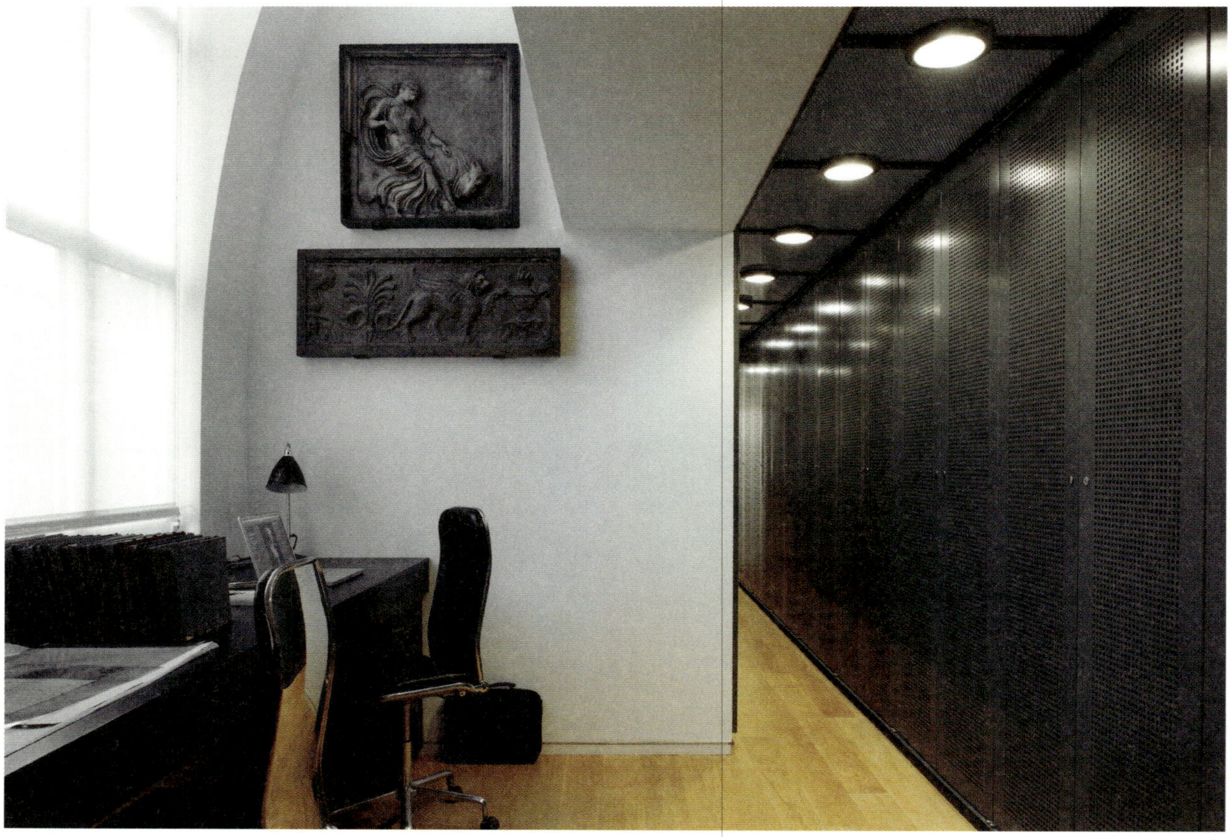

Fig. 276
Dame Jillian Sackler Archive Room (designed by Alex Dobbs), 2010.
Photograph by Paul Highnam.
Royal Academy of Arts, London

Fig. 277
Brian Delf, Cutaway showing proposed Sackler Gallery (designed by Foster Associates), *c.* 1990.
Royal Academy of Arts, London, 15/2047

to draw attention to the ceiling paintings; and installing a pair of beautifully proportioned revolving doors in place of Jackson's intrusive porters' kiosks.[187] There could have hardly been a clearer message to its visitors that the Academy had turned a new page thanks to the sale of the Leonardo cartoon. There might even perhaps have been an underlying suggestion that it was grateful for the support of those members of the public who had contributed to the National Art Collection Fund's appeal to secure the cartoon for the nation. If so, it would have marked a turning point, the moment when the Academy began to regain the support of the public for what it was founded to achieve 250 years ago. It was to be entirely due to the strength of this support that it would become capable once again of undertaking building work on a scale comparable to what had been carried out at Burlington House a century earlier.

THE 1990–91 SACKLER GALLERY development scheme was driven primarily by the need to upgrade the environmental conditions in the former Diploma Gallery in order to qualify for government indemnity (Fig. 277). Rather than attempt to adapt the existing Victorian structure to these requirements, the Academy took the bold step of commissioning Sir Norman Foster, an associate member since 1983, to design new exhibition galleries within the existing space. Reminiscent of Louis Kahn's barrel-vaulted Kimbell Art Museum in Fort Worth, Texas, but with a slot at the apex of the vault containing adjustable louvres to modulate the daylight, Foster's Sackler Gallery is just the right size to offer a viable curatorial alternative to the majestic sweep of the Main Galleries. Quietly expressive of function in the best mid-twentieth-century modernist tradition, the Gallery's calm aesthetic offsets the hi-tech drama of the visitor's ascent to reach it through the narrow gap between the south wall of Smirke's Main Galleries and the north front of Burlington House (Figs 278, 279).

In this forgotten space Foster had been able to address the other major problem of the existing top-floor galleries, that of circulation. Previously these galleries, in common with Cadbury-Brown's recently installed library,

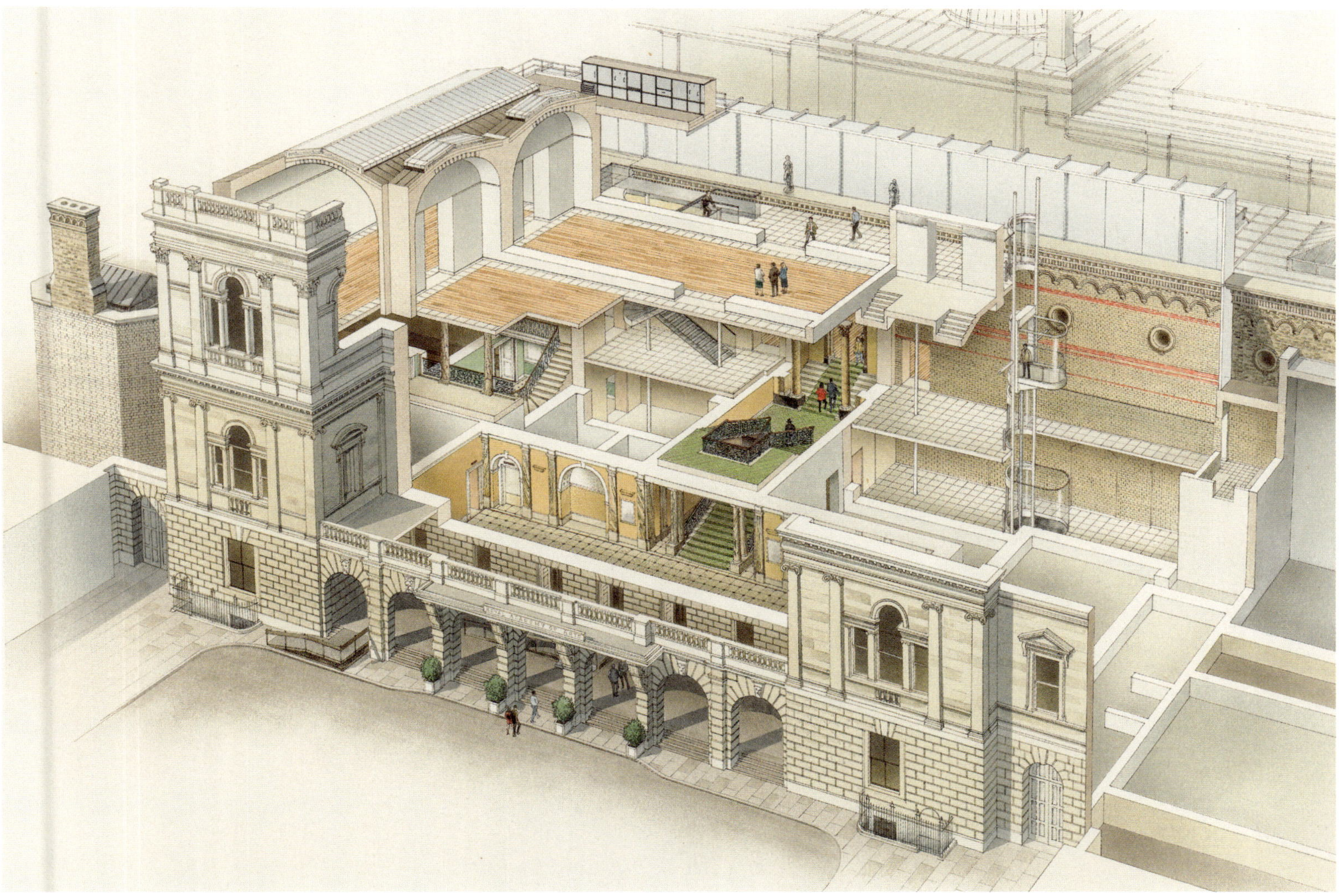

Fig. 278
Foster Associates and Julian Harrap, North front restoration and lift, 1991.
Photograph by Dennis Gilbert.
Foster + Partners, London

Fig. 279
Sydney Smirke, Royal Academy exhibition galleries: south elevation, eastern half, 1867.
Royal Academy of Arts, London, 07/942

could only be reached by means of a badly lit staircase or, worse still, a manually operated 1951 Keighley birdcage lift.[188] Together these took up a good deal of valuable space in the former ticket office on the ground floor, two-thirds of what later became the Tennant Gallery on the first floor, the library undercroft on the mezzanine floor, and the upper part of the library print room on the top floor. Foster's solution was to delicately insert new means of access between the two façades, exposing both to uninterrupted view. Having sailed up the north front of Burlington House in a glass lift, or bravely climbed a glass staircase floating in space with no visible means of support (Fig. 280), visitors emerge on to a sculpture court bathed in opalescent light diffused through industrial-sized sheets of opaque white glass. Taking advantage of Smirke's weathered Portland stone cornice as a ready-made plinth on which to display sculpture and casts from the Academy's collection, the Dame Jillian Sackler Sculpture Landing included until very recently a chapel-like area at its westernmost end in which was installed – on the south wall behind bullet-proof glass – Michelangelo's *Taddei Tondo* (Fig. 281).

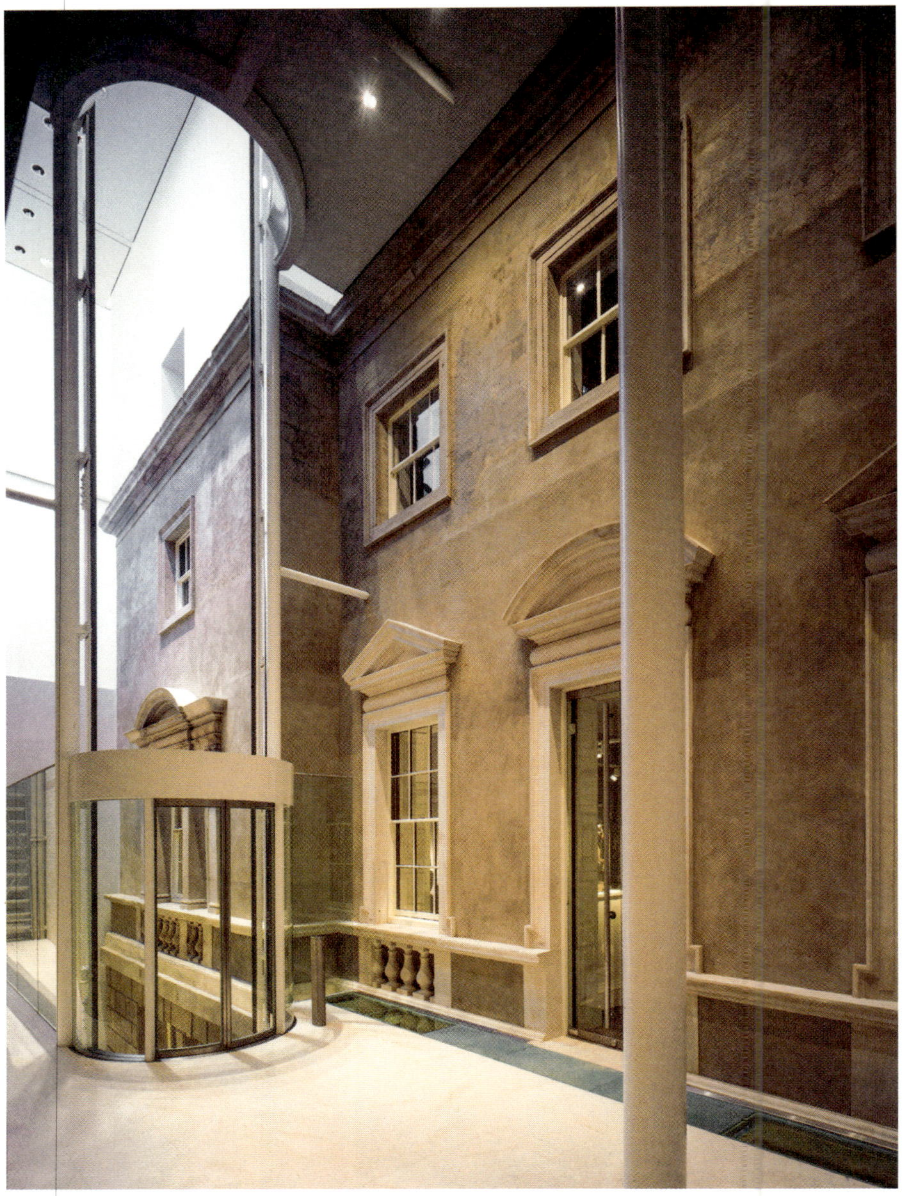

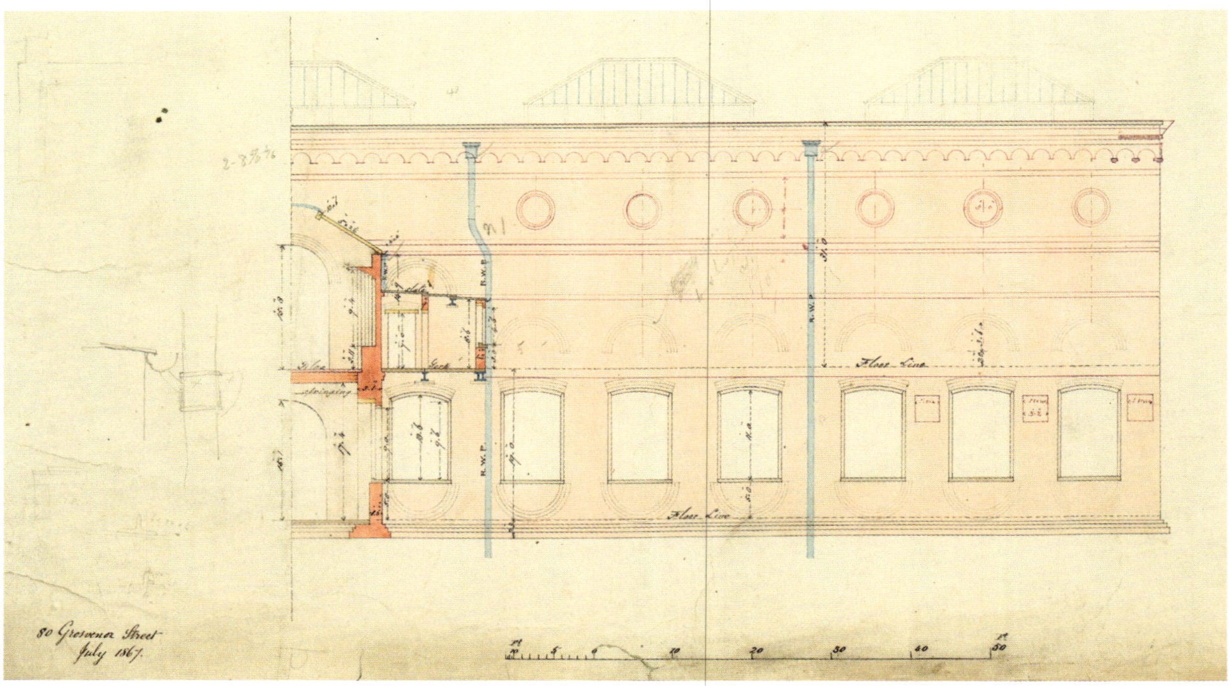

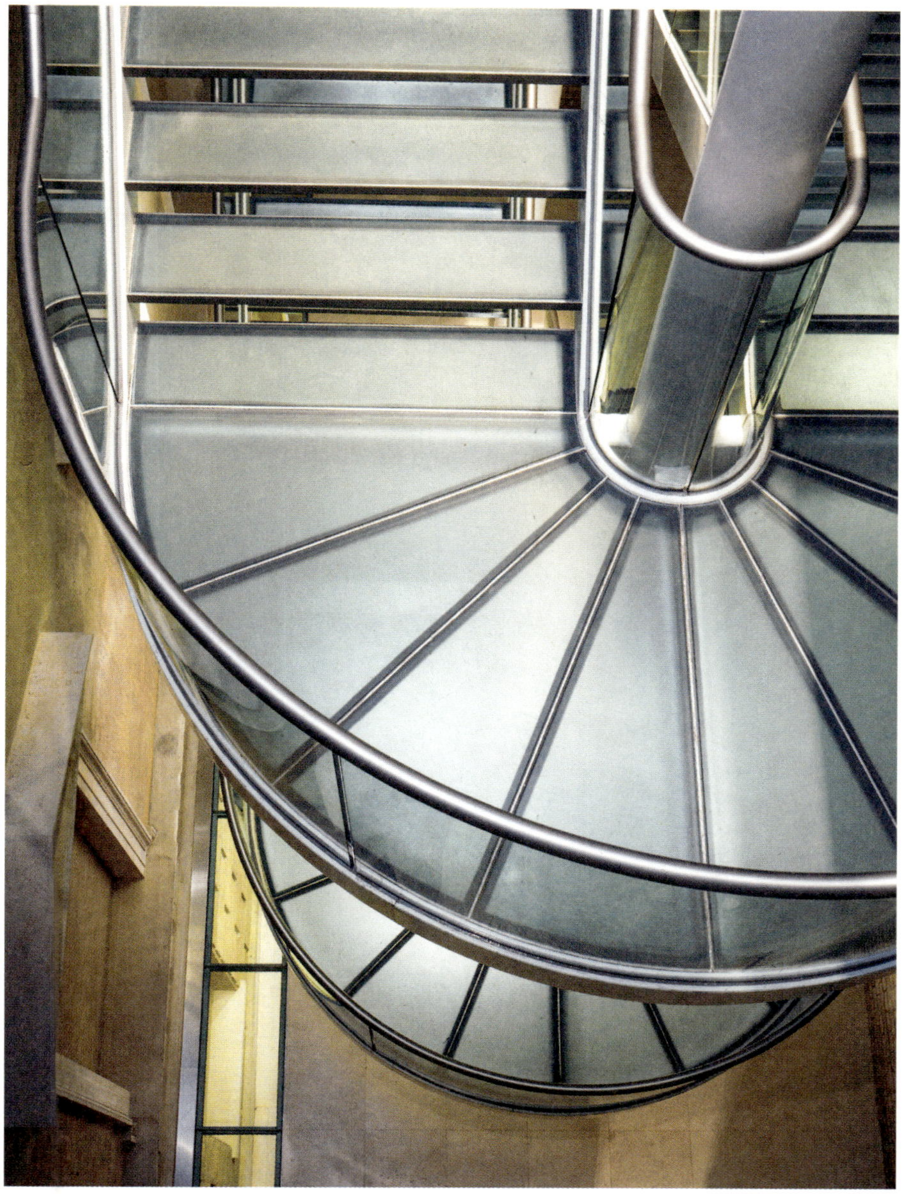

Fig. 280
Foster Associates, Glass stairs to the Sackler Gallery landing, 1991.
Photograph by Dennis Gilbert.
Foster + Partners, London

Foster's stroke of genius lay not so much in using this hidden 'gap' between the buildings to improve vertical circulation – almost every architect before him had exploited this space in one way or another – but rather in exposing the whole of it to full view. Although like many galleries and museums in the late twentieth century the Academy had turned to hi-tech architecture to signal its embrace of the future, the effect of this exposure was to confront the past. For what Julian Harrap's meticulous restoration of the opposing façades reveals in the end is the true price the house had paid for its preservation. Here indeed was 'High Victorian cruelty', made all the more striking by the obliviousness of Smirke's sheer brick wall and the extraordinary care that had now been taken over the points of conjunction between old and new (see above, Figs 239, 279).

Foster's bold but historically respectful intervention at Burlington House won unanimous acclaim from architectural critics and historians alike, and its success may well have helped shape the approach that won his firm not only the 1992 competition for the reconstruction of the Reichstag in Berlin, but also the commission not long afterwards for the Queen Elizabeth II Great Court at the British Museum. Although the idea of converting Sir Robert Smirke's lost quadrangle into the hub of the Museum was proposed as far back as the 1970s, there is little doubt that its eventual development by the Foster team in the late 1990s owed something to the way exposing the Sackler 'gap' at Burlington House had succeeded in turning architecture outside in.

The British Library's move to St Pancras in 1997 also freed up space for new display galleries to be built beneath the Great Court, enabling the exhibitions of the British Museum's ethnographic collections in 6 Burlington Gardens to return to the Bloomsbury fold. As had happened almost a hundred years earlier, when it became known early in 1996 that the current occupants were scheduled to leave, the Academy lost no time in making its interest known to the government. This time it demonstrated the seriousness of its intentions by commissioning Michael Hopkins & Partners 'to investigate the potential for linking Burlington Gardens to the Royal Academy and for accommodating within the existing building an Auditorium, an Architecture Gallery and the other necessary facilities.'[189] Armed with the results of the Hopkins strategic study, by the end of 1996 the Academy was able to issue a 50-page illustrated booklet, *Royal Academy of Arts: A Vision for Burlington Gardens*, in which it proposed an outline scheme 'to reintegrate Burlington House and Burlington Gardens' and explained in some detail how it would use the latter building to consolidate and expand its education and exhibition programmes to meet the needs and expectations of an 'Academy for the twenty-first century'. Although it was to be another four years before it completed the purchase of the building's freehold and a further three before it could enjoy vacant possession, the Academy's proposal that it should be allowed to 'reintegrate' 6 Burlington Gardens into the Burlington House site was buoyed by three new factors in its favour. Firstly, Pennethorne's building had been accorded Grade II* listing in January 1970, which meant that

Fig. 281
Foster Associates, Sackler Gallery landing with Michelangelo's *Taddei Tondo*, 1991. Photograph by Dennis Gilbert.

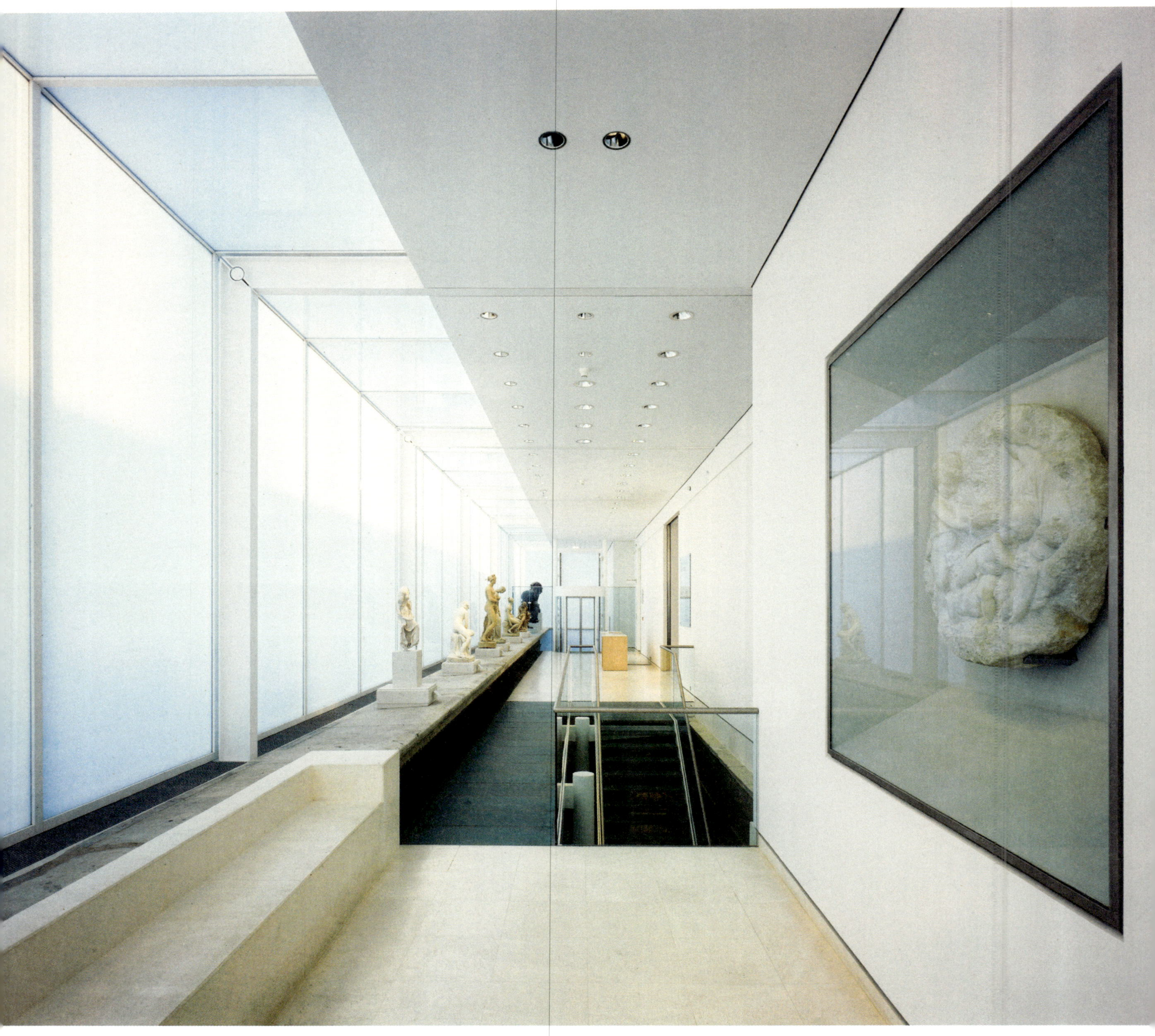

demolition for redevelopment of the site was no longer an option; secondly, the 27 years in which the building had been used by the Museum of Mankind had fully demonstrated its suitability as an exhibition venue; and thirdly, after the privatisation of the government's Property Services Agency (effectively the successor to the Ministry of Public Buildings and Works), in the mid-1990s the freehold was now vested in the Secretary of State for National Heritage. For the first time in its existence it was possible to make a case for the building's future that took into proper account its location, its history, its intrinsic architectural quality, and its most appropriate long-term use.

In 1998 Sir Michael Hopkins RA won the first competition for the Academy's Burlington Gardens reunification project with a spectacular design for joining the Smirke and Pennethorne buildings seamlessly along their common axes at both gallery and basement level (Fig. 282). In the 57-foot-wide space between their back-to-back façades Hopkins proposed to create a great glass-ceilinged 'Forum', not unlike Foster's luminescent enclosure of the space between the Main Galleries and Burlington House. However, although the Academy's *Vision* document had proposed 'a new courtyard … bounded on all sides by the studios of the RA Schools' that could be 'a beautiful and secluded place at the heart of the Academy',[190] it was not clear that this vast atrium opening off Gallery VI would serve any practical purpose beyond that of physically connecting the two buildings. Estimated to cost around £80 million to build, the Hopkins scheme was abandoned after the Heritage Lottery Fund turned down a £20 million grant application on the grounds of insufficient need.

There was to be a silver lining to this disappointment in that the one element of Hopkins's masterplan that was carried out – the repaving of the Burlington House courtyard in 2002 – did more to improve this unique space than anything else since the Academy moved to Burlington House. Employing varieties of natural stone that harmonised with the masonry of the surrounding buildings, Hopkins's reintroduction of traditional granite setts in place of the municipal tarmac (and before that wooden paving blocks) that the Ministry of Works had insisted on, marked the return of a characteristic feature of the original Burlington House forecourt. Renamed the Annenberg Courtyard in honour of the principal donors to the project, the American ambassador Walter Annenberg and his wife Leonore, what had deteriorated into little more than a car park became a piazza, complete with a gentle *cordonata* leading to elegant stone ramps under Smirke's subtly disencumbered entrance portico, a large flagstone platform in the centre for changing displays of sculpture, and a family-friendly fountain in which small children can enjoy paddling on hot summer

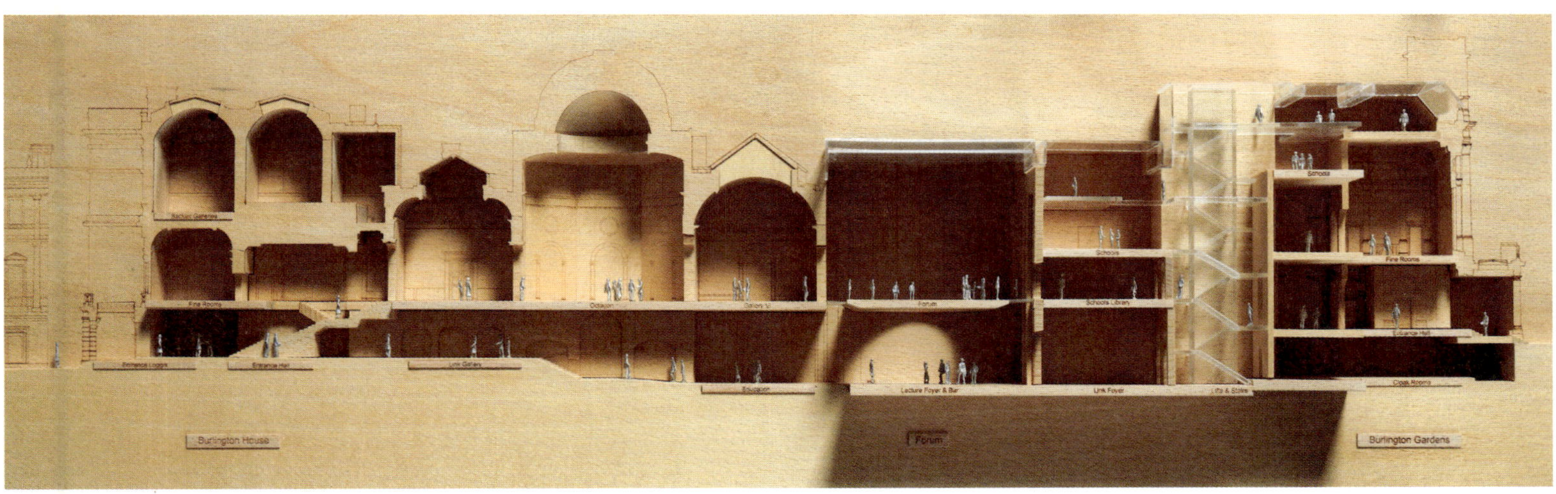

Fig. 282
Sir Michael Hopkins, Design for Burlington Gardens development: part of model showing longitudinal section, 1997.
Royal Academy of Arts, London, 09/2578

days. The seventeen water jets and eleven up-lights of the fountain are seemingly arranged at random in front of Alfred Drury's 1931 statue of Reynolds but in fact correspond to the position of the planets, moon and bright stars at midnight on his birthday (16 July 1723). Based on an idea proposed by Ian Ritchie RA and researched by Steve Bell of HM Nautical Almanac Office, it represents one of the more unexpected bonuses of a happy collaboration between the government, the Royal Academy and the courtyard societies that is probably unique in the history of the site.

It was obvious in the aftermath of the abandonment of the Hopkins scheme that the Academy needed both to prioritise what it wanted to achieve by acquiring 6 Burlington Gardens and to find a more pragmatic way of linking it to Burlington House that avoided disturbing the integrity of the Main Galleries or the privacy of the Schools. As a result, three things became much clearer. Firstly, that before embarking on any expensive alterations, it would be wise for the Academy to follow the Museum of Mankind's example and use 6 Burlington Gardens in the best way that it could while ensuring that it at least covered its costs. Accordingly, it was decided to trial the building's capacity to meet the institution's ongoing needs for additional exhibition, retail, office and storage space, and thereafter to buy time to fundraise for a major capital project by letting the west wing to a prestigious contemporary art gallery in need of premises close to Cork Street, Haunch of Venison between March 2009 and November 2011 and the Pace Gallery since September 2012. Secondly, it became apparent that of the prospective benefits of reintegrating the site adumbrated in the 1996 *Vision* document, that of using the space between the buildings to 'improve the facilities of the Royal Academy Schools' was not only the most obvious, but also the most likely to attract sponsorship. Thirdly, this being the case, it made more sense to tackle the problem of how to connect the buildings not just in formal abstract terms but as part of a properly developed masterplan for expanding and reorganising the accommodation of the Schools generally.

With this latter aim in mind, in 2003–04 the Academy's in-house architectural team led by Peter Schmitt prepared a feasibility scheme in which it was proposed that the extended bank of studios at the back of the Schools should be replaced by a free-standing three-storey block of new studios with top-floor offices set back sufficiently to create a lightwell for the main range of studios within the existing building.[191] Integral to the scheme was a proposal to establish a new route to Burlington Gardens down the east flank of the Main Galleries (Fig. 283). The ghost of the counterpart to the Burlington Arcade that never got built, this forgotten canyon-like alleyway running along the Albany boundary wall had been Smirke's original choice for the main entrance to the Schools from Burlington Gardens, an idea that was almost certainly abandoned because the Academy had no right of way on that side of the University's building (see above, Fig. 241). Whether or not anyone was aware of this historical precedent, its principal advantage now was the same as it would have been in 1869, namely that it provided the Schools not only with an independent entrance from the street but also, for the first time in their history, an appropriate visual presence on the site.

It was on the basis of the favourable reception of a development of the Academy's in-house scheme that in September 2004 Sir Colin St John Wilson RA was selected 'in competition with two other candidates as architect to prepare a design for the rehabilitation & extension of the accommodation for the Schools', and that the scope of his brief 'extended to the inclusion of proposals for an 'East Link' to permit access between Burlington House and the Albany to a new dedicated entrance for the Schools & thence north to Burlington Gardens.'[192] The attractiveness of the scheme as developed by Wilson in design and content derived from three principal outcomes: firstly, by raising Shaw's mansard roof structure 'on a platform above its present location' and shifting it 'further north to sit on the line of the present fence' it would be possible to enlarge the area of studio space at the existing basement level and still preserve the nineteenth-century character of the Schools; secondly, the new entrance courtyard would provide public access not only to a permanent Schools exhibition gallery but also to a basement-level lecture

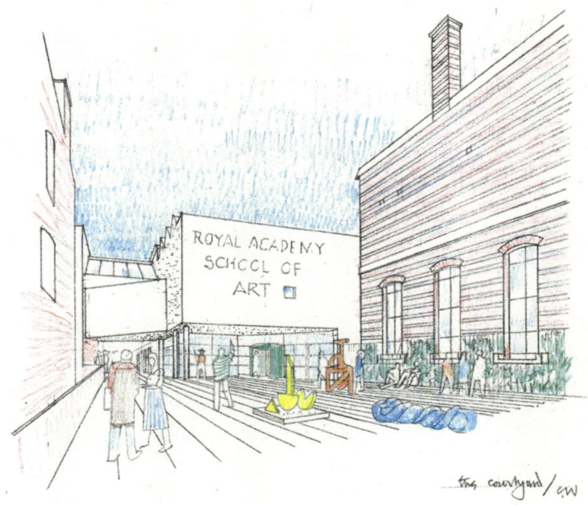

Fig. 284
Sir Colin St John Wilson, Royal Academy of Arts and 6 Burlington Gardens, proposed east link and new RA Schools: perspective sketch, 2004.
Royal Academy of Arts, London

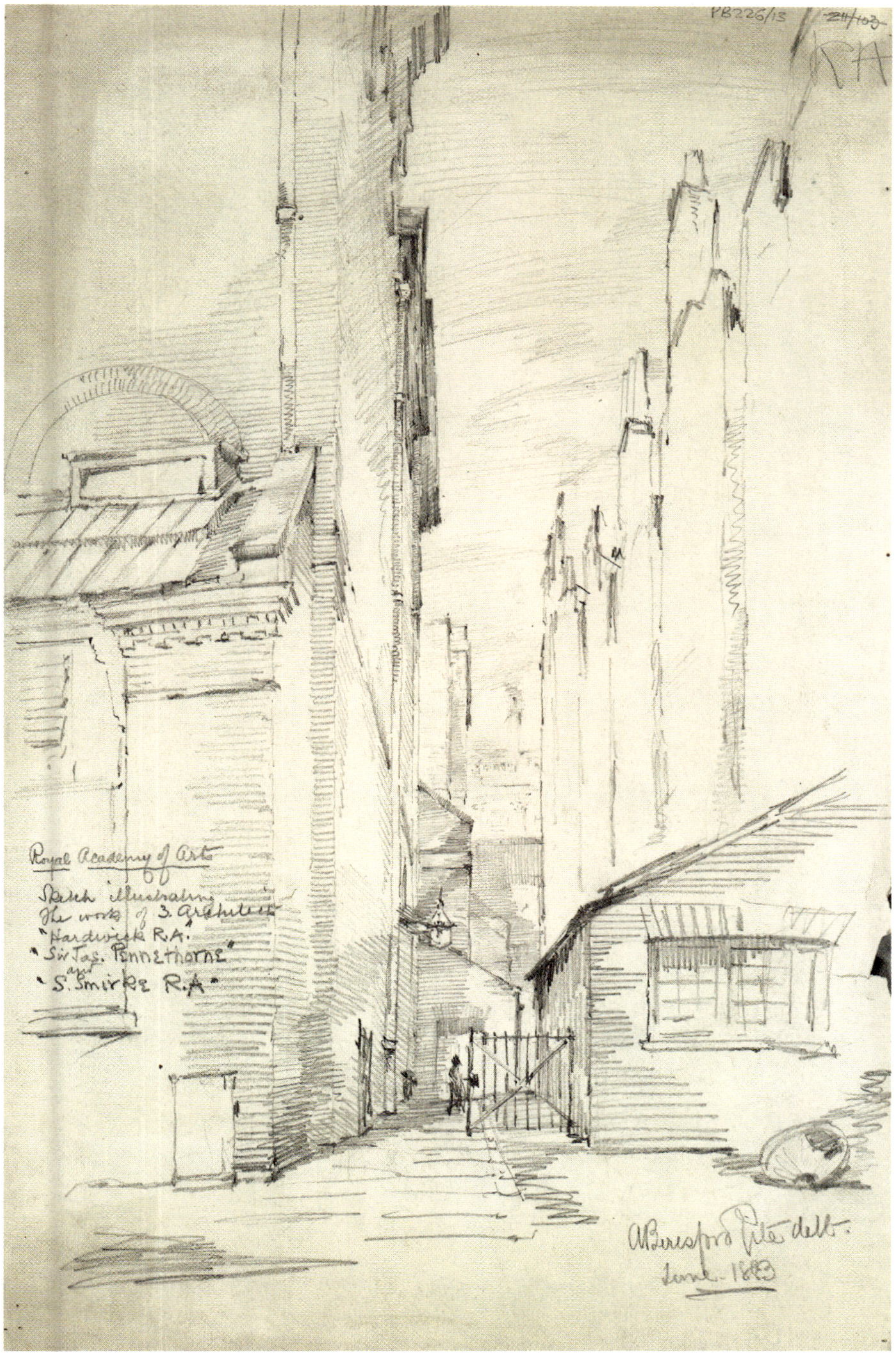

Fig. 283
Arthur Beresford Pite, View from the south-east corner of the Royal Academy's exhibition galleries, looking north, 1883.
RIBA Collections, PB 226/13

room for use out-of-hours without risk of disturbance to the work of the Schools; and thirdly, an 'East Link Galleria, glazed overhead but open at each end', would enable visitors to approach the Schools with equal ease from Burlington House or Burlington Gardens (Fig. 284).[193] Wilson was all too aware that the success or failure of the project hung on making the East Link 'compelling both in design and in what it houses, in order to give the visitor a reason for moving down it, and to establish a powerful connection between Burlington House and Burlington Gardens.'[194] Lining the link with casts of the Parthenon frieze could only go so far in drawing people in, especially on a gloomy winter's day when the Burlington Arcade might seem to promise a more cheerful route to or from Piccadilly. Of particular concern therefore, was the fact, as Wilson emphasised, that 'the quality and enjoyability of this space very much hinge on the viability of the attachment of the glazed roof to Albany.'[195] Sadly, neither this critical issue nor the project as a whole came much closer to being tested before Wilson's death on 14 May 2007 aged 85.

Although the 'East Link' had considerable support both within and beyond the Academy, there were those who felt that it ought to be possible, despite the changes in level dictated by the incline of the site, to create a more direct and logical link between two symmetrical buildings built on the same axis. There were also those who, while appreciating the importance of extending and improving the facilities of the Schools, were equally concerned to protect their unique atmosphere and character, and not convinced that modern studios would necessarily be an improvement on the tried and tested Victorian model. Then there were those who saw the 'reintegration' of the site as the perfect opportunity for the Academy to demonstrate in architectural terms that its Schools were the heart of the institution and deserved better than the backyard they had occupied since they

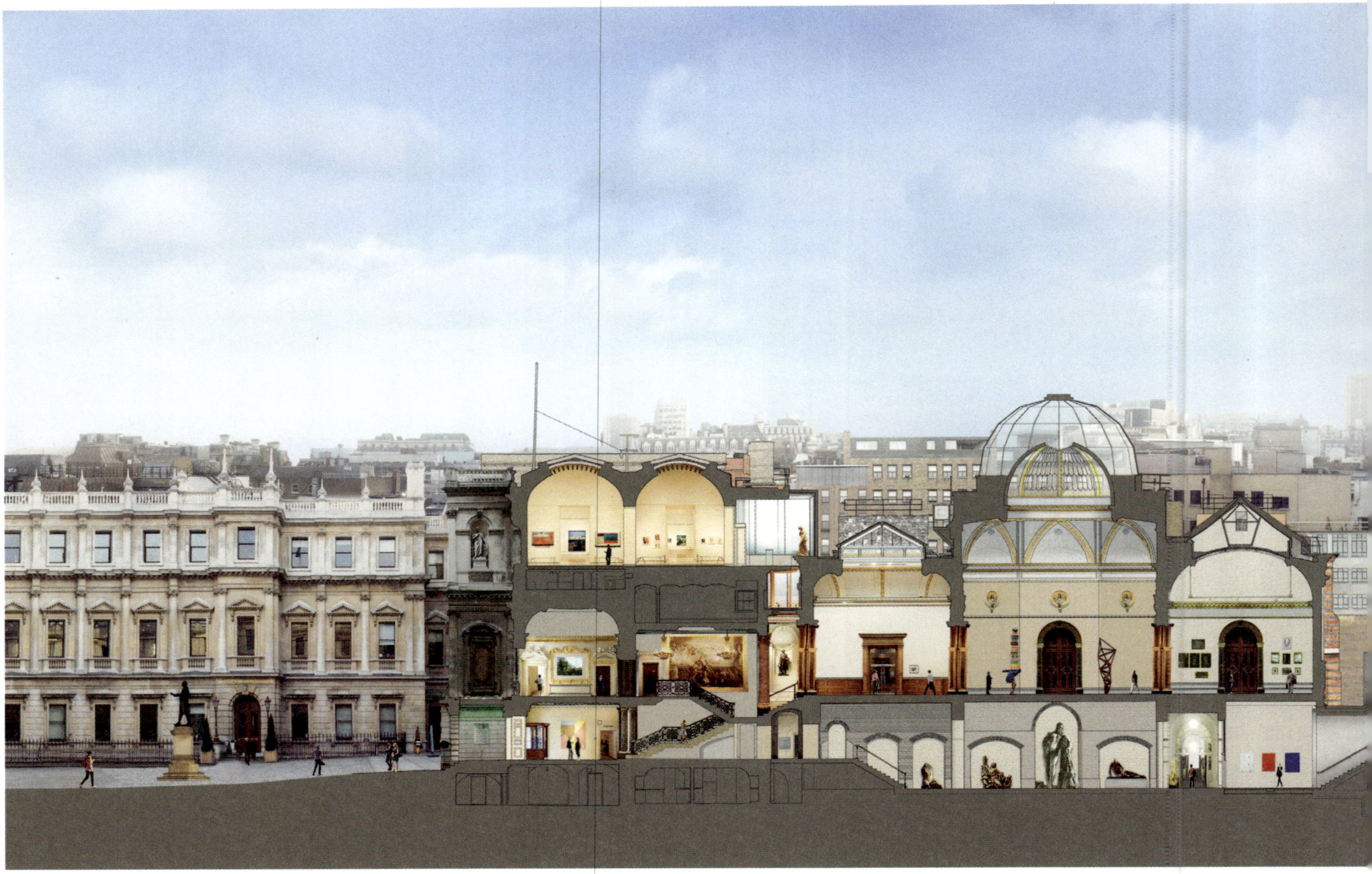

moved to Burlington House. While welcoming the improved facilities promised in the Wilson plan, this school of thought worried that resiting the entrance to the Schools on the east as opposed to the west periphery would do nothing to reduce the impression that they were a separate entity – an impression inadvertently reflected in the new name they had been given in one of Wilson's perspective sketches. And finally, there were those who thought that it was high time the Academy finally made up its mind about what difference it wanted 6 Burlington Gardens to make, not just to the Schools but to the public generally and to its future.

In 2008, the appointment of David Chipperfield Architects to develop a masterplan for the site marked the moment when the utopian expectation that somehow joining up Burlington House with Burlington Gardens could solve all the Academy's space problems did not just evaporate but gradually, and not without pain, crystallised into a project that focussed solely on what was both possible and essential (Figs 285, 286). It was part of a process for ensuring that nothing more is done than needs to be done, which is one of the hallmarks of Chipperfield's approach to the renovation of historic buildings. It was also part of a process that required and enabled the Academy to rethink how it related to its visitors through its building, not merely in terms of the facilities it could now offer but through a new configuration of the public areas within it.

This new relationship is evident the moment one enters Burlington House, where for the first time there is no longer a feeling that one is being funnelled up the stairs to the galleries. Instead of squeezing down narrow passages to reach other destinations, there is a sense of being invited to explore the interior of the house. As a result, the north façade as revealed by Foster no longer seems like a full-size architectural model, but rather the real front of a real house overlooking the garden down which Lord Burlington and William Kent walked almost 300 years ago. The path they would have taken now leads to a different kind of garden, one in which, however, they would have felt very much at home. The continuity with the past that is such a source of strength to the Academy

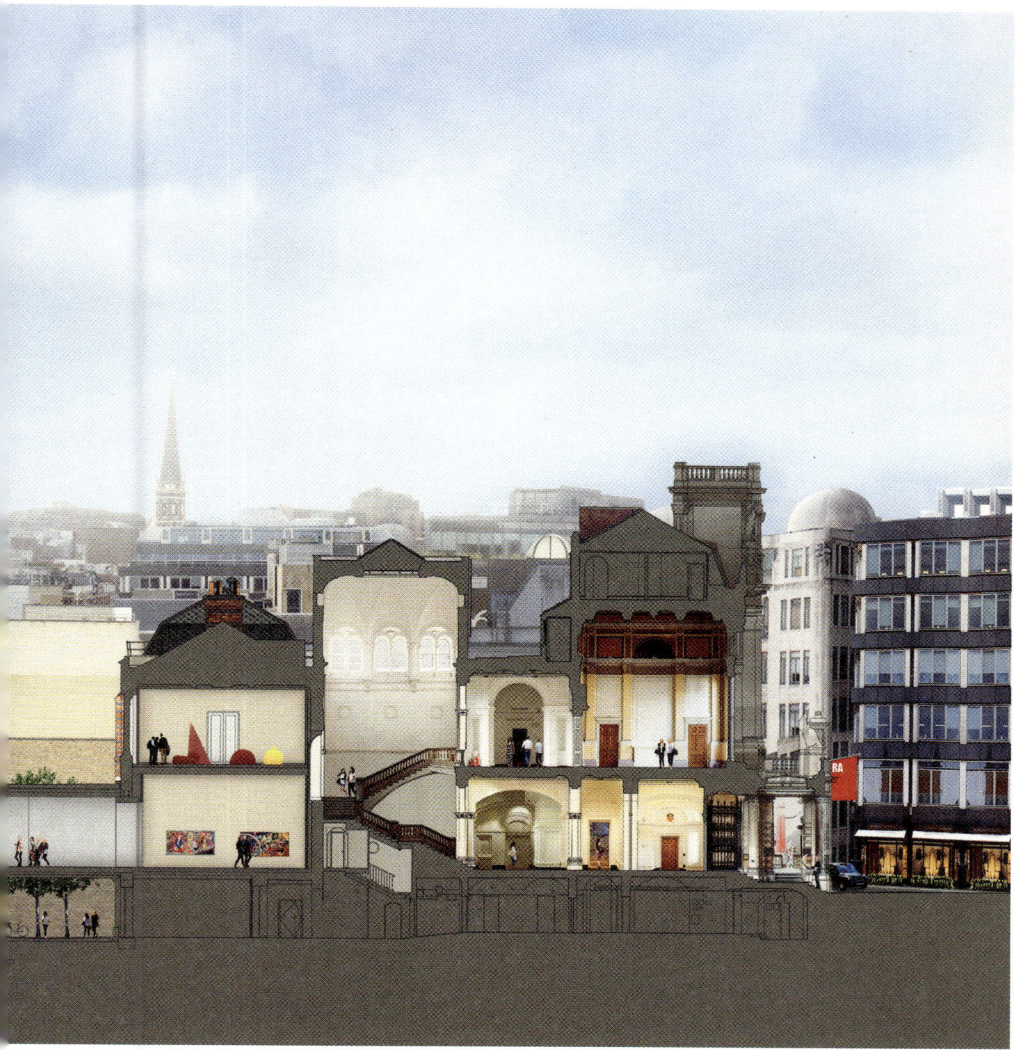

Fig. 287 (overleaf)
The Weston Studio, within the Royal Academy Schools, showing the Weston Bridge

Fig. 288 (p.295)
The Weston Bridge, designed by Sir David Chipperfield and completed in 2018 to link Burlington House to Burlington Gardens, seen from below

Fig. 285
David Chipperfield Architects, Cross-section through the Royal Academy of Arts and 6 Burlington Gardens renovation: rendering by Hayes Davidson, 2015.
Royal Academy of Arts, London

Fig. 286
David Chipperfield Architects, Burlington House and 6 Burlington Gardens: renovation plan, 2018.
David Chipperfield Architects

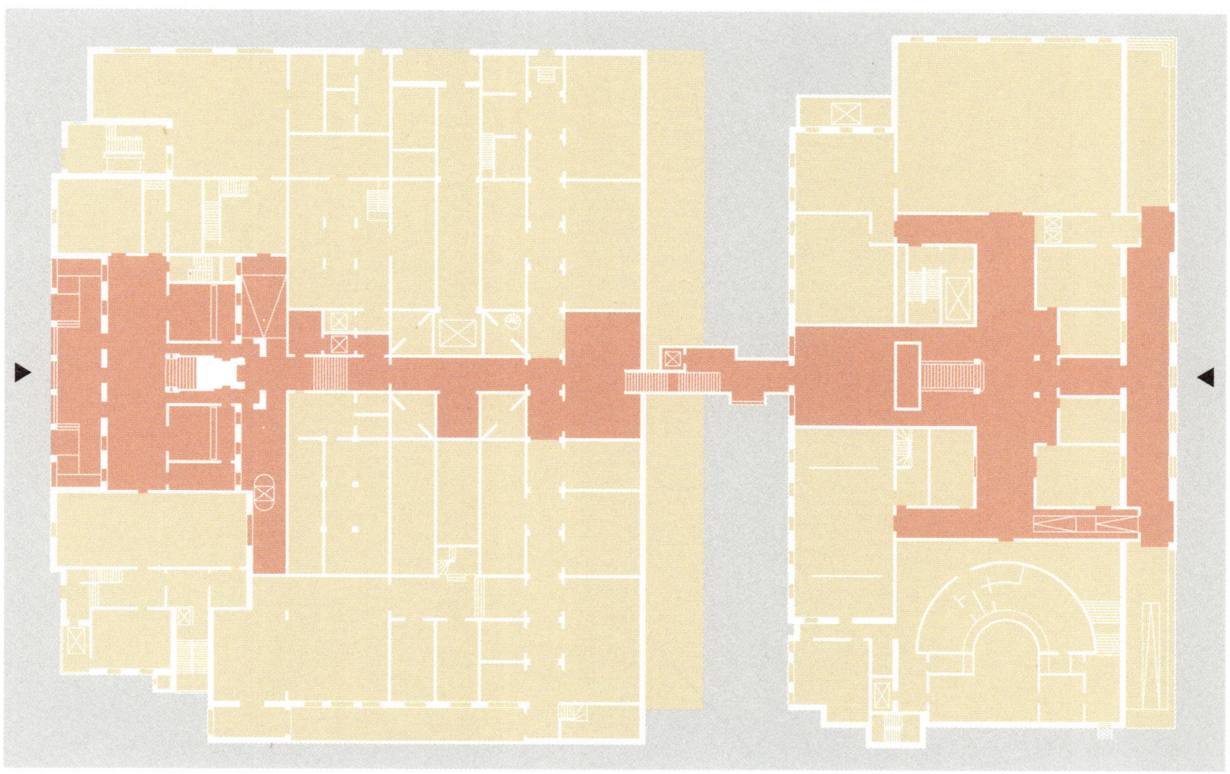

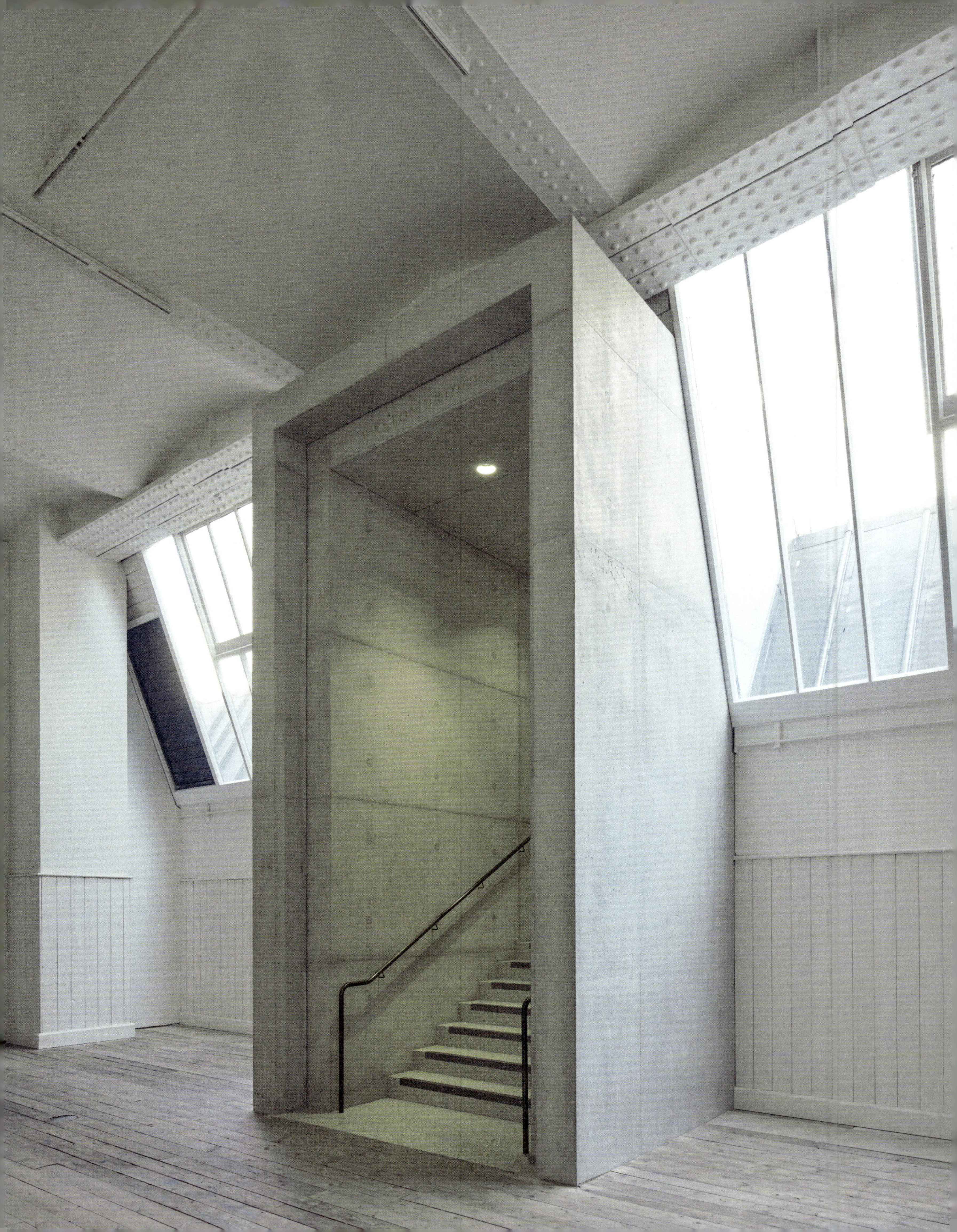

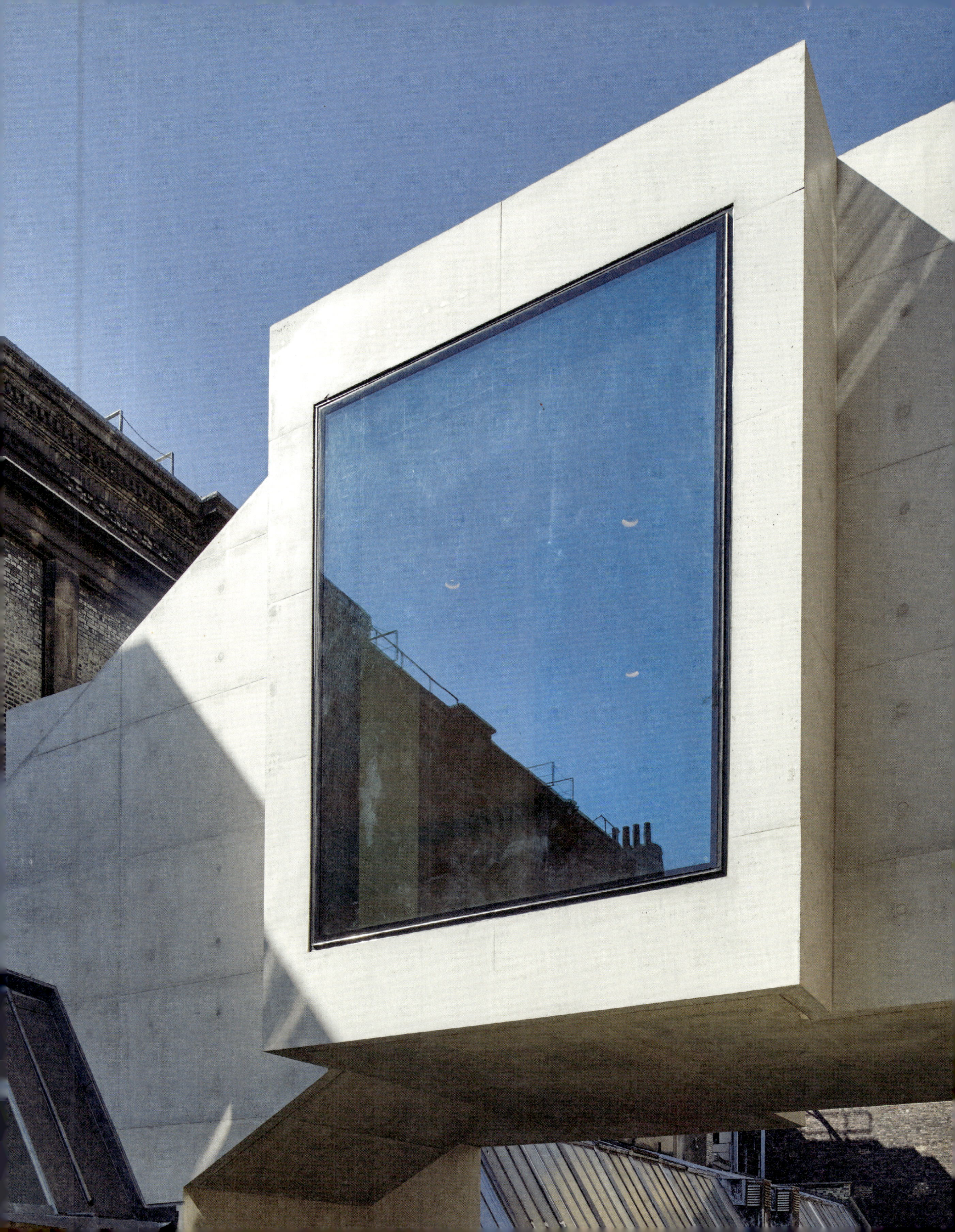

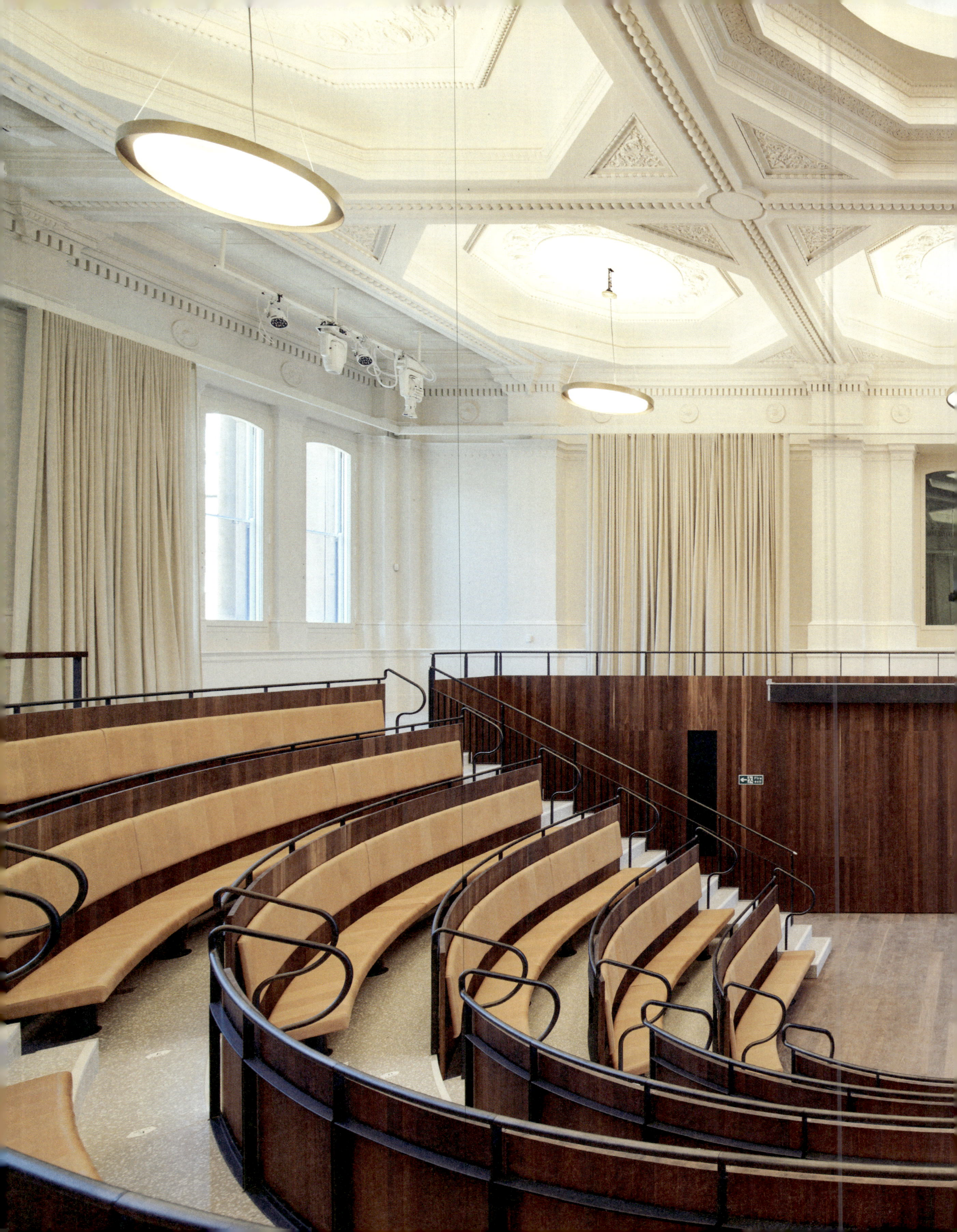

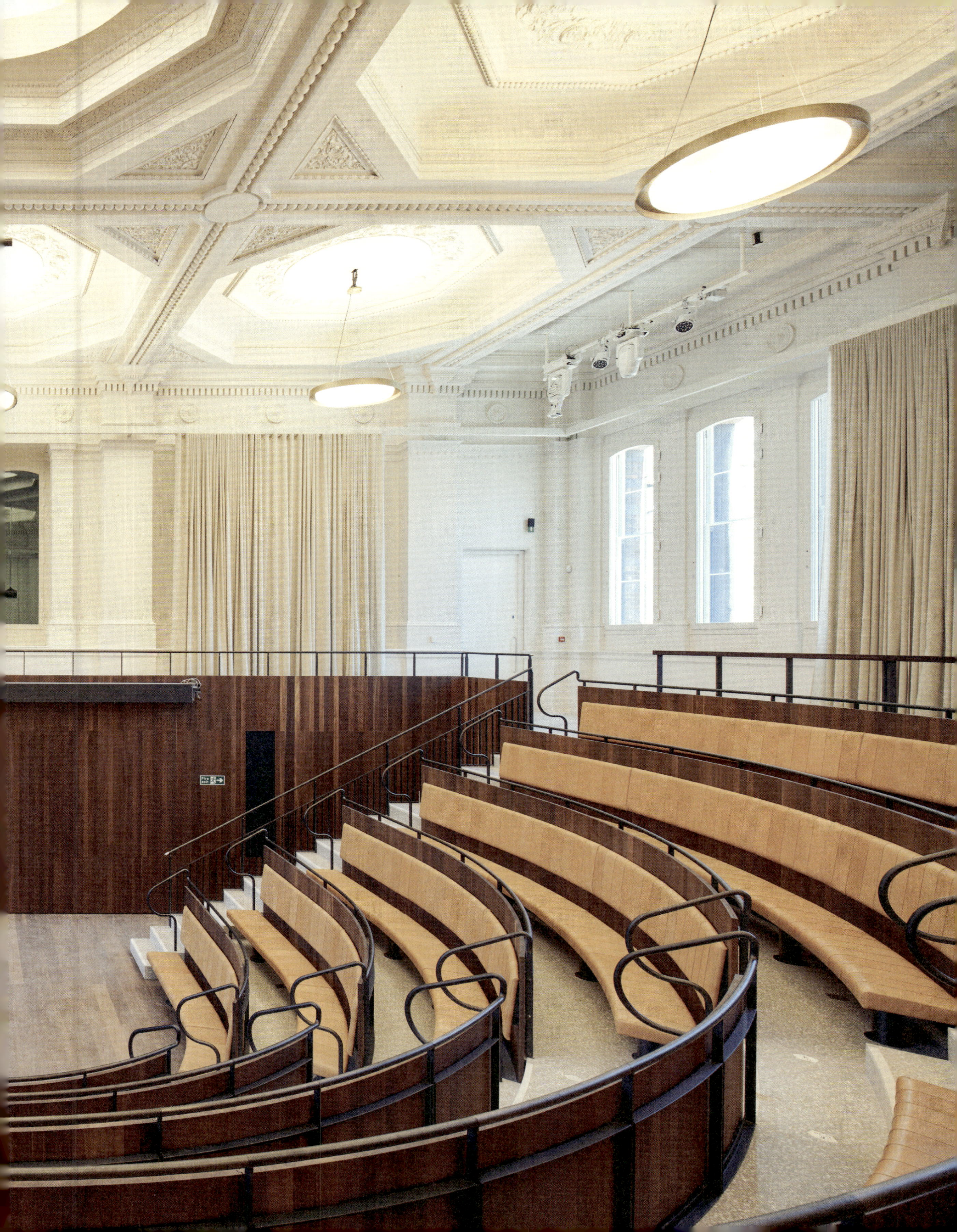

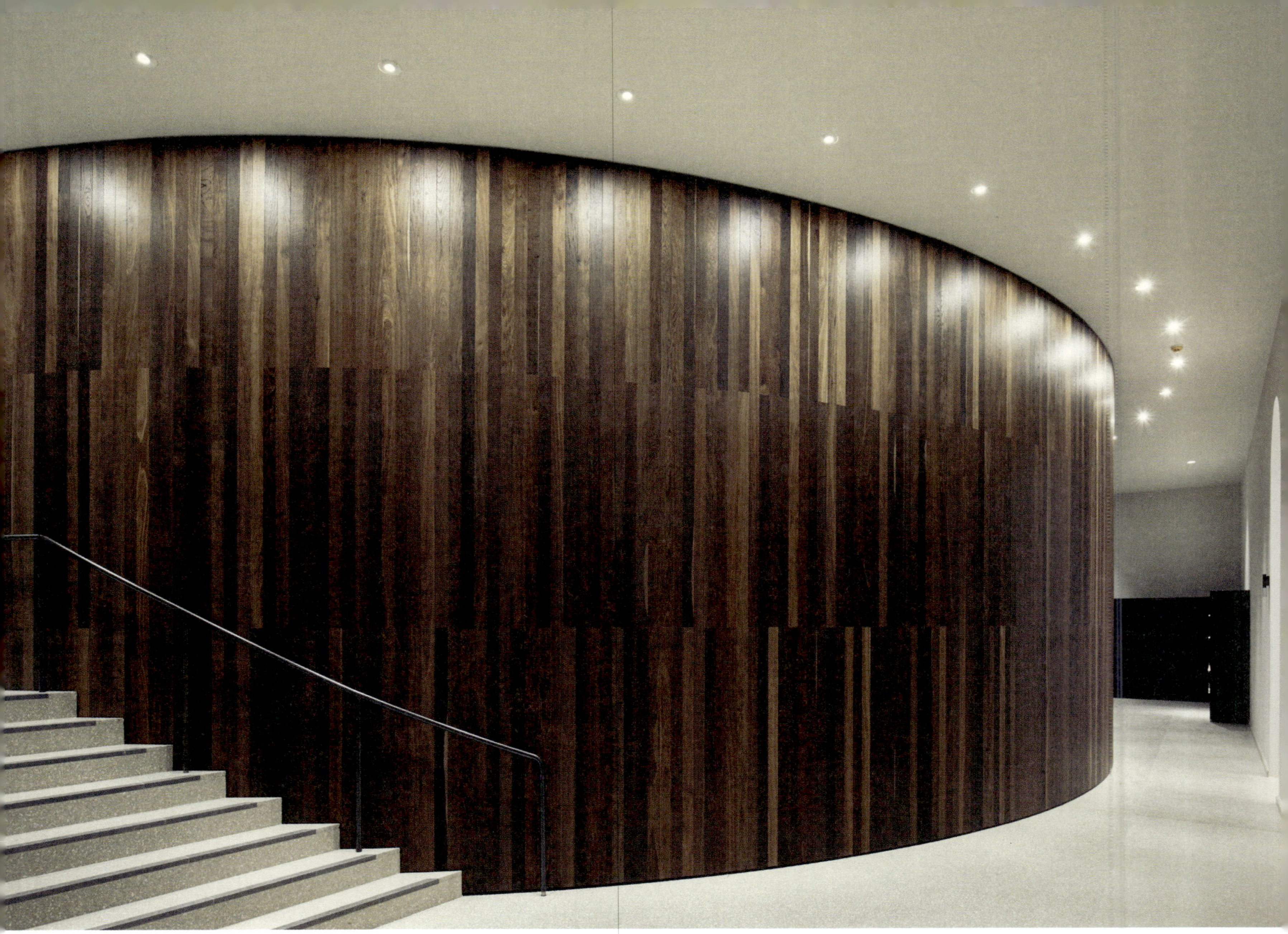

Fig. 289 (previous pages)
The Benjamin West Lecture Theatre, designed by Sir David Chipperfield and completed in 2018, can seat an audience of more than 200

Fig. 290
The approach to the Benjamin West Lecture Theatre

Fig. 291
One of the three Gabrielle Jungels-Winkler Galleries at Burlington Gardens, designed by Sir David Chipperfield and inaugurated in 2018 with the exhibition 'Tacita Dean: Landscape'

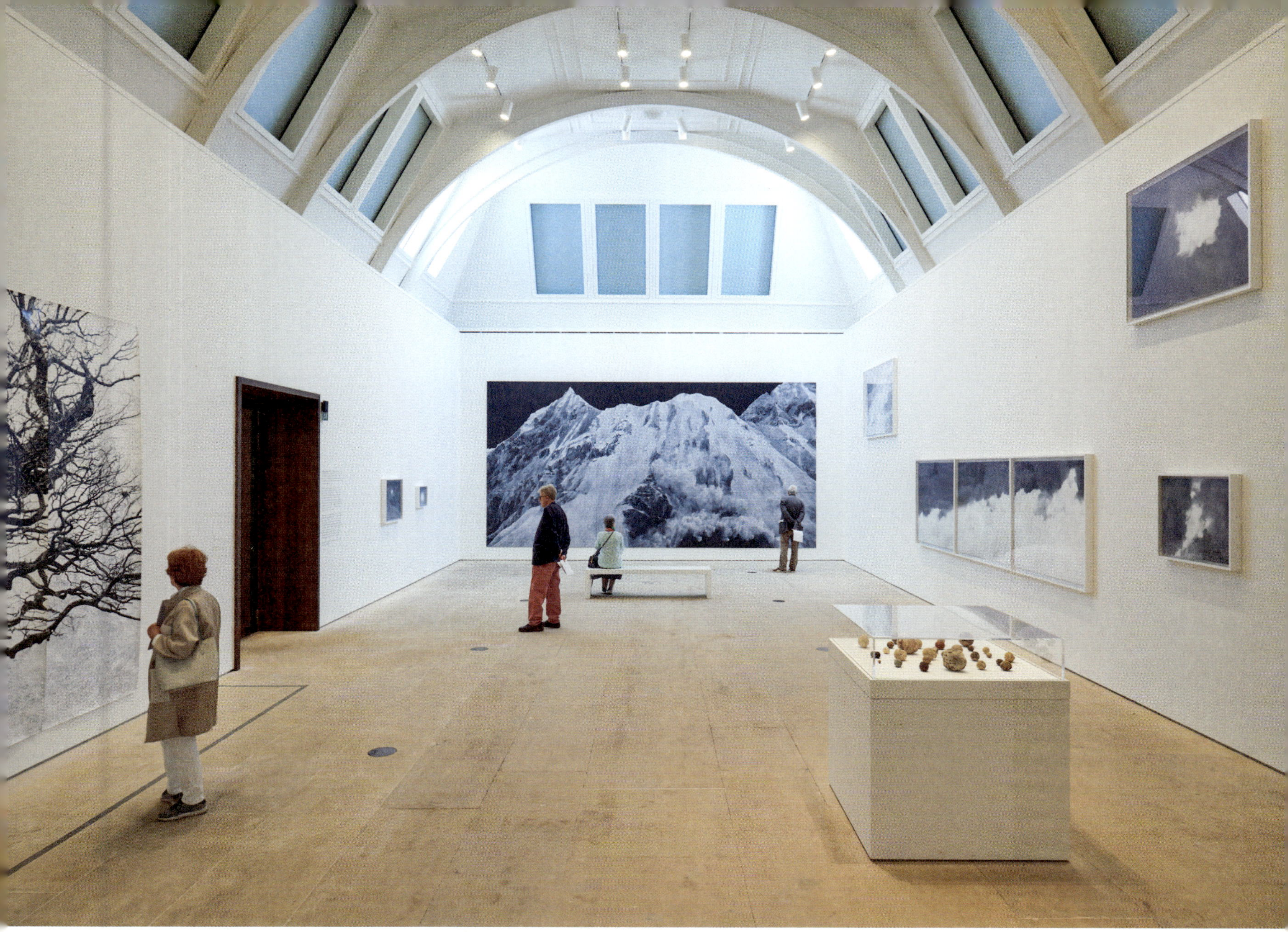

in the present is brought to life here in the Vaults and Schools' Corridor by eighteenth- and nineteenth-century plaster casts displayed not as institutional relics or memorabilia but as the vital teaching tools that enabled the Academy to become the most successful art school in the country. The continuity of past and present in the work of the Schools can be seen also in their new permanent gallery space (Fig. 287), for this in essence performs the function of the lost 'Annex', Smirke's original lean-to structure along the north wall, which E. M. Barry had altered in 1877 to provide 'a proper place for hanging the students & probationers' drawings'.

Whether deliberate or not, continuity of a different sort is evident in Chipperfield's polished concrete bridge spanning the space between the Schools and the south front of Pennethorne's building, for this bold exposition of the similar juncture that lies hidden in the bridge between Burlington House and the Main Galleries is in its way a tribute to the pragmatism of Smirke's building and the tradition of Victorian civil engineering generally (Fig. 288). However, suggesting such a comparison also points up an essential difference for, unlike his Victorian predecessor, Chipperfield has no wish or need to disguise what has been done. Within 6 Burlington Gardens itself, Chipperfield's intervention is neither a redevelopment nor a restoration, but rather a *renovation* designed to enable the Academy to give the building a new lease of life. While this quite rightly puts the architecture first, in the sense that the building's original form is allowed to dictate what can be reasonably expected of it (a parameter that past alterations failed to respect with disastrous consequences), it also bestows on the Academy the freedom and responsibility to make the best use of it that it can. Thus, with the kitting out of new top-lit exhibition spaces and provision of the first ever dedicated workshop space for the Academy's Learning Department, there is little doubt Chipperfield's 'renewal' of the building will help relieve many current constraints on the Academy's increasingly ambitious public and artistic programmes (Fig. 291).

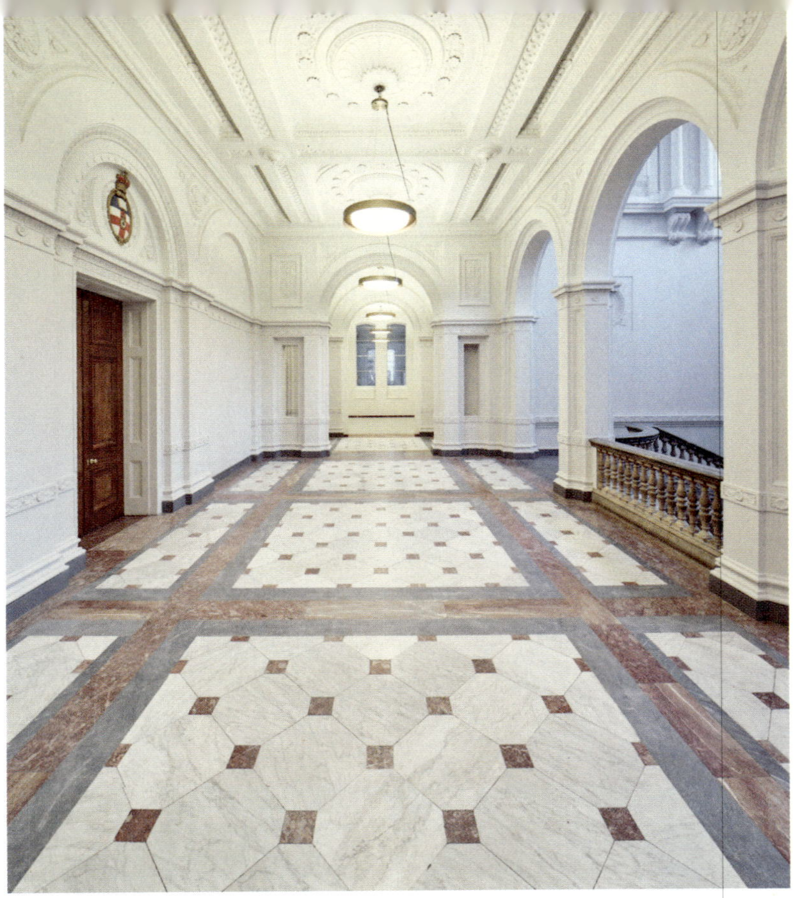

Fig. 292
The first-floor landing at Burlington Gardens, looking towards the Benjamin West Lecture Theatre and the Dorfman Architecture Court

Fig. 293
The Dorfman Senate Rooms, Burlington Gardens, restored by Julian Harrap in 2018

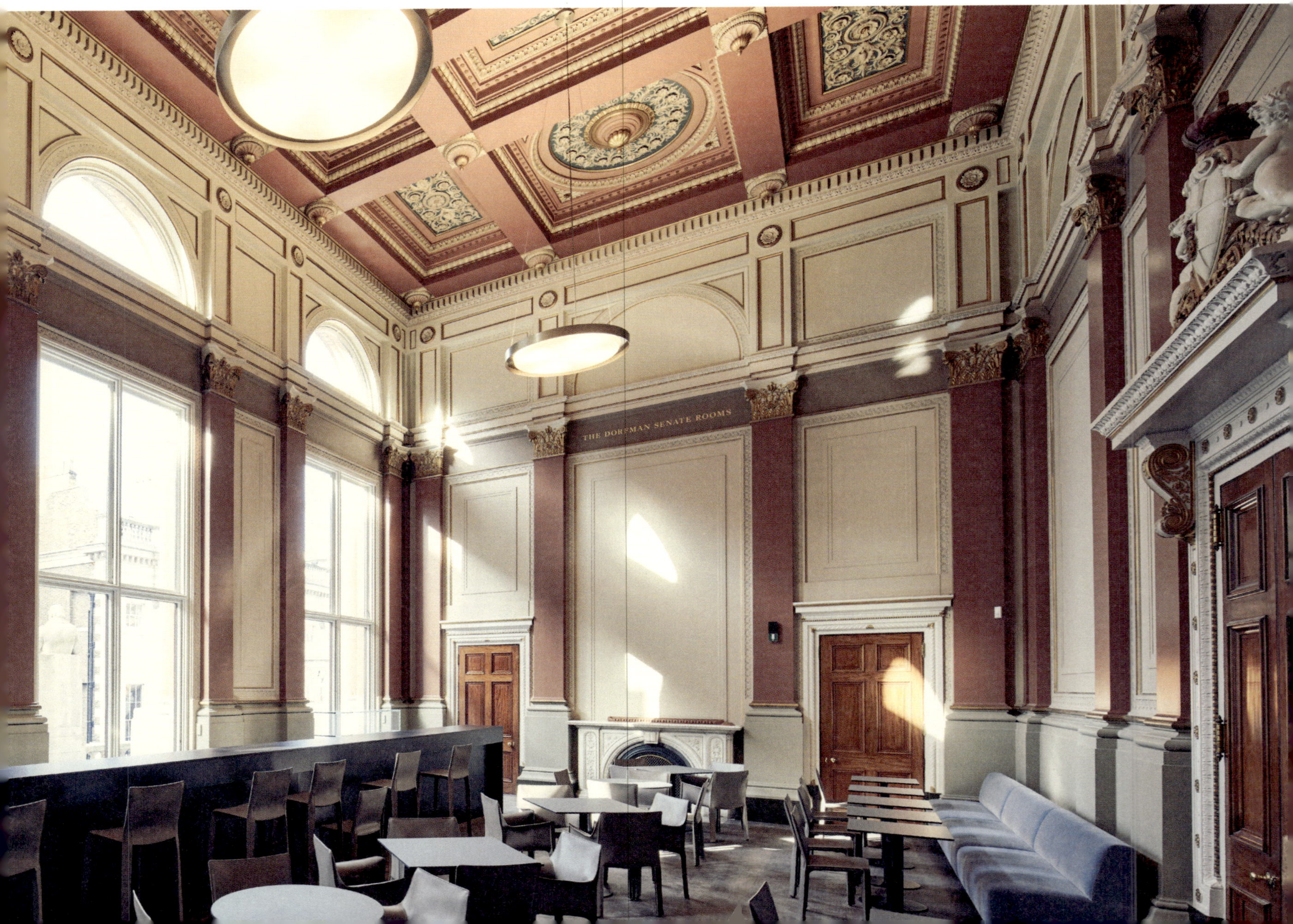

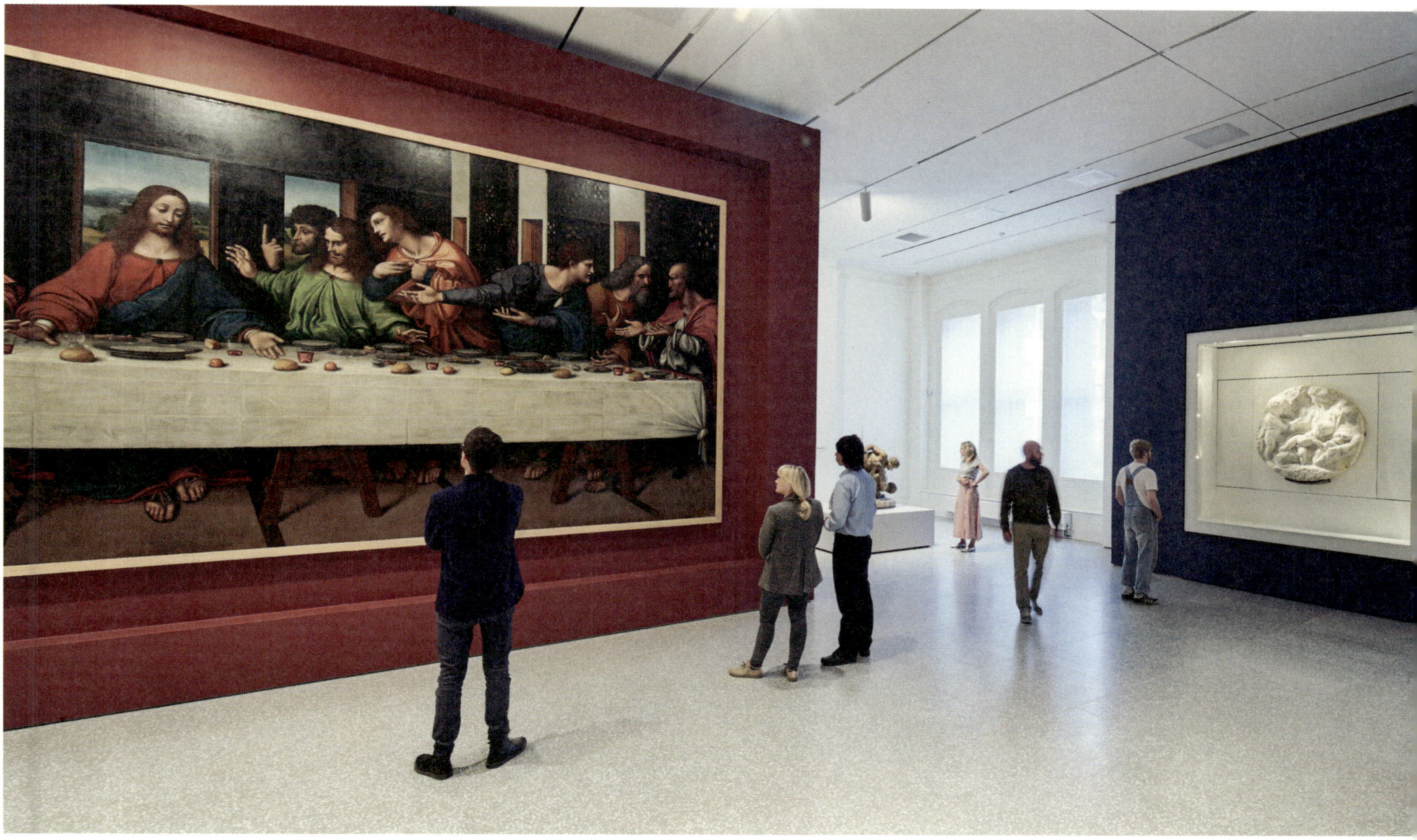

From an historical perspective, the most important contribution of 6 Burlington Gardens is that it allows the Academy to fulfil two promises made when it first moved to Burlington House. One of these promises – Francis Grant's undertaking to Lord John Manners in August 1866 that its art collection would be on permanent public display – had been forgotten when it was decided not to reinstall the Diploma Gallery after World War II. There is some poetic justice, therefore, in the fact that the inaugural exhibition in the new Collections Gallery was selected by Christopher Le Brun, the Academy's current president, and reunited for the first time two of the star attractions of the West Diploma Gallery when it first opened to the public on 14 January 1878 – Giampietrino's copy of Leonardo's *Last Supper* and Michelangelo's *Taddei Tondo* (Fig. 294). The Academy's other promise, a promise that it made to itself but failed to keep a century and a half ago, has finally borne fruit in Chipperfield's magnificent Lecture Theatre, which not only occupies the same footprint and two-thirds of the volume of its great predecessor but is once again the showpiece of the building (Figs 289, 290).

The coincidence of significant anniversaries connecting the Royal Academy to Burlington House is so striking that a Higher Power seems to have been at work. Thus 2018 marks not only the 250th anniversary of the founding of the Academy but also the 350th anniversary of the year the gout-stricken 1st Earl of Burlington was carried over the threshold of his new house, and the 150th anniversary of the fine building weather that enabled Messrs Jackson & Shaw to meet their targets. Today Burlington House is so indelibly associated with the Royal Academy that for most visitors it *is* the Academy. As we have seen, there are dangers in such synonyms – buildings can all too easily become a lazy logo, a forbidding mask, a barrier to change. No. 6 Burlington Gardens has pointed the RA in a new direction, and that can only be a good thing.

Fig. 294
The Collections Gallery, designed by Sir David Chipperfield and completed in 2018, displays some of the Academy's greatest treasures, among them Giampietrino's near-contemporary copy of Leonardo's *Last Supper* and Michelangelo's *Taddei Tondo*

Fig. 295 (overleaf)
The ceiling above the staircase of the Wohl Entrance Hall at Burlington Gardens, restored in 2018

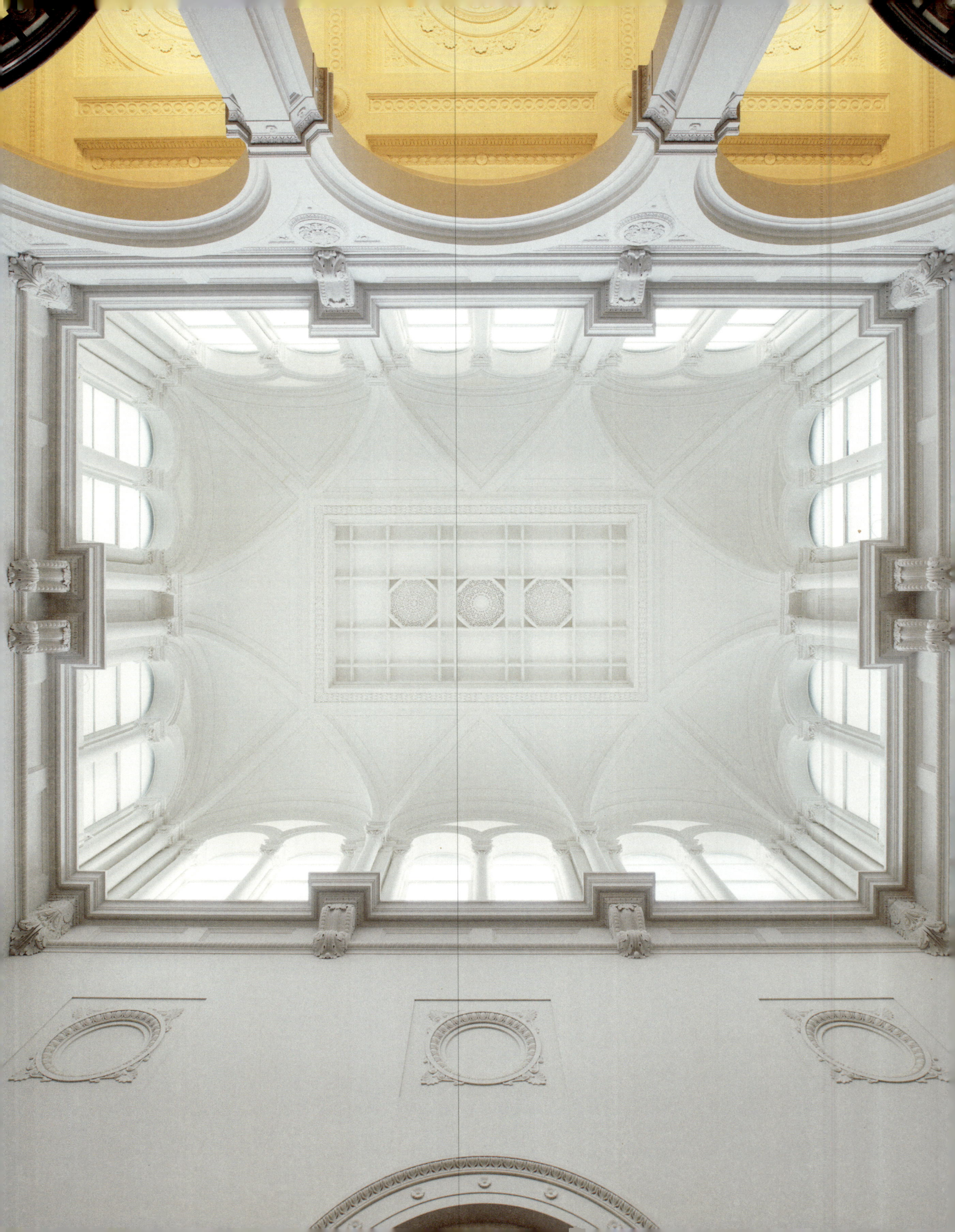

NOTES

1

SIR JOHN DENHAM (pp. 20–39)

1 Recollection of Josias Howe, Denham's fellow student at Trinity College, Oxford, as recorded by John Aubrey in *'Brief Lives', Chiefly of Contemporaries, Set Down by John Aubrey Between the years 1669 & 1696*, ed. Andrew Clark, Oxford, 1898, vol. I, p. 217.

2 F. H. W. Sheppard (gen. ed.), *Survey of London: Volumes 31–32, Parish of St James, Westminster, Part 2: North of Piccadilly*, London, 1963, chap. XXIII, 'Burlington House: Stone Conduit Close' [by P. A. Bezodis and Walter Ison], p. 390.

3 PRO CP25/2/690/18 CHASII TRIN [Feet of Fines Files Henry VIII–Victoria/Middlesex]; see also Sutton deeds, box 1, bundle 2, 18 January 1666/67 and undated plan (cited in Sheppard 1963, chap. XXI, p. 574, n. 9).

4 PRO C10/162/76 [Court of Chancery: Six Clerks' Office]. The claimants were: Joshua Marshall, bricklayer; Maurice Emmett [jun.], bricklayer; Isaac Corner, bricklayer; Henry Wilkins, carpenter; Peter Brent, plumber; and George Drew, smith. Of these only Wilkins is not known to have been an employee, or the son of an employee at the Office of Works during Denham's tenure as Surveyor General (1660–69).

5 H. M. Colvin (gen. ed.), *The History of the King's Works: Volume 5, 1660–1782*, London, 1976, p. 445.

6 http://www.pepysdiary.com/diary/1665/02/20/ Accessed 20 December 2016.

7 C. L. Kingsford, *The Early History of Piccadilly, Leicester Square, Soho & Their Neighbourhood: Based on a Plan Drawn in 1585*, Cambridge, 1925, p. 15.

8 PRO C66/3065, no. 17 [Patent Rolls]. 23 August 1664.

9 H. M. Colvin, *A Biographical Dictionary of British Architects 1600–1840*, 3rd ed., New Haven and London, 1995, pp. 777–78.

10 'Pickadilly Hall' probably occupied the site where William Hunter was to build his house and anatomical museum in 1767, the façade of which still exists. For an authoritative account of other, less convincing theories that have been proposed to account for the district's name, see Sheppard 1963, chap. II, 'The Early History of Piccadilly', pp. 32–40.

11 R. T. Gunther (ed.), *The Architecture of Sir Roger Pratt… Now Printed for the First Time from his Note-books*, Oxford, 1928, p. 144.

12 PRO C54/4165, nos 18–20 [Close Rolls]. 24 August 1664. Conveyed the westernmost part of Stonebridge Close to Sir William Pulteney; the eight acres to the east of that to Lord John Berkeley; and the seven acres of Stone Conduit Close to the east of Clarendon's plot jointly to Denham and Pulteney. See Sheppard 1963, chap. XXI, 'Sackville Street: Stone Conduit Close', p. 342.

13 It is perhaps significant in this regard that the other Crown leases granted to Denham around this time all involved land that required improvement or development of some kind, *viz.*: a portion of the 'Bedford Levell Fennes, not farre from Peterborough' granted by the Duke of York, probably in 1664 when Denham was elected to serve as bailiff of the Bedford Level Corporation (Samuel Wells, *The History of the Drainage of… the Bedford Level*, London, 1830, vol. I, p. 457; Denham's will, proved 9 May 1670 [PROB 11/332/618]); 'a parcel of waste land and oosey ground in Sussex' on the Selsey peninsula (warrant granted 17 July 1665 [William A. Shaw, *Calendar of Treasury Books: vol. I, 1660–1667*, London, 1904, p. 674]); '2,500 acres of waste lands in the parishes of Walpole and Walsoken, co. Norfolk' (warrant granted 8 August 1664 [M. A. E. Green (ed.). *Calendar of State Papers, Domestic Series, of the Reign of Charles II: 1663–64*, London, 1862, pp. 558, 661]); and 'Land under St. James' Park-wall, being lately a highway from Charing Crosse to ye Pallace of St. James, 218 foot in length & about 39 in bredth … under on rental of 26 l., with l[i]b[er]ty to build within 3 years …' (granted March 1663, PRO SP29/70, no. 70, f. 160 [Secretaries of State: State Papers Domestic, Charles II: Letters and papers]; Green 1862, pp. 88, 94). In each case (apart from the last-mentioned, which does, however, seem to have been connected in some way with the grant of a plot for Sir Philip Warwick to build himself a house on the same disused road), Denham's leases were held in partnership with former royalist associates or a family member, namely his longstanding friend William Ashburnham, his son-in-law Sir William Morley, and his prospective neighbour on Piccadilly, Lord John Berkeley.

14 Pulteney-Sutton estate deeds, box 2, bundle 6, 29 August 1664 (cited in Sheppard 1963, chap. XXIII, p. 577, n. 3).

15 Green 1862, p. 25. In this building licence Denham and Pulteney's plot is described as 'bounded by London highway to the South, by the Easte of Clarendons Walke to the west, by the house and ground of John Emlin, Brickmaker, towards the East, and by a field called Crabtree Field towards the North contg. in length five hundred and sixty foot or thereabouts, and that Proportion in depth …' (see Soane Museum, 'Court Orders of Sir Christopher Wren', ff. 39–40, published in *The Wren Society*, vol. 18, 1941, p. 32).

16 E. S. de Beer (ed.), *The Diary of John Evelyn*, London, 2006, 19 October 1661, p. 392.

17 Roland Fréart de Chambray, *A Parallel of the Antient Architecture with the Modern*, translated by John Evelyn, London, 1664, 'The Epistle Dedicatory', p. [9].

18 Fréart 1664, pp. [9–10].

19 PRO SP29/75, No. 27.

20 PRO C66/3005, Part 3.

21 Sir John Fielding, *A Brief Description of the Cities of London and Westminster*, London, 1776, p. 18.

22 http://www.pepysdiary.com/diary/1667/06/14/ Accessed 20 December 2016.

23 Brendan O Hehir, *Harmony from Discords: A Life of Sir John Denham*, Berkeley and Los Angeles, 1968, p. 124. Berkeley and Clarendon had also been longstanding political enemies during the Interregnum. http://www.oxforddnb.com.ezproxy2.londonlibrary.co.uk/view/article/2217 Accessed 20 December 2016.

24 PRO C66/3065, no. 17.

25 PRO SP44/16, pp. 235–38.

26 Sheppard 1963, chap. XXI, 'Sackville Street: Stone Conduit Close', p. 342.

27 PRO CP25/2/690/18 CHASII TRIN. Pulteney is named as a party to the sale of Denham's house.

28 1st Earl of Burlington's diary, 16 April 1668 (Chatsworth, Devonshire Collections, Cork MSS, Miscellaneous, box 1).

29 Brendan O Hehir, *Expans'd hieroglyphicks: A Critical Edition of Sir John Denham's Coopers Hill*, Berkeley and Los Angeles, 1969, p. 21.

30 Quoted from the dedication of 'The Rival Ladies' to Roger, Earl of Orrery, in J. H. Smith, D. Macmillan, and V. A. Dearing (eds), *The Works of John Dryden: vol. VIII, Plays*, Berkeley and Los Angeles, vol. VIII, p. 100.

31 Clark 1898, vol. I, pp. 219–20.

32 O Hehir 1968, pp. 1–2.

33 O Hehir 1969, 'Coopers Hill', "A" Text (1642), ll. 28–40.

34 Johannes Kip's engraving of Leonard Knyff's celebrated bird's-eye view, the earliest-known representation of Denham's house after its completion for the 1st Earl of Burlington in summer 1668, seriously foreshortens its distance from the road. Forming part of a series of similar views of royal palaces and noblemen's seats first published by David Mortier in *Britannia Illustrata* (London, 1707), it bears an engraved dedication to the then owner of the house, Charles Boyle, 2nd Earl of Burlington, datable on internal evidence to between January 1698 and late summer 1699.

35 Sheppard 1963, chap. XXIII, p. 391.

36 Gunther 1928, p. 260.

37 Gunther 1928, p. 60.

38 Colvin 1976, p. 8.

39 O Hehir 1968, p. 170, n. 38.

40 Gunther 1928, p. 149.

41 O Hehir 1968, pp. 187–99.

42 Letter dated 14 April 1666 from Sir Stephen Fox to Sir George Lane in Dublin, in Historical Manuscripts Commission, *The Manuscripts of the Marquis of Ormonde: New Series, vol. III*, compiled by C. L. Falkiner, London, 1904, p. 217.

43 Colvin 1976, p. 445; O Hehir 1968, p. 200, n. 31.

II

THE EARLS OF BURLINGTON AND CORK (pp. 40–73)

1 Chatsworth, Devonshire Collections, Cork MSS, Miscellaneous, box I.

2 Copy of 1st Earl of Burlington's will (TNA, PROB 11/448).

3 Toby Barnard, 'Land and the Limits of Loyalty: The Second Earl of Cork and First Earl of Burlington (1612–98)', in T. Barnard and J. Clark, *Lord Burlington: Architecture, Art and Life*, London and Rio Grande, 1995, p. 172.

4 Laurence Hyde to Countess of Burlington, 11 June 1670 (BL Add MS 75355, Althorp Papers, vol. lv, B5/13).

5 Copy of 1st Earl of Burlington's will (TNA, PROB 11/448).

6 NLI, MS 13227, letter of 2nd Earl of Burlington, quoted in Barnard 1995, p. 195.

7 Abstract of Duke of Devonshire's title, recital of deed of 3 May 1670 (Chatsworth, Devonshire Collections, Devonshire MSS).

8 See the anonymous map of *c.* 1710 reproduced in Sheppard 1963, pl. 3b.

9 City of Westminster Archive Centre, St James's Piccadilly, Vestry Minute Book, vol. I, D1756, 10 April 1694.

10 'Cork Street and Savile Row Area: Introduction', in Sheppard 1963, pp. 442–455. *British History Online* http://www.british-history.ac.uk/survey-london/vols31-2/pt2/pp442-455 [accessed 12 March 2017].

11 4 Geo. I, c. 11, private; *Journals of the House of Lords*, vol. XX, pp. 580–81, 591, 612, 634, 663.

12 Lady Shelburne to Alexander Murray, 20 June 1705 (PRONI, D2860/9/3), quoted in Rachel Wilson, *Elite Women in Ascendancy Ireland 1690–1745: Imitation and Innovation*, Woodbridge, 2015, pp. 76–77.

13 Joseph Waite to Richard Musgrave, 9 September 1707 (Chatsworth, Joseph Waite's letter book (Ireland and Yorkshire), Burlington MSS, Miscellaneous, box 1), quoted in Wilson 2015, p. 84; TNA, PROB 11/475 (copy of 2nd Earl of Burlington's will).

14 Toby Barnard, *A New Anatomy of Ireland: The Irish Protestants, 1649–1770*, New Haven and London, 2003, p. 208.

15 Juliana, Dowager Countess of Burlington to Roger Power, Richard Bagge and Thomas Baker, 7 October 1704 (NLI, MS 43, 361/2), quoted in Wilson 2015, p. 63.

16 The Act of Parliament enabling Juliana to sell an entailed portion of her husband's estate in 1705 to pay his debts gave rise to rumours that 'the sense of what he had done struck him so severely for the great wrong he had done his family, that he could not die in peace before he had obtained their pardon' – see letter from Sir Richard Grosvenor 4th Bt. to Peter Shakerley, 5 June 1705 (Eaton Hall, Grosvenor Papers, Papers of 4th Bt., Misc. Papers), quoted in D. Hayton, E. Cruickshanks, S. Handley (eds), *The History of Parliament: The House of Commons 1690–1715*, Woodbridge, 2002, s.v. Boyle, Hon. Charles I (1660–1704). It was to foil such stories of family dissension no doubt that Juliana had commissioned Mary Pix's *A Pastoral Elegy on the Death of the Rt. Hon. The Earl of Burlington* (London, 1704), the last lines of which read: 'In vain, thy aking Sighs, thy ceasless moan, / In vain, for Daphnis to the Grave is gone, / And never can revive but in his lovely Son.'

17 Joshua Dawson to Catherine O'Brien, 12 March 1717/18 (NLI, MS 45, 346/3), quoted in Wilson 2015, p. 83.

18 *The Wren Society*, VI (1929), p. 78; George Vertue, *Notebooks*, vol. I, in *The Walpole Society*, XVIII (1929–30), p. 38.

19 G. Knox, 'Antonio Pellegrini and Marco Ricci at Burlington House and Narford Hall', *The Burlington Magazine*, vol. 130, no. 1028 (November 1988), pp. 846–53. Knox's reconstruction assumes that by 'hall' both Thornhill and Vertue must be referring to the Saloon. However, as Tim Knox was the first to point out, there is no necessity to discount the usual meaning of the word 'hall' since the entrance hall of Burlington House at this date corresponded closely with the Saloon directly above it, both in terms of floor dimensions and window/door apertures; see T. A. J. Knox, 'The Decorative History of the Private Rooms of Burlington House', unpublished report for Royal Academy of Arts, May 1998, pp. 4–5. The context makes it is unlikely that both Thornhill and Vertue were thinking of Palladio's specialised use of the word, for which see below.

20 G. Knox, *Antonio Pellegrini, 1675–1741*, Oxford, 1995, p. 52.

21 Samuel Garth (ed.), *Ovid's Metamorphoses in Fifteen Books. Translated by the Most Eminent Hands. Adorn'd with Sculptures*. London, 1717. Juliana must have supported this edition particularly generously being the only dedicatee to sponsor not only a frontispiece illustrating 'The Transformation of Scylla' but an additional plate, 'The Story of Vertumnus and Pomona' (see Book XIV, plates facing pp. 481 and 500).

22 Wilson 2015, pp. 85–86.

23 Copy of 2nd Earl of Burlington's will (TNA, PROB 11/475).

24 Papers of the Virtuosi of St Luke, 1697–*c.* 1743, BL Add MS 39167; for details of Graham's long membership see https://artworld.york.ac.uk/sourceView.do?sourceUrn=5.2238&br=no

25 G. Knox, 'Sebastiano Ricci at Burlington House: a Venetian decoration "alla Romana"', *The Burlington Magazine*, vol. 127, no. 990 (September 1985), p. 609.

26 Reproduced in John Cornforth, 'A Pantheon in Piccadilly', *Country Life*, 1 April 2004, p. 75.

27 Knox 1985, p.609.

28 J. Lees-Milne, *Earls of Creation: Five Great Patrons of Eighteenth-Century Art*, London, 1962, p. 112.

29 Jacques Carré, *Lord Burlington (1694–1753): le connaisseur, le mécène, l'architecte*, Clermont-Ferrand, 1993, Appendice III, p. 518.

30 Carré 1993, p. 117.

31 For circumstantial but as yet inconclusive evidence that the 3rd Earl was a prominent Jacobite and that Chiswick House constituted a coded expression of his loyalty to the Stuart cause, see Jane Clark, 'Lord Burlington is here', in Barnard 1995, pp. 251–310. So far no-one has suggested that Burlington House might harbour similar secrets.

32 'A Short Accompt of Mr James Gibbs Architect and of Several things he built in England &c. after his returne from Italy', in 'A Manuscri[pt] by Mr. Gibbs Memorandums, &c.', p. 90 (Sir John Soane's Museum, London).

33 Sheppard 1963, chap. XXIII, 'Burlington House: Stone Conduit Close' [by P. A. Bezodis and Walter Ison], p. 398.

34 John Macky's comparison of the Burlington House colonnade with 'the Portico to the Church of St. Peter at Rome, from whence his Lordship I suppose took the Model', was probably a fairly typical contemporary response ([John Macky], *A Journey through England*, 2nd edition, London, 1722, vol. I, p. 190).

35 HMC, Stuart, vol. II, p. 93.

36 Colen Campbell, *The Third Volume of Vitruvius Britannicus*, London, 1725, p. 7.

37 'Messrs Graham & Colliers Joynt Accounts', July 1719–July 1722, record of receipt dated 11 September [1719] (Chatsworth, Devonshire Collections, Burlington MSS, Miscellaneous, box 1).

38 PRO, C11/2435/8.

39 Richard Graham's dedication of this edition to the 3rd Earl concludes: '... And I congratulate my Countrey-men, upon the happy Prospect they have, of saving themselves the Trouble and Expence of a Journey to Rome, or Paris, for the study of those Arts, which they may find in their utmost Perfection at BURLINGTON-HOUSE.'

40 See Kent's letter to Massingberd dated 10 December 1719, in Carol Blackett-Ord, 'Letters from William Kent to Burrell Massingberd from the Continent, 1712–1719', *Walpole Society Annual*, vol. 63 (2001), p. 107.

41 John Harris, *The Palladian Revival: Lord Burlington, His Villa and Garden at Chiswick*, London, 1994, p. 68.

42 Kent to Massingberd, 19[?] January 1720, in Blackett-Ord 2001, p. 107.

43 Pauline Plummer and Peter Schmitt, 'The rediscovery of the lost ceiling decorations in the Saloon at Burlington House', in R. Gowing and R. Pender (eds), *All Manner of Murals: The History, Techniques and Conservation of Secular Wall Paintings*, London, 2007, p. 166.

44 See R. Graham and J. Collier to 3rd Earl of Burlington, 17 September 1719 (Chatsworth, Devonshire Collections, Burlington MSS, CS1/154.0). Although the Earl outgrew Campbell's imitative neo-Palladianism there is no real evidence for a breakdown in their relationship. Campbell was still living rent-free at No. 3 Great Burlington Street in 1726 according to a 'Half years Rent-roll of Burlington Garden' dated Lady day 1725 [i.e. 25 March 1725/6] (London Metropolitan Archives Q/CML/8/1).

45 Kent to Massingberd, 19[?] January 1720, in Blackett-Ord 2001, p. 107.

46 Colvin 1995, p. 210. Cf. engraving of cross-section of central hall at Wanstead, in Colen Campbell, *Vitruvius Britannicus*, vol. I, London, 1715, pl. 26.

47 J. Leoni, *The Architecture of A. Palladio; in Four Books*, 3rd ed., London: printed for A. Ward [*et al.*], 1742, Book I, chapter XXI, p. 26.

48 Ian C. Bristow, 'Report on Paint Samples taken from the Fine Rooms, Burlington House', 2001 (Royal Academy Archives FAC/2010/2/10).

49 W. Kent, *The designs of Inigo Jones ... with some additional designs*, London [for Lord Burlington], 1727, vol. I, pl. 72.

50 Kent to Massingberd, 3 June 1720, in Blackett-Ord 2001, p. 109.

51 John Gay, 'Epistle to the Right Honourable Paul Methuen', lines 57–62; first published in Gay's *Poems on several Occasions* (1720), which was illustrated by Kent and heavily subsidised by the 3rd Earl of Burlington.

52 Colvin 1995, p. 366.

53 For the origins of this story see J. T. Smith, *Nollekens and his Times*, London, 1828, vol. II, pp. 206–08.

54 Quoted in Colvin 1995, p. 393.

55 Kent to Massingberd, 30 January 1721, in Blackett-Ord 2001, p. 108 (misdated 1720).

56 Knox, 1998, pp. 40–41.
57 Plummer and Schmitt in Gowing 2007, pp. 162–64.
58 An almost exact replica of this doorcase survives in No. 9 Henrietta Street, Dublin. The façade of this house, which was built *c.* 1731 for Thomas Carter, a friend and associate of the 3rd Earl, was modelled on the latter's design for No. 30 Old Burlington Street.
59 On John Carter's life, character and achievements, see Colvin 1995, pp. 228–29. A copy of Carter's letter applying for permission to draw the colonnade, together with Samuel Ware's note of authorisation dated 12 September 1815, is preserved in the RIBA Drawings Collection (ref. DC/Ware, S./ L6/5). Ware instructed his clerk of the works Thomas Dudly, to 'request Mr. Carter to confine himself to that part only.'
60 On a probable connection between Kent's painting and the initiation in September 1720 of the project to publish Jones's designs, see Eileen Harris, *British Architectural Books and Writers 1556–1785*, Cambridge, 1990, p. 250.
61 'Voiage d'Angleterre, d'Hollande et de Flandre' (National Art Library, Victoria and Albert Museum, London, MSL/1912/1255).
62 The only basis for this assertion appears to be Sir Thomas Robinson's comment in a letter to the Earl of Carlisle dated 24 December 1733 in which he reports that 'Lord B ... is quite quitted London, sent for all his pictures from Burlington House, and is making very great and beautiful additions to Chiswick' (HMC, *Carlisle MSS*, p. 125). As Jane Clark has pointed out, 'he may have wanted to give Robinson the impression that he was retiring from central activities yet from all surviving documents it is clear that life went on at Burlington House as usual' (in Barnard 1995, p. 309). It is quite possible in fact that some rearrangement of his pictures at Burlington House had become necessary as a consequence of the Prince of Wales's purchase in 1732 of Carlton House, Pall Mall, where the Dowager Countess Juliana had been living since her son had inherited it from his uncle Lord Carleton in March 1725.
63 'John Ferrett's Account Currant with the Right Hon[ble] The Earl of Burlington', 1745–53 (Chatsworth, Devonshire Collections, Burlington MSS, BU/3/2/14).
64 W. Chambers, *A Treatise on Civil Architecture*, London: printed for the author, 1759, p. 63. Apart from Campbell's ground-plan in the third volume of *Vitruvius Britannicus* (1725) there is no further evidence to suggest that the re-entrant angle arcades linking the service wings to the main building apparently shown there, were ever in fact executed (see Shepherd 1963, p. 404).
65 'John Ferrett's Account Currant with the Right Hon[ble] The Earl of Burlington', 1745–53 (Chatsworth, Devonshire Collections, Burlington MSS, BU/3/2/14).
66 Kent to 3rd Earl of Burlington, 12 September 1745 (Chatsworth, Devonshire Collections, Burlington MSS, CS1/206.9).

III

THE CAVENDISH FAMILY (pp. 74–141)

1 Rent valuation of Burlington House, John Soane to Samuel Ware, 20 November 1811 (Chatsworth, Devonshire MSS, Currey Papers, L/86/1).
2 Sheppard 1963, chap. XXIII, 'Burlington House: Stone Conduit Close' [by P. A. Bezodis and Walter Ison], p. 402n.
3 Giles Worsley, *The British Stable*, New Haven and London, 2004, p. 141.
4 [John Bowack], *The Antiquities of Middlesex*, part 1, London: printed for S. Keble [*et al.*], 1705, p. 21.
5 John Gwynn, *London and Westminster improved; illustrated by plans. To which is prefixed, a Discourse on Publick Magnificence*, London: printed for the author, 1766, p. 82.
6 Chambers 1759, p. 69.
7 Horace Walpole, *Anecdotes of Painting in England ... volume the fourth*, Strawberry-Hill: printed by T. Kirgate, 1771, p. 109.
8 Sheppard 1963, p. 406.
9 'Inventory of the Goods & Chattels at Burlington House 1770' (Chatsworth, Devonshire MSS, vellum-bound 4to ledger; photocopy held in RA Library).
10 Sir Anthony T. Abdy to 3rd Duke of Portland, 2 April 1771 (University of Nottingham, Manuscripts and Special Collections, PwF 3).
11 J. Hinchcliffe to 3rd Duke of Portland, 2 June 1771 (University of Nottingham, Manuscripts and Special Collections, PwF 5134).
12 David Wilkinson, *The Duke of Portland: Politics and Party in the Age of George III*, Basingstoke, 2003, p. 62.
13 See Richard Horwood, *Plan of the cities of London and Westminster* ... [London: R. Horwood, 1792–99], section B published 22 June 1792.
14 '26 Bills and abstracts of bills from various tradesmen, mostly for work done on Burlington House' (University of Nottingham, Manuscripts and Special Collections, Pl F5/4/232/1-18). For Carr's reference to 'the new Mahogany doors in Burlington House' see his letter to Portland dated 6 March 1776 (*ibid.*, PwF 2546). For transcripts of the relevant bills see Knox 1998, appendix 5.
15 John Carr to 3rd Duke of Portland, 27 October 1771 (University of Nottingham, Manuscripts and Special Collections, PwF 2539).
16 Richard Dixon to 3rd Duke of Portland, 8 May 1772, 30 March 1774, 25 January 1775 (University of Nottingham, Manuscripts and Special Collections, PwF 3369-3371). See also references to Dixon's workmen in the Duchess of Portland's letters to her husband dated 31 August and 2 September 1771 regarding an attempted burglary at Burlington House (*ibid.*, PwF 10601–10602).
17 Colvin 1995, pp. 306–07, *s.v.* Joseph Dixon; http://ghgraham.org/richarddixon1724.html
18 RA Collection Inv. Nos 06/2194–2197, 06/4378.
19 On Portland as the 'fountain head' of the Home Office's network of government spies, see Wilkinson 2003, pp. 124–30.
20 The carver and gilder Solomon Hudson charged a total of £51 15s. on 29 September 1775 for carving (but *not* gilding) waterleaf and 'rich' impost and architrave mouldings on the window shutters and soffits of the 'Middle Room principle Story', i.e. the Saloon (University of Nottingham, Manuscripts and Special Collections, Pl F5/4/232/10).
21 The monumental stonemason John Devall charged £90 on 19 July 1776 for 'a Chimney Piece in the Center Room North Front' composed of 'Statuary and Sienna Marble. The tablet Carved with Antique Vase, Goats heads and Festoons of Drapery, Pillasters with Rams Heads and Drops of Natural Flowers tied with ribbands two pateras on the Blocks two Members Enriched in the Cornice & one in the Moulding to inside of the Chimney the fluted Frieze Inlaid, with Sienna, Including a Statuary Marble Slab and Black Marble Covings' (University of Nottingham, Manuscripts and Special Collections, Pl F5/4/232/6).
22 Knox 1998, pp. 14–16.
23 'Particulars of the State of Burlington House and the premises thereunto belonging surveyed July 10th and 13th 1782' (University of Nottingham, Manuscripts and Special Collections, Pl F5/15/3/5). This report was prepared by Portland's steward Richard Norris as a consequence of Lord George Cavendish taking on the house in March that year.
24 3rd Duke of Portland to 5th Duke of Devonshire, 17 July 1807 (Chatsworth, Devonshire MSS, CS5/1928).
25 See J. Carter, Sketch survey of Burlington House, 1st-floor plan with rooms numbered 1–10 (Fig. 49; RA Coll. Inv. No. 06/2157 verso); *ibid.*, details of room 'No. 6', i.e. bedroom to west of middle anti-room in north range (06/2155); *ibid.*, details of 'No. 8', i.e. north-east anti-room according to sketch plan, but more probably the north-west 'Pillar Bed Room' (06/2158); *ibid.*, sketch of carved gilt Kent-style pedimented pier glass and console table with elaborate curved scroll legs and garlanded apron, apparently in room 'No. 10', i.e. the Ball Room (06/2157 recto).
26 Adam Price to 3rd Duke of Portland, 18 November 1772 and 4 February 1773 (University of Nottingham, Manuscripts and Special Collections, PwF 7884, 7887).
27 'An Inventory of Sundry Household Goods and Chattels being the property of his Grace the Duke of Devonshire and his Grace the Duke of Portland at Burlington House in Piccadilly taken the 20th day of April 1812 and following days' (Chatsworth, Devonshire Collections, Devonshire MSS, L/52/11). To judge from the following barbed comment in the press, Portland continued to spend considerable sums on altering and redecorating the house during his second tenure: 'The Duke of Portland is much to be commended, for the expensive work he is now doing at Burlington House. His humble friends, the Blue and Buff, say otherwise – The gold leaf, in such quantity on the walls, they think might be laid where it is more wanted. – Several Tradesmen in St James's and St George's parish, happen to think the same' (*World*, 13 September 1787).
28 'Masons Work Done for His Grace the Duke of Portland at Burlington House John Devall' (University of Nottingham, Manuscripts and Special Collections, Pl F5/4/232/6); for a reference to the 'large cast iron Buzaglo Stove and pipe' in the 'Entrance Hall', see the 1812 inventory cited above.
29 Wilkinson 2003, pp. 72–73.
30 Sir William Gell refers to 'stalls of penny ballads' outside Burlington House in a letter to his father Philp Gell in 1808 (Derbyshire Record Office, D25/50/20).
31 Wilkinson 2003, p. 27.
32 David Cannadine, 'The Landowner as Millionaire: Finances of the Dukes of Devonshire, *c.* 1800–*c.* 1926', *Agricultural History Review*, 25, no. 2 (1977), pp. 79–80.

For Devonshire's income from the Burlington Gardens estate see rent-rolls for 1796–8 (Chatsworth, Devonshire MSS, Currey papers, L/16/24; see also rent-roll *c.* 1800 in box 73, bundle 1, cited in *Survey of London*, 'Cork Street and Savile Row Area', fn. 109).

33 See Richard Wooding, 'Description of the several designs herewith submitted for converting the scite of Ground now occupied by Burlington House, into Building Ground', and his accompanying letter to John Heaton dated 16 March 1808 (Royal Academy Archives, Record Sheet No. 185).

34 See RA Coll. Inv. Nos 07/205 and 18/995.

35 Neil Bingham, 'Humphry and John Adey Repton's unexecuted design for Burlington Place, Piccadilly', *London Gardener, or The Gardener's Intelligencer*, 12 (2006–2007), p. 12.

36 See John Heaton's 'Cash Account with the Duke of Devonshire' for his annual payment of 'Mr Ware's Bill' between 1804–11 (Chatsworth, Devonshire MSS, AS/902).

37 Samuel Ware to John Heaton, 26 July 1814 (Chatsworth, Devonshire MSS, Currey Papers, L/86/1).

38 Ware used the same method of comparing three hypothetical development schemes when he came to value the Burlington House property for Lord George Cavendish in 1826 (Chatsworth, Devonshire MSS, AS/1593; for the correct date of this valuation see Charles Compton Cavendish's 'Mem: B. H.' dated 5 December 1853 (Chesham Papers).

39 See RA Coll. Inv. No. 07/382.

40 The Whites charged a total of £381 18s. (paid on 3 February 1812) for these designs, the valuations based upon them dated 17 July 1810, their earlier 1807–08 proposals, and the design requested by the Duke later in 1810 (Chatsworth, Devonshire MSS, Currey Papers, L/86/1).

41 *Ibid.*; see the Whites' two Burlington House valuations dated 17 July 1810: 'No. 1 £50,237 18s.' based on retaining and 'modernising in part' the main house and offices; 'No. 2 £48,507 18s.' based on converting the main house into two dwellings and replacing the east and west offices with three houses on each side.

42 A prospectus for building a new Italian opera house on the grounds of Burlington House appeared in the *Morning Chronicle* on 23 January 1811.

43 John Heaton to Lord George Cavendish, 21 November 1811 (Chatsworth, Devonshire MSS, Currey Papers, L/86/1).

44 See the schedule of Portland's debts dated 13 July 1809, by which time they amounted to £120,959 in tradesmen's' bills and undischarged bonds and £379,666 in mortgages (University of Nottingham, Manuscripts and Special Collections, Pl F5/13/4/72).

45 5th Duke of Devonshire to Marquess of Hartington, 10 June 1811 (Chatsworth, Devonshire MSS, CS5/2008).

46 Stamp duty was paid on Porden, Saunders and Soane's valuation reports (Chatsworth, Devonshire MSS, Currey Papers, L/86/1). Unstamped fair copies were also made (*ibid.*, AS/3101).

47 'Report & Valuation of Rent for Burlington House, Offices & Garden', 21 November 1811 (Sir John Soane's Museum).

48 Soane's fervent admiration of Burlington House and fear that it was 'doomed' to destruction found particularly eloquent expression in his fifth Royal Academy lecture, first delivered on 9 January 1812 (see David Watkin, *Sir John Soane: Enlightenment Thought and the Royal Academy Lectures*, Cambridge, 1996, p. 564).

49 Philip Hunt and A. H. Smith, 'Lord Elgin and his Collection', *Journal of Hellenic Studies*, vol. 36 (1916), p. 313.

50 Hunt 1916, p. 316.

52 *Life of Benjamin Robert Haydon, Historical Painter, From his Autobiography and Journals*, edited and compiled by Tom Taylor, 2nd ed., 3 vols, London, 1853, vol. 1, p. 150.

52 J. T. Smith, *Nollekens and His Times*, 2 vols, London, 1828, pp. 293–94.

53 Hunt 1916, pp. 314–16.

54 Hunt 1916, p. 314.

55 Hunt 1916, pp. 318–19, 332–34.

56 'Fete at Burlington-House', *The Times*, 22 June 1814, p. 3.

57 'Masqued Ball at Burlington House', *The Morning Post*, 4 July 1814.

58 *The Morning Chronicle*, 30 June 1814.

59 'Masquerade at Burlington House. (From a Correspondent.)', *The Morning Post*, 8 July 1814.

60 'Mr. Sadler's Balloon', *The Morning Post*, 16 July 1814.

61 See notices and long reports in *The Morning Chronicle*, 22 June, 27 and 30 July, 1 August 1814; *The Morning Post*, 16, 23 and 30 July 1814; *The Times*, 30 July 1814.

62 Samuel Ware to John Heaton, 26 July 1814 (Chatsworth, Devonshire MSS, Currey Papers, L/86/1).

63 Lord George Cavendish, 'Alterations proposed to be made in Burlington House', memorandum endorsed 26 Sept: 1811 (Chatsworth, Devonshire MSS, Currey Papers, L/86/1).

64 Ware to Heaton, 26 July 1814 (*ibid.*).

65 Lord George Cavendish to 6th Duke of Devonshire, 31 August 1811 (Chatsworth, Devonshire MSS, CS6/26).

66 Although Lord George purchased Burlington House on 25 March 1815, the transaction was not completed until 15 December that year because it involved cancellation of the Duke's current debts to him of £73,688 18s. 6d.; for details see 'Account between His Grace the Duke of Devonshire and the Right Hon[ble] Lord G.H. Cavendish 1815' (Chatsworth, Devonshire MSS, AS/655/bundle 5).

67 James Abercromby to 6th Duke of Devonshire, 7 June 1824 (Chatsworth, Devonshire MSS, CS6/974); *Three Howard Sisters: Selections from the Writings of Lady Caroline Lascelles, Lady Dover and Countess Gower*, edited by Maud, Lady Leconfield, revised and completed by John Gore, London, 1955, p. 200n.

68 Samuel Ware to John Heaton, 12 April 1815 (Chatsworth, Devonshire MSS, Currey Papers, L/86/1).

69 Thomas Dudly's 'Account Book' recording payments to 'self and son ... on Acct. of Burlington House' between 5 April 1815 and 10 April 1819, is preserved in the Chesham Papers.

70 *News*, 5 March 1815, quoted in Hunt 1916, p, 319 n. 304.

71 Francis Bickley, *The Cavendish Family*, London, 1911, p. 275.

72 George Selwyn to Lord Carlisle, 13 March 1782 (*The Manuscripts of the Earl of Carlisle, preserved at Castle Howard*, Historical Manuscripts Commission, 15th Report, Appendix Pt. VI, London, 1897, p. 593).

73 Lady George Cavendish, 'Various Memorandums', 1782 (Chatsworth, Devonshire MSS, DF 31/1/2/1).

74 The brilliant but reclusive scientist Henry Cavendish (1731–1810) was the elder son of Charles Cavendish (1704?–1783), a younger brother of the 2nd Duke of Devonshire. Although they only met once a year, Lord George was appointed the executor and principal beneficiary of his distant cousin's will, inheriting all his personal property and approximately £270,000 in funds (see C. Jungnickel and R. McCormmach, *Cavendish*, Philadelphia, Penn., 1996, p. 361).

75 The attribution to J. C. Nattes was made by Edward Croft-Murray (see Sheppard 1963, p. 408n.). Formerly part of the Gardner Collection, this series of drawings is held in the Metropolitan Prints Collection of the London Metropolitan Archives (ref. SC/P2/WE/01/0345-0370), and can be accessed online at http://collage.cityoflondon.gov.uk

76 Samuel Ware, 'A general statement of the works performed ...', 2 May 1818 (Chatsworth, Devonshire MSS, Currey Papers, L/86/1).

77 Lord George Cavendish, 'Alterations proposed ...', 26 September 1811 (*ibid.*).

78 John Britton and A. C. Pugin, *Illustrations of the Public Buildings of London*, London, 1825, vol. 1, pp. 98–99.

79 See RA Coll. Inv. No. 06/4340. Evidence of the erasure of the window columns can be seen in the overlay to this drawing.

80 S. Ware, *A Treatise of the Properties of Arches, and their Abutment Piers: containing Propositions for describing geometrically the Catenaria, and the Extradosses of all Curves*, London, 1809. Two folio albums of plans, drawings and prints of bridges and aqueducts, mostly by Ware himself, together with an octavo notebook of memoranda, newspaper cuttings and views relating to bridges and canals, owned and probably compiled by Ware, are in the British Library (BL 1802.c.17; 1397.f.37).

81 Mears's bill of £259 15s. for supplying on 24 February 1817 'Two Faggoted Parabola Bars to support the Grand Staircase Ornamented with Egg and Tongue mouldings fitted with tap screws', and of £316 11s. 8d. in April 1819, for 'eighty-seven feet four inches of Ornamental Railing for Grand Staircase @ £3 12s. 6d. per foot', came to slightly more than the £575 8s. 11d. that James Millbourne had charged on 28 November 1818 for gilding the new ball room 'in Oil Gold Varnished' (Chesham Papers, bundle of 'Bills not included in Messrs. Woolcot & Browning's Accounts').

82 Samuel Ware to 4th Duke of Portland, 6 June 1818 (University of Nottingham, Manuscripts and Special Collections, PwH 1174); see also letter from John Wilson dated 30 May 1818, explaining the method of applying the new stucco (*ibid.*, PwH 1173).

83 See penultimate first-floor plan showing proposed alterations (RA Coll. Inv. No. 06/4328).

84 *Ex info* Neil Bingham, who has recently identified some of the acanthus ornament shown in Nattes's drawing with full-size drawings of examples designed by Ware (see Neil Bingham, 'The Regency transformation of Burlington House, Piccadilly: The architectural drawings of Samuel Ware in the Royal Academy of Arts', in Susanna Avery-Quash and Kate Redford (eds), *The Georgian London Town House: Building, Collecting and Display*, London and New York (forthcoming).

85 See James Millbourne's 'Account to Jan[y] 1st 1818' (Chesham Papers).

86 There is a slightly confected appearance to the composition consonant with its having been assembled to some degree from pre-existing elements. The Greek-key panel in the architrave may have been added by Ware since he made a separate drawing relating to this feature (see RA Coll. Inv. No. 06/4817).

87 See bill dated 24 April 1816 for £10 charged by Thomas Foy and other 'Bow Street Officers' for daily attendances at Burlington House between 18 and 27 March 1816 (Chesham Papers).

88 Samuel Ware, 'A general statement of the works performed ...', 2 May 1818 (Chatsworth, Devonshire MSS, Currey Papers, L/86/1).

89 Samuel Ware to Lord George Cavendish, 18 August 1820 (Chatsworth, Devonshire MSS, Currey Papers, L/86/1); copy of Henry Luttrell, Henry Sandford, Alexander Copland, Richard White (Albany trustees) to Samuel Ware, 18 August 1820 (*ibid.*).

90 Samuel Ware to Lord George Cavendish, 7 October 1820 (*ibid.*).

91 *Gentleman's Magazine*, vol. LXXXVII, pt 2 (September 1817), p. 272.

92 Samuel Ware, 'Report of the Rents and Advantages arising from the Erection of Two Entrance Facades and a Double Row of Shops ...', 5 May 1815 (Royal Academy Archives, Record Sheet 540).

93 On 14 October 1817 Mears supplied 'Iron Palisade Railing for the Front in Piccadilly' (£130 18s. 7d.), '2 Large Gates to match' (£28 0s. 7d.), and '16 Lamp Irons for Railing in Front' (£90 7s. 4d.). (Chesham Papers, bundle of 'Bills not included in Messrs. Woolcot & Browning's Accounts').

94 See Mears's bill for £2 5s. dated 11 November 1818. Two of Mears's men installed 'A Pair of Bracket Gates for Grand Entrance' on 9 May 1817 for £15 9s. 10d. plus 11s. labour (*ibid.*).

95 See Mears's bill for £1 5s. dated 23 November 1818 (*ibid.*).

96 'London's Palais Royal', *The Morning Post*, 4 December 1817.

97 Samuel Ware to Lord George Cavendish, 23 July 1824 (Chatsworth, Devonshire MSS, Currey Papers, L/86/1).

98 'Law Report. Court of Chancery, Tuesday 27 April [1819], Burlington Arcade – Bennet, Odell and others v. Lord George Cavendish and others', *The Times*, 28 April 1819.

99 Samuel Ware to Lord George Cavendish, 23 June 1819 (Chatsworth, Devonshire MSS, Currey Papers, L/86/1).

100 *The Morning Post*, 3 Nov. 1817. *The History of Parliament: the House of Commons 1790–1820*, ed. R. G. Thorne, Woodbridge, 1986, s.v. Cavendish, Lord George Augustus Henry (1754–1834).

101 *The Morning Post*, 8 May 1815.

102 Sheppard 1963, p. 412, citing St James's parish rate-books (Westminster Archives Centre).

103 *The Morning Post*, 29 May 1820.

104 *The Morning Post*, 11 December 1819.

105 For press notices and brief descriptions of some of these social events, which were held from May to July, see *The Morning Post*, 29 May, 10 July 1820; 13 and 18 June, 2 and 9 July 1821; 6 May, 5 and 22 June and 6 July 1822.

106 'An Inventory and Valuation of All the Household furniture, Wearing apparel, Linen, Crockery, Glass, China, Plate, Books, Wine, Kitchen requisites, Horses, Carriages, and sundry other effects at Burlington House, Piccadilly', pp. 7–10 (Chesham Papers). Inventory taken on 28 June 1834 by Stow, Preston & Lyttelton, adjusted and appraised 20 April 1835.

107 'After the Concert, about the hour of two, the Visitants promenaded through the Rooms of State, and were particularly struck with the inimitable statue of the Venus de Medicis, which acquisition was obtained in Rome since the last season. Among the other novelties, the Mosaic table, an unique of prodigious size and inestimable value, attracted much attention. The party did not break up till three o'clock.' *The Morning Post*, 14 May 1825. Unfortunately, Gibson's *Shepherd Boy* had not yet arrived from Rome, as is clear from Lord George's letter to Gibson on 7 May 1825 urgently inquiring after the sculpture (Royal Academy Archives, GI/1/60). Its safe arrival and warm reception in London was reported in Lord George's letter to the sculptor dated 17 November 1825 (*ibid.*, GI/1/61).

108 A copy of Seguier's valuation dated 10 July 1834 is included in Stow, Preston & Lyttelton's inventory cited above (note 106).

109 Copy of George Augustus Henry Cavendish, 1st Earl of Burlington's will (TNA, PROB 11/1832/186).

110 See unsigned 'Elevation of the Screen Wall of Burlington House towards Piccadilly, showing how it may be converted into Shops', *c.* 1836 (RA Coll. Inv. No. 06/5749).

111 'Burlington Arcade', unsigned memorandum of rental income dated 'Burlington Street, July 6th 1831' (Chatsworth, Devonshire MSS, Currey Papers, L/86/1).

112 C. N. Cumberlege, 'Report upon the mode of appropriating to Building Purposes certain portions of the ground belonging to Burlington House', 26 April 1836 (Royal Academy Archives, Record Sheet 539).

113 For this alternative scheme see RA Coll. Inv. No. 07/709.

114 For these schemes see RA Coll. Inv. Nos 07/711 and 07/712.

115 Site plan showing building plots on garden and behind colonnade, dated October 1846 (Chesham Papers).

116 Survey plan showing building plots behind western quadrant of colonnade (undated); block plan for two cross-streets off Burlington Gardens, dated January 1847 (Chesham Papers).

117 Single-sheet undated memorandum beginning '1 / What could I obtain in Rent if I added ...' (Chesham Papers).

118 Private Act 12 & 13 Victoria I, c. 21: 'An Act for removing doubts relative to the powers of granting building leases contained in the will of the Rt. Hon. George Augustus Henry, Earl of Burlington' (Parliamentary Archives, HL/PO/PB/1/1849/12 and 13 VI n 235).

119 See Henry Cavendish's 'Observation' dated 13 June 1849, beginning 'If my brother would wisely give up his resolution of residing in Burlington House, ...' included in a draft letter to Charles's agent John Simpson (Chesham Papers). For a block-plan of the proposed garden square, see RA Coll. Inv. No. 07/728.

120 *The Builder*, 5 April 1851, p. 221.

121 Mayhew was probably unaware that in December 1849 Cavendish had made an unsuccessful attempt to interest the government in the offer of 'a portion of the site at the present time, and perhaps the reversion of the whole at a future period'; and that Cumberlege had prepared a proposal showing how the National Gallery might be rebuilt on Burlington Gardens and extended to form an eastern counterpart to the Burlington Arcade (see Cumberlege to Earl of Carlisle, Commissioner of the Office of Woods and Forests, 10 December 1849, with enclosed plan, TNA WORK 12/283).

122 George Tarlington to John Simpson, 18 February 1853 (Chesham Papers).

123 See Tarlington to Simpson, 12 February 1853, endorsed with comments by recipient (Chesham Papers).

124 Charles Cavendish, 'Mem: B. H.' dated 5 December 1853 (Chesham Papers).

125 Cavendish to Simpson, 31 July 1853 (Chesham Papers).

126 'Town and Table-Talk on Literature, Art, &c.', *Illustrated London News*, 28 January 1854.

127 Simpson to Lord Dacre, 18 November 1853, draft letter (Chesham Papers).

128 Charles Cavendish to John Simpson, 15 December 1853; Simpson to Cavendish, 19 December 1853, draft letter (Chesham Papers).

129 W. Longbourne to Simpson, 10 December 1853; Dacre to Simpson, 6 December 1853; Cavendish 'Mem: B. H.' 5 December 1853 (Chesham Papers).

130 Dacre to Simpson, 22 December 1853 (Chesham Papers).

IV

HER MAJESTY'S OFFICE OF WORKS (pp. 142–211)

1 *The Builder*, 22 April 1854, p. 206. Six months later *The Builder* had more fun at the expense of the Office of Works when their artist was refused entry to the courtyard. An undaunted paparazzo, 'B. Sly' made a drawing instead from the top floor of the house opposite. See *The Builder*, 28 October 1854, pp. 558–59.

2 Gladstone to Lord John Russell, 1 November 1853 (TNA, PRO/22/11B, f.79).

3 'Copy of Treasury Minute, 24 March 1854' (TNA, WORK 12/283).

4 Royal Society, Council Minutes, 22 June 1852, p. 221.

5 Hansard, House of Commons, 26 July 1854, vol. 135, c. 798.

6 Hansard, House of Commons, 26 July 1854, vol. 135, cc. 798–799.

7 Negley Harte, *The University of London 1836–1986: An Illustrated History*, London and Atlantic Highlands, N.J., 1986, p. 102.

8 See statement relating to cleaning charges signed and dated by Office of Works employee J. R. S. Cox, 8 February 1856, in response to House of Commons order of 4 February 1856 'for a Return of any Sums spent on any part of Burlington House since its Conveyance' (TNA, WORK 12/283).

9 Copy of Sabine, Murchison, Playfair to Rothman, and reply, 14 January 1856 (Royal Society Archives, MS/755/1–2).

10 Molesworth's plans may have progressed further than his successor was prepared to admit since, presumably at Hall's request, the record of both these payments was suppressed in a later draft of the return from the Office of Works to the Commons order of 4 February 1856. For both early and late drafts of the latter document, see TNA, WORK 12/283.

11 *Illustrated London News*, 5 May 1855, p. 447.

12 *The Times*, 29 June 1855, p. 10.

13 Wrottesley to Wilson, 14 January 1856 (TNA, T1/6029A/18994).

14 Draft or copy of Wrottesley to Duke of Argyll, 30 April 1856 (Royal Society Archives, MS/755/5).

15 Wilson to Wrottesley, 22 May 1856 (Royal Society Archives, MS/755/6).

16 Copy of Wilson to Senate of the University of London, 3 June [1856] (Royal Society Archives, MS/755/8).

17 Hansard, House of Commons, 6 June 1856, vol. 142, cc. 1132–1133.

18 *The Jubilee of the Chemical Society of London ... Together with an Account of the History and Development of the Society, 1841–1891*, London, 1891, 'Meeting places of the Society', p. 157.

19 Royal Society, Council Minutes, 'Report of Burlington House Arrangements Committee', 5 December 1856, pp. 376–77.

20 See *Hampshire Advertiser and Salisbury Guardian*, 29 August 1857, p. 6. This presumably included the George Caley collection of quadrupeds, birds and reptiles from New South Wales purchased with funds donated by members of the Society in 1818 (see A. T. Gage, *A History of the Linnean Society of London*, London, 1938, p. 125).

21 'The New Home of the Royal Society in Burlington-House', *The Morning Post*, 2 May 1857.

22 Royal Society, Council Minutes, 5 December 1856, p. 377.

23 Royal Society, Council Minutes, 'Report to the Council from the Library Committee', 14 January 1858, pp. 419–20.

24 Thomas Bell, Presidential Address, *Journal of the Proceedings of the Linnean Society: Zoology*, vol. 1, London, 1857, p. xxxiii.

25 Office of Works to C. R. Weld, 30 March 1857 (Royal Society Archives, MSS/755/19); Royal Society, Council Minutes, 6 May 1858, p. 432. The Linnean and Royal societies were told at the same time that there was no point in reseeding the lawn as a building for the Patent Law Commission was about to be erected on the northern half of the garden (Gage 1938, pp. 50, 61).

26 *The Builder*, 14 March 1857, p. 153. According to this report the large meeting room was 77 feet long, 42 feet wide, and about 30 feet high. The 'Lower Library', which was described by *The Builder* as 'a room of good size, but comparatively low', was ordered to be fitted out 'with the gallery of the present upper library [at Somerset House] along the side and end wall not occupied by windows' and with bookshelves below 'enclosed to the height of the gallery with wired doors.' (Royal Society, Council Minutes, 'Report of Burlington House Arrangements Committee', 5 December 1856, p. 377). The principal contractors were Messrs Myers and Smith of Pimlico.

27 Gage 1938, p. 53; *Jubilee of the Chemical Society of London*, p. 171.

28 Gage 1938, p. 167.

29 For the outcome see Royal Society, Council Minutes, 'Report ... from the conference of the Officers of the Royal, Linnean and Chemical Societies', 14 January 1858, p. 416.

30 Royal Society, Council Minutes, letter from Office of Works dated 11 May 1858, p. 436.

31 Royal Society, Council Minutes, 10 May 1860, p. 60; and 20 December 1860, p. 75.

32 See draft return from the Office of Works to the Commons order of 4 February 1856 (TNA, WORK 12/283).

33 Royal Society, Council Minutes, 14 July 1859, p. 28.

34 RGS meetings at Burlington House were accorded regular detailed coverage by *The Morning Chronicle* from 11 November 1857 onwards; for the Canadian Rockies see the issue of 6 February 1859; for the search for the Franklin Expedition see *The Standard*, 15 November 1859; for the source of the Nile see *Daily News*, 16 June 1859; for news of Dr Livingstone see *Essex Standard*, 1 May 1860 and *Illustrated London News*, 8 February 1868, p. 144.

35 Gage 1938, pp. 54–56.

36 Geological Society, Council Minutes, 22 April 1857, pp. 108–109 (GSL CM 1/8).

37 Geological Society Archives, Hardwick to Leonard Horner, 5 May 1857 (GSL COM/H/3/3/5); draft memorial to Lord Palmerston, 8 May 1857 (GSL COM/H/ 3/3/6).

38 Wilson to Horner, 11 December 1857 (GSL Letterbook 1857–59, No. 156).

39 The true source of this celebrated quote was disputed by Lord Elcho who claimed during the course of a debate in the House of Commons that it had been fathered on Peel by Acton Smee Ayrton MP to bolster his argument against resiting the National Gallery (see Hansard, House of Commons, 8 June 1866, vol. 184, c. 64).

40 *The Times*, 11 June 1866, p. 9. Cf. Alexander Beresford Hope's comment in the Commons: 'he was glad that Government had purchased the garden of Burlington House. It was, however, useless to anybody except the sparrows, and he thought Government ought to produce a proper plan for utilizing it, and making it available to the public' (Hansard, House of Commons, 19 June 1857, vol. 146, c. 81).

41 'Mr [Henry] Drummond', Hansard, House of Commons, 19 June 1857, vol. 146, cc. 82–83.

42 *The Standard*, 29 June 1857, p. 7; *The Morning Post*, 7 July 1857, p. 4.

43 Hansard, House of Commons, 4 June 1858, vol. 150, c. 1580.

44 Hansard, House of Commons, 4 June 1858, vol. 150, c. 1583.

45 Hansard, House of Commons, 8 February 1859, vol. 152, c. 181.

46 Hansard, House of Lords, 4 March 1859, vol. 152, cc. 1241–49

47 Hansard, House of Lords, 4 March 1859, vol. 152, cc. 1249-53.

48 TNA, T1/6223A/2CC 21929.

49 Alfred Barry, *The Life and Work of Sir Charles Barry, R.A., F.R.S.* London, 1867, pp. 281–84; Matthew Digby Wyatt, 'On the Architectural Career of the Late Sir Charles Barry', *The Builder*, 2 June 1860, p. 344.

50 TNA, WORK 2/30, pp. 243–44.

51 TNA, T1/6223A/19527.

52 Internal Treasury memo, R. C. Griffiths to J. P. Carswell, 10 December 1962 (TNA, T227/2009).

53 See M. H. Port, *Imperial London: Civil Government Building in London 1850–1915*, New Haven and London, 1995, p. 96.

54 Copy of letter from Horner to Gladstone per Sir Roderick Murchison, 12 May 1860, headed 'Application from the Geological Society to be transferred to Burlington House' (GSL COM/H/3/3).

55 Treasury to Murchison, 19 June 1860 (GSL COM/H/3/3).

56 Hansard, House of Commons, 16 August 1860, vol. 160, c. 1360.

57 Sheppard 1963, 'Burlington House', p. 414, citing G. E. Cokayne and H. A. Doubleday *et al.* (eds), *Complete Peerage of England, Scotland, Ireland, Great Britain and the United Kingdom*, 2nd ed., vol. IX, London, 1936, s.v. Mount-Temple.

58 Hansard, House of Commons, 1 July 1861, vol. 164, c. 155.

59 Hansard, House of Commons, 16 July 1861, vol. 164, c. 1020.

60 Hansard, House of Commons, 14 February 1862, vol. 165, cc. 273–74.

61 Hansard, House of Commons, 5 June 1863, vol. 171, cc. 408, 417.

62 Hansard, House of Commons, 18 June 1863, vol. 171, c. 1048.

63 Hansard, House of Commons, 7 July 1863, vol. 171, c. 356.

64 Hansard, House of Commons, 15 April 1864, vol. 174, c. 1079.

65 J. L. E. Dreyer and H. H. Turner (eds), *History of the Royal Astronomical Society, 1820–1920*, London, 1923, p. 122.

66 'Mr [William] Cowper', Hansard, House of Commons, 6 June 1864, vol. 175, c. 1298.

67 House of Lords, *Select Committee on Public Institutions*, Parliamentary Papers [181] XVI, 1860, qq. 350–51, 395–97, 429–42.

68 *Commissioners appointed to inquire into the present position of the Royal Academy in relation to the Fine Arts*, Parliamentary Papers [3205] XXVII, 1863, p. xxi.

69 Philip Guedalla (ed.), *Gladstone and Palmerston* (The Palmerston Papers), London, 1928, 262, 10 June 1863.

70 Southampton University Archives, Broadlands Papers, HA/J/2 [no date] (cited in Port 1995, p. 90).

71 Pennethorne to Cowper, 23 November 1861 (TNA, WORK 12/432).

72 *The Standard*, 11 April 1859, p. 3.

73 G. Basalla, W. Coleman, R. H. Kargon (eds), *Victorian Science: A Self-portrait From the Presidential Addresses of the British Association for the Advancement of Science*, Garden City, N.Y., 1970, p. 52.

74 Gordon L. Herries Davies, *Whatever is Under the Earth: The Geological Society of London 1807 to 2007*, London, 2007, p. 133. Permission for this use of the 'Great Hall' had to be obtained also from the University.

75 Banks & Barry were able to claim at least a moral right to the commission on the grounds of the government's abandonment of their 1859 scheme. In return they reduced their bill for the work they had done on the latter from £5,007 to £1,575 (see Hansard, House of Commons, 18 February 1867, vol. 185, cc. 501–02).

76 *Minutes of the Senate of London University*, 1863, pp. 86–87.

77 Hansard, House of Commons, 6 June 1864, vol. 175, cc. 1303–14.

78 Hansard, House of Commons, 13 June 1864, vol. 175, cc. 1637–39.

79 *Minutes of the Senate of London University*, 1864, pp. 49–53, 93; and 1870, pp. 91–93; TNA, WORK 2/28, pp. 380–81.

80 Hansard, House of Commons, 2 June 1865, vol. 179, cc. 1209–16; *Minutes of the Senate of London University*, 1865, pp. 96–97.

81 *Minutes of the Senate of London University*, 1866, p. 2.

82 Hansard, House of Commons, 30 April 1866, vol. 183, cc. 184–96.

83 *The Times*, 17 May 1866, p. 7.

84 *The Builder*, 9 June 1866, p. 430.

85 *The Times*, 30 May 1866, p. 9.

86 Hansard, House of Lords, 17 May 1866, vol. 183, cc. 1035–36.

87 Hansard, House of Commons, 23 July 1866, vol. 184, cc. 1303–22.

88 Hansard, House of Commons, 5 June 1868, vol. 192, cc. 1183–84. A copy of the sale catalogue is held in the City of Westminster Archive Centre (Gardner Box 48, No. 38).

89 Percy Fitzgerald, *London City Suburbs as They Are Today*, London, 1893, pp. 222–23.

90 Cf. *The Builder*, 20 October 1883, p. 512.

91 L.C.C. Architect's Department, Historic Buildings Section file (cited in Sheppard 1963, p. 418, n. 206).

92 Seated above the portico are Newton, Bentham, Milton, and Harvey carved by Joseph Durham ARA, representing the four faculties of the University, *viz.* Science, Law, Arts, and Medicine; standing on the central roof balustrade are six representatives of ancient classical learning, *viz.* Galen, Cicero and Aristotle by J. S. Westmacott, and Plato, Archimedes and Justinian by W. F. Woodington (elected ARA 1876); on the east wing are six learned foreigners of modern times, Galileo, Goethe, and Laplace by E. W. Wyon on the balustrade, and in the ground-storey niches, Leibnitz, Cuvier, and Linnaeus by Patrick MacDowell; the corresponding statues on the west wing are their English equivalents, [William or John] Hunter, David Hume, and Humphry Davy by Matthew Noble on the balustrade, and Adam Smith, John Locke, and Francis Bacon by William Theed junior in the niches. Selected by the University's New Building Committee and agreed by the Senate, Tribonian, John Dalton and Shakespeare were originally chosen instead of Justinian, Davy and Hume. Although the Senate stood their ground when Manners ventured to query their choice of Bentham to represent English law, his suggestion that Shakespeare would have been better placed over the portico as representative of the arts rather than of modern knowledge, led to a copy of Peter Scheemakers's statue of the Bard being placed instead on the main staircase, on the grounds that he was 'not a man of University education'. (University of London, *Minutes of the Senate*, 1868, 4 March, p. 23, 1 April, pp. 25–26; *The Times*, 9 May 1870; *Illustrated London News*, 14 May 1870).

93 *The Daily Telegraph*, 12 May 1870, press cutting, University of London, Senate House Library, RC 28/11/6.

94 George Grote to W. E. Gladstone, 5 April 1865, printed University of London, *Minutes of the Senate*, 19 April 1865, pp. 28–29.

95 Grote to the Earl Russell, undated draft printed *ibid.*, 22 October 1865, pp. 96–97.

96 Hansard, House of Commons, 2 June 1865, vol. 179, c. 1215.

97 William Cowper to Treasury, 31 December 1864 (TNA WORK 2/28, pp. 380–81).

98 Hansard, House of Commons, 30 April 1866, vol. 183, c. 192.

99 'Memorandum respecting the General Plans and Designs for the Front towards Burlington Gardens', associated with a letter from Pennethorne to the registrar dated 23 June 1870 presenting 'the three Designs made successively for the University of London', University of London, *Minutes of the Senate*, 20 July 1870, pp. 91–93. These drawings are currently untraced.

100 J. Pennethorne, 'University of London: Design for Halls and Apartments: Plans & Sections' (TNA WORK 33/1745). This is a group of six drawings stitched together showing basement, ground-, first- and attic-floor plans and longitudinal and transverse sections, but no elevations.

101 'Memorandum', *ibid.*, p. 92.

102 Cowper subsequently admitted that this was his reason for delaying any decision on the elevation – see Hansard, House of Commons, 5 April 1867, vol. 186, c. 1247.

103 'Memorandum', *ibid.*, p. 92.

104 *Ibid.*, p. 92.

105 RIBA *Sessional Papers, 1871–72* (1872), p. 59.

106 Hansard, House of Commons, 5 April 1867, vol. 186, cc. 1243–44.

107 'Memorandum', *ibid.*, p. 92.

108 *The Times*, 9 May 1870, p. 6.

109 'I have requested Mr. Pennethorne to send the alternative elevations. In so doing I think it right to add that, while anxious to consult the convenience and wishes of the Senate on all practical points, I am not prepared to discuss other questions with them. The Building is now making substantial and satisfactory progress, and it is my duty to see that nothing is allowed to interfere with their early and economical completion.' Lord John Manners to Lord Granville, 22 March 1867, private letter (University of London, Senate House Library, RC 28/8).

110 *The Times*, 15 May 1867, p. 9.

111 'Memorandum', *ibid.*, p. 92.

112 It is not known how much of the half-constructed building had to be taken down as a result of the new design. The gothic detailing on the south front, which had probably reached a height of just under nineteen feet from the basement windows, was presumably allowed to remain *in situ* because it was not visible from a public highway; cf. contract tender drawing of 'Details of Windows on South Front' dated 13 February 1867 and initialled 'J.P. 23.6. 69' (TNA WORK 33/1771).

113 Hansard, House of Commons, 5 April 1867, vol. 186, c. 1235.

114 'Memorandum', *ibid.*, pp. 92–93.

115 University of London, *Minutes of the Senate*, 1867, 27 March, p. 27.

116 Dr John Storrar to W. B. Carpenter, 11 June 1867 (University of London, Senate House Library, RC 28/9).

117 *Ibid.*

118 'Memorandum', *ibid.*, p. 93.

119 *Daily News*, 16 May 1867.

120 University of London, *Minutes of the Senate*, 1867, 27 November, p. 87.

121 Hansard, House of Commons, 9 July 1867, vol. 188, c. 1263.

122 University of London, *Minutes of the Senate*, 1864, 6 July, pp. 52–53.

123 *The Times*, 15 May 1867, p. 9.

124 *The Times*, 9 May 1870, p. 6. See also a comment in *The Bradfield Observer* that 'At present the tone of the building is too white' (12 May 1870, p. 12) and a description in *The Graphic* of the lecture theatre as 'a finely proportioned room, but ostentatiously plain' (21 May 1870).

125 *The Daily Telegraph*, 12 May 1870, press cutting, University of London, Senate House Library, RC 28/11/6.

126 *The Times*, 9 May 1870, p. 6

127 'Londinensis', *Pall Mall Gazette*, 29 November 1869.

128 See Pennethorne's note referring to 'Bookcase Contract Decr. 28th 1869' in relation to Spanish mahogany bookcases and sham doors in the rooms east and west of the Senate Room (TNA WORK 33/1785).

129 Hansard, House of Commons, 8 April 1867, c. 1267.

130 George Russell to George Grote, 10 January 1871, printed in University of London, *Minutes of the Senate*, 1871, 18 January, p. 3.

131 *Ibid.*, pp. 3–4.

132 Milman to Office of Works, 25 October 1888, copy (University of London, Senate House Library, RC 28/12).

133 Royal Academy of Arts, *Annual Report from the Council ... for the Year 1890*, London, 1891, pp. 5–6.

134 Royal Academy of Arts, *Annual Report from the Council ... for the Year 1891*, London, 1892, pp. 5–6.

135 *Ibid.*, p. 5.

136 Royal Academy of Arts, General Assembly Minutes, 19 July 1900, p. 81.

137 On the fundamental disagreements of the two organising societies over the objectives of the expedition see Bernard E. Leake, *The Life and Work of Professor J. W. Gregory FRS*, London, 2011, pp. 65–70.

138 C. Russell Peacock, memo to Secretary of War Cabinet Committee on Accommodation, 26 July 1919 (TNA WORK 12/233). This was a revision of the scheme under consideration in 1913 (Treasury Letter 5937/13, 30 May 1913).

139 Sir Lionel Earle to the Secretary of the Treasury, 24 October 1919 (TNA WORK 12/233).

140 For references to William Poel's use of the Burlington Gardens lecture theatre for experimental stage performances, see *The Times*, 22 November 1900; for an account of his production of *Richard II* on 11 November 1899, see Margaret Shewring, *Shakespeare in Performance: King Richard II*, Manchester, 1996, p. 71.

141 'The Headquarters of the R.I.B.A.', memorandum sent by MacAlister to Earle, 8 March 1924 (TNA WORK 12/287).

142 'Burlington Gardens: Uneconomic utilization', confidential MS. memo signed and dated 'AD 15/3/24' (TNA WORK 12/287).

143 'The R.I.B.A. and the Civil Service Commission Building in Burlington Gardens', typescript memo of RIBA Council's 'definite' offer, undated but associated with abortive meeting on 18 January 1928 (TNA WORK 12/287).

144 For the vigorous case put up by the Civil Service Commission to remain at 6 Burlington Gardens see Sir Stanley Leathes's five-page letter to Sir Arthur Durrant, 26 August 1927 (TNA WORK 12/287).

145 Typescript memo to Assistant Secretary [i.e. W. Leitch] signed and dated 'H.L.D. 29 July, 1927' (TNA WORK 12/287).

146 Earle to Scott, 25 January 1928 (TNA WORK 12/287).

147 Leitch to Earle, MS memo dated 29 June 1927 (TNA WORK 12/287).

148 Earle to Leitch, *ibid.*

149 Scott to Earle, 31 January 1928 (TNA WORK 12/287).

150 Earle to Leitch, typescript note dated 24 Feb. 1928 (TNA WORK 12/287).

151 H. C. Bradshaw to Earle, 24 April 1928 (TNA BP 2/76).

152 RFAC, 'Draft letter to H.M. Office of Works with reference to the desirability of developing the site of No. 6 Burlington Gardens' (TNA BP/2/76).

153 H. C. Bradshaw to Earle, 24 April 1928 (TNA BP 2/76).

154 Earle to Leitch, typescript note dated 24 February 1928 (TNA WORK 12/287).

155 Earle to First Commissioner, typescript note dated 27 April 1928, copied to W. Leitch (TNA WORK 12/287).

156 Typescript note signed and dated 'F.E.C. 3rd August 1928' (TNA WORK 12/287).

157 Lamb to Earle, 1 August 1929 (TNA WORK 12/287).

158 Director of Lands & Accommodation to Secretary, typescript memo dated 6 July 1931; 'Section thro'

Gallery No. 6 looking W shewing proposed Extension', signed and dated 'Reginald Blomfield, R.A., June 1931.' (TNA WORK 12/287).

159 Leitch to Treasury, 22 October 1932, regarding possible plans to dispose of 6 Burlington Gardens site for development; see also drawing of plan and section of proposed extension of Gallery 6 and Architecture Gallery over West Yard, signed and dated 'E.L. Lutyens R.A. Oct. 1932' (TNA WORK 12/287).

160 Lord Robbins to Harold Macmillan, 30 May 1963 (TNA WORK 12/475). For the Ministry's unenthusiastic response to Sir Mortimer Wheeler's proposal and low opinion of the quality of Arnold Mitchell's British Academy Council Room, see the report of its Historic Buildings Division advisor H. G. Yexley dated 5 December 1966 (TNA WORK 12/890).

161 See press cuttings in file TNA T227/2490.

V

THE ROYAL ACADEMY OF ARTS (pp. 212–297)

1 James Pennethorne to Lord John Manners, 31 July 1866 (TNA WORK 12/285 [formerly Ministry of Works file OA 2/12803 pt. 1]).

2 Grant's second wife Isabella Norman was the niece of the 5th Duke of Rutland, father of Lord John Manners. On Grant's social connections see Catherine Wills, *The Life and Work of Sir Francis Grant, P.R.A.* (unpublished Ph.D. thesis, Courtauld Institute of Art, 1988), chapter 10.

3 Hansard, House of Commons, 15 May 1868, vol. 192, c. 391.

4 'Smirke's conversion, of 1872–3, was of High Victorian cruelty.' Simon Bradley and Nikolaus Pevsner, *London 6: Westminster* (Pevsner Architectural Guides). New Haven and London, 2003, p. 488.

5 Grant to Cowper, 22 June 1866 (TNA WORK 12/285).

6 Cowper to Treasury, 7 April 1866, transcript (TNA WORK 2/30, pp. 7–8).

7 Grant to Cowper, 26 March 1866, copy (*ibid.*, pp. 8–12).

8 RAA, General Assembly Minutes, 20 February 1866, pp. 312–13.

9 Transcript of Cowper to J. P. Knight RA, secretary of the Academy, 18 November 1865 (*ibid.*, 18 December 1865, p. 259).

10 RAA, Council Minutes, 17 May 1866, p. 287; General Assembly Minutes, 19 May 1866, pp. 340–43.

11 RAA, General Assembly Minutes, vol. VI, Appendix, p. 21.

12 George Jones's Commonplace Book (RAA/Acc./2005/28, p. 45).

13 RAA, General Assembly Minutes, 19 May 1866, p. 342; *ibid.*, 18 June 1866, p. 349.

14 Francis Grant, 'Statement ... made to the General Assembly of the Royal Academy of Arts, 29 August 1866', transcribed in 'Correspondence relative to the New Site for the Royal Academy of Arts on the Burlington House Estate' (RAA/PRA/2/1, pp. 2–3).

15 *Ibid.*, p. 3.

16 Grant to Gen. Sir Charles Grey, Wednesday [1 Augist 1866], transcript (*ibid.*, letter no. 5, p. 11).

17 'Minutes of Committee appointed [by General Assembly] on March 27th 1850', 2nd meeting, 12 April 1850 (RAA/GA/8/6/1, p. [5]).

18 *Ibid.*, p. [10], partial transcript of letter from Sir Robert Smirke, RA treasurer, to George Jones, RA keeper, 10 April 1850. After referring to Burlington House, Smirke went on, 'But upon this part of the subject, Hardwick can I have no doubt assist you well, and pray do not for an hour delay getting from him all the assistance it may be in his power to give you'.

19 RAA, General Assembly Minutes, 25 March 1859, pp. 11–12.

20 Hansard, House of Commons, 6 June 1864, vol. 175, c. 1310.

21 For an early use of the phrase see C. M. Westmacott, *A Descriptive and Critical Catalogue of the* [55th] *Exhibition of the Royal Academy*, London, [1823], p. 21.

22 Lord Derby to Grant, 11 August 1866, transcribed in 'Correspondence relative to the New Site for the Royal Academy of Arts on the Burlington House Estate' (RAA/PRA/2/1, letter no. 6, pp. 13–15). *The Times*, 16 August 1866, p. 8; *Illustrated London News*, 18 August 1866, p. 159.

23 The day after the article in *The Times* appeared, the treasurer of the Royal Society, William Allen Miller, wrote what was presumably a pretty stiff letter to Lord Derby, who duly passed it on to the Office of Works (for 10 Downing Street's letter in reply, see G. Barrington to W. Allen Miller, 21 August 1866, Royal Society Archives, MS/755/23).

24 [James Pennethorne], 'Memorandum respecting the General Plans and Designs for the Front towards Burlington Gardens', printed in University of London, *Minutes of the Senate*, 1870, 20 July, p. 92.

25 Pennethorne to Manners, 31 July 1866 (TNA WORK 12/285). Manners also ignored Pennethorne's own idea for a 'completion of the whole design upon the principle shown by the enlarged plan herewith transmitted, at a cost to the Public of £100,000, or say £110,000 if the Colonnade there shewn next Piccadilly be included.'

26 Hansard, House of Commons, 5 April 1867, vol. 186, c. 1241.

27 Manners to General Edward Sabine, 19 May 1868 (Royal Society Archives, MS/755/31).

28 Manners to Treasury, 24 August 1866; Treasury to Manners, 13 September 1866, transcripts (TNA WORK 2/30, pp. 205–06, 220).

29 *The Times*, 22 October 1856, letter signed 'Vicinus'.

30 Sydney Smirke to Banks & Barry, 8 October 1866 (RIBA Drawings and Archive Collections, BaFam/1/8/1).

31 Banks & Barry to Council of Royal Astronomical Society, 20 October 1866, photocopy (Society of Antiquaries Archive, 'Solicitors' Bundle', Burlington House High Court case, 20–29 January 2004); Banks & Barry to H. M. Jenkins, Assistant Secretary, Geological Society, 26 November 1866 (Geological Society Archives, GSL/COM/H/3/3).

32 'Burlington House Committee', minutes of meeting held 21 November 1866; Jenkins to Banks & Barry, 22 November, 1866, copy (Geological Society Archives, GSL/COM/H/3/3).

33 Memorandum [by Philip Hardwick] dated 19 March 1859 on the 'accommodation that will be required by the Royal Society in a new Building' (Royal Society Archives, MM/13/66).

34 Royal Society, Minutes of Council, 2 July 1868, pp. 429–30. The chemists' earlier 'memorial' on the subject had been rejected by the Council on 18 June 1868. While the president and officers stated that they were prepared to give 'such an arrangement as they deem suitable and which shall not involve an alteration in the Architect's plans ... their best consideration', nothing could come of the idea since the two societies were not neighbours in the new building. Ironically, it was at the Royal Society's request that a communicating double door was opened in 1934 between their first-floor apartments and those of the Geological Society (*ex info* Caroline Lam).

35 Society of Antiquaries, Council Minutes, 6 November 1866, p. 210.

36 Sydney Smirke to Banks & Barry, 10 November 1866 (RIBA Drawings and Archive Collections, BaFam/1/8/3).

37 Sydney Smirke to Banks & Barry, 6 December 1866 (RIBA Drawings and Archive Collections, BaFam/1/8/4).

38 Grant to Manners, 11 December 1866 (TNA WORK 12/285).

39 Banks & Barry to Manners, 18 December 1866 (TNA WORK 12/285).

40 Hansard, House of Commons, 12 March 1868, vol. 190, cc. 1454-5.

41 C. W. Cope to Banks & Barry, 10 December 1866 (RIBA Drawings and Archive Collections, BaFam/1/13)

42 Manners to Grant, 12 December 1866, copy (TNA WORK 12/285).

43 Grant to Banks & Barry, 11 March [1867] (RAA/MIS/GR/6).

44 Grant to Banks & Barry, 16 March 1867 (RAA/MIS/GR/9/1).

45 Grant to Banks & Barry, various dates, late February to 1 April 1867 (RAA/MIS/GR/7–15).

46 Grant to Banks, 'Tuesday' [April 1867] (RAA/MIS/GR/16/1–2).

47 Grant to Banks, undated, probably late April 1867 (RAA/MIS/GR/17).

48 *The Builder*, 25 March 1871, p. 218. The contract for the foundations was awarded to Trollope and Sons, who tendered for £10,865 and began work in November 1868. Mansfield & Price, who had quoted £128,803 for the superstructure, began work in October 1869, but defaulted in March 1871. Messrs Perry & Co. of Bow signed a new contract on 3 May 1871.

49 Sir Henry Dale, PRS, 'Anniversary Address, 30 November 1943' (*Proceedings of the Royal Society*, A, vol. 182 (1944), p. 240.

50 Banks & Barry to Jenkins, 15 June 1868 (Geological Society Archives, GSL/COM/H/3/3).

51 Burlington House Committee, minutes of meeting held 17 April 1867 (Geological Society Archives, GSL/COM/H/3/3).

52 Letters to the editor, *The Times*, 7 May 1872, p. 4.

53 A Treasury summary of the new Burlington House building costs totalling £160,838 19s. (ref. 1213/74) included a contract 'for carving (Mr. Sansom) £5,843' (TNA T1/7382A 049586). Three designs for lace were registered at the Patent Office in the joint names of Josiah Handford and Samuel Samson of Nottingham on 1 March 1855 (TNA BT 44/31 Design Nos 9941–3). Samuel Sansom's bill for modelling a Corinthian capital for Lewis Vulliamy at Westonbirt House in 1867 is among the Vulliamy Papers in the RIBA Drawings and Archive Collection (VuL/47/5).

54 Grant to Gen. Sir Charles Grey, Wednesday [1 August 1866], transcript (RAA/PRA/2/1, letter no. 5, p. 11).

55 It is indicative that the 1863 Royal Commission had made no recommendations in relation to the Academy's collection or library. However, this omission was noticed in a follow-up to an editorial article on 'Reform of the Royal Academy' published in the *Illustrated London News* in July 1864. Complaining that the Academy's 'collection has been jealously concealed from the public and even a large number of the students in the Academy itself only see it occasionally', the article also questioned why its library 'cannot be opened under the charge of a curator … to all students of art, whether practical or literary, upon conditions as easy as those of that very serviceable and well-managed library attached to the South Kensington Museum.' In the author's opinion 'this continued concealment when the Academy will be at liberty to build itself galleries three or four times larger than those at present occupied will be inexcusable.' (*Illustrated London News*, 23 July 1864, p. 104).

56 Grant to Manners, 4 August 1866 (TNA WORK 12/285).

57 Royal Academy of Arts, Council Minutes, 29 April 1851, p. 346. The memorial was delivered in July 1851 (*ibid.*, 16 July 1851, p. 351).

58 Royal Academy, General Assembly Minutes, 16 December 1864, pp. 213–15.

59 Sydney Smirke to Banks & Barry, 10 November 1866 (RIBA Drawings and Archive Collections BaFam/1/8/3).

60 Grant to Gen. Sir Charles Grey, Wednesday [1 August 1866], transcript (RAA/PRA/2/1, letter no. 5, p. 11).

61 John Gardiner, solicitor of the Board of Works, to Manners, 17 December 1866 (TNA WORK 12/285).

62 Pennethorne to Manners, 31 July 1866 (TNA WORK 12/285).

63 Hansard, House of Commons, 5 April 1867, vol. 186, c. 1233.

64 Grant to Banks & Barry, [1 April 1867] (RAA/MIS/GR/9/15).

65 Grant to Ayrton, 'Tuesday 30' [January 1872] (TNA WORK 12/285).

66 Banks & Barry to Ayrton, 28 February 1871 (TNA WORK 12/285).

67 Ayrton to Grant, 29 February 1872 (*ibid.*)

68 Royal Academy, Council Minutes, 17 December 1872, p. 315. In the event, Calder Marshall and Weekes took responsibility for the statues of Michelangelo and Titian, and Flaxman and Raphael respectively; those of Leonardo, Reynolds and Wren were assigned to Edward Stephens ARA, and those of Phidias and Wykeham to Joseph Durham ARA.

69 *Ibid.*, 21 January 1873, p. 325

70 Nine days later the assistant secretary of the Royal Society wrote in his journal: 'Today the last of the trees, the old elms on our lawn, was felled. For five years I have seen them bud and leaf in spring, have heard the starlings, thrushes and sparrows; now all is havoc. The University building has risen above its basement. Nearly all the trees were hollow' (*The Journals of Walter White*, London, 1898, pp. 203–04, entry dated 29 March 1867).

71 Royal Academy of Arts, *Annual Report from the Council … for the Year 1867*, London, 1868, Appendix no. 9, p. 38.

72 Royal Academy of Arts, *Annual Report from the Council … for the Year 1867* (London, 1868), Appendix no. 9, p. 38; *Annual Report from the Council … for the Year 1868*, London, 1869, Appendix no. 9, p. 41.

73 *Ibid.*, p. 9.

74 *Ibid.*, p. 41.

75 For details of the progress of the work, see the RA treasurer's consolidated ledger of 'Accounts of the New Building & Works at Burlington House' (RAA/TRE/10/1). Payments to specialist suppliers and craftsmen are listed by date but only rarely is specific work identifiable. The original bills have not survived.

76 The comparative plan and section and a preliminary design for the Lecture Room with no doorway leading from the Octagon and a south-facing auditorium (inscribed 'Plan No. 2') are in the RIBA Drawings Collection (SC 95/17/1; SC 95/18/10). The authors of the *Survey of London* noted that 'other early drawings by Smirke (in the library of the Royal Institute of British Architects) proposed a domed skylight over tiers of seats in a hemicycle with a semi-circular exterior wall, apparently projecting into the present gallery IX' (Sheppard 1963, p. 427); these were not however included in the 1976 printed catalogue of the RIBA Drawings Collection and are now untraced.

77 'Accounts of the New Building & Works at Burlington House' (RAA/TRE/10/1).

78 *Ibid.*

79 *Illustrated London News*, 8 May 1869, p. 470.

80 *Illustrated London News*, 30 January 1869, p. 122; *Daily News*, 1 May 1869.

81 For details of 'The South door into the Lecture Room', see Smirke's drawing no. 117 dated February 1869 (RA Coll. Inv. 07/1388).

82 Royal Academy of Arts, *Annual Report from the Council … for the Year 1869*, London, 1870, pp. 10–11.

83 *The Times*, 1 May 1869, p. 12.

84 *Daily News*, 1 May 1869.

85 *Illustrated London News*, 8 May 1869, p. 470; *Pall Mall Gazette*, 26 May 1869.

86 *The Standard*, 3 May 1869, p. 3.

87 Royal Academy, General Assembly Minutes, 19 July 1869, pp. 20–21.

88 Smirke to Pennethorne, 20 August 1869 (TNA WORK 12/285).

89 Pennethorne to Layard, 23 August 1869 (TNA WORK 12/285).

90 Royal Academy, Council Minutes, 27 February 1871, p. 177; 17 July 1871, p. 206.

91 Royal Academy, Council Minutes, 6 February 1872, p. 255.

92 *The Daily Telegraph*, 12 May 1870, press cutting, University of London, Senate House Library, RC 28/11/6.

93 Grant to Sabine, 25 May [1868] (Royal Society Archives, MM 11/133).

94 Sabine to unidentified, possibly the assistant secretary Walter White, 26 May 1868 (Royal Society Archives, MM 11/134).

95 Banks & Barry [to Walter White], 2 June 1868 (Royal Society Archives, MS/755/34).

96 W. B. Carpenter to Alfred Austin, 9 July 1868, printed University of London, *Minutes of the Senate*, 1868, 13 July, pp. 55–56.

97 Grant to Barry, 20 June 1868 (RAA/MIS/GR/19).

98 Royal Academy, General Assembly Minutes, 2 January 1867, p. 375.

99 Royal Academy of Arts, *Annual Report from the Council … for the Year 1869*, Appendix no. 8, p. 38.

100 For Smirke's withdrawal from the Building Committee and the looming contention over 'the large amount introduced in our Report for prospective alterations', see Richard Westmacott's letters to J. P. Knight, 10 and 27 March 1869 (RAA/SEC/3/12).

101 'With regard to the soirées, of course if you wish it, you might hold them in our rooms – But I shoud have thought you woud hold them as heretofore in your present rooms in Burlington House, which when the screen is put up, with doors at the top of the stairs, will be as private & completely at your disposal as in times past.' Grant to Sabine, 27 May 1868 (Royal Society Archive, MM/11/135).

102 Grant to Douglas Galton, Director of Works, Office of Works, 2 December [1872] (British Library, Add. 59847, f. 89).

103 Philip's bill 'for carving at the entrance porch of the R. Academy' amounted to £312 (Royal Academy, Council Minutes, 17 March 1874, p. 40).

104 'Accounts of the New Building & Works at Burlington House' (RAA/TRE/10/1); Royal Academy, Council Minutes, 28 October 1873, p. 413.

105 Statement of proposed works on roof of Burlington House, signed and dated 'Sydney Smirke, RA Dec: 30, 1871' (Royal Society Archives, MM/13/73).

106 Grant to Ayrton, 29 February 1872 (TNA WORK 12/285). Despite Grant's assurance, the window in the west screen-wall was built as, and remains to this day, a dummy.

107 'Additions & Alterations to Burlington House' (RAA/TRE/10/1).

108 'Statement relative to the subject of the future progress of the new works', signed & dated 'Sydney Smirke Feb[y] 11. 1873.' (RAA/SEC/10/80/1).

109 Royal Academy, Council Minutes, 24 June 1873, p. 373.

110 Royal Academy of Arts, *Annual Report from the Council … for the Year 1870*, London, 1871, p. 6.

111 Royal Academy of Arts, *Annual Report from the Council … for the Year 1873*, London, 1876, p. 10.

112 *Ibid.*, pp. 9–10.

113 *The Sunday Times*, 28 February 1869, p. 2.

114 *The Standard*, 11 May 1869, p. 5.

115 Royal Academy, Council Minutes, 20 November 1873, pp. 425–26.

116 'I have (as promised) ascertained from Perry that he will put up for you when you are ready a scaffold framework from the nearest angle window of old B. House (the Linneans' Room) to the angle window in New Building & furnish a small travelling truck on rails between window and window, for £25 to £30 not to exceed the latter.' Barry to Walter White, 23 January 1873 (Royal Society Archives, MS/755/52). On 3 July 1873 the Council of the Linnean Society gave permission for this rail-bridge to be constructed in September that year.

117 Royal Academy, Council Minutes, 16 December 1873, p. 434.

118 Royal Academy of Arts, *Annual Report from the Council … for the Year 1873*, London, 1876, p. 9.

119 Royal Academy, Council Minutes, 3 November 1874, p. 105.

120 'It was decided that the paintings from the ceilings in Trafalgar Square should be placed in the ceilings of the Hall & Refreshment Room at Burlington House'. (Royal Academy, Council Minutes, 11 April 1874, p. 52). Assuming this decision was acted upon, these paintings were not replaced after Smirke's alteration of the Entrance Hall that autumn, since they were subsequently rediscovered in the basement in 1899. In February 1874 the Board of Works granted permission for a notice board of about 3 feet by 2 feet to be put

up 'inside the archway leading to Burlington House, to 'contain Notices of Exhibitions, Lectures, Meetings, &c.' (Royal Academy, Council Minutes, 13 and 24 January 1874, 19 February 1874, pp. 7, 9 and 28).

121 *Richard Redgrave, C.B., R.A.: a memoir compiled from his diary by F.M. Redgrave*, London, 1891, p. 330.

122 Landseer to Grant, 2 May 1869 (National Art Library Special Collections, 86.RR.38).

123 Grant to Sabine, 6 June [1868] (Royal Society Archives, MM/11/136).

124 Royal Academy, Council Minutes, 22 December 1873, pp. 439–40.

125 'The Instrument of Foundation', article VIII, printed in Sidney C. Hutchison, *The History of the Royal Academy 1768–1986*, London, 1986, p. 247.

126 Grant to Sir Thomas Biddulph, 11 February 1874, transcript (Royal Academy, General Assembly Minutes, 26 February 1874, p. 177).

127 Royal Academy, General Assembly Minutes, 15 January 1874, p. 174; *ibid.*, 26 February 1874, p. 178.

128 Royal Academy, Council Minutes, 16 June 1874, pp. 75–76; *ibid.*, 1 June 1875, p. 194.

129 *Ibid.*, 12 January 1875, p. 130.

130 *Ibid.*, 25 March 1875, p. 168.

131 Royal Academy of Arts, *Annual Report from the Council ... for the Year 1875*, London, 1878, pp. 5–6. Mr Fahey's tumble down the stairs, which he blamed on loose coconut matting, had been reported to the Council on 9 June 1875. At the time Barry had been asked to investigate 'the propriety of putting up a balustrade the whole length of the stairs in the centre.' (Royal Academy, Council Minutes, 9 June 1875, pp. 197–98).

132 Royal Academy, Council Minutes, 23 December 1875, p. 243.

133 *Ibid.*, 11 January 1876, p. 4.

134 *Ibid.*, 25 January. 1876, p. 11.

135 *Ibid.*, 7 November 1876, p. 82.

136 *Ibid.*, 13 February 1877, p. 115.

137 Royal Academy, General Assembly Minutes, 21 March 1877, pp. 273–74; *ibid.*, 24 November 1877, p. 278.

138 *Ibid.*, 12 December 1876, p. 95.

139 *Ibid.*, 9 January 1877, pp. 102–03.

140 *Ibid.*, 23 January 1877, p. 108.

141 *Ibid.*, 9 January 1877, pp. 102–03.

142 Royal Academy, General Assembly Minutes, 2 December 1878, p. 318.

143 *Ibid.*, 7 March 1879, p. 332.

144 E. M. Barry to George Richmond, 8 March 1879 (RAA/397/GRI/3/512).

145 E. M. Barry to George Richmond, 12 March 1879 (RAA/397/GRI/3/515).

146 Royal Academy, Council Minutes, 27 January 1880, p. 8.

147 The source is G. W. Burnett's account in [Sir] Leslie Stephen's *Dictionary of National Biography* (vol. III, London, 1885, p. 316), which, although lacking in objectivity as far as Barry's character was concerned, was probably based on an eye-witness's recollection of the event.

148 Royal Academy, Council Minutes, 18 November 1879, p. 202.

149 *Ibid.*, p. 206.

150 Royal Academy of Arts, *Annual Report from the Council ... for the Year 1881*, London, 1882, p. 66.

151 *Ibid.*, p. 33.

152 *Ibid.*, p. 66.

153 Royal Academy, Council Minutes, 28 March 1882, p. 215. Shaw's letter of resignation is dated 18 March 1882 (RAA/SEC/4/120/2). Leighton urged him to reconsider but he stood by his decision, replying that 'he had thought the whole question over very carefully & must persist in his determination of resigning the office.' (Council Minutes, 5 April 1882, pp. 218–19).

154 Andrew Saint, *Richard Norman Shaw*, rev. ed., New Haven and London, 2010, p. 265.

155 Andrew Saint (ed.), 'Norman Shaw's letters: a selection', *Architectural History*, vol. 18 (1975), p. 69, no. 9.

156 Shaw to President and Council, 1 July 1880 (RAA/SEC/7/7/2/1).

157 Saint 2010, pp. 265, 269.

158 Shaw to president and Council, 1 July 1880 (RAA/SEC/7/7/2/1). Shaw also suggested that the new Refreshment Room might be used as a lecture room, pointing out that 'it would be on about the same level as the Schools, and a way in could easily be made for them' and that the 'present approach to the Lecture room through trap doors in the floor of the Water Colour room could then be done away with.'

159 Royal Academy, Council Minutes, 28 February 1882, pp. 204–05.

160 Royal Academy of Arts, *Annual Report from the Council ... for the Year 1884*, London, 1885, pp. 6–7.

161 Royal Academy of Arts, *Annual Rreport from the Council ... for the Year 1885*, London, 1886, pp. 5–6.

162 Royal Academy, Council Minutes, 28 February 1882, p. 204.

163 Royal Academy, Council Minutes, 9 May 1882, pp. 227–28.

164 Royal Academy, Council Minutes, 28 February 1882, p. 204.

165 The idea was explored again by Sir T. G. Jackson in May 1908 and by Sir Edwin Lutyens in October 1932; for the former's report on his proposal with accompanying sketches dated 20 May 1908, see 'General Committees', RAA/PC/7/4; for Lutyens's scheme, which also included an extension northward of Gallery VI, see his drawing in TNA WORK 12/287.

166 'Proposed New Buildings', Royal Academy of Arts, *Annual Report from the Council ... for the Year 1883*, London, 1884, Appendix no. 11, pp. 62–64.

167 *Ibid.*, p. 64.

168 'Alteration and Enlargement of the Schools. Memorandum from the Council, with Plan and Estimates', printed sheet, [1885] (RAA/SEC/22/6).

169 Royal Academy of Arts, *Annual Report from the Council ... for the Year 1883*, London, 1884, pp. 15–16.

170 'Additions & Alterations to Burlington House: New Galleries, &c.', RA treasurer's account-book (RAA/TRE/10/1).

171 The last expenditure on Shaw's works – for the removal of a 'disused cesspool under the entrance porch' – brought their total cost in May 1886 to £37,477 19s. (*Annual Report from the Council ... for the Year 1886*, London, 1887, pp. 5–6). The building contractor George Jackson's original tender, accepted by the General Assembly on 7 August 1883, had been for £20,183.

172 Royal Academy, Council Minutes, 27 November 1876, p. 91.

173 E. W. Gosse, 'The Diploma Gallery at the Academy', *Pall Mall Gazette*, 10 October 1883.

174 Royal Academy, Council Minutes, 17 March 1874, p. 41.

175 Royal Academy of Arts, *Annual Report from the Council ... for the Year 1891*, London, 1892, pp. 6–7.

176 J. E. Hodgson and F. A. Eaton, *The Royal Academy and its Members, 1768–1830*, London, 1905; Lamb 1935; Hutchison 1968. The Council had given Hodgson and Eaton permission in 1889 'to make use of any pictures and documents belonging to the Academy for the purposes of a series of articles to be written by them on the History of the Academy and its Members.' (*Annual Report from the Council ... for the Year 1889*, London, 1890, p. 7).

177 Royal Academy of Arts, *Annual Report from the Council ... for the Year 1899*, London, 1900, p. 8.

178 *Ibid.*, pp. 8–9.

179 Sheppard 1963, p. 421.

180 'Additions & Alterations to Burlington House: Entrance Hall', RA treasurer's account-book (RAA/TRE/10/1).

181 No documentary evidence has been found to support the assertion in Sheppard 1963 that 'the arched openings to the cloakroom (north-west) and to the Diploma Gallery staircase (north-east) [*sic*] were certainly due to Jackson' (Sheppard 1963, p. 421). The reference to the 'Diploma Gallery staircase' is an error; the corresponding opening on the east side is that of the ticket office.

182 'Additions & Alterations to Burlington House: Entrance Hall', RA treasurer's account-book (RAA/TRE/10/1).

183 Royal Academy of Arts, *Annual Report from the Council ... for the Year 1899*, London, 1900, p. 7.

184 Blomfield to President and Council, 26 April 1927 ('General Committees', RAA/PC/7/4).

185 Royal Academy of Arts, *Annual Report from the Council ... for the Year 1927*, London, 1928, p. 7.

186 This staircase 'leading from the north-west corner of the Library to the passage communicating directly with the Schools' had been constructed in 1888 (see Royal Academy of Arts, *Annual Report from the Council ... for the Year 1888*, London, 1889, p. 7).

187 For details of Erith's proposed make-over of the entrance hall and Reynolds Room, not all of which was carried out, see his report dated 3 August 1962, extracts from which are quoted in Lucy Archer's monograph *Raymond Erith, Architect*, Burford, 1985, pp. 98–99, 176.

188 Denis Serjeant, 'The Diploma Gallery Stair and Lift: an interim report on suggested improvements', February 1985 (RA Library).

189 *Royal Academy of Arts: A Vision for Burlington Gardens*, [London, 1996], p. 34.

190 *Ibid.*, p. 34.

191 Peter Schmitt, 'Scheme for Schools and East Link to Burlington Gardens', interoffice memo to Royal Academy Executive Committee, 6 January 200 (RA Library).

192 Colin St John Wilson, 'Report on the design for the Schools at the Royal Academy' [*c.* November 2004], p. 2 (RA Library).

193 *Ibid.*, pp. 14, 17.

194 *Ibid.*, p. 12.

195 *Ibid.*, p. 17.

SELECTED BIBLIOGRAPHY AND FURTHER READING

MONOGRAPHS AND EXHIBITION CATALOGUES

Lucy Archer, *Raymond Erith, Architect*, Burford, Oxfordshire, 1985

Barbara Arciszewska, *The Hanoverian Court and the Triumph of Palladio: the Palladian Revival in Hanover and England c. 1700*, Warsaw, 2002

Barbara Arciszewska, *Classicism and Modernity: Architectural Thought in Eighteenth-Century Britain*, Warsaw, 2010

Dana Arnold (ed.), *Belov'd by Ev'ry Muse: Richard Boyle, 3rd Earl of Burlington and 4th Earl of Cork*, London, 1994

Dana Arnold (ed.), *The Metropolis and its Image: Constructing Identities for London, c. 1750–1950*, Oxford, 1999

Philip Ayres, *Classical Culture and the Idea of Rome in Eighteenth-Century England*, Cambridge, 1997

Nicolas Barker, *The Devonshire Inheritance: Five Centuries of Collecting at Chatsworth*, exhib. cat., Alexandria, Virginia, 2003

T. Barnard and J. Clark, *Lord Burlington: Architecture, Art and Life*, London and Rio Grande, 1995

T. Barnard, *A New Anatomy of Ireland: The Irish Protestants, 1649–1770*, New Haven and London, 2003

Alfred Barry, *The Life and Work of Sir Charles Barry, R.A., F.R.S.*, London, 1867

George Basalla, William Coleman, Robert H. Kargon (eds), *Victorian Science: A Self-Portrait from the Presidential Addresses of the British Association for the Advancement of Science*, Garden City, N.Y., 1970

Bernard H. Becker, *Scientific London*, London, 1874 (reprinted 1968)

Francis Bickley, *The Cavendish Family*, London, 1911

Neil Bingham, *Samuel Ware and the Creation of the Great Staircase, Burlington House, Piccadilly*, exhib. cat., London, 2008

Michael Borozdin-Bidnell, *Absolute Architecture: English Palladianism in the Long Eighteenth Century*, exhib. cat., London, 2008

Burlingtonia: Historical Notes about Burlington House, Piccadilly, and Neighbourhood, London, 1878

Jacques Carré, *Lord Burlington (1694–1753): le connaisseur, le mécène, l'architecte*, Clermont-Ferrand, 1993

E. Beresford Chancellor, *A History of the Squares and Palaces of London*, reprinted London, 2012

Stefan Collini, *Public Moralists: Political Thought and Intellectual Life in Britain, 1850–1930*, Oxford, 1991

H. M. Colvin, *The History of the King's Works: Vol. v 1660–1782*, London, 1976

H. M. Colvin, *A Biographical Dictionary of British Architects 1600–1840*, 3rd ed., New Haven and London, 1995; rev. ed., New Haven and London, 2008

Edward Corp (ed.), *Lord Burlington: The Man and his Politics: Questions of Loyalty*, Lewiston, New York, 1998

Allan Cunningham, *The Lives of the Most Eminent British Painters, Sculptors, and Architects*, vol. iv, London, 1831

Gordon L. Herries Davies, *Whatever is Under the Earth: The Geological Society of London 1807 to 2007*, London, 2007

J. L. E. Dreyer and H. H. Turner, *History of the Royal Astronomical Society 1820–1920*, London, 1923

Joan Evans, *A History of the Society of Antiquaries*, Oxford, 1956

James Fenton, *School of Genius: A History of the Royal Academy of Arts*, London, 2006

Terry Friedman, *James Gibbs*, New Haven and London, 1984

A. T. Gage, *A History of the Linnean Society of London*, London, 1938

H. S. Goodhart-Rendell, *English Architecture since the Regency: An Interpretation*, London, 1954

R. T. Gunther (ed.), *The Architecture of Sir Roger Pratt*, Oxford, 1928

Marie Boas Hall, *All Scientists Now: The Royal Society in the Nineteenth Century*, Cambridge, 1984

Eileen Harris assisted by Nicholas Savage, *British Architectural Books and Writers 1556–1785*, Cambridge, 1990

John Harris, *The Palladians*, London, 1981

John Harris, *The Palladian Revival: Lord Burlington, His Villa and Garden at Chiswick*, exhib. cat., London, 1994

John Harris, *William Kent, 1685-1748: A Poet on Paper*, exhib. cat., London, 1998

Negley Harte, *The University of London 1836–1986: An Illustrated History*, London and Atlantic Highlands, N.J., 1986

Brendan O Hehir, *Harmony from Discords: A Life of Sir John Denham*, Berkeley and Los Angeles, 1968

Brendan O Hehir, *Expans'd Hieroglyphicks: A Critical Edition of Sir John Denham's Coopers Hill*, Berkeley and Los Angeles, 1969

Charles Hind (ed.), *New Light on English Palladianism: Papers given at the Georgian Group Symposium 1988*, London, 1990

Charles Hind and Vicky Wilson (eds.), *Palladian Design: The Good, The Bad and the Unexpected*, exhib. cat., London, 2015

Sidney C. Hutchison, *The Homes of the Royal Academy*, London, 1956

Sidney C. Hutchison, *The History of the Royal Academy 1768–1986*, London, rev. ed., 1986

Basil H. Johnson, *Berkeley Square to Bond Street: The Early History of the Neighbourhood*, London, 1952

The Jubilee of the Chemical Society of London: Record of the Proceedings together with an Account of the History and Development of the Society, 1841–1891, London, 1896

C. Jungnickel and R. McCormmach, *Cavendish*, Philadelphia, 1996

F. G. Kenyon, *The British Academy: The First Fifty Years*, London, 1952

Pamela D. Kingsbury, *Lord Burlington's Town Architecture*, London, 1995

C. L. Kingsford, *The Early History of Piccadilly, Leicester Square, Soho & their Neighbourhood*, Cambridge, 1925

George Knox, *Antonio Pellegrini 1675–1741*, Oxford, 1995

Walter Lamb, *The Royal Academy: A Short History of its Foundation and Development to the Present Day*, London, 1935 (rev. ed., 1951)

G. D. Leslie, *The Inner Life of the Royal Academy with an Account of its Schools and Exhibitions principally in the Reign of Queen Victoria*, London, 1914

James Lees-Milne, *Earls of Creation: Five Great Patrons of Eighteenth-Century Art*, London, 1962

James Lees-Milne, *The Bachelor Duke: A Life of William Spencer Cavendish, 6th Duke of Devonshire*, London, 1991

D. W. Logan, *The University of London: An Introduction*, rev. ed., London, 1956

William C. Lubenow, *'Only Connect': Learned Societies in Nineteenth-Century Britain*, Woodbridge, 2015

Maynard Mack, *Alexander Pope: A Life*, New Haven and London, 1985

Robin Middleton, Gerald Beasley, Nicholas Savage *et al.*, *The Mark J. Millard Architectural Collection: Volume II British Books*, Washington, D.C. and New York, 1998

Rowan Moore and Dennis Gilbert, *Sackler Galleries, Royal Academy: Architects, Foster Associates*, London, 1992.

Timothy Mowl, *William Kent: Architect, Designer, Opportunist*, London, 2006

John W. Papworth and Wyatt Papworth, *Museums, Libraries, and Picture Galleries, Public and Private*, London, 1853

David Pearce, *London's Mansions: The Palatial Houses of the Nobility*, London, 1986

M. H. Port, *Imperial London: Civil Government Building in London 1850–1915*, New Haven and London, 1995

Alan Powers and James Dunnett, *Elegant Variation: The Architecture of H. T. Cadbury-Brown, R.A.*, London, 2006

Norman Price, *Somerset House: A Biography of a Building*, [London, 1970]

Andrew Saint, *Richard Norman Shaw*, rev. ed., New Haven and London, 2010

Peter Schmitt and Owen Hopkins, *Burlington House: A Brief History*, London, [2010]

F. H. W. Sheppard (gen. ed.), *Survey of London: Volumes 31–32, Parish of St James, Westminster, Part 2: North of Piccadilly*, London, 1963

G. S. Street, *The Ghosts of Piccadilly*, London, 1907

Howard E. Stutchbury, *The Architecture of Colen Campbell*, Manchester, 1967

John Gordon Sutherland, *Burlington House and the Royal Academy: Historical and Biographical Notes*, London, 2002

Robert Tavernor, *Palladio and Palladianism*, New York, 1991

Simon Thurley, *Men from the Ministry: How Britain Saved its Heritage*, New Haven and London, 2013

Geoffrey Tyack, *Sir James Pennethorne and the Making of Victorian London*, Cambridge, 1992

Giles Waterfield, *The People's Galleries: Art Museums and Exhibitions in Britain 1800–1914*, New Haven and London, 2015

Susan Weber (ed.), *William Kent: Designing Georgian Britain*, New Haven and London, 2013

H. B. Wheatley, *Round About Piccadilly and Pall Mall*, London, 1870
Mortimer Wheeler, *The British Academy 1949–1968*, London, 1970
Roger White (ed.), *Lord Burlington and his Circle: Papers given at the Georgian Group Symposium, 22 May 1982*, London, 1982
Walter White, *The Journals of Walter White, Assistant Secretary of the Royal Society*, London, 1898
David Wilkinson, *The Duke of Portland: Politics and Party in the Age of George III*, Basingstoke, 2003
Michael I. Wilson, *William Kent: Architect, Designer, Painter, Gardener, 1685–1748*, London and Boston, 1984
Rachel Wilson, *Elite Women in Ascendancy Ireland 1690–1745: Imitation and Innovation*, Woodbridge, 2015
Rudolf Wittkower, *Palladio and English Palladianism*, London, 1974 (reprint, London and New York, 1989)
Horace B. Woodward, *The History of the Geological Society of London*, London, 1907
Giles Worsley, *Architectural Drawings of the Regency Period, 1790–1837*, London, 1991
Giles Worsley, *Classical Architecture in Britain: The Heroic Age*, New Haven and London, 1994

ESSAYS AND JOURNAL ARTICLES

Megan Aldrich, 'The Victorian Craces, *c.* 1830–1899', in M. Aldrich (ed.), *The Craces: Royal Decorators 1668–1899*, exhib. cat., London and Brighton, 1990, pp. 53–136
Philip Ayres, 'Pope's Epistle to Lord Burlington: the Vitruvian analogies', *Studies in English Literature 1500–1900*, 30 (1990), pp. 429–44
Neil Bingham, 'Humphry and John Adey Repton's unexecuted design for Burlington Place, Piccadilly', *London Gardener, or The Gardener's Intelligencer*, 12 (2006–07), pp. 11–19
Neil Bingham, 'The Regency transformation of Burlington House: The architectural drawings of Samuel Ware in the Royal Academy of Arts', in Susanna Avery-Quash and Kate Redford (eds), *The Georgian London Town House: Building, Collecting and Display*, London and New York (forthcoming)
Philip Booth, 'Speculative housing and the land market in London 1660–1730: four case studies', *Town Planning Review*, 51, no. 4 (October 1980), pp. 379–98
John Britton, 'An account of Burlington House', in J. Britton and A. Pugin, *Illustrations of the Public Buildings of London*, vol. 1, London, 1825, pp. 95–101
John M. Brydon (*et al.*), 'York Water-Gate, Temple Bar and the colonnade of old Burlington House', *RIBA Proceedings*, 2nd series, vol. 1, no. 11 (26 March 1885), pp. 148–54
Arthur Cates, 'A biographical notice of the late Sir James Pennethorne', *Sessional Papers of the Royal Institute of British Architects*, vol. 22 (1871–72), pp. 53–69
E. Beresford Chancellor, 'An unrecognized masterpiece' [i.e. 6 Burlington Gardens], *Architects' Journal*, 66 (14 Dec. 1927), pp. 772–74
Jane Clark, 'The mysterious Mr. Buck', *Apollo*, 129 (May 1989), pp. 317–22
Jane Clark, 'Lord Burlington is here', in T. Barnard and J. Clark, *Lord Burlington: Architecture, Art and Life*, London and Rio Grande, 1995
H. M. Colvin, 'Lord Burlington and the Office of Works', in H. M. Colvin, *Essays in English Architectural History*, New Haven and London, 1999
John Cornforth, 'Tribute to Burlington', *Country Life*, 168 (6 November 1980), pp. 1658–59
John Cornforth, 'A Pantheon in Piccadilly', *Country Life*, 198 (1 April 2004), pp. 74–79
Matthew Craske, 'From Burlington Gate to Billingsgate: James Ralph's attempt to impose Burlingtonian classicism as a canon of public taste', in Barbara Arciszewska and Elizabeth McKellar (eds), *Articulating British Classicism: New Approaches to Eighteenth-Century Architecture*, Aldershot, 2004, pp. 97–118
Edward Croft-Murray, 'Decorative paintings for Lord Burlington and the Royal Academy', *Apollo*, 89 (January 1969), pp. 11–21
J. Mordaunt Crook, 'Sydney Smirke: the architecture of compromise', in: Jane Fawcett (ed.), *Seven Victorian Architects*, London, 1970
T. Durrant, 'History of Burlington House', *London Society Journal*, 393 (September 1971), pp. 36–40
Alexander Echlin and William Kelley, 'A Shaftesbury agenda? Lord Burlington, Lord Shaftesbury and the intellectual origins of English Palladianism', *Architectural History*, 59 (2016), pp. 221–52
Julian Harrap, 'Restoration of the historic fabric of Burlington House and the Main Galleries, Royal Academy of Arts', *Journal of Architectural Conservation*, vol. 1, no. 1 (March 1995), pp. 70–87
John Harris, 'Burlington House: the Royal Academy and Norman Foster triumph', *Apollo*, 133 (June 1991), pp. 406–08
John Harris, 'The transformation of Lord Burlington: From the Palladio and Jones of his time to the modern Vitruvius', in Dana Arnold (ed.), *The Georgian Villa*, Stroud, 1996
Richard Hewlings, 'The statues of Inigo Jones and Palladio at Chiswick House', *English Heritage Historical Review*, vol. 2 (2007), pp. 70–83
Naill Hobhouse, 'Academic exercise', *Architectural Review*, vol. 233, no. 1391 (January 2013), pp. 70–73
Christopher Hussey, 'Burlington House, Piccadilly: the home of the Royal Academy of Arts', *Country Life*, 55 (3 May 1924), pp. 694–702
Christopher Hussey, 'The young Lord Burlington', *Country Life*, 133 (30 June 1960), p. 1494
Walter Ison, 'The architecture of Burlington House', *Apollo* (January 1969), pp. 4–10
Fiske Kimball, 'Burlington *Architectus*', parts 1 and 2, *RIBA Journal*, 3rd series, vol. 34 (15 October 1927), pp. 674–93; vol. 35 (12 November 1927), pp. 14–16
George Knox, 'Sebastiano Ricci at Burlington House: a Venetian decoration "alla Romana"', *The Burlington Magazine*, vol. 127, no. 990 (September 1985), pp. 601–09
George Knox, 'Antonio Pellegrini and Marco Ricci at Burlington House and Narford Hall', *The Burlington Magazine*, vol. 130, no. 1028 (November 1988), pp. 846–53
D. C. Martin, 'Former homes of the Royal Society', *Notes and Records of the Royal Society of London*, vol. 22 (1967), pp. 12–19
T. G. A. Nelson, 'Pope, Burlington, architecture, and politics: a speculative revisionist view', *Eighteenth-Century Life*, vol. 21, no. 1 (1997), pp. 45–61
Christopher Neve, 'The "Tondo" in a new setting: the Private Rooms at Burlington House', *Country Life*, 157 (13 March 1975), pp. 628–29
Benedict Nicolson, 'Sebastiano Ricci and Lord Burlington', *The Burlington Magazine*, 105 (March 1963), pp. 88, 121–23, 125
John Julius Norwich, 'The Royal Academy of Arts', *Interiors* (September 1982), pp. 160–71
Steven Parissien, John Harris, and H. M. Colvin, 'Narford Hall, Norfolk', *Georgian Group Journal* (1987), pp. 49–61
H. F. Pfister, 'Burlingtonian architectural theory in England and America', *Winterthur Portfolio*, 11 (1976), pp. 123–51
Pauline Plummer and Peter Schmitt, 'The rediscovery of the lost ceiling decoration in the Saloon at Burlington House', in R. Gowing and R. Pender (eds), *All Manner of Murals: The History, Techniques and Conservation of Secular Wall Paintings*, London, 2007
C. H. Reilly, 'Old Burlington House, Piccadilly', *Country Life*, 13 January 1923, pp. 37–40
Jane Rendell, 'Thresholds, passages and surfaces: touching, passing and seeing in the Burlington Arcade', in Alex Coles (ed.), *The Optic of Walter Benjamin*, London, 1999
Albert Richardson, 'A painter's views on architecture', *Country Life*, 5 July 1962, p. 14
Andrew Saint (ed.), 'Norman Shaw's letters: a selection', *Architectural History*, vol. 18 (1975), pp. 60–85
Spencer Savage, 'The homes of the Linnean Society of London', *Proceedings of the Linnean Society*, Session 145 (1932–33), part 2, pp. 56–61
Clare Sherriff, 'Arnold Mitchell (1863–1944): "Fecundity" and "Versatility" in an early twentieth-century architect', *Architectural History*, vol. 55 (2012), pp. 199–235
A. H. Smith, 'Lord Elgin and his collection', *Journal of Hellenic Studies*, XXXVI (1916)
R. Phené Spiers, 'Burlington House, Piccadilly', *Architectural Review*, 16 (October 1904), pp. 149–57
R. Phené Spiers, 'Alterations to Burlington House', *Architectural Review*, (September 1911), pp. 122–26
John Steegman, 'The Royal Academy's second founder: Sir Francis Grant's crucial role', *Country Life*, 7 June 1962, pp. 1372–73
Geoffrey Tyack, "A gallery worthy of the British people': James Pennethorne's designs for the National Gallery, 1845–1867', *Architectural History*, vol. 33 (1990), pp. 120–34
H. B. Wheatley, 'The Royal Society', *Country Life*, 32 (20 July 1912), pp. 84–88
Rudolf Wittkower, 'The Earl of Burlington and William Kent', *York Georgian Society*, Occasional Paper no. 5 (1948)

PHOTOGRAPHIC ACKNOWLEDGEMENTS

All works of art are reproduced by kind permission of the owners. Every attempt has been made to trace the photographers of works reproduced. Specific acknowledgements are as follows:

PHOTOGRAPHIC CREDITS

DawkinsColour/John Bodkin: pp. 4–5

© James Harris; p. 302

Kew, The National Archives: Figs 176, 177, 188, 196, 198, 201, 202, 203, 204, 205, 206, 207, 208, 214, 215, 216, 217, 220, 221, 222, 227

© 2018 Leigh Goodsell: Fig. 20

London, Bridgeman Images Figs 3, 7, 8 (© British Library Board. All Rights Reserved); 16, 125 (© Devonshire Collection, Chatsworth / Reproduced by permission of Chatsworth Settlement Trustees); 17 (© National Trust Photographic Library); 22 (© Chiswick House, London); 53 (The Portland Collection, Harley Gallery, Welbeck Estate, Nottinghamshire)

London, © The Trustees of the British Museum: Figs 5, 9, 10, 43, 44, 52, 103, 115, 121, 141, 151, 152, 159, 211

London, By Courtesy of the Trustees of Sir John Soane's Museum: Figs 28, 29, 30, 75

London, © Crown copyright: UK Government Art Collection: Figs 4, 40

London, David Chipperfield Architects: Figs 286, 287, 288

London, © Dennis Gilbert/VIEW: Figs 278, 280, 281

London, © Felix Rosenstiel's Widow & Son Ltd: Fig. 178

London, courtesy Foster + Partners: Figs 230, 278, 280

London, © The Linnean Society of London: Figs 153, 154, 242

London, London Metropolitan Archives (City of London): Figs 46, 57, 76, 77, 78, 80, 81, 82, 110, 142, 184, 270

London, © Mary Evans Picture Library/Illustrated London News Ltd: Figs 160, 161, 175, 183, 186, 189, 191, 192, 194, 195

London, © National Portrait Gallery: Fig. 228

London, Parliamentary Archives: Figs 162, 163, 164, 165, 166, 167, 168, 169, 170, 171, 172, 173, 174

London, RIBA Collections: Figs 6, 21, 31, 32, 33, 34, 35, 36, 37, 38, 41, 47, 48, 51, 86, 150, 179, 180, 197, 199, 219, 200, 223, 224, 225, 236, 241, 243, 244, 245, 266, 283; 257 (Martin Charles)

London, © Royal Academy of Arts: Figs: 12, 13, 14, 15, 18, 26, 60, 61, 65, 67, 68, 69, 70, 89, 90, 95, 102, 105, 116, 117, 118, 126, 127, 128, 137, 138, 139, 140, 144, 218, 234, 235, 240, 281, 284, 285, 272, 289

London, © Royal Academy of Arts. Photo: Prudence Cuming Associates Limited: Figs 11, 39, 45, 49, 54, 55, 58, 59, 62, 63, 64, 66, 71, 72, 73, 74, 85, 84, 85, 87, 88, 91, 92, 93, 94, 97, 98, 99, 100, 101, 104, 106, 107, 109, 111, 112, 113, 114, 119, 120, 122, 123, 124, 129, 130, 133, 134, 143, 145, 146, 147, 148, 149, 181, 182, 187, 212, 213, 226, 229, 230, 231, 232, 233, 236, 237, 238, 246, 247, 248, 249, 250, 251, 252, 253, 254, 255, 256, 258, 259, 259, 260, 261, 262, 265, 268, 269, 271, 273, 274, 275, 276, 277, 279, 282

London, © Royal Academy of Arts. Photo: John Hammond © Copyright protected: Figs 23, 24, 25, 50, 108

London, © Royal Academy of Arts. Photo: Paul Highnam © Copyright protected: Fig. 135

London, Royal Academy of Arts. Photo: Marcus Leith © Copyright protected: Fig. 42

London, Royal Academy of Arts. Photo: Russell Westwood: Figs 263, 267

London, Royal Collection Trust © Her Majesty Queen Elizabeth II, 2018: Figs 2, 56, 155

London, © Royal Geographical Society: Fig. 210

London, © The Royal Society: Figs 156, 157, 158, 185

London: © The Samuel Courtauld Trust, The Courtauld Gallery: Fig. 1

London, Reproduced with the permission of Senate House Library, University of London: Figs 193, 208

Fraser Mar: pp. 2–3

Rory Mulvey: pp. 6, 7, 8, 9, 10–11, 12–13; Figs 287, 288, 289, 290, 291, 292, 293, 294

Northamptonshire, From the collection at Althorp: Fig. 19

Oxford, Image produced with permission of ProQuest, as part of the John Johnson Collection, www.proquest.com: Fig. 132

Private collection: Fig. 190

© Städel Museum – ARTOTHEK: Fig. 79

Swindon, © National Trust Images: Fig. 27, 136; 131 (Charles Thomas)

Maciej Urbanek: Fig. 264

COPYRIGHT

H. T. Cadbury-Brown © artist's estate: Figs 273, 274, 275
© David Chipperfield Architects: Fig. 286
© Michael Craig-Martin, courtesy Gagosian Gallery: Fig. 289
© Hayes Davidson: Fig. 285
© Richard Davies: Fig. 239
© Russell Westwood estate: Figs 265, 267

INDEX

Page numbers in *italic* refer to the illustrations